Lecture Notes in Computer Science   10436

Commenced Publication in 1973
Founding and Former Series Editors:
Gerhard Goos, Juris Hartmanis, and Jan van Leeuwen

Editorial Board

More information about this series at http://www.springer.com/series/7410

Joaquin Garcia-Alfaro · Guillermo Navarro-Arribas
Hannes Hartenstein · Jordi Herrera-Joancomartí (Eds.)

Data Privacy Management, Cryptocurrencies and Blockchain Technology

ESORICS 2017 International Workshops, DPM 2017
and CBT 2017, Oslo, Norway, September 14–15, 2017
Proceedings

Springer

Editors
Joaquin Garcia-Alfaro
Télécom SudParis
Evry
France

Hannes Hartenstein
Karlsruhe Institute of Technology
Karlsruhe
Germany

Guillermo Navarro-Arribas
Department of Information
  and Communications Engineering
Autonomous University of Barcelona
Bellaterra
Spain

Jordi Herrera-Joancomartí
Autonomous University of Barcelona
Bellaterra
Spain

ISSN 0302-9743   ISSN 1611-3349 (electronic)
Lecture Notes in Computer Science
ISBN 978-3-319-67815-3   ISBN 978-3-319-67816-0 (eBook)
DOI 10.1007/978-3-319-67816-0

Library of Congress Control Number: 2017953409

LNCS Sublibrary: SL4 – Security and Cryptology

Printed on acid-free paper

This Springer imprint is published by Springer Nature
The registered company is Springer International Publishing AG
The registered company address is: Gewerbestrasse 11, 6330 Cham, Switzerland

Foreword from the DPM 2017 Program Chairs

This volume contains the proceedings of the 12th Data Privacy Management International Workshop (DPM 2017), held in Oslo, Norway, during September 14–15, 2017, in conjunction with the 22nd European Symposium on Research in Computer Security (ESORICS) 2017. The DPM series started in 2005 when the first workshop took place in Tokyo (Japan). Since then, the event has been held in different venues: Atlanta, USA (2006); Istanbul, Turkey (2007); Saint Malo, France (2009); Athens, Greece (2010); Leuven, Belgium (2011); Pisa, Italy (2012); Egham, UK (2013); Wroclaw, Poland (2014); Vienna, Austria (2015); and Crete, Greece (2016).

The aim of DPM is to promote and stimulate the international collaboration and research exchange in areas related to the management of privacy-sensitive information. This is a very critical and important issue for organizations and end-users. It poses several challenging problems, such as translation of high-level business goals into system-level privacy policies, administration of sensitive identifiers, data integration and privacy engineering, among others.

For this workshop edition we received 51 submission, and each one was evaluated on the basis of significance, novelty, and technical quality. The Program Committee, formed by 41 members, performed an excellent task and with the help of an additional 18 referees all submissions went through a careful review process (three or more reviews per submission). In the end, 16 full papers were accepted for presentation at the event. In addition, the program was completed with a keynote talk given by Vicenç Torra (University of Skövde, Sweden) on integral privacy (privacy models and disclosure risk).

We would like to thank everyone who helped organize the event, including all the members of the Organizing Committee of both ESORICS and DPM 2017.

Our gratitude goes also to Pierangela Samarati, Steering Committee Chair of the ESORICS Symposium, for all her arrangements to make possible the satellite events, and Socratis Katsikas, Workshops Chair of ESORICS 2017. Last but by no means least, we thank all the DPM 2017 Program Committee members, additional reviewers, all the authors who submitted papers, and all the workshop attendees.

Finally, we want to acknowledge the support received from the sponsors of the workshop: Institut Mines-Telecom (Telecom SudParis), CNRS Samovar UMR 5157 (R3S team), Universitat Autonoma de Barcelona, UNESCO Chair in Data Privacy, Universitat Rovira i Virgili, and project TIN2014-55243-P from the Spanish MINECO.

August 2017

Joaquin Garcia-Alfaro
Guillermo Navarro-Arribas

Organization

12th International Workshop on Data Privacy Management — DPM 2017

Program Committee Chairs

Joaquin Garcia-Alfaro   Telecom SudParis, Paris-Saclay University, France
Guillermo Navarro-Arribas   Universitat Autònoma de Barcelona, Spain

Program Committee

Günes Acar	KU Leuven, Belgium
Jordi Casas-Roma	Universitat Oberta de Catalunya, Spain
Jordi Castella-Roca	Universitat Rovira i Virgili, Spain
Frederic Cuppens	Telecom Bretagne, France
Nora Cuppens-Boulahia	Telecom Bretagne, France
Josep Domingo-Ferrer	Universitat Rovira i Virgili, Spain
Christian Duncan	Quinnipiac University, USA
Sara Foresti	Università degli Studi di Milano, Italy
Sebastien Gambs	Université du Québec à Montréal, Canada
Paolo Gasti	New York Institute of Technology, USA
Marit Hansen	Unabhängiges Landeszentrum für Datenschutz, Germany
Jordi Herrera-Joancomarti	Universitat Autònoma de Barcelona, Spain
Masahiro Inuiguchi	Osaka University, Japan
Marc Juarez	KU Leuven, Belgium
Florian Kammueller	Middlesex University London, UK
Hiroaki Kikuchi	Meiji University, Japan
Evangelos Kranakis	Carleton University, Canada
Maryline Laurent	Telecom SudParis, Paris-Saclay University, France
Giovanni Livraga	Università degli Studi di Milano, Italy
Javier Lopez	University of Malaga, Spain
Brad Malin	Vanderbilt University, USA
Chris Mitchell	Royal Holloway, UK
Tarik Moataz	Brown University, USA
Refik Molva	EURECOM, France
Anna Monreale	University of Pisa, Italy
Jordi Nin	BBVA Data & Analytics, Spain

Melek Önen	EURECOM, France
Cristina Pérez-Solà	Universitat Autònoma de Barcelona, Spain
Silvio Ranise	FBK, Security and Trust Unit, Trento, Italy
Kai Rannenberg	Goethe University, Germany
Yves Roudier	Université de Nice, France
Pierangela Samarati	Università degli Studi di Milano, Italy
David Sanchez	Universitat Rovira i Virgili, Spain
Claudio Soriente	Telefonica Research and Development, Spain
Matthias Templ	Vienna University of Technology, Austria
Vicenç Torra	University of Skövde, Sweden
Yasuyuki Tsukada	Kanto Gakuin University, Japan
Alexandre Viejo	Universitat Rovira i Virgili, Spain
Jens Weber	University of Victoria, Canada
Lena Wiese	University of Göttingen, Germany
Nicola Zannone	Eindhoven University of Technology, The Netherlands

Steering Committee

Josep Domingo-Ferrer	Universitat Rovira i Virgili, Spain
Joaquin Garcia-Alfaro	Telecom SudParis, Paris-Saclay University, France
Guillermo Navarro-Arribas	Universitat Autònoma de Barcelona, Spain
Vicenç Torra	University of Skövde, Sweden

Additional Reviewers

Carles Anglès-Tafalla
Monir Azraoui
Sergi Delgado-Segura
Gerardo Fernandez
José Maria de Fuentes
Akos Grosz
Paolo Guarda
Daniel Homann
Ibrahim Lazrig

Wanpeng Li
Fatma Al Maqbali
Ana Nieto
Jose A. Onieva
Alfredo Rial
Sara Ricci
Ruben Rios
Jordi Ribes-González
Hari Siswantoro

Foreword from CBT 2017 Program Chairs

This volume contains the proceedings of the First International Workshop on Cryptocurrencies and Blockchain Technology (CBT 2017) held in Oslo, Norway, on September 14, 2017, in conjunction with the 22nd European Symposium on Research in Computer Security (ESORICS) 2017.

Since the appearance of Bitcoin in 2009, a plethora of new cryptocurrencies and other blockchain-based systems have been proposed and deployed. While some of them are slightly different copies of Bitcoin, others propose interesting improvements or new usages of the underlying blockchain technology. Owing to their construction as blockchain-based systems, security and dependability aspects need to be rigorously designed and analyzed. The goal of the CBT workshop is to provide a forum for researchers in this area to carefully analyze current systems and propose new ones in order to create a scientific background for the solid development of new cryptocurrencies and blockchain technology systems.

In response to the call for papers, we received 27 submissions that were carefully reviewed by the Program Committee comprising 15 members and by additional reviewers. Each submission received at least three reviews. The Program Committee selected six papers as full papers (resulting in an acceptance rate of about 22%) and four short papers for presentation at the workhop. The selected papers cover aspects of identity management, smart contracts, soft- and hardforks, proof-of-works and proof-of-stake as well as on network layer aspects and the application of blockchain technology for secure concert/event ticketing.

Furthermore, the workshop was enhanced by the keynote offered by Prof. Roger Wattenhofer, a talk that was made possible thanks to the sponsorship of Blockchain Inc.

We would like to thank all the authors who submitted papers to CBT 2017 and the Program Committee and the additional reviewers who worked hard to review the submissions and discussed the final program. We would also like to thank the ESORICS workshop chair Sokratis Katsikas and his team as well as the ESORICS organizers for putting faith in us and in the topic of cryptocurrencies and blockchain technology.

We hope that you find the proceedings of CBT 2017 interesting and inspiring and that there will be follow-ups of the CBT workshop in the coming years.

Jordi Herrera-Joancomartí
Hannes Hartenstein

First International Workshop on Cryptocurrencies and Blockchain Technology CBT 2017

Program Committee Chairs

Hannes Hartenstein	Karlsruher Institut für Technologie, Germany
Jordi Herrera-Joancomartí	Universitat Autònoma de Barcelona, Spain

Program Committee

Rainer Böhme	Universität Innsbruck, Austria
Jeremy Clark	Concordia University, Canada
Christian Decker	Blockstream, USA
Joaquin Garcia-Alfaro	Telecom SudParis, Paris-Saclay University, France
Arthur Gervais	ETH, Switzerland
Man Ho Au	The Hong Kong Polytechnic University, SAR China
Ghassan Karame	NEC Research, Germany
Stefan Katzenbeisser	Technische Universität Darmstadt, Germany
Patrick McCorry	UCL, UK
Shin'ichiro Matsuo	BSafe.network and Keio University, Japan
Guillermo Navarro-Arribas	Universitat Autònoma de Barcelona, Spain
Mariusz Nowostawski	NTNU, Norway
Cristina Pérez-Solà	Universitat Autònoma de Barcelona, Spain
Roger Wattenhofer	ETH, Switzerland

Steering Committee

Rainer Böhme	Universität Innsbruck, Austria
Joaquin Garcia-Alfaro	Telecom SudParis, Paris-Saclay University, France
Hannes Hartenstein	Karlsruher Institut für Technologie, Germany
Jordi Herrera-Joancomartí	Universitat Autònoma de Barcelona, Spain

Additional Reviewers

Svetlana Abramova	Shinichi Miyazawa	Paulina Pesch
Sergi Delgado-Segura	Ken Naganuma	Kazue Sako
Michael Fröwis	Till Neudecker	Oliver Stengele

Contents

Short Papers

Privacy, Logics, and Computational Models

A Proof Calculus for Attack Trees in Isabelle

Florian Kammüller[1,2(✉)]

[1] Middlesex University London, London, UK
`f.kammueller@mdx.ac.uk`
[2] Technische Universität Berlin, Berlin, Germany

Abstract. Attack trees are an important modeling formalism to identify and quantify attacks on security and privacy. They are very useful
as a tool to understand step by step the ways through a system graph
that lead to the violation of security policies. In this paper, we present
how attacks can be refined based on the violation of a policy. To that end
we provide a formal definition of attack trees in Isabelle's Higher Order
Logic: a proof calculus that defines how to refine sequences of attack
steps into a valid attack. We use a notion of Kripke semantics as formal
foundation that then allows to express attack goals using branching time
temporal logic CTL. We illustrate the use of the mechanized Isabelle
framework on the example of a privacy attack to an IoT healthcare system.

1 Introduction

Identifying attacks and quantifying the attacker is a major challenge in security
engineering. Attack trees are a simple classical approach but they still thrive in
practical applications. One of the reasons is their simplicity and transparency to
the user; the other is that their notion of attack analysis is a natural mechanism
of a gradual approach to understanding security risks. In this paper, we provide
a formal basis for attack trees in the interactive theorem prover Isabelle: a proof
calculus for attack trees using a notion of refinement and attack validity. An
existing emulation of modelchecking [6] provides a Kripke semantics for the proof
calculus for attack trees. We introduce the proof calculus and the underlying
mechanisation of the Kripke semantics. Finally, we illustrate the application of
the presented Isabelle formalisation of attack trees on a case study from the
health care sector which is the target of the CHIST-ERA project SUCCESS [3].

The main novelty of this paper is a mechanized theory for attack trees using
Kripke structures to provide a state based foundation for the attack sequences as
well as enabling the combination with the branching time logic CTL to facilitate
detection and analysis of attacks.

The paper first introduces attack trees, Kripke structures, and attack tree
refinement (Sect. 2) before presenting the proof calculus (Sect. 3). Section 4 then
summarises the Isabelle Insider framework that can be used as an application of
the attack tree formalisation. A health care system Insider attack is introduced
and used as an illustrative example for the application of Isabelle attack trees
and Kripke structures.

© Springer International Publishing AG 2017
J. Garcia-Alfaro et al. (Eds.): DPM/CBT 2017, LNCS 10436, pp. 3–18, 2017.
DOI: 10.1007/978-3-319-67816-0_1

2   Attack Trees and Kripke Structures

2.1   Attack Trees

Attack Trees [16] are a graphical tree-based design language for the stepwise investigation and quantification of attacks. We believe that attack trees are a succinct way of representing attacks and thus not only useful as an immediate tool to quantify the attacker as part of a security analysis but also a good way of making security and privacy risks transparent to users. In attack trees [13,16], the root represents a goal, and the children represent sub-attacks. Sub-attacks can be alternatives for reaching the goal (disjunctive node) or they must all be completed to reach the goal (conjunctive node). Figure 1 illustrates the clarity of this graphical formalism by giving an example of an attack tree for opening a safe [16]. Leaf nodes represent the basic actions in an attack. Nodes of attack trees can be adorned with attributes, for example costs of attacks or probabilities which allows quantification of attacks (not used in the example). Sub-trees can be combined disjunctively (or-nodes) or conjunctively (and-nodes).

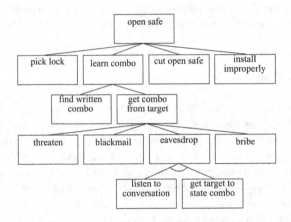

Fig. 1. Attack tree example illustrating mainly disjunctive nodes for alternative attacks refining the root node "open safe" and one conjunctive node for "eavesdrop".

As much as this clarity is encouraging to employ the formalism in the early stages of a security engineering process, it is also abstract and may lead to ambiguities. Therefore, it is desirable to lay foundations for attack trees that help us to use them not only to grasp intuitive attacks but to provide a foundation that helps to disambiguate and verify the intuition.

There are excellent foundations available based on graph theory [13]. They provide a very good understanding of the formalism, various extensions (like attack-defense trees [12] and differentiations of the operators (like sequential conjunction (SAND) versus parallel conjunction [5]) and are amply documented in the literature. These theories for attack trees provide a thorough foundation for the formalism and its semantics. The main problem that adds complexity to the semantical models is the abstractness of the descriptions in the nodes. This leads to a variety of approaches to the semantics, e.g. propositional semantics, multiset semantics, and equational semantics for ADtrees [12]. The theoretical foundations allow comparison of different semantics, and provide a theoretical framework to develop evaluation algorithms for the quantification of attacks.

Surprisingly, the use of an automated proof assistant, like Isabelle, has not been considered despite its potential of providing a theory and analysis of attacks simultaneously. The essential attack tree mechanism of disjunction and conjunction in tree refinement is relatively simple. The complexity in the theories is caused by the attempt to incorporate semantics to the attack nodes and relate the trees to actual scenarios. This is why we consider the formalisation of a foundation of attack trees in the interactive prover Isabelle since it supports logical modeling and definitions of datatypes very akin to algebraic specification but directly supported by semi-automated analysis and proof tools.

2.2   Attack Tree Datatype in Isabelle

The attack trees formalisation including Kripke structures is formalised in Isabelle's Higher Order Logic. All sources are available online [7]. This Isabelle formalisation constitutes a tool for proving security properties using the assistance of the semi-automated theorem prover [11]. Isabelle is an interactive proof assistant based on Higher Order Logic (HOL). Applications can be specified as so-called object-logics in HOL providing reasoning capabilities for examples but also for the analysis of the meta-theory. An object-logic contains new types, constants and definitions. These items reside in a theory file, *e.g.*, the file AT.thy contains the object-logic for attack trees. This Isabelle Insider framework is a *conservative extension* of HOL. This means that an object logic does not introduce new axioms and hence guarantees consistency.

Attack trees have already been integrated as an extension to the Isabelle Insider framework [9,15] but with a limited scope to conjunctive nodes only and no added semantics to construct a proof calculus. In the current paper, we not only generalise the attack trees for arbitrary state systems but also properly extend to disjunctive nodes.

The principal idea is that base attacks are defined as a datatype and attack sequences as lists over them. Base attacks consist of actor's moves to locations, performing of actions and stealing of credentials stored at locations as expressed in the following datatype definition.

```
datatype baseattack = Goto "location"
                     | Perform "action"
                     | Credential "location"
```

The following datatype definition **attree** defines attack trees. The simplest case of an attack tree is a base attack. Attacks can also be combined as the conjunction or disjunction of other attacks. The operator $\oplus_\vee$ creates or-trees and $\oplus_\wedge$ creates and-trees. And-attack trees $l\oplus_\wedge^s$ and or-attack trees $l\oplus_\vee^s$ combine lists of attack trees l either conjunctively or disjunctively on the attack goal s. The attack goal s is of arbitrary type α. It can be instantiated simply to the type **string** to represent the attack goal "informally" by an attack name. However, we can here also instantiate to a predicate type thereby enabling a constructive predicative description of the attack state using logic.

```
datatype attree = BaseAttack "baseattack" ("𝒩 (_)")
                | AndAttack "attree list" "α"   ("_ ⊕^(-)_∧")
                | OrAttack  "attree list" "α"   ("_ ⊕^(-)_∨")
```

The functions **get_attseq** and **get_attack** are corresponding projections on attack trees returning the entire attack sequence or the final attack (the root), respectively. They are needed for defining the rule for attack refinement in Sect. 2.4.

2.3   Kripke Structures

Due to the expressiveness of Higher Order Logic (HOL), Isabelle allows us to formalise within HOL the notion of Kripke structures and temporal logic by directly encoding the fixpoint definitions for each of the CTL operators [6]. To realize this, a change of the considered system's state needs to be incorporated into Isabelle. A relation on system states is defined as an inductive predicate called **state_transition**. It introduces the syntactic infix notation I $\rightarrow_i$ I' to denote that system state I and I' are in this relation.

```
inductive state_transition :: [state, state] ⇒ bool  ("_  →ᵢ _")
```

The definition of this inductive relation is given by a set of specific rules which are, however, not yet necessary to understand the notion of a Kripke structure and attack trees. They can be left out for the moment and will be introduced in Sect. 4.1, when we present the application of a healthcare Insider attack.

The set of states of a Kripke structure can be defined as the set of states reachable by the state transition from some initial state, for example, **Istate**.

```
Example_states ≡ { I. Istate →ᵢ^* I }
```

The relation $\rightarrow_i$^* is the reflexive transitive closure – an operator supplied by the Isabelle theory library – applied to the relation $\rightarrow_i$.

The **Kripke** constructor combines a set of states, like the above example, and an initial state into a Kripke structure that is the graph formed by the closure over the state transition relation $\rightarrow_i$ starting in the initial state.

```
Example_Kripke ≡ Kripke Example_states {Istate}
```

When we now try to verify that some global security policy, say **global_policy**, holds for all paths globally in the example system, this can be expressed as follows in our Isabelle embedding of Kripke structures and branching time logic CTL [6].

```
Example_Kripke ⊢ AG global_policy
```

The relation $\rightarrow_i$ provides a transition between states of a system. State transitions transform a state into another state by actions that change this state. In the human centric systems that we focus on, these actions are executed by actors. By contrast for attack trees, we have not yet explicitly introduced an effect on the system's state but we equally investigate and refine attacks as sequences of actions eventually mapping those actions onto sequences of base attacks. In the current approach, we use the Kripke models as the *semantics* for the attack tree analysis. More precisely, the sequences of attack steps that are eventually found by the process of refining an attack, need to be checked against sequences of state transitions possible in the Kripke structure that consists of the graph of system state changes.

Technically, we need a slight transformation between sequences of steps of the system's state changing relation $\rightarrow_i$ and sequences of actions of actors leading to states where policies are violated. We simply annotate the state transitions by actions. Then, sequences of actions naturally correspond to the paths that determine the way through the Kripke structure and can be one-to-one translated into attack vectors.

Formally, we simply define a relation very similar to $\rightarrow_i$ but with an additional parameter added as a superscript after the arrow.

```
inductive state_step ::  [state, action, state] ⇒ bool  ("_ →(-) _")
```

We define an iterator relation `state_step_list` over the `state_step` that enables collecting the action sequences over state transition paths.

```
inductive state_step_list :: [state, action list, state] ⇒ bool
              ("_ →(-) _")
where
  state_step_list_empty: I →[] I |
  state_step_list_step : [ I →[a] I'; I' →l I'' ]
                         ⟹ I →a#l I''
```

With this extended relation on states we can now trace the action sequences. Finally, a simple translation of attack sequences from the attack tree model to action sequences can simply be formalised by first defining a translation of base attacks to actions.

```
primrec transform :: baseattack ⇒ action
where
  transform_move:     transform (Goto l') = move |
  transform_get:      transform (Credential l') = get |
  transform_perform:  transform (Perform a) = a
```

From this we define a function `transf` for transforming sequences of attacks.

```
primrec transf :: baseattack list ⇒ action list
where
  transf_empty : transf [] = [] |
  transf_step:   transf (ba#l) = (transform ba)#(transf l)
```

2.4   Attack Refinement

The main construction concept for attack trees is *refinement* defined by an inductive predicate `refines_to` syntactically represented as the infix operator $\sqsubseteq$. Intuitively, refinement corresponds to developing an attack tree from the root to the leaves (see Fig. 2). Refinement is an order relation on sub-trees of an attack tree formalising this intuition. There are rules `trans` and `refl` making the refinement a preorder; the rule `refineI` shows how attack vectors can be integrated into the refinement process by extending an abstract attack into a conjunctive sequence of more concrete attacks. The term `sublist_rep l a (get_attseq A)` replaces an attack `a` by the attack sequence `l` in the attack sequence of attack tree `A` given by its leaves. The definition of this function is a straightforward recursive list function and omitted here for brevity [7]. The rule `refineO` defines how an attack `A` can be refined into a disjunction of attacks `as` if each of these attacks refines `A`. The complete definition of the inductive definition of attack tree refinement is given in Table 1.

Table 1. Attack tree refinement: inductive definition containing defining rules.

```
inductive refines_to :: [attree, state, attree] ⇒ bool  ("_ ⊑₍.₎ _")
  where
  refineI: ⟦ I →ᵢ* I'; I' →ˡ' I''; transf l = l';
             sublist_rep l a (get_attseq A) = (get_attseq A');
             get_attack A = get_attack A' ⟧ ⟹ A ⊑ᵢ A' |
  refineO: ∀ A' ∈ set(as). A ⊑ᵢ A' ∧ get_attack A = s ⟹ A ⊑ᵢ as ⊕ᵥˢ |
  trans:   ⟦ A ⊑ᵢ A'; A' ⊑ᵢ A'' ⟧ ⟹ A ⊑ᵢ A'' |
  refl :   A ⊑ᵢ A
```

An application can be seen in Sect. 4.3 where we apply the attack tree analysis to the health care case study.

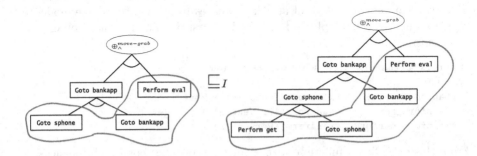

Fig. 2. Attack refinement for healthcare case study (see also Sect. 4.3).

The refinement of attacks allows the expansion of top level abstract attacks into longer sequences or disjunctions. Ultimately, we need to have a notion of when a sufficiently refined sequence of attacks is valid. This notion is provided by the *proof calculus* for attack trees which allows the deduction of validity of attacks expressed formally as $I, h \vdash a$ saying that in the state I the actor h can perform attack a. The proof calculus integrates attack tree refinement and is presented in the following Sect. 3.

3   Proof Calculus

The proof calculus for attack trees provides a notion of validity of an attack tree with respect to a given system and an attacker. The definition of the proof calculus for attack trees is given in Tables 2 and 3.

For individual attack steps, it presupposes a definition of the behaviour of an attacker in a system given by the **enables** predicate to set off the derivation of valid base attacks (rules **att_act**, **att_goto**, **att_cred**). This **enables** predicate is treated here as an abstract predicate over the state describing whether an actor is entitled by the policy to execute a specific action. In the application example in the following section, we will see an example for a concrete definition for this enables predicate in the Isabelle Insider framework.

The rule **att_ref** states that an abstract attack that can be refined into a valid concrete attack is itself valid. The rule **att_comp_and** defines how an attack **as** $\oplus_\wedge^{s'}$ can be conjoined with a valid conjunctive attack **as'** $\oplus_\wedge^{s}$ into a larger conjunctive attack **as @ as'** $\oplus_\wedge^{s}$. The operator **@** is the Isabelle list operator for appending two lists. In this rule, the system state **I** before the first attack needs to allow a state transition **I** $\rightarrow^*$ **I'** to the state **I'** before the second attack. Since Isabelle is a Higher Order Logic theorem prover, the variables **I**, **I'** are higher order variables. This permits a flexible instantiation within a derivation and a gradual development of concrete states that exhibit corresponding pre-conditions and post-conditions of attacks. Since we use the reflexive transitive closure $\rightarrow^*$ (available in Isabelle as a constructor of relations) the rule also allows the pre-states and post-states **I**, **I'** to be identical. Thus, we can in one rule express sequential and concurrent conjunctive attacks. We do not need a separate rule for SAND as in other foundations for attack trees, e.g. [5]. The rule for disjunctive composition uses universal quantification to express that a list of disjunctive attacks needs to have the same pre-state and post-state (these states **I**, **I'** are fixed by the same quantifier) in order to be unified in an "or" attack tree. The rule **att_comp_and** defines how two and-sequences of attacks can be added to one larger attack.

As a consequence of introducing also or-attacks for attack trees, we naturally create the need to define how or-attacks and and-attacks relate to each other. We therefore extend the inductive definition with the distribution rules presented in Table 3.

An advantage of using an interactive theorem prover like Isabelle is that the rules of the inductive definition can be used to derive within the theorem prover. This avoids introducing inconsistencies but in general also enables the development of meta-theory, i.e., theoretical consequences of the definitions of

Table 2. Proof calculus for attack trees: main part

```
inductive is_and_attack_tree :: [state, actor, attree] ⇒ bool
        ("_, _ ⊢ _")
where
  att_act: enables I l h a ⟹ I , h ⊢ 𝒩(Perform(a)) |
  att_goto: enables I l h (move) ⟹ I, h ⊢ 𝒩(Goto l) |
  att_cred: enables I l h (get) ⟹ I, h ⊢  𝒩(Credential l) |
  att_ref: ⟦ A ⊑ᵢ A'; I, h ⊢ A' ⟧ ⟹ I, h ⊢ A |
  att_and_one: I, h ⊢ a  ⟹ I, h ⊢ [a] ⊕ˢ∧  |
  att_comp_and: ⟦ I, h ⊢  as ⊕ˢ∧; I →* I'; I', h ⊢  as' ⊕ˢ∧ ⟧
             ⟹ I, h ⊢ as @ as' ⊕ˢ∧ |
  att_comp_or:  ⟦ ∀ a ∈ (set(as)). I, h ⊢ a ∧ get_attack a = s ⟧
             ⟹ I, h ⊢ as ⊕ˢ∨
  ...
```

Table 3. Proof calculus for attack trees: distributivity rules

```
...
att_and_distr_left: I, h ⊢ ( [a,(as ⊕ˢ∨)] ⊕ˢ∧)
           ⟹ I, h ⊢ ((map (λ x. [a, x]⊕ˢ∧) as) ⊕ˢ∨) |
att_and_distr_right: I, h ⊢ ( [(as ⊕ˢ∨),a] ⊕ˢ∧)
           ⟹ I, h ⊢ ((map (λ x. [x, a] ⊕ˢ∧) as) ⊕ˢ∨) |
att_or_distr_left: I, h ⊢ ((map (λ x. [a, x]⊕ˢ∧) as) ⊕ˢ∨)
           ⟹ I, h ⊢ ( [a,(as ⊕ˢ∨)] ⊕ˢ∧) |
att_or_assoc_right: I, h ⊢ ((map (λ x. [x, a] ⊕ˢ∧) as) ⊕ˢ∨)
           ⟹ I, h ⊢ ( [(as ⊕ˢ∨),a] ⊕ˢ∧)
```

the concepts, here attack trees. For example, standard rules, like associativity rules, for attack trees can be derived. But also other rules, like for example a "one-step" composition rule for and-attacks adding just a single attack a at the front of an attack sequence as using the cons-operation # on lists.

```
lemma att_comp_and_cons:  ⟦ I, h ⊢  a ; I', h ⊢ as ⊕ˢ∧; I →* I' ⟧
             ⟹ (I, h ⊢ (a # as) ⊕ˢ∧)
```

In this paper, we base the definitions of system, actors, their behaviour, and the corresponding state transitions on the Isabelle Insider framework. The presented proof calculus for attack trees is easily applicable to other models of applications by exchanging the behaviour predicate and using the corresponding state transition relation. The calculus only considers attacks by single actors. An extension to sets of actors can be defined in a straightforward manner based on this calculus.

4   Application: Insider Attack in IoT Healthcare

In this section, we finally illustrate how the proof calculus for attack trees is applied to an example. We instantiate the formalism to the Isabelle Insider framework that supports the representation of infrastructures as graphs with actors and policies attached to nodes. These infrastructures are the *states* of the Kripke structure for the attack trees. This section gives a brief summary of the main relevant parts of the Isabelle Insider framework: actions, actors, infrastructures, behaviour and state transition relation. We next give a summary of our health care case study before illustrating how the attack tree analysis is performed on it using the attack tree mechanism.

4.1   Isabelle Insider Framework

The Isabelle Insider framework [11] is based on a logical process of sociological explanation [4] inspired by Weber's *Grundmodell*, to explain Insider threats by moving between societal level (macro) and individual actor level (micro).

The interpretation into a logic of explanation is formalized in the Isabelle Insider framework [11]. The micro-level and macro-level of the sociological explanation give rise to a two-layered model in Isabelle, reflecting first the psychological disposition and motivation of actors and second the graph of the infrastructure where nodes are locations with actors associated to them. Security policies can be defined over the agents, their properties, and the infrastructure graph; properties can be proved mechanically with Isabelle.

In the Isabelle/HOL theory for Insiders, one expresses policies over actions get, move, eval, and put. The framework abstracts from concrete data – actions have no parameters:

```
datatype action = get | move | eval | put
```

The human component is the *Actor* which is represented by an abstract type actor and a function Actor that creates elements of that type from identities (of type string):

```
typedecl actor
type_synonym identity = string
consts Actor :: string ⇒ actor
```

Policies describe prerequisites for actions to be granted to actors given by pairs of predicates (conditions) and sets of (enabled) actions:

```
type_synonym policy = ((actor ⇒ bool) × action set)
```

Policies are integrated with a graph into the infrastructure providing an organisational model where policies reside at locations and actors are adorned with additional predicates to specify their 'credentials', and a predicate over locations to encode attributes of infrastructure components:

```
datatype infrastructure = Infrastructure
                "igraph" "location ⇒ policy set"
                "actor ⇒ bool" "location ⇒ bool"
```

These local policies serve to provide a specification of the 'normal' behaviour of actors but are also the starting point for possible attacks on the organisation's infrastructure. The `enables` predicate specifies that an actor `a` can perform an action `a'∈ e` at location `l` in the infrastructure `I` if `a`'s credentials (stored in the tuple space `tspace I a`) imply the location policy's (stored in `delta I l`) condition `p` for `a`:

```
enables I l a' ≡ ∃ (p,e) ∈ delta I l. a' ∈ e
                ∧ (tspace I a ∧ lspace I l ⟶ p(a))
```

This definition of the behaviour for the Insider framework allows to define the rules for the state transition relation of the Kripke structure (see Sect. 2.3) for each of the actions. Here is the rule for move.

```
move: ⟦ G = graphI I; a @_G l; l ∈ nodes G;
        l' ∈ nodes G; a ∈ actors_graph(graphI I);
        enables I l (Actor a) move;
        I' = Infrastructure (move_graph_a a l l'
            (graphI I))(delta I)(tspace I)(lspace I)
      ⟧ ⟹ I →_i I'
```

4.2 Health Care Case Study

The case study we use as a running example in this paper is a simplified scenario from the context of the SUCCESS project for Security and Privacy of the IoT [3]. A central topic of this project for the pilot case study is to support security and privacy when using cost effective methods based on the IoT for monitoring patients for the diagnosis of Alzheimer's disease. As a starting point for the design, analysis, and construction, we currently develop a case study of a small device for the analysis of blood samples that can be directly connected to a mobile phone. The analysis of this device can then be communicated by a dedicated app on the smart phone that sends the data to a server in the hospital.

In this simplified scenario, there are the patient and the carer within a room together with the smart phone.

We focus on the carer having access to the phone in order to support the patient in handling the special diagnosis device, the smart phone, and the app.

The insider threat scenario has a second banking app on the smart phone that needs the additional authentication of a "secret key": a small electronic device providing authentication codes for one time use as they are used by many banks for private online banking.

Assuming that the carer finds this device in the room of the patient, he can steal this necessary credential and use it to get onto the banking app. Thereby he can get money from the patient's account without consent.

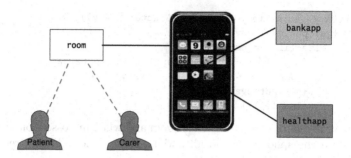

Fig. 3. Health care scenario: carer and patient in the room may use smartphone apps.

4.3   Health Care Case Study in Isabelle Insider Framework

We only model two identities, `Patient` and `Carer` representing a patient and his carer. We define the health care scenario in the locale `scenarioHealthcare`. The syntax `fixes` and `defines` are keywords of locales that we drop together with the types for clarity of the exposition from now on. The double quotes `''s''` represent strings in Isabelle/HOL. The global policy is 'no one except the patient can use the bank app':

```
fixes global_policy :: [infrastructure, identity] ⇒ bool
defines  global_policy I a ≡  a ≠ ''Patient'' ⟶
                ¬(enables I bankapp (Actor a) eval)
```

The graph representing the infrastructure of the health care case study has the following locations: (0) smart phone, (1) room, (2) bank app, and (3) health app: In order to define the infrastructure, we first define the graph representing the scenario's locations and the positions of its actors. The actors patient and carer are both initially in room. The graph is given as a set of nodes of locations and the actors residing at certain locations are specified by a function associating lists of nodes with the locations.

```
ex_graph ≡
  Lgraph {(room, sphone), (sphone, healthapp),
         (sphone, bankapp)}
        (λ x. if x = room then
              [''Patient'', ''Carer''] else [])
```

In the following definition of local policies for each node in the office scenario, we additionally include the parameter G for the graph. The predicate @$_G$ checks whether an actor is at a given location in the graph G.

```
local_policies G  ≡
  (λ x. if x = room then {(λ y. True,{get, put, move})}
    else (if x = sphone then
    {((λ y. has (y, ''PIN'')), {put,get,eval,move}), (λ y. True, {})}
        else (if x = healthapp then
```

```
{((λ y. (∃ n. (n @_G sphone) ∧ Actor n = y)),
  {get,put,eval,move})}
    else (if x = bankapp then
      {((λ y. (∃ n. (n @_G sphone) ∨ (n @_G bankapp)
        ∧ Actor n = y ∧ has (y, ''skey''))),
        {get,put,eval,move})}
      else {}))))
```

In this policy, any actor can move to the room and when in possession of the PIN can move onto the sphone and do all actions there. The following restrictions are placed on the two other locations.

healthapp: to move onto the healthapp and perform any action at this location, an actor must be at the position sphone already;

bankapp: to move onto the bankapp and perform any action at this location, an actor must be at the position sphone already and in possession of the skey.

The possession of credentials like PINs or the skey is assigned in the infrastructure as well as the roles that actors can have. We define this assignment as predicate over actors being true for actors that have these credentials. For the health care scenario, the credentials express that the actors Patient and Carer possess the PIN for the sphone but Patient also has the skey.

```
ex_creds ≡
  (λ x. if x = Actor ''Patient'' then
            has (x,''PIN'') ∧ has (x, ''skey'')
        else (if x = Actor ''Carer'' then
            has (x, ''PIN'') else True))
```

The graph and credentials are put into the infrastructure hc_scenario.

```
hc_scenario ≡ Infrastructure
                ex_graph (local_policies ex_graph)
                ex_creds ex_locs
```

4.4 Attack Tree Analysis

System states in the application to the Insider framework are given by infrastructures. The initial state corresponds to the above hc_scenario; following states are introduced by applying the state transition function. We introduce the following definitions to denote changes to the infrastructure. A first step towards critical states is that the carer gets onto the smart phone. We first define the changed infrastructure graph.

```
ex_graph' ≡ Lgraph
              {(room, sphone), (sphone, healthapp),
               (sphone, bankapp)}
              (λ x. if x = room
                    then [''Patient''] else
                      (λ x. if x = sphone
                            then [''Carer''] else []))
```

The dangerous state has a graph in which the actor `Carer` is on the bankapp.

```
ex_graph'' ≡  Lgraph
                {(room, sphone), (sphone, healthapp),
                 (sphone, bankapp)}
                (λ x. if x = room
                        then [''Patient''] else
                        (λ x. if x = bankapp
                                then [''Carer''] else []))
```

The critical state of the credentials is where the carer has the skey as well.

```
ex_creds' ≡
  (λ x. if x = Actor ''Patient'' then
              has (x,''PIN'') ∧ has (x, ''skey'')
         else (if x = Actor ''Carer'' then
              has (x, ''PIN'') ∧ has (x, ''skey'')
              else True))
```

We use these changed state components to define a series of infrastructure states.

```
hc_scenario'   ≡ Infrastructure
                   ex_graph (local_policies ex_graph)
                   ex_creds' ex_locs
hc_scenario''  ≡ Infrastructure
                   ex_graph'(local_policies ex_graph')
                   ex_creds' ex_locs
hc_scenario'''≡ Infrastructure
                   ex_graph''(local_policies ex_graph'')
                   ex_creds' ex_locs
```

We next look at the abstract attack that we want to analyse before we see how Kripke structures and temporal logic support the analysis.

The abstract attack is stated as [Goto bankapp, Perform eval] $\oplus_{\wedge}^{move-grab}$. The following refinement encodes a logical explanation of how this attack can happen by the carer taking the skey, getting on the phone, on the bankapp and then evaluating.

[Goto bankapp, Perform eval] $\oplus_{\wedge}^{move-grab}$
$\sqsubseteq_{hc\_scenario}$
[Perform get, Goto sphone, Goto bankapp, Perform eval] $\oplus_{\wedge}^{move-grab}$

This refinement is proved by applying the rule **refineI** (see Sect. 2.4). In fact, this attack could be *found* by applying **refineI** and using interactive proof with Isabelle to instantiate the higher order parameter ?l in the following resulting subgoal.

hc_scenario $\rightarrow^{\mathrm{transf}(?l)}$ hc_scenario'''

This proof results in instantiating the variable ?l to the required attack sequence [Perform get, Goto sphone, Goto bankapp, Perform eval].

So far, we have used the combination of a slightly adapted notion of the state transition of the Kripke structures to build a model for attack refinement of attack trees. We can further use the correspondence between Kripke structures and attack trees to find attacks. We first define the Kripke structure for the health case scenario representing the state graph of all infrastructure states reachable from the initial state.

```
hc_states ≡ { I. hc_scenario →ᵢ* I }
hc_Kripke ≡ Kripke hc_states {hc_scenario}
```

Since it is embedded into Isabelle [6], we may use branching time logic CTL to express that the global policy (see Sect. 4.3) holds for all paths globally.

```
hc_Kripke ⊢ AG {x. global_policy x ''Carer''}
```

Trying to prove this must fail. However, using instead the idea of invalidation [10] we can prove the negated global policy.

```
hc_Kripke ⊢ EF {x. ¬ global_policy x ''Carer''}
```

The interactive proof of this EF property means proving the theorem

```
hc_Kripke ⊢ EF {x. enables x bankapp
                      (Actor ''Carer'') eval}
```

This results in establishing a trace l that goes from the initial state hc_scenario to a state I such that enables I bankapp (Actor ''Carer'') eval. This I is for example hc_scenario''' and the action path get, move, move is a side product of this proof. Together with the states on this path the transf function delivers the required attack path [Perform get, Goto sphone, Goto bankapp, Perform eval].

5   Conclusion

Summarizing, we have provided a mechanized foundation for attack trees. The semantics of attack trees has been defined using an embedding of modelchecking in Isabelle leading to a proof calculus for attack trees. We illustrated the benefits on a health care case study of an Insider attack using the semantics on the Isabelle Insider framework infrastructures as our system state but this state model can be replaced by other suitable state models to apply Isabelle attack trees and Kripke structures.

There is a range of observations concerning the relation between attack trees and Kripke structures in Isabelle that we presented in this paper and whose conception, construction, and demonstration represents our contribution.

– Kripke structures can be used as the underlying semantics for state based systems interpreting the attacks, i.e., providing semantics for attack trees.
– Therefore, the state transition relation can be used to define refinement steps in the refinement part of a proof calculus for attack trees.

- Higher Order Logic variables for pre-states and post-states of an attack step can be dynamically derived in applications of our proof calculus.
- Temporal logic formulas in the branching time logic CTL can be used in our Isabelle framework extension supporting the detection of attacks.
- The attack tree proof calculus serves as a logical basis to judge the validity of an attack in a given model.
- The attack tree proof calculus can be applied to case studies as demonstrated on an IoT health care application case study.

Clearly relevant to this work are the Isabelle Insider framework and its extensions [6,8,9,11] but also the related experiments with the invalidation approach for Insider threat analysis using classic implementation techniques like static analysis and implementation in Java [15] or probabilistic modeling and analysis [2].

We believe that the combination of Kripke structures and attack trees is novel in the way we tie these concepts up at the foundational level. Considering the simplicity of this pragmatically driven approach and the relative ease with which we arrived at convincing results, it seems a fruitful prospect to further explore this combination. Beyond the mere finding of attack vectors in proofs, the expressivity of Higher Order Logic will allow developing meta-theory that in turn can be used for the transfer between state based reasoning and attack tree analysis.

The presented foundation of attack trees in Isabelle is consistent with the existing foundations [5,12,13] but instead of providing an on paper mathematical foundation it provides a direct formalisation in Higher Order Logic in the proof assistant. This enables the application of the resulting framework to case studies and does not necessitate a separate implementation of the mathematical foundation in a dedicated tool. Clearly, the application to case studies requires user interaction. However, the formalisation in Isabelle supports not only the application of the formalised theory but furthermore the consistent development of meta-theorems thus guaranteeing consistency at all levels. In addition, dedicated proof automation by additional proof of supporting lemmas is straightforward and even code generation is possible for executable parts of the formalisation.

In comparison to the existing foundations [5,12,13], the presented attack tree framework only covers a portion of available extensions for attack trees. For example, it does not support attack-defense trees, i.e., the integration of defenses within the attack tree. This is a straightforward future development. Other work on attack trees includes the extension of the formalism by probabilities and time [1]. To support this quantitative analysis, automated verification techniques using modelchecking with the UPPAAL system and timed automata are applied as well [14]. This direct application of modelchecking provides automated analysis of attack trees but unlike our proof theory for attack trees it does not allow any proofs about attack trees. Thereby, the consistency and partially also the adequacy of the model is not guaranteed. However, we believe that a complementary use of these works with our more expressive formalisation is fruitful for developing secure systems from early requirements.

References

1. Arnold, F., Hermanns, H., Pulungan, R., Stoelinga, M.: Time-dependent analysis of attacks. In: Abadi, M., Kremer, S. (eds.) POST 2014. LNCS, vol. 8414, pp. 285–305. Springer, Heidelberg (2014). doi:10.1007/978-3-642-54792-8_16

2. Chen, T., Kammüller, F., Nemli, I., Probst, C.W.: A probabilistic analysis framework for malicious insider threats. In: Tryfonas, T., Askoxylakis, I. (eds.) HAS 2015. LNCS, vol. 9190, pp. 178–189. Springer, Cham (2015). doi:10.1007/978-3-319-20376-8_16

3. CHIST-ERA. Success: Secure accessibility for the internet of things (2016). http://www.chistera.eu/projects/success

4. Hempel, C.G., Oppenheim, P.: Studies in the logic of explanation. Philos. Sci. **15**, 135–175 (1948)

5. Jhawar, R., Kordy, B., Mauw, S., Radomirović, S., Trujillo-Rasua, R.: Attack trees with sequential conjunction. In: Federrath, H., Gollmann, D. (eds.) SEC 2015. IFIP AICT, vol. 455, pp. 339–353. Springer, Cham (2015). doi:10.1007/978-3-319-18467-8_23

6. Kammüller, F.: Isabelle modelchecking for insider threats. In: Livraga, G., Torra, V., Aldini, A., Martinelli, F., Suri, N. (eds.) DPM/QASA -2016. LNCS, vol. 9963, pp. 196–210. Springer, Cham (2016). doi:10.1007/978-3-319-47072-6_13

7. Kammüller, F.: Isabelle insider framework with Kripke structures, CTL, attack trees and refinement (2017). https://www.dropbox.com/sh/rx8d09pf31cv8bd/AAALKtaP8HMX642fi04Og4NLa?dl=0

8. Kammüller, F., Kerber, M., Probst, C.: Towards formal analysis of insider threats for auctions. In: 8th ACM CCS International Workshop on Managing Insider Security Threats, MIST 2016. ACM (2016)

9. Kammüller, F., Nurse, J.R.C., Probst, C.W.: Attack tree analysis for insider threats on the IoT using Isabelle. In: Tryfonas, T. (ed.) HAS 2016. LNCS, vol. 9750, pp. 234–246. Springer, Cham (2016). doi:10.1007/978-3-319-39381-0_21

10. Kammüller, F., Probst, C.W.: Invalidating policies using structural information. In: IEEE Security and Privacy Workshops (SPW). IEEE (2013)

11. Kammüller, F., Probst, C.W.: Modeling and verification of insider threats using logical analysis. IEEE Syst. J. Special Issue Insider Threats Inf. Secur., Digit. Espionage, Counter Intell. **11**, 534–545 (2017)

12. Kordy, B., Mauw, S., Radomirovic, S., Schweitzer, P.: Attack-defense trees. J. Logic Comput. **24**(1), 55–87 (2014)

13. Kordy, B., Piètre-Cambacédès, L., Schweitzer, P.: Dag-based attack and defense modeling: don't miss the forest for the attack trees. Comput. Sci. Rev. **13–14**, 1–38 (2014)

14. Kumar, R., Ruijters, E., Stoelinga, M.: Quantitative attack tree analysis via priced timed automata. In: Sankaranarayanan, S., Vicario, E. (eds.) FORMATS 2015. LNCS, vol. 9268, pp. 156–171. Springer, Cham (2015). doi:10.1007/978-3-319-22975-1_11

15. Probst, C.W., Kammüller, F., Hansen, R.R.: Formal modelling and analysis of socio-technical systems. In: Probst, C.W., Hankin, C., Hansen, R.R. (eds.) Semantics, Logics, and Calculi. LNCS, vol. 9560, pp. 54–73. Springer, Cham (2016). doi:10.1007/978-3-319-27810-0_3

16. Schneier, B.: Secrets and Lies: Digital Security in a Networked World. Wiley, New York (2004)

Confidentiality of Interactions in Concurrent Object-Oriented Systems

Olaf Owe$^{(\boxtimes)}$ and Toktam Ramezanifarkhani

Department of Informatics, University of Oslo, Oslo, Norway
{olaf,toktamr}@ifi.uio.no

Abstract. We consider a general concurrency model for distributed systems, based on concurrent objects communicating by asynchronous methods. This model is suitable for modeling of modern service-oriented systems, and gives rise to efficient interaction avoiding active waiting and low-level synchronization primitives such as explicit signaling and lock operations. This concurrency model has a simple semantics and allows us to focus on information flow at a high level of abstraction, and allows realistic analysis by avoiding unnecessary restrictions on information flow between confidential and non-confidential data. We formalize our approach by introducing a high-level language for this concurrency model, and we provide a secrecy-type system to capture inter-object communication. We prove soundness based on an operational semantics, which includes runtime secrecy levels.

Keywords: Concurrent objects · Asynchronous methods · Communication patterns · Information flow · Secrecy · Confidentiality · Distributed systems · Inter-object leakage

1 Introduction

Programming languages can provide fine-grained control for security issues because they allow accurate and flexible security information analysis of program components [8]. In particular, to specify and enforce information-flow policies, the effectiveness of language-based techniques has been established. Secure information flows are often expressed by semantic models of program execution in the form of a *noninterference* policy. Noninterference stipulates that manipulation and modification of confidential data should be allowed in programs, as long as their visible outputs do not improperly reveal information about the confidential data. Attackers are assumed to be able to view "low" information. The usual method for showing that noninterference holds is to demonstrate that the attacker cannot observe any difference between two executions that differ only in their confidential input [7]. However, attackers may also see intermediate outputs [1] and observe the progress of the program, e.g., absence or presence

Work supported by the IoTSec and DiversIoT projects, the Norw. Research Council.

J. Garcia-Alfaro et al. (Eds.): DPM/CBT 2017, LNCS 10436, pp. 19–34, 2017.
DOI: 10.1007/978-3-319-67816-0_2

of the next observable value, which leads to the concept of progress-sensitive noninterference [1].

In this paper, we are interested in service-oriented and object-oriented systems at a high level of abstraction, and consider the setting of distributed concurrent objects communicating by asynchronous methods calls. We focus on efficient interaction, including non-blocking calls and high-level mechanisms for process control, suitable for modern service-oriented systems. Our notion of noninterference reflects the non-deterministic nature of interacting concurrent objects.

Fields are encapsulated by objects and remote access is forbidden. Thus, fields are non-observable, and the (typically) illegal flows in the sense of assignment of confidential values to non-confidential variables inside objects are not critical.

To formalize our approach we introduce a high-level imperative language based on the chosen concurrency model. This language is derived from the object-oriented language *Creol* [12]. We define an extension of Creol called *SeCreol*, adding awareness of secrecy levels as well as secrecy type information. We define an operational semantics, and prove that our secrecy-type system is sound with respect to the operational semantics, ensuring that every well-typed program of our language satisfies the proposed non-interference property.

2   Object-Oriented Distributed Systems in SeCreol

We consider concurrent, distributed objects where each object has its own execution thread. An object does not have access to the internal state variables of other objects. Communication is only by method calls, allowing asynchronous and synchronous communication, implemented by means of asynchronous message passing. In order to avoid undesirable waiting in the distributed setting, we allow mechanisms for non-blocking method calls. By means of a suspension mechanism, unfinished method invocations in an object may be placed on the object's process queue, for instance while waiting for a response from another object. The process will be enabled when then object receives the response. This allows flexible interleaving of incoming calls and (enabled) suspended processes. Internally in an object, there is at most one process executing at any time. Objects reflect concurrent system components, while data structure inside an object is defined by data types using functional programming.

A *SeCreol* program consists of a number of interfaces and classes (with the last class being the "main" class). An interface may have a number of super-interfaces and method declarations. A class C takes a list of class parameters cp, defines fields w, and has an optional initialization part followed by method definitions. Class parameters cp are like fields apart from being initialized through the **new** statement. Class parameters, the implicit class parameter this, and the implicit method parameter caller are read-only. A class may implement a number of interfaces, and for each method of an interface it is required that the class implements the method such that the type and secrecy level information is respected. Additional methods may be defined in a class as well, but these may not be called from outside the class. All variables and parameters are typed by data types or interfaces. Classes are not allowed as types, which means that an object can only be seen through an interface, and therefore, remote access to fields nor methods that are not exported through an interface is not allowed. Thus shared variable concurrency is avoided. With respect to security analysis, fields are then not observable, and observable behavior is limited to interactions by means of method-oriented communication.

Expressions e and functions f are side-effect free, and $\bar{e}$ is a (possibly empty) expression list, comma-separated. Statements include standard constructs for assignment, skip, if, while, object generation, and sequential composition. The *simple call* statement $e!m(\bar{e})$ is like message passing; a message is sent to the object expressed by e (the callee) indicating that it should execute method m (when the callee is free to do this) with a list of actual parameters $\bar{e}$. Thus the current object is not blocked, and will not wait for the return value. If the return value is desired by the calling object, it may use the *blocking call* statement $v := e.m(\bar{e})$ or the *non-blocking call* statement **await** $v := e.m(\bar{e})$. The latter call statement forces the caller object to suspend the current process, allowing it to continue with any enabled suspended process in its process queue or handle incoming calls. Similarly, the conditional await statement **await** e suspends, placing the current process on the process queue. This process is enabled when the Boolean condition e is satisfied. The considered core language allows high-level and yet efficient method-based interaction, supporting both passive and active waiting. The operational semantics of SeCreol is given in Sect. 4.

The language is strongly typed, and a typing system can be given in the style of [13]. A variable is typed either by an interface or by a data type, called *object variable* or *data variable*, respectively. The runtime value of an object variable is an object identity (or null), and that of a data variable is a data value. Data variables are passed by value and object variables are passed by reference (i.e., the object identity is passed by value). Note that all object expressions are typed by an interface, except this, which is typed by the enclosing class. In a well-typed program, we may assume that each call is annotated by the interface/class of the callee, as in $o.m_I(\ldots)$ where I contains a declaration of m.

Secrecy Levels. We enrich the typing system with *secrecy levels*. Secrecy levels range over $\mathcal{L}$ of basic secrecy descriptions with ordering $\sqsubseteq$, such that $(\mathcal{L}, \sqsubseteq)$ is a lattice, i.e., a partially ordered set with *meet* ($\sqcap$), *join* ($\sqcup$), a top element $\top$ and bottom element $\perp$. Higher in the lattice means more secure. A lattice may be indexed by object identities for controlling access rights. This would be essential at runtime for controlling object secrecy; however, in our static analysis we will not use levels indexed by identities, since there is limited static knowledge about object identities.

In a program, all declarations of fields, formal parameters, and return values are given a secrecy level, with level Low as default (if none is specified). Local variables do not have a declared secrecy level; their level starts as Low but may change after each statement. At runtime, objects are assigned a secrecy level that protects against unauthorized changes. Such a protected part is typical in policy enforcement research [6]. The statically assigned level of a formal data parameter represents the maximal level of any actual parameter. The declared secrecy level of an object variable expresses the secrecy of the object identity, which is typically *low*, reflecting that object *identities* (as such) are considered non-secret, whereas the runtime secrecy level of an object gives more detailed information, for instance about the access rights of the object.

The static analysis is class-based, and therefore the analysis is based on the (statically) declared levels, and not the runtime object levels. However, the language allows specification of restrictions on the secrecy level of a new object (as in x:=new C():Low) which determines the initial runtime secrecy level of the generated object. At runtime an object generated by the statement x:=new C():l will get the level $l \sqcap l_{this}$ where l_{this} is the level of the parent object. Note that $l \sqcap l_{this} \sqsubseteq l_{this}$, ensuring that the secrecy level of the generated object will not exceed that of the parent object. As an object encapsulates local data and fields, these are not accessible from outside of the object, and we do not need static control of write access to fields of an object. In a program, the runtime secrecy level of an object can be tested using the $\sqsubseteq$ operation.

In the static analysis, we consider all possibilities for levels that can be assigned at runtime. This allows us to detect a maximal secrecy level for each program variables at a given point in a program (see Sect. 3).

3   Secrecy-Type System

Our analysis is done class-wise, which is possible since remote access to fields is forbidden and since all object interaction is done by methods declared in an interface. This means that limitations on information flow between high and low variables (such as $v_{High} := v_{Low}$ and $v_{High} := v_{Low}$) are not needed. However, we rely on level information about fields before and after suspension, maintained in a way similar to a class invariant. The secrecy analysis of a class only depends on that class declaration, related interfaces, and the class parameter declaration of instantiated classes.

We assume a well-typed program and assume each method call $e.m(\ldots)$ is augmented by annotating the method name m by the interface of the callee e (as in $e.m_I(\ldots)$), or the enclosing class when e is this. The secrecy-type system for classes and methods are shown in Fig. 1. The confidentiality of a class definition Cl is formalized by judgments of the form

$$\vdash Cl \ \mathbf{ok}$$

expressing that the class definition obeys the confidentiality rules. And the confidentiality of a method definition M is formalized by judgments of the form

$$C \vdash M \ \mathbf{ok}$$

where C is the enclosing class. The confidentiality of a *statement* s is formulated by considering judgments of the form

$$C \vdash [\Gamma, pc] \ s \ [\Gamma', pc']$$

$$\frac{C \vdash M_i \text{ ok}, \quad \text{for each } M_i \in \overline{M}}{\vdash \textbf{class } C(\overline{cp} : \overline{U})\{\overline{w} : \overline{U}'; \ \overline{M}\} \text{ ok}} \text{ (S-\textsc{class})}$$

$$\frac{C \vdash [\Gamma_C[\overline{y} \mapsto \mathcal{L}(\overline{U}), \overline{x} \mapsto \textsf{Low}], \textsf{Low}] \ s \ [\Gamma, pc]}{C \vdash [\Gamma, pc] \ e :: l' \quad l' \sqsubseteq l \quad \Gamma[\overline{w}] \sqsubseteq \Gamma_C[\overline{w}]}{C \vdash T{:}l \ m(\overline{y} : \overline{U})\{\textbf{var } \overline{x} : \overline{T}; s; \textbf{return } e\} \text{ ok}} \text{ (S-\textsc{method})}$$

Fig. 1. SeCreol confidentiality type system for classes and methods where Γ_C denotes the declared secrecy levels for class parameters and fields, in class C, and Γ expresses confidentiality information at a particular program point.

where Γ is a mapping binding variable names to confidentiality levels for a given program point, and pc is the confidentiality level of the current program point. As Γ and pc depends on the program point, we let the "pre-binding" $[\Gamma, pc]$ denote the bindings in the pre-state of s and the "post-binding" $[\Gamma', pc']$ those in the post-state of s. Moreover, for a class C we let the mapping Γ_C represent the *declared* secrecy levels of fields and class parameters, as given in the class definition, i.e., if the secrecy level of a field w is declared as l, the binding $w \mapsto l$ is included in Γ_C. The notation $\Lambda[I, m, i]$ denotes the level of the ith parameter of the method as *declared* in interface I, and similarly for classes. For a class C, we let C also denote the class constructor (initialization code). In contrast, Γ expresses confidentiality information depending on a particular program point. Since Γ-levels of class fields can increase and decrease, the type rules insist that at the end of each method (and at each suspension point) their resulting levels should not exceed the declared secrecy levels. This allows us to assume the declared levels at method start and after suspension.

Map Notation. A finite mapping M is given by a set of bindings $z_i \mapsto value_i$ for a finite set of disjoint identifiers z_i, the *domain*. The empty map is denoted $\emptyset$. Map look-up is written $M[z]$. A map update, written $M[z \mapsto d]$, is the map M updated by binding z to d, regardless of any previous bindings of z. Similarly $M[S]$ denotes M updated with a set S of (disjoint) bindings. And the map composition $M + M'$ is the map M overwritten by M' (on the common domain).

According to Rule S-CLASS in Fig. 1, confidentiality of each class is satisfied, or simply is ok, if the confidentiality of each method is satisfied. The confidentiality of a method (see Rule S-METHOD) is satisfied if its body satisfies confidentiality, starting with the declared level bindings (for fields and class parameters, method parameters, and local variables) and with Low as starting pc level, and resulting in some binding $[\Gamma, pc]$ such that Γ respects the declared field and class parameter bindings levels (i.e., $\Gamma[z] \sqsubseteq \Gamma_C[z]$ for each field/class-parameter z) and such that the returned value respects the declared output level of the method. As stated before, we check $\Gamma[z] \sqsubseteq \Gamma_C[z]$ because the secrecy level of program variables is allowed to be changed at different program points.

The SeCreol secrecy-type system for expressions and statements is shown in Figs. 2 and 3, respectively. These figures present typing rules describing which secrecy type is assigned to each occurrence of an expression and program variable. The confidentiality of expressions and right-hand-sides rhs, given in Fig. 2, are formulated by judgments of the form

$$C \vdash [\Gamma, pc] \, rhs :: l$$

where l is the resulting confidentiality level of rhs. The rules check that each occurrence of an actual parameter (or return value) respects the declared level of the corresponding formal parameter (or method return level), and that fields and class parameters respect the corresponding declared levels at suspension points and at method returns. In our formalization this is checked by premises in the rules; thus if these premises cannot be derived, the program will not satisfy the secrecy rules. Note that each statement may adjust Γ, but only **if** and **while** statements may affect pc. Thus the level of variables and pc may differ at different program points, which for example means that a call that is acceptable at one program point, might be unacceptable at another point.

Rule S-EXP states that the confidentiality of an expression e is achieved by $\Gamma[e] \sqcup pc$, where pc represents the context level of the current program branch. Thus a low level expression occurring in a program branch with level pc, gets pc as its level, since it may reveal context information. We define $\Gamma[e]$ as follows: For a constant c (including null, this, *void*, and caller) $\Gamma[c]$ is Low (i.e., $\bot$), $\Gamma[e \sqsubseteq e']$ is High (i.e., $\top$), and for other kinds of expressions (including function applications) $\Gamma[e]$ is defined as $\sqcup_{v \in e} \Gamma[v]$, where v ranges over the variables textually occurring in e, and $\Gamma[v]$ is its level recorded in Γ. (For simplicity, we here ignore so-called sanitizer functions, i.e., special functions resulting in a lower level than an input.)

Moreover, object identities are not confidential, thus object variables are typically declared with a Low level. However, the level of such variables in Γ is affected by the branch level pc as other program variables. Thus the resulting level of object creation is pc as object identities as such are considered Low. For the right-hand-side of a call or new construct, corresponding to the other rules in Fig. 2, each actual parameter is required to have a level not exceeding the declared level of the corresponding formal parameter. The resulting level of the call's right-hand-side is the declared return level of the method, joined with the current context level pc. We observe that $C \vdash [\Gamma, pc] \, rhs :: l \Rightarrow pc \sqsubseteq l$, which means the rhs level is always at least as high as pc. This can be easily proved by looking at each case of a right-hand-side rhs in the rules.

(S-EXP)
$$C \vdash [\Gamma, pc] \, e :: \Gamma[e] \sqcup pc$$

(S-NEW)
$$\frac{C \vdash [\Gamma, pc] \, e_i :: l_i \quad l_i \sqsubseteq \Gamma_{C'}[cp_i]}{C \vdash [\Gamma, pc] \, (\textbf{new } C'(\bar{e}) : l) :: pc}$$

(S-CALL)
$$\frac{C \vdash [\Gamma, pc] \, e_i :: l_i \quad l_i \sqsubseteq \Lambda[I, m, i]}{C \vdash [\Gamma, pc] \, e.m_I(\bar{e}) :: \Lambda[I, m] \sqcup pc}$$

(S-SELFCALL)
$$\frac{C \vdash [\Gamma, pc] \, e_i :: l_i \quad l_i \sqsubseteq \Lambda[C, m, i]}{C \vdash [\Gamma, pc] \, \textsf{this}.m(\bar{e}) :: \Lambda[C, m] \sqcup pc}$$

Fig. 2. SeCreol secure-type system for expressions and right-hand-sides.

According to the secure-type system for statements in Fig. 3, a simple call does not change Γ nor pc, but the actual parameter levels must respect the declared levels of the corresponding formal parameters (as above). And we have

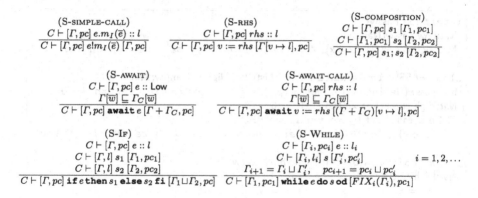

Fig. 3. SeCreol secure-type system for statements.

$C \vdash [\Gamma, pc]$ *skip* $[\Gamma, pc]$. For an assignment, object creation statement, or call, $v := rhs$, with level l for rhs, the level of v in Γ is changed to l, which could imply a downgrade or an upgrade (or no change) of level. The pc is not modified since such a statement is considered efficiently terminating without any branching.

For an **await** statement we must ensure that the declared levels of all fields and class parameters are respected, since the suspension may cause other processes to continue, for which we assume these declared levels. Levels of local variables will remain after an **await** statement since local variables are not affected by other processes. We therefore use map composition $(+)$ in the post-state of an await to overwrite the levels of fields and class parameters by the declared levels (Γ_C). For simplicity we consider only Low await conditions. In the case of a suspending call, the effect of the assignment part is added after the map composition since this assignment happens after suspension.

Rule S-IF lifts the pc level of each branch by the level of the test. This will make all expressions occurring in both branches at least as high as the if-test. Thereby implicit leakage is avoided. Since the static analysis does not know which branch is taken at runtime, the resulting value of Γ for each variable is calculated as the highest level of each branch. An **if** statement without an else-branch is like an **if** statement with skip in the else-branch. The treatment of **while** is similar to an **if** statement without an else-branch, except that the static analysis cannot predict how many times the branch is iterated. Each iteration may lift the levels in Γ or pc. However, a loop will have a finite number of program variables and since there is a finite number of static levels, there is a minimal fixpoint reachable in a finite number of approximations (typically i equal to one or two). Rule S-WHILE reflects this fixpoint calculation.

The secrecy typing ensures that there is no flow from high values to low values, and that values evaluated in an if-branch with a high test are high (since they may depend on the test), and similarly for values evaluated inside a while-loop with a high test. Thus the values of low variables in any program state do not depend on high inputs. Furthermore, this ensures that for each call (and return) generated by o the values of parameters declared as low do not depend

```
interface Passw{
  Nat:Low passw(Nat:High x)// store password, return a ref number
  Nat:High check(Nat:Low x)// check validity of password given ref
}
class PASSW implements Passw{ List[Nat]:High p:=empty; Nat n:=0;
  Nat passw(Nat:High x){p:=append(p,x); n:=n+1; return n}// return index
  Nat:High check(Nat x){Nat:High c:=0;
    if p ⊑ caller and 1≤x≤n then c:=p[x]fi;
    return c}//for High callers the value in p is returned (if any)
}
class TEST(Passw o){ Nat:High xh; Nat:Low xl;
  Nat:High test(Nat x){  xh ↦ High . Note: all others are Low
       xl := x;           xl ↦ Low
       x := o.check(x);   x ↦ High
       xh := xl;          xh ↦ Low . Note: suspension is ok even with x high
       await true;        xh ↦ High, x ↦ High . Note: all others are Low
       xh := o.passw(x);  xh ↦ Low . Note: the call is ok with x high
       await x:=o.check(xh); x ↦ High . Note: the call is ok since xh now is Low
       return x           Note: return is ok with x High, since xh ⊑ High ∧ xl ⊑ Low.
}}
```

Fig. 4. An example showing a password protection class and a test program. In the latter, level changes in fields and local variables are indicated to the right in each line.

on high inputs. We provide a proof of this in Sect. 5, based on a semantics that includes runtime secrecy levels.

Example. A small example is given in Fig. 4 to illustrate possible changes in the levels of fields (xh and xl) and local variables (x). The implementation of *Passw* uses an if-test to check $p \sqsubseteq$ caller before returning a high value in *check*. A test class with non-trivial secrecy typing is added. Here, level changes are written to the right of each line, not repeating unchanged information. The program satisfies the rules for confidentiality, i.e., the program does not leak information in its explicit output and respects field levels at return/await statements. Note that the lowering of xh was needed to make the *check* call allowed, that the higher level of the local variable x was maintained over the await (since x is local), that the higher level of x was acceptable in the *passw* call, and that the high level of x is allowed at the return point (after which x is deallocated).

4   Operational Semantics

The operational semantics is given in Fig. 5. We explain the main elements, while a more detailed explanation is given in the extended version [16]. A runtime configuration of a system is a multiset of objects and messages (using blank-space as the binary multiset constructor). Each rule in the operational semantics deals with only one object *o*, and possibly messages, reflecting that we deal with concurrent distributed systems communicating asynchronously. When a subconfiguration $\mathcal{C}$ can be rewritten to a $\mathcal{C}'$, this means that the whole configuration $\ldots \mathcal{C} \ldots$ can be rewritten to $\ldots \mathcal{C}' \ldots$, reflecting interleaving semantics. Each object o is responsible for executing all method calls to o as well as self-calls. An object has at most one active process, reflecting a method execution, and a sequence of suspended processes organized in a process queue PQ. Remote calls and replies are handled by messages. Objects have the form

$$o : \mathbf{ob}(\delta, \overline{s})$$

where o is the object identity, δ is the current object state, and $\overline{s}$ is a sequence of statements ending with a **return**, representing the remaining part of the active process, or **idle** when no active process. A message has the form

$$\mathbf{msg}\ o \rightarrow o'.m(\overline{e})$$

representing a call with o as caller, o' callee, and $\overline{e}$ actual parameters, or

$$\mathbf{msg}\ o \leftarrow o'.(u, d)$$

representing a completion event where d is the returned value and u the identity of the call. The operational rules reflect small-step semantics. For instance, the rule for skip is given by $o : \mathbf{ob}(\delta, \mathbf{skip}; \overline{s}) \longrightarrow o : \mathbf{ob}(\delta, \overline{s})$, saying that the execution of *skip* has no effect on the state δ of the object. A while loop is handled by expanding while b do s od to if b then s; while b do s od fi upon execution of the while-statement. The semantics of an if-statement without an else-part is equivalent to if b then s else skip fi.

The operational semantics uses some additional variables, like PQ for holding the process queue and nextId for generating unique identities for calls. These appear as fields in the operational semantics. Furthermore, this is handled as an implicit class parameter, while callId and caller appear as implicit method parameters, holding the identity of a call and its caller, respectively. The operational semantics uses an additional *query* statement, [**await**] **get** u, for dealing with the termination of call/await call statements. The query **get** u is blocking while waiting for the method response with identity u, and **await get** u is a suspending query.

The state of an object is given by a twin mapping, written $(\alpha|\beta)$, where α is the state of the field variables (including PQ, nextId) and class parameters $\overline{cp}$ (including this), and β is the state of the local variables and formal parameters (including callId and caller) of the current process. Look-up in a twin mapping, $(\alpha|\beta)[z]$, is simply given by $(\alpha + \beta)[z]$. The notation $\alpha[z := e]$ abbreviates $\alpha[z \mapsto alpha[e]]$, and the notation $(\alpha|\beta)[v := e]$ abbreviates **if** v in β **then** $(\alpha \mid \beta[v \mapsto (\alpha|\beta)[e]])$ **else** $(\alpha[v \mapsto (\alpha|\beta)[e]] \mid \beta)$, where in is used for testing domain membership.

The *process queue* PQ is the queue of suspended processes, of form $(\beta, \overline{s})$. The operations $enq(PQ, p)$ and $deq(PQ, \alpha)$ are used to add a process p to the queue, and to select an *enabled* process (if any) from the queue, respectively. The latter results in the sequence $(p; PQ')$ of the selected enabled process p and

ASSIGN :
$o : \mathbf{ob}(\delta, v := e; \bar{s})$
$\rightarrow o : \mathbf{ob}(\delta[v := e], \bar{s})$

IF-TRUE :
$o : \mathbf{ob}(\delta, \mathbf{if}\ b\ \mathbf{then}\ \overline{s1}\ \mathbf{else}\ \overline{s2}\ \mathbf{fi}; \bar{s})$
$\rightarrow o : \mathbf{ob}(\delta, pcs := push(pcs, l); \overline{s1}; pcs := pop(pcs); \bar{s})$
$\mathbf{if}\ \delta[b] = true_l$

IF-FALSE :
$o : \mathbf{ob}(\delta, \mathbf{if}\ b\ \mathbf{then}\ \overline{s1}\ \mathbf{else}\ \overline{s2}\ \mathbf{fi}; \bar{s})$
$\rightarrow o : \mathbf{ob}(\delta, pcs := push(pcs, l); \overline{s2}; pcs := pop(pcs); \bar{s})$
$\mathbf{if}\ \delta[b] = false_l$

WHILE :
$o : \mathbf{ob}(\delta, \mathbf{while}\ b\ \mathbf{do}\ \overline{s1}\ \mathbf{od}; \bar{s})$
$\rightarrow o : \mathbf{ob}(\delta, \mathbf{if}\ b\ \mathbf{then}\ \overline{s1};\ \mathbf{while}\ b\ \mathbf{do}\ \overline{s1}\ \mathbf{od}\ \mathbf{fi}; \bar{s})$

NEW :
$o : \mathbf{ob}(\delta, v := \mathbf{new}\ C(\bar{e}) : l; \bar{s})$
$\rightarrow o : \mathbf{ob}(\delta[v := o', \bar{s})$
$o' : \mathbf{ob}(\delta_C[\mathsf{this} \mapsto o', \overline{cp} \mapsto \delta[\bar{e}]], init_C)$
$\mathbf{where}\ o' = (fresh, o.level \sqcap l),$ for a globally fresh reference $fresh$

SIMPLE CALL:
$o : \mathbf{ob}(\delta, a!m(\bar{e}); \bar{s})$
$\rightarrow o : \mathbf{ob}(\delta[\mathsf{nextId} := next(\mathsf{nextId})], \bar{s})$
$\mathbf{msg}\ o \rightarrow \delta[a].m(\delta[\mathsf{nextId}, \bar{e}])$

CALL :
$o : \mathbf{ob}(\delta, [\mathbf{await}]\ v := a.m(\bar{e}); \bar{s})$
$\rightarrow o : \mathbf{ob}(\delta, a!m(\bar{e}); [\mathbf{await}]\ v := \mathbf{get}\ \delta[\mathsf{nextId}]; \bar{s})$

START :
$\mathbf{msg}\ o' \rightarrow o.m(u, \bar{c})$
$o : \mathbf{ob}((\alpha|\beta'), \mathbf{idle})$
$\rightarrow o : \mathbf{ob}((\alpha|(\beta[\mathsf{caller} \mapsto o', \mathsf{callId} \mapsto u, \bar{y} \mapsto \bar{c}])), \bar{s})$
$\mathbf{where}\ m$ is statically bound to $(m, \bar{y}, \beta, \bar{s})$ in the class of this

RETURN :
$o : \mathbf{ob}(\delta, \mathbf{return}\ e)$
$\rightarrow o : \mathbf{ob}(\delta, \mathbf{idle})$
$\mathbf{msg}\ \delta[\mathsf{caller}] \leftarrow \delta[\mathsf{this}].(\delta[\mathsf{callId}], \delta[e])$

QUERY :
$\mathbf{msg}\ o \leftarrow o'.(u, c)$
$o : \mathbf{ob}(\dots [\mathbf{await}]\ v := \mathbf{get}\ u \dots)$
$\rightarrow o : \mathbf{ob}(\dots v := c \dots)$

AWAIT :
$o : \mathbf{ob}(\delta, \mathbf{await}\ b; \bar{s})$
$\rightarrow o : \mathbf{ob}(\delta, \bar{s})$
$\mathbf{if}\ \delta[b] = true_l$

CONTINUE :
$o : \mathbf{ob}((\alpha|\beta'), \mathbf{idle})$
$\rightarrow o : \mathbf{ob}((\alpha[PQ \mapsto rest])|\beta), \bar{s})$
$\mathbf{if}\ deq(\alpha[PQ], \alpha) = ((\beta, \bar{s}); rest)$

SUSPEND :
$o : \mathbf{ob}((\alpha|\beta), \bar{s})$
$\rightarrow o : \mathbf{ob}((\alpha[PQ \mapsto enq(\alpha[PQ], (\beta, \bar{s}))], \varepsilon), \mathbf{idle})$
$\mathbf{if}\ \bar{s}$ starts with $\mathbf{await}$

Fig. 5. Operational rules reflecting small-step semantics of SeCreol with secrecy levels.

the remainder of the queue PQ' (depending on the specific scheduling policy), or the empty sequence *empty* if no process is enabled. A process $(\beta, \bar{s})$ is *enabled* if it starts with an enabled statement. A conditional **await** is enabled if the condition evaluates to true (in state $\alpha|\beta$), and an **await** call statement is not enabled unless reduced by the QUERY rule. All other statements are enabled.

The given language fragment may be extended with constructs for local (stack-based) method calls, e.g., by using the approach of [12].

Runtime Secrecy Levels. We here explain the secrecy aspects of the operational semantics. We assume a program that has passed the secrecy typing, and therefore the operational semantics does not include explicitly checks for confidentiality errors during reduction. However, we prove that any secrecy level obtained at runtime is less or equal to the one calculated by the static secrecy typing. This property, called *secrecy soundness*, is formalized in the next section. This guarantees that the static secrecy level checks will be satisfied at run-time, even when based on the runtime secrecy levels. And non-interference is then proved.

At runtime the evaluation of an expression e gives a secrecy tag l, in addition to a (normal) value d. We let the tagged value d_l denote this result, and let c denote tagged values. We let $d_l.tag$ be l. If this value is assigned to a program variable v, the binding $v \mapsto d_l$ is added to the state. The state of an object is given by a twin-mapping as above, but the values of variables are now bound to tagged values. Thus the values appearing in the extended semantics are all tagged. Each object identifier has the form of a pair (oid, l) where oid is a normal object identifier and l is the secrecy level of the object. We refer to the secrecy level of an object o by the meta-notation $o.level$, letting $(oid, l).level$ be l. For data values c, we define $c.level$ by $c.tag$. The secrecy semantics uses an additional variable pcs in each method, reflecting the context secrecy level of enclosing if- and while-branches. (pcs is local since it must be retrieved after suspension.) And pcs is a stack of levels reflecting the levels of the enclosing if- and while-branches, such that the top of the stack is the innermost branch.

The evaluation of an expression e in a state δ is denoted $\delta[e]$, where the value is evaluated ignoring tags, and the tag is defined by $level(pcs) \sqcup_i v_i.tag$, where $\sqcup_i v_i.tag$ is the join of the tags of all variables occurring in e, and where $level(pcs)$ is the join of all levels in the stack pcs. This assumes strictness of all functions in the language, i.e., the level of $f(\bar{c})$ is simply $\sqcup_i c_i$. The special expression $e \sqsubseteq e'$ is evaluated by $\delta[e].level \sqsubseteq \delta[e'].level$ and with tag as defined above. (Other kinds of non-strict functions are for simplicity ignored here.) The runtime secrecy level of a variable v in an execution state will be less or equal to that of the static level in a corresponding program point. There are several reasons for this. For instance, there can be many calls to the same method, some with actual parameters of less secrecy level than for other calls. And at the start of a method, the static analysis will assume the declared secrecy level for fields, whereas at runtime the levels might be less. Similarly, any expression may have a lower level at runtime since the variables involved might have a lower level than in the static analysis.

5   Theoretical Results

In order to relate runtime states to those of the static secrecy typing, we use statement labels. Following [15], each basic statement and each if- and while-condition in a given program is tagged by a unique statement label (i.e., statement number) n appearing as a superscript (when needed).

The result of the secrecy analysis can be captured by a mapping SL (Static Level) such that $SL(C,n)$ gives the binding environment of the pre-state of statement n in class C. Thus $SL(C,n)[v]$ is the level statically assigned to variable v in this state by the secrecy typing analysis, and $SL(C,n)[pc]$ is the level statically assigned to pc in this state. If an execution reaches a configuration where a C object is about to execute a basic statement s^n, and similarly for another execution, we say that the two pre-states of n are low equal if the values of all variables v such that $SL(C,n)[v]$ is Low are equal in the two pre-states.

In the operational semantics, the level information at time t (i.e., the number of execution steps) in an execution is captured by a function $RT(t)$ returning the executing object (of form $o : \mathbf{ob}(\delta, \overline{s})$) such that $RT(t).class$ is its class, and $RT(t).label$ is the label of the statement to be executed, and $RT(t)[v]$ is the secrecy level of variable v, i.e., the level of $\delta[v]$. Similarly, $RT(t)[pc]$ is the level of pc in this state, and $RT(o)[pcs]$ is the level of the stack pcs given by $\sqcup_i pcs[i]$ where i ranges over all indexes in the stack. The following theorem ensures that the evaluation of variables and expressions at runtime gives levels that are less or equal to those of the static analysis.

Theorem 1 (Soundness).   *At any time t in an execution where the active object $RT(t)$ is of the form $o : \mathbf{ob}(\delta, s^n; \overline{s})$ of class C, then*

(i) the levels of δ are less or equal to the corresponding ones in $SL(C,n)$, i.e., $\delta[v] \sqsubseteq SL(C,n)[v]$ for all program variables v and $level(\delta[pcs]) \sqsubseteq SL(C,n)[pc]$.

(ii) if $C \vdash [\Gamma, pc]\, e :: l$ and $\delta[e] = d_{l'}$ for an expression e, then $l' \sqsubseteq l$.

Proof. We use induction on the time t, and may assume that the conclusion holds up to a given time t and must ensure that it holds in the next state. We first note that (i) implies (ii) because the static level of an expression e is given by the join of the static levels of all variables in e and of pc, whereas the runtime level of e is given by the join of the runtime levels of all variables in e and of $level(\delta[pcs])$. By (i) the latter cannot exceed the former since the runtime level of each variable v cannot exceed the static level of v, and since the runtime level of pcs cannot exceed the static level of pc.

It remains to show that (i) holds in the next state. Consider all basic statements that modify the state (of the active object). For an assignment $v := e$ the new runtime level of v is the runtime level of e evaluated in the current state. This level is less than the static level of e by (ii), thus the conclusion holds in this case. Similar arguments apply to all assignment-like statements, such as new and call statements, in which cases the assignment to the implicit and unobservable object variable $nextId$ is unproblematic. The operational rules for skip and return give no state change. The operational rules for continue and suspend give a twin state where fields are not changed. In the case of suspend, the local state is empty (ignoring the PQ which is not a program variable), and in the case of continue, the local state is reset to an old state, for which we may use the induction hypothesis. The rules for if and while give a next state (after evaluating the condition) that is the same as before except that the *pcs* level may be raised. We need to show $level(\delta[pcs]) \sqsubseteq SL(C, n)[pc]$. This follows by (ii) since the condition is evaluated in the object state of time t. The discussion of the rule for await is similar.   □

In our context of message-based systems, we define non-interference by:

Definition 1 (Non-interference). *Non-interference means that if two executions reach the pre-state of a basic statement s^n with configurations C_1 and C_2, respectively, such that $C_1 =_{Low} C_2$, then the observable output resulting from execution of s^n on the two configurations, will be the same.*

The output *of a basic statement s is the message (**msg**) generated by the operational rule for s, if any, and otherwise empty. The observable part of a message is the values of parameters/method results declared as Low in the method declaration (as detected by the secrecy-type analysis).*

Theorem 2 (Non-interference). *A program that is secrecy-type correct will satisfy non-interference.*

Proof. We consider all basic statements. The ones generating output are the call statements and the return statement. The output of a call statement is given by the rule for SIMPLE CALL, and the observable output is the values of the parameters of m for which the declared level is Low. Since this parameter information is static, the sublist of Low parameters have the same length for two executions. Consider a call statement with label n of a given class C. Each parameter expression e_i of a low parameter has a static level l, which by Theorem 1 must be less than the runtime level l' of the evaluation of $RT(t)[e_i]$ for any execution at time t, where $RT(t)$ has an active object of the given class and with label n. Since the states of the two executions are low equal, the values of any expression with a low runtime label must be the same since only low variables are used on the evaluation (otherwise the runtime label could not be low). Therefore the value of each such e_i must be the same in the two executions. Similarly, the values of any return expression e evaluated in different pre-states of the same statement n are equal if the resulting runtime level is low, provided the two pre-states are low equal. Since static low level implies runtime low level, the two pre-states give the same observable output. The above discussion applies also to object identities since the only observable relation over object identities with low output is equality.

The argument above can be extended to **new** statements and any basic statement. It follows that the new state of all variables is low equal for two executions after a basic statement since each basic statement is deterministic (apart from generated object identities). Thus we have also shown that low equality of states is preserved by all basic statements.   □

Note that the code `if b then o!m1() else o!m2() fi` leaks the outcome
of the if-test to object o. To deal with such implicit leakage, one may define
a stronger notion of non-interference involving communication events. This is
studied in [17] defining *interaction non-interference* and showing that this can
be enforced by static analysis involving communication traces.

6   Related Work

A number of complications arise from the different concurrency and communication models [3,19]. For imperative concurrent programs, the multi-thread, shared
variable, and channel-based paradigms have been studied [18]. These paradigms
give non-trivial privacy challenges. For instance the channel paradigm gives intri-
cate timing leaks, based on observations of channel size [4,18]. In our paradigm,
an object's process queue and queue of incoming calls are encapsulated and are
non-observable (as well as their size). There are several works on static checking
of noninterference for active objects communicating by asynchronous methods,
including [10,11] and work based on [9], but with different goals, assumptions,
and results ([9] with other forms of noninterference). Kammüller [11] considers
a functional language with futures, with a different treatment of methods. To
preserve confidentiality, we have considered Multilevel Security(MLS) which is a
well-established concept for confidentiality while the goal of multilateral security
in [10] is useful to satisfy complex and very different sets of policies in distributed
computer systems. The multilateral security of [10] is relevant for our operational
semantics. In our setting, instead of the traditional concept of public and private
methods in [11], we use interfaces to control visibility of methods. Moreover, our
approach is not dependent on the concept of futures. In addition, in [11] remote
method calls are considered side-effect free which guarantees that no information from the caller side is leaked. Therefore, although secure down-calls are
supported in [11], interaction noninterference is not preserved.

Our paradigm is based on a simple, compositional semantic model, which
gives flexible analysis of program variables, including fields and communicated
values, and of synchronization mechanisms, thereby reducing the amount of false
positives. Scheduling-related primitives are included in our high-level language;
this enables further static analysis than in [3]. Compared to [3], we consider
more high-level concurrency constructs such as asynchronous calls and suspension mechanisms. A complementary work on SeCreol [17] focuses on indirect
leakage caused by observations of network traffic, where enforcement of network-
level non-interference is handled by means of static trace analysis. It assumes a
similar secrecy typing system, but without including an operational semantics
with secrecy levels nor a soundness proof of the secrecy typing.

While most of the related work aim at preventing traditional progress-
insensitive non-interference, we are considering progress-sensitive non-
interference, where an attacker can indirectly observe the progress of an object,
caused by e.g. process termination or suspension (assuming termination proofs
of while loops). Another aim of that paper is minimizing the Trusted Computing Base (TCB) by not trusting the compiler and using Proof-Carrying Code

(PCC). Moreover, [3,11] prevent all flows from secret to public variables, while in our setting this is not necessary. In addition, for explicit flows, we also consider interaction between objects such as if secret then call fi for different method calls.

Dynamic checking of runtime access control, which has been done in the Java virtual machine and the .NET runtime systems, provides useful guarantee especially in the application of dynamic code involvements like mobile code. For example, in [2] static permissions are assigned to classes based on code origin, and when untrusted code calls trusted code, then the permission is checked using the run-time stack, while our approach is static. However, we aim at an extension to runtime checks in future work.

7 Conclusion

We have considered a model for concurrent object-oriented systems suitable for distributed service-oriented systems. The concurrent objects may communicate confidential and non-confidential information, restricting confidential information to method parameters/returns declared as safe for confidential information. The language is high-level and includes process control and suspension, without explicit signaling and locking operations. Objects are imperative and non-deterministic. We introduce a type and effect system and prove a noninterference property, as well as soundness of the secrecy typing system. Due to hiding and encapsulation, we do not impose unnecessary restrictions on information flow inside objects. The language has a compositional semantics and supports compositional program reasoning [5]; and the process control mechanisms include primitives typically part of an operating system. This allows class-wise secrecy analysis that goes beyond what is normally possible by static checking. The absence of futures simplifies the analysis. As shown in a complimentary work [16], one can deal with implicit leakage caused by network level observations of observable aspects of communicated messages.

The Creol concurrency model is adopted by the ABS language [14], and the work here can be extended to ABS by considering *object groups*, which impose concurrency restrictions, and *futures*, which may give rise to implicit information leakage. We have presented a more high-level language without (explicit) futures and object groups, which simplifies the formalization. We are initiating an implementation based on a Creol interpreter in Maude. The ABS tool support will be used for an ABS implementation.

References

1. Askarov, A., Hunt, S., Sabelfeld, A., Sands, D.: Termination-insensitive noninterference leaks more than just a bit. In: Jajodia, S., Lopez, J. (eds.) ESORICS 2008. LNCS, vol. 5283, pp. 333–348. Springer, Heidelberg (2008). doi:10.1007/978-3-540-88313-5_22
2. Banerjee, A., Naumann, D.A.: Stack-based access control and secure information flow. J. Funct. Program. **15**(02), 131–177 (2005)

3. Barthe, G., Rezk, T., Russo, A., Sabelfeld, A.: Security of multithreaded programs by compilation. In: Biskup, J., López, J. (eds.) ESORICS 2007. LNCS, vol. 4734, pp. 2–18. Springer, Heidelberg (2007). doi:10.1007/978-3-540-74835-9_2

4. D. Devriese and F. Piessens. Noninterference through secure multi-execution. In: 2010 IEEE Symposium on Security and Privacy (SP), pp. 109–124. IEEE (2010)

5. Din, C.C., Dovland, J., Johnsen, E.B., Owe, O.: Observable behavior of distributed systems: component reasoning for concurrent objects. J. Logic Algebr. Program. **81**(3), 227–256 (2012)

6. Erlingsson, U.: The inlined reference monitor approach to security policy enforcement. Ph.D. thesis, Cornell University, Ithaca, NY, USA (2004). AAI3114521

7. Goguen, J.A., Meseguer, J.: Unwinding and inference control. In: IEEE Symposium on Security and Privacy, p. 75 (1984)

8. Heintze, N., Riecke, J.G.: The SLAM calculus: programming with secrecy and integrity. In: Proceedings of POPL 1998, pp. 365–377. ACM (1998)

9. Hodges, S.J., Jones, C.B.: Non-interference properties of a concurrent object-based language: proofs based on operational semantics. In: Freitag, B., Jones, C.B., Lengauer, C., Schek, H.J. (eds.) Object Orientation with Parallelism and Persistence, pp. 1–22. Springer, Boston (1996). doi:10.1007/978-1-4613-1437-0_1

10. Kammüller, F.: A semi-lattice model for multi-lateral security. In: Di Pietro, R., Herranz, J., Damiani, E., State, R. (eds.) DPM/SETOP -2012. LNCS, vol. 7731, pp. 118–132. Springer, Heidelberg (2013). doi:10.1007/978-3-642-35890-6_9

11. Kammüller, F.: Confinement for active objects. Int. J. Adv. Comput. Sci. Appl. (IJACSA) **6**(2), 246–260 (2015)

12. Johnsen, E.B., Owe, O.: An asynchronous communication model for distributed concurrent objects. Softw. Syst. Model. **6**(1), 35–58 (2007)

13. Johnsen, E.B., Owe, O., Creol, I.C.Y.: A type-safe object-oriented model for distributed concurrent systems. Theor. Comput. Sci. **365**(1–2), 23–66 (2006)

14. Johnsen, E.B., Hähnle, R., Schäfer, J., Schlatte, R., Steffen, M.: ABS: a core language for abstract behavioral specification. In: Aichernig, B.K., de Boer, F.S., Bonsangue, M.M. (eds.) FMCO 2010. LNCS, vol. 6957, pp. 142–164. Springer, Heidelberg (2011). doi:10.1007/978-3-642-25271-6_8

15. Nielson, F., Nielson, H.-R., Hankin, C.L.: Principles of Program Analysis. Springer, Heidelberg (1999). doi:10.1007/978-3-662-03811-6

16. Owe, O., Ramezanifarkhani, T.: Static enforcement of confidentiality of interactions in concurrent object-oriented systems. Technical report, Department of Informatics, University of Oslo, Norway (2017). An extended version of this paper. http://heim.ifi.uio.no/olaf/Papers/SeCreolReport.pdf

17. Ramezanifarkhani, T., Owe, O., Tokas, S.: A secrecy-preserving language for distributed and object-oriented systems, March 2017 (submitted)

18. Sabelfeld, A., Mantel, H.: Static confidentiality enforcement for distributed programs. In: Hermenegildo, M.V., Puebla, G. (eds.) SAS 2002. LNCS, vol. 2477, pp. 376–394. Springer, Heidelberg (2002). doi:10.1007/3-540-45789-5_27

19. Sabelfeld, A., Myers, A.C.: Language-based information flow security. IEEE J. Sel. Areas Commun. **21**, 5–19 (2003)

Using Oblivious RAM in Genomic Studies

Nikolaos P. Karvelas[1]([✉]), Andreas Peter[2], and Stefan Katzenbeisser[1]

[1] TU Darmstadt, Darmstadt, Germany
karvelas@seceng.informatik.tu-darmstadt.de
[2] University of Twente, Enschede, The Netherlands

Abstract. Since the development of tree-based Oblivious RAMs by Shi et al. it has become apparent that privacy preserving outsourced storage can be practical. Although most current constructions follow a client-server model, in many applications, such as Genome Wide Association Studies (GWAS), it is desirable that multiple entities can share data, while being able to hide access patterns not only from the server, but also from any other entities that can access parts of the data. Inspired by the efficiency and simplicity of Path-ORAM, in this work, we study an extension of Path-ORAM that allows oblivious sharing of data in a multi-client setting, so that accesses can be hidden from the server and from other clients. We address various challenges that emerge when using Path-ORAM in a multi-client setting, and prove that with adequate changes, Path-ORAM is still secure in a setting, where the clients are semi-honest, do not trust each other, but try to learn the access patterns of each other. We demonstrate our ORAM construction in a GWAS setting. Our experiments show that in databases storing 2^{23} data blocks (corresponding to a database holding 2^{17} blocks per client, capable of storing human genome in the form of SNPs, for 100 clients), the average query time is less than 7 s, yielding a secure and practical solution.

Keywords: Path-ORAM · Multiple clients · Genomic privacy

1 Introduction

As cloud applications continue to grow in popularity, outsourcing sensitive data to remote servers has become common practice, and with it, significant ramifications to users' privacy have been induced. While encryption plays a central role in data protection and privacy, it has become apparent that simply employing encryption is not enough to protect sensitive data, since significant information leakage can already occur when a remote server merely observes the clients' access patterns. Take, for example, the case of genomic data: it is foreseeable, that in the future, genomic data will be stored as part of patients' electronic health records. This has the benefit that large sets of genomic data will also be available to research institutions, which will have the opportunity to carry out genomic tests, such as Genome Wide Association Studies (GWAS), on large datasets. In this setting, a third party, such as a medical research center (further called an investigator), could be granted access to specific parts of multiple

© Springer International Publishing AG 2017
J. Garcia-Alfaro et al. (Eds.): DPM/CBT 2017, LNCS 10436, pp. 35–52, 2017.
DOI: 10.1007/978-3-319-67816-0_3

patients' genomic data, which he could analyze in a study. Clearly, in such a setting encryption is not enough to protect the interests of both the participants and the research center: even with encrypted data, the server can observe which portions of the genome are accessed, and deduce vital information, such as which test has been run, or what disease a patient is suspected to suffer from.

Inspired by the above scenario, in this work, we ask ourselves if an ORAM solution can be found, that guarantees access pattern hiding not only against the server, but also against fellow clients. We answer this question in a positive way, by extending the highly efficient Path-ORAM [15] so that it can support multiple clients who access parts of a specific database, and share them with each other. At the same time, access pattern privacy is guaranteed both against the server and against other clients who share parts of the database.

The problem of constructing a privacy preserving multi-client storage solution has been explored in a number of works, namely [1,4,7,10,11]. In a privacy preserving multi-client storage, each client has his own data (all stored in a single ORAM) and is free to share only parts of his data with other clients. In [4] the authors propose a solution, where a data owner can delegate rights to read or write some of his data items to other clients. This solution is based on the square-root ORAM [5] and thus suffers from heavy communication complexity. Equally important, it requires the data owner to be constantly online, thus restricting the applicability of the solution. The construction in [7] avoids this drawback, but suffers from high storage requirements on the client side. In a recent work of Maffei et al. [10], a multi-client ORAM is proposed, which is based on Path-ORAM [15] and achieves security guarantees against a malicious server. Regarding the security against the clients, however, the main focus lies on anonymity, i.e., unlinkability of a given operation on a datablock and a client, among the set of clients who have access to that specific data-block. Further, the construction does not guarantee hiding access patterns between clients who share data, as privacy leakage can occur due to the stash or due to the position map. Facing a similar problem, Backes et al. [1] examined the problem of access pattern anonymity in a multi-client ORAM, and proposed two constructions that achieve this goal. Both proposed solutions do not deal with the privacy leakage occurring between the multiple clients, and therefore cannot be applied in the scenario we are looking at. In our work, we sacrifice user anonymity, in order to build a solution that guarantees access pattern privacy between all involved parties. We leave adding user anonymity to our current solution as future work.

In this work, we focus on the development of an ORAM that allows multiple clients to store their data on a server and share *parts of their data* with each other. At the same time, the system protects the access pattern privacy of the clients, not only against the server, but also against other clients. In our solution, we assume K semi-honest clients, with each of them storing up to N blocks of data. Every client encrypts his datablocks with his individual encryption key, and all encrypted datablocks are stored in a classical Path-ORAM of height $\log N$, with Z blocks per node. The resulting K Path-ORAM trees are merged on each node, resulting in a Path-ORAM of height $\log N$ with ZK blocks per node. At this point, in every node, blocks of all the clients can be found. After a number of data accesses (that also include block sharing), the blocks found in every node are eventually shuffled, and due to the presence of shared blocks, it can happen that some clients have more blocks in a node than others. Thus, we end up with a "blurred" version of the originally merged client trees. To differentiate our construction from a simple concatenation of Path-ORAM trees, where each client is allocated a fixed number of blocks in every node, we will refer to our construction as Blurry-ORAM. Sharing a data block between two clients is done by having the original block owner change the private key under which the block is encrypted and handing over this new key to the client. Our ORAM construction is very efficient and achieves full privacy, i.e., provides access pattern hiding against both the server and other clients. In Table 1 we sum up properties of the existing multi-client ORAM constructions, show their communication complexity and recall if they allow access pattern privacy against other clients, allow for anonymous accesses or sharing of data between the clients. To our knowledge, our construction is the first to allow data sharing between clients in an ORAM, and to guarantee access pattern hiding not only against the server, but also against other clients.

To this end, our solution is directly applicable to the case of GWAS: multiple clients store their encrypted genomic data in a Blurry-ORAM and give partial access to multiple investigators. The investigators can then access only specific parts of the clients' sequenced genome, without leaking any information about the parts they are interested, to any other investigators. Indeed, our experiments showed that our construction is efficient, as retrieving one block in a database where 100 clients store their whole genome in the form of Single Nucleotide Polymorphisms (SNPs) and they share parts of it with 10 investigators, can be done on average in 14.94 s.

1.1 Organization of the Paper

The rest of the paper is organized as follows: in Sect. 2, we describe the functionality we want to achieve, and define the security of the protocol. In Sect. 3, we recall the Path-ORAM protocol, and we describe our architecture. In Sect. 4, we examine the stash occupancy by our protocol, and analyze the time and space requirements of our solution. In Sect. 5, we analyze the security of our construction. In Sects. 6 and 7, we apply our solution to the case of genomic studies, and present our experimental results. We conclude with open problems and future work in Sect. 8.

2   System Model

In our ORAM construction we consider one server and multiple clients. Both the server and the clients are assumed to be semi-honest, i.e., they try to extract as much information possible about the data belonging to other clients, but they never deviate from the protocol. Each client stores his data on the server,

Table 1. Comparison of multi-client ORAM solutions; A.P.H. stands for Access Pattern Hiding, N: Number of blocks per client, G: Number of groups, K: Number of clients.

Solution	Communication complexity	A.P.H. against server	A.P.H. against clients	Client anonymity	Data sharing
[4]	$O(\sqrt{N}\log^2 N)$ (amort.)	✓	✗	✗	✓
[7]	$O(\log^2 N)$	✓	✗	✗	✓
[11]	$O(\log^2 N)$ to $O(\log^5 N)$	✓	✗	✗	✓
[10]	$O(G\log^2 N)$	✓	✗	✓	✓
[1]	$O(\log^2(KN))$	✓	✗	✓	✗
This work	$O(K\log^2 N\log(\log N))$	✓	✓	✗	✓

partitioned in N blocks of fixed size B, and each block is identified by a unique identifier id. Thus, we consider a block as a tuple (id, dat), with id being a unique identifier and dat the actual data. In the following we will abuse this notation, and, for ease of presentation, denote by id_i^j the block with identifier id_i, that belongs to client j, without referring to the actual data of the block, unless it is crucial for the description.

2.1 Functionality

Since we want to build a multi-client ORAM solution that allows block sharing between the clients, our architecture must support operations for reading, writing, sharing and revoking access to shares. The operations used in our construction are defined as follows:

Init(λ): The Init operation is run by every client, takes as input a security parameter λ and outputs an encryption/decryption key pair, which the client uses to encrypt and decrypt his datablocks.

Read(id_i^j, enc_key, dec_key): The read operation is a protocol run between a client cli_j and the server. It returns the block identified by id_i^j or NULL, if the block was not found (for example, if a client queries for a block to which he does not have access rights).

Write(id_i^j, enc_key, dec_key, dat): The write operation is a protocol executed between a client cli_j and the server. It is similar to the read operation, as it returns the block with identifier id_i^j, but overwrites its contents with dat, in case the read operation was successful.

Share(cli_i, cli_j, id_u^i, enc_key, dec_key): The share operation is a protocol run between the server and the clients cli_i and cli_j. The goal is to make the block with identifier id_u^i, which is accessible by client cli_i, also accessible (for read, write, share and revoke) to client cli_j.

Revoke(cli_i, cli_j, id, enc_key, dec_key): The revoke operation is a protocol run between the server and a client cli_i. For a block with identifier id that can be accessed by clients cli_i and cli_j, the purpose of this operation is to disallow cli_j from further being able to access (read, write, share or revoke) block id. Note, that the revoke operation is not recursive and disallows only one specific client (client cli_j) all further access to the block; thus, after a revoke operation, all other clients, to whom the revoked client granted access in the past, are still allowed to read, write, share and revoke the particular block.

2.2 Definitions

In order to argue about the security of our scheme, we first need to define the notion of a view (or access pattern). We do this in the following definitions, that are tailored towards our setting of extended ORAM functionality, that allows block sharing between clients.

Definition 1. *A data request is a tuple of the form* $(\mathsf{op}, \mathsf{id}, \mathsf{dat}, \mathsf{cli}_j)$ *where* $\mathsf{op} \in \{\mathsf{Read}, \mathsf{Write}, \mathsf{Share}, \mathsf{Revoke}\}$, id *is the block's identifier, and* dat *is the data to be written. If* $\mathsf{op} = \mathsf{Read}$, *then* $\mathsf{dat} = \mathsf{NULL}$ *and* $\mathsf{cli}_j = \mathsf{NULL}$. *If* $\mathsf{op} = \mathsf{Write}$, *then* $\mathsf{cli}_j = \mathsf{NULL}$. *If* $\mathsf{op} \in \{\mathsf{Share}, \mathsf{Revoke}\}$, *then* $\mathsf{dat} = \mathsf{NULL}$ *and* cli_j *is the client with which the block will be shared or from whom the sharing will be revoked.*

Definition 2. *A data request sequence is a tuple of the form* $(x_1, x_2, \ldots, x_l)$, *where each* x_i *is a data request. The number* l *of data requests in a data request sequence is called the data request sequence's length.*

Definition 3 (View). *Let* X *be a data request sequence of length* l. *We call the view (or access pattern) induced by* X, *everything that the server sees during the execution of* X *(often referred to also, as the protocol's transcript).*

Definition 4 (Shared Block). *In a multi-client ORAM construction that allows data sharing between clients, we call a block* id_i *shared if at least two clients have access to it.*

2.3 Security Properties

We consider a semi-honest server and semi-honest clients that do not collude with each other, or with the server. Thus, all involved parties try to gain as much information possible (e.g., which data blocks were read or written by which client, how many blocks are shared with whom, etc.) by examining the views of the access transactions. As far as the security against the server is concerned, we follow the classical access pattern privacy definition [15]:

Definition 5 (Client-to-Server Privacy). *We say that a multi-client ORAM protocol provides client-to-server privacy, if any two views of a client induced by data request sequences of the same length, are computationally indistinguishable by the server.*

Hiding the access patterns against the server is already a non-trivial problem, so it is no surprise that when multiple clients are present, the situation becomes much more involved. Suppose that two clients share blocks with each other, and that one of them, the attacking client, acquires views of the other client's accesses (for example by eavesdropping the communication channel). The views potentially include datablocks that the attacker shares with the attacked client and he thus can decrypt. Therefore, traditional proof techniques used in the simple client-server model (showing, for example indistinguishability of these views) cannot be adapted directly to the multi-client case, due to the fact that the adversary can potentially read parts of the view. In our security model, which is based on the IND-CPA paradigm and detailed in Definition 6, we let the adversary have "oracle" access to any operations on blocks he does not have access to. In the challenge phase, the adversary issues two data request sequences on blocks that he does not have access to (ultimately, we are interested in breaking the access pattern privacy for blocks that the adversary cannot see), and Share and Revoke operations can also be included, as long as they do not result in the adversary gaining or losing access to blocks, after their execution. Observe that the notion described here, resembles exactly the adversary's ability to read parts of the views that do not belong to him, and can thus help him to (potentially) gain information about blocks he does not have access to. Further, remark that the problem we are dealing with has little to do with client anonymity as opposed to other works in the literature like [1, 10, 11], where the identity of the clients accessing the oram is protected. Here we model and want to minimize the privacy leakage potentially appearing between clients who *share parts of their data*, about the parts of the data they *do not* share. Having these in mind, we can now define access pattern privacy in a multi-client ORAM construction as follows:

Definition 6 (Client-to-Client Privacy). *We say that a multi-client ORAM protocol which allows sharing of blocks between the clients provides client-to-client privacy (i.e., hides the access patterns of a client against other semi-honest clients), if for every PPT adversary $\mathcal{A}$, the advantage of winning the IND-CQA game, described in Table 2, is negligible in the security parameter.*

3   Blurry-ORAM Construction

3.1   Review of Path-ORAM

Our starting point is the Path-ORAM construction of Stefanov et al. [15], where a client stores N blocks of data in a binary tree structure of N leaves, with each node holding Z blocks. If less than Z real blocks are stored in a node, then the node is filled with fake blocks. Real and fake blocks are encrypted under a semantically secure encryption scheme, ensuring that encryptions of real and fake blocks are indistinguishable. Since each tree node can hold up to a constant amount of Z blocks, for N real blocks, $Z(2N - 1) - N$ fake blocks are stored

Table 2. The IND-CQA game.

Initialization: The challenger runs the Init algorithm and creates the public/private key pairs for all the clients except the adversary. The adversary runs the Init algorithm, creates his own private/public key pair and sends his public key to the challenger. The challenger uploads every client's encrypted data blocks to the ORAM and the adversary uploads his own data blocks

---

Pre-challenge phase: For polynomially many (in the security parameter) times, the adversary runs any data request (may it be read, write, share or revoke) on any blocks of his choosing. For blocks he has access to, he executes the data request with the challenger. For blocks that the adversary does not have access to, he gets "oracle" access and receives by the challenger the view yielded by the corresponding data request of this operation

---

Challenge: The challenge phase consists of two steps
1. The adversary chooses two data request sequences (drs_c^0, drs_c^1) and sends them to the challenger. The data request sequences may include read or write requests on blocks that the adversary does not have access to, and share or revoke operations that do not result in the adversary gaining or losing access to blocks
2. The challenger chooses randomly a bit b, runs drs_c^b and returns the view to the adversary

---

Post-challenge phase: Similar to the pre-challenge phase, with the restriction that no share or revoke operation on the blocks included in the challenge phase are allowed

---

Guess: The adversary guesses which data request was ran by the challenger during the challenge phase, and outputs a bit b'. He wins the game if $b' = b$

---

in the structure. Each real block is mapped to a leaf of the tree, and every time the client wants to retrieve one of his elements, he downloads the whole path from the root node to the respective leaf; the client is guaranteed to find the desired block in one of the nodes along this path. The client then chooses randomly a new leaf, re-maps the retrieved block to this leaf, and places it in the node closest to the leaf, which is the common ancestor of the retrieved element's previous and new mappings, if there is enough space in its buckets. Otherwise the block is moved to higher and higher levels, until a node with enough space is found. It can happen (in fact, this event occurs with probability 1/2 during every remapping) that the only common ancestor of the two leaves is the root node. Thus, the root may quickly get filled up with elements in which case, a small auxiliary storage, called a *stash*, is used to store the element instead. Furthermore, for every real block replaced in the path's node, a fake block is put in its position and all blocks in every accessed node are rerandomized. The resulting path is then uploaded to the server, while the stash (due to its small size) is stored directly on the client. In order for the client to know to which leaf an element is mapped in the tree, the client must store a table (called *position map*) that grows linear with the amount of elements he has outsourced to the server, but as shown in [12] can be recursively stored in smaller Path-ORAMs, until a Path-ORAM of constant size is reached.

3.2   Construction of Blurry-ORAM

In our setting, we consider K clients, who store their data on a data structure
residing on a remote server. Every client stores a maximum number of N real
blocks and their corresponding fakes, just like in Path-ORAM. How the clients'
data is laid on the remote data structure is of grave importance: The easiest way
to do this, would be to construct a tree with KN leaves and assign every block
to one of those leaves, as in a Path-ORAM. However, such a solution affects the
stash size in a way that renders the underlying Path-ORAM inoperable, due to
an exceedingly big stash size. The reason for this is the following: assume that
each node of the tree can hold Z blocks and that all clients' blocks are uniformly
distributed in the tree. Assume further, that every client can access only those
blocks that belong to him or are shared with him. Then, in every path, a client
can only find on average $Z/K \log(KN)$ blocks belonging to him, as opposed to
$Z \log N$ blocks that he would find if he had stored his blocks in a single client
Path-ORAM. This means that it will be more difficult for the client to put the
element he read back into the path, which will eventually force him to use his
stash more often. We indeed observed this behavior experimentally.

In contrast, in Blurry-ORAM we store the clients' blocks differently: we let
each of the K clients store his N blocks in a separate binary tree with N leaves,
where each node holds ZK blocks, as can be seen in Fig. 1. Every block (real or
fake) is encrypted using the client's public key, but in such a way that the block
can be re-randomized without knowledge of the owner's public key (using for
example the encryption scheme proposed in [6]). Further, we employ a homomorphic encryption scheme, which is IND-CPA and IK-CPA secure. The latter
notion is referred to as 'key privacy', introduced in [2] and is modeled similarly
to the IND-CPA game, but in the challenge phase, the adversary sends a message and two keys to the challenger. The challenger then, chooses one of the
two keys, and encrypts the message under this key and the adversary wins, if he
can tell under which key the ciphertext presented to him was encrypted. This
way, the property is achieved that all blocks (real and fake) belonging to a client,
are indistinguishable for anyone but the client who can decrypt them. Note here,
that the ElGamal encryption scheme (which we use in the implementation of our
construction) has all the required properties, i.e. it is homomorphic, and is both
IND-CPA and IK-CPA secure. As our construction is based on Path-ORAM, it
inherits the need of using a stash, since there is a chance that during an access,
some blocks cannot be put back in the downloaded path. For blocks that belong
solely to one client each client locally maintains a stash (called localstash in the
rest of the paper). The bounds on Path-ORAM stash size apply here. However, it
might happen that blocks shared between clients cannot be written back into the
path. For this case we maintain a so-called "commonstash", which will contain
all the encrypted shared blocks that could not fit into the tree. The size of this
commonstash can be upper bounded, as we show in Sect. 4. The commonstash
is initially filled with encrypted fake items, so that the server cannot observe if
shared blocks have been added or removed, and remains stored on the server;
each client retrieves this stash before he performs any operation. Furthermore,

we use a dedicated private key for the fake blocks on the commonstash, so that the clients can distinguish between fake and real blocks in the commonstash.

Unfortunately, however, this ability of the clients can be a source of privacy leakage: once client cli_i notices that after a client's cli_j access, a shared datablock has been moved on the commonstash, cli_i immediately knows that in the last accessed path, all blocks of cli_j are real. Therefore, we must make sure that the commonstash remains as small as possible. We achieve this by changing the way the Read operation is performed – due to lack of space, we give here only a brief overview of the algorithm, and refer the reader to the full version of the paper, in [8] for details. In order for a client to read a block id, he first finds the leaf i, to which id is mapped. The client then downloads the commonstash and *two* paths[1]: One determined by the leaf i (which we will from then on call the "original" path), and the "symmetric" path, which is the path leading to the symmetric leaf of i, when considering as symmetry axis the line that cuts the leaf level into two parts of equal size. The client then identifies the blocks he has access to (real, fake and shared). This is done by having the client iterate on his keys, and checking for every block, if he can decrypt it – as we detail however in Sect. 7.2, this can be done more efficiently, by using the properties of homomorphic schemes. By construction, one of these blocks is guaranteed to be the block that the client is looking for. Consequently, the client copies the real and shared blocks of his in a local list, along with the blocks in his localstash, and replaces his real, shared and fakes in the paths, with empty placeholders. The client can now use all the empty placeholders in the paths for his eviction. First the client evicts all shared blocks, trying to store them as deep down in either of the paths as possible. If a shared block cannot fit in any of the paths, it replaces a fake block in the commonstash. Subsequently, he evicts in a similar manner those blocks that are not shared. If there is not enough space in the paths, the localstash is used. The client then fills up the remaining placeholders with fake elements, and finally re-randomizes all the blocks in the paths and the commonstash. The paths and the commonstash are then sent back to the server. Indeed, using these ideas, we observed during our experiments (cf. Sect. 7) that the stash sizes were very small, with the commonstash being almost empty during all our experiments, even when we let Z as small as 2.

In our construction, sharing a block between clients is straightforward: Suppose client cli_i wants to share block id_u with client cli_j; cli_i retrieves his block id_u (by means of Read operation, which changes also the block's path assignment), re-encrypts the block with a new key and uploads the block to the server. Finally, cli_i hands over to cli_j the *new key* and *the new index of the leaf to which* id_u is mapped. In a similar way, revocation of access rights is performed: If cli_i wants to revoke access rights of block id_u from cli_j, cli_i changes the key under which block id_u is encrypted (again by reading block id_u, and thus changing its path assignment) and informs other clients about the change of key and of path

---

[1] Adopting directly the eviction from [12], which also involves reading two paths, would unnecessarily degrade the protocol's performance, since we would have to store smaller ORAMs of size $\log(KN)$ in every node.

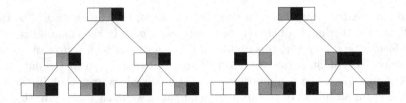

Fig. 1. Path-ORAMs of three clients, concatenated together, forming the initialization of Blurry-ORAM, on the left (blocks of different clients have different colors), and a Blurry-ORAM state after some accesses (the 'blurred' version of the multiple Path-ORAMs), on the right.

assignment. Note here, that cli_i and cli_j can share multiple blocks under the same key, thus forming *groups* of shared datablocks. This way, more clients can share only one key for a whole set of blocks.

Storing the Position Map. In order to save space, in ORAM constructions that use a position map, such as [12–15], the position map is stored recursively on the server, in smaller ORAMs, $ORAM_1, \ldots, ORAM_k$, where $ORAM_1$ stores the positions of the data and $ORAM_k$ is of constant size. In a multi-client ORAM allowing data sharing, at least $ORAM_2, \ldots, ORAM_k$ must be accessible by all clients. But in such a case, any client can infer that a position has been changed in $ORAM_1$, by noticing the changes in $ORAM_2$, thus trivially breaking the access pattern privacy of other clients, regardless if they share their data or not. In order to avoid this potential leakage, in Blurry-ORAM we store the clients' position maps in the following way: Every client stores a position map for his own blocks in a classic Path-ORAM on the server. Similarly, we store a position map in a separate ORAM for every group of shared datablocks to which all the members of the group have access. In order further to prevent the server from knowing whether a client is asking for a shared block (which the server can see by observing the position maps being accessed), all clients must access all the position maps for every access they make, even if they cannot decrypt blocks from certain position maps. In such a case, the client simply downloads a path, re-encrypts it and uploads it.

4 Analysis

4.1 Stash Size

As mentioned above, it is important that the commonstash remains very small. For this reason, the client first evicts all shared blocks found in the downloaded paths. Clearly, however, this does not guarantee that shared blocks never need to be stored outside the tree, and surely the greater the amount of shared blocks, the greater the probability that the commonstash will be used. We thus have to place a restriction on the amount of shared blocks. Suppose that in a Blurry-ORAM with N leaves, and K clients, each client shares at most m blocks. Since every client has a fixed amount of buckets that he can use in every node of the Blurry-ORAM, we could simulate every client's data as being stored in a single Path-ORAM, in which the client stores $N+m$ real blocks in a tree with N leaves. Since during eviction we let the shared items take the place of real items that belong to the client and we first push these shared items into the structure, in essence we treat these m blocks as the real blocks and all other blocks as fakes. Thus, in order to examine the commonstash size, we can simulate a Blurry-ORAM by a Path-ORAM, in which a client stores m real blocks in a tree with N leaves. Based on the proof of [15] we can estimate the probability of using a stash of size $O(\log \log N)$ for $m = \log^2 N$, by following the same argumentation as in the classical Path-ORAM, adjusting the number of leaves of the tree. These ideas are summarized in the following lemmata:

Lemma 1. *For a data request sequence α in a Blurry-ORAM with K clients, each having N blocks and sharing $O(\log^2 N)$ blocks, with $Z = 5$ buckets per client per node, that uses a commonstash of size R, the probability that the size of the commonstash during a data request sequence α exceeds R during one of the requests is bounded by $\mathsf{Prob}[\mathsf{st}(\mathsf{Blurry} - \mathsf{ORAM}_L^Z)[\alpha] > R] \leq 1.002 \cdot (0.5006)^R$.*

We can further use the above lemma in order to show that, in case $O(\log^2 N)$ blocks are shared, the commonstash does not grow larger than $O(\log \log N)$. The proof follows the one given in [15] and is thus omitted.

Proposition 1. *For a Blurry-ORAM of height $L = \log N$, $Z = 5$ buckets per client, per node, $O(\log^2 N)$ blocks shared by every client, and a data request sequence α, of length $N + \log^2 N$, the probability that the commonstash st exceeds the size R, after a series of load/store operations that correspond to α, is at most $\mathsf{Prob}[\mathsf{st}(\mathsf{Blurry} - \mathsf{ORAM}_L^Z)[\alpha] > R] = 14 \cdot (0.6002)^R$.*

The above lemmata show that, as long as the amount of the shared elements is in $O(\log^2 N)$, the commonstash will remain small. We observed this behaviour also during our simulations, where the commonstash was never used (cf. Sect. 7).

4.2 Time and Space Requirements

Based on the observations made earlier in this section, we can now analyze the time and space requirements of our protocol. A client that participates in $O(\log N)$ groups needs $O(\log N)$ space for the keys and $O(\log N)$ for the position maps (given the recursive position map storage). The client also needs to store his private stash, which follows the bounds provided in Proposition 1, and is thus limited to $O(\log N)$. Each time the client performs a data request, he downloads two paths of size $O(\log N)$, and the commonstash, which is in the worst case of size $O(\log \log N) \in O(\log N)$. Thus, the amount of space needed during protocol execution for the client is $O(\log N)$.

As far as the computational complexity of the client is concerned, recall that the client has to iterate on his $O(\log N)$ keys for each of the downloaded blocks found in the paths, thus the computational complexity is $O(\log^2 N)$. Note that since we have restricted the amount of shared items to $O(\log N)$ per client, there is a total $O(K \log N) \in O(\log N)$ position maps from each of which a client will read and rerandomize a path during a query.

Suppose that a client shares $N - 1$ blocks of his with K clients. Instead of holding a different key for every group, the client can share all the common blocks with all the clients, using only one key, and create smaller position maps only for the blocks that are not shared with all of the clients. Thus, each smaller position map will not exceed a size of $O(\log N)$, which means that for every query, the client will have to dedicate $O(\log^2 N \log(\log N))$ time for the recursive position map accesses.

5 Security

Proposition 2. *Blurry-ORAM achieves Client-to-Server Privacy.*

Proof (sketch). Recall that the position map and stash of every client are stored in exactly the same way as in the classical Path-ORAM. The commonstash is of fixed size and re-randomized every time a data request is performed by a client. Thus, it is easy to see, that the security of Blurry-ORAM against the server can be reduced to the security of Path-ORAM.

Proving that our construction achieves access pattern privacy against clients is more involved and is done by showing that Blurry-ORAM satisfies Definition 6. To do this, however, we must first make sure that the commonstash is empty. Indeed, recalling Lemma 1 we see that the size of the commonstash is very small with high probability. Thus, we can show the following proposition, which we prove in the paper's full version, found in [8]:

Proposition 3. *Assuming that the commonstash is empty, Blurry-ORAM achieves Client-To-Client privacy, if the used encryption scheme $\mathcal{E}$ is both IND-CPA and IK-CPA secure.*

The main proof idea is that we assume the existence of a PPT adversary that breaks the Client-To-Client privacy, by winning the IND-CQA game with non-negligible advantage, and we then construct an algorithm that by carefully crafting the views the adversary creates, as well as the views he is given through oracle access to other clients' data requests, he implants the IND-CPA or the IK-CPA challenge in the IND-CQA challenge, and can break the encryption scheme's semantic security, or its IK-CPA property, thus yielding a contradiction.

6 Application to Genomic Studies

We return to our motivating scenario of genomic studies, and we give a brief overview of the techniques used to store and query genomic data. A sequenced human genome is a set of approximately 3.3 billion characters, out of which only around 1% seem to be relevant. This specific part of the genome is typically stored in the form of Single Nucleotide Polymorphisms (SNPs), which are the positions in the sequenced genome of an individual which differ from what is known as the reference genome – and what is believed to be a representative example of a human genome.

Once a donor's SNPs have been determined, they are stored in biobanks, alongside those of other individuals, and can be used for various tests. These tests range from simple paternity and ancestry tests, to complex genome wide association studies. In the latter, the sequenced genome of multiple DNA donors is examined, and associations between specific parts of the human genome and various diseases are made. To do this, a biostatistician (in the following called an investigator) examines parts of the genome of multiple DNA samples that are suspected to be associated with a specific disease. Further, the investigator consults a table indicating whether if a DNA donor suffers from the disease or not, and thus can extract the probability that a particular DNA region (or SNP) is correlated with the disease. As pointed out in [9], estimating this probability in a privacy preserving way, can be done efficiently, using Secure Two Party Computation (STC) protocols. However, privacy leakage can occur, while the investigator retrieves the required SNPs (since the biobank can link parts of the genome to various diseases). Dealing with this leakage against the biobank is the main contribution of [9]. However, the authors in that solution, do not deal with the privacy leakage that may occur if multiple investigators are allowed to perform tests. To this end, our solution can be applied: By extending the highly efficient Path-ORAM construction, to a multi-client setting (where now a client might be a DNA donor or an investigator) so that information leakage between the participating entities is eliminated, we can substitute the ORAM used in [9] with Blurry-ORAM. This way, not only do we improve the computational complexity of the construction, we also improve the security guarantees. Observe here, that changing the ORAM construction of [9] does not affect either the security or the performance of the STC protocol used to evaluate the correlation probability. Since retrieving the relevant genome parts in a privacy preserving way is the bottleneck of [9], we focus the evaluation on this part.

Note also that the honest-but-curious and non-colluding assumption in this setting is realistic, since the investigators might get permission from the DNA donors to share specific parts of the DNA between them. At the same time, the investigators and the biobank would not jeopardise their reputation, by colluding with each other (Fig. 2).

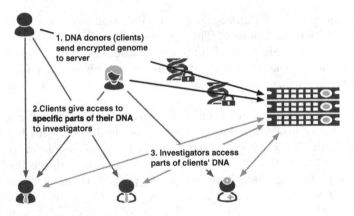

Fig. 2. Clients upload their encrypted genome on a Blurry-ORAM structure (step 1), give to investigators access to parts of it (step 2), which the latter access (step 3)

7 Experimental Results

7.1 Experimental Setup

We implemented Blurry-ORAM on a Virtual Machine running Ubuntu Version 16.10 with 8 cores and 16 GB of RAM, hosted on a 2x Xeon E5 2620v2 server with 12 Cores (24HT) and 64 GB of RAM, using VMWare ESXi 6 for the virtualization. For the client we used a desktop PC equipped with an AMD FX(tm)-8350 Eight-Core Processor and 24 GB of RAM, running on Ubuntu Desktop Version 16.04. As backend on the server, we used MySQL version 5.7.16. The code was compiled using $g{+}{+}$ version 6.2.0, for the cryptographic backend we used the OpenSSL library, version 1.0.2, and the experiments were ran on a 1 Gbit LAN network. Note that using as many cores as possible is crucial in boosting the efficiency of our construction: After the client has identified the blocks he can decrypt, he can perform the eviction in parallel, with the rerandomization of all other blocks, using all available cores.

7.2 Instantiation

Throughout the description of our architecture (cf. Sect. 3.2), we have assumed a public key encryption scheme that provides indistinguishability of keys, indistinguishability of ciphertexts (so that fake blocks are indistinguishable from real ones), and allows re-randomization of ciphertexts without knowledge of the public key. We achieve these properties using a variant of the ElGamal encryption scheme on elliptic curves: For a given block B, we store as its encryption the tuple (c_0, c_1, c_2, c_3), where $(c_0, c_1) = \mathsf{Enc}_k(B)$ and $(c_2, c_3) = \mathsf{Enc}_k(1)$. Thus for a client who has s_k as one of his secret keys, in order to check if a block belongs to him, he simply checks if $c_2^{s_k} = c_3$, instead of performing a costly decryption. Rerandomization without knowledge of the public key can also be easily done, due to the homomorphic properties, by using the ideas from [6].

7.3   Experiments

Using the techniques proposed in [3], one can efficiently store a patient's genome, by using roughly 2^{17} SNPs. Using an elliptic curve over a prime field $G(p)$ with p of size 256 bits, we can map a SNP to a single point of the elliptic curve. Typically for elliptic curve cryptography, mapping a plaintext to a point of the elliptic curve is not a trivial task. This is usually solved by concatenating random noise to the plaintext so that it can be mapped to a point of the elliptic curve. Indeed, doing this and using 16 bits of randomness for every block, we were able to map all the plaintexts we had, to points of the elliptic curve. Observe also, that for every SNP, we needed maximally 17 bits to represent the identifier and 16 bits of randomness to do the mapping to the elliptic curve. This left us with 223 bits, which provide adequate space to store the SNP, using the techniques described in [3].

In our simulations, therefore, we stored the SNPs of 100 clients, resulting in a database that stores a total of 2^{23} blocks (2^{17} SNPs per client, enough to hold a human genome stored in the form of SNPs as described in [3]). We then allowed multiple investigators access specific parts of the stored genomic data. We assume that every client distributed a different key to every investigator, so that neither other clients, nor investigators could learn anything about datablocks they would not have access to. The top left graph of Fig. 3 shows the performance of our construction: we performed 10 rounds of 1000 queries and measured the time needed for every query, depending on the number of keys a client has access to. The time needed for each query is affected by the number of investigators present (since decryption is attempted with all the client's keys), and varies from 6.48 s on average, when only one investigator is present to 63.01 s when 100 investigators are present.

In a similar setting, we varied the number of clients storing their data, (again with use 2^{17} SNPs per client), while 100 investigators were present, each one of them using a different key. We performed 10 rounds of 1000 queries. The results are presented in the top right graph of Fig. 3. We observe that, when 10 clients were present, the average time for a query was 6.9 s, when 50 clients were present, the average time was 31.40 s and when 100 clients were present, the average time for a query was 63.01 s.

In the lower left graph of Fig. 3 we examined how the number of datablocks affects the performance of our construction. We instantiated our construction with 50 clients and 10 investigators (i.e., 10 keys per client) and stored 2^{15}, 2^{16} and 2^{17} datablocks per client. We performed again 10 rounds of 1000 queries and measured an average query time of 6.92 s, 7.42 s and 7.71 s, when each client stored 2^{15}, 2^{16} and 2^{17} datablocks, respectively.

As we have seen in Sect. 5, the occupancy of the commonstash plays a very important role for client-to-client privacy. To experimentally assess the size of the stashes, we performed 10 rounds of 2^{17} queries (i.e., access of all blocks) in the database of 100 clients with 2^{17} blocks, 1000 keys each, and set $Z = 2$, i.e. 2 blocks per client per node. We examined the sizes of the localstash and the commonstash. The results are shown in the bottom right graph of Fig. 3, where

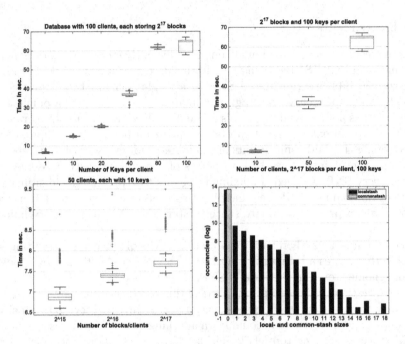

Fig. 3. Performance of Blurry-ORAM, when varying the number of keys (top left), and varying the number of clients (top right) in the scenario of storing the SNPs. Performance of Blurry-ORAM when varying the number of datablocks per client (bottom left). Sizes of the local- and commonstash for $Z = 2$ with each client sharing 1000 blocks and storing 2^{17} blocks (bottom right).

we see that the commonstash was *never* used. On the other hand, the localstash attained once a maximum occupancy of 20 blocks.

The previous experiment focused on storing all SNPs, which store only of the positions where a human's genome differs from the reference genome. Now we examine the applicability of the solution to databases storing full genomes. Using elliptic curves as described above, we can store the approximately 3d9 characters, using 2^{23} blocks per client, with each block storing approximately 128 characters[2]. We ran a series of 10 rounds of 1000 queries in a database with 2, 4 and 8 clients that share 10 blocks. The results are shown in the left graph of Fig. 4, where we see that the average query time was 50 s, 55 s, 60 s respectively. In a similar manner, we ran 10 rounds of 1000 queries in a database storing the whole genome of 8 clients, that share 10, 50 and 100 blocks and the results. The right graph of Fig. 4 shows that the average query time was 4.11, 6.98 and 11.26 respectively in this case, thus yielding a practical solution.

---

[2] Note that since the genome's alphabet consists only of the four letters A, T, G, C, we only need 2 bits to represent each letter of the alphabet.

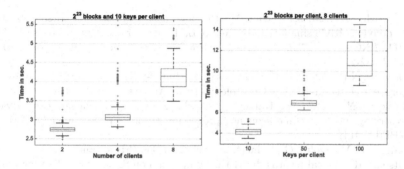

Fig. 4. Blurry-ORAM performance, when varying the number of clients (left), and the number of keys per client (right). The experiment used $Z = 2$, and allowed each client to store 2^{23} blocks.

8   Conclusion

In this work, we developed an ORAM construction that allows multiple clients to store their data on a remote server, share parts of it with each other, and access it in a way that protects their privacy both against the server, and other clients. We formalized the notion of access pattern privacy in a multi-client setting, and inspired by the GWAS case, we showed that our construction is practical. We leave as future work, extending our security model against colluding and malicious clients, as well as combining ideas of other multi-client ORAM constructions, in order to achieve client anonymity as well.

Acknowledgments. This work has been funded by the DFG as part of project S5 within the CRC 1119 CROSSING, and by the Netherlands Organisation for Scientific Research (NWO) in the context of the CRIPTIM project.

References

1. Backes, M., Herzberg, A., Kate, A., Pryvalov, I.: Anonymous RAM. In: ESORICS 2016 (2016)
2. Bellare, M., Boldyreva, A., Desai, A., Pointcheval, D.: Key-privacy in public-key encryption. In: Boyd, C. (ed.) ASIACRYPT 2001. LNCS, vol. 2248, pp. 566–582. Springer, Heidelberg (2001). doi:10.1007/3-540-45682-1_33
3. Brandon, M.C., Wallace, D.C., Baldi, P.: Data structures and compression algorithms for genomic sequence data. Bioinformatics **25**, 1731–1738 (2009)
4. Franz, M., Williams, P., Carbunar, B., Katzenbeisser, S., Peter, A., Sion, R., Sotakova, M.: Oblivious outsourced storage with delegation. In: Danezis, G. (ed.) FC 2011. LNCS, vol. 7035, pp. 127–140. Springer, Heidelberg (2012). doi:10.1007/978-3-642-27576-0_11
5. Goldreich, O., Ostrovsky, R.: Software protection and simulation on oblivious RAMs. J. ACM **43**, 431–473 (1996)
6. Golle, P., Jakobsson, M., Juels, A., Syverson, P.: Universal re-encryption for mixnets. In: Okamoto, T. (ed.) CT-RSA 2004. LNCS, vol. 2964, pp. 163–178. Springer, Heidelberg (2004). doi:10.1007/978-3-540-24660-2_14

7. Goodrich, M.T., Mitzenmacher, M.: Privacy-preserving access of outsourced data via oblivious RAM simulation. In: Aceto, L., Henzinger, M., Sgall, J. (eds.) ICALP 2011. LNCS, vol. 6756, pp. 576–587. Springer, Heidelberg (2011). doi:10.1007/978-3-642-22012-8_46

8. Karvelas, N.P., Peter, A., Katzenbeisser, S.: Blurry-ORAM: a multi-client oblivious storage architecture. IACR Cryptology ePrint Archive, p. 1077 (2016)

9. Karvelas, N., Peter, A., Katzenbeisser, S., Tews, E., Hamacher, K.: Privacy-preserving whole genome sequence processing through proxy-aided ORAM. In: WPES (2014)

10. Maffei, M., Malavolta, G., Reinert, M., Schröder, D.: Privacy and access control for outsourced personal records. In: IEEE Symposium on Security and Privacy (2015)

11. Mayberry, T., Blass, E.O., Noubir, G.: Multi-user oblivious RAM secure against malicious servers. IACR Cryptology ePrint Archive (2015)

12. Shi, E., Chan, T.-H.H., Stefanov, E., Li, M.: Oblivious RAM with $O((\log N)^3)$ worst-case cost. In: Lee, D.H., Wang, X. (eds.) ASIACRYPT 2011. LNCS, vol. 7073, pp. 197–214. Springer, Heidelberg (2011). doi:10.1007/978-3-642-25385-0_11

13. Stefanov, E., Shi, E.: Oblivistore: High performance oblivious distributed cloud data store. In: NDSS 2013 (2013)

14. Stefanov, E., Shi, E., Song, D.X.: Towards practical oblivious RAM. In: NDSS 2012 (2012)

15. Stefanov, E., van Dijk, M., Shi, E., Fletcher, C.W., Ren, L., Yu, X., Devadas, S.: Path ORAM: an extremely simple oblivious RAM protocol. In: CCS 2013 (2013)

Privacy and Encrypted Search

Towards Efficient and Secure Encrypted Databases: Extending Message-Locked Encryption in Three-Party Model

Yuuji Furuta[1]([⊠]), Naoto Yanai[1], Masashi Karasaki[2], Katsuhiko Eguchi[2], Yasunori Ishihara[1], and Toru Fujiwara[1]

[1] Osaka University, 1-5 Yamadaoka, Suita, Osaka 565–0871, Japan
yanai@ist.osaka-u.ac.jp
[2] Nippon Telegraph and Telephone West Corporation,
3-15 Bamba-cho, Chuo-ku, Osaka 540–8511, Japan

Abstract. In database systems with three parties consisting of a data owner, a database manager and a data analyst, the data owner uploads encrypted data to a database and the data analyst delegated by the data owner analyzes the data by accessing to the database without knowing plaintexts. In this work, towards an efficient and secure scheme whose encryption can be processed in real time, we extend message-locked encryption (Bellare et al. [2]), where parts of ciphertexts are generated from their plaintexts deterministically. In particular, we introduce both delegations of relational search between ciphertexts from a data owner to a data analyst, and re-encryption of ciphertexts such that ciphertexts of the message-locked encryption become truly probabilistic against a database manager. We call the scheme *message-locked encryption with re-encryption and relational search*, and formalize the security, which is feasible and practical, in two cases, i.e., any relationship in a general setting and only an equality test in a restricted setting. Both settings are useful from a standpoint of trade-offs between the security and the efficiency. We also propose an instantiation with the equality test between ciphertexts.

Keywords: Message-locked encryption · Encrypted database · Re-encryption · Relational search · Three-party model

1 Introduction

1.1 Backgrounds and Research Problem

Motivation for Three-Party Model. In recent years, there are several big data services whereby a data owner stores data in a storage server and outsources a job of analysis to an expert. For example, in the life-science area, a research institute corresponding to a data analyst analyzes genome data provided by each user corresponding to a data owner (and its centralized control center) via

© Springer International Publishing AG 2017
J. Garcia-Alfaro et al. (Eds.): DPM/CBT 2017, LNCS 10436, pp. 55–69, 2017.
DOI: 10.1007/978-3-319-67816-0_4

a computational resource such as Amazon EC2 to process a large amount of the data. These services provide potential advantages to both data owner and expert since the owner has data but not an analysis skill and vice versa. Such a situation is modeled as a *three-party* model between a data owner who stores data in a cloud, a database manager who manages a storage, and a data analyst to whom the data owner outsources a job. These data are often provided per second in real time because a large number of patients may exist in the above life-science area. Since big data services need a large amount of data in general to discover a new fact as soon as possible, processing and analyzing the data in real time is necessary.

Problem Statement. We describe more details of the three-party model below. First, each data is generated per second by a data owner, and the owner adds the data in a database in real time. Next, an analyst specified by the data owner analyzes the data via the database. In such a situation, the data owner often want to give the database manager no information on the stored data. Furthermore, the data owner may also want to hide any information other than the results of the analysis, i.e., not only plaintexts but also their substrings and related keywords, from the data analyst. For example, in the life-science area described above, the data analyst needs to know the number of patients with the same sick. However, the analyst may not know their personal information, e.g., names and addresses. Here, the results of the analysis mean results of relational searches between ciphertexts, e.g., ciphertexts such that the number of occurrences is greater than some threshold. Meanwhile, the owner may want to add new data in the database in real time, and sometimes receives information about the analysis from the analyst. That is, there are two standpoints in the three-party model, i.e., the confidentiality of data and the efficiency of processing data in real time. We summarize the scenario described above in Fig. 1.

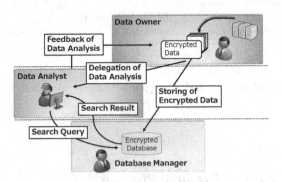

Fig. 1. Our targeting three-party model

We note that conventional encryption schemes are not useful for the above analysis. In particular, the schemes satisfy either one of the two standpoints. First, several cryptographic schemes [5,7,15,17] can satisfy the confidentiality since they can compute plaintexts without their knowledge. However, their computational costs are heavy, and are inefficient in dealing with data added in real time. Meanwhile, symmetric searchable encryption [18] can provide fast encryption and analysis of encrypted data by searching a specified keyword without decryption. Although the symmetric searchable encryption can satisfy the efficiency, the scheme forces a user who searches data, i.e., a data analyst, to know the keyword. Hence, the scheme cannot satisfy the confidentiality in the three-party model.

Message-Locked Encryption (MLE) and Its Limitations. In this work, we focus on *message-locked encryption (MLE)* [2] whose encryption keys are generated by plaintexts as a potentially suitable and efficient scheme for processing encrypted data. This cryptographic scheme can generate ciphertexts whose equality can be checked without knowledge of their plaintexts even if the ciphertexts are generated by different signers. Namely, ciphertexts between two parties, e.g., a sender and a receiver, can be analyzed. Especially, the scheme proposed by Bellare et al. [2] has been constructed by well-known building blocks such as hash functions and a standard symmetric key encryption scheme, e.g., SHA-2 and AES. Hence, their scheme is also able to provide fast encryption.

Although one might think that the above problem statement in the three-party model can be overcome by the use of MLE, we need to solve the following problem about MLE. First, since the motivation of MLE is deduplication to decrease the size of a cloud storage storing ciphertexts, MLE is discussed in two-party model between a sender and a receiver. That is, processing encrypted data in the three-party model is out of the scope of the original work. Hence, a new MLE scheme suitable in the three-party model is necessary. However, such an extension of MLE is non-trivial. Loosely speaking, whereas a feasible and meaningful definition is necessary, the security of variants of MLE is weaker than that of standard cryptographic schemes. More specifically, results of the analysis of data is leaked to a data analyst in the three-party model while an adversary against MLE is disallowed to know plaintexts to be encrypted. To avoid this dilemma, an extension of MLE in the three-party model and its security should be discussed carefully.

1.2   Our Contribution

In this paper, we extend MLE to a scheme suitable in the three-party model by introducing re-encryption from a data owner to a data analyst and search of relationships between ciphertexts. We call the extended scheme *message-locked encryption with re-encryption and relational search (MLERERS)*, and also show its instantiation which generates ciphertexts probabilistically. This essentially contributes to processing encrypted data by searching relationships such as frequency analysis. Furthermore, by formalizing the above features, subsequent works can analyze the security rigorously via our formalization.

We briefly describe our main idea of the extension of MLE in the three-party model. A data owner first converts ciphertexts of MLE, i.e., first-level ciphertexts, to fully probabilistic ciphertexts, i.e., second-level ciphertexts by a re-encryption key. The data owner then outsources analysis of data to a data analyst by sending the data analyst the re-encryption key. Next, the data analyst generates a trapdoor by the re-encryption key for any search of a relationship between ciphertexts, and then a database manager receiving the trapdoor extracts search results of first-level ciphertexts. By generating such a trapdoor securely, the database manager cannot extract the re-encryption key and the raw first-level ciphertexts from the search results.

We formalize the security in the situation described above. The main technical problem of this formalization is to define a feasible and practical security. We note that achieving a perfect security, where a database manager obtains no information about results in search, seems to be impossible: because a data analyst knows nothing about plaintexts (and their keywords) to be searched and has no ciphertexts themselves in local. That is, for any search, the database manager can know that ciphertexts meet some relationships via the search although the manager does not know its condition and raw ciphertexts. Instead of such a perfect security, our security definition guarantees that "any search in the past" does not affect search of newly added data. Intuitively, our security is feasible since a data analyst can potentially generate ciphertexts unsuitable for known trapdoors. Moreover, the security is practical since a database manager extracts nothing about a new ciphertext. We also define the unforgeability of trapdoors to guarantee the security strictly. Note that we define the security from two settings, i.e., any search as the general setting and only equality tests as the restricted setting. We mention that both settings are useful: in particular, the equality tests are enough in the sense of providing frequency analysis and more efficient, while wider searches are available for the former scheme. See Sect. 4 for more details.

We also propose an instantiation with equality tests under the security described above. Our scheme is an extension of the randomized convergent encryption scheme by Bellare et al. [2] in the model of MLERERS. This scheme can be instantiated by standard cryptographic tools such as AES and SHA-2. See Sect. 5 for more details.

1.3   Related Works

Message-Locked Encryption and its Re-encryption. To the best of our knowledge, there are several MLE schemes [1,8,11,12] which probabilistically generate ciphertexts fully in the sense that all parts of the ciphertexts are random. However, these schemes are discussed in two-party model and are still insufficient in the three-party model. Meanwhile, Lei et al. [11] and Li et al. [12] have proposed re-encryption schemes for MLE, and their works are the closest to our work. However, their schemes do not target the three-party model and a receiver designated by a re-encryption key can obtain plaintexts. Namely, our work is not implied by their works.

Searchable Encryption. Another scheme close to our work is searchable encryption. There are two classifications of searchable encryption, i.e., symmetric searchable encryption [18] and publicly encrypted keyword search [4]. We note that, the limitation described in Sect. 1.1 exist in both schemes. Meanwhile, several efficient schemes suitable for real-time data have been proposed in the symmetric searchable encryption. For instance, Ogata et al. [14] proposed a scheme utilizing only hash functions. In addition, there are several schemes [9,13] with dynamic update of encrypted dataset. These ideas are close to our instantiations.

2 Preliminaries

In this section, we define mathematical backgrounds to understand our work. Hereafter, we denote by ϵ a negligible function.

Symmetric Key Encryption. A symmetric key encryption scheme is defined as follows: a key generation algorithm KG takes a security parameter n as input and outputs a secret key sk; an encryption algorithm Enc takes sk and a plaintext m as input and outputs a ciphertext c; a decryption algorithm Dec takes sk and c as input and outputs m. The correctness of the scheme is defined as, for any n, m and $sk \leftarrow KG(1^n)$, $m = Dec(sk, Enc(sk, m))$.

Next, we recall the indistinguishablity against a chosen plaintext attack [10], IND-CPA for short. The security is defined as the following game between a challenger C and an adversary A, which are probabilistic polynomial time algorithms. C generates a secret key $sk \leftarrow KG(1^n)$ for a given n. Given n and access to an oracle $Enc(sk, \cdot)$, A outputs a pair (m_0, m_1) of plaintexts. Next, C chooses a random bit $b \leftarrow \{0,1\}$ and computes a challenge ciphertext $c \leftarrow Enc(sk, m_b)$. C then gives c to A. A is given access to the oracle $Enc(sk, \cdot)$ again, and finally outputs a bit $b' \in \{0,1\}$. In this game, an advantage of A is defined as $Adv^{SK}_{IND\text{-}CPA,A}(1^n) = |Pr[b' = b] - \frac{1}{2}|$. We say that a scheme is IND-CPA secure if the advantage is negligible, i.e., $Adv^{SK}_{IND\text{-}CPA,A}(1^n) \leq \epsilon(1^n)$.

Message Locked Encryption (MLE). We recall the definition of MLE and a source as its basic notion by Bellare et al. [2]. First, a source M generates $(m_0, ..., m_{N-1}, Z)$, where $m_0, ..., m_{N-1}$ are vectors in $\{0,1\}^*$, $Z \in \{0,1\}^*$ is any auxiliary information, and N is the number of operands in the source. Let len be the length of a message from the source. For instance, for all $i \in [\lambda(1^n)]$ and all $j \in [0, N-1]$, where λ is a function to represent the number of messages in the source, a string $m_j[i]$ has length $len(1^n, i)$. A guessing probability of messages by M is assumed to be negligibly small although we omit the detail due to the page limitation.

An MLE scheme is then defined by the following algorithms: a parameter generation algorithm P takes a security parameter 1^n as input and outputs a parameter P; a key generation algorithm K takes P and a plaintext m and outputs a secret key k; an encryption algorithm E takes (P, k, m) as input and outputs a ciphertext c; a decryption algorithm D takes (P, k, c) as input and outputs a plaintext m; a tag generation algorithm T takes (P, c) as input and outputs a tag T. The correctness of a MLE scheme is defined as follows, where $MsgSp_{MLE}$ described below means a MLE-valid source in [2]: for any security parameter 1^n and any message $m \in MsgSp_{MLE}$, $P \leftarrow \mathcal{P}(1^n)$, $m = \mathcal{D}(\mathcal{K}(P, m), \mathcal{E}(\mathcal{K}(P, m)))$ and, for any messages $m, m' \in MsgSp_{MLE}$ such that $m = m'$, $\mathcal{T}(P, \mathcal{E}(\mathcal{K}(P, m), m)) = \mathcal{T}(P, \mathcal{E}(\mathcal{K}(P, m'), m'))$ hold.

The security of an MLE scheme is defined as privacy against chosen distribution attacks (PRV-CDA) and tag consistency [2]. The former is the confidentiality of data and the latter is a notion for deduplication. The security discussion in the rest of this paper deals with the former feature, and we omit the latter notion due to the page limitation. Intuition of the PRV-CDA security is that ciphertexts are indistinguishable unless messages are predictable. According to Bellare et al. [2], there is no MLE scheme classical security notion such as IND-CPA because secret keys are generated by messages to be encrypted. That is, an adversary can easily obtain secret keys if the messages are predictable. Therefore, the PRV-CDA security is the best possible notion although messages are required to be unpredictable. The PRV-CDA security is defined via the following game: A challenger $\mathcal{C}$ generates $\mathcal{P}(1^n)$ for a given n, and choses a bit $b \leftarrow \{0, 1\}$. Next, $\mathcal{C}$ generates $(\mathbf{m}_0, \mathbf{m}_1, Z) \leftarrow \mathcal{M}(1^n)$ and, for all $i \in [1, |\mathbf{m}_b|]$, computes $C[i] \leftarrow \mathcal{E}(P, \mathcal{K}(P, \mathbf{m}_b[i]), \mathbf{m}_b[i])$. Given n and $C[i]$ for all $i \in [1, |\mathbf{m}_b|]$, $\mathcal{A}$ outputs a guess b'. In this game, an advantage of $\mathcal{A}$ is defined as $Adv_{PRV\text{-}CDA, \mathcal{M}, \mathcal{A}}^{MLE}(1^n) = |Pr[b = b'] - \frac{1}{2}|$. We say that an MLE scheme is PRV-CDA secure if the advantage is negligible, i.e. $Adv_{PRV\text{-}CDA, \mathcal{M}, \mathcal{A}}^{MLE}(1^n) \leq \epsilon(1^n)$.

3 Our Motivating Three-Party Model

In this section, we describe a three-party model as our motivating scenario. First, we define three parties and their requirements in this model.

3.1 Entities in Three-Party Model

There are three entities in the model as follows:

Data Owner is able to access to any plaintext. The owner stores encrypted data in a database and delegates its analysis to other users.

Database Manager receives encrypted data from the data owner, and provides an encrypted database. The manager also returns responses to queries by a data analyst.

Data Analyst is delegated analysis of data by the data owner, and accesses to the database by issuing search queries. The analyst then receives responses from the database.

3.2 Requirements in the Three-Party Model

We describe requirements in the three-party model below. The main motivation described in Sect. 1.1 is to discuss extension of MLE and its security suitable for the following requirements.

Real-Time Processing for Encryption. A database system deals with a large amount of data which is added per second in real time. To process such kind of data, a cryptographic scheme should be able to dynamically update the database, i.e., without re-construction. It should also be able to provide fast encryption.

Prevention of Undesirable Extraction of Plaintexts and Searchability for Data Analyst. A data analyst specifies a rule of analysis for ciphertexts, and then queries the rule to a database. Here, the data analyst can obtain only the results, but not plaintexts themselves stored in the database and their related keywords. In other words, the data analyst needs to search only by relationships between ciphertexts, e.g., the number of occurrences or a series of the same ciphertexts. In general, storing plaintexts in local may pose an unnecessary risk to the data analyst, e.g., the accountability and compensation to the data owner. Meanwhile, the results themselves are necessary for the data analyst to analyze data.

Data Confidentiality against Database Manager. Since a malicious server may exists, the confidentiality of data against a database manager should be guaranteed. That is, we regard the confidentiality against a database manager as the same level against an adversary, and discuss whether information about plaintexts are leaked from ciphertexts. Meanwhile, we tolerate that the database manager obtains results in search.

Decryption via Feedback from Data Analyst. A data owner may want to decrypt ciphertexts in a database via feedback of analysis of data from a data analyst. Then, the data owner needs to keep the capability of decryption in the database even after delegating analysis of the data.

4   Message Locked Encryption with Re-encryption and Relational Search

In this section, we introduce re-encryption and searchability of relationships between ciphertexts in MLE. We call this scheme *message-locked encryption with re-encryption and relational search (MLERERS)*. We first define a syntax of MLERERS and show that the syntax meets the three-party model described in the previous section. Next, we formalize its security more precisely. These are the main contribution in this work.

4.1   Syntax

A message-locked encryption scheme with re-encryption and relational search (MLERERS) is defined via the following ten algorithms.

Parameter Generation $\mathcal{P}$ takes a security parameter 1^n and outputs a parameter P.

Key Generation $\mathcal{K}$ takes P and a message m and outputs a key K.

Re-encryption Key Generation $\mathcal{RKG}$ takes P and outputs a re-encryption key RK.

Encryption $\mathcal{E}$ takes P, m and K, and outputs a first-level ciphertext C.

Re-encryption $\mathcal{RE}$ takes P, C and RK, and outputs a second-level ciphertext C'.

Tag $\mathcal{T}$ takes C, and outputs a tag T.

Trapdoor Generation $\mathcal{TG}$ takes P, RK and a query condition X to search relationships between ciphertexts, and outputs a trapdoor $t(RK)$.

Re-encryption Test $\mathcal{RT}$ takes a set $\mathcal{C}'$ of second-level ciphertexts and a list of trapdoors $t(RK)$, and outputs its resulting set $Data$ of ciphertexts.

Second-level Decryption $\mathcal{RD}$ takes RK and a second-level ciphertext C' and outputs a first-level ciphertext C.

Decryption $\mathcal{D}$ takes P, K and a first-level ciphertext C, and outputs a message m. If any error happens, It outputs an error symbol $\perp$.

(Note 1) The re-encryption test algorithm $\mathcal{RT}$ searches ciphertexts for a given trapdoor with any condition X. This is a generic definition and, when only equality tests are executed, the following algorithm can be defined as a simpler algorithm. Here, input X in the trapdoor generation algorithm $\mathcal{TG}$ is omitted in the following simpler algorithm.

Equal $\mathcal{EQ}$ takes two ciphertexts (C_1', C_2') and a list of trapdoors $t(RK)$, and outputs *true* or *false* as equality.

Correctness. We say that a scheme is correct if the following conditions hold, where $MsgSp_{MLE}$ is a MLE-valid source in [2]: for any security parameter n, any message $m \in MsgSp_{MLE}$ and $P \leftarrow \mathcal{P}(1^n)$, $m = \mathcal{D}(P, \mathcal{K}(P, m), \mathcal{E}(P, m, \mathcal{K}(P, m)))$ holds; for any $RK \leftarrow \mathcal{RK}(P)$, $C = \mathcal{RD}(P, RK, \mathcal{RE}(RK, C))$ holds; and for any $RK \leftarrow \mathcal{RK}(P)$, $Data_X = \mathcal{RT}(\mathcal{C}', \mathcal{TG}(P, RK, X))$ holds where $Data_X$ is a subset of $\mathcal{C}'$ which meets the condition X.

(Note 2) The correctness of a scheme with the equal algorithm $\mathcal{EQ}$ is defined as, instead of the above third condition, $true = \mathcal{EQ}(\mathcal{E}(P, m, \mathcal{K}(P, m)), \mathcal{E}(P, m', \mathcal{K}(P, m')), \mathcal{TG}(P, RK))$ holds if and only if $m = m'$ holds.

We summarize the flow of algorithms in MLERERS in Fig. 2.

(Note 3) We note that MLERERS is suitable for the three-party model described in the previous section. First, the encryption algorithm and the re-encryption algorithm encrypt each input individually, and hence MLERERS can support real-time processing by dynamically updating a database. Next, a data owner stores data in the database after executing the re-encryption algorithm, and then delegates analysis of the data to a data analyst by sending the re-encryption key. Next, the data analyst generates trapdoors by the re-encryption key, and sends a database manager the trapdoors. The database manager executes the re-encryption test algorithm by the use of the given trapdoors, and returns a set of data corresponding to the relation to the data analyst. Here, the database manager cant obtain neither plaintexts nor first-level ciphertexts, and hence

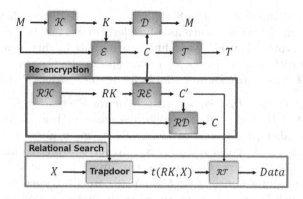

Fig. 2. Flow of MLERERS

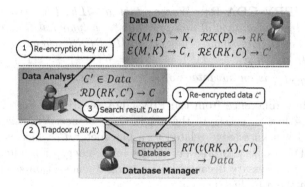

Fig. 3. MLERERS in the three-party model

MLERERS can provide the data confidentiality against a database manager. Moreover, the data analyst can decrypt only second-level ciphertexts to first-level ciphertexts. This means that both prevention of undesirable extraction of plaintexts and searchability for the data analyst can be achieved. We summarize the algorithms described above in Fig. 3.

4.2 Definition of Security

We define security of MLERERS in this section, where that with the equal algorithm $\mathcal{EQ}$ can also be defined by replacing $\mathcal{RT}$ in the following definition with $\mathcal{EQ}$.

Security Definition of First-Level Ciphertext. The security of first-level ciphertexts captures a situation in which a data analyst cannot distinguish ciphertexts of the message-locked encryption. Intuitively, the security is an extension of the security definition of PRV-CDA in Sect. 2 in the sense that a view of an adversary is identical to that in Sect. 2; more specifically, we discuss a situation whereby a challenger just outputs a first-level ciphertext C for any message m with an encryption key K. We define two notions in this security, *privacy against chosen distribution attacks for re-encryption (PRV-CDA-R)* and *strong privacy against chosen distribution attacks for re-encryption (PRV$-CDA-R)*.

Privacy against Chosen Distribution Attack for Re-Encryption (PRV-CDA-R). The PRV-CDA-R is defined via the following game with a challenger and an adversary: A challenger C generates $P \leftarrow \mathcal{P}(1^n)$ for a given n, and chooses a bit $b \leftarrow \{0,1\}$. $\mathcal{A}$ is given n and access to an a re-encryption key generation oracle $\mathcal{O}_{RK}(P)$. Next, C generates $(\mathbf{m}_0, \mathbf{m}_1, Z) \leftarrow \mathcal{M}(1^n)$ and, for all $i \in [1, \lambda(1^n)]$, computes $C[i] \leftarrow \mathcal{E}(P, \mathcal{K}(P, \mathbf{m}_b[i]), \mathbf{m}_b[i])$. C then gives $C[i]$ to $\mathcal{A}$ for all $i \in [1, |\mathbf{m}_b|]$. Next, $\mathcal{A}$ is given access to the re-encryption key generation oracle $\mathcal{O}_{RK}(P)$ again. Finally, $\mathcal{A}$ outputs a guess b'.

Definition 1 (PRV-CDA-R). *We say that a MLERERS scheme achieves PRV-CDA-R if an advantage of any probabilistic polynomial time adversary $\mathcal{A}$ in the game is negligibly small. That is, a MLERERS scheme achieves PRV-CDA-R if $Adv_{PRV\text{-}CDA\text{-}R,\mathcal{M},\mathcal{A}}^{MLERERS}(1^n) = \left| \Pr[b = b'] - \frac{1}{2} \right| \leq \epsilon(1^n)$ holds, where $Adv_{PRV\text{-}CDA\text{-}R,\mathcal{M},\mathcal{A}}^{MLERERS}$ is an advantage of $\mathcal{A}$ in the game.*

(Note) The main difference from the PRV-CDA security in Sect. 2 is whether an adversary $\mathcal{A}$ has an access to the oracle $\mathcal{O}_{RK}$ or not. Via accessing to the oracle, $\mathcal{A}$ can learn knowledge related to a parameter P, which is never given in the PRV-CDA security. Moreover, oracles for re-encryption and second-level decryption are unnecessary because, by receiving re-encryption keys from $\mathcal{O}_{RK}$, $\mathcal{A}$ can perform them by his-/herself.

Strong Privacy against Chosen Distribution Attack for Re-Encryption (PRV$-CDA-R). The PRV$-CDA-R is defined similarly as the PRV-CDA-R security except for generating challenge ciphertexts. In particular, by utilizing a source such that $(m, Z) \leftarrow \mathcal{M}(1^n)$, a challenger generates $C_1[i]$ by running $\mathcal{E}(\mathcal{K}(\mathbf{m}[i]), \mathbf{m}[i])$. C also generates $C_0[i] \leftarrow \{0,1\}^{|C_1[i]|}$ randomly, and then gives $C_b[i]$ to $\mathcal{A}$ for $i \in [1, \lambda(1^n)]$. We say that a MLERERS scheme achieves PRV$-CDA-R if an advantage in the game is negligibly small. We omit the full definition due to the page limitation.

Security Definition of Second-Level Ciphertexts. Next, we define the security of second-level ciphertexts. The security is a requirement against a database manager, and captures a situation where the manager cannot distinguish a second-level ciphertext corresponding to first-level ciphertexts. The security is an extension from the IND-CPA security in the sense that a view of an adversary is identical to that of a symmetric key encryption: in particular, we discuss a situation whereby a challenger just outputs a second-level ciphertext from first-level ciphertexts as plaintexts with a key RK. We then define *indistinguishablity against chosen plaintext attacks for re-encryption (IND-CPA-R)* and *indistinguishablity against chosen ciphertext attacks for re-encryption (IND-CCA-R)*.

Indistinguishablity against Chosen Plaintext Attacks for Re-Encryption (IND-CPA-R). The security is defined as the following game between a challenger $\mathcal{C}$ and an adversary $\mathcal{A}$: $\mathcal{C}$ generates a parameter $P \leftarrow \mathcal{P}(1^n)$ for a given n and a re-encryption key $RK \leftarrow \mathcal{RK}(P)$. Given n, P and accesses to a re-encryption oracle $\mathcal{O}_{RE}(RK, \cdot)$ and a tag generation oracle $\mathcal{O}_{TG}(RK, \cdot)$, $\mathcal{A}$ outputs a pair (C_0, C_1) of ciphertexts with the same length. Next, $\mathcal{C}$ chooses a random bit $b \leftarrow \{0, 1\}$ and computes a challenge second-level ciphertext $C' \leftarrow \mathcal{RE}(RK, C_b)$. $\mathcal{C}$ then gives C' to $\mathcal{A}$. $\mathcal{A}$ is given access to $\mathcal{O}_{RE}(RK, \cdot)$, and finally outputs a bit $b' \in \{0, 1\}$.

Definition 2 (IND-CPA-R). *We say that a MLERERS scheme achieves IND-CPA-R if the advantage of any probabilistic polynomial time adversary $\mathcal{A}$ in the game is negligibly small. That is, a MLERERS scheme achieves IND-CPA-R if $Adv_{IND\text{-}CPA\text{-}R,\mathcal{A}}^{MLERERS}(1^n) = \left| \Pr[b = b'] - \frac{1}{2} \right| \leq \epsilon(1^n)$ holds, where $Adv_{IND\text{-}CPA\text{-}R,\mathcal{A}}^{MLERERS}$ is an advantage of $\mathcal{A}$.*

Indistinguishablity against Chosen Ciphertext Attacks for Re-Encryption (IND-CCA-R). The security is defined similarly as the IND-CPA-R security except that an adversary $\mathcal{A}$ can access to a second-level decryption oracle $\mathcal{O}_{RD}$[1]. More precisely, $\mathcal{A}$ can receive first-level ciphertexts by requesting second-level ciphertexts to the oracle $\mathcal{O}_{RD}$. We omit the full definition due to the page limitation.

Security Definition of Trapdoors. A data analyst delegated by a data owner generates trapdoors for any relation to search in a encrypted database. If an adversary can extract knowledge of a re-encryption key RK or can forge trapdoors $t(RK)$ by the re-encryption test algorithm $\mathcal{RT}$ for any condition X, the adversary is able to search any relation between ciphertexts. To prevent such an attack, trapdoors have to be secure. In particular, we define *onewayness of trapdoors* and *unforgeability of trapdoors* below.

Onewayness of Trapdoors. The onewayness of trapdoors guarantees preventing an adversary from extracting a re-encryption key via given trapdoors. We define the security as the following game between a challenger $\mathcal{C}$ and an adversary $\mathcal{A}$: $\mathcal{C}$ generates a parameter $P \leftarrow \mathcal{P}(1^n)$ for a given n and then generates a re-encryption key $RK \leftarrow \mathcal{RK}(P)$. $\mathcal{A}$ is given n, P and access to a trapdoor generation oracle $\mathcal{O}_{TG}(RK, \cdot)$. $\mathcal{A}$ then outputs a re-encryption key RK'.

Definition 3 (Onewayness of Trapdoor). *We say that a MLERERS scheme achieves the onewayness of trapdoors if the advantage of any probabilistic polynomial time adversary $\mathcal{A}$ in the game is negligibly small. That is, a MLERERS scheme achieves the onewayness of trapdoors if $Adv_{TR,\mathcal{A}}^{MLERERS}(1^n) = |\Pr[RK = RK']| \leq \epsilon(1^n)$ holds, where $Adv_{TR,\mathcal{A}}^{MLERERS}$ is an advantage of $\mathcal{A}$.*

Unforgeability of Trapdoors. The unforgeability of trapdoors is a stronger security notion than the onewayness with respect to trapdoors. The security is defined as follows: $\mathcal{C}$ generates a parameter $P \leftarrow \mathcal{P}(1^n)$ for a given n, and then generates

---

[1] Note that the IND-CCA security of a standard symmetric key encryption scheme has been defined by Katz and Lindel [10] by introducing the decryption oracle.

a re-encryption key $RK \leftarrow \mathcal{RK}(P)$ and a set $\mathcal{C}'$ of second-level ciphertexts. $\mathcal{A}$ is given P and access to a trapdoor generation oracle $\mathcal{O}_{TG}(RK, \cdot)$. Here, we denote by $PreX$ a set of conditions which are queried by $\mathcal{A}$ to $\mathcal{O}_{TG}(RK, \cdot)$. $\mathcal{A}$ then outputs a pair $(t'(RK), X)$ of a trapdoor and a condition.

Definition 4 (Unforgeability of Trapdoors). *We say that a MLERERS scheme achieves the unforgeability of trapdoors if the advantage of any probabilistic polynomial time adversary $\mathcal{A}$ in the game is negligibly small. That is, a MLERERS scheme achieves the unforgeability of trapdoors if $Adv_{TRU,\mathcal{A}}^{MLERERS}(1^n) = |\Pr[\mathcal{RT}(\mathcal{C}', \mathcal{TG}(P, RK, X)) = \mathcal{RT}(\mathcal{C}', t'(RK, X)) \wedge X \notin PreX]| \leq \epsilon(1^n)$ holds, where $Adv_{TRU,\mathcal{A}}^{MLERERS}$ is an advantage of $\mathcal{A}$.*

5   Instantiation of MLERERS with Equality Tests

In this section, we show the concrete construction with equality tests.

5.1   The Algorithms

Let SKE be a symmetric key encryption scheme consisting of a key generation algorithm $SKE.K$, an encryption algorithm $SKE.E$ and a decryption algorithm $SKE.D$. We also denote by $\mathcal{H}$ a family of collision-resistant hash functions, by $\bigoplus$ XOR operation and by $||$ a concatenation of any two elements. Moreover, let $\ell(1^n)$ be a length of output of a hash function, and let $Data$ be a set of ciphertexts stored in a database. In the scheme, we also assume that each file is indexed as unique identifier $i \in \mathbb{Z}$ without loss of generality.

Parameter Generation $\mathcal{P}$: Choose a hash function H from $\mathcal{H}$ and a symmetric key encryption scheme SKE. Return $P = (H, SKE)$.

Key Generation $\mathcal{K}(P, m)$: Return $K = H(P, m)$.

Re-encryption Key Generation $\mathcal{RKG}(P)$: Randomly choose $RK \leftarrow \{0, 1\}^{\ell(1^n)}$, and return RK.

Encryption $\mathcal{E}(P, K, m)$: Randomly choose $L \leftarrow \{0, 1\}^{\ell(1^n)}$, and compute $T = \mathcal{H}(P, K)$. Then, compute $C_1 \leftarrow SKE.E(L, m)$ and $C_2 = L \bigoplus K$. Finally, return $C = C_1 || C_2 || T$.

Re-encryption $\mathcal{RE}(P, C, RK)$: Parse C as $C_1 || C_2 || T$, and compute $T' = T \bigoplus \mathcal{H}(RK || i)$. Return $C' = C_1 || C_2 || T'$.

Tag $\mathcal{T}(C)$: Parse C as $C_1 || C_2 || T$, and return T as a tag.

Trapdoor Generation $\mathcal{TG}(P, RK)$: Randomly choose $r \leftarrow \{0, 1\}^{\ell(1^n)}$ and compute $t(RK || i) = \mathcal{H}(RK || i) \bigoplus \mathcal{H}(r)$ for any $i \in |Data|$. Return $t(RK || i)$ as a trapdoor.

Equal $\mathcal{EQ}(C_i, C_{i'}, t(RK))$: Parse C_i as $C_{i,1} || C_{i,2} || T_i'$, $C_{i'}$ as $C_{i',1} || C_{i',2} || T_{i'}'$ and $t(RK)$ as $t(RK || i)$ and $t(RK || i')$. For i and i', compute $T_i = T_i' \bigoplus t(RK || i)$ and $T_{i'} = T_{i'}' \bigoplus t(RK || i')$, respectively. Then, check if $T_i = T_{i'}'$. If so, return *true*. Otherwise, return *false*.

Second-Level Decryption $\mathcal{RD}(RK, C')$: Parse C' as $C_1 || C_2 || T'$, and compute $T = T' \bigoplus H(RK || i)$. Then, return $C = C_1 || C_2 || T$

Decryption $\mathcal{D}(P, K, C)$: Parse C as $C_1 \| C_2 \| T$, and compute $L = C_2 \oplus K$. Then, compute $m = SKE.D(L, C_1)$ and $T' = H(P, H(P, m))$. If $T' \neq T$, then return $\perp$ as error. Otherwise, return m.

5.2 Security Analysis

In this section, we discuss the security proposed in the previous section. Due to the page limitation, we briefly describe the results in the analysis.

PRV\$-CDA-R for First-Level Ciphertexts. The proposed scheme achieves PRV\$-CDA-R if a symmetric key encryption is secure in the sense of key recovery security and one-time real-or-random security [16] and a hash function is modeled as a random oracle. Although we omit the notions and the detail, the proof of the proposed scheme is almost the same as that of the randomized convergent encryption scheme by Bellare et al. [2]. Intuitively, the view of an adversary in the PRV-CDA-R game with the proposed scheme is identical to that against the randomized convergent encryption scheme except for generation of re-encryption keys. Moreover, the generation of re-encryption keys is exactly identical to a generation of random strings. Hence, in a similar manner as the proof in [2], we can construct a reduction algorithm to the symmetric key encryption scheme from the proposed scheme by generating random strings for the re-encryption key generation oracle.

IND-CPA-R for Second-Level Ciphertexts. The proposed scheme is IND-CPA-R if a symmetric key encryption scheme is IND-CPA and a hash function is modeled as a random oracle. In particular, by setting an encryption oracle of the symmetric key encryption as a challenge re-encryption key in the proposed scheme, a reduction algorithm to the symmetric key encryption scheme can forward queries to any first-level ciphertext by an adversary to the re-encryption oracle in the symmetric key encryption scheme. Moreover, via the random oracle, the reduction algorithm can identify any pair of a plaintext and a ciphertext including a tag, and can then generate a trapdoor for any index by generating a random number. Then, the reduction algorithm can simulate the oracles in the IND-CPA-R security. Hence, the reduction algorithm can succeed the guess in the IND-CPA game by which the adversary succeeds the guess in the IND-CPA-R game.

Onewayness of Trapdoors. The proposed scheme achieves the onewayness of trapdoors if a hash function has preimage resistance, where an input of the hash function cannot be computed from an output. In particular, $t(RK)$ is computed as $\mathcal{H}(RK \| i) \oplus \mathcal{H}(r)$, where r is a random number generated by a data analyst. This r is not given to a database manager, and the database manager cannot extract $\mathcal{H}(RK \| i)$ from $t(RK)$. Moreover, since a hash function has the preimage resistance, an adversary cannot also extract RK from $\mathcal{H}(RK \| i)$.

6   Conclusion

In this work, we proposed a new framework called message-locked encryption with re-encryption and relational search (MLERERS) by extending MLE to the three-party model. Our main ideas were to re-encrypt ciphertexts of MLE and to provide the capability of search of relationships between ciphertexts by generating trapdoors from a re-encryption key. Hence, a data analyst can search relationships between ciphertexts while a database manager cannot extract anything for newly added data. We formalized the security of MLERERS to encourage analysis of the security in subsequent works and showed the concrete construction with equality tests.

Our future work is to implement the proposed scheme. As described in Sect. 1, big data services often require users to deal with a large amount of data in real time, and hence we evaluate the performance of the proposed scheme rigorously via implementation. Another future work is to extend the capability of search in an instantiation of MLERERS. Although our definition captured search of any relationship, our concrete scheme provided equality tests. Thus, we plan to propose an instantiation with the capability of search of any relationship.

Acknowledgments. We would like to thank Taisuke Yamauchi in NIPPON TELE-GRAPH AND TELEPHONE WEST CORPORATION for his support.

References

1. Abadi, M., Boneh, D., Mironov, I., Raghunathan, A., Segev, G.: Message-locked encryption for lock-dependent messages. In: Canetti, R., Garay, J.A. (eds.) CRYPTO 2013. LNCS, vol. 8042, pp. 374–391. Springer, Heidelberg (2013). doi:10.1007/978-3-642-40041-4_21
2. Bellare, M., Keelveedhi, S., Ristenpart, T.: Message-locked encryption and secure deduplication. In: Johansson, T., Nguyen, P.Q. (eds.) EUROCRYPT 2013. LNCS, vol. 7881, pp. 296–312. Springer, Heidelberg (2013). doi:10.1007/978-3-642-38348-9_18
3. Bellare, M., Desai, A., Pointcheval, D., Rogaway, P.: Relations among notions of security for public-key encryption schemes. In: Krawczyk, H. (ed.) CRYPTO 1998. LNCS, vol. 1462, pp. 26–45. Springer, Heidelberg (1998). doi:10.1007/BFb0055718
4. Boneh, D., Crescenzo, G., Ostrovsky, R., Persiano, G.: Public key encryption with keyword search. In: Cachin, C., Camenisch, J.L. (eds.) EUROCRYPT 2004. LNCS, vol. 3027, pp. 506–522. Springer, Heidelberg (2004). doi:10.1007/978-3-540-24676-3_30
5. Boneh, D., Sahai, A., Waters, B.: Functional encryption: definitions and challenges. In: Ishai, Y. (ed.) TCC 2011. LNCS, vol. 6597, pp. 253–273. Springer, Heidelberg (2011). doi:10.1007/978-3-642-19571-6_16
6. Chen, R., Mu, Y., Yang, G., Guo, F.: BL-MLE: block-level message-locked encryption for secure large file deduplication. IEEE Trans. Inf. Forensics Secur. **10**(12), 2643–2652 (2015)
7. Gentry, C.: Fully homomorphic encryption using ideal lattice. In: Proceedings of STOC 1999, pp. 169–178. ACM (2009)

8. Jiang, T., Chen, X., Wu, Q., Ma, J., Susilo, W., Lou, W.: Towards efficient fully randomized message-locked encryption. In: Liu, J.K.K., Steinfeld, R. (eds.) ACISP 2016. LNCS, vol. 9722, pp. 361–375. Springer, Cham (2016). doi:10.1007/978-3-319-40253-6_22

9. Kamara, S., Papamanthou, C.: Parallel and dynamic searchable symmetric encryption. In: Sadeghi, A.-R. (ed.) FC 2013. LNCS, vol. 7859, pp. 258–274. Springer, Heidelberg (2013). doi:10.1007/978-3-642-39884-1_22

10. Katz, J., Lindell, Y.: Introduction to Modern Cryptography. Chapman and Hall/Crc Cryptography and Network Security Series, pp. 82–104. Chapman and Hall/CRC, Boca Ration (2007)

11. Lei, L., Cai, Q., Chen, B., Lin, J.: Towards efficient re-encryption for secure client-side deduplication in public clouds. In: Lam, K.-Y., Chi, C.-H., Qing, S. (eds.) ICICS 2016. LNCS, vol. 9977, pp. 71–84. Springer, Cham (2016). doi:10.1007/978-3-319-50011-9_6

12. Li, J., Qin, C., Lee, P.P.C., Li, J.: Rekeying for encrypted deduplication storage. In: Proceedings of DSN 2016, pp. 618–629. IEEE (2016)

13. Naveed, M., Prabhakaran, M., Gunter, C.A.: Dynamic searchable encryption via blind storage. In: Proceedings of IEEE S&P, pp. 639–654. IEEE (2014)

14. Ogata, W., Koiwa, K., Kanaoka, A., Matsuo, S.: Toward practical searchable symmetric encryption. In: Sakiyama, K., Terada, M. (eds.) IWSEC 2013. LNCS, vol. 8231, pp. 151–167. Springer, Heidelberg (2013). doi:10.1007/978-3-642-41383-4_10

15. Okamoto, T., Takashima, K.: Fully secure functional encryption with general relations from the decisional linear assumption. In: Rabin, T. (ed.) CRYPTO 2010. LNCS, vol. 6223, pp. 191–208. Springer, Heidelberg (2010). doi:10.1007/978-3-642-14623-7_11

16. Rogaway, P., Bellare, M., Black, J., Krovetz, T.: OCB: a block-cipher mode of operation for efficient authenticated encryption. In: Proceedings of ACM CCS 2001, pp. 196–205. ACM (2001)

17. Shi, E., Chan, T.-H.H., Rieffel, E.G., Chow, R., Song, D.: Privacy-preserving aggregation of time-series data. In: Proceedings of NDSS 2011 (2011)

18. Song, D., Wagner, D., Perrig, A.: Practical techniques for searches on encrypted data. In: Proceedings of IEEE S&P 2000, pp. 44–55. IEEE (2000)

Searchable Encrypted Relational Databases: Risks and Countermeasures

Mohamed Ahmed Abdelraheem[1(✉)], Tobias Andersson[1],
and Christian Gehrmann[2]

[1] RISE SICS AB, Lund, Sweden
{mohamed.abdelraheem,tobias.andersson}@ri.se
[2] Lund University, Lund, Sweden
christian.gehrmann@eit.lth.se

Abstract. We point out the risks of protecting relational databases via Searchable Symmetric Encryption (SSE) schemes by proposing an inference attack exploiting the structural properties of relational databases. We also show that record-injection attacks mounted on relational databases have worse consequences than their file-injection counterparts on unstructured databases. Moreover, we discuss some techniques to reduce the effectiveness of inference attacks exploiting the access pattern leakage existing in SSE schemes.

1 Introduction

One of the practical solutions for searching on encrypted data is provided by Searchable Symmetric Encryption (SSE) schemes. The very first such scheme was proposed by Song et al. in [19]. Later, Curtmola et al.'s [12] introduced two security notions for SSE schemes, namely, the non-adaptive semantic security definition and the adaptive semantic security definition. Subsequent SSE schemes [6–8] are all based on Curtmola et al.'s security model. The price of the efficiency offered by SSE schemes comes at the cost of leaking the frequency of each keyword after it has been queried. This makes them vulnerable to inference attacks [5,14] which recovers the issued queries by combining its access pattern leakage by background information about the protected dataset. Most of the proposed SSE schemes are designed to protect unstructured document datasets such as emails or a backup of anyve files. However, recently two SSE schemes proposed by Cash et al. [6,7] are designed to efficiently run and protect relational databases where they achieved a query speed comparable to the unprotected MySQL (release 5.5) [6,7].

In addition to SSE schemes, there are several practical solutions proposed to execute SQL queries on an encrypted database. Recently, Popa et al. proposed CryptDB as a solution to protect confidentiality for applications using SQL databases [18]. CryptDB uses column-level encryption to encrypt the database tables. To enable equality searches, CryptDB uses deterministic encryption. Order preserving encryption (OPE) is used to enable range and comparison queries on

© Springer International Publishing AG 2017
J. Garcia-Alfaro et al. (Eds.): DPM/CBT 2017, LNCS 10436, pp. 70–85, 2017.
DOI: 10.1007/978-3-319-67816-0_5

encrypted data. OPE is the weakest encryption scheme used in CryptDB whose design concept is based on the trade-off between functionality and confidentiality. Recently, Naveed et al. [17] mounted inference attacks that recovered the plaintext from CryptDB's columns protected by deterministic encryption and order preserving encryption schemes.

Another line of research in preserving database privacy is achieved by distributing and fragmenting the database table across two or more servers [2,9,11] using vertical fragmentation where the table's columns are partitioned across the servers. Privacy in the scheme proposed in [2] is provided under the assumption that the two cloud servers are unable to communicate directly with each other. However, privacy in the work proposed in [9,11] is achieved without this assumption where encryption is used as little as possible and fragmentation is used to provide security by breaking the associations among the attributes and also to provide functionality by keeping most attributes in plaintext. In the scheme proposed in [10], privacy is preserved by using fragmentation only and no encryption is employed. This comes at the cost of saving sensitive data in the clear at the data owner, i.e. the client. All these privacy constraints schemes provide efficiency and functionality but at the cost of having plaintext fields and only encrypting sensitive data which makes them vulnerable to be attacked by an adversary with background information about the database. Also adding or modifying a record reveals the relation among the fragments to passive adversary monitoring the fragments.

Comparing the above methods for searching on encrypted data in terms of security, one can see that SSE schemes offer better security than deterministic or order preserving encryption schemes since they do not leak the frequency of a keyword before querying it. They also provide better security than the data fragmentation method via privacy constraints [9] since they encrypt all the plaintext data and they can also securely manage a dynamic database [6].

However, SSE schemes suffer from leaking the access pattern of a queried keyword which make them vulnerable to inference attacks as demonstrated by Islam et al. [14] and Cash et al. [5]. In this paper, we study the effect of these inference attacks as well as the recent file-injection attacks [21] on relational databases. We also propose a suitable inference control to safeguard relational databases secured via SSE schemes from being completely recovered by strong adversaries with background knowledge about the relational database.

Our Contribution. We exploit the properties of relational databases and propose an inference attack [5,14] targeting relational databases. We also study the injection attacks [21] in the context of relational databases protected via SSE schemes. We propose the use of privacy constraints [2,9,11] to distribute the encrypted index of an SSE scheme into several fragments or servers to reduce the effectiveness of inference attacks exploiting the access pattern leakage [5,14] which is inherent in SSE schemes. Note that the privacy constraints as defined in [2,9,11] were mainly used to depart completely from the use of encryption or to use encryption as less as possible. However, in this paper we propose using them to strengthen the security of SSE schemes against inference attacks.

Related Work. Query recovery attacks exploiting the access pattern leakage of SSE schemes were proposed by Islam et al. [14] and recently improved by Cash et al. [5]. Both attacks assume background knowledge in the form of joint frequencies between keywords and were proposed mainly to deal with unstructured datasets. However, in this work we propose an inference attack called Relational-Count that uses only knowledge about the frequency of keywords in the target relational database. We show that this might lead to complete record-recovery attacks. Moreover, we propose the use of privacy constraints as an additional countermeasure that should be used together with padding to reduce the effectiveness of inference attacks. The recently proposed file-injection attack by Zhang et al. [21] recovers only a set of keywords in encrypted document and could be prevented by limiting the content of each injected file. However, in this paper we show that record-injection attacks have more severe consequences than file-injection attacks since they can achieve full record recovery on relational databases protected via SSE schemes. Moreover, record-injection attacks cannot be simply prevented by limiting the content of an injected record as done to prevent file-injection attacks [21] since that would hinder the addition of complete records to the protected relational databases.

Organization of the Paper. Section 2 gives a brief overview about SSE schemes. In Sect. 3, we give a brief overview about inference attacks and propose a new inference attack targeting relational databases. In Sect. 4, we point out the security risks of protecting relational databases via SSE schemes where we show that inference attacks and record-injection attacks can fully recover a significant number of database records. In Sect. 5, we propose the use of privacy constraints as an inference control and countermeasure to reduce the risk of inference attacks.

2 Background

Definition. An SSE scheme takes as inputs a plaintext database index together with the client's secret keys and outputs an encrypted and frequency-hiding database index where the keywords are encrypted using a deterministic encryption algorithm and the document/records identifiers are encrypted using a randomized algorithm. When the SSE-protected database is a relational database (i.e. searchable encrypted relational databases), a keyword w_i will represent an attribute-value pair which points to a cell in the relational database (i.e. $w_i = (attribute_i : v_i)$ where $attribute_i$ refers to the column name or attribute name and v_i refers to the value of the attribute). All recent SSE schemes follow the adaptive security definition proposed by Curtmola et al. [12] where security is achieved against an honest-but-curious server.

Leakage Profile. An SSE scheme leaks the *access pattern*: the result size of the query and the document/record IDs corresponding to the queried keyword w_i and also leaks the *search pattern*: the fact that whether two searches are the same or not.

Passive Attacks on SSE Schemes. Two passive attacks against SSE schemes exploiting the access pattern leakage have been proposed recently by Islam et al. [14] and later developed by Cash et al. [5]. These passive attacks are inference attacks mounted by an honest-but-curious server who knows the distribution of the dataset under attack or knows a significant number of the client's plaintext documents.

Active Attacks on SSE Schemes. Another class of attacks outlined by Cash et al. [5] are the chosen-document attacks and the chosen-query attacks. Both attacks are mounted by an active adversary who is somehow capable of deceiving the client into including her own chosen-document into the documents set as well as into choosing her favorite queries respectively. Recently, Zhang et al. [21] presented a concrete description of a chosen-document attack (file-injection) where the attacker is able to recover all the queries without any prior knowledge about the client's dataset under attack. The equivalent of file-injection in the context of searchable encrypted relational databases is record-injection and it has worse consequences that go beyond query recovery, namely, full record recovery or partial record recovery (cf. Sect. 4.2).

3 Inference Attacks

Inference attacks are mounted on SSE schemes to recover the plaintext of encrypted keywords involved on previous queries issued by the client and observed by the attacker. This kind of attack is called *query recovery* and was proposed by Islam, Kuzu and Kantarcioglu (IKK) in [14]. Their attack, known in the literature as the IKK attack, targets the strongest kinds of SSE schemes which are those proved to be secure under the adaptive security definition. The IKK attack models the problem of recovering the unknown keywords as an optimization problem solved using a simulated annealing algorithm. Recently, Cash et al. [5] improved the IKK by proposing another inference attack, called the *Count attack*, that is simpler and more efficient than the IKK attack. The Count attack assumes knowledge about the joint frequency of any two keywords as well as the frequency of each keyword in the dataset under attack.

However, in this section, we propose an inference attack that assumes only that the attacker knows the frequency of each keyword (attribute-value pair). We call our attack, the *Relational-Count attack*. Our attack targets relational databases by exploiting their structural properties. First we describe the Count attack and then describe the Relational-Count attack.

The Count Attack. The Count attack [5] assumes knowledge about the *joint frequency (or co-occurrence count)* of any two plaintext keywords $w_i, w_j \in W$ where W is the set of all unique keywords in the target database. It also assumes knowledge about the occurrence of each keyword w (attribute-value pair) over all the database documents/records, say $size(w)$. Assume that the number of unique keywords (or attribute-value pairs) indexed by an SSE scheme is m. Then the attacker uses the joint frequency knowledge to construct an $m \times m$ matrix

M where its entry $M[i,j]$ holds the co-occurrence value or the joint frequency of having the ith unique keyword and jth unique keyword together in the database indexed by the SSE scheme under consideration. The constructed matrix M represents the background knowledge of the attacker about the encrypted database. Using the access pattern leakage, the attacker also constructs another matrix C that represents the observed joint frequency between any two queries intercepted by the attacker. Obviously, any keyword w with unique result size will be easily recovered when queried since the size of the result set of its query q, $size(q)$, will be known to the attacker who will use the knowledge about the frequency or occurrence of each keyword w to find the keyword whose frequency matches the result size of q (i.e. find a keyword w such that $size(q) = size(w)$). The unique counts approach will recover all the queries corresponding to keywords with unique result sizes which can be significant in some databases. A query q with non-unique result size is recovered by creating a candidate list consisting of all keywords with the same result size as q and then discarding the wrong keywords from the candidate list by comparing the observed joint frequency between q and any previously recovered query q_k with the prior known joint frequency between c_i and w_k where c_i is the candidate keyword under consideration and w_k is the recovered keyword corresponding to q_k. If they are unequal (i.e. $C[q, q_k] \neq M[c_i, w_k]$), then c_i will be discarded from the candidate list.

The Relational-Count Attack. Similar to the Count attack, our attack assumes that the attacker has knowledge about the frequency of each attribute-value pair which allows the attacker to recover the queries with unique result sizes and to add a candidate list for each query with non-unique result size. However, unlike the Count attack, we do not assume that the attacker has any knowledge about the joint frequencies between attribute-value pairs. Instead, we use the following simple observation about the structural properties of relational databases to filter out the wrong candidates.

Observation 1. *If the joint frequency (or the co-occurrence count) between any two different queries (tokens) is non-zero, then their corresponding attribute names are different.*

In other words, the joint frequency between two queries with the same attribute name is zero. The observation should be clear from the fact that each relational database record has only one value for each column or attribute name. This observation allows us to reduce the list of candidates for a given query with non-unique result size. Assume that there is an unknown query q_i with non-unique result size, then one can see that a candidate keyword $w_j = (a_j : v_j)$, where a_j is the attribute name and v_j is its value, will be discarded if there is a previously recovered query q_k whose attribute name is a_j and whose joint frequency with q_i is non-zero. In other words, If $C[q_i, q_k] \neq 0$, then discard w_j, where C is the observed joint frequency matrix. This is because the right candidate keyword must have the same attribute name as the unknown query q_i. Next, we apply the Count attack and the Relational-Count attack on searchable encrypted relational databases.

4   Risks of Using Searchable Encrypted Relational Databases

In this section, we point out three risks that might occur when protecting relational databases via SSE schemes. The first risk is breaking query privacy by a passive adversary with knowledge about the target relational database represented in the form of joint frequencies between attribute-value pairs and the frequency of each attribute-value pair (i.e. knowledge of all the database records). This means that the attacker here is only interested in recovering queries to break query privacy. The second risk is the possibility of complete record recovery attack by a passive adversary who has knowledge about the frequency distribution of attribute-value pairs. The third risk is the possibility of complete record recovery via record-injection attacks performed by an active adversary with no prior knowledge about the target database.

4.1   Query and Record Recovery Attacks

One can see that inference attacks on searchable encrypted relational databases will probably lead to a partial or full record recovery since query recovery directly translates to partial record recovery in this case. Thus, inference attacks that do not require the knowledge of all the database records but only the frequency distribution of attribute-value pairs, such as our Relational-Count attack, are more interesting from the attacker's point's of view since they extend the attacker's goal from only breaking query privacy by performing query recovery as done in the Count attack to gaining new knowledge through partial or full record recovery.

In the following, we apply the Count and Relational-Count attacks on searchable encrypted relational databases. Our goal is to firstly break query privacy using the Count attack which employs a strong attacker who knows almost all the database records (i.e. so the attacker is able to compute joint frequencies between attribute-value pairs and frequencies of attribute-value pairs) and then secondly recover complete records using our Relational-Count attack which employs a weaker attacker who knows only the frequency distribution of the attribute-value pairs of the target database.

Data Sets. We mount the Count attack over the Census dataset [16], the Bank dataset [3] and the Adult dataset [15]. These are real world datasets from the UCI Machine Learning Repository [13]. The Census dataset consists of 299285 records, 40 columns, and 3993 distinct attribute-value pairs when we exclude the 8 missing attribute-value pairs (in total there are 4001 attribute-value pairs but we do not consider the empty or missing values in our keywords set). The Bank dataset consists of 4521 records, 17 columns, and 3720 distinct attribute-value pairs. The Adult dataset consists of 32561 records, 14 columns, and 498 distinct attribute-value pairs.

Query Generation. We used a standard single-keyword SSE scheme where a Bitmap encrypted index is used similar to the single-keyword Bitmap index scheme described in [1,14,20] to transform each target relational database into a separate searchable encryption relational database. We conducted four experiments per each target dataset where different sets of random queries within the target protected database are issued in each experiment. The access pattern leakage (result size + retrieved record IDs) of each query is intercepted by a passive attacker who combines this knowledge with background knowledge about the dataset and then execute the Count or the Relational-Count attacks described above to recover the queries.

Query Recovery via the Count Attack. Table 1 shows the query recovery results on the three datasets. Three experiments are conducted for each dataset. One can see that when the number of issued queries increases, the rate of query recovery also increases. For example, the Census dataset contains 3993 unique attribute-value pairs and only 77.60% are recovered when 600 queries are issued. But when all queries are issued as shown in the 3rd experiment, we see that a high percentage of queries (≈98.1%) are recovered in the Census dataset. So query privacy is completely broken by the Count attack. Note that the record recovery rate will be high but the attacker here is only concerned about query recovery and not record recovery since we assume that the attacker already knows all the database records.

Table 1. Query recovery results on different relational databases. All queries are issued in the 3rd experiment. Results are averaged over 3 tests, where queries are chosen randomly, in the 1st and 2nd experiments. 455/600 indicates an average of 455 queries out of 600 issued queries were recovered successfully using the Count attack.

Exp. no	Census data set	Bank data set	Adult data set
1	455/600	300/600	135/150
2	1432/1500	1237/1500	230/250
3	3917/3993	3460/3720	466/498

Record Recovery via the Relational-Count Attack. We applied our attack on the three relational databases described above. Table 2 shows that our attack recovers only 757 queries out of 3993 queries whereas the Count attack recovers 3917 queries out of 3993 queries. Thus, our attack is not as effective as the Count attack. However, our attack assumes that the attacker only knows the frequency distribution of the attribute-value pairs which is a more realistic assumption that could hold in practice. Table 3 shows that the 757 queries recovered in the Census dataset allowed us to recover 447 complete records in the Census dataset whereas the 122 queries recovered in the Bank dataset allowed us to recover only recover 1 complete database record in the Bank dataset. The Bank dataset also has 989 records where 64.99–52% (9–11 attributes) of the attributes are recovered. The results on the Census displayed in Table 3 show that even recovering as few as 757/3993 queries allows us to learn a high percentage of records in the Census data set. For example 109433 records are recovered where only between

Table 2. The table shows the total number of queries recovered in three relational databases when all the queries are issued and the Relational-Count attack is used. The unique recovery column shows the number of queries recovered whose result sizes are unique and the non-unique recovery column shows the number of queries whose result sizes are non-unique which are recovered using the Relational-Count attack.

Data set	Unique recovery	Non-unique recovery	Total
Adult dataset	155	81	236/498
Bank	97	25	122/3720
Census	531	226	757/3993

Table 3. The table shows the number of records recovered with the percentage of attributes recovered (record recovery rate) in each record when all queries are executed in the SSE-protected Bank and Census datasets together. 100% Rec. means all attributes are recovered, 95–85% Rec. means all attributes are recovered except 5–15% of them have not been recovered, and so on. The entry 708/4521 indicates that around 84.99–74% attributes (i.e. 13–14 attributes out of 17 attributes) of 708 records out of 4521 records of the Bank dataset are recovered. Note that the bank dataset has 989 records where 64.99–52% (i.e. 9–11 attributes) of the attributes are recovered which is not shown in the table. 4521 ≡ total number of records for the Bank dataset and 299285 ≡ total number of records for the Census dataset.

Data set	100% Rec.	95–85% Rec.	84.99–74% Rec.	73.99–65% Rec.
Bank	1/4521	39/4521	997/4521	2495/4521
Census	447/299285	109433/299285	131253/299285	58152/299285

2 and 6 attributes are missing. This could enable a strong attacker that uses machine learning to predict the missing values given the 757 records that are fully recovered. We have not investigated this possibility and we leave it for future work. Note that we can recover only 149 complete records from the Census dataset after recovering only the 531 attribute-value pairs with unique result sizes compared to recovering 447 complete records when we resolve the attribute-value pairs with non-unique result sizes using our Relational-Count attack. This shows the effect of our Relational-Count attack in recovering complete database records.

4.2   Record-Injection Attacks

Zhang et al.'s non-adaptive file-injection binary attack [21] cannot be applied exactly in searchable encrypted relational databases since we are dealing with a structured text governed by a relational database rather than unstructured text. Depending on the relational database under attack, there might be a large number of records needed to be injected in order to recover all the possible encrypted queries if the database contains attributes whose values are variables (not discrete) with a big range. However, if the attacker is concerned about a small subset of attribute-value pairs. Then the attacker can inject a number of records by focusing on some attributes whose values are discrete with a small range as noted in [21]. This will reduce the number of injected records and will lead to query recovery and consequently partial record recovery without any prior knowledge.

We focus here on non-adaptive record injections as adaptive injection attacks need background knowledge about the target encrypted database and they can be prevented by using a forward secure SSE scheme [4]. Similar to Zhang et al. [21], we assume that the attacker can identify the record ID of each injected record. Let D be a relational database with n records and m attributes or columns where each attribute is denoted by a_i and its cardinality is denoted by $|a_i|$, $1 \leq i \leq m$. Assume that the number of records need to be injected in D in order to cover the whole attribute-value pair space $|W|$ or a target subset of attribute-value pairs S is l. Suppose that $R = r_1 r_2 \cdots r_l$ is the search result on the injected records regarding an observed query q, where $r_i = 1$ iff the ith injected record is part of the result set of the query q, otherwise $r_i = 0$. Clearly $l \geq |a_i|$ for all i, otherwise the injected records will not recover all the values of the attribute a_i. Assume that there are t attributes $(a_1, \cdots, a_t)$ with the same cardinality d, then in order to cover all the $d \cdot t$ values one can construct a mapping that assigns each attribute-value pair to a unique search result string on the injected records by simply injecting $d \cdot t$ records as follows. Let the first d records contain all the values of the 1st attribute (i.e. $a_{11}, a_{12}, \cdots, a_{1d}$) and the other attributes belonging to S are empty. Also, let the second d records contain all the values of the 2nd attribute (i.e. $a_{21}, a_{22}, \cdots, a_{2d}$) and the other attributes belonging to S are empty and so on until the last and tth d records contain all the values of the tth attribute and the other attributes belonging to S are empty. Now one can see that the search result on the injected records regarding any attribute-value pair in S will yield a binary string with Hamming weight one where the location of the i-th active bit in the binary string indicates that the attribute value is located at position $i \mod d$ (or last position if $i \mod d = 0$) in the $\lceil i/d \rceil$th attribute.

However, one can inject l records, where l is much less than $d \cdot t$, by injecting t columns of length l where the search results of all the attribute-value pairs in a single column have active bits at different positions and all the possible search results representing all attribute-value pairs are disjoint. In other words, we need to separate the l-bit binary strings where each l-bit corresponds to a search result into t disjoint sets where each set S_j has d elements representing the d attribute-value pairs of the jth column (note that all the t columns have the same cardinality). Each element in S_j is an l-bit binary string representing a search result of an attribute-value pair belonging to the jth column. Assume that all the elements of S_j have the same Hamming weight w_j. Assume also that d divides l. Then, w_j must be $\leq l/d$ in order to have a valid set S_j representing unique search results. The number of l-bit binary strings of Hamming weight i is $\binom{l}{i}$. Therefore, one can look for the smallest l satisfying the inequality $\binom{l}{l/d} + \cdots + \binom{l}{1} \geq d \cdot t$ and the same time construct a one-to-one mapping between the l-bit binary strings of S_j representing the unique search results and the injected columns C_j of length l for all $1 \leq j \leq t$.

Concrete Example. The Census dataset discussed above, has 7 attributes with cardinality 3. By setting $t = 7$ and $d = 3$ in the above inequality, one can see that $l = 6$ is the smallest integer to satisfy it. Now we need to divide all the 6-bit binary vectors with Hamming weight ≤ 2 (since $l/d = 6/3 = 2$) into 7 disjoint sets where each set S_j holds three (since $d = 3$) 6-bit binary vectors that have different active positions. The elements of S_j must contain binary vectors of Hamming weight two or one as otherwise we will not be able to cover all the $d \cdot t = 3 \cdot 7 = 21$ attribute-value pairs. One can see that $S_1 = \{100000, 010000, 001000\}$ is a set whose binary strings can represent the search results corresponding to the attribute-value pairs injected in the column $C_1 = \begin{bmatrix} a_{11} \ a_{12} \ a_{13} \ ? \ ? \ ? \end{bmatrix}^T$ where '?' means an empty entry and T is the transpose operator. Let C_1 be the first column injected in our records. When one searches for a_{11}, a_{12} and a_{13} the search results on the injected records will be 100000, 010000 and 001000 respectively. Now, from S_1 we could generate another valid search results set S_2 by looking at the other possible binary strings of Hamming weight one representing valid search results. There are exactly 3 other possible binary strings, namely, 000100, 000010 and 000001. So $S_2 = \{000100, 000010, 000001\}$ and it represents the search results corresponding to the attribute-value pairs injected in the column $C_2 = \begin{bmatrix} ? \ ? \ ? \ a_{21} \ a_{22} \ a_{23} \end{bmatrix}^T$. Let C_2 be the second column injected in our records. Now we consider search results whose binary strings have Hamming weight 2 such as $S_3 = \{110000, 001100, 000011\}$ which represents the attribute-value pairs injected in the column $C_3 = \begin{bmatrix} a_{31} \ a_{31} \ a_{32} \ a_{32} \ a_{33} \ a_{33} \end{bmatrix}^T$. Let C_3 be the third column injected in our records. Thus we have three sets and we need to construct another four sets in order to obtain seven sets that cover all the search results of the 21 attribute-value pairs. One set S_3 has three binary strings of Hamming weight 2. So there remains another $\binom{6}{2} - 3 = 15 - 3 = 12$ binary strings of Hamming weight 2 and we need to divide them into 4 sets S_4, S_5, S_6 and S_7 where each set has 3 elements which have different positions for the active bits similar to S_3. Note that each binary string in S_3 have four non-active bits, so interchanging the location of an active bit with the location of a non-active bit will yield a new binary string but we need to interchange the location of active bits with the location of non-active bits for all the binary strings of S_3. So the four sets, S_4, S_5, S_6 and S_7, can be obtained by permuting the locations of active bits within each element in S_3. To do so, we need to consider the elements of S_3 as columns of a matrix M_3 where the first column is $\begin{bmatrix} 1 \ 1 \ 0 \ 0 \ 0 \ 0 \end{bmatrix}^T$, the second column is $\begin{bmatrix} 0 \ 0 \ 1 \ 1 \ 0 \ 0 \end{bmatrix}^T$ and the last column is $\begin{bmatrix} 0 \ 0 \ 0 \ 0 \ 1 \ 1 \end{bmatrix}^T$. In each column of M_3, there are four locations to move the active bits in order to get a new valid and unique column. However, we want all the new columns to have active bits at different positions in order to form valid and unique search results (e.g. $S_i \ i \geq 4$). To construct the set S_4, we change the positions of the active bits in M_3 by multiplying it by a 6×6 permutation matrix, P_{π_4} where the first and third rows of the 6×6 identity matrix I_6 are permuted and also the second and fifth rows are permuted.

In cyclic notation, the permutation π_4 can be written as follows $\pi_4 = (13)(25)$. Now, $M_4 = P_{\pi_4} \times M_3$. The first column of M_4 is $\begin{bmatrix} 0\,0\,1\,0\,1\,0 \end{bmatrix}^T$. The second column is $\begin{bmatrix} 1\,0\,0\,1\,0\,0 \end{bmatrix}^T$ and the last column is $\begin{bmatrix} 0\,1\,0\,0\,0\,1 \end{bmatrix}^T$. The columns of M_4 form valid search results and thus $S_4 = \{001010, 100100, 010001\}$. Its corresponding injected column is $C_4 = \begin{bmatrix} a_{41}\ a_{42}\ a_{43}\ a_{41}\ a_{43}\ a_{42} \end{bmatrix}^T$. Similarly, we form another 6×6 permutation matrix, P_{π_5} by interchanging the first and fourth rows and also interchanging the second and the sixth rows in the identity matrix I_6. In cyclic notation, the permutation π_5 can be written as follows $\pi_5 = (14)(26)$. The columns of $M_5 = P_{\pi_5} \times M_3$ gives us $S_5 = \{0000101, 101000, 010010\}$. Its corresponding injected column is $C_5 = \begin{bmatrix} a_{51}\ a_{52}\ a_{51}\ a_{53}\ a_{52}\ a_{53} \end{bmatrix}^T$. S_6 is obtained from the columns of $M_6 = P_{\pi_6} \times M_3$ where P_{π_6} is a permutation matrix obtained by interchanging the rows of the identity matrix corresponding to the cyclic permutation $\pi_6 = (15)(24)$. $S_6 = \{000110, 011000, 100001\}$ and its corresponding injected column is $C_6 = \begin{bmatrix} a_{61}\ a_{62}\ a_{62}\ a_{63}\ a_{63}\ a_{61} \end{bmatrix}^T$. Finally, S_7 is obtained from the columns of $M_7 = P_{\pi_7} \times M_3$ where P_{π_7} is a permutation matrix obtained by interchanging the rows of the identity matrix corresponding to the cyclic permutation $\pi_7 = (16)(23)$. $S_7 = \{001001, 010100, 100010\}$ and its corresponding injected column is $C_7 = \begin{bmatrix} a_{71}\ a_{72}\ a_{73}\ a_{72}\ a_{71}\ a_{73} \end{bmatrix}^T$. Thus, we can inject only $l = 6$ records instead of $l = d \cdot t = 3.7 = 21$ records in order to cover all the 7 attributes with the same cardinality 3 in the Census dataset. Table 4 shows the injected 6 records formed by injecting 7 columns yielding unique search results.

Table 4. The table shows that for each attribute-value a_{ij} we have a unique search result on the injected records. Injecting 6 records to cover 7 attributes each with 3 attribute-value pairs. A query for the attribute-value a_{21} will yield the search result 000100 on the injected records while a query for the attribute-value a_{71} will yield the search result 100010.

No	a_1	a_2	a_3	a_4	a_5	a_6	a_7
1	a_{11}	?	a_{31}	a_{41}	a_{51}	a_{61}	a_{71}
2	a_{12}	?	a_{31}	a_{42}	a_{52}	a_{62}	a_{72}
3	a_{13}	?	a_{32}	a_{43}	a_{51}	a_{62}	a_{73}
4	?	a_{21}	a_{32}	a_{41}	a_{53}	a_{63}	a_{72}
5	?	a_{22}	a_{33}	a_{43}	a_{52}	a_{63}	a_{71}
6	?	a_{23}	a_{33}	a_{42}	a_{53}	a_{61}	a_{73}

Discussion. It is clear that once an attacker is able to inject records then record-injection will lead to query recovery and eventually could lead to full record recovery. The above record injection attack works under the assumption that the attacker can identify the record identifiers of the injected records. This assumption was also adopted by Zhang et al. [21]. If the client updates one record at a time, then the attacker will always be able to identify the identifier of an injected records based on the time at which it is stored in the server.

However, if the client does only batch updates, then an attacker could inject records in a certain way such that each attribute-value pair has a unique number of appearances in all the injected records. The file-injection countermeasure proposed by Zhang et al. [21] which restricts the number of keywords per document to a certain threshold T (e.g. $T \ll |W|/2$) cannot be applied here since a relational database record has a certain number of keywords (attribute-value pairs) equivalent to its number of attributes and any restriction would hinder the work of any application using the searchable encrypted relational database. So one needs to use a forward secure SSE scheme such as the one proposed in [4] in order to protect relational databases against adaptive injection attacks (Note that the above described attacks are non-adaptive attacks but an adaptive injection attacks similar to the one proposed in [21] can easily be realized).

5   Countermeasures Against Attacks on SSE Schemes

Countermeasures against inference attacks must be used in order to reduce the their effectiveness. A well known technique is *padding* which is proposed in [5,14] as a potential countermeasure to reduce the effectiveness of inference attacks. Basically, during the setup of the encrypted database, the client adds dummy record (or document) IDs to each attribute-value pair (or keyword) in the index in order to hide the actual frequency of the keyword. Also, the client adds an encrypted dummy record (or document) corresponding to each dummy ID added in the index. Later, during search, the client filters out the dummy records (or documents). Experiments in [5], show that a padding level that increases the index size by 15% for a real world sample dataset and 30% for another real world sample dataset, does not affect the success rate of the generalized Count attack [5] which is a slight improvement of the Count attack. It basically does not depend on resolving queries with unique frequency which will not exist in a padded SSE scheme but it initially guesses these queries. The detection of a wrong guess is done during the co-occurrence testing phase which does equality matches in a window or a range of a fixed size to nullify the noise coming from the dummy records (or documents) causing false co-occurrence count values. Thus, the generalized Count attack presented in [5] suggests that padding alone does not reduce the effectiveness of inference attacks as matches in a range can be done through the observed co-occurrence matrix. The effect of our Relational-Count attack can be reduced by padding to reduce the number of attribute-value pairs with unique result sizes. So we focus here on preventing the Count attack.

Countermeasure Against the Count Attack. In addition to reducing the effectiveness of the actual query result size by padding, one might think of reducing the effectiveness of the queries' observed joint frequency matrix C by forcing the observed joint frequency between some queries to be zero. One can see that if q_i and q_j are distributed in different fragments according to a defined privacy constraints, then $C[q_i, q_j]$ will be zero when each query is executed in only one fragment and the fragments are not allowed to interact with each other to evaluate any query. Now an equality match or a window equality match with the joint frequency knowledge-matrix $M[s_i, t_j]$ as done in [5] will never happen which will significantly reduce the effectiveness of the Count attack. This can be done by applying vertical fragmentation to a relational database table according to a pre-defined set of *privacy constraints* on its columns.

The aim behind the privacy constraints is hiding the association among the attributes which means that there should be no joint appearance of the attributes in the privacy constraints [2,9,11]. For example, consider the relation of the following attributes about patients in a hospital: Name, Date of Birth (DOB), Disease, Medical Doctor (MD), and ZIP. Now one can define the following privacy constraints $c_1 = \{$Name, DOB$\}$, $c_2 = \{$Name, Disease$\}$, $c_3 = \{$Name, ZIP$\}$, $c_4 = \{$Name, MD$\}$, $c_5 = \{$DOB, ZIP, Disease$\}$ and $c_6 = \{$DOB, ZIP, MD$\}$. Now a privacy constraint prevents some columns from being together, so the privacy constraint $c_1 = \{$Name, DoB$\}$ prevents the Name column or attribute from being together in one fragment with the DoB column since they might reveal together more information about a specific person if one of them is recovered using an inference attack. We note that the privacy constraints should be used to produce the minimal amount of fragments possible using the heuristic algorithm proposed in [9]. For instance, a valid minimal fragmentation for the relation and privacy constraints defined above is the following $\mathcal{F} = \{\mathcal{F}_1 = \{$Name$\}$, $\mathcal{F}_2 = \{$DoB,ZIP$\}$, $\mathcal{F}_3 = \{$Disease,MD$\}\}$. After applying the fragmentation, we need to ensure that each query is executed in only one fragment in order to prevent an attacker monitoring all the fragments (or collaborative honest-but-curious fragment servers) from gaining any information about the correlation of the records between any two fragments which will obviously break the pre-defined the privacy constraints set by the data owner. Moreover, we need to have different record IDs for the same original record at each fragment in order to achieve security against an attacker monitoring all fragments (or collaborative honest-but-curious fragment servers) and also apply secure random shuffling for the fragment's records. After that, we can apply the same SSE scheme in each fragment using a different key. This ensures that applying inference attacks on each fragment is not effective since the encrypted attributes within each fragment does not provide sufficient information if they are recovered. Note that the generalized Count attack is effective in each fragment and it could probably recover entire records in each fragment. However, the fragments are defined according to the privacy constraints which means that the recovered records are unlinkable and thus will not reveal useful information. If all fragments are recovered, the attacker will not be able to link or combine them to recover the original record before fragmentation. This is because each fragment is shuffled differently and each fragment's record has a different record ID secretly pointing to the same original record.

Security Gain. Vertical fragmentation using privacy constraints prevents full record recovery but the fragmented SSE scheme will still leak the access pattern inside each fragment as well as leaking the attribute of the queries in each fragment. We performed one experiment to show the security gain when we employ vertical fragmentation via privacy constraints. We split the Bank dataset into three fragments. The first fragment contains five attributes, namely, "age", "job", "marital", "education" and "duration". The second fragment contains seven attributes, namely, "default", "balance", "housing", "loan", "contact", "day" and "month". The third fragment contains five attributes, namely, "campaign", "pdays", "previous", "poutcome" and "y". The Count attack was not able to resolve 130/961 queries in the first fragment, 1264/2405 queries in the second fragment, and 105/354 queries in the third fragment. In total, there are 1499/3720 queries that have not been recovered in all the three fragments compared to only, $3620 - 3460 = 260$, queries that have not been recovered when vertical fragmentation is not employed as shown in Table 1 where 3460/3720 queries are recovered. The increased number of unresolved queries after fragmentation shows the impact of vertical fragmentation as an effective countermeasure in reducing the strength of the Count attack. We note here that in some scenarios, vertical fragmentation alone might not be enough to prevent the Count attack, for example in a small dataset such as the Adult dataset, the Count attack will always recover most of the fragments and the security gain will only be in preventing the attacker from linking the recovered records and combine them to recover one or more original records. Such a gain can be useful to reduce the effect of the Relational-Count attack where record recovery is the one of the attacker's goals. However, an attacker who is able to perform the Count attack is concerned only about query recovery and not record recovery. Therefore, we need to employ padding also as an additional countermeasure needed to reduce the effectiveness of the Count attack.

Privacy Constraints vs. Record Injection Attacks. Privacy constraints can not prevent record injection attacks but they can reduce their effectiveness since the attacker will not be able to re-construct and combine the recovered fragments to form the original plaintext records even if all the records of each fragment are recovered since each fragment has a different record ID secretly pointing to the same original record before fragmentation. Note that an attacker injecting records that do not have any prior knowledge about the target database will not be able to link and combine the fragmented records in case all fragments are recovered.

Performance Gain. The drawback with the fragmentation approach is in the extra computational work done when a multi-keyword query whose keywords or attribute-value pairs exist in different fragments. But this can be improved using a fragmentation algorithm which takes usage data into account [11] which will allow us to find a suitable minimal fragmentation providing efficient execution for multi-keyword queries and the same time meeting the security demands set by the privacy constraints.

6   Conclusion

In this paper, we pointed out that inference and record-injection attacks pose a real threat to searchable encrypted relational databases. We proposed the use of privacy constraints together with padding on top of any SSE scheme in order to reduce the effectiveness of the inference attacks proposed in [5, 14].

References

1. Abdelraheem, M.A., Gehrmann, C., Lindström, M., Nordahl, C.: Executing boolean queries on an encrypted bitmap index. In: Proceedings of the 2016 ACM on Cloud Computing Security Workshop, pp. 11–22. ACM (2016)
2. Aggarwal, G., Bawa, M., Ganesan, P., Garcia-Molina, H., Kenthapadi, K., Motwani, R., Srivastava, U., Thomas, D., Xu, Y.: Two can keep a secret: a distributed architecture for secure database services. In: CIDR 2005 (2005)
3. Portuguese banking institution. Bank marketing data set (2014). https://archive. ics.uci.edu/ml/datasets/Bank+Marketing. Accessed June 2017
4. Bost, R.: σοφος: forward secure searchable encryption. In: CCS 2016 (2016)
5. Cash, D., Grubbs, P., Perry, J., Ristenpart, T.: Leakage-abuse attacks against searchable encryption. In: Proceedings of CCS 2015 (2015)
6. Cash, D., Jaeger, J., Jarecki, S., Jutla, C.S., Krawczyk, H., Rosu, M.-C., Steiner, M.: Dynamic searchable encryption in very-large databases: data structures and implementation. IACR Cryptology ePrint Archive, 2014:853 (2014)
7. Cash, D., Jarecki, S., Jutla, C., Krawczyk, H., Roşu, M.-C., Steiner, M.: Highly-scalable searchable symmetric encryption with support for boolean queries. In: Canetti, R., Garay, J.A. (eds.) CRYPTO 2013. LNCS, vol. 8042, pp. 353–373. Springer, Heidelberg (2013). doi:10.1007/978-3-642-40041-4_20
8. Chase, M., Kamara, S.: Structured encryption and controlled disclosure. In: Abe, M. (ed.) ASIACRYPT 2010. LNCS, vol. 6477, pp. 577–594. Springer, Heidelberg (2010). doi:10.1007/978-3-642-17373-8_33
9. Ciriani, V., De Capitani di Vimercati, S., Foresti, S., Jajodia, S., Paraboschi, S., Samarati, P.: Fragmentation and encryption to enforce privacy in data storage. In: Biskup, J., López, J. (eds.) ESORICS 2007. LNCS, vol. 4734, pp. 171–186. Springer, Heidelberg (2007). doi:10.1007/978-3-540-74835-9_12
10. Ciriani, V., De Capitani di Vimercati, S., Foresti, S., Jajodia, S., Paraboschi, S., Samarati, P.: Keep a few: outsourcing data while maintaining confidentiality. In: Backes, M., Ning, P. (eds.) ESORICS 2009. LNCS, vol. 5789, pp. 440–455. Springer, Heidelberg (2009). doi:10.1007/978-3-642-04444-1_27
11. Ciriani, V., De Capitani Di Vimercati, S., Foresti, S., Jajodia, S., Paraboschi, S., Samarati, P.: Combining fragmentation and encryption to protect privacy in data storage. ACM Trans. Inf. Syst. Secur. (TISSEC) (2010)
12. Curtmola, R., Garay, J., Kamara, S., Ostrovsky, R.: Searchable symmetric encryption: improved definitions and efficient constructions. In: Proceedings of the 13th ACM Conference on Computer and Communications Security, pp. 79–88. ACM (2006)
13. Center for Machine Learning and Intelligent Systems. University of California, Irvine. https://archive.ics.uci.edu/ml/datasets.html. Accessed June 2017
14. Islam, M.S., Kuzu, M., Kantarcioglu, M.: Access pattern disclosure on searchable encryption: ramification, attack and mitigation. In: NDSS (2012)
15. Kohavi, R., Becker, B.: Adult data set (1996). https://archive.ics.uci.edu/ml/machine-learning-databases/adult/. Accessed June 2017
16. Lane, T., Kohavi, R.: Census-income (KDD) data set (2000). https://archive.ics. uci.edu/ml/machine-learning-databases/census-income-mld/. Accessed June 2017
17. Naveed, M., Kamara, S., Wright, C.V.: Inference attacks on property-preserving encrypted databases. In: Proceedings of CCS 2015 (2015)
18. Popa, R.A., Redfield, C., Zeldovich, N., Balakrishnan, H.: Cryptdb: protecting confidentiality with encrypted query processing. In: Proceedings of the Twenty-Third ACM Symposium on Operating Systems Principles, pp. 85–100. ACM (2011)

19. Song, D.X., Wagner, D., Perrig, A.: Practical techniques for searches on encrypted data. In: 2000 IEEE Symposium on Security and Privacy, S&P 2000, Proceedings, pp. 44–55. IEEE (2000)
20. van Liesdonk, P., Sedghi, S., Doumen, J., Hartel, P., Jonker, W.: Computationally efficient searchable symmetric encryption. In: Jonker, W., Petković, M. (eds.) SDM 2010. LNCS, vol. 6358, pp. 87–100. Springer, Heidelberg (2010). doi:10.1007/978-3-642-15546-8_7
21. Zhang, Y., Katz, J., Papamanthou, C.: All your queries are belong to us: the power of file-injection attacks on searchable encryption. Cryptology ePrint Archive, Report 2016/172

Private Verification of Access on Medical Data: An Initial Study

Thaís Bardini Idalino[1], Dayana Spagnuelo[2(✉)], and Jean Everson Martina[3]

[1] School of Electrical Engineering and Computer Science,
University of Ottawa, Ottawa, Canada
[2] Interdisciplinary Centre for Security Reliability and Trust (SnT),
University of Luxembourg, Luxembourg, Luxembourg
dayana.spagnuelo@uni.lu
[3] Departamento de Informática e Estatística,
Universidade Federal de Santa Catarina, Florianópolis, Brazil

Abstract. Patient-centered medical systems promote empowerment of patients, who can decide on the accesses and usage of their personal data. To inspire a sense of trust and encourage the adoption of such systems, it is desired to allow one to verify whether the system has acted in accordance with the patients' preferences. However, it is argued that even audit logs and usage policies, normally used when verifying such property, may already be enough for one to learn sensitive information, e.g., the medical specialists a given patient has visited in the past. This is not only damaging for the patients, but is also against the interests of the medical system, which may lose back the trust earned and gain a bad reputation. Verifiability should not come at the expense of patients' privacy. It is, therefore, imperative that these systems take necessary precautions towards patient's information when providing means for verifiability. In this work we study how to realize that. In particular, we explore how searchable encryption techniques could be applied to allow the verification of systems in a private fashion, providing no information on patient's sensitive data.

Keywords: Verifiability · Audit · Compliance · Privacy · Searchable encryption · Patient-centered medical systems

1 Introduction

Verification is, by the pure meaning of the word, "the process of establishing the truth, accuracy, or validity of something"[1]. Verifiability is regarded in literature as a property desired in many information systems (e.g., [11,12,25]). It is also presented as one of the properties composing the principle of transparency, which is said to promote accountability and to realize people's right to privacy [36].

Verifiability has been studied as a mean for compliance with data access and usage policies [31]. It is presented from two perspectives: preventative and

---

[1] Definition taken from the Online Oxford Dictionaries.

© Springer International Publishing AG 2017
J. Garcia-Alfaro et al. (Eds.): DPM/CBT 2017, LNCS 10436, pp. 86–103, 2017.
DOI: 10.1007/978-3-319-67816-0_6

detective. The preventative ensures that policies are enforced in IT operations. Thus non-compliant actions are prevented from even happening. The detective approach focus in validating the actions a posteriori.

The two approaches are not conflicting. In fact both can be combined in a way that the detective approach gives evidences that preventative techniques are in place and working properly. In some cases the combination of the two approaches is even mandatory. For example, medical systems usually need to be flexible and allow for emergency exceptions, such as break-the-glass. In these systems the preventative approach alone cannot enforce compliance. Detective approaches need to be in place in order to verify for obligations after the exceptional accesses happened.

In the medical systems domain, verifiability (also called auditability) has been explored with regard to access control (e.g., [14,24]). Even though there are solutions proposed for verifying access of personal data in medical systems (e.g., [20,21,32,33]), to the best of our knowledge, none do that while ensuring the details about patient's information are kept confidential [20,37]. In fact, according to Butin and Le Métayer [7], this is the most commonly used argument against verifiability in the context of personal data protection.

Allowing patients to manually verify compliance with policies is possible, but is not ideal. It would overwhelm them with the technical charge. A good verifiability solution in the medical domain should be *automatically executed*. To demonstrate good faith and commitment towards the fair use of personal data, it is desired that medical systems allow the verification process to be executed *independently*. In a way that the patient can choose to trust the system with the verification task, or to execute it with an external auditing tool. Moreover, it is imperative that the verifying solution ensures the *privacy of the subjects involved*. No personal and private information should be leaked during the verification process, even if unintentionally. However, those requirements are not easily achieved together. Commonly, verifiability solutions imply in the disclosure of information while privacy advocates the opposite. The independent verification requirement, while fostering the trust on the system may also become a privacy vulnerability if proper measures are not in place.

In this work we demonstrate how independent verifiability can be realized in a private fashion. We model an initial theoretical solution for detective compliance through verifiability in a patient-centered medical system. We use searchable encryption techniques for that. Our scheme allows for the access logs from medical system to be independently checked by a third party tool without leaking private information. It also protects the verification conditions by encrypting the queries executed by this third-party. Moreover, empowering users with the ability of privately checking compliance with access policies, helps supporting the confidence these users have in the system.

In what follows we present the related works and review the literature on searchable encryption techniques in Sect. 2. In Sect. 3 we contextualize and present the basic concepts on medical systems, and in Sect. 4 we model the requirements and the entities involved in our scheme. Section 5 deepens into the details of our scheme, while in Sect. 6 we present a high-level analysis of the complexity and security of our proposal. Finally, in Sect. 7 we conclude our work and present the future directions.

2   Related Works

A survey from Reuben et al. [31] classifies the existing automated audits for privacy compliance verification. They study several solutions and separate them according to their auditing goals. The authors highlight three main goals: 1. *audit for ex-post obligations* – which regards compliance with after-the-fact obligations that cannot be verified beforehand, such as mandatory deletion of data after a fixed amount of time; 2. *audit for permitted exceptions* – which includes exceptional actions that happen in case of emergency (break-the-glass policies); and 3. *audits for access legitimacy* – which intends to demonstrate compliance with the data owner's preferences.

Audits for ex-post obligations do not necessarily imply on disclosure of personal data. In fact Butin and Le Métayer [7] propose a formal framework for verifying compliance in a privacy friendly way. They check compliance with data protection policies based on logs free of any personal data. However, they are not able to demonstrate compliance with access policies. They only verify properties such as "delete requests are fulfilled before expiration of request fulfillment delay", and "no personal data should appear in an abstract state after its global deletion delay has expired".

Audits for permitted exceptions and for access legitimacy pose more challenge for the privacy of personal and sensitive data. In most of the cases they mandate the analysis of audit logs, which contain information on *who* accessed *what kind* of information from *whom* [20,37]. In this work we intend to demonstrate how one could conduct these kind of audits in a private manner. For this purpose we show a model to automatically verify the latter (access legitimacy). Our scheme is capable of identifying accesses that do not match the user's preferences. Which can be later manually investigated for permitted exceptions (break-the-glass policies, for example). Automatic verification of permitted exceptions in a private manner would require a more in-depth study that is outside of the scope of our work. It will be subject of our future work.

In [20] authors point out security and privacy issues involved in making access policies and audit logs available in medical domain. They advocate that policies and logs, even though not containing personal and sensitive information (only references to it), may be enough for revealing details that should be kept private. Someone in possession of such policies and logs can gain knowledge of what kind of treatment a patient has received in the past, or what types of medical data are available. Authors advocate that by properly controlling the access to policies and logs it is possible to solve this privacy issue. They propose an adapted Information Accountability Framework [15] in which only the patient (data owners), medical professionals and medical authorities (e.g., government agency conducting audits) can access the policies and logs with restrictions according to their roles.

However, this work is not suitable to be applied to our context. In [20] independent auditing processes, one of our goals, are not considered. Even if this work was adapted to allow independent verification, the principle of privacy would still not be realized. External entities would still have access to more information than necessary to the purpose of verification. Restricted access control when applied in an uncontrolled environment (possibly insecure) does not suffice to prevent leakage of personal information.

While in [20] the confidentiality of sensitive information is realized only by controlling access to policies and logs, Walters et al. [37] propose a different solution for the problem: to operate on encrypted audit logs.

In [37], authors assume a scenario in which a system is being audited but the controllers of the system do not wish to share information from the audit logs with other entities. Similarly, the authors also believe it is possible to learn sensitive details about the system and the users by analyzing the logs. For example, one can instantly learn what actions were conducted by a given user. The authors build an scheme for conducting searches in encrypted audit logs. For each log registered, the system should define a few keywords with which this log can be found. It then distributes searching capabilities for those keywords only to specific authorized persons. Each log is encrypted with a key that can only be retrieved by persons that possess searching capabilities for, at least, one of its keywords. Consequently, this scheme only allows authorized persons to decrypt the audit logs.

The audit process presented in [37] cannot be fully independent though. It relies on the system providing searching capabilities to the auditor for the given set of actions he or she can audit. Despite that, this scheme is also not in accordance with the privacy principle. In our scenario, in order to verify compliance with the patient's preferences the auditor would search for log entries matching the set of allowed actions and be able to decrypt them, in detriment of the patient's privacy. Ideally the external entity should not be able to decrypt, only learning whether or not a given log entry matches a search (and consequently is an allowed action) would suffice.

There are several other works that, similarly to the one mentioned above, suggest schemes for privately processing personal data. The majority of those use searchable encryption techniques for that. In what follows we present the most relevant of those works while reviewing basic concepts of the technique.

2.1 Searchable Encryption

Searchable encryption (SE) techniques were initially introduced in the context of outsourced databases. With the growth of the amount of data generated, came an increasing need for outsourced options to store it. However, one cannot fully trust outsourced databases and may want to keep its data confidential. One possible solution to guarantee confidentiality involves encrypting the data before the storage on the database. Only the ones in possession of the key can decrypt it and learn its contents. However, denying the database access to the information increases the difficulty of performing queries and selectively retrieving data.

Searchable encryption techniques try to approach this problem by allowing the database to execute queries on encrypted data.

Search on encrypted data was initially introduced by Goldreich and Ostrovsky [18], and Song et al. [35]. It is, to this day, an active research area with three main research directions [5]: to improve efficiency; to improve security; and to enhance the expressiveness of the search. Usually we see a trade-off between them. For example, guaranteeing a stronger *security* usually compromises the *efficiency*.

An important scheme based on searchable encrypted index was first presented by Goh [17] and later considered in other works (i.e. [8,29,30] and many others). For each encrypted data, keywords are extracted and those are used to generate an encrypted index. In the outsourced database scenario, the indexes are generated by the client and sent with the respective encrypted data to the database. Later, the client can send an encrypted query and the indexes will help the database/server to search over the encrypted data without the need of decryption. Indexes and queries should not leak information about the encrypted data, while guaranteeing that clients obtain what they are searching for.

There are specific techniques for searching on public key [2,3,16] and symmetric key [10,17,35] encrypted data. The last one is known as searchable symmetric encryption (SSE). Several works presented solutions for searching single keywords [9,10,37]. Other schemes propose a search using more expressive keyword searches, such as conjunctions [4,6,19,34], ranges [4,34], or even dealing with keyword occurrence frequency [6]. This improves the expressiveness and security of searches, as opposed to perform several single-keyword searches and combining the results [29]. A few even more expressive schemes support general Boolean searches with conjunction, disjunction and negation of keywords in disjunctive normal form (DNF) and/or conjunctive normal form (CNF) [8,13,23,26,29,30]. We demonstrate later that these works are of a special interest since it is possible to model our problem into queries in a disjunctive normal form (DNF).

Symmetric searchable encryption are usually applied to scenarios where data owners want to query their own encrypted data stored in some third party server. In our work we propose the use of SSE techniques in a slightly different scenario, where data owners (patients) share their data with medical services and use SSE to independently verify accesses, while guaranteeing the confidentiality of their personal data.

It is necessary to note though, that we have a few different (and more relaxed) requirements in comparison to the conventional application of SSE in outsourced data storage. The first is related to the amount of data stored, searched and returned: while outsourced data applications may have to deal with large amounts of data, our application deals only with the event registers (logs) related to one specific patient (as shown in Sect. 3). We assume these logs to be in a smaller scale. This implies that the use of SSE algorithms with non-optimal search time is not prohibitive in our application. Second, the patient already has access to all encrypted data and uses the verifier only for auditing. Therefore, if the search returns all the data, which is an expected result for the cases where no violation of the policy was made, we can save on communication and avoid returning everything again to the client, i.e. we can return just a positive message instead.

3   Technical Aspects of Medical Systems

The term "medical systems" is broad and encompasses several types of systems with different goals: clinical data management systems, telemedicine systems, hospital information systems, pharmaceutical, etc. In our work we only distinguish those which are patient-centered. The goal of these systems is to allow the patient to be in control of the personal data being processed. From this point on we refer to patient-centered systems simply as *medical systems*.

One example of a patient-centered medical system is Microsoft HealthVault[2], an online platform that allows users to gather, use and share health information. The information stored in the system can be provided manually by the user; or automatically by mobile applications or compatible medical devices. In this system the users are able to control which information is stored, deleted, and who will be able to access or edit their data [28]. Other example is the national Dossier de Soins Partagé[3] (Shared Care Dossier in English) from Luxembourg. In this system the goal is to facilitate the communication between health professionals intervening with a patient. Health data is uploaded to the system by authorized institutions, e.g., laboratories and hospitals, and shared with a default set of persons (the patient, the doctor assigned to him or her and the team related to them). But similarly to the Microsoft HealthVault, the patients have full control over sharing of data, being able even to revoke the default access privileges.

Generally speaking we can assume these patient-centered medical systems to adopt a discretionary access control system (DAC) [22]. In DAC systems the owner of a resource, in our case the patient, may grant or revoke access to other entities (users) based on their identities. We do not affirm that every patient-centered medical system implements DAC exactly as described in [22]. We just claim their access control method resembles DAC and could be modelled using it. For the sake of simplicity we assume discretionary access control policies as a set of fixed size clauses as shown in Eq. (1), where id_i is the identity of the person authorized to realize an action $action_j$ on the patient's data.

$$\pi = \{(id_i, action_j)\} \tag{1}$$

It is, however, unrealistic to assume one access control system to be the perfect fit for every variation of medical systems. We do not attempt doing that. We instead chose to model our solution based on DAC systems to demonstrate that private verification can be accomplished even in systems implementing highly malleable and granular access control mechanisms. We present arguments to

---

[2] https://www.healthvault.com/.

[3] https://www.esante.lu/portal/fr/espace-patient/le-dsp-au-quotidien,199.html?

endorse this claim in Sect. 5. And later, in Sect. 7, we discuss how our solution can also handle other types of policies richer in attributes.

Our simplified policy is only suitable to represent patient-centered medical systems though. In general these systems do not handle the definition of pre-conditions, post-conditions, obligations and other more complex policies that may be found in other types of medical system. To add more representativeness to the verification one could also explore revocation of access rights, which would mandate clauses to be time anchored. However, this is out of our scope. We restrict ourselves to the study of static policies and verification without temporal aspects.

Every action a person realizes on the patient's data, whether authorized or not, should be registered as an event in the audit logs. Similarly to how we defined the policies, we do for the register of events. We do not go into details on how they are in fact implemented because that may vary in different implementations. But according to a recent work [38] which surveys log files in the medical domain, it is reasonable to assume at least the following attributes would have to be registered in order to provide verifiability: 1. event identification ($action$) – the action performed; 2. date and time (t); 3. actor identification (id) – who performed the action; 4. object identification (ob) – the data that suffered the actions. Some standards are more complete and consider more attributes (i.e., RFC 3881 [27]), but in general these four attributes are commonly observed in medical systems [38]. We assume the register of events simply as the set of logs as displayed in Eq. (2).

$$L = \{(action, t, id, ob)\} \tag{2}$$

4   Model Description

As described in Sect. 3, our scenario assumes a patient-centered medical system. Users of such a system should be able to verify whether their data has been accessed in compliance to the access policy. We assume three different players:

- **Medical System:** Stores patient's data, which can be accessed by its owner (the patient), and few predetermined professionals. This decision is agreed with the patient through an access policy.
- **Patient:** May want to verify if specific statements of the policy are being enforced, or search for possible violations.
- **Verifier:** Third party tool or mechanism responsible for verifying compliance of the medical system with regard to specific statements of the agreed policy.

Additionally, we also assume the ideal solution would take into consideration the following requirements:

- **Automated verification:** The medical system should provide means for the patients to avoid the overburden of manually verifying logs;
- **Independent audit:** Allowing a third party to verify compliance with privacy policies demonstrates good faith and commitment towards the fair use of personal data;

- **Privacy:** During the auditing, patients' privacy should be ensured – only the strictly necessary information to determine compliance should be disclosed. From this information one should not be able to infer any personal details about the patients.

Patients should access and be able to export logs of actions performed on their data. However, data and the logs are private and should only be accessed by its owner (the patient) and a few designated medical staff. Therefore, both patient and the medical system are interested on keeping communications confidential. We chose to encrypt data with a symmetric key that is only known by the medical system and the patient. Keys differ for each patient of the system.

Patients may require the logs related to their data to check if the agreed policy is being followed. They can decrypt all logs received and verify by themselves, or they have the option to execute this task with an independent verifier. For that, the patient simply redirects the encrypted logs to the verifier. Since the verifier does not have access to the key used for encryption, a (good) traditional symmetric encryption is enough to guarantee that this verifier will not learn any information about the events these logs represent. Finally, in order to allow the verifier to operate over the encrypted logs while protecting the patient's privacy, we propose the use of symmetric searchable encryption (SSE).

4.1   Trust Model

The medical system we model is assumed to be honest, but not trustworthy. In systems that implement break-the-glass, for example, the policy may be relaxed and this can cause abuses. It may also be the case that the access control mechanism implemented does not flawlessly represent the policy agreed prior the disclosure of data. In both cases the medical system does not act ill-intentioned, but the patients' data can still be misused, and this may cause mistrust. Hence, the medical system's goal is to regain the trust of its users. This is realized by allowing them to independently verify whether the system has acted in compliance with the agreed policy. By doing that, we also avoid requiring the patient to place major trust in one single entity.

Our attacker model also assumes an honest-but-curious verifier, which will not actively behave dishonestly, but my retain any information disclosed to it. We also assume an external attacker, who will try to extract or infer information on the patients. The attacker is assumed to have access to the verifier, and any information exchanged between the other players. Because our goal is to demonstrate how independent verifiability can be achieved in a private manner (without leaking any sensitive information), we are only interested in what an attacker can learn through the use of the verifier. The capabilities of the attacker towards the medical system are not explored in this work.

In order to avoid a possible collusion between medical system and verifier, we suggest the implementation of several verifiers by different entities. In this way, the patients can double-check with different verifiers in case of suspicion. Verifiers would avoid collusion with medical systems in order to maintain reputation, and medical systems would avoid collusion with verifiers as that can be identified by other verifiers. Verifiers can also be tested by the users with a set of logs and policies for which the expected results are known. Even though these approaches do not demonstrate the verifier correctness, they provide stronger evidences that can be used as criteria to support the choice of verifier.

It is important to note that we do not investigate into the matter of how to ensure the logs' accuracy and integrity. This topic is out of the scope of our work. We assume the medical system is honest and has its own reliable and trustworthy logging mechanism, and that it securely stores and handles data and logs. The following section presents in details our proposal for verification using searchable encryption.

5   Solving Verification with Searchable Encryption

Symmetric searchable encryption (SSE) schemes are popular in cloud settings. Data owners store encrypted data in an outsourced database, perform encrypted queries, and receive the encrypted data they searched for. We propose the use of SSE in a different setting: to verify whether the medical system is compliant to the access policy agreed with the patient. This verification is done through an external and independent audit. In our scenario, the verifier plays the role of the outsourced cloud service (even though it is not necessarily remote) and the patient is the data owner. We have added a third role played by the medical system, that is responsible for encrypting the data and generating the search indexes.

Next we present our scheme dividing it into the encryption of logs and index generation, the query generation and policy verification.

5.1   Encryption and Index Generation

For each patient that requires his or her logs, the medical system performs a *key agreement* process, where system and patient agree on a symmetric key k to be used for encryption and decryption. After that, the medical system encrypts each log individually and generates an index for each one of them, summarizing its content. The index includes all the *keywords* that can be searched in the encrypted data. Specifically for our scenario, the index of a log should contain the keywords related to the policy, such as the *action* registered by that log and the identity *id* of the user who performed the action (see Eq. (2)). The index generation depends on the SSE method used, but a common requirement is that no *keyword* in the index should be exposed. This is usually achieved by encrypting or through the use of scrambling-related techniques [6, 13, 17, 29]. We abstract the process of encryption and index generation in Algorithm 1.

Algorithm 1. EncryptLogs($logs[n]$)

Input: array of $logs$ with n entries
for each $i \in \{1, \ldots, n\}$ **do**
    c[i] = Enc($k, logs[i]$)
    keywords = extractKeywords($logs[i]$)
    index[i] = generateIndex(k, keywords)
end for
Output: c, index

5.2 Query Generation

The medical system sends indexes and encrypted logs to the patient, who can redirect this information to the verifier for auditing purposes. On the patient's side, the main computation is related to the query generation. The query indicates which clauses the patient wants to verify. By generating one query containing each clause in the policy π (see Eq. (1)), it is possible to determine compliance. We present here Algorithm 2 as a generic algorithm for query generation.

In a traditional SSE approach, the data owner would generate an encrypted query and the database should simply execute this query over the indexes and return the respective encrypted data that matches the search. We adopt a similar approach. Here we assume that the patient has access to the policy agreed with the medical system. The patient then generates an encrypted query that contain the clauses from the policy, in order to check if the actions registered in the logs comply with the policy agreed. If the policy and the key used to encrypt the logs and indexes do not change, this query could also be further reused by the same patient.

We represent our query as a Boolean expression in a disjunctive normal form (DNF). We assume a simple policy containing only a set of s *identities* and t *actions* as *keywords*, and relations in the format $(id_i, action_j)$ representing a clause of the policy allowing a person identified by id_i to execute $action_j$. To search for all logs that match the policy, the patient can generate a query in the DNF form as follows: $(id_{i_1} \wedge action_{j_1}) \vee \ldots \vee (id_{i_s} \wedge action_{j_t})$, where $(id_i \wedge action_j)$ is an allowed relation of the policy.

We abstract the query generation with a call to *"generate query"*. The details of this generation depend on the SSE method, but it basically identifies the clauses from the DNF expression and perform specific computations depending on the method used. Since we don't want the verifier to obtain information about the encrypted logs, some computation must be performed on the query as well to guarantee its confidentiality. This is a reasonable assumption considering that several SSE algorithms already guarantee that by using encryption or scrambling-based techniques [8, 23, 29]. As an example, the query generation by Moataz and Shikfa [29] consists on converting keywords to vectors, and applying consecutive multiplications, sums and divisions to them. The confidentiality in this case is guaranteed by incorporating random integers in the query computation (see [29, Sect. 4.2] for more details).

Note that the query generation is quite flexible, since it allows the patient to search for a range of different options. For example, he or she can search for all logs that match the policy, for some combination of specific clauses from the policy, or even for logs that do not match the policy by simply negating the search expression. It is important to note that most SSE schemes (specially the most traditional ones) search for single keywords on encrypted data. Here we require the use of a more expressive SSE that supports Boolean queries, such as the solutions proposed in [8,23,29]. Algorithm 2 summarizes the process of query generation.

Algorithm 2. GenerateQuery(π)

Input: Policy $\pi = \{(id_i, action_i)\}$ with m clauses
DNF = empty string
for each $i \in \{1, \ldots, m\}$ **do**
    DNF = DNF $\|(id_i \wedge action_i)$
    if $i \neq m$ **then**
        DNF = DNF $\|\vee$
    end if
end for
$\mathcal{Q}$ = generateQuery(DNF)
Output: $\mathcal{Q}$

Recall that we created indexes for the encrypted logs with the keywords $(id_i, action_j)$ contained in each log. The verifier can then search through the logs indexes and identify the ones that match at least one of the conjunctions $(id_i \wedge action_j)$ from the query. Here we considered small policy clauses, but if necessary, we can easily adapt the query to be more expressive. For example, by considering extra information such as identification of the objects that suffered the actions. In order to incorporate extra keywords in the search, these keywords also need to be incorporated in the policy and during the generation of the logs' indexes.

5.3 Policy Verification

After the verifier receives the encrypted logs, respective indexes, and the query $\mathcal{Q}$, it has enough information to perform the verification for policy compliance. The search process consists on going through the encrypted logs to find the ones that match the query. For each log, the verifier obtains the corresponding index and use it to check if it matches the query. Here we call this comparison "test" and the logs that "pass" the test are added to the vector of results. If a log pass a test, it means that this log contains at least all the keywords from one of the conjunctions of the query, which represents compliance with one of the clauses of the policy.

Note that the search depends on the SSE method as well. Some constructions propose visiting each encrypted data and its indexes [29], while others present some more efficient search methods [13,23,30]. After the search, the verifier sends to the patient a list of encrypted logs that match the query. As logs, indexes, and queries are encrypted, the verifier is not able to learn anything about the confidential information. As an example, the verification by Moataz and Shikfa [29] consists on visiting every index and comparing it to the query. Generally speaking, every index is multiplied by the query and the ones that output a result equals to "1" correspond to logs that satisfy at least one clause from the policy. Algorithm 3 summarizes the our verification process.

Algorithm 3. Search($Q, c[n], index[n]$)

Input: Encrypted query Q, vector c with n encrypted logs, and their indexes
  for each $i \in \{1, \ldots, n\}$ do
    $r = \text{test}(Q, index[i])$
    if $r = $ **true** then
      $result.\text{add}(c[i])$
    end if
  end for
Output: $result$

The results can be simplified by returning the number of logs that match the query, or a custom message for the special cases, such as "All logs match your query", or "No logs match your query". If further investigation is desired, Algorithm 3 can easily be adapted to return the logs that caused a mismatch. If the patient is interested in learning the cause for the mismatch he or she can decrypt those logs (using the key k) and understand what event is not compliant to the policy. Alternatively, these logs could be redirected to the medical system in order to inquire for a justification. How to better display and interpret the results, or how to request for justification are definitely relevant issues, but we understand they would require a research on their own. We refrain from delving into those matter in this work.

6   Complexity and Security Analysis

Several searchable encryption schemes are designed for the settings of big data applications, where there is a large amount of encrypted data and it is, for example, unfeasible to search through every single record. Our scenario is slightly different and some of the assumptions in those settings are not applicable here. In what follows we discuss how technical aspects of SSE methods impact our solution. We first examine aspects of computational complexity of those methods (Subsect. 6.1) and later we discuss about their security (Subsect. 6.2).

6.1   Complexity

The efficiency of our scheme is directly related to the efficiency of the SSE method used. However, the use of non-optimal SSE methods, such as [8,29], while prohibitive for big data applications, is acceptable in our scenario. In fact, SSE techniques are very well suited for our application. Our verifier processes only the audit logs related to one specific patient. These logs are assumed to be small pieces of data and in a much smaller scale than in cloud settings. Consequently, the efficiency problems presented in outsourced databases are not applicable here. Moreover, the generation of keywords in our application does not require complex calculations. The keywords are defined by the policy and logs, and can be automatically extracted from those.

Other more efficient SSE methods, such as the ones with sub-linear search time [23,30], could also be considered here. In this case, the efficiency would depend on the query we are searching for. When searching for all logs that match the policy, it is expected the result to be close to the total amount of logs n. Hence, our search complexity will end up being close to $O(n)$ as well. However, when searching for the logs that *do not* match the policy, or that match some specific patters, we should expect a small number of results. In this case, methods that have search time close to the number of results may be the right choice. We assume the complexity of our worst-case scenario to be $O(n)$.

Intuitively one would tend to believe that the most efficient SSE methods on the literature are the best fit. However, there are trade-offs on these methods that need to be consider. Some of these methods use complicated structures and increase the spacial complexity, and others end up revealing parts of sensitive information. For a more extensive discussion on the trade-offs related to expressiveness of the query, efficiency, and security, the reader may want to refer to [5]. The choice of the method is not straightforward, it needs to be carefully studied. However, we suggest that in cases where the number of logs (n) is reasonable, it is a good practice to prioritize secure over efficient methods, even if they offer search complexity of $O(n)$.

6.2   Security

The confidentiality of personal information in our scheme is provided by the chosen symmetric key encryption algorithm. To avoid brute force and the most common attacks it is recommended to use encryption algorithms that have at least 112 bits of security (i.e. AES) [1]. Moreover, the use of deterministic encryption algorithms commonly implies in the leakage of patterns [5]. Therefore, the most secure SSE schemes are usually non-deterministic.

The security of the scheme is not only given by the encryption algorithm though, it also depends on the security of the SSE method itself. The SSE methods in the literature present a concern on the amount of information that can be inferred by the results of the search. Although they do not reveal directly the content of the encrypted data, the majority of these schemes will not prevent probabilistic analysis if the same data is repeatedly searched. This is a problem common to any application of this nature.

In our application the verifier returns all the results that match an specific query. This means that the verifier knows which encrypted logs are being returned, but not their plain content. The same applies to the attacker we consider in our model, since we assume it has access to the verifier and any exchanged message. There are SSE methods that aim to hide all information. In this way, the verifier is not even able to detect which logs are being returned to the data owner. However, these SSE methods are usually based on oblivious RAMs (ORAMs), and are not efficient in practice (for more details, see survey [5]).

We understand that the searches will usually be related to the logs that match or do not match the policy. By analyzing the number of results from an specific query one could guess which search was performed. The search with several results is likely to be a search for all logs that match the policy, and the search with a few results is probably for the logs that do not match the policy. In this sense the verifier (or attacker) would be able to identify which logs match/do not match the policy, but would not be able to learn their content. We do not consider this as a threat to our scheme. A well chosen encryption algorithm would make sure that encrypted logs and queries are not available in plain text (they are encrypted or scrambled depending on the SSE scheme). Nonetheless, it is important to consider this case when applying our solution to other scenarios.

It is also important to note that any technical limitation of the underlying schemes (symmetric encryption or SSE) also reflects on a limitation of our proposed solution. We can cite, for example, the case of compromised or revoked private keys. In this case every data encrypted with that key is assumed to be compromised as well. A known solution to neutralize the potential damage is to reduce the lifetime of the key, and for example, use session keys instead of a single private key. In our scenario this solution would come at the cost of recalculating the queries, which could no longer be reused. This is the classical trade-off between efficiency and security.

Furthermore, a slight modification of our scheme is also needed to cope with the problem of compromised keys. Compromising one session key is enough for breaking privacy, even if forward and backwards secrecy are maintained, and no other message is obtained. The damage cause by compromising one session key is proportional to the amount of logs encrypted with that key. Therefore, to minimize this problem, only a small subset of logs should be verified at a time, i.e. the logs of the day or past week. Note that the maximum number of logs that are encrypted by the same session key is determined by the security guarantees required for specific applications of our scheme.

7 Discussion and Conclusion

In this work we modeled a scheme for verifying data access in the context of patient-centered medical systems. Our scheme is based on Symmetric Searchable Encryption methods and suggests how to meet the three requirements we deem imperative in the medical context: 1. *automated verification* – patients should not be required to manually verify audit logs; 2. *independent audit* – demonstrates the honest intentions of the medical system and helps building reputation; and 3. *privacy* – protects the right for privacy of the patients.

We propose the introduction of an entity for auditing the *Medical System* on behalf of the *Patient*. This entity is the *Verifier*. The implementation of the verifier as a Transparency Enhancing Tool controlled by the patient or by a third party would suffice to accomplish requirements for automated independent audit (requirements 1 and 2).

The privacy principle poses the biggest challenge as it conflicts with the other two requirements. To be able to verify whether a system acted in compliance with a given policy the verifier needs access to audit logs. However, those logs may reveal private information about the patients [20,37]. Revealing them is outside of the patient's interest. But not revealing them would mean the patient needs to trust the medical system with the verification. Obliging the patient to place major trust in one single entity. In this paper we demonstrate that Symmetric Searchable Encryption (SSE) can be adapted to provide the right balance between the requirements.

By using SSE methods we allow the verifier to operate on encrypted logs. In this way the interests of the patient are protected. Our scheme defines that compliance is achieved whenever a log entry matches, at least, one clause in the policy. This is possible since the policy describes every allowed action in the system. The SSE method allows then the verifier to search for those matches over encrypted audit logs and the obfuscated policy clauses. This ensures the verifier, and consequently the attacker, will not learn any sensitive information. The only information the one can learn is the number of logs that match (or not) a given search. This is, however, acceptable in our scheme since the logs are encrypted and indistinguishable from each other, and the policy is obfuscated. We understand that this is a necessary trade-off between privacy and verifiability in medical systems. Moreover, this does not violate requirement 3, which foresees a *minimal* disclosure to determine compliance.

One may question the simplicity of our policy model. Only the identity of the actor and the action executed are considered. This was deliberately done to simplify the description. Our model supports other types of access control policies and any number of attributes. This can be realized by computing extra keywords in the indexes and conjunctions of the query. The model we propose can handle the verification of actors' roles, attributes, sections of personal data, for example. Given the medical system supports such attributes in its policy and register them in the audit logs.

At this stage, our proposal is limited to the identification of log entries that match and the ones that do no match a given policy. The latter can then be manually investigated for permitted exceptions (break-the-glass policies), or other events also relevant in medical systems, such as delegation. Including these events in our verifier is a natural evolution of our proposal. As our next step we plan to investigate this matter.

We also foresee the formalization of our scheme as a future work. A good starting point is the work from Butin and Le Métayer [7]. We plan to extend that model now accounting for access legitimacy. To do so we will have to take a more careful look into the representation of events (logs) and authorized actions (policy), and to define protocols for obtaining and transferring these data between the players. We will also need to investigate deeper on the SSE schemes in order to select the most suitable ones. The extension of searching capabilities is directly dependant on the evolution of these schemes.

Finally, another interesting evolution of our work is to allow the verification of data access even in the presence of a dishonest medical systems. A possible starting point is to study how to ensure the logs integrity and accuracy. This is important to prevent medical systems from intentionally removing or altering logs that do not comply with the policy.

Acknowledgments. Thais Bardini Idalino acknowledges funding granted from CNPq-Brazil [233697/2014-4]. Dayana Spagnuelo's research is supported by the Luxembourg National Research Fund (FNR), AFR project 7842804 - TYPAMED. The authors would also like to thank Dr. Gabriele Lenzini and Prof. Peter Y.A. Ryan for contributing to this work with relevant discussions and valuable advice.

References

1. Barker, E.: NIST Special Publication 800-57 Part 1 Revision 4—Recommendation for Key Management (Part 1: General) (2016)
2. Boneh, D., Di Crescenzo, G., Ostrovsky, R., Persiano, G.: Public key encryption with keyword search. In: Cachin, C., Camenisch, J.L. (eds.) EUROCRYPT 2004. LNCS, vol. 3027, pp. 506–522. Springer, Heidelberg (2004). doi:10.1007/978-3-540-24676-3_30
3. Boneh, D., Raghunathan, A., Segev, G.: Function-private identity-based encryption: hiding the function in functional encryption. In: Canetti, R., Garay, J.A. (eds.) CRYPTO 2013. LNCS, vol. 8043, pp. 461–478. Springer, Heidelberg (2013). doi:10.1007/978-3-642-40084-1_26
4. Boneh, D., Waters, B.: Conjunctive, subset, and range queries on encrypted data. In: Vadhan, S.P. (ed.) TCC 2007. LNCS, vol. 4392, pp. 535–554. Springer, Heidelberg (2007). doi:10.1007/978-3-540-70936-7_29
5. Bösch, C., Hartel, P., Jonker, W., Peter, A.: A survey of provably secure searchable encryption. ACM Comput. Surv. (CSUR) **47**(2), 18 (2015)
6. Bösch, C., Tang, Q., Hartel, P., Jonker, W.: Selective document retrieval from encrypted database. In: Gollmann, D., Freiling, F.C. (eds.) ISC 2012. LNCS, vol. 7483, pp. 224–241. Springer, Heidelberg (2012). doi:10.1007/978-3-642-33383-5_14
7. Butin, D., Le Métayer, D.: Log analysis for data protection accountability. In: Jones, C., Pihlajasaari, P., Sun, J. (eds.) FM 2014. LNCS, vol. 8442, pp. 163–178. Springer, Cham (2014). doi:10.1007/978-3-319-06410-9_12
8. Cash, D., Jarecki, S., Jutla, C., Krawczyk, H., Roşu, M.-C., Steiner, M.: Highly-scalable searchable symmetric encryption with support for boolean queries. In: Canetti, R., Garay, J.A. (eds.) CRYPTO 2013. LNCS, vol. 8042, pp. 353–373. Springer, Heidelberg (2013). doi:10.1007/978-3-642-40041-4_20
9. Chang, Y.-C., Mitzenmacher, M.: Privacy preserving keyword searches on remote encrypted data. In: Ioannidis, J., Keromytis, A., Yung, M. (eds.) ACNS 2005. LNCS, vol. 3531, pp. 442–455. Springer, Heidelberg (2005). doi:10.1007/11496137_30
10. Curtmola, R., Garay, J., Kamara, S., Ostrovsky, R.: Searchable symmetric encryption: improved definitions and efficient constructions. J. Comput. Secur. **19**(5), 895–934 (2011)

11. Dreier, J., Giustolisi, R., Kassem, A., Lafourcade, P., Lenzini, G.: A framework for analyzing verifiability in traditional and electronic exams. In: Lopez, J., Wu, Y. (eds.) ISPEC 2015. LNCS, vol. 9065, pp. 514–529. Springer, Cham (2015). doi:10.1007/978-3-319-17533-1_35

12. Dreier, J., Jonker, H., Lafourcade, P.: Defining verifiability in e-auction protocols. In: Proceedings of the 8th ACM SIGSAC Symposium on Information, Computer and Communications Security, pp. 547–552. ACM (2013)

13. Fisch, B.A., Vo, B., Krell, F., Kumarasubramanian, A., Kolesnikov, V., Malkin, T., Bellovin, S.M.: Malicious-client security in blind seer: a scalable private DBMS. In: 2015 IEEE Symposium on Security and Privacy (SP), pp. 395–410. IEEE (2015)

14. Flores, A.E., Vergara, V.M.: Functionalities of open electronic health records system: a follow-up study. In: 6th International Conference on Biomedical Engineering and Informatics, pp. 602–607. IEEE (2013)

15. Gajanayake, R., Sahama, T.R., Lane, B., Grunwell, D.: Designing an information accountability framework for eHealth. In: IEEE Healthcom 2013 15th International Conference on E-Health Networking, Application and Services. Instituto Superior de Ciências Sociais e Políticas - Technical University of Lisbon, Lisbon, Portugal, June 2013. https://eprints.qut.edu.au/60690/

16. Gentry, C.: A fully homomorphic encryption scheme. Ph.D. thesis, Stanford University (2009)

17. Goh, E.J., et al.: Secure indexes. IACR Cryptology ePrint Archive 2003, 216 (2003). http://eprint.iacr.org/2003/216

18. Goldreich, O., Ostrovsky, R.: Software protection and simulation on oblivious RAMs. J. ACM (JACM) 43(3), 431–473 (1996)

19. Golle, P., Staddon, J., Waters, B.: Secure conjunctive keyword search over encrypted data. In: Jakobsson, M., Yung, M., Zhou, J. (eds.) ACNS 2004. LNCS, vol. 3089, pp. 31–45. Springer, Heidelberg (2004). doi:10.1007/978-3-540-24852-1_3

20. Grunwell, D., Gajanayake, R., Sahama, T.: The security and privacy of usage policies and provenance logs in an information accountability framework. In: Proceedings of the Eighth Australasian Workshop on Health Informatics and Knowledge Management (HIKM2015), vol. 164, pp. 33–40. Australian Computer Society (2015)

21. Haas, S., Wohlgemuth, S., Echizen, I., Sonehara, N., Müller, G.: Aspects of privacy for electronic health records. Int. J. Med. Inf. 80(2), e26–e31 (2011)

22. Hu, V.C., Ferraiolo, D., Kuhn, D.R.: Assessment of access control systems. US Department of Commerce, National Institute of Standards and Technology (2006)

23. Kamara, S., Moataz, T.: Boolean searchable symmetric encryption with worst-case sub-linear complexity. In: Coron, J.-S., Nielsen, J.B. (eds.) EUROCRYPT 2017. LNCS, vol. 10212, pp. 94–124. Springer, Cham (2017). doi:10.1007/978-3-319-56617-7_4

24. King, J.T., Smith, B., Williams, L.: Modifying without a trace: general audit guidelines are inadequate for open-source electronic health record audit mechanisms. In: Proceedings of the 2nd ACM SIGHIT International Health Informatics Symposium, pp. 305–314. ACM (2012)

25. Kremer, S., Ryan, M., Smyth, B.: Election verifiability in electronic voting protocols. In: Gritzalis, D., Preneel, B., Theoharidou, M. (eds.) ESORICS 2010. LNCS, vol. 6345, pp. 389–404. Springer, Heidelberg (2010). doi:10.1007/978-3-642-15497-3_24

26. Kurosawa, K.: Garbled searchable symmetric encryption. In: Financial Cryptography, vol. 2014, pp. 234–251 (2014)

27. Marshall, G.: Security audit and access accountability message XML. Technical report, RFC 3881 (2004)
28. Microsoft: Microsoft Privacy Statement (2017). https://privacy.microsoft.com/en-gb/privacystatement. Accessed 15 May 2017
29. Moataz, T., Shikfa, A.: Boolean symmetric searchable encryption. In: Proceedings of the 8th ACM SIGSAC symposium on Information, Computer and Communications Security, pp. 265–276. ACM (2013)
30. Pappas, V., Krell, F., Vo, B., Kolesnikov, V., Malkin, T., Choi, S.G., George, W., Keromytis, A., Bellovin, S.: Blind seer: a scalable private DBMS. In: 2014 IEEE Symposium on Security and Privacy (SP), pp. 359–374. IEEE (2014)
31. Reuben, J., Martucci, L.A., Fischer-Hübner, S.: Automated log audits for privacy compliance validation: a literature survey. In: Aspinall, D., Camenisch, J., Hansen, M., Fischer-Hübner, S., Raab, C. (eds.) Privacy and Identity 2015. IAICT, vol. 476, pp. 312–326. Springer, Cham (2016). doi:10.1007/978-3-319-41763-9_21
32. Røstad, L.: An initial model and a discussion of access control in patient controlled health records. In: 2008 Third International Conference on Availability, Reliability and Security, ARES 2008, pp. 935–942. IEEE (2008)
33. Seneviratne, O., Kagal, L.: Enabling privacy through transparency. In: 2014 Twelfth Annual International Conference on Privacy, Security and Trust (PST), pp. 121–128. IEEE (2014)
34. Shi, E., Bethencourt, J., Chan, T.H., Song, D., Perrig, A.: Multi-dimensional range query over encrypted data. In: 2007 IEEE Symposium on Security and Privacy, SP 2007, pp. 350–364. IEEE (2007)
35. Song, D.X., Wagner, D., Perrig, A.: Practical techniques for searches on encrypted data. In: 2000 IEEE Symposium on Security and Privacy, S&P 2000, Proceedings, pp. 44–55. IEEE (2000)
36. Spagnuelo, D., Lenzini, G.: Transparent medical data systems. J. Med. Syst. **41**(1), 8 (2017)
37. Waters, B.R., Balfanz, D., Durfee, G., Smetters, D.K.: Building an encrypted and searchable audit log. NDSS **4**, 5–6 (2004)
38. Wickramage, C., Sahama, T., Fidge, C.: Anatomy of log files: implications for information accountability measures. In: 2016 IEEE 18th International Conference on e-Health Networking, Applications and Services (Healthcom), pp. 1–6. IEEE (2016)

Data Privacy, Data Mining, and Applications

Default Privacy Setting Prediction by Grouping User's Attributes and Settings Preferences

Toru Nakamura[1]([⊠]), Welderufael B. Tesfay[2], Shinsaku Kiyomoto[1], and Jetzabel Serna[2]

[1] KDDI Research, Inc., Saitama, Japan
{tr-nakamura,kiyomoto}@kddi-research.jp
[2] Chair of Mobile Business and Multilateral Security, Goethe University Frankfurt, Theodor-W.-Adorno-Platz 4, 60323 Frankfurt Am Main, Germany
{welderufael.tesfay,jetzabel.serna}@m-chair.de

Abstract. While user-centric privacy settings are important to protect the privacy of users, often users have difficulty changing the default ones. This is partly due to lack of awareness and partly attributed to the tediousness and complexities involved in understanding and changing privacy settings. In previous works, we proposed a mechanism for helping users set their default privacy settings at the time of registration to Internet services, by providing personalised privacy-by-default settings. This paper evolves and evaluates our privacy setting prediction engine, by taking into consideration users' settings preferences and personal attributes (e.g. gender, age, and type of mobile phone). Results show that while models built on users' privacy preferences have improved the accuracy of our scheme; grouping users by attributes does not make an impact in the accuracy. As a result, services potentially using our prediction engine, could minimize the collection of user attributes and based the prediction only on users' privacy preferences.

Keywords: Privacy preference · Privacy setting · Machine learning

1 Introduction

Usage of personal data is increasing as it is believed to promote innovation. However, it also raises privacy concerns. In many cases, a service delivered to users is provided with embedded privacy functionality that can limit the sharing of personal data by the user in specific scenarios or given situations. For instance, Facebook provides the user with the privacy setting functionality that enable users to manage which other users can browse his/her posts, pictures, etc. Similarly, modern smartphones (e.g. Android and iPhone) provide users the possibility to control which applications can access different resources including personal or privacy related data. In future, such settings may be used not only for permitting to provide personal data but also for deciding some privacy level such as anonymization level. Generally speaking, personal data is anonymized in

© Springer International Publishing AG 2017
J. Garcia-Alfaro et al. (Eds.): DPM/CBT 2017, LNCS 10436, pp. 107–123, 2017.
DOI: 10.1007/978-3-319-67816-0_7

higher level, the usability becomes lower. So if starting with the most privacy-friendly pre-setting, the users may not be able to use high quality services unless they manually change their settings. However, many users do not change the privacy settings, either because of the effort required or due to the lack of a proper understanding of privacy settings. Thus, to address this, general frameworks, such as PDS (Personal Data Store) [4] and PPM (Privacy Policy Manager) [14] have emerged, which provide the user with a generic privacy manager for various types of personal data and service providers.

When providing a privacy function, the default settings are very important because many users may not spend the time and effort to set their privacy preferences adequately. It is especially difficult to manually configure appropriate privacy settings as the combinations of service providers, types of personal data, and the applications for personal data have become so vast. Hence, it is important to simplify this task of setting privacy-preserving default preferences by providing tailoring mechanisms that will address individual privacy concerns and translate these concerns into personalized privacy settings to users.

In our initial efforts to overcome this, we proposed a conceptual design and a mechanism based on a Support Vector Machine (SVM) for the automatic generation of personalized privacy settings [17]. In our basic approach we have designed a questionnaire of 80 questions that considered the combination of 16 different data types shared for 5 different utilization purposes and services. The basic approach delivered a minimal set of (5) questions to each user at registration time, and from the user's answers, it predicted the default privacy settings for each user.

In this paper, we present a more advanced scheme and a prototype that improve the accuracy of the privacy setting prediction, based on the grouping of users' attributes and setting preferences. Thus, the contribution of this paper is twofold. First, we present an extension and improvement of previous work [17], which was focused on selecting optimal and minimal number of questions to predict the privacy settings. In this work, we further elaborate and give an in-depth analysis on the improvement mechanisms by considering user attributes and privacy preferences. Second, to showcase the applicability of the proposed models, we implemented a prototype of the prediction engine in R using SVM based models in order to predict user privacy settings.

The rest of the paper is organized as follows. Section 2 provides an overview of related work in the area of privacy preferences. Section 3 describes the main methodology and approach of the SVM-based prediction scheme proposed in [17] and the questionnaires designed and used to derived initial settings database. Section 4 describes the experimental evaluation for both user attributes and privacy preferences. Section 5 discusses the results of the evaluation. Section 6 draws the main conclusions and points out future directions for research.

2   Related Work

In privacy policy management the burden of checking on and maintaining privacy policies has been identified as a major issue. In one study, Madejski *et al.* [15]

showed that a serious mismatch existed between intentions for privacy settings and real settings in an online social network service. Users are commonly required to check the privacy policies of a given service offered by a service provider before starting to use the service. Thus, each service provider prepares a privacy policy for each service. Because it is frequently the case that users must check a large number of privacy policies, it becomes irksome and difficult to understand. Consequently, users are not able to determine or customise the privacy policies for themselves. Furthermore, if a user does not agree with the privacy policy of a service, the user simply cannot use the service.

In this regard, Solove suggested that the privacy self-management model cannot achieve its objectives, and it has been pushed beyond its limits, while privacy law has been relying too heavily upon the privacy self-management model [20]. Moreover, other studies such as the experimental study conducted by Acquisti and Grossklags [1] demonstrated users' lack of knowledge about technological and legal forms of privacy protection when confirming privacy policies. Their observations suggest that several difficulties obstruct individuals in their attempts to protect their own private information, even those concerned about and motivated to protect their privacy. This was reinforced by authors in [18] who also supported the presumption that users are not familiar with technical and legal terms related to privacy. Moreover, it was suggested that users' knowledge about privacy threats and technologies that help to protect their privacy is inadequate [12]. In this regard, Guo and Chen [11] proposed an algorithm to optimise privacy configurations based on desired privacy level and utility preference of users.

Fang et al. [9,10] have proposed a privacy wizard for social networking sites. The purpose of the wizard is to automatically configure a user's privacy settings with minimal effort required by the user. The wizard is based on the underlying observation that real users conceive their privacy preferences based on an implicit structure. Thus, after asking the user a limited number of carefully chosen questions, it is usually possible to build a machine learning model that accurately predicts the user's preferences. This approach is very similar to ours. The difference is the target dataset. Fang et al. treated real data of Facebook, so the variety of the items was limited and the number of the participants is small. We treat more general data items and the number of the participants is larger because our approach does not focus on a specific service such as Facebook.

Some languages to describe privacy policies have been presented in [3,7,8]. Backes et al. examined some comparisons of enterprise privacy policies using formal abstract syntax and semantics to express the policy contents [2]. Tondel and Nyre [22] proposed a similarity metric for comparing machine-readable policies. There is some existing research about learning privacy preferences. Berendt et al. [5] emphasised the importance of privacy preference generation and Sadah et al. [19] suggested that machine learning techniques have the power to generate more accurate preferences than users themselves in a mobile social networking application. Tondel et al. [21] proposed a conceptual architecture for learning privacy preferences based on the decisions a user makes in their normal interactions on the web. They suggested that learning of privacy preferences has the

Table 1. Types of personal data

No.	Data type
1	Addresses and telephone numbers
2	Email addresses
3	Service accounts
4	Purchase records
5	Bank accounts
6	Device information (e.g., IP addresses, OS)
7	Browsing histories
8	Logs on a search engine
9	Personal info (age, gender, income)
10	Contents of email, blog, twitter etc.
11	Session information (e.g., Cookies)
12	Social Info. (e.g., religion, volunteer records)
13	Medical Info.
14	Hobby
15	Location Info.
16	Official ID (national IDs or license numbers)

Table 2. Usage purposes

No.	Data purpose
A	Providing the service
B	System administration
C	Marketing
D	Behavior analysis
E	Recommendation

potential to increase the accuracy of preferences without requiring users to have a high level of knowledge or willingness to invest time and effort in their privacy. Kelley *et al.* [13] showed preferences for a mobile social network application. Preference modeling for eliciting preferences was studied by Bufett and Fleming [6]. Mugan *et al.* [16] proposed a method for generating persona and suggestions intended to help users incrementally refine their privacy preferences over time.

3 SVM Based Privacy Setting Prediction Scheme

This section introduces the SVM-scheme used as the basis of our approach, as well as the questionnaires designed in order to get the initial privacy settings database.

3.1 Design of Questionnaires

We designed a questionnaire survey focused on the acceptability from users to provide personal data, considering a combinations of 16 data types (cf. Table 1) for 5 utilization purposes (cf. Table 2). The data types and usage purposes were selected from the items defined in P3P [23]. In this work, we prioritized to make them close to P3P categories. We recognize that there are some misleading and uneasy to understand points, hence we will modify them next evaluation.

Table 3. Distribution of participants

Gender	Age	Ratio (%)
Male	20s	10.0
Male	30s	10.0
Male	40s	10.0
Male	50s	10.0
Male	Over 60	10.0
Female	20s	10.0
Female	30s	10.0
Female	40s	10.0
Female	50s	10.0
Female	Over 60	10.0

Table 4. Distribution of types of mobile phone

Mobile phone	Ratio (%)
iPhone	23.5
Android	30.0
Others	1.71
Not smart phone	44.9

Additionally, other attributes related to demographics and type of mobile device used were considered because they might have possibility to find any special features in the groups separated with them.

We collected responses from 10,000 Japanese participants and they answered our questionnaires by web-based system. As it is shown in Table 3 the distribution of the participants was uniform over all the categories. Each participant evaluated all 80 combinations of types of personal data and usage purposes on a Likert scale of 1 to 6 ("1" for strongly disagree, and "6" for strongly agree.). The distribution of mobile devices used by participants is shown in Table 4. Table 5 shows the distribution of the results. As can be observed from Table 5, the percentage decreases with the increasing acceptance of providing personal data. For the sake of simplicity, the obtained results were merged initially into the following three classes on a scale from 0 to 2, i.e.: i) 1 & 2 into scale 0; ii) 3 & 4 into scale 1; and, iii) 5 & 6 into scale 2. In future, we also plan to perform experiments using a different merging approach. The differences between questions are shown in Fig. 1.

Table 5. Distribution of result

Likert scale	1	2	3	4	5	6	Total
Number	317497	238826	145952	67629	24583	5513	800000
Ratio	0.3969	0.2985	0.1824	0.08454	0.03073	0.006891	1

3.2 Comparison Based on Attributes

The trend based on the attributes of participants is shown in Fig. 2. Between genders, the trend for males is more positive than for females, that is, the ratios for answering "2" (means positive for providing personal data) and "1" (means

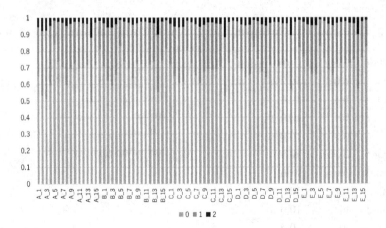

Fig. 1. Differences between questions

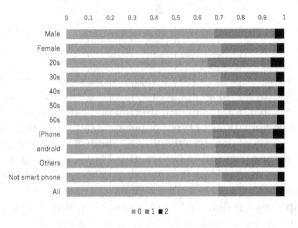

Fig. 2. Tendency on attributes

neutral) for males are about 1% and 2% higher than those for females, respectively. Based on age, the most positive age group is in their 20s, while the most negative group is in their 40s. The ratios for those answering "2" and "1" in their 20s are about 3% and 6% higher than for those in their 40s, respectively. For the type of mobile phone, the ratio for answering "2" for iPhone users is about 1% higher than that for Android users, while the others are similar.

3.3 SVM-based Prediction Scheme

This paper considers as a basis only the first SVM-based scheme introduced in [17] and evaluates the change of accuracy when the dataset is either grouped by user attributes or grouped by user setting preferences. Thus, we used the same dataset detailed in Sect. 3.1 for the evaluation. A high level description of the prediction scheme is shown in Fig. 3. The main procedure is as follows:

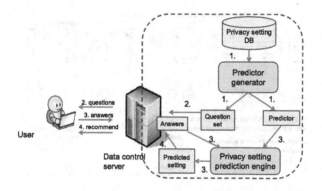

Fig. 3. The framework of our prediction scheme

1. An existing user settings database is the input to a prediction model generator in order to generate an optimal question set and the prediction model.
2. A user is provided with the question set (5 questions).
3. The user's answers to the selected questions are then the input to the prediction model so that the privacy setting prediction engine generates the corresponding (personalized) prediction values.
4. The prediction values are then recommended to the user.

The abstract of the prediction-model-generating algorithm is shown in Fig. 4. The prediction-model-generating algorithm is detailed below.

1. The existing user settings database is split into learning data and test data.
2. Questions are randomly selected for prediction.
3. SVM models are generated for the rest of the questions (75) in the learning data by using selected questions in the learning data as feature vectors.
4. The SVM models that were created in the previous step are evaluated using the test data.
5. The process is repeated to evaluate for an adequate number of combinations of questions, and the combination of questions achieving the highest accuracy as the selected questions is adopted.

4   Experimental Evaluation

Appropriate parameters need to be chosen such as the number of learning data, test data, items for prediction of answers, and combinations of items for evaluation in order to efficiently make experiments in various conditions. Generally, if a greater number of learning data items and combinations of items for evaluation are used for prediction, higher accuracy can be expected, but meanwhile, the processing time (especially critical for generating the SVM model) is also increasing.

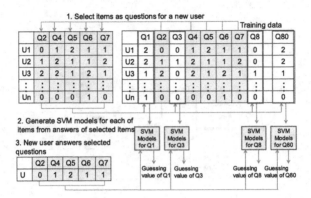

Fig. 4. The abstract of our prediction algorithm

Table 6. Experiment settings

OS	Windows8.1
Memory	8 GB
CPU	intel core i7-4770 @ 3.40 GHz
Language, Library	R, e1071(SVM), doSNOW(Multi core processing)

A preliminary experiment was performed for choosing the appropriate values for these parameters. The experimental parameters are shown in Table 6. This experiment was performed using parallel processing with two machines. In this experiment, the parameters of SVM were not adjusted, and the default parameters such that $\gamma = 0.2$ and $cost = 1$ were always used.

In order to discover an adequate number of samples of combinations of items and finding the most suitable combination for prediction of answers, the accuracy is evaluated by varying the number of samples of combinations from 1,000 to 10,000 in increments of 1,000 and fixing the number of learning data, test data, and items for prediction of answers at 100, 50, and 5, respectively. Learning data and test data were randomly chosen from the original dataset twice and called dataset A and dataset B. For each dataset, we randomly choose samples of combinations of items, evaluate all combinations, and find the best combination and its accuracy. After five evaluations, we regard the average of accuracy of the five evaluations as the accuracy of the dataset. The results show that 10,000 samples of combinations are sufficient because the maximum differences in accuracy in dataset A and B are only about 0.46% and 0.67%, Fig. 5.

As a second step, in order to discover an adequate number of test data, the accuracy is evaluated by varying the number of test data from 500 to 5,000 in increments of 250 and fixing the number of learning data, items for prediction, samples of combinations of items at 100, 5, and 10,000, respectively. Learning data from the original dataset are randomly chosen 14 times, as samples of combinations of items, and called datasets A to N. For each dataset, we randomly

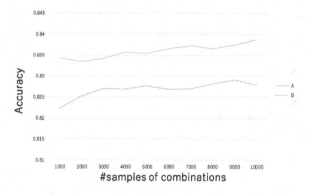

Fig. 5. Influence of the number of samples of combinations

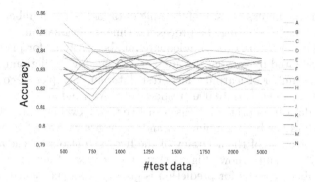

Fig. 6. Influence of the number of test data

choose test data from original dataset for ten times, evaluate all combinations of items, and find the best combination and its accuracy. After ten evaluations, we regard the average of accuracy of the ten evaluations as the accuracy of the dataset. The result is shown in Fig. 6. The result shows that 1,000 test data are sufficient because the variance is about 0.00007 when the number of test data is 750, the variance is about 0.00001 when the number of test data is 1,000, and the variance does not decrease much with further increases of the number of test data above 1,000.

For learning data, the accuracy is evaluated by varying the number of learning data from 50 to 500 and fixing the number of test data, items for prediction of answers, samples of combinations of items at 1,000, 5, and 10,000, respectively. Test data are randomly chosen from the original dataset five times, as samples of combinations of items, and called datasets A to E. For each dataset, we randomly choose learning data from original dataset for ten times, evaluate all combinations of items, and find the best combination and its accuracy. After ten evaluations, we regard the average of accuracy of the ten evaluations as the accuracy of the dataset. The results show (Fig. 7) that the accuracy linearly

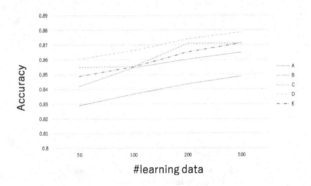

Fig. 7. Influence of the number of learning data

increases with the increase in size of learning data, hence the number of learning data is set to 100, considering the processing time for evaluation.

Finally, in order to discover an adequate number of items for prediction, the accuracy is evaluated by varying the number of items for prediction from 2 to 10 and fixing the number of learning data, test data, and samples of combinations of items at 100, 1,000, and 10,000, respectively. We randomly choose learning data and test data from original dataset for five times, evaluate all combinations of items, and find the best combination and its accuracy. After five evaluations, we regard the average of the accuracy of the five evaluations as the accuracy of the dataset. The results show (Fig. 8) that the increase of accuracy is reduced when the number of items for prediction is greater than six, hence the number of items for prediction is set at five.

From the previous results, the parameters in this experiment are set as shown in Table 7. Note that the SVM parameters are not adjusted, and the default SVM parameters are used such that $\gamma = 0.2$ and $cost = 1$ both in this section and in Sect. 4.1 and 4.2.

Regarding the computation time, the process of selecting the best combination of items from 10,000 combinations, requires about 4,013 seconds with a single-core computation in the environment shown in Table 6. Using the same setup, the process of generating the prediction requires about 0.32 s. Note that, the process of choosing the best combination does not affect the user experience, thus, even with larger numbers it could be neglected; furthermore, the overall computation time could be reduced by using parallel computation.

4.1   Evaluation by Attributes Grouping

In this section, the original data set is grouped by the participants' attributes such as gender, age, and type of mobile phone. The accuracy is evaluated in order to generate the prediction model from the grouped data set. The parameters used for the evaluations are the same as in Sect. 4. Note that the size of learning data or test data does not decrease even if the data set is divided into small subsets. Learning data and test data are randomly chosen from the grouped

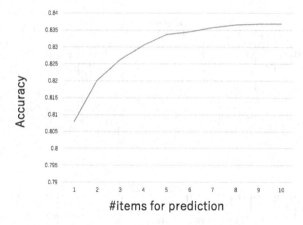

Fig. 8. Influence of the number of items for prediction

Table 7. Parameters in this experiment

# learning data	100
# test data	1000
# items for prediction	5
# samples of combinations	10000
γ (Parameter on SVM)	0.2
cost (Parameter on SVM)	1.0

subset 10 times, as samples of combinations of items, and the average of the accuracy is evaluated in the 10 trials. The result is shown in Table 8. Note that on the type of mobile phone, the item "other smart phone" is omitted because the number is too small.

According to the results, in all the cases where the original data set is grouped by gender, age, and type of mobile phone, the total accuracy decreases compared to the original approach (data set not grouped), though there are some categories in which the accuracy increases.

4.2   Evaluation by Privacy Preferences

We selected the K-means algorithm, and used it to observe the participants' answer preferences. The number of clusters is varied between 1 and 10. For instance, the case where the number of clusters is 4 is shown in Fig. 9.

The results show that there are two characteristic clusters: Cluster 1 and Cluster 4. The participants in Cluster 1 tend to answer "0" (means negative), and the participants in Cluster 4 tend to answer "1" (means neutral) for almost all the questions. It is easy to determine to which cluster a person belongs, e.g., Cluster 1, Cluster 4, or another cluster, because it is only necessary to ask

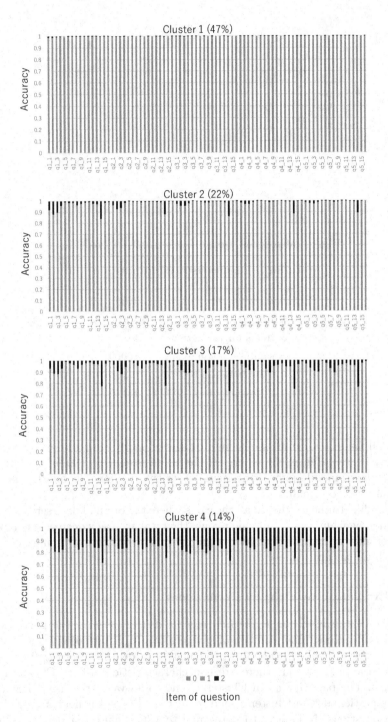

Fig. 9. Tendency of each cluster

Table 8. Accuracy by grouping by attributes

Not grouping		Accuracy
	Total	**0.8415**
Gender	Male	0.8364
	Female	0.8348
	Total	**0.8356**
Age	20s	0.8073
	30s	0.8421
	40s	0.8519
	50s	0.8511
	Over 60	0.8243
	Total	**0.8353**
Type of mobile phone	iPhone	0.8248
	Android	0.8282
	Other smart phone	
	Not smart phone	0.8445
	Total	**0.8325**

his/her basic privacy attitude directly, for example, "Would you prefer that your personal data never be provided at all?". If accuracy is improved by grouping the original data set by clustering on the answer preferences, it may be possible to improve our scheme by adding only one question that may determine to which cluster a person belongs. Hence in the next subsection, the case is evaluated with the original data set divided into Cluster 1, Cluster 4, and the other clusters, and each prediction model is generated for each cluster.

4.3 Evaluation by Grouping of Clusters

The parameters used for the evaluations are the same as for Sects. 4 and 4.1. Learning data and test data are randomly chosen 10 times from the grouped subset, as samples of combinations of items, and the average of the accuracy is evaluated in the 10 trials. The case when applying the prediction model from the whole data set to each cluster is compared with the case when applying each prediction model from the data set grouped by each cluster to each cluster. The result is shown in Table 9.

Results in Table 9 show that the improvement in accuracy is less than 1% for Cluster 1 and Clusters 2+3, while the improvement for Cluster 4 is about 5% and the total improvement is about 1%.

Table 9. Evaluation in grouping by clustering

Cluster	Using model from all data (Previous scheme [17])			Using models from divided data		
	Accuracy	Ratio	Accuracy × Ratio	Accuracy	Ratio	Accuracy × Ratio
1	0.9698	47.10%	0.456776	0.9738	47.10%	0.45866
2+3	0.7088	38.50%	0.272888	0.7126	38.50%	0.274351
4	0.7767	14.40%	0.111845	0.8237	14.40%	0.118613
		Total	**0.841509**		**Total**	**0.851624**

5   Discussion

Results based on privacy preferences (Sect. 4.2) show that it is possible to improve the accuracy of the prediction scheme by grouping based on clustering of the answer preferences and generating prediction models for each cluster. However, results based on users' attributes (Sect. 4.1) show no improvement, this may be, because there are less differences in the answer preferences tendency among the different categories of users. For instance, the answer preferences for those aged in their 20s and 40s show no significant difference, as it can be obeserve in Fig. 10.

Table 10. Evaluation in the case dividing Cluster 2 and 3

Cluster	Using model from all data (Previous scheme [17])			Using models from divided data		
	Accuracy	Ratio	Accuracy × Ratio	Accuracy	Ratio	Accuracy × Ratio
1	0.9698	47.10%	0.4568	0.9738	47.10%	0.4587
2	0.7617	21.50%	0.1638	0.7855	21.50%	0.1689
3	0.6420	17.00%	0.1091	0.6768	17.00%	0.1151
4	0.7767	14.40%	0.1118	0.8237	14.40%	0.1186
		Total	**0.8415**		**Total**	**0.8612**

Regarding the results in Sect. 4.2, accuracy is improved for Cluster 4; however, no significant improvement is obtained for Cluster 1 and Clusters 2+3. The reason why the accuracy is not improved for Cluster 1 may be that sufficiently high accuracy was already achieved from using the prediction model generated from the whole data set because the ratio of answering "0" (i.e., negative) is very high (about 96.8%). The reason the accuracy is not improved for Clusters 2+3 may be that the prediction model is generated from mixed data with two clusters with different tendencies. Results of the additional evaluations, where Clusters 2+3 are split into Cluster 2 and Cluster 3 from the evaluation are shown in Table 10. These results show an improvement of accuracy of about 2.4% and 3.4% for Clusters 2 and 3, respectively. These results raise the possibility for

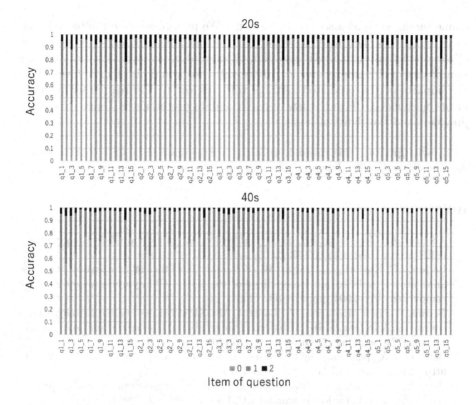

Fig. 10. Tendencies of 20s and 40s

improving the accuracy by subdividing the clusters even further based on the answer preferences.

6   Conclusions

In this paper, we proposed and evaluated the applicability of SVM-based models to predict default privacy settings of users at the time of registration to service providers. Furthermore, we evaluated the improvement in accuracy of a privacy setting prediction scheme when the machine learning data sets were grouped based on users' attributes and setting preferences. First, we evaluated the case where the data sets were grouped by gender, age, and type of mobile phone; however, the accuracy was not improved. In terms of privacy protection, this result shows that the collection of additional user attributes could be minimized. We then evaluated our scheme by grouping privacy setting preferences using the K-means algorithm, from the results we could observe an improvement in accuracy. Future work will focus on enhancing the prediction accuracy, for instance by trying a different combination when merging the classes. We also plan to trial the model in real world scenarios; i.e. by integrating our prediction engine to an online service such as a social network site. We plan to analyze the behavior of users and collect their feedback regarding the usefulness and expected accuracy of the prediction engine. We also plan to execute some statistical tests on the significance of this improvement. Additionally, we would also like to investigate the impacts of the predicted settings with respect to the regulatory requirements, such as GDPR or the law of personal data protection in Japan, of service providers and the rights of users.

Acknowledgment. This research work has been supported by JST CREST Grant Number JPMJCR1404, Japan.

References

1. Acquisti, A., Grossklags, J.: Privacy and rationality in individual decision making. IEEE Secur. Priv. **3**(1), 26–33 (2005)
2. Backes, M., Karjoth, G., Bagga, W., Schunter, M.: Efficient comparison of enterprise privacy policies. In: Proceedings of the 2004 ACM symposium on Applied computing, SAC 2004, pp. 375–382 (2004)
3. Bekara, K., Ben Mustapha, Y., Laurent, M.: XPACML extensible privacy access control markup langua. In: 2010 Second International Conference on Communications and Networking (ComNet), pp. 1–5 (2010)
4. Bell, G.: A personal digital store. Commun. ACM **44**(1), 86–91 (2001). http://doi.acm.org/10.1145/357489.357513
5. Berendt, B., Günther, O., Spiekermann, S.: Privacy in e-commerce: Stated preferences vs. actual behavior. Commun. ACM **48**(4), 101–106 (2005)
6. Buffett, S., Fleming, M.W.: Applying a preference modeling structure to user privacy. In: Proceedings of the 1st International Workshop on Sustaining Privacy in Autonomous Collaborative Environments (2007)
7. Cranor, L.: P3P: making privacy policies more useful. IEEE Secur. Priv. **1**(6), 50–55 (2003)
8. Dehghantanha, A., Udzir, N., Mahmod, R.: Towards a pervasive formal privacy language. In: 2010 IEEE 24th International Conference on Advanced Information Networking and Applications Workshops (WAINA), pp. 1085–1091 (2010)
9. Fang, L., Kim, H., LeFevre, K., Tami, A.: A privacy recommendation wizard for users of social networking sites. In: Proceedings of the 17th ACM conference on Computer and communications security, pp. 630–632. ACM (2010)
10. Fang, L., LeFevre, K.: Privacy wizards for social networking sites. In: Proceedings of the 19th international conference on World wide web, pp. 351–360. ACM (2010)
11. Guo, S., Chen, K.: Mining privacy settings to find optimal privacy-utility tradeoffs for social network services. In: 2012 International Conference on Privacy, Security, Risk and Trust (PASSAT) and 2012 International Confernece on Social Computing (SocialCom), pp. 656–665 (2012)
12. Jensen, C., Potts, C., Jensen, C.: Privacy practices of internet users: self-reports versus observed behavior. Int. J. Hum.-Comput. Stud. **63**(1–2), 203–227 (2005)
13. Kelley, P.G., Hankes Drielsma, P., Sadeh, N., Cranor, L.F.: User-controllable learning of security and privacy policies. In: Proceedings of the 1st ACM workshop on Workshop on AISec, AISec 2008, pp. 11–18 (2008)

14. Kiyomoto, S., Nakamura, T., Takasaki, H., Watanabe, R., Miyake, Y.: PPM: privacy policy manager for personalized services. In: Cuzzocrea, A., Kittl, C., Simos, D.E., Weippl, E., Xu, L. (eds.) CD-ARES 2013. LNCS, vol. 8128, pp. 377–392. Springer, Heidelberg (2013). doi:10.1007/978-3-642-40588-4_26
15. Madejski, M., Johnson, M., Bellovin, S.: A study of privacy settings errors in an online social network. In: 2012 IEEE International Conference on Pervasive Computing and Communications Workshops (PERCOM Workshops), pp. 340–345 (2012)
16. Mugan, J., Sharma, T., Sadeh, N.: Understandable learning of privacy preferences through default personas and suggestions (2011)
17. Nakamura, T., Kiyomoto, S., Tesfay, W.B., Serna, J.: Personalised privacy by default preferences - experiment and analysis. In: Proceedings of the 2nd International Conference on Information Systems Security and Privacy, ICISSP, vol. 1, pp. 53–62 (2016)
18. Pollach, I.: What's wrong with online privacy policies? Commun. ACM **50**(9), 103–108 (2007)
19. Sadeh, N., Hong, J., Cranor, L., Fette, I., Kelley, P., Prabaker, M., Rao, J.: Understanding and capturing people's privacy policies in a mobile social networking application. Pers. Ubiquit. Comput. **13**(6), 401–412 (2009)
20. Solove, D.J.: Privacy self-management and the consent paradox. In: Harvard Law Rev. **126** (2013)
21. Tondel, I., Nyre, A., Bernsmed, K.: Learning privacy preferences. In: 2011 Sixth International Conference on Availability, Reliability and Security (ARES), pp. 621–626 (2011)
22. Tøndel, I.A., Nyre, Å.A.: Towards a similarity metric for comparing machine-readable privacy policies. In: Camenisch, J., Kesdogan, D. (eds.) iNetSec 2011. LNCS, vol. 7039, pp. 89–103. Springer, Heidelberg (2012). doi:10.1007/978-3-642-27585-2_8
23. W3C: The platform for privacy preferences 1.0 (P3P1.0) specificati. In: Platform for Privacy Preferences (P3P) Project (2002)

δ-privacy: Bounding Privacy Leaks in Privacy Preserving Data Mining

Zhizhou Li[1(✉)] and Ten H. Lai[2]

[1] The Voleon Group, Berkeley, USA
lizhizhou@gmail.com
[2] The Ohio State University, Columbus, USA
lai@cse.ohio-state.edu

Abstract. We propose a new definition for privacy, called δ-privacy, for privacy preserving data mining. The intuition of this work is, after obtaining a result from a data mining method, an adversary has better ability in discovering data providers' privacy; if this improvement is large, the method, which generated the response, is not privacy considerate. δ-privacy requires that no adversary could improve more than δ. This definition can be used to assess the risk of privacy leak in any data mining methods, in particular, we show its relations to differential privacy and data anonymity, the two major evaluation methods. We also provide a quantitative analysis on the tradeoff between privacy and utility, rigorously prove that the information gains of any δ-private methods do not exceed δ. Under the framework of δ-privacy, it is able to design a pricing mechanism for privacy-utility trading system, which is one of our major future works.

1 Introduction

Privacy is a high-profile public issue that attracts attention from the entire society. Information collectors and/or processors, such as Internet business, market consulting companies, and governments, are eager to collect as much information as they could to discover people's behavioral patterns. They acquires information from a large number of people, then extract useful knowledges (e.g., statistics and patterns) from the data set using statistical methods and/or data mining techniques. However, data mining on genuine data would be harmful to data privacy, data providers are not willing to commit their sensitive data to a untrusted data collector.

The goal of privacy preserving data mining is to extract knowledge from a data set, while maintaining data contributor's privacy. However, there is a tradeoff between knowledge discovering and privacy preservation: the more knowledge discovered from the data set, the higher possibility that the privacy is leaked. To preserve privacy, a data mining method should hide a certain amount of information before giving them to public.

This work was done while this author was studying in The Ohio State University.

© Springer International Publishing AG 2017
J. Garcia-Alfaro et al. (Eds.): DPM/CBT 2017, LNCS 10436, pp. 124–142, 2017.
DOI: 10.1007/978-3-319-67816-0_8

There are two major classes of privacy protection methods in knowledge discovering, one is input perturbation, which pre-process the input data to "de-privatize" them, then extract knowledge from the modified data; the other is output perturbation, which generates the true result on the original data set, but modify it before publishing.

Input Perturbation. Input perturbations are also called data anonymity, the idea was first proposed by Sweeney [23]. A database is divided into different equivalence classes with a "identifying tag," records that fit the identifying information will fall into that class. Then those classes, along with the original private data from each record, are published. In that case, even if an adversary knew a target's identifying information and locates it in a equivalence class, he cannot determine which one is it because there are multiple records having the same identifying tag.

Sweeney proposed a rule for grouping similar records, called k-anonymity [23], it requires each class to hold at least k records, such that even if an adversary can identify that a target falls in one class, he only has $1/k$ chance to identify the target record in the class. However, having k entries in a class is not enough, if everyone in a class has the same private data, an adversary can still learn the secret. l-diversity [17] is proposed based on k-anonymity, requiring that each equivalence class should contain k records and l distinct values of private data. t-closeness principle [13] is then developed based on k-anonymity and l-diversity, it further requires the distribution of private data in a equivalence class should be *close* to that in the whole data set. See Definition 10 for more details.

Output Perturbation. Instead of modifying the input data, output perturbation methods modify the data mining results. *Differential privacy* [6, 7] is a privacy constraint on how to change the true result to prevent privacy leak. The result should be "de-privatized" such that any adversary is not able to distinguish whether it is generated from a data set that contains the target record, or from a data set that does *not* contain the target. If the target is not in a data set, the data mining result does not contain any information about the target, therefore, adversary is not able to learn any privacy of the target from such a unrelated result; if a data mining result "looks like" such a unrelated result, an adversary is not likely to discover useful fact about the target either.

Our Contribution. In this paper, we propose a metric that measures the largest possible privacy leak in a knowledge discovering process, and provide a new definition of privacy, called δ-privacy, that restricts the privacy leak in a data mining process. Compared with existing privacy definitions, δ-privacy is from an adversary's perspective; by studying adversaries' behavior, we can tell how they are going to harm privacy, that is the most direct way to assess the risk of privacy leak. Under this framework, we are able to tell the data providers what's the risk that their secret is learned by an adversary, and in the meantime, we can tell the data collectors how much information they could acquire. We also show the following:

1. Our framework can be used to evaluate any privacy preserving data mining algorithms; in particular, we show the relation between δ-privacy and existing privacy definitions, namely, if a method satisfy ϵ-differential privacy [6], it will also satisfy δ-privacy with $\delta = \epsilon$ (Lemma 2); if a data anonymity method satisfies t-closeness [13] w.r.t. variational distance, it also satisfies δ-privacy with $\delta = t$ (Lemma 3).
2. Utility and privacy are zero-summed in the sense that the maximum utility gained by the data processor is bounded by the maximum privacy leak allowed (Theorem 1). To obtain more information from the data set, data processors need to ask the data provider to increase the privacy loss limit, i.e., δ. To the best of our knowledge, this is the first work that quantitatively proves this idea.

Informally speaking, if a data mining method is δ-private, then any *partial privacy* of data providers are protected, in the sense that no adversary can tell the secret much better than random guessing. We model a partial privacy of a target record r as a binary-valued function priv on r. An adversary discloses the secret fact by calculating priv(r). We assume that the adversary is *well-informed*, he is aware of all publicly accessible information of r, he knows the intrinsic knowledge of priv, i.e., the distribution of priv over the records in the database. He makes queries to the database, obtains result m (which is generated by a privacy preserving data mining method) to discover more knowledge, then he outputs one bit as the prediction of priv(r). We say the data mining result reveals privacy if given m, the adversary can compute priv(r) with higher success rate versus that before he gets the result. More generally, an adversary $\mathcal{A}$ computes priv(r); his success rate increases after he gets m. This difference in probability is the improvement of $\mathcal{A}$ after getting m, it reflects how much privacy $\mathcal{A}$ learns from m. We use this difference as the indicator of privacy leak and say a data mining method is δ-private if the privacy leak is always smaller than δ.

Our research focus on large scale databases, which enroll enough samples from the real world. Therefore, the distribution of priv(r) over the records in the database is close to that over the whole human population. This distribution is an important prior knowledge for adversaries to predict priv on a particular target.

The utility of a data mining method is the quantity of information that one could learn from the data mining result, while the utility gain is the utility minus the intrinsic utility, which can be achieved without querying. This research shows that privacy loss and utility gain are zero-summed, the maximum knowledge that can be extracted is no more than δ. To get more utility, data processor should convince (using money) the data providers to increase the limit of privacy leak. This enables "privacy trading" in the future: data providers can put a price tag on their data based on the risk of privacy leak, and the data user can determine the amount of information to purchase based on how much utility he could get from the data mining process.

2 Preliminaries

Records and Tables. A record is composed of fields, each field contains one attribute of the record. More specifically, a record is a member of a Cartesian product $\mathcal{F} \triangleq \mathcal{F}_1 \times \mathcal{F}_2 \times \cdots \times \mathcal{F}_k$, where $\mathcal{F}_i$ is a finite set of all possible values for a field. A table $\mathcal{X}$ is a collection of records. There are 2 different types of fields:

1. identifiers, such as name, social security number, or other information that uniquely identifies a record in the database, or quasi-identifiers, such as address, sex, etc. which can help to, albeit not uniquely, identify a record in the database.
2. sensitive data, the information that the data contributors want to keep secret from the public.

Take the farmer's survey database (Table 1) as an example, gender, age, zip code, and owned acres are quasi-identifiers, the combination of those fields can be used to identify a farmer. Note that those fields are accessible to public: gender and age are not considered secret to a farmer; his address and how many acres he owns are available in county auditor. If an attacker knows a farmer in person, he is able to get all those facts. On the other hand, the rented acres and rental rates are sensitive fields in this database, they are not publicly accessible. Also, because they are directly related to farmers' income, farmers would like to keep them secret. In this paper, we consider identifiers and quasi-identifiers as *public fields*, which are accessible to public, and consider sensitive data as *secret fields*, which should be kept secret from the public.

Table 1. The Original Farmers Database. In this table, gender, age, zip code and owned acres are quasi-identifiers; rented acres and rental rate are considered secret.

Gender	Age	Zip_code	Owned_acres	Rented_acres	Rental_rate
Female	43	43111	100	120	130
Male	37	42102	551	1100	140
Male	35	43110	120	91	125
Male	56	43208	625	110	180
Male	31	43315	220	630	175
Male	51	43111	64	0	NA
Female	45	43102	250	2000	200
Male	37	43215	320	1200	200
Male	41	43215	580	400	170
Male	25	43102	200	200	150

Queries. A query is a question or request for information to the database management system (or database for short). We regard it as step-by-step instructions which retrieve information and/or discover knowledge from the database.

Traditionally, when given a query, the database follows the all instructions in the query, then returns the result as response.

In our research, there is no constraint on the query, an adversary can ask any question. Also, the adversary is allowed to ask multiple questions, and the same question can be asked for multiple times. See Sect. 4 for more discussion.

Privacy-Preserving Data Mining Methods. We regard a privacy preserving data mining method $\mathcal{M}$ as a mechanism to generate responses to queries. $\mathcal{M}(\mathsf{q}, \mathcal{X})$ takes as input one query q and a database $\mathcal{X}$, it produces a result of q, but that result should not reveal privacy of the records in $\mathcal{X}$. Obviously, if it exactly follows the instructions in q as a traditional database does, it is not safe to data providers' privacy because adversaries can design queries to retrieve secret data he wants. To protect privacy, $\mathcal{M}$ would either (1) follow the instructions in q but add noise to the result, or (2) follow the instructions but perform them over the de-privatized table, or (3) takes other possible approaches that would not follow the instructions but still generate a response.

Usually, $\mathcal{M}$ is a randomized algorithm, the message generated by it is a random variable. We denote by

$$m \leftarrow \mathcal{M}(\mathsf{q}, \mathcal{X})$$

the messages/transcripts generated by $\mathcal{M}$ and sent to $\mathcal{A}$.

3   Attacker Model

To define privacy, we first discuss what information an adversary wants to learn, and what prior knowledge he already has. In our discussion, we always assume that an adversary, who wants to disclose *partial privacy* of records in the database, is *well informed*, which means (1) he knows all the *public information*, e.g., the identifying information, of the target, and (2) he holds *intrinsic knowledge*, i.e., he know how normal people behave. To discover more knowledge about the target, he makes query to a database, which runs privacy preserving data mining algorithms to answer queries. Finally, he makes a judgment on the target. In this section, we will explain the above concepts.

What to Learn. In a database, sensitive fields contains private information of a record. If any adversary is able to learn any partial information about a secret field (not necessarily the whole field), it is considered a privacy leak. Take the farmers' survey as example (see Table 1), rented acres and rental rates are secret fields. Adversaries may not know exactly how many acres a farmer rents, but they are more interested in partial information like "does Bob rent over 200 acres" or "is Alice's rental rate in between 90 to 110 dollars" or "is Eve's rental acres below average." Conceptually, a partial privacy is a statement about the records in the database. If an adversary can correctly determine whether the statement is true or false, we say the adversary discloses the partial privacy of the target record.

We model such partial privacy as *privacy predicates*. A privacy predicate priv : $\mathcal{F} \mapsto \{0, 1\}$ is a binary-valued function, its input is a record r (including all fields), its output is either true or false on some statement about r. If the statement is true, then $\mathsf{priv}(r) = 1$, otherwise $\mathsf{priv}(r) = 0$. An adversary is then an algorithm computing $\mathsf{priv}(r)$ based on his knowledge about r.

Not every predicate is a privacy predicate. Computing priv on r should involve at least one bit in the sensitive fields; predicates that can be computed using only public information are not private. We will precisely define privacy predicates in Definition 1. They should not be computed by any *well-informed* adversary, who holds the public information of the target record, as well as the intrinsic knowledge of the privacy, which we will discuss below.

Public Information. Public information of a record consists of (quasi-) identifying fields of the record. We denote the public information as a function $\mathsf{pub} : \mathcal{F}_1 \times \cdots \times \mathcal{F}_k \mapsto \mathcal{F}_1 \times \cdots \times \mathcal{F}_l$ that maps a record to its public fields, where fields $\mathcal{F}_1, \ldots, \mathcal{F}_l$ are (quasi-)identifiers, and $\mathcal{F}_{l+1}, \ldots, \mathcal{F}_k$ are sensitive fields. Public information is assumed accessible to adversaries. In the farmer survey, the public information of a farmer are her/his gender, age, owned acres and zip code. Those information are considered not private, for example, a curious neighbor of Bob is potentially an attacker of Bob. He knows the Bob's age and location, and he can learn the farmer's ownership information from county auditor. These information are not private to Bob's neighbor. Any information that is derivable from those fields are not considered private.

Once an adversary knows a target's public information, he is able to perform queries to discover more particular information about the target. For example, if Bob's zip code is 43111, adversaries design query like "what is the average rental rate in area of zip code 43111", where *zip code 43111* is used to confined the search range.

Public information function $\mathsf{pub}(r)$ is "one-wayed": it is easy to compute given r, but given $\mathsf{pub}(r)$, it is hard to recover all fields of r. We assume that at least some "hardcore" bits in the sensitive fields $\mathcal{F}_{l+1} \times \cdots \times \mathcal{F}_k$ are not computable given $\mathsf{pub}(r)$, otherwise, if every bit in the sensitive fields is computable given the public information, we say the database contains no secret. See "Comments on Privacy Predicates and Hardcore Predicates" on Page 8 for more discussion on the one-wayness of public informations.

Intrinsic Knowledges. Intrinsic knowledges are also referred to as common knowledges, existing knowledge or prior knowledges. These knowledges are about the privacy itself, they may come from the nature of priv, or from the perception of behaviors of general people, or from social statistics, etc. Intrinsic knowledges are of great importance in predicting priv on a particular target. For example, the rental rates are from 0 to 500 dollar per acre, and this knowledge is a common sense for all people, so the fact "is Bob's rental rate less than 800" becomes trivial because every adversary can answer it with 100% success rate. Another example is, an experienced market analyst is aware that most rental rates are below 400 dollars with only a few exceptions, then he can answer the question "is Bob's rental rate less than 400" with high success rate.

We use the probability distribution of priv(r) over $r \in \mathcal{X}$ to represent the intrinsic knowledge about priv:

$$p^{\mathsf{priv}} \triangleq \Pr[\mathsf{priv}(r) = 0 | r \leftarrow \mathcal{X}],$$

which we may simplify to p when understood. This knowledge is known to all adversaries. Take the experienced market analyst as example again, he knows that 98% of the rental rates are less than 400 dollar, that is, $\Pr[\mathsf{priv}(r) = 1] = 0.98$ for $r \in \mathcal{X}$. When he tries to predict the rental rate of a particular person in the database (say, Bob), suppose he does not know anything particular about Bob, he will refer to his intrinsic knowledge about priv (i.e., 98% farmers' rental rate is less than 400) and predicts that Bob has rental rate under 400, as most people do. This strategy is obviously better than random guessing. In this example, the probability of priv$(r) = 1$ over all people plays an important role in predicting priv on a particular person.

A very important assumption in our discussion is that the database is large-scaled and it is equipped with real world data. Generally speaking, if a database enrolls enough samples from the entire population, the distribution of priv over the database would be close enough to that over the entire population, the latter is what we call the "intrinsic knowledge." Intrinsic knowledge is considered public to a well-informed adversary.

Information that is not yet known. Although a well-informed adversary has a good sense of common knowledge, he does not know anything about any specific record(s). As a counter example, suppose $\mathcal{A}$ knew his friend Bob was enrolled in the database $\mathcal{X}$, and he also knew Bob's rental rate is around 140 to 180 dollars (this fact is considered a personal secret, it is not *common* for every farmer); when given question "is Bob's rental rate greater than 140?" he was quite confident to answer *yes*, regardless of the rental rate distribution in $\mathcal{X}$. The second example is, the fact "area of zip code 43113 has rental rate from 200 to 350 dollar per acre" is not considered a common knowledge either, because this fact does not apply to all farmers. Actually, such knowledges are what $\mathcal{A}$ wants to learn in a data mining process. After he knows this kind of knowledge, he is able to make better prediction on priv(r). We required that a well-informed adversary only knows the general information over *all* records; he does not hold any specific information on any record(s), before he makes queries to the database. See Sect. 4 for more discussion on what information $\mathcal{A}$ has before and after the knowledge discovering process.

Defining Privacy Predicate. More formally, a well informed adversary $\mathcal{A}$ knows the public information pub(r) on a target record r, as well as the overall distribution of priv(r) over $r \in \mathcal{X}$. He wants to predict priv(r) on target r. We denote as $r \leftarrow \mathcal{X}$ that r is chosen from $\mathcal{X}$ at uniform random. Let $\Omega(\cdot)$ be the big Ω notation, denote $|\mathcal{X}|$ the number of records in the table. Let $p = \Pr[\mathsf{priv}(r) = 0 | r \leftarrow \mathcal{X}]$ (therefore, $1-p = \Pr[\mathsf{priv}(r) = 1 | r \leftarrow \mathcal{X}]$); p represents the distribution of priv over $r \in \mathcal{X}$. We define privacy predicate as one that no adversary can compute it better than random guessing, even they know pub(r) and p.

Definition 1 (Privacy Predicate). *A predicate* priv *is a privacy predicate if (1) it is efficiently computable from r, and (2) there exists a function in $\Omega(|\mathcal{X}|)$ such that for any well informed, probabilistic polynomial time adversary $\mathcal{A}$,*

$$\Pr_{r \leftarrow \mathcal{X}} [\mathcal{A}(\mathsf{pub}(r), p) = \mathsf{priv}(r)] \leq \max\{p, 1 - p\} + \frac{1}{\Omega(|\mathcal{X}|)}. \qquad (1)$$

Remark. If priv is a privacy predicate, no adversary can predict it better than random guessing, even if they know the public information of the target. That is, the success rate of any adversary given the public information $\mathsf{pub}(r)$ is less than $\max_{\mathcal{A}} \{\Pr_{r \leftarrow \mathcal{X}} [\mathcal{A}(p) = \mathsf{priv}(r)]\} = \max\{p, 1 - p\}$, the best success rate in guessing $\mathsf{priv}(r)$, without $\mathsf{pub}(r)$. See "maximum success rate in guessing" for more discussion. It is required that $\mathsf{priv}(r)$ involves at least some bits in the sensitive fields, those bits are not predicable given $\mathsf{pub}(r)$.

Definition 1 only considers adversaries $\mathcal{A}(\mathsf{pub}(r), p)$ who never make query to the database before. After getting data mining result $m \leftarrow \mathcal{M}$ from method $\mathcal{M}$, an adversary $\mathcal{A}(\mathsf{pub}(r), p, m)$ gains new knowledge, then he makes a better judgment on $\mathsf{priv}(r)$. See Sect. 4 for more details.

Maximum Success Rate in Guessing. Given the distribution of a predicate priv over $\mathcal{X}$, the best strategy of guessing $\mathsf{priv}(r)$ (without any information of r, merely guessing) for a randomly chosen input is simply returning the majority bit b in $\{\mathsf{priv}(r)|r \in \mathcal{X}\}$, which yields a success rate equal to the ratio of b in all $\mathsf{priv}(r)$. It is not hard to see that other guessing strategies have lower success rate, that is,

$$\max_{\mathcal{A}} \left\{ \Pr_{r \leftarrow \mathcal{X}} [\mathcal{A}(p) = \mathsf{priv}(r)] \right\}$$
$$= \max_{b \in \{0,1\}} \left\{ \Pr_{r' \leftarrow \mathcal{X}} [\mathsf{priv}(r') = b] \right\}$$
$$= \max\{p, 1 - p\} \qquad (2)$$

that's because, if $\mathcal{A}$ does not know any information about r, he can only output a random bit. Suppose $\mathcal{A}$ outputs 0 with probability q, and 1 with probability $1 - q$. By calculating the success rate of $\mathcal{A}$:

$$\Pr[\mathcal{A} = \mathsf{priv}(r)]$$
$$= \Pr[\mathcal{A} = 0, \mathsf{priv}(r) = 0] + \Pr[\mathcal{A} = 1, \mathsf{priv}(r) = 1]$$
$$= q \cdot p + (1 - q) \cdot (1 - p)$$
$$= 1 - q - p + 2qp$$
$$= p - (2p - 1)(1 - q) = (1 - p) - q(1 - 2p) \qquad (3)$$

we have if $p > 0.5$ then he gets the maximum rate p with $q = 1$, otherwise if $p < 0.5$ then he gets the maximum $1 - p$ with $q = 0$. That means, $\mathcal{A}$ will get the best success rate when it always returns the majority bit in $\{\mathsf{priv}(r)|r \in \mathcal{X}\}$.

Comments on Privacy Predicates and Hardcore Predicates. Readers with knowledge on cryptography may have been aware that the definition of a privacy predicate is superficially similar to that of a hardcore predicate. Informally, public information function $\mathsf{pub}(r)$ is "one-wayed" in the sense that it is hard to compute r given $\mathsf{pub}(r)$[1], privacy predicate can be viewed as its "hardcore predicate." Indeed, hardcore predicate is a special form of privacy predicate. Assume that there exists a one-way function $f : \{0,1\}^n \mapsto \{0,1\}^*$ with a hardcore predicate $h : \{0,1\}^n \mapsto \{0,1\}$, then for any PPT adversary $\mathcal{A}$, and x sampled from the universe $\{0,1\}^n$ at uniform random, there exists a negligible function negl such that

$$\Pr_{x \leftarrow \{0,1\}^n} [\mathcal{A}(f(x)) = h(x)] < \frac{1}{2} + \mathsf{negl}(|x|). \tag{4}$$

Due to its definition, distribution of $\{h(x)\}$ is $50 : 50$ for $x \leftarrow \{0,1\}^n$, where each possible x is equally chosen. Compare Eq. (4) to Eq. (1), a hardcore predicate is indeed a privacy predicate with $p = 0.5$ and $\mathcal{X} = \mathcal{F} = \{0,1\}^n$. Notice that if $\mathcal{X} = \{0,1\}^n$, then $|\mathcal{X}| = 2^{|x|}$. If $\mathsf{negl}(|x|) = 2^{-|x|}$ (a typical choice of negligible function), then $\mathsf{negl}(|x|) = \frac{1}{|\mathcal{X}|} \in \frac{1}{\Omega(|\mathcal{X}|)}$, still satisfies Eq. (1).

However, secret predicate priv is not a hardcore predicate of pub. priv and pub's input are records sampled from $\mathcal{X}$, but the records in $\mathcal{X}$ is not necessarily evenly distributed over the universe $\mathcal{F}$: some values in $\mathcal{F}$ are never chosen to $\mathcal{X}$ and some may be chosen multiple times. As a result, the distribution of $\{\mathsf{priv}(r)|r \in \mathcal{X}\}$ is not $50 : 50$ for most priv.

In next section, we will define δ-privacy. Our intuition is, if $\mathcal{A}$'s success rate increases a lot after he gets a response from $\mathcal{M}$, we say $\mathcal{M}$ reveals too much information. δ-privacy is defined as even after the adversary gains new knowledge from data mining, his success rate in predicting $\mathsf{priv}(r)$ is not much higher (limited by δ) than before.

4 δ-privacy

We provide a new privacy definition for privacy preserving data mining, called δ-privacy. δ-privacy protects all partial secrets in the following sense: a well-informed adversary $\mathcal{A}$ makes a guess on $\mathsf{priv}(r)$; then he makes a query to the database, gets a response from a privacy preserving data mining method $\mathcal{M}$, from which he learns new knowledge about r; then he makes a new judgment on $\mathsf{priv}(r)$. The second prediction is supposed to have higher success rate compared with that before he makes a query; δ-privacy requires that the extra success rate is limited by δ, for any privacy predicate priv.

To better illustrate the above idea, we design a game between adversary $\mathcal{A}$ and a privacy preserving data mining method $\mathcal{M}$ as follow.

---

[1] If f is a one-way function, then given $f(x)$, it is hard to compute an x' such that $f(x') = f(x)$. But by definition of pub, given $\mathsf{pub}(r)$, it is not hard to find a $r' \in \mathcal{F}$ such that $\mathsf{pub}(r') = \mathsf{pub}(r)$, therefore, pub is not a one-way function. See Chap. 6 of [5] or Chap. 6 of [12] for rigorous definition of one-way functions and hardcore predicates.

Game 1. Game of Privacy Preserving Data Mining.

1: Target record $r \leftarrow \mathcal{X}$ is chosen at uniform random.
2: $\mathcal{A}$ is given the public information $\mathsf{pub}(r)$.
3: $\mathcal{A}$ chooses a privacy predicate priv.
4: $\mathcal{A}$ is given the probabilities $\{p, 1-p\}$ of distributions of $\mathsf{priv}(r')$ over $r' \in \mathcal{X}$.
5: $\mathcal{A}(\mathsf{pub}(r), p)$ predicts $\mathsf{priv}(r)$.
6: $\mathcal{A}$ makes query $\mathsf{q} = \mathsf{q}^{\mathsf{priv},\mathsf{pub}(r)}$.
7: $\mathcal{M}$ is given the query q and the database $\mathcal{X}$. It returns a result m to $\mathcal{A}$.
8: $\mathcal{A}(\mathsf{pub}(r), p, m)$ makes a new judgement on $\mathsf{priv}(r)$.

In the above game, the adversary gets the public information of r and the intrinsic knowledge of priv, we say he becomes a well informed adversary at step 4; he makes the first judgment at step 5. After that, he starts a knowledge discovering process, retrieves more information from the database. Finally, based on all information he receives in the game, he computes $\mathsf{priv}(r)$.

The success rate of prediction made in step 8 should not be much higher than that of the guess made in step 5; if the gap is large, which means $\mathcal{A}$ performs much better in computing $\mathsf{priv}(r)$ after he gets m, we say m discloses excessive information/privacy. The difference

$$\Pr_{r \in \mathcal{X}} \left[\mathcal{A}(\mathsf{pub}(r), p, m) = \mathsf{priv}(r) | m \leftarrow \mathcal{M}(\mathsf{q}, \mathcal{X}) \right]$$

$$- \Pr_{r \in \mathcal{X}} \left[\mathcal{A}(\mathsf{pub}(r), p) = \mathsf{priv}(r) \right]$$

is the extra success rate after $\mathcal{A}$ gets a response from $\mathcal{M}$. We also notice that before $\mathcal{A}$ makes any query to the database, the best possibility $\mathcal{A}(\mathsf{pub}(r), p)$ can achieve is $\max\{p, 1-p\}$, as shown in Eq. (1). We use the following difference to capture the probability gain (in successfully computing $\mathsf{priv}(r)$) after $\mathcal{A}$ discovers new knowledge from the database:

$$\Pr_{r \in \mathcal{X}} \left[\mathcal{A}(\mathsf{pub}(r), p, m) = \mathsf{priv}(r) | m \leftarrow \mathcal{M}(\mathsf{q}, \mathcal{X}) \right]$$

$$- \max\{p, 1-p\}. \tag{5}$$

Intuitively, this difference is the amount of privacy leaked to the adversary. For the purpose of protecting privacy, this difference should be small. δ-privacy is then defined as no adversary can gain extra success rate more than δ.

Definition 2 (δ-privacy). *Let* priv *be a privacy predicate. Suppose a computationally bounded adversary* $\mathcal{A}$ *is given* $\mathsf{pub}(r)$ *of some* $r \in \mathcal{X}$, *and let* $p = \Pr[\mathsf{priv}(r) = 0 | r \leftarrow \mathcal{X}]$ *denote the distribution of* $\mathsf{priv}(r)$ *over* $r \in \mathcal{X}$. *$\mathcal{A}$ makes query* q *and obtains response* m *from a privacy preserving data mining method* $\mathcal{M}$. *$\mathcal{A}$ outputs a bit to predict* $\mathsf{priv}(r)$. *$\mathcal{M}$ is said to preserving δ-privacy if there exists a positive real number δ, for any privacy predicate* priv,

$$\Pr_{r \leftarrow \mathcal{X}} \left[\mathcal{A}(\mathsf{pub}(r), p, m) = \mathsf{priv}(r) | m \leftarrow \mathcal{M}(\mathsf{q}, \mathcal{X}) \right]$$

$$\leq \max\{p, 1-p\} + \frac{1}{\Omega(|\mathcal{X}|)} + \delta, \tag{6}$$

where, on the left hand side, the probability of $\mathcal{A}$ successfully computing $\mathsf{priv}(r)$ depends on the random coin used by $\mathcal{M}$.

Remark. For the ease of presentation, we sometimes may omit the term $1/\Omega(|\mathcal{X}|)$ in our discussion. Also, we only consider the case that $\delta \in (0, \frac{1}{2}]$, because if $\delta > \frac{1}{2}$, $\max\{p, 1 - p\} + \delta$ exceeds 1, the formula will be always true.

Variants of δ-Privacy. The privacy Definition 2 introduces a absolute bound on the privacy leaks. This constraint can also be in other mathematical forms, the following variant introduces a relative bound, which depends on the intrinsic knowledge of the secret.

Definition 3 (δ-privacy-variant-I). *Let the notations be the same with those in Definition 2. The variant I of δ-privacy requires that for all computationally bounded adversaries in Game 1,*

$$\Pr_{r \leftarrow \mathcal{X}} [\mathcal{A}(\mathsf{pub}(r), p, m) = \mathsf{priv}(r) | m \leftarrow \mathcal{M}(\mathsf{q}, \mathcal{X})]$$

$$\leq \left(\max\{p, 1 - p\} + \frac{1}{\Omega(|\mathcal{X}|)} \right) \cdot \exp(\delta). \tag{7}$$

Dealing with Multiple Queries. Note that in Game 1, step 6 and 7 can be repeated multiple times, that is, we allow the adversary to make multiple queries, and to adaptively choose queries. If the queries are different, we can consider them as one big query, and that will be just the same with the single query case.

Another case is $\mathcal{A}$ makes the same queries for multiple times. As mentioned above, $\mathcal{M}(\mathsf{q}, \mathcal{X})$ is a random variable (r.v.). To learn the distribution of this r.v., adversaries may make the same query q for multiple times to get more samples. The more samples he gets, the more detailed he learns about the distribution, then he is able to use the distribution of $\mathcal{M}$ to predict $\mathsf{q}(\mathcal{X})$ and hence $\mathsf{priv}(r)$. There are three strategies to deal with multiple queries:

1. $\mathcal{M}$ will always return the same answer for the same query. An example for this is the anonymized table (Definition 10): once the anonymized table is published, adversaries run the query on the (deterministic) anonymized table, that is equivalent to a method $\mathcal{M}$ that always output the same answer to the same query.
2. $\mathcal{M}$ returns the same answer by maintaining a hash table, with the key being the input pair $\langle \mathsf{q}, \mathcal{X} \rangle$ and the value being the output m; when a request is made to $\mathcal{M}$, it first checks the hash table. If the request is new, $\mathcal{M}$ generates a new answer m, add it to the hash table and returns it; otherwise, it returns the existing answer. Such a method requires a large amount of storage space if there are many different queries and/or the database $\mathcal{X}$ is updated frequently. Also, this method may be not safe either: if $\mathcal{X}$ is updated frequently, and each update is small (such that the changes of $\mathsf{q}(\mathcal{X})$ is small in each update), adversaries may still have a good estimation on $\mathsf{q}(\mathcal{X})$.

3. $\mathcal{M}$ generates a new answer to every request. That means adversary is able to learn the distribution of $\mathcal{M}(q, \mathcal{X})$. It implicitly requires that even if $\mathcal{A}$ knows the distribution of $\mathcal{M}(q, \mathcal{X})$, he does not know $q(\mathcal{X})$, or the relationship between $q(\mathcal{X})$ and $\mathcal{M}(q, \mathcal{X})$.

5   Tradeoff Between Privacy and Utility

In this section, we will discuss the relation between privacy and utility. Intuitively, the need for privacy is incompatible with the need for utility: to protect privacy, a data provider wishes to hide information, while a data user wishes to collect as much information as he could. We provide a quantitative analysis for the tradeoff between privacy and utility, showing that the amount of information gain is bounded by the largest possible privacy loss of the data provider. To get more information, the data user should negotiate with the data provider to increase the limit of privacy leak.

The utility of a data mining method is how much knowledge can be discovered from its results. If the result is generated by a privacy preserving data mining method $\mathcal{M}(q, \mathcal{X})$, its utility should be measured by the "distance" to the true result $q(\mathcal{X})$. More precisely, the output of $\mathcal{M}(q, \mathcal{X})$ is a random variable; the utility is the closeness between the random variable and the true value $q(\mathcal{X})$. Intuitively, if $\mathcal{M}(q, \mathcal{X})$ is close to $q(\mathcal{X})$, the result is likely to be useful, otherwise it is not.

Some literatures (e.g., [24]) employ the *entropy* of $\mathcal{M}(q, \mathcal{X})$ to estimate utilities for perturbation-based methods. The idea behind is, the more "concentrated" are the results (which are drawn from $\mathcal{M}(q, \mathcal{X})$, the closer they are to the real result $q(\mathcal{X})$. However, this definition is correct if and only if the true answer is always at the "center" of the random variable, it does not apply to all methods.

Utility of a Data Mining Method. Before we define the utility of a method $\mathcal{M}$ on query q and database $\mathcal{X}$, we first introduce one kind of adversaries called *honest users* to determine the utility of a method. An honest user is a deterministic algorithm that, given the answer of $q(\mathcal{X})$, he correctly computes a knowledge knlg, where knlg $: \mathcal{F} \mapsto \{0, 1\}$. More specifically, we define an honest user $\tilde{A} = \tilde{A}^{knlg}$ as an adversary who takes part in the Game 2. He would like to compute a knowledge predicate (a privacy predicate) knlg on some $r \in \mathcal{X}$. He is an honest user if he always wins the game, that is, $\tilde{A}$ designs query $q = q^{knlg, pub(r)}$, after he receives the true result of $q(\mathcal{X})$, he returns one bit as result such that

$$\tilde{A}(pub(r), q(\mathcal{X})) = knlg(r) \tag{8}$$

for any $\mathcal{X}$, any choice of $r \in \mathcal{X}$, and any appropriately chosen knlg.

Existence of Honest Users. Note that such honest user and knlg may not always exist; if $pub(r)$ is not unique, $\tilde{A}$ may not win the game with probability 1. For example, assume that there are two records r and r' which have the same public information, but one's rental rate is 150 and the other is 250. Then $\tilde{A}$ may only

Game 2. Game of Honest User.

1: A target record r is chosen uniformly at random from the database $\mathcal{X}$.
2: User $\tilde{A}$ is given the public information $\mathsf{pub}(r)$.
3: User $\tilde{A}$ chooses a knowledge predicate knlg.
4: Based on knlg, $\tilde{A}$ designs query $\mathsf{q} = \mathsf{q}^{\mathsf{knlg},\mathsf{pub}(r)}$.
5: An oracle $\mathcal{O}$ responses to $\tilde{A}$ with the true result of $\mathsf{q}(\mathcal{X})$.
6: $\tilde{A}$ outputs a bit b.
7: User $\tilde{A}$ wins the game if $b = \mathsf{knlg}(r)$.

have $\frac{1}{2}$ chance in computing knowledge predicate "does r's rental rate greater than 200", no matter how $\tilde{A}$ designed the query $\mathsf{q}^{\mathsf{knlg},\mathsf{pub}(r)}$. We assume here that the public information $\mathsf{pub}(r)$ is unique in database $\mathcal{X}$, so that such intelligent adversaries always exist.

Loosely speaking, we can think of a honest user as a person who lives in a world that people trust each other, he will treat any result given to him as the true $\mathsf{q}(\mathcal{X})$ and computes $\mathsf{knlg}(r)$ from it. Now suppose we replace the oracle $\mathcal{O}$ by a privacy preserving method $\mathcal{M}$, $\tilde{A}$ remains innocent. Game 2 becomes the Game 1 (on Page 10), with knlg being priv.

Definition 4 (*Utility of a Single Result* m). *Given a single result $m \leftarrow \mathcal{M}(\mathsf{q}, \mathcal{X})$, the utility of m with respect to a honest user $\tilde{A} = \tilde{A}^{\mathsf{knlg}}$ is defined by a function $u_{\tilde{A}}$:*

$$u_{\tilde{A}}(r, m) = \begin{cases} 1 \; if \tilde{A}(\mathsf{pub}(r), m) = \mathsf{knlg}(r) \\ 0 \; otherwise \end{cases} \tag{9}$$

If an honest user $\tilde{A}$ correctly computes knlg given m, we say that m is useful ($u_{\tilde{A}}(m) = 1$), otherwise it is not ($u_{\tilde{A}}(m) = 0$).

Given results from $\mathcal{M}(\mathsf{q}, \mathcal{X})$, $\tilde{A}$ evaluates the utilities of single results, we define the utility of the method as the expectation of utilities.

Definition 5 (*Utility of* $\mathcal{M}(\mathsf{q}, \mathcal{X})$). *The utility (with respect to $\tilde{A} = \tilde{A}^{\mathsf{knlg}}$) of a method $\mathcal{M}$ on query q and data set $\mathcal{X}$ is defined as the expected utility of the random variable $\mathcal{M}(\mathsf{q}, \mathcal{X})$:*

$$\mathcal{U}_{\tilde{A}}(\mathcal{M}(\mathsf{q}, \mathcal{X})) \triangleq E[u_{\tilde{A}}(r, m) | r \leftarrow \mathcal{X}, m \leftarrow \mathcal{M}(\mathsf{q}, \mathcal{X})]$$
$$= \sum_{r,m} u_{\tilde{A}}(r, m) \times \Pr[r \leftarrow \mathcal{X}, \mathcal{M}(\mathsf{q}, \mathcal{X}) = m] \tag{10}$$

Notice that the intrinsic knowledge $p = p^{\mathsf{knlg}}$ of knlg also provides some "utility": even without querying to $\mathcal{M}$, there are adversaries that can achieve some utility, which we refer to as intrinsic utility. Assume, w.l.o.g., that $p > 0.5$. We fix an adversary (denoted as $\mathcal{A}' = \mathcal{A}^{\mathsf{knlg}}$) which outputs 0 with probability 1 (that is, $\mathcal{A}'(r, m) = 0$ for all r and m). We define the intrinsic utility as the expected utility evaluated by $\mathcal{A}'$ (perhaps with a little abuse of notation):

Definition 6 (*Intrinsic Utility of* knlg). *The intrinsic utility of knowledge predicate* knlg *is defined as the expected utility evaluated by a user* $\mathcal{A}' = \mathcal{A}^{\text{knlg}}$

$$\mathcal{U}_{\mathcal{A}'}(1) \triangleq E[u_{\mathcal{A}'}(r,1)|r \leftarrow \mathcal{X}] \tag{11}$$

The reason we employ the special user $\mathcal{A}'$ to define intrinsic utility is this user is the one that achieves the largest possible utility among all guessing users, see "maximum success rate in guessing", Page 8 for more information.

The intrinsic utility is the one that obtained by a user without querying to $\mathcal{M}$, we define the utility gain of a method $\mathcal{M}$ on q and $\mathcal{X}$ as the utility of $\mathcal{M}(q, \mathcal{X})$ (w.r.t. $\tilde{\mathcal{A}}^{\text{knlg}}$) minus the intrinsic utility of knlg.

Definition 7 (Utility Gain of $\mathcal{M}(q, \mathcal{X})$). *The utility gain (w.r.t. $\tilde{\mathcal{A}}^{\text{knlg}}$) of* $\mathcal{M}(q, \mathcal{X})$ *is the difference between the utility of the method minus the prior utility of* knlg, *that is,*

$$\mathcal{G}_{\tilde{\mathcal{A}}}(\mathcal{M}(q, \mathcal{X})) \triangleq \mathcal{U}_{\tilde{\mathcal{A}}}(\mathcal{M}, q, \mathcal{X}) - \mathcal{U}_{\mathcal{A}'}(1), \tag{12}$$

the (value of) utility of $\mathcal{M}(q, \mathcal{X})$ *depends on the choice of* $\tilde{A}$.

The utility gain reflects how much information is gained from the data mining method. Intuitively, the larger is the gain, the better is the result. However, we show the following theorem, saying that the largest possible utility gain of a δ-private method, can not exceed the amount of privacy loss, namely, δ.

Theorem 1. *If* $\mathcal{M}$ *is* δ-*private, then*

$$\mathcal{G}_{\tilde{\mathcal{A}}}(\mathcal{M}(q, \mathcal{X})) \le \delta + \frac{1}{\Omega(|\mathcal{X}|)}$$

for all q, *all* $\mathcal{X}$, *all* knlg *and all* $\tilde{\mathcal{A}}$.

Remark. We can achieve a similar result for δ-privacy-variant-I (but in different mathematics form). This theorem is an important result that shows the relation between privacy and utility: they are zero-summed in the sense that the utility gain is always less than the amount of largest possible privacy leak. Suppose a user wants to learn some knowledge knlg, he wants to get Δ utility gain versus his intrinsic knowledge, he have to ask his data providers to increase the privacy leak limit to at least Δ.

The Theorem also depicts a framework for potential privacy trading. Data providers can consider "selling" their private data, the price is the largest possible privacy leak; and data processors can purchase those data based on how much information they can learn from them.

6 The Relations Between δ-privacy and Other Existing Privacy Definitions

In this section, we will discuss the relationship between δ-privacy and existing privacy definitions, namely, differential privacy and data anonymity. We will show that differential privacy (with parameter δ) implies δ-privacy-variant-I, and t-closeness w.r.t. variational distance implies δ-privacy with $t = \delta$.

6.1   A Supporting Lemma

We will show a lemma used in the proof Lemmas 2 and 3. Reader may proceed to the next sections for now and come back for this lemma later.

We will show that if two random variables $\mathcal{Y}_1$ and $\mathcal{Y}_2$ are *close*, then the r.v.'s generated by running $\mathcal{A}$ on $\mathcal{Y}_1$ and $\mathcal{Y}_2$ are still close.

Denote $\mathcal{A}(\mathcal{Y})$ the binary-valued random variable generated by randomized algorithm $\mathcal{A}$, whose input is sampled from discrete random variable $\mathcal{Y}$. We argue that if the distance between two random variables $\mathcal{Y}_1$ and $\mathcal{Y}_2$ is less than δ, then $\mathcal{A}(\mathcal{Y}_1)$ and $\mathcal{A}(\mathcal{Y}_2)$ also have distance less than δ. On the other hand, if for all algorithm $\mathcal{A}$, $\mathcal{A}(\mathcal{Y}_1)$ and $\mathcal{A}(\mathcal{Y}_2)$ are close, then $\mathcal{Y}_1$ and $\mathcal{Y}_2$ must be close to each other.

A very important question arises: how to define the distance of two random variables? There are many way to define it, for example, variational distance, Kullback-Leibler distance, Earth Mover's Distance, just to name a few. In this paper, we use the variational distance to define statistical distance of two random variables.

Definition 8 (Variational Distance of Two Random Variables [15]).
Suppose $\mathbf{P}_1$ *and* $\mathbf{P}_2$ *are probability distribution functions (p.d.f.) of two discrete random variables (with respect sample space* Ω_1 *and* Ω_2*). The two random variables are statistically close if for some* $\delta > 0$,

$$\sup_{S \subseteq \Omega_1 \cup \Omega_2} |\mathbf{P}_1(S) - \mathbf{P}_2(S)| \leq \delta.$$

If the random variables are discrete ones, the above formula becomes

$$\max_{S \subseteq \Omega_1 \cup \Omega_2} \left\{ \sum_{y \in S} (\mathbf{P}_1(y) - \mathbf{P}_2(y)) \right\} \leq \delta. \tag{13}$$

Variation distance is the maximum difference between the probabilities that two p.d.f.'s can assign to the same event.

Lemma 1. *Suppose* $\mathcal{A}$ *is a randomized algorithm whose output is one bit,* $\mathcal{Y}_1$ *and* $\mathcal{Y}_2$ *are two discrete random variables with sample space* Ω. $\mathcal{A}(\mathcal{Y}_1)$ *and* $\mathcal{A}(\mathcal{Y}_2)$ *satisfy*

$$\Pr\left[\mathcal{A}(\mathcal{Y}_1) = b\right] \leq \Pr\left[\mathcal{A}(\mathcal{Y}_2) = b\right] + \delta \tag{14}$$

for $b = 0, 1$ *if and only if the variational distance of* $\mathcal{Y}_1$ *and* $\mathcal{Y}_2$ *are less than* δ, *i.e., for any subset* $S \subseteq \Omega$,

$$\Pr\left[y \in S | y \leftarrow \mathcal{Y}_1\right] \leq \Pr\left[y \in S | y \leftarrow \mathcal{Y}_2\right] + \delta. \tag{15}$$

Lemma 1 will be used to show the relationship between δ-privacy and differential privacy, and between δ-privacy and t-closeness. Note that even if Eq. (14) is true for both $b = 0$ and 1, it does not imply that

$$\Pr[\mathcal{A}(y) = f(y) | y \leftarrow \mathcal{Y}_1] \leq \Pr[\mathcal{A}(y) = f(y) | y \leftarrow \mathcal{Y}_2] + \delta$$

is true for all binary valued function f.

Corollary 1. *Let algorithm $\mathcal{A}$, random variables $\mathcal{Y}_1$ and $\mathcal{Y}_2$, sample space Ω be the ones defined in Lemma 1. The random variables $\mathcal{A}(\mathcal{Y}_1)$ and $\mathcal{A}(\mathcal{Y}_2)$ satisfy*

$$\Pr\left[\mathcal{A}(\mathcal{Y}_1) = b\right] \leq \Pr\left[\mathcal{A}(\mathcal{Y}_2) = b\right] \times \exp(\delta) \tag{16}$$

if and only if for any set $S \subseteq \Omega$,

$$\Pr\left[y \in S | y \leftarrow \mathcal{Y}_1\right] \leq \Pr\left[y \in S | y \leftarrow \mathcal{Y}_2\right] \times \exp(\delta). \tag{17}$$

6.2 Relation to Differential Privacy

In this section, we will show the relation between differential privacy and δ-privacy. If a privacy preserving data mining method is differentially private (with parameter ϵ), then it is δ-private-variant-I with parameter $\delta = \epsilon$. But on the other hand, a method satisfies δ-privacy does not necessarily mean it satisfies δ-differential privacy. That means, in terms of the maximum privacy leak, δ-differential privacy is more secure than δ-privacy, which, by Theorem 1, gives less flexibility in getting utility.

Differential privacy [6] is one of the most influential definition of privacy, which is widely adopted by output perturbation methods. It captures the idea that the result of the query should not leak information of any person, as if the target person were not included in the table.

Definition 9 (differential privacy *[6]*). *An algorithm $\mathcal{M}$ is said to satisfy ϵ-differential privacy if for all database $\mathcal{X}$ and $\mathcal{X}_1$ which only differ in one record, and for any set S of possible outcomes,*

$$\Pr\left[m_1 \in S | m_1 \leftarrow \mathcal{M}(\mathsf{q}, \mathcal{X}_1)\right]$$
$$\leq \Pr\left[m \in S | m \leftarrow \mathcal{M}(\mathsf{q}, \mathcal{X}) \in S\right] \times \exp(\epsilon). \tag{18}$$

Lemma 2. *If $\mathcal{M}$ satisfies ϵ-differential privacy, it also satisfies ϵ-privacy-variant-I.*

Remarks. Lemma 2 shows that if a method is ϵ-differential privacy, then it is ϵ-private-variant-I, however, the reverse is not necessarily true: a method is δ-private is not necessarily δ-differentially-private.

6.3 Relation to Data Anonymity

Data anonymity is family of privacy preserving data mining methods. In this section, we will show that if a data anonymity method is t-close w.r.t. variational distance (which is the strongest requirement in the series), it is δ-private with $\delta = t$.

Instead of answering to queries, data anonymity methods publish a modified table for everyone to query on. Records in the database are grouped into equivalence classes sharing a same identifying tag, their secret fields remain unchanged.

Using the (original) public information of a target record, an adversary can locate the target to a specific class by the tags on the classes, but he does not know which one in the class is the target, since everyone in the group looks the same.

It is required that in each equivalence class, the distribution of the sensitive data is close to that of the entire table, otherwise, if for some class, the distribution is greatly different from that of the entire table, an adversary can conclude that targets in this class have special properties that other records do not have.

Definition 10 (t-closeness [13]). *An equivalence class is t-close to the whole table if the distance between the following two distributions is no more than a threshold t: the distribution of sensitive data in that equivalence class, and the one in the whole table. An anonymized table is t-close to the original table if all equivalence classes are t-close to the whole table.*

The definition of t-closeness does not specify how to measure the divergence of two distributions. In the following lemma, we will show that data anonymity methods satisfies t-closeness w.r.t. variational distance (Definition 8), then it is δ-private:

Lemma 3. *A privacy preserving method $\mathcal{M}$ publishes an anonymized table with equivalence classes, it is δ-private if the variational distance between the distribution of sensitive data in any equivalence class, and the distribution of sensitive data in the whole table, is no more than δ.*

7   Conclusion

In this paper, we proposed δ-privacy, a new privacy definition for privacy preserving data mining. By analyzing adversaries' behaviors, δ-privacy directly tells the data provider the risk of privacy leak in a data mining process. We show that existing data privacy analysis mechanisms are also compatible to ours; actually, our method can be applied to any data mining process, not limited to particular ones. Another important contribution of our work is, we mathematically shows that the amount of information extracted from a data mining process does not exceed the amount of possible privacy loss; this idea seems not surprising, but to the best of our knowledge, we are the first one to rigorously prove this conjecture. A potential application for this is, we can develop a pricing system for "data trading," data providers could sell their data, get compensated based on their (possible) privacy loss; on the other hand, data users could purchase data based on the amount of information they could get. This trading system is possible under our δ-privacy framework.

References

1. Agrawal, R., Srikant, R.: Privacy-preserving data mining. SIGMOD Rec. **29**(2), 439–450 (2000). http://doi.acm.org/10.1145/335191.335438
2. Brenner, H., Nissim, K.: Impossibility of differentially private universally optimal mechanisms. In: FOCS, pp. 71–80. IEEE Computer Society (2010)
3. Brickell, J., Shmatikov, V.: The cost of privacy: destruction of data-mining utility in anonymized data publishing. In: Proceedings of the 14th ACM SIGKDD International Conference on Knowledge Discovery and Data Mining, KDD 2008, pp. 70–78. ACM, New York (2008)
4. Cormode, G., Procopiuc, C., Shen, E., Srivastava, D., Yu, T.: Empirical privacy and empirical utility of anonymized data. In: 2013 IEEE 29th International Conference on Data Engineering Workshops (ICDEW), pp. 77–82, April 2013
5. Delfs, H., Knebl, H.: Introduction to Cryptography - Principles and Applications. Information Security and Cryptography. Springer, Heidelberg (2007)
6. Dwork, C.: Differential privacy: a survey of results. In: Agrawal, M., Du, D., Duan, Z., Li, A. (eds.) TAMC 2008. LNCS, vol. 4978, pp. 1–19. Springer, Heidelberg (2008). doi:10.1007/978-3-540-79228-4_1
7. Dwork, C., McSherry, F., Nissim, K., Smith, A.: Calibrating noise to sensitivity in private data analysis. In: Halevi, S., Rabin, T. (eds.) TCC 2006. LNCS, vol. 3876, pp. 265–284. Springer, Heidelberg (2006). doi:10.1007/11681878_14
8. Dwork, C., Pottenger, R.: Toward practicing privacy. J. Am. Med. Inform. Assoc. **20**(1), 102–108 (2013). http://jamia.bmj.com/content/20/1/102.abstract
9. Ganta, S.R., Kasiviswanathan, S.P., Smith, A.: Composition attacks and auxiliary information in data privacy. In: Proceedings of the 14th ACM SIGKDD International Conference on Knowledge Discovery and Data Mining, KDD 2008, pp. 265–273. ACM, NY, USA (2008). http://doi.acm.org/10.1145/1401890.1401926
10. Ghosh, A., Roughgarden, T., Sundararajan, M.: Universally utility-maximizing privacy mechanisms. In: Proceedings of the Forty-first Annual ACM Symposium on Theory of Computing, STOC 2009, pp. 351–360. ACM, NY, USA (2009). http://doi.acm.org/10.1145/1536414.1536464
11. Gupte, M., Sundararajan, M.: Universally optimal privacy mechanisms for minimax agents. In: Proceedings of the Twenty-ninth ACM SIGMOD-SIGACT-SIGART Symposium on Principles of Database Systems, PODS 2010, pp. 135–146. ACM, NY, USA (2010). http://doi.acm.org/10.1145/1807085.1807105
12. Katz, J., Lindell, Y.: Introduction to Modern Cryptography. Chapman & Hall/Crc Cryptography and Network Security Series. Chapman & Hall/CRC, Boca Raton (2007)
13. Li, N., Li, T.: t-closeness: Privacy beyond k-anonymity and -diversity. In: Proceedings of IEEE 23rd International Conference on Data Engineering (ICDE 2007) (2007)
14. Li, T., Li, N.: On the tradeoff between privacy and utility in data publishing. In: Proceedings of the 15th ACM SIGKDD International Conference on Knowledge Discovery and Data Mining, KDD '09, pp. 517–526. ACM, NY, USA (2009). http://doi.acm.org/10.1145/1557019.1557079
15. Lin, J.: Divergence measures based on the shannon entropy. IEEE Trans. Inform. Theory **37**(1), 145–151 (1991)
16. Lindell, Y., Pinkas, B.: Privacy preserving data mining. In: Bellare, M. (ed.) CRYPTO 2000. LNCS, vol. 1880, pp. 36–54. Springer, Heidelberg (2000). doi:10.1007/3-540-44598-6_3

17. Machanavajjhala, A., Gehrke, J., Kifer, D., Venkitasubramaniam, M.: L-diversity: privacy beyond k-anonymity. In: Proceedings of the 22nd International Conference on Data Engineering, ICDE 2006, p. 24 (2006)
18. McSherry, F., Mironov, I.: Differentially private recommender systems: Building privacy into the net. In: Proceedings of the 15th ACM SIGKDD International Conference on Knowledge Discovery and Data Mining, KDD 2009, pp. 627–636. ACM, NY, USA (2009). http://doi.acm.org/10.1145/1557019.1557090
19. McSherry, F.D.: Privacy integrated queries: an extensible platform for privacy-preserving data analysis. In: Proceedings of the 2009 ACM SIGMOD International Conference on Management of Data, SIGMOD 2009, pp. 19–30. ACM, NY, USA (2009). http://doi.acm.org/10.1145/1559845.1559850
20. Parra-Arnau, J., Rebollo-Monedero, D., Forn, J.: Measuring the privacy of user profiles in personalized information systems. Future Gener. Comput. Syst. **33**, 53–63 (2014). http://www.sciencedirect.com/science/article/pii/S0167739X1300006X, special Section on Applications of Intelligent Data and Knowledge Processing Technologies; Guest Editor: Dominik lzak
21. Peters, F., Menzies, T., Gong, L., Zhang, H.: Balancing privacy and utility in cross-company defect prediction. IEEE Trans. Softw. Eng. **39**(8), 1054–1068 (2013)
22. Rebollo-Monedero, D., Parra-Arnau, J., Diaz, C., Forn, J.: On the measurement of privacy as an attackers estimation error. Int. J. Inf. Secur. **12**(2), 129–149 (2013). http://dx.doi.org/10.1007/s10207-012-0182-5
23. Sweeney, L.: K-anonymity: a model for protecting privacy. Int. J. Uncertain. Fuzziness Knowl.-Based Syst. **10**(5), 557–570 (2002). http://dx.doi.org/10.1142/S0218488502001648
24. Venkatasubramanian, S.: Measures of anonymity. In: Aggarwal, C.C., Yu, P.S. (eds.) Privacy-Preserving Data Mining. ADBS, vol. 34. Springer, Boston (2008). doi:10.1007/978-0-387-70992-5_4

Threshold Single Password Authentication

Devriş İşler$^{(\boxtimes)}$ and Alptekin Küpçü

Koç University, İstanbul, Turkey
{disler15,akupcu}@ku.edu.tr

Abstract. Passwords are the most widely used form of online user authentication. In a traditional setup, the user, who has a *human-memorable low entropy password*, wants to authenticate with a login server. Unfortunately, existing solutions in this setting are either non-portable or insecure against many attacks, including phishing, man-in-the-middle, honeypot, and offline dictionary attacks. Three previous studies (Acar et al. 2013, Bicakci et al. 2011, and Jarecki et al. 2016) provide solutions secure against offline dictionary attacks by additionally employing a *storage provider* (either a cloud storage or a mobile device for portability). These works provide solutions where offline dictionary attacks are impossible as long as the adversary does not corrupt *both* the login server and the storage provider.

For the first time, improving these previous works, we provide a more secure generalized solution employing *multiple* storage providers, where our solution is proven secure against offline dictionary attacks as long as the adversary does not corrupt the login server and *threshold-many* storage providers. We define ideal and real world indistinguishability for threshold single password authentication (Threshold SPA) schemes, and formally prove security of our solution via ideal-real simulation. Our solution provides security against all the above-mentioned attacks, including *phishing, man-in-the-middle, honeypot, and offline dictionary attacks*, and requires *no* change on the server side. Thus, our solution can immediately be deployed via a browser extension (or a mobile application) and support from some storage providers. We further argue that our protocol is efficient and scalable, and provide performance numbers where the user and storage load are only a few milliseconds.

Keywords: Password based authentication · Threshold secret sharing · Dictionary attack · Phishing

1 Introduction

Passwords are the most widely used form of online user authentication. In a traditional password based authentication, there are two parties: the *user* who has a *human-memorable low entropy password* and the *login server* that creates an account for the user and keeps the user's account information (e.g. $<$*username, hash(password)*$>$) to authenticate the user later when she wants

© Springer International Publishing AG 2017
J. Garcia-Alfaro et al. (Eds.): DPM/CBT 2017, LNCS 10436, pp. 143–162, 2017.
DOI: 10.1007/978-3-319-67816-0_9

to login. Another related field includes password authenticated key exchange (PAKE) protocols, where a user and a server desire to establish a *secure and authenticated channel* via a shared secret password [3,6,7,19,20]. Passwords are also employed in password-protected secret sharing (PPSS) techniques, where the user stores her credential(s) on a server or among multiple servers [5,8,9,16]. The server(s) verify that the user is legitimate before giving an access to the stored secret, and this authentication is done via passwords.

The existence of servers' adversarial behaviors such as *phishing, man-in-the-middle*, and *honeypot* attacks, where the adversarial server tries to trick the user to willingly reveal her password (unaware of the attack), as well as *offline dictionary attacks* that can be mounted by the server or hackers obtaining the server database are commonly known and powerful attacks on users' passwords. Unfortunately, all the above-cited constructions, where the server stores the user's password as plain text or the hash of the password, lose security against such attacks. Indeed, such attacks are very prevalent, and recent studies even propose improved offline dictionary attacks [24]. The damage of the successful attack is increased dramatically if the user reuses the same password to register with more than one login server, which is a common practice [13].

Our focus in this paper is on password based authentication secure against those attacks. Consider the following approaches:

– **Traditional insecure approach:** Store the output of a deterministic (hash) function of the password at the login server. The user's password is easily compromised in the current traditional approach against adversarial servers (e.g. phishing, man-in-the-middle, honeypot). Moreover, it is directly vulnerable to offline dictionary attacks by hackers obtaining the login server database, since recomputing the output of the deterministic function and comparing against the database enables such offline dictionary attacks.
– **Secure but non-portable approach:** Store a verification key at the login server, where the corresponding secret key is blinded by the user's password and stored on the user's machine or USB device. When the keys are generated independent of the password, such an approach will protect the user against the mentioned attacks. Unfortunately, this approach is not user friendly in the contemporary setting where each user owns multiple devices or employs public terminals, as this incurs portability issues (even with USB storage employed, note that not all devices have USB ports).[1]
– **Secure and usable approach:** Store the verification key at the login server and securely store the corresponding secret key blinded by some function of user password at storage provider(s) *different* from the login server. Such a *storage provider* can be a cloud storage or mobile device (as opposed to a non-portable location above). This was first observed and the first solution

---

[1] Non-cloud-based password managers also fall into this setting.

was constructed by Acar et al. [1] (with their patent application dating 2010 [2]), and later also used by Jarecki et al. [17] and also Bicakci et al. [4].[2]

The only known provably secure (against offline dictionary attacks) and usable password based authentication or PAKE systems are the Acar et al. [1] (with their patent application dating 2010 [2]) and Jarecki et al. [17] solutions (Bicakci et al. [4] present a solution idea briefly, but without a formal security proof). They include a single storage provider (which is either a cloud storage or a mobile device) for the secret storage. The underlying assumption is that the protocol is secure unless the login server and the storage provider are corrupted by the same adversary. Thus, when the same adversary corrupts both the login server and the storage provider, or they simply collude, they can mount an offline dictionary attack to find the user password. Any weaker adversary can always perform an *online attack*; however, online attacks are not big threats due to several reasons. Firstly, they are inherently many orders of magnitude slower compared to offline attacks due to network delays. Secondly, the honest login servers and storage providers will block the adversary after several unsuccessful attempts, or limit the rate of such attempts.

For the first time, we present a **single password authentication (SPA)** protocol that can employ possibly *more than one* storage provider (any combination of cloud or mobile devices). In our **Threshold SPA** solution, we employ a total of n storage providers, and a threshold $1 \leq t \leq n$. This setting serves two purposes. Firstly, for an adversary to be able to successfully mount an offline dictionary attack, he must corrupt the login server *in addition to* t storage providers. Secondly, to login, the user must access t storage providers out of n; thus availability can be balanced against security easily by setting these parameters. While the underlying techniques are different, in terms of security, the previous solutions correspond to setting $t = n = 1$.

Delving deeper, Acar et al. [1] discuss in one paragraph that it is possible to convert their solution to employ more than one storage provider using secret sharing. Unfortunately, when done in a straightforward manner, this results in an insecure solution in the sense that corrupting the login server and *only one* storage provider will still enable the adversary to perform an offline dictionary attack. As mentioned earlier, they employ the storage provider to store the secret key needed for authentication. This secret key is protected by the password. When this secret is simply shared among multiple storage providers, there needs to be a mechanism to prevent the login server to obtain these shares from the storage providers, as otherwise the adversarial login server can simply request these shares and perform an offline dictionary attack. To prevent this, only the entity knowing the password should be able to retrieve these shares, meaning that there needs to be another password based authentication mechanism also done at the storage provider side, creating a recursive problem, needing further storage providers indefinitely. If traditional password based authentication approaches

---

[2] Cloud-based password managers are related to this setting, but almost all of them employ the user master password for authenticating with their own servers, hence having the same insecurities there.

are employed instead, then this password based authentication subprotocol will enable the login server to collude with only one storage provider to mount the offline dictionary attack, since the user only has a single password and hence the same authentication is employed at every storage provider. Moreover, their one paragraph extension idea lacks any formal proof where we give a formal proof for Threshold SPA for the first time.

In our solution, while the user still has only a single password, **our protocol provably ensures that the following adversaries will be completely unsuccessful:**

- An adversary that controls threshold-many storage providers (but not the login server).
- An adversary that controls less than threshold-many storage providers *in addition to* the login server.
- An adversary who successfully mounts a phishing, man-in-the-middle, or honeypot attack.

We assume that if any party is corrupted by an adversary once, it remains corrupted (which is realistic, since the adversary can install backdoors on a system once corrupted). Our solution only fails against a local adversary (such as a keylogger on the user's computer), since it can sniff the password. Our **contributions** are as follows:

1. We **define** a general structure of threshold single password authentication (Threshold SPA) systems and propose the **first construction** with a formal proof.
2. We formally present **ideal and real world** definitions for security of Threshold SPA protocols, for the first time in the literature.
3. We **formally prove** the security of our Threshold SPA solution via ideal-real simulation, showing impossibility of **offline dictionary attacks**.
4. Our Threshold SPA method is also secure against **phishing and man-in-the-middle attacks** during authentication, after a secure registration, and **honeypot attacks** during registration and authentication.
5. We present **performance** evaluation numerically, showing that our techniques are easily applicable with today's hardware.
6. Our construction does **not require any change** at the login server side and can work with a variety of storage providers (e.g. mobile devices and cloud providers).

Overview: Our solution achieves full threshold security as follows: We create a salt as the secret *independent* of the password pwd and compute verification information as the hash of salt, password, and login server domain name ls ($Hash(salt\|pwd\|ls)$). Then, the verification information is shared with the login server whereas the salt is secret shared. But, these shares are not directly sent to the storage providers. We employ a layer of encryption to hide each share, and this encryption employs an oblivious pseudorandom function (OPRF) F output over the password pwd as its key. Moreover, each storage provider will use a different key k_i for the OPRF, and thus each share will be encrypted with the corresponding $F_{k_i}(pwd)$ as the key. This means, the storage providers also hold essentially no information regarding the password. This is true because as first observed by Acar et al. [1] (for this discussion simply assume one time pad is employed for encryption, though they discuss in further detail how a block cipher can be employed), when a random value (such as the secret key or shares) is encrypted with the password or any deterministic value derived from the password (such as hash or OPRF over the password), an offline dictionary attack is impossible without knowing what the decryption needs to reveal since any password in the dictionary would yield a valid plaintext.

Later, for authentication, the user interacts with threshold-many servers using the OPRF protocol, reconstructs the original secret salt after decryption with her correct password, and then computes the verification information as $Hash(salt||pwd||ls)$ and sends it along with her username to the login server. Only when the login server and at least threshold-many storage providers collude they can reconstruct the secret salt by trying different passwords, and calculate the hashes offline. Otherwise, offline dictionary attacks are impossible. Consider, for example, the adversarial login server potentially colluding with $t-1$ storage providers. He needs to interact online through the OPRF protocol with at least one honest storage provider to be able to reconstruct the secret salt, which can be rate/attempt limited. Moreover, consider that threshold-many storage providers are colluding while the login server is honest. Even though they can reconstruct a secret salt, since all passwords yield to a valid (in terms of format) secret salt, they can only try to authenticate online with the login server to verify whether or not the secret salt they constructed is the correct one. Again, this can easily be rate/attempt limited.

2   Related Work

Traditional password-based authentication takes place between two parties (a *user* and a *login server*). However, Boyen [5] showed that any password-based authentication between a user and a login server is vulnerable to an *offline dictionary attack* by the login server (or hackers obtaining its database). Tatlı [24] improved offline dictionary attacks on password hashes to find some additional passwords assumed to be strong and complex.

Ford et al. [14] suggest a *password hardening* protocol where the user, holding a weak-password *pwd*, interacts with one or more servers by blinding the password to create a secret credential (to decrypt, or authenticate herself to a login server, etc.) from shares received by the hardening server(s) (which is like storage providers). The hardening server(s) cannot learn anything about the password and the secret unless all of them collude. During the authentication, for each login server, the user runs the password hardening protocol to retrieve the same secret as in the registration by communicating with hardening servers. The solution proposed do not have a formal proof and requires interaction with all of the servers to be able to reconstruct the secret. MacKenzie et al. [20]

propose a threshold PAKE where the password is secure unless threshold-many servers collude. [20] requires servers to know each other. [18] proposes to create a password file storing false passwords called *honeywords* per user account. In case the adversary steals the password file, and mistakenly employs a honeyword, the system is alerted.

Mannan et al. [21] propose to secure user's password from untrusted user computer (malicious browser) assuming the server holds the user password. Camenish et al. [10] distribute the password verification over multiple servers to secure the password against server compromise where the server keeps the hash of username and password $hash(username \| password)$. PwdHash [22] produce a different password for each login server by simply computing the hash of the password and login server domain where the hash is a pseuodorandom function of the domain keyed with the user password $H(password, domain) = PRF_{password}(domain)$ and the server stores the hash value. The discussed solutions do not provide security against offline dictionary attack in case the server database is compromised. Increasing the number of parties by adding storage provider(s) is one way to help prevent offline dictionary attacks.

Acar et al. [1] (with their patent application dating 2010 [2]) present the first provably secure single password authentication protocols where the user employs a cloud or mobile storage provider to keep her secret to prevent offline dictionary attacks. The user's password is secure against offline dictionary attacks unless the storage provider and the server are colluding. Their mobile device based solution inputs the password to the device, and hence provides security against *malware* on the public terminal. They provide security against *phishing* indirectly because the user identifier used at the storage provider depends on the server name. Since the phishing site name is *different* from the actual login server name, the retrieval of the user secret fails. Our main differences are to enable a fully secure threshold construction for the first time, without requiring any changes at the login server, making our solution much easier to deploy.

Following Acar et al. [1], Jarecki et al. [17] provided a device enhanced password authenticated key exchange protocol employing a mobile device storage. Similar to [1], their protocol is secure against offline dictionary attacks assuming the login server and the mobile device are not colluding. They provide a recovery procedure in case the device is lost. They leave threshold authentication as future work, which is what we achieve.

Bicakci et al. [4] discuss briefly a single password solution employing a storage provider for unique blind signatures (similar to Acar et al. [1]), but they neither delve into the details of their solution nor present a security proof. Nevertheless, we are influenced by their work in terms of requiring no change at the login server, and achieve to distribute the storage provider for the first time.

3   Preliminaries

Let $\lambda \in N$ be security parameter. A probabilistic polynomial time (PPT) algorithm A is a probabilistic algorithm taking 1^λ as an input and has running time bounded by a polynomial in λ. We say that a function $negl(\lambda)$ is negligible if for every positive polynomial $poly(\lambda)$ there exists a $\lambda' \in N$ such that $\forall \lambda > \lambda'$ $negl(\lambda) < 1/poly(\lambda)$.

Hash Function: A hash function H is a deterministic function from an arbitrary size input to a fixed size output, denoted $H : \{0,1\}^* \to \{0,1\}^l$. The hash function is assumed to be *collision resistant* if it is hard to find two different inputs $x \neq y$ that hash to the same output $H(x) = H(y)$.

Oblivious Pseudorandom Function (OPRF): A psuedorandom function (PRF) F is a function that takes two inputs: a secret function key k and an input x to compute on, and outputs $F_k(x)$. A function chosen randomly from a PRF family (a PRF with random key k) is secure if it is distinguishable from a random function with the same domain and range with only negligible probability for all PPT distinguishers given oracle access. An Oblivious PRF (OPRF) [15] is a protocol between two parties (*sender* and *receiver*) that securely computes $F_k(x)$ where the k and x are the inputs of *sender* and *receiver*, respectively, such that the sender learns *nothing* from the interaction and the receiver learns $F_k(x)$.

Symmetric Encryption Scheme: consists of three PPT algorithms: $KeyGen(1^\lambda)$ generates a secret key sk, $Enc_{sk}(msg)$ encrypts the message using the secret key and outputs the ciphertext c. The decryption algorithm $Dec_{sk}(c)$ uses the secret sk to decrypt the ciphertext c, and outputs the original message msg. The encryption scheme we use need to be semantically secure.

Threshold Secret Sharing (TSS): consists of two PPT algorithms $<s_1, ..., s_n> \leftarrow TSS(S)$ to create the n shares of the secret S, and for a threshold t we use $S \leftarrow TSSRecon(s_1, ..., s_t)$ to reconstruct the original secret. We employ the methodology of Shamir [23]. The security is that less than threshold many shares provide theoretically no information regarding the original secret.

4   Threshold Single Password Authentication

In a Threshold SPA protocol, there are three types of players. There are **users** who register with one or more **login servers** using (possibly) the same password, and later on authenticate with these login servers. For this purpose, the users store some secret information (that is needed for authentication with the login servers) at one or more **storage providers**. The main objective of a Threshold SPA solution is to protect the user's password against offline dictionary attacks by the storage providers, the login servers, and many other adversaries (including phishing sites). Figure 1 shows an overview of the **registration** and **authentication** phases of a Threshold SPA protocol, considering a single user who registers with a login server and stores the secret at n storage providers. Threshold in this context refers to the fact that the user must communicate with some subset (defined by the threshold) of storage providers to facilitate authentication with the login server. It furthermore refers to the security of the solution: An offline dictionary attack is possible only when the adversary controls the login server *and* at least threshold many storage providers.

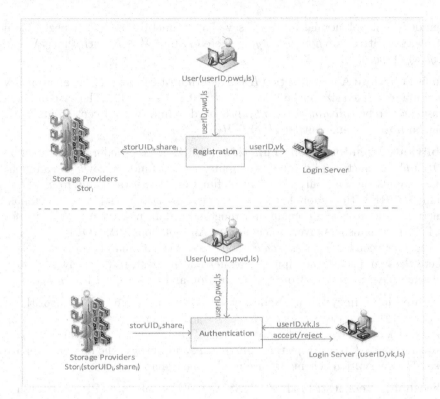

Fig. 1. Threshold-SPA Overview. The registration and authentication protocols are separated by the dashed line.

The **registration** phase is for the user to register with the login server and store the secret among storage providers. The user registers with the login server whose domain is ls using a low-entropy password pwd (only secure against online attacks). The login server obtains the user's verification information vk and identifier $userID$ such that the login server can authenticate the legitimate user whenever the user wants to login. The user further stores some secret information $share_i$ with the storage providers, in a distributed manner. Some identifier $storUID_i$ is associated with this secret to facilitate later retrieval. More formally we have the following multi-party protocol:

Registration

1. **The user's inputs** are a user name $userID$ for the login server whose domain is ls, and a password pwd.
2. **Each storage provider receives as output** an identifier $storUID_i$ and a share $share_i$ and stores the data received in the database. This share is what the user wants to store among the storage providers depending on the Threshold SPA protocol. The identifier is employed for later retrieval of the stored share.

3. **The login server receives as output** an identifier *userID* and a server verification information based on user's password *vk* of the user, and stores them in his database. The verification information *vk* is used by the login server to verify the user during the authentication phase.

The **authentication** phase is for the user who remembers the user name *userID* and the password *pwd* to authenticate herself to the login server with domain *ls* by interacting with *threshold-many* (*t*) storage providers to retrieve and reconstruct the secret needed for authentication. Of course, in general it is possible that $t = n$ and hence all storage providers may need to be contacted.

Authentication

1. **The user's inputs** are as before: the user name *userID*, the password *pwd*, and the domain *ls* of the login server to authenticate with.
2. **The login server's inputs** include the user identifier *userID*, as well as the verification information *vk* corresponding to the user, and its domain *ls*.
3. **Each storage provider's inputs** are the share *share$_i$* that they hold for that user and the identifier *storUID$_i$* of that user.
4. **The login server outputs** accept or reject. The domain name *ls* is employed to prevent phishing/man-in-the-middle attacks.

4.1   Security Definition

We define the *ideal world* and the *real world* for a Threshold SPA protocol, in the spirit of Canetti [11].

Ideal World: The ideal world consists of a user $\mathcal{U}$, a login server $\mathcal{LS}$, *n-many* storage providers $\mathcal{SP} = (Stor_1, Stor_2, \ldots, Stor_n)$ (realize that $\mathcal{SP}$ denotes the set of storage providers), and the universal trusted party $\mathcal{TP}$ **(which is not a real entity, and only exists in the ideal world)**.

Registration

1. $\mathcal{U}$ sends *<userID, pwd>* to $\mathcal{TP}$.
2. $\mathcal{TP}$ computes the necessary steps to obtain the shares *share$_i$* and identifiers *storUID$_i$*, and the verification information *vk*.
3. $\mathcal{TP}$ sends *<userID, vk>* to $\mathcal{LS}$ and *<storUID$_i$, share$_i$>* to each storage provider in $\mathcal{SP}$.

Authentication

1. $\mathcal{U}$ sends *<userID, pwd>* to $\mathcal{TP}$.
2. $\mathcal{TP}$ sends *userID* to $\mathcal{LS}$ for login request.
3. $\mathcal{TP}$ sends *storUID$_i$* to *at least threshold-many* storage providers in $\mathcal{SP}$ for retrieving the secret shares (wlog. assume all storage providers are employed).
4. $\mathcal{SP}$ send their shares *share* = {*share$_1$, share$_2$, \ldots, share$_t$*}.
5. $\mathcal{TP}$ calculates the verification information *vk* using the shares from the $\mathcal{SP}$ and the *pwd* from $\mathcal{U}$, and sends *vk* to $\mathcal{LS}$.

Real World: The real world consists of a user $\mathcal{U}$, a login server $\mathcal{LS}$, and storage providers $\mathcal{SP} = (Stor_1, Stor_2, \ldots, Stor_n)$. There is no universal trusted party $\mathcal{TP}$ for a real world protocol π for the threshold-single password authentication. The parties $\mathcal{U}$, $\mathcal{LS}$, and $\mathcal{SP}$ are involved in the real execution of the protocol π.

Definition 1 (Secure Threshold Single Password Authentication). *Let π be a probabilistic polynomial time (PPT) protocol for a threshold single password authentication. We say that π is secure if for every non-uniform PPT real world adversary $\mathcal{A}$ attacking π, there exists a non-uniform PPT ideal world simulator $\mathcal{S}$ such that for both registration and authentication phases, the real and ideal world interactions and outputs are computationally indistinguishable;*

$$\{IDEAL_{\mathcal{S}(aux)}(userID, pwd, ls, \lambda)\} \equiv_c \{REAL_{\pi,\mathcal{A}(aux)}(userID, pwd, ls, \lambda)\}$$

where $aux \in \{0,1\}^*$ denotes the auxiliary input, and λ is the security parameter.

Note that such an ideal world definition assumes secure and authenticated channels between parties. Furthermore, as there is only a single login server in the ideal world, it does not include phishing (this is why *ls* domain is not part of the ideal world). But it provides security against offline dictionary attacks. In Sect. 5.2 we discuss the security of our solution for attacks like phishing not covered by this ideal model definition.

5   Threshold SPA Construction

Our Threshold SPA construction is represented visually in Fig. 2 (*registration phase*) and Fig. 3 (*authentication phase*). It is also described below.

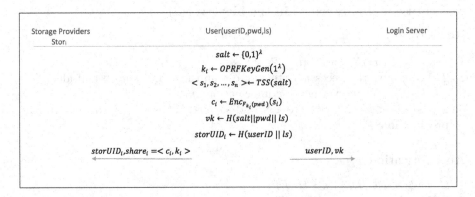

Fig. 2. Threshold SPA construction registration phase

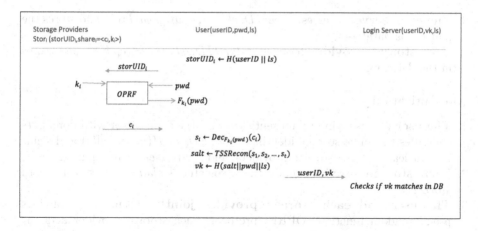

Fig. 3. Threshold SPA construction authentication phase

Registration

1. **The user**
   (a) generates a random *salt* as $salt \leftarrow \{0,1\}^{\lambda}$
   (b) generates one *OPRF* key per storage provider as $k_i \leftarrow OPRFKeyGen(1^{\lambda})$.
   (c) runs threshold secret sharing construction scheme on *salt* to create the secret share for each storage provider $<s_1, s_2, ..., s_n> \leftarrow TSS(salt)$.
   (d) encrypts each share using *oblivious pseudorandom function* of the password *pwd* using generated *OPRF* key of each storage provider obtaining $c_i \leftarrow Enc_{F_{k_i}(pwd)}(s_i)$.
   Remark: Since the secret shares are random bitstrings, offline dictionary attacks on these encryptions are impossible. Therefore, in our solution, even all the storage providers,without the help of the login server, they cannot break the security.
   (e) computes verification information for the login server via a collusion-resistant hash function as $vk = H(salt||pwd||ls)$
   Remark: Salt is a randomstring with size of security parameter. For that reason, the login server, without colluding at least *t-many* storage provider, cannot perform a successful dictionary attack.
   (f) computes the same identifier for all storage providers via a collusion-resistant hash function as $storUID_i \leftarrow H(userID||ls)$.
   Remark: This identifier is only used to retrieve the correct values from the storage providers that serve multiple clients. Remember that *ls* is the domain name of the server the user is registering/connected to (e.g. *ls* = paypal.com).
   (g) sends $<userID, vk = H(salt||pwd||ls)>$ to the login server, and $<storUID_i, share_i = (c_i, k_i)>$ to each storage provider.
   (h) can forget all the data she computed that are cumbersome for her to remember (e.g. K, $k_{i=1,..,n}$).

2. **The login server** receives $<userID, vk = H(salt||pwd||ls)>$, and stores the pair in his database.
3. **Each storage provider** receives $<storUID_i, share_i = (c_i, k_i)>$ and stores in the database.

Authentication

1. **The user** who is trying to authenticate with the login server with domain ls computes the same storage identifier $storUID_i \leftarrow H(userID||ls)$ and sends it to at least t-*many* storage providers, and sends $userID$ to login server.
2. **Each storage provider** finds the associated $<share_i = (k_i, c_i)>$ with $storUID_i$.
3. **The user and each storage provider jointly** execute the oblivious pseudorandom function (OPRF) protocol. Each storage provider acts the sender and the user acts as the receiver in these protocol executions. The user obtains the OPRF value (with key k_i) of the password $F_{k_i}(pwd) \leftarrow OPRF(pwd, k_i)$ as the output.
   Remark: The $OPRF$ result is received *only* by the user.
4. **Each storage provider** sends c_i to the user.
5. **The user** decrypts each ciphertext c_i using the corresponding OPRF output already received to obtain the secret shares $s_i \leftarrow Dec_{F_{k_i}(pwd)}(c_i)$ and computes threshold secret sharing reconstruction algorithm to reconstruct the secret $salt \leftarrow TSSRecon(s_1, s_2, ..., s_t)$.
   Remark: Even when at least threshold-many storage providers collude and reconstruct the ciphertext *salt* of the original secret salt by trying different passwords in the dictionary, they still need to try the resulting salts *online* against the login server, since each password in the dictionary would result in a valid *salt* when decrypting shares S.
6. **The user** computes the verification information as $vk = H(salt||pwd||ls)$ and sends $<userID, vk = H(salt||pwd||ls)>$ to the login server.
7. **The login server** looks up the verification information vk associated with $userID$, and it accepts the response if and only if the vk sent by the user same as the vk in the database.[3]
   Remark: The domain name of the login server ls in the hash is to prevent a phishing/man-in-the-middle attacks. This attack prevention is discussed in Sect. 5.2 in details.

5.1   Security Proof

Theorem 1. *Our Threshold SPA protocol is secure according to Definition 1 against any non-uniform PPT adversary $\mathcal{A}$ corrupting* **the login server $\mathcal{LS}$ and (t-1) many storage providers $\mathcal{SP}_c$**, *assuming that the threshold secret sharing construction is secure, encryption scheme is semantically-secure, the oblivious pseudorandom function is secure, and the hash function is collision resistant.*

---

[3] Or a hashed version of vk can be stored in the database, as usual.

Proof. The simulator $\mathcal{S}$ simulates honest parties in the real world (which are the user $\mathcal{U}$ and $n-t+1$ storage providers denoted by $\mathcal{SP}_h = \{Stor_{i_h}\}$ where $i_h = t, ..., n$ wlog. since all storage providers in our solution are identical) and corrupted parties in the ideal world (which are the login server $\mathcal{LS}$ and $t-1$ storage providers denoted by $\mathcal{SP}_c = \{Stor_{i_c}\}$ where $i_c = 1, ..., t-1$). $\mathcal{S}$ behaves as follows:

Registration Phase:

1. $\mathcal{S}$ receives $<userID, vk = H(salt||pwd||ls), \{storUID_i, share_i = (c_i, k_i)\}_{i=1,...,t-1}>$ from $\mathcal{TP}$.
   Remark: Since $\mathcal{S}$ simulates $\mathcal{LS}$ and $\mathcal{SP}_c = \{Stor_{i_c}\}_{i_c=1,...,t-1}$ in the ideal world, $\mathcal{S}$ receives whatever they receive from $\mathcal{TP}$. Because of the symmetry of the actions of the storage providers in our construction, which ones are corrupted by the adversary does not change anything in the proof as long as the number of corrupted storage providers is below the threshold.
2. $\mathcal{S}$ sends $<userID, vk = H(salt||pwd||ls)>$ to the adversarial $\mathcal{LS}$ in the *real world*.
3. $\mathcal{S}$ follows the protocol as a user choosing a random password pwd' from the dictionary and a secret share s_{i_c}' for each corrupted storage provider, and sends $<storUID_{i_c}, share_{i_c} = (c_{i_c}', k_{i_c})>$ where $c_{i_c}' = Enc_{F_{k_i}(pwd')}(s_{i_c}')$ to each adversarial storage provider $\{Stor_{i_c}\}_{i_c=t,...,n}$.
   Remark: Adversarial storage providers receive encrypted shares of random values with the random password pwd'. There is no efficient way for adversarial storage providers to distinguish this from real behavior since one more storage provider needs to be corrupted to mount a successful offline dictionary attack. For our protocol, all $storUID_i$ values are the same.
4. $\mathcal{S}$ stores all the data in its database.

Authentication Phase:

1. $\mathcal{S}$ receives $<\{storUID_i\}_{i=1,...,t-1}>$ from $\mathcal{TP}$.
   Remark: In general, since $\mathcal{TP}$ may pick any (threshold size) subset of storage providers to work with, and so not all adversarial storage providers may need to be contacted. We are assuming the most powerful adversary here, therefore suppose that all adversarial storage providers are contacted.
2. $\mathcal{S}$ sends $storUID_{i_c}$ to each storage provider $Stor_{i_c}$ where $i_c = 1, ..., t-1$.
   Remark: While $\mathcal{S}$ could already contact the $\mathcal{TP}$ regarding the storage providers at this point (since it already possesses the necessary shares), this may be distinguishable by the adversary. It is possible that the adversarial storage providers will not provide correct values in the real world, and hence the real authentication may fail. The simulator must ensure in that case that the ideal authentication also fails. The following steps are hence necessary for indistinguishability.
3. $\mathcal{S}$ executes the OPRF protocol with each $\{Stor_{i_c}\}_{i_c=1,...,t-1}$ using the password pwd', and receives $p_{i_c} = F_{k_{i_c}}(pwd')$ and also c_{i_c} from each real $Stor_{i_c}$.

4. $\mathcal{S}$ checks whether or not each $\{Stor_{i_c}\}_{i_c=1,\ldots,t-1}$ used the correct corresponding $share_{i_c} = (c_{i_c}, k_{i_c})$ values. $\mathcal{S}$ already possesses the correct values obtained
from $\mathcal{TP}$ during registration in the database. For each p_{i_c}, c_{i_c} received from
$Stor_{i_c}$, $\mathcal{S}$ does the following: Using the corresponding c'_{i_c}, k_i stored in its
database during registration, it computes $p_i = F_{k_i}(pwd')$ locally and checks
whether or not $p_{i_c} = p_i$ and $c_{i_c} = c'_{i_c}$. There are two cases for each $Stor_{i_c}$:

  (a) **Case 1: Correct** $share_{i_c} = (c_{i_c}, k_{i_c})$ **employed by the adversary in
  the real protocol.** $\mathcal{S}$ detects this by verifying that $p_{i_c} = p_i$ and $c_{i_c} = c'_{i_c}$. Therefore, $\mathcal{S}$ sends (c_i, k_i) in its database to $\mathcal{TP}$ where c_i, k_i was
  sent by $\mathcal{TP}$ during the registration.

  (b) **Case 2: Incorrect** $share_{i_c} = (c_{i_c}, k_{i_c})$ **employed by the adversary
  in the real protocol.** $\mathcal{S}$ detects this by verifying that $p_{i_c} \neq p_i$ or $c_{i_c} \neq c'_{i_c}$.

    i. If $p_{i_c} = p_i$ and $c_{i_c} \neq c'_{i_c}$, $\mathcal{S}$ sends (c_{i_c}, k_i) to $\mathcal{TP}$, where k_i was in its
    database.

    ii. If $p_{i_c} \neq p_i$, $\mathcal{S}$ generates a random OPRF key $k'_i \neq k_i$, and sends
    (c_i, k'_i) to $\mathcal{TP}$ where c_i sent by $\mathcal{TP}$ during registration.
    Remark: Even though $\mathcal{S}$ does not have any knowledge about k_{i_c} used
    by $Stor_{i_c}$, he can easily understand if each $Stor_{i_c}$ used the correct
    input k_i by computing the OPRF locally using k_i in the database.
    Then, if incorrect k_{i_c} or c_{i_c} are employed in the real protocol, $\mathcal{S}$ also
    sends incorrect values to $\mathcal{TP}$, in which case both the real and ideal
    responses will fail.

5. $\mathcal{TP}$ calculates and sends the verification information vk and $userID$ to $\mathcal{S}$
based on the $\{c_i, k_i\}_{i=1,\ldots,t-1}$ received from $\mathcal{S}$, together with (at least) one
(c_i, k_i) pair from one of the remaining $n-t+1$ honest storage providers to reach
the threshold t.
Remark: $\mathcal{TP}$ employs the ideal user provided password in the ideal world.
Therefore, if the adversarial storage providers in the real world acted honestly
meaning that the simulator provided correct c_i, k_i pairs, then the calculated
verification information will be valid, since it is computed using the actual
password. On the other hand, if the storage providers acted maliciously in
the real world, $\mathcal{S}$ would have detected this in the previous step, and would
have provided wrong pairs to $\mathcal{TP}$ in the ideal world, so in both worlds the
response will be invalid.

6. $\mathcal{S}$ forwards $<userID, vk>$ to the adversarial $\mathcal{LS}$ in the real world.

Claim. The view of adversary $\mathcal{A}$, controlling the login server $\mathcal{LS}$ and $t-1$ storage providers $\mathcal{SP}_c$, in his interaction with the simulator $\mathcal{S}$ is indistinguishable
from the view of his interaction with a real honest party.

Proof. $\mathcal{S}$ acts differently while sending shares c'_i calculated based on randomly
chosen pwd' instead of sending actual c_i (sent by $\mathcal{TP}$) calculated based on actual
password pwd and executing the $OPRF$ with the $Stor_{i_c}$ using the password
pwd' chosen randomly because $\mathcal{S}$ does not have the correct password. If $\mathcal{A}$ can
distinguish these behaviors, then we can construct another adversary $\mathcal{A}'$ which

breaks either the OPRF construction or TSS construction. We skip this relatively straightforward reductions for the sake of space, but intuitively;

1. **Reduction 1:** The OPRF security ensures that the sender (the adversarial storage providers) cannot distinguish the receiver (the simulated user) input, whether it is the actual password pwd or another randomly chosen password pwd'. Such a reduction will be a hybrid proof, where if at least one adversarial storage provider distinguishes the simulator from the real user, that can be used to distinguish the OPRF receiver input.
2. **Reduction 2:** The TSS security ensures that less than threshold many providers cannot reconstruct the secret and also cannot check if the shares are indeed related to the same secret. Intuitively, if adversarial storage providers can distinguish the simulator, who employs random secret shares during the registration, from the real user, then that can be used to break the security of the underlying threshold secret sharing scheme.

Moreover, even though $\mathcal{A}$ knows the verification information $vk = H(salt\|pwd\|ls)$ and $\{c_i, k_i\}_{i=1,...,t-1}$ from the registration, $\mathcal{A}$ cannot perform an offline dictionary attack on the password because he needs one more (c_i, k_i) to reach the threshold t to reconstruct the secret $salt$. This part can be informationa theoretically secured if an information theoretically secure threshold secret sharing scheme (e.g. Shamir [23]), semantically secure encryption scheme and collision resistant hash function are employed.

Theorem 2. *Our Threshold-SPA protocol is secure according to Definition 1 against any non-uniform PPT adversary $\mathcal{A}$ corrupting threshold many (t) storage providers $\mathcal{SP}_c$, assuming that the threshold secret sharing construction is secure, encryption scheme is semantically-secure, the oblivious pseudorandom function is secure, and the hash function is collision resistant.*

Proof. The simulator $\mathcal{S}$ simulates honest parties (which are the login server $\mathcal{LS}$ n-t storage providers denoted by $SP_h = \{Stor_{ih}\ where\ ih = t+1, ..., n-t\ wlog.\}$ the user $\mathcal{U}$) in the real world and corrupted parties (which are n storage providers denoted by $\mathcal{SP}_c = \{Stor_{i_c}\}_{i_c=1,...,t}$) in the ideal world. $\mathcal{S}$ behaves as follows:

Registration Phase

1. $\mathcal{S}$ receives $<storUID_i, share_i = (c_i, k_i)>$, where $i = 1, ..., t$ from $\mathcal{TP}$. $\mathcal{S}$ follows the protocol as a user choosing a random password pwd' from the dictionary and a secret share s_{i_c} for each corrupted storage provider, and sends $<storUID_{i_c}, share_{i_c} = (c'_{i_c}, k_{i_c})>$ where $c'_{i_c} = Enc_{F_{k_i}pwd'}(s'_{i_c})$ to ℓ-many adversarial storage providers $\{Stor_{i_c}\}_{i_c=1,...,\ell}$ and for the rest, it sends $<storUID_{i_c}, share_{i_c} = (c_i, k_i)>$ in the real world
2. $\mathcal{S}$ stores the all the data in its database.

Authentication Phase

1. S receives $\{storUID_i\}_{i=1,\dots,t}$ from $\mathcal{TP}$.
   Remark: If more than t-many storage providers (e.g. t+1) are corrupted then they can employ a successful offline dictionary attack by taking advantage of TSS. Since a wrong password would result wrong shares (from decryption by the wrong password) and two reconstruction results of these shares (e.g. two different combinations of t+1 shares) will be two different salts. If the password is correct, then the reconstruction of the combinations will result same salt.
2. S sends $storUID_{i_c}$ to each $Stor_{i_c}$ where $i_c = 1, \dots, t$.
3. S executes OPRF protocol with each $\{Stor_{i_c}\}_{i_c=1,\dots,t}$ using the password pwd', and receives $p_{i_c} \leftarrow OPRF(pwd', k_{i_c})$ and c_{i_c} from each $Stor_{i_c}$ in real.
4. S checks whether or not each $\{Stor_{i_c}\}_{i_c=1,\dots,t}$ used the correct corresponding $share_{i_c} = (c_{i_c}, k_{i_c})$ values. S already holds the correct corresponding values during registration in the database. For each (p_{i_c}, c_{i_c}) received from $Stor_{i_c}$, S does the following: Using the corresponding c_i, k_i stored in its database during registration, it computes $p_i = F_{k_i}(pwd')$ locally and checks whether or not $p_{i_c} = p_i$, $c_{i_c} = c_i$ for corresponding $t - \ell$ $Stor_{i_c}$ and $c_{i_c} = c'_{i_c}$ for ℓ many $Stor_{i_c}$. There are two cases for each $Stor_{i_c}$:

   (a) **Case 1: Correct $share_{i_c} = (c_{i_c}, k_{i_c})$ employed by the adversary in the real protocol.** S detects this by verifying that $p_{i_c} = p_i$ and $c_{i_c} = c'_{i_c}$ for ℓ-many $Stor_{i_c}$ and $c_{i_c} = c_i$ for n-ℓ-many $Stor_{i_c}$. Therefore, S sends (c_i, k_i) in its database to $\mathcal{TP}$.

   (b) **Case 2: Incorrect $share_{i_c} = (c_{i_c}, k_{i_c})$ employed by the adversary in the real protocol.** S detects this by verifying that $p_{i_c} \neq p_i$ or $c_{i_c} \neq c'_{i_c}$ for ℓ-many $Stor_{i_c}$ and $c_{i_c} \neq c_i$ for t-ℓ-many $Stor_{i_c}$.
      i. If $p_{i_c} = p_i$ and $c_{i_c} \neq c_i$ are sent by $\alpha - many$ $Stor_{i_c}$ and $p_{i_c} = p_i$ and $c_{i_c} \neq c'_{i_c}$ are sent by $\beta - many$ $Stor_{i_c}$, S sends $\alpha + \beta$ many (c_{i_c}, k_i) to $\mathcal{TP}$, where k_i was in its database, in case $\alpha + \beta \geq n - t + 1$. Otherwise, meaning that $\alpha + \beta = t$, S sends $\alpha + \beta$ many (c_i, k_i) to $\mathcal{TP}$.
      ii. If $p_{i_c} \neq p_i$, S generates a random OPRF key $k'_i \neq k_i$, and sends (c_{i_c}, k'_i) to $\mathcal{TP}$.
      Remark: Even though S does not have any knowledge about k_{i_c} used by $Stor_{i_c}$, he can easily understand if each $Stor_{i_c}$ used the correct input k_i by computing the OPRF locally using k_i in the database. Then, if incorrect k_{i_c} or c_{i_c} are employed in the real protocol, S also sends incorrect values to $\mathcal{TP}$, in which case both the real and ideal responses will fail. On the other hand, if t values were correct in the real protocol, responses in ideal and real worlds will be both valid.
5. S will not receive anything from $\mathcal{TP}$, and hence halts.

Claim. The view of adversary $\mathcal{A}$, controlling t-many storage providers $\mathcal{SP}_c$, in his interaction with the simulator S is indistinguishable from the view of his interaction with a real honest party.

Proof. $\mathcal{S}$ acts differently while sending ℓ-many shares c_i' calculated based on randomly chosen pwd' instead of sending actual c_i (sent by $\mathcal{TP}$) calculated based on actual password pwd and executing the $OPRF$ with the $Stor_{i_c}$ using the password pwd' chosen randomly because $\mathcal{S}$ does not have the correct password. If $\mathcal{A}$ can distinguish this behavior, then we can construct another adversary $\mathcal{A}'$ which breaks either the OPRF construction (as in *Theorem* 1) or password based encryption scheme.

If adversarial storage providers can distinguish the simulator, who employs ℓ random secret shares and $t-\ell$ actual shares during the registration, from the real user, than it can distinguish actual secret share c_i based on pwd from chosen random share c_{i_c}' based on pwd', that can be used to break the security of the underlying encryption scheme. Moreover, $\mathcal{A}$ can compute $s_{i_c} \leftarrow Dec_{F_{k_{i_c}}(pwd^*)}(c_{i_c})$ for each pwd^* in the dictionary, then compute the threshold secret sharing reconstruction algorithm to reconstruct the $salt^* \leftarrow TSSRecon(s_1, s_2, ..., s_t)$. For $\mathcal{A}$ to verify if $salt^*$ (and hence pwd^*) is correct, he needs to have actual verification information $vk = H(salt||pwd||ls)$ to compare, which he does not have, since only the login server has that information.

5.2 Further Analysis

Phishing protection: We consider a strong phishing attack with man-in-the-middle between the user and the login server during authentication (not registration). This means, the user registered with a legitimate server with ls (e.g. ls = paypal.com), but now is trying to authenticate with an attacker with ls' (e.g. ls'=paypat.com). Therefore, during registration, the user computed $storUID_i \leftarrow H(userID||ls)$, but now for authentication, $storUID_i' \leftarrow H(userID||ls')$ values are computed instead. Thus, honest storage providers will not proceed with the OPRF protocol if a phishing domain ls' is used. Even when all storage providers are corrupted by the phishing attacker and the correct salt is obtained, remember that the original registered $vk \leftarrow H(salt||pwd||ls)$, whereas during attack, the user will send $vk' \leftarrow H(salt||pwd||ls')$ to the attacker. This means the phishing/man-in-the-middle attacker cannot authenticate with the original login server on the user's behalf. Furthermore, because of the security of salt, the adversary cannot obtain any information about the user password, unless threshold-many storage providers are also corrupted.

Handling different domains of the same login server: Ross et al. [22] suggest an approach that enables recognizing that amazon.com.de and amazon.co.uk accounts belong to the same login server and one registration is indeed enough. Using the same approach for setting ls values, we can also enable the user to authenticate with any one of the valid domains of the login server.

Remembering the storage providers: The human user is not required to remember the storage providers. There are several easy solutions. As addressed by Camenisch et al. [9], the user can remember only a few storage providers who can help direct to other storage providers. Alternatively, a browser extension or a mobile device may remember the list of storage providers employed. Finally, if all storage providers in the whole system are employed by all users, such a public list can be employed, and t of them may be contacted by the user for any given authentication attempt. Observe that publicly listing storage providers does not affect cryptographic security. Our ideal model allows the adversary to know all the storage providers. Therefore, their identities are not hidden when protecting against offline dictionary attacks.

6   Performance Evaluation

In this section, we discuss performance evaluation for the user and storage providers. Since the login server acts the same as current servers, we did not discuss its efficiency. Performance measurement is processed on a standard laptop machine with Intel Core(TM) i7-5600U CPU 2.60 GHz, 8.00 GB RAM, and 64-bit OS. For our implementation, we choose AES [12], OPRF in [17], and TSS [23] with various thresholds. Table 1 shows the computational performance of the authentication and registration phases. For the registration, the storage providers *do not* compute anything, only receive and store some value. Finally, the user can communicate with the storage providers in parallel, which decreases the network round trip to 1.5 rounds per authentication, which should be added to the login total time in practice.

Table 1. Performance evaluation of Threshold SPA (in milliseconds)

	User (Reg.)	User (Auth.)	Storage provider	Login total
1–1 Threshold	0.85	1.14	0.35	1.50
3–6 Threshold	2.84	2.83	0.70	3.53
5–10 Threshold	4.46	3.99	1.30	5.30

7   Conclusion

Recent studies [1,4,17] introduced cloud or mobile storage providers to secure passwords against offline dictionary attacks currently prevalent in password-based authentication systems. They provided solutions that ensure that as long as the adversary does not corrupt the login server and the storage provider together, offline dictionary attacks will be prevented. For the first time, in this paper, we provide novel techniques to ensure that multiple storage providers can be employed, and the adversary now must corrupt the login server *and threshold-many* storage providers to be able to mount an offline dictionary attack. We provided an ideal and real world security definition and presented an ideal-real simulation proof. We further ensure phishing, man-in-the-middle, and honeypot attacks are also thwarted. Lastly, our construction employs efficient symmetric key primitives and can easily work with today's hardware, even on mobile devices.

Acknowledgements. We thank Prof. Jens Groth from University College London for his valuable comments and discussions that greatly improved the manuscript, and acknowledge the support of TÜBİTAK (the Scientific and Technological Research Council of Turkey) under project numbers 114E487 and 115E766, European Union COST Action IC1306, and the Royal Society of UK Newton Advanced Fellowship NA140464.

References

1. Acar, T., Belenkiy, M., Küpçü, A.: Single password authentication. Comput. Netw. **57**(13), 2597–2614 (2013)
2. Belenkiy, M., Acar, T., Morales, H., Küpçü, A.: Securing passwords against dictionary attacks (2015). US Patent 9,015,489
3. Bellovin, S.M., Merritt, M.: Encrypted key exchange: password-based protocols secure against dictionary attacks. In: Proceedings of the 1992 IEEE Computer Society Symposium on Research in Security and Privacy, pp. 72–84. IEEE (1992)
4. Bicakci, K., Atalay, N.B., Yuceel, M., van Oorschot, P.C.: Exploration and field study of a browser-based password manager using icon-based passwords. In: Workshop on Real-Life Cryptographic Protocols and Standardization (2011)
5. Boyen, X.: Hidden credential retrieval from a reusable password. In: Proceedings of the 4th International Symposium on Information, Computer, and Communications Security, pp. 228–238. ACM (2009)
6. Boyen, X.: HPAKE: password authentication secure against cross-site user impersonation. In: Garay, J.A., Miyaji, A., Otsuka, A. (eds.) CANS 2009. LNCS, vol. 5888, pp. 279–298. Springer, Heidelberg (2009). doi:10.1007/978-3-642-10433-6_19
7. Boyko, V., MacKenzie, P., Patel, S.: Provably secure password-authenticated key exchange using Diffie-Hellman. In: Preneel, B. (ed.) EUROCRYPT 2000. LNCS, vol. 1807, pp. 156–171. Springer, Heidelberg (2000). doi:10.1007/3-540-45539-6_12
8. Camenisch, J., Enderlein, R.R., Neven, G.: Two-server password-authenticated secret sharing UC-secure against transient corruptions. In: Katz, J. (ed.) PKC 2015. LNCS, vol. 9020, pp. 283–307. Springer, Heidelberg (2015). doi:10.1007/978-3-662-46447-2_13
9. Camenisch, J., Lehmann, A., Lysyanskaya, A., Neven, G.: Memento: how to reconstruct your secrets from a single password in a hostile environment. In: Garay, J.A., Gennaro, R. (eds.) CRYPTO 2014. LNCS, vol. 8617, pp. 256–275. Springer, Heidelberg (2014). doi:10.1007/978-3-662-44381-1_15
10. Camenisch, J., Lehmann, A., Neven, G.: Optimal distributed password verification. In: Proceedings of the 22nd ACM SIGSAC Conference on Computer and Communications Security, pp. 182–194. ACM (2015)
11. Canetti, R.: Security and composition of multiparty cryptographic protocols. J. Cryptology **13**(1), 143–202 (2000)
12. Daemen, J., Rijmen, V.: The Design of Rijndael: AES-The Advanced Encryption Standard. Springer, Heidelberg (2013)
13. Florencio, D., Herley, C.: A large-scale study of web password habits. In: Proceedings of the 16th International Conference on World Wide Web, pp. 657–666. ACM (2007)
14. Ford, W., Kaliski, B.S.: Server-assisted generation of a strong secret from a password. In: Proceedings of the IEEE 9th International Workshops on Enabling Technologies: Infrastructure for Collaborative Enterprises (WET ICE 2000), pp. 176–180. IEEE (2000)

15. Freedman, M.J., Ishai, Y., Pinkas, B., Reingold, O.: Keyword search and oblivious pseudorandom functions. In: Kilian, J. (ed.) TCC 2005. LNCS, vol. 3378, pp. 303–324. Springer, Heidelberg (2005). doi:10.1007/978-3-540-30576-7_17

16. Jarecki, S., Kiayias, A., Krawczyk, H.: Round-optimal password-protected secret sharing and T-PAKE in the password-only model. In: Sarkar, P., Iwata, T. (eds.) ASIACRYPT 2014. LNCS, vol. 8874, pp. 233–253. Springer, Heidelberg (2014). doi:10.1007/978-3-662-45608-8_13

17. Jarecki, S., Krawczyk, H., Shirvanian, M., Saxena, N.: Device-enhanced password protocols with optimal online-offline protection. In: Proceedings of the 11th ACM on Asia Conference on Computer and Communications Security, pp. 177–188. ACM (2016)

18. Juels, A., Rivest, R.L.: Honeywords: making password-cracking detectable. In: Proceedings of the 2013 ACM SIGSAC Conference on Computer & Communications Security, pp. 145–160. ACM (2013)

19. Katz, J., Ostrovsky, R., Yung, M.: Efficient password-authenticated key exchange using human-memorable passwords. In: Pfitzmann, B. (ed.) EUROCRYPT 2001. LNCS, vol. 2045, pp. 475–494. Springer, Heidelberg (2001). doi:10.1007/3-540-44987-6_29

20. MacKenzie, P., Shrimpton, T., Jakobsson, M.: Threshold password-authenticated key exchange. In: Yung, M. (ed.) CRYPTO 2002. LNCS, vol. 2442, pp. 385–400. Springer, Heidelberg (2002). doi:10.1007/3-540-45708-9_25

21. Mannan, M., van Oorschot, P.C.: Using a personal device to strengthen password authentication from an untrusted computer. In: Dietrich, S., Dhamija, R. (eds.) FC 2007. LNCS, vol. 4886, pp. 88–103. Springer, Heidelberg (2007). doi:10.1007/978-3-540-77366-5_11

22. Ross, B., Jackson, C., Miyake, N., Boneh, D., Mitchell, J.C.: Stronger password authentication using browser extensions. In: Usenix Security, Baltimore, MD, USA, pp. 17–32 (2005)

23. Shamir, A.: How to share a secret. Commun. ACM **22**(11), 612–613 (1979)

24. Tatli, E.I.: Cracking more password hashes with patterns. IEEE Trans. Inf. Forensics Secur. **10**(8), 1656–1665 (2015)

Towards a Toolkit for Utility and Privacy-Preserving Transformation of Semi-structured Data Using Data Pseudonymization

Saffija Kasem-Madani$^{(\boxtimes)}$, Michael Meier$^{(\boxtimes)}$, and Martin Wehner

University of Bonn, 53113 Bonn, Germany
{kasem,mm,wehner}@cs.uni-bonn.de
https://net.cs.uni-bonn.de/wg/itsec/staff/

Abstract. We present a flexibly configurable toolkit for the automatic pseudonymization of datasets that keeps certain utility. The toolkit could be used to pseudonymize data in order to preserve the privacy of data owners while data processing and to meet the requirements of the new European general data protection regulation. We define some possible utility requirements and corresponding utility options a pseudonym can meet. Based on that, we define a policy language that can be used to produce machine-readable utility policies. The utility policies are used to configure the toolkit to produce a pseudonymized dataset that offers the utility options. Here, we follow a confidentiality-by-default principle. I.e., only the data mentioned in the policy is transformed and included in the pseudonymized dataset. All remaining data is kept confidential. This stays in contrast to common pseudonymization techniques that replace only personal or sensitive data of a dataset with pseudonyms, while keeping any other information in plaintext. If applied appropriately, our approach allows for providing pseudonymized datasets that includes less information that can be misused to infer personal information about the individuals the data belong to.

Keywords: Privacy · Pseudonymization · Data utility · Confidentiality · Policy language · Utility requirements

1 Introduction

Pseudonymizing privacy-relevant datasets is done to keep the contained privacy-relevant information confidential. On the other hand, the pseudonymized data should keep some of its original utility for fulfilling the use case. Consider the following application scenario: multiple sensors want to share log file content with a centralized analysis entity for obtaining knowledge of indicators of possible network attacks. They want to hide the privacy-relevant information contained in the log file data. On the other hand, they are interested in the results of the analysis the centralized analysis entity would provide. Hence, certain utility of

© Springer International Publishing AG 2017
J. Garcia-Alfaro et al. (Eds.): DPM/CBT 2017, LNCS 10436, pp. 163–179, 2017.
DOI: 10.1007/978-3-319-67816-0_10

the data must be kept. On the other hand, they want to keep person-identifiable information contained in the logfiles confidential. In order to solve the resulting conflict between privacy and utility requirements, the sensors agree with the analysis entity on the required utility options the data should fulfill. Then, they transform the data into a pseudonymized dataset with utility options that meet the formulated requirements.

Another motivating example is the data processing of IoT devices in smart buildings. Consider a simple smart building that consists of actors holding one of the roles *system administrator* and *employee*. The sensors include a *door* to the building that permits entrance using an employee's smart card. For that, a *smart card reader* is included. When an employee makes use of the smartcard reader, it gathers *working time data* with the employee's ID eID, the time of entrance t_e and the time of leave t_l, storing (eID, t_e) and (eID, t_l), respectively. For simplicity, we assume that presence time equals working time. On receiving a signal from the smartcard reader's site, it immediately activates the door to allow for entrance or leave. The data is stored for three purposes: Working time data is collected for tracking the total hours of work of each employee (purpose 1) and for reproducing the exact working times for conflict resolution (purpose 2). The times employees enter and leave the building are also collected to be able to reconstruct the presence of individuals in certain time intervals, e.g. in case of theft detection (purpose 3). While some of the data is processed and stored locally on sensors side's registers, e.g. the signals the barrier receives for activation, some other data, e.g. the working time information is sent to a centralized database. Despite the fact that not all the data is collected and stored on a centralized system, the administrators are allowed to access the data. Obviously, the collected data is person-identifiable and prone to be misused for other purposes. A curious administrator may use the working time data to infer the daily routine of an employee, including habits like starting to work the same time every day [28]. This clearly contradicts the stated purposes the data have been collected for. Moreover, the use of data containing person-identifiable information is legally restricted [9].

In this work, we present a tool that transforms textual data into a representation that meets certain, purpose-specific utility requirements without revealing the privacy-relevant plaintext. We call that data transformation *pseudonymization with utility options*. Our contribution is as follows:

1. We define a categorization of utility requirements a pseudonymized dataset can meet.
2. We present an XML-based policy language that allows for a precise definition and machine-readable formulation of the defined utility requirements in a so-called utility policy.
3. We present a pseudonymization toolkit that allows for
   - a definition of utility requirements using the XML policy language;
   - a transformation of a given file that contains semi-structured data into a data representation in an XML structure that can be referenced by a utility policy;
   - generating a pseudonymized dataset with utility options according to the utility policy.

Note that the goal of this work is not to trade-off privacy for utility. We aim at providing pseudonymized datasets that makes it difficult to an attacker to retrieve privacy-relevant information while keeping desired utility. This is done by carefully selecting utility options that a pseudonymized dataset should provide. Compared to providing access to the plaintext data, the resulting pseudonymized dataset keeps most of the contained information confidential. Compared to sanitizing data by identifying and removing any privacy-relevant information, our technique provides only information that is necessary for the computation. This makes it harder for an attacker to use such a pseudonymized dataset to re-identify persons. However, we must point out that our goal is not to anonymize data.

The rest of this work is structured as follows: After introducing notions and cryptographic facts required for this work in Sect. 2, related work is reviewed in Sect. 3. We describe the construction of pseudonyms with utility options in Sect. 4. The architecture of the pseudonymization toolkit is described in Sect. 5. In Sect. 6, the security requirements for a system that processes and stores pseudonymized datasets is discussed. Finally, the work is concluded and future work is discussed in Sect. 7.

2   Preliminaries

To enhance the understanding of the approach presented in this work, we shortly introduce the relevant basic notions.

We consider a dataset D being a semi-structured set of plaintext data entries d_i, $1 \leq i \leq n$, where n is the number of data entries in D. Each data entry consists of data items d_{ij}, $j \in \{1, \cdots, m_i\}$, where m_i is the number of data items of the data entry d_i. A pseudonym of a data item d_{ij} contained in a data entry $d_i \in D$ is a sequence of l_{ij} utility tags, i.e. $(u_1(d_{ij}), \cdots u_{l_{ij}}(d_{ij}))$, each of them consisting of possibly multiple strings. Its construction depends on the utility it is intended to represent. The set of all pseudonyms of all data items d_{ij} and all data entries d_i contained in D is the pseudonymized superset of D,

$$\mathcal{P}(D) = \bigcup_{i=1}^{n} \bigcup_{j=1}^{m_i} p(d_{ij}).$$

The set of pseudonyms that fulfill a subset of utility requirements is called a pseudonymized dataset $P(D)$, where $P(D) \subseteq \mathcal{P}(D)$. In the following, we use the abbreviation UR for utility requirement, and PsD for pseudonymized dataset. Depending on the utility options required, cryptosystems may be used to generate pseudonyms. A symmetric cryptosystem is a cryptosystem that utilizes the same key k for encryption and decryption. In an asymmetric cryptosystem, a public key k_{pub} and a corresponding private key k_{priv} are used for encryption and decryption, respectively. Original data is referred to as plaintexts, and encrypted data as ciphertexts. A cryptosystem is called deterministic if, given a plaintext p and a key k, the output is always the same ciphertext $c(p)$, independently from the execution of the cryptographic algorithm. Its output only relies on the given input plaintext and the key. Otherwise, the cryptosystem is called probabilistic [13]. A homomorphic cryptosystem produces ciphertexts that allow for executing operations on them. These operations produce encrypted results of corresponding homomorphic operations on the underlying plaintexts. If the homomorphic operation on the plaintexts is an addition or multiplication, the cryptosystem is called additively homomorphic or multiplicatively homomorphic, respectively. Homomorphic cryptosystems that allow for the execution of simple operations, like addition or multiplication, are called partially homomorphic (PH). Somewhat and threshold homomorphic cryptosystems (SWH) allow for the execution of functions of limited deep on the ciphertexts [3,4]. Fully homomorphic cryptosystems (FH) produce ciphertexts that can be used for arbitrary computation [12]. Due to their impracticability for our use cases, we are not considering SWH and FH cryptosystems here and omit an explanation.

The AES is an example of a symmetric, deterministic cryptosystem [7]. The Paillier cryptosystem is an asymmetric, probabilistic, additively homomorphic cryptosystem [20]. The RSA cryptosystem in its unpadded version is asymmetric and deterministic [23]. The ElGamal cryptosystem is asymmetric and probabilistic [11]. Both RSA and ElGamal cyptosystems are multiplicative homomorphic.

3 Related Work

Saving some specific utility of structured data while keeping the plaintext content confidential has been well-studied for different usage scenarios. For SQL databases, Popa et al. have introduced CryptDB [21], a confidentiality-preserving database system that enables for SQL querying encrypted database content. For that, it provides certain, database-utility preserving encryption schemes. In contrast to our work, it only encrypts database entries that have been identified as sensitive. Any other data is kept in plaintext. Among other reasons, this increases the probability of successful inference and correlation attacks [18]. Also, the whole approach is database-specific. For processing textual data, CryptDB requires fundamental conceptual adjustments.

Analogous to our approach on textual data, Bkakria et al. [25] present a flexible, policy-based configuration of utility-preserving encryption of relational structured data. It includes the detection of conflicting goals in a policy and algorithms that propose conflict resolution.

LidSec [14] is a use-case independent pseudonymization framework for the preparation of textual data for data sharing. The data consists of so-called entities of possibly multiple features. One can choose for each entity feature whether it should be kept in plaintext or removed. Other possibilities include suppressing, i.e. replacing the value of a feature with a pseudonym, or removing an entity completely. Different data formats can be used. In contrast to our work, the pseudonyms generated here provide a comparably limited variety of utility options, e.g. the ability to check whether underlying plaintexts are equal. For more utility, the affiliated data has to be represented in plaintext.

FLAIM [27] is an open-source log data sanitization tool for privacy-respecting information sharing. FLAIM uses sanitization rules that technically define how to treat the data. While the goal of our approach is to reach reversible anonymization using pseudonymization, the goal of FLAIM is to anonymize data in a utility-preserving way. Moreover, our utility policy approach allows for describing the desired utility of a PsD without the need to describe the pseudonymization technique.

Flegel et al. [10] describe how to preserve the privacy of involved individuals when sharing security incident-related information in an early warning system (EWS). After analyzing the URs of each party involved in the EWS, they define pseudonyms consisting of linkability and disclosability tags to achieve privacy-respecting linkability and disclosability, respectively. In contrast to our approach, their approach is use-case dependent and does not include the definition of pseudonyms that allow for performing mathematical operations.

There exist several approaches to pseudonymize textual data for reversible, context-based confidentiality of privacy-relevant information [2,19,22]. All these approaches have in common that they are application-dependent. Different from our approach, almost all of them do not provide a policy that clearly indicates the desired and achieved utility of the PsD. This makes it hard to estimate the quality of a PsD and to extend the utility after the data has been pseudonymized once. Also, the definition of the pseudonymization mechanism depends on the utilized pseudonymization techniques rather than the desired utility.

Several privacy policy languages for various different purposes have been introduced [15,17,29]. To the best of our knowledge, none of the introduced languages can be utilized for the definition of URs for certain data items of a dataset.

4   Utility Requirements and Construction of Pseudonyms with Utility Options

Given a semi-structured data file and the URs as an input, the pseudonymization toolkit automatically generates and outputs a file that contains the PsD.

To construct a PsD of a semi-structured set of data entries D, the purposes of processing must be identified. Based on the analysis of the purposes, the URs for each d_{ij} are defined. For each d_{ij}, one or more utility tags will be constructed based on the defined URs. This is done by applying appropriate mechanisms to d_{ij}. The resulting pseudonym $p(d_{ij})$ is then a sequence of all constructed utility tags. For each UR, $p(d_{ij})$ includes a utility tag $u_l(d_{ij})$ that offers the corresponding utility option of d_{ij}. In case cryptographic parameters are required, they will be included in the belonging utility tags.

4.1   Utility Requirements

In the following, we present a definition and classification of the utility options which a pseudonym can support to meet corresponding URs.

Linkability. A pseudonym $p(d_{ij}) \in P(D)$ of a plaintext $d_{ij} \in D$ is linkable with respect to a relation r, i.e. fulfills the UR "linkability w.r.t. r", if, given another pseudonym $p(d_{xy})$ that is linkable w.r.t. the same relation r, one can determine whether the underlying plaintexts d_{ij} and d_{xy} are in a certain relation r or not. This can be modeled by a function $f : (P(D), P(D)) \rightarrow \{0, 1\}$ with

$$f(p(d_{ij}), p(d_{xy})) \begin{cases} 1, & \text{if}(d_{ij}, d_{xy}) \in r \quad (1) \\ 0, & \text{else} \quad (2) \end{cases}$$

Linkability w.r.t. a relation r is available on a set of pseudonyms P, if the aforementioned function f is defined on all pseudonyms of P.

Disclosability. A pseudonym $p(d_{ij}) \in P$ of a plaintext $d_{ij} \in D$ is disclosable, i.e. fulfills the UR "disclosability", if a mapping $p^{-1}(p(d_{ij})) = d_{ij}$ is defined for $p(d_{ij})$.

Mathematical Operations. A mathematical operation $+$ is available on a set of pseudonyms P, if there is a corresponding operation $*$ that can be applied to each pair of pseudonyms $p(d_{xy}), p(d_{ij}) \in P$ with

$$p(d_{ij}) * p(d_{xy}) = p(d_{ij} + d_{xy})$$

for all plaintexts $d_{xy}, d_{ij} \in D$ with pseudonyms in P, and there is a mapping $p^{-1} : P \rightarrow D$ with

$$p^{-1}(p(d_{ij} + d_{xy})) = d_{ij} + d_{xy}$$

for all $p(d_{ij}), p(d_{xy}) \in P$.

Binding the Accessibility of the Utility Options. The accessibility of a utility option in a PsD can be bound to certain roles a subject in the system may hold, or to a purpose that has to be fulfilled. Hence, the utility of a pseudonym $p(d_{ij})$ itself underlies access control mechanisms.

In the Smart Building example stated in the Introduction, the URs of the stated purposes are as follows:

- Purpose 1: "How many hours has employee x worked?"
  UR 1:
  - The accountant must be able to disclose the employee's ID eID to create the payroll.
  - The accountant must be able to calculate the working hours of each day by calculating the differences between the corresponding entrance and leaving times t_e, t_l to create the payroll.
- Purpose 2: "At what time has employee x entered and left the building, respectively?" (conflict resolution).
  UR 2:
  - The conflict resolver of the company must be able to disclose eID, t_e and t_l to prove the entrance and leaving times used for calculating the working hours in case an employee has not consented the payroll.
- Purpose 3: "Who of the employees has been present during a time interval T?" (theft detection).

UR 3:

- When a detected theft is likely to have happened in a certain time interval $T = [t_i, t_j]$, the security responsible of the company must be able to disclose t_e and t_l to identify the presence of employees in that time interval, i.e. all employees with last $t_e < t_j$ and last $t_l > t_i$. He also must be able to disclose all eID that correspond to suspicious timestamps.

4.2   Pseudonym Construction

The pseudonyms are constructed as sequences of utility tags, where each utility tag is used to provide a certain, well-defined utility option. We give example mechanisms that can be used to generate utility tags of a pseudonym.

Pseudonyms with Linkability options. Selecting an appropriate mechanism for generating pseudonyms that are linkable depends on the desired relation r. A simple example for the linkability option is linkability with respect to equality. Here, pseudonyms are generated such that for two given pseudonyms $p(d_{ij})$ and $p(d_{xy})$ of d_{ij} and d_{xy}, $f(p(d_{ij}), p(d_{xy})) = 1$ implies $d_{ij} = d_{xy}$, and $f(p(d_{ij}), p(d_{xy})) = 0$ implies $d_{ij} \neq d_{xy}$. Pseudonyms that are linkable w.r.t. equality can be obtained by generating a utility tag $u(d_{ij})$ of d_{ij} using a symmetric block cipher. For a fast and secure utility tag and pseudonym generation, e.g. AES may be utilized as a pseudonymization function. To prevent the disclosure of d_{ij}, the symmetric key has to be kept secret.

The notion for a pseudonym with a utility tag for linkability w.r.t. equality for d_{ij} would be $p(d_{ij}) = (\cdots, u_=(d_{ij}), \cdots)$. In case AES is used for the generation, $u_=(d_{ij}) = (AES_{k_=}(d_{ij}))$. Note that the key $k_=$ is not rolled out with the utility tag.

Pseudonyms with the Disclosability option. To generate a disclosable pseudonym of d_{ij}, one may utilize a symmetric encryption scheme using a key k_{discl}. To obtain a unique disclosable pseudonym for each d_{ij}, randomization is included. One possibility is to append a nonce $n_{d_{ij}}$ of fixed, known length to each plaintext under consideration before encrypting. k_{discl} is made accessible to an entity that is responsible for managing the disclosure of the plaintext of d_{ij}. This is to ensure that only making use of the disclosability option makes plaintext information available.

The notion for a pseudonym with a utility tag for disclosability for d_{ij} would be $p(d_{ij}) = (\cdots, u_{discl}(d_{ij}), \cdots)$. In case AES is used for the generation, $u_{discl}(d_{ij}) = (AES_{k_{discl}}(d_{ij}|n_{d_{ij}}), k_{discl})$. Note that the key k_{discl} is rolled out within the utility tag. To prevent the misuse of this utility option, a secure handling of the key in the processing system is required.

Pseudonyms with the Mathematical Operation option. In this work, the utility option for a UR "mathematical operation" is implemented using homomorphic encryption. To apply the mathematical operation "addition" on data items d_{ij} from a subset $D_+ \subseteq D$, we use the Paillier cryptosystem [20] using the same public key $k_{+_{pub}}$ for generating the corresponding utility tags of all the d_{ij}. The resulting pseudonym p_{ij} includes a utility tag $u_+(d_{ij})$ that can be homomorphically added with other utility tags $u_+(d_{xy})$. The result of the homomorphic addition is an encrypted sum. To decrypt the sum, access to the private key k_{+priv} that corresponds to k_{+pub} is required.

The notion for a pseudonym with a utility tag for the addition operation for d_{ij} would be $p(d_{ij}) = (\cdots, u_+(d_{ij}), \cdots)$. In case the Paillier cryptosystem is used for the generation, $u_+(d_{ij}) = (Paillier_{k_{+pub}}(d_{ij}), k_+ = (k_{+pub}, k_{+priv}))$. Note that the key $k_+ = (k_{+pub}, k_{+priv})$ is rolled out within the utility tag. Due to the construction of homomorphic cryptosystems, k_{+priv} can be used to decrypt the pseudonyms and hence, allows for disclosure of the plaintexts d_{ij}. Also, k_{+pub} can be used to malleableize $u_+(d_{ij})$, i.e. for a known plaintext x, generating a utility tag $u_+(x)$ and homomorphically add it to a given $u_+(d_{ij})$, yielding $u_+(d_{ij}+x)$. Subtracting x from the decrypted sum would reveal d_{ij}. Thus, there is the need for a secure handling of the public and private key on the processing system.

For the utility option of the mathematical operation "multiplication", the ElGamal cryptosystem is utilized similarly.

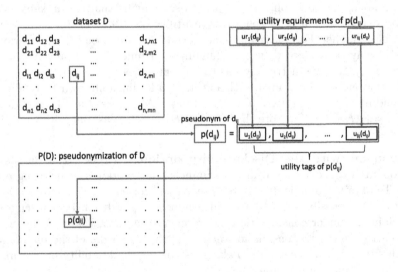

Fig. 1. Structure of a PsD with utility options.

Pseudonyms with utility options bound to roles or purposes. For controlling the access to a utility option of a pseudonym $P(d_{ij})$, the matching utility tag $u(d_{ij})$ can be bound to a role or purpose. For that, it is probabilistically encrypted. The decryption key can be accessed only by a subject holding that certain role, or is proving to fulfill the dedicated purpose, respectively. This additional encryption introduces a layer of access control on the pseudonyms. To obtain a probabilistic encryption of a utility tag, we use a symmetric block cipher, e.g. AES, together with a nonce of fixed known length for generating each utility tag. The goal of using probabilistic encryption is to prevent a possible attacker from detecting duplicate plaintexts by checking encrypted utility tags and hence, gaining a benefit that might rise the success probability of a correlation attack using background knowledge.

The key used for role or purpose binding of the availability of a utility option of a utility tag must be securely stored and processed in the system.

Summarizing, a PsD $P(D)$ of a dataset D can be considered as a set

$$P(D) \subseteq \bigcup_{i=1}^{n} \bigcup_{j=1}^{m_i} p(d_{ij}).$$

Each utility option of each d_{ij} addressed in the utility policy is represented in the PsD as a utility tag. This results in a pseudonym of d_{ij} being a sequence of utility tags $u_k(d_{ij})$, i.e.

$$p(d_{ij}) = (u_1(d_{ij}), \cdots, u_{l_{ij}}(d_{ij})),$$

where l_{ij} is the number of utility tags required for meeting all URs defined for $p(d_{ij})$. I.e., l_{ij} equals the number of URs. The strings required to offer a single utility option are summarized in one utility tag. Figure 1 shows the structure of a PsD with utility options.

Note that for each utility tag, corresponding cryptographic parameters may be required for security reasons. In order to prevent a misuse of the utility options offered by a PsD, the parameters have to be treated carefully in the processing systems.

Note that generating pseudonyms with utility options may have side effects that lead to a disclosure of unwanted information by combining the knowledge gained from different utility options. For that, the definition of the URs has to be done very carefully and respecting the principle of data minimization and purpose binding [9] together with a strict access control.

In the example of the Introduction, data produced in a simple smart building could be pseudonymized according to each described UR stated in Sect. 4.1. This would result in utility tags constructed as follows:

Req. 1: Tracking the total number of hours of an employee.

Utility tags:

- eID is probabilistically encrypted using a purpose-specific key k_1 that is only accessible for that purpose. The result is $el_{k_1}(eID)$.
- Every working day, t_e and t_l are used to generate pseudonyms that preserve distances within a limited time interval, e.g. using the functions described in [16]. The result is $ed(t_e)$ and $ed(t_l)$, respectively. As soon as the smartcard reader gathers an employee's leave, it calculates the difference of $ed(t_e)$ and $ed(t_l)$, yielding $ed(t_l - t_e)$. For purpose binding, the result is encrypted using k_1 to $el_{k_1}(ed(t_l - t_e))$.

Req. 2: Resolving conflicts about the working hours between an employee and the company.

Utility tags: eID, t_e and t_l are probabilistically encrypted using a purpose-specific key k_2 that is only accessible for that purpose. The result is $(e1_{k_2}(eID), e1_{k_2}(t_e), e1_{k_2}(t_l))$. On conflicts, only conflict-resolving subjects in the system can access the key and hence decrypt and access the plaintext values.

Req. 3: Suspect identification after theft detection.

Utility tags: eID, t_e and t_l must be probabilistically encrypted using a purpose-specific key k_3. The result is $(e1_{k_3}(eID), e1_{k_3}(t_e), e1_{k_3}(t_l))$. To identify suspects, only security responsible subjects can access the key and decrypt and access the plaintext values. The PsD is then

– for the time stamps t_e and t_l:
  $u_1(t_e, t_l) = (e1_{k_1}(ed(t_e)), e1_{k_1}(ed(t_l)), e1_{k_1}(ed(t_l - t_e)), k_1))$
  $u_2(t_e, t_l) = (e1_{k_2}(t_e), e1_{k_2}(t_l)), k_2)$. $u_3(t_e, t_l) = (e1_{k_3}(t_e), e1_{k_3}(t_l)), k_3)$. Note that each value of the utility tag is generated as soon as the corresponding plaintext value occurs.
  The result is $p(t_e, t_l) = (u_1(t_e, t_l), u_2(t_e, t_l), u_3(t_e, t_l))$;
– for the employee's ID eID: $p(eID) = (u_1(eID), u_2(eID), u_3(eID))$.
  $u_1(eID) = (e1_{k_1}(eID), k_1)$,
  $u_2(eID) = (e1_{k_2}(eID), k_2)$, and
  $u_3(eID) = (e1_{k_3}(eID), k_3)$;

k_1 is only accessible to the accountant for payroll generation, k_2 is only accessible to the conflict resolver in case of conflicts, and k_3 is only accessible to the security responsible in case of theft detection.

5   Architecture

The pseudonymization toolkit consists of a policy builder, an input transformation tool, and a pseudonymization tool that utilizes pseudonymization functions. Given a semi-structured data file and the URs as an input, the pseudonymization toolkit automatically generates and outputs a pseudonymized data file (Fig. 2).

The Transformation Tool

The toolkit accepts data of arbitrary semi-structured data formats as an input. In order to allow the pseudonymization tool to address the data items and apply the corresponding pseudonymization rules on each addressed data item, the transformation tool generates an XML structured representation of the input dataset. It identifies the data entries and generates an XML node for each data entry. For each identified data item of a data entry, a corresponding sub-node is generated in the XML representation.

The transformation tool includes Python scripts [24] as plug-ins for different semi-structured data formats, including JSON [6], YAML [1], CSV [26] and the content of electronic health records written in HL7 compatible formats [8].

The Policy Builder

The policy builder is the human interface to the toolkit. It provides a GUI for passing the file that contains the plaintext data D and inserting the URs that have to be provided by each data item. With the input, it generates a machine-readable policy using the specific XML based policy language.

The Policy Language

A utility policy has two purposes. Firstly, it serves as a machine-readable, yet human-comprehensible documentation of the URs for a PsD of a dataset D. Secondly, the pseudonymization tool infers the configuration required for generating a PsD that meets the formulated URs from the policy. Here, a configuration of the pseudonymization tool is the selection of appropriate mechanisms and parameters, e.g. cryptographic keys, to generate an appropriate PsD of D.

The policy language consists of XML-based syntax. A utility policy has the parent tag <utility_policy>.

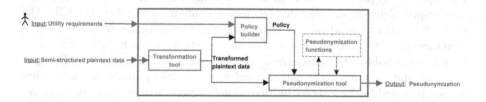

Fig. 2. Dataflow of the toolkit.

Addressing a dataset and data entries. The dataset is addressed with the child tag <dataset id="f">, where f is the identifier of the file that contains the dataset. Each data entry d_i that contains data items to be represented in the PsD by pseudonyms is addressed by an annotating child tag <dataentry>. The data item d_{ij} is represented by the XML tag of the column it belongs to. To define a UR for a single d_{ij}, the id attribute of the tag <dataentry> is set to the number of the containing data entry. We call this referencing method "individual addressing". To address all data items of the same type in a dataset, e.g. all data items of the type <time>, the tag <time> is used. The id attribute of <dataentry> is set to all. We call this referencing method "tag-based addressing". Note that a data item can only be referenced by its position and tags, and not by its value. To address data by value-based properties, the tagging must indicate these properties.

Formulation of the policy rules. The rules that define the URs for a pseudonym of d_{ij} are annotated with the child tag <utility>.

Utility options. A <utility> rule contains the child tag <option> that defines whether the utility option is of the type linkability, disclosability or mathematical operation. To annotate these utility options, the values `linkability`, `disclosability`, or `mathematical operation` are included, respectively.

For denoting the relation of linkability options, the child tag <relation> of <utility> is used. The child tag <operation> indicates the intended mathematical operation.

Binding a utility option to a role or purpose. The utility option defined in a <utility> rule can be bound to a role or purpose using the child tag `binding` of `utility`. For role binding, the `binding` is extended with an attribute `type`. The value of `type` is either set to `role` or `purpose`. The value of the <binding> tag is set to a system-based identifier of the intended role or purpose, respectively. An example of a XML utility policy is given on our website[1]. A utility policy can be addressed by extending the <utility_policy> tag with the `id` attribute.

The Pseudonymization Tool

The input of the pseudonymization tool is a utility policy file and an XML structured input plaintext dataset file. The tool is configured based on the URs. For each UR, it selects an appropriate pseudonymization function from the pool of pseudonymization functions. It applies the functions to each data entry mentioned in the policy and writes the PsD output into an XML structured output file. Only data entries with matching rules in the utility policy are pseudonymously included in the PsD output file. Data entries with no matching rules are omitted in the PsD. Note that the provided mathematical operation "addition" is homomorphic and requires access to the corresponding Paillier public and private key. For that, the key is included in the utility tag. On deployment, it must be ensured that the key is stored and accessed securely.

6   Security Requirements

The goal of this work is to present a flexible, almost use-case independent pseudonymization toolkit. The system architecture must provide means that provide security against a realistic, well-defined attacker model. Here, we assume the honest-but-curious adversarial model. For that, the system architecture must fulfill the following conditions:

Data minimization. Depending on the usage scenario, (possibly multiple) parties may be involved in the definition of the URs a PsD $P(D)$ should fulfill. We assume that the parties agree on the minimum possible set of URs. This includes that the data holder would only provide pseudonyms of data entries of D with utility options that are required for fulfilling the computation purpose. I.e., the parties under consideration strictly follow the principle of data minimization.

---

[1] https://net.cs.uni-bonn.de/wg/itsec/staff/saffija-kasem-madani/appendix/.

Access control on the pseudonyms. Whenever required, the parties of the system agree on clear purposes the utility options should be used for. This implies purpose-based access control on the utility tags of a pseudonym, i.e. purpose binding. If necessary, the utility options should be made accessible to certain, well-defined roles. This leads to a role-based access control on the utility tags of the pseudonyms. The access control comprises keys, salts and nonces contained in the utility tags. We assume that the system architecture provides means of secure key storage and access.

Secure decryption management. The system ensures that the private keys are only used for enabling a utility of a pseudonym according to the formulated utility policy. This includes trusted means that ensure that no plaintexts of D are revealed unless it is required to meet a well-defined disclosure condition. In order to fulfill this security requirement, hardware security modules may be utilized.

7 Evaluation

The goal of our evaluation is to elaborate the overhead of utilizing a PsD with utility options instead of a plaintext dataset described and to compare the overhead caused by different utility options. For that, we have considered the time and space consumption of the PsD of different utility options during generation and utilization. We have examined the utility options disclosability, linkability w.r.t. equality, mathematical operation "addition", and mathematical operation "multiplication". Each of the utility options has been considered with binding to a purpose/role, and without binding. We have run our experiments on a Microsoft Windows 10 Home 64-bit system with a Intel(R) Core(TM) i7-4500U CPU and a 1.80 GHz clock rate, a 8 GB RAM and a hard disk drive. We have followed the BSI[2] recommendations for key and block sizes [5]. The key and block sizes are as follows: To generate a utility tag for the utility option "disclosablity", we have performed an AES encryption with a 128-bit salt and a 128-bit key and 128-bit block size. For linkability w.r.t. equality, we have used a SHA2 hash function of 256 bit length. For the mathematical operation "addition", we have used a Paillier encryption with a key and block size both of 2048 bits. For multiplication, we have used an ElGamal encryption with 2048 bits for both key and block sizes. For binding, we have re-encrypted each generated utility tag with an AES encryption with 128 bit for both key and block size. Overall, we have considered a utility tag that is disclosable without being bound to a role/purpose to be a plaintext.

For the evaluation, we have generated a CSV file that contains a simulated log of the working times of six different simulated employees. The file consists of 250 data entries. Each data entry consists of three data items: the employee's ID, the time he started to work, and the time he finished his work. We have generated

---

[2] Bundesamt für Sicherheit in der Informationstechnik: German Federal Office for Information Security.

Table 1. Space consumption for PsD with different utility options.

Utility/Option	With binding	Without binding
Disclosability	188.9%	100%
Linkability w.r.t. equality	572.12%	240.69%
Mathematical operation "addition"	8586.31%	3266.90%
Mathematical operation "multiplication"	8665.55%	3283.83%

Table 2. Pseudonym generation: time consumption in seconds for pseudonymizing all data items of a file that contains 250 entries with three data items for each entry.

Utility/Option	Without binding	With binding
Disclosability	0.264	19.212
Linkability w.r.t. equality	0.311	31.517
Mathematical operation "addition"	2015.674	2643.181
Mathematical operation "multiplication"	66.635	90.365

PsD of one utility option for each data item, i.e. each data item contained in the CSV file is represented by a pseudonym that consists of one utility tag. Depending on the desired utility option, it took between 0.26 s (including a plaintext for an unbound disclosable data item) and 44 min (bound addition) to generate the pseudonyms. Table 2 shows the time consumed for pseudonymizing the whole dataset.

We compared the size of the XML representation of plaintext CSV file, i.e. the plaintext after being transformed to an XML-tagged file to the size of the PsD file in its XML representation. Here, we omitted the key sizes. For unbound disclosability, we simply keep the plaintext. The remaining utility options lead to file sizes between 1.8-fold for unbound linkability w.r.t. equality, and 86-fold for bound addition. The detailed space consumptions are listed in Table 1.

We consider the generation of a PsD being a process that is done once before rolling out data. Thus, we conclude that the space and time consumption for generating a PsD is feasible. In the related work, we could identify that Flegel et al. stated comparably small ressource consumptions for their approach [10]. In contrast to their work, our approach allows for various utility options. This comes together with the use of cryptographic mechanisms that are highly time and space consuming. Summarizing, we believe that there is the possibility of optimizations in future work.

8   Conclusions and Future Work

We have presented a toolkit for pseudonymization with utility options. It allows for the formulation of URs in a machine-readable utility policy of a PsD. Based on the utility policy, it generates an XML structured PsD that fulfills the URs.

To this stage of research, we have identified three types of URs and formulated corresponding constructs in the policy language. Therefore, the policy language can be used to formulate matching policies. We aim at identifying more URs and extend the policy language to serve them as well. Based on the future findings, we would extend the toolkit to produce PsDs with more utility.

Formulating URs of a PsD and balancing them with the privacy requirements of the individuals the data belong to requires experience and knowledge about the possible privacy implications of rolling out pseudonymized data. For example, a pseudonym with the utility option "disclosability" may lead to the disclosure of personal information. Therefore, it is important to balance between the need for privacy and the need for utility. Some combinations of utility options that may be contained in a PsD may be prone to correlation attacks. Building upon the presented work, one may develop technologies that enhance privacy-respecting selections of URs. Future work would also include a study about privacy risks implied by different combinations of utility tags for a data item. A deeper knowledge of these implications would enable us to design recommendations on how to combine URs to achieve appropriate utility policies for certain application scenarios.

At this stage of research, the toolkit provides a graphical user interface (GUI) that allows a user to formulate a policy by clicking desired URs in a multi-step process. The GUI allows to combine arbitrary URs for each data item in a dataset to formulate a utility policy. On the other hand, there is no guidance that enhances the user in choosing the URs that are appropriate for the current use case. Therefore, the user must have some experience to be able to formulate appropriate utility policies. We aim at providing use-case dependent combinations of URs that can be used as templates for the formulation of utility policies. One possible example is a template that consists of the URs that come from the need of applying a certain algorithm on the pseudonymized data.

We have presented a comparably simple usage scenario in the Internet of Things. There, we identified three requirements that have resulted in pseudonyms for the timestamps' tuples consisting of two different utility tags, and pseudonyms for the employee's ID consisting of three utility tags. Considering the increased storage space caused by the cryptographic outputs, we believe that there is potential for optimization. In future work, our goal is to study and implement those optimizations.

We have shown how the availability of the utility option of a utility tag can be bound to a specific purpose or role using symmetric encryption. Utilizing asymmetric cryptography may ease the key deployment and management. However, it may imply higher storage and processing costs.

When decryption is required for making a utility option of a pseudonym available, mechanisms that ensure that the decryption key is securely accessed and utilized are required as well. One may extend this work to include safe decryption mechanisms.

References

1. Ben-Kiki, O., Evans, C., Ingerson, B.: Yaml Ain't Markup Language (yaml) Version 1.1. yaml.org. Technical report (2005)
2. Biskup, J., Flegel, U.: On pseudonymization of audit data for intrusion detection. In: International Workshop on Designing Privacy Enhancing Technologies: Design Issues in Anonymity and Unobservability, pp. 161–180. Springer-Verlag, New York Inc., New York (2001). http://dl.acm.org/citation.cfm?id=371931.371988
3. Boneh, D., Gentry, C., Halevi, S., Wang, F., Wu, D.J.: Private database queries using somewhat homomorphic encryption. In: Jacobson, M., Locasto, M., Mohassel, P., Safavi-Naini, R. (eds.) ACNS 2013. LNCS, vol. 7954, pp. 102–118. Springer, Heidelberg (2013). doi:10.1007/978-3-642-38980-1_7
4. Brakerski, Z., Gentry, C., Vaikuntanathan, V.: (Leveled) fully homomorphic encryption without bootstrapping. In: Proceedings of the 3rd Innovations in Theoretical Computer Science Conference, ITCS 2012, NY, USA, pp. 309–325 (2012). http://doi.acm.org/10.1145/2090236.2090262
5. BSI: Kryptographische Verfahren: Empfehlungen und Schlüssellangen. Technische Richtlinie TR-02102-1, Bundesamt fur Sicherheit in der Informationstechnik (2017)
6. Crockford, D.: The application/json media type for javascript object notation (json) 2006a (2006). http://tools.ietf.org/html/rfc4627
7. Daemen, J., Rijmen, V.: AES proposal: Rijndael (1999)
8. Dolin, R.H., Alschuler, L., Boyer, S., Beebe, C., Behlen, F.M., Biron, P.V., Shabo, A.: HL7 clinical document architecture, release 2. J. Am. Med. Inf. Assoc. **13**(1), 30–39 (2006)
9. Regulation (EU) 2016/679 of the European Parliament and of the Council of 27 April 2016 on the protection of natural persons with regard to the processing of personal data and on the free movement of such data, and repealing Directive 95/46/EC (General Data Protection Regulation). Official Journal of the European Union L119/59, May 2016. http://eur-lex.europa.eu/legal-content/EN/TXT/?uri=OJ:L:2016:119:TOC
10. Flegel, U., Hoffmann, J., Meier, M.: Cooperation enablement for centralistic early warning systems. In: Proceedings of the 2010 ACM Symposium on Applied Computing, SAC 2010, NY, USA, pp. 2001–2008 (2010). http://doi.acm.org/10.1145/1774088.1774509
11. ElGamal, T.: A public key cryptosystem and a signature scheme based on discrete logarithms. In: Blakley, G.R., Chaum, D. (eds.) CRYPTO 1984. LNCS, vol. 196, pp. 10–18. Springer, Heidelberg (1985). doi:10.1007/3-540-39568-7_2
12. Gentry, C., et al.: Fully homomorphic encryption using ideal lattices. In: STOC, vol. 9, pp. 169–178 (2009)
13. Goldwasser, S., Micali, S.: Probabilistic encryption. J. Comput. Syst. Sci. **28**(2), 270–299 (1984)
14. Heurix, J., Khosravipour, S., Tjoa, A.M., Rawassizadeh, R.: LiDSec- A lightweight pseudonymization approach for privacy-preserving publishing of textual personal information. In: 2012 Seventh International Conference on Availability, Reliability and Security, pp. 603–608 (2011)
15. Kasem-Madani, S., Meier, M.: Security and Privacy Policy Languages: A Survey, Categorization and Gap Identification. arXiv preprint arXiv:1512.00201 (2015)
16. Kerschbaum, F.: Distance-preserving Pseudonymization for timestamps and spatial data. In: Proceedings of the 2007 ACM Workshop on Privacy in Electronic Society, WPES 2007, NY, USA, pp. 68–71 (2007). http://doi.acm.org/10.1145/1314333.1314346

17. Kumaraguru, P., Calo, S.: A survey of privacy policy languages. In: Workshop on Usable IT Security Management (USM 2007): Proceedings of the 3rd Symposium on Usable Privacy and Security. ACM (2007)

18. Naveed, M., Kamara, S., Wright, C.V.: Inference attacks on property-preserving encrypted databases. In: Proceedings of the 22nd ACM SIGSAC Conference on Computer and Communications Security, CCS 2015, NY, USA, pp. 644–655 (2015). http://doi.acm.org/10.1145/2810103.2813651

19. Neubauer, T., Riedl, B.: Improving patients privacy with pseudonymization. Stud. Health Technol. Inf. **136**, 691 (2008)

20. Paillier, P.: Public-key cryptosystems based on composite degree residuosity classes. In: Stern, J. (ed.) EUROCRYPT 1999. LNCS, vol. 1592, pp. 223–238. Springer, Heidelberg (1999). doi:10.1007/3-540-48910-X_16

21. Popa, R.A., Redfield, C.M.S., Zeldovich, N., Balakrishnan, H.: CryptDB: protecting confidentiality with encrypted query processing. In: Proceedings of the Twenty-Third ACM Symposium on Operating Systems Principles, SOSP 2011, NY, USA, pp. 85–100 (2011). http://doi.acm.org/10.1145/2043556.2043566

22. Riedl, B., Neubauer, T., Goluch, G., Boehm, O., Reinauer, G., Krumboeck, A.: A secure architecture for the pseudonymization of medical data. In: The Second International Conference on Availability, Reliability and Security, ARES 2007, pp. 318–324. IEEE (2007)

23. Rivest, R.L., Shamir, A., Adleman, L.: A method for obtaining digital signatures and public-key cryptosystems. Commun. ACM **21**(2), 120–126 (1978)

24. Rossum, G.: Python Reference Manual. Technical report, Amsterdam, The Netherlands (1995)

25. Schaad, A., Bkakria, A., Kerschbaum, F., Cuppens, F., Cuppens-Boulahia, N., Gross-Amblard, D.: Optimized and controlled provisioning of encrypted outsourced data. In: 19th ACM Symposium on Access Control Models and Technologies, SACMAT 2014, London, ON, Canada, 25–27 June 2014, pp. 141–152 (2014). http://doi.acm.org/10.1145/2613087.2613100

26. Shafranovich, Y.: Common format and MIME type for comma-separated values (csv) files (2005)

27. Slagell, A., Lakkaraju, K., Luo, K.: FLAIM: a multi-level anonymization framework for computer and network logs. In: LISA 2006: Proceedings of the 20th conference on Large Installation System Administration, p. 6. USENIX Association, Berkeley (2006)

28. Wendzel, S.: How to increase the security of smart buildings? Commun. ACM **59**(5), 47–49 (2006). http://doi.acm.org/10.1145/2828636

29. Zhao, J., Binns, R., Van Kleek, M., Shadbolt, N.: Privacy languages: are we there yet to enable user controls? In: Proceedings of the 25th International Conference Companion on World Wide Web, WWW 2016 Companion, pp. 799–806. International World Wide Web Conferences Steering Committee, Republic and Canton of Geneva, Switzerland (2016). http://dx.doi.org/10.1145/2872518.2890590

User Privacy

Privacy Dashcam – Towards Lawful Use of Dashcams Through Enforcement of External Anonymization

Paul Wagner[1], Pascal Birnstill[2(✉)], Erik Krempel[2], Sebastian Bretthauer[1,3], and Jürgen Beyerer[1,2]

[1] Karlsruhe Institute of Technology, Karlsruhe, Germany
paul.wagner@student.kit.edu, sebastian.bretthauer@kit.edu
[2] Fraunhofer IOSB, Karlsruhe, Germany
{pascal.birnstill,erik.krempel,juergen.beyerer}@iosb.fraunhofer.de
[3] Goethe University Frankfurt, Frankfurt, Germany

Abstract. Dashcams are small, dashboard mounted camera systems that continuously monitor the area around a vehicle and record video images on a portable storage device. According to many data protection authorities, dashcams constitute surveillance systems that are operated by private individuals in public places. By continuously acquiring personal data they interfere disproportionately with the right of informational self-determination. One approach to make dashcams compliant to data protection law is to automatically identify personal information – at least pedestrian's faces and license plates – in the captured video image and subsequently disguise them. Even though appropriate anonymization methods exist, high computational costs prevent their use in portable dashcams. This article presents a new approach that enforces the anonymization of encrypted dashcam videos on a dedicated computer system, before the user gets access to the videos. To accomplish this, classified images are safeguarded by usage control techniques on the way from the camera to the anonymization component. By applying the developed system, any existing dashcam can ultimately be enhanced by privacy protection capabilities.

1 Introduction

Dashcams are small cameras that are installed on dashboards and behind windscreens of cars. During the recent years they became increasingly popular in many parts of the world, including Europe. Drivers expect dashcam footage to simplify claim settlement in case of traffic accidents as well as to proof their innocence. Simultaneously the spread of dashcams is accompanied by a controversy regarding data protection. For example, dashcams can be seen as mobile surveillance systems, which can hardly be operated legitimately by private individuals in public places. Furthermore all existing types of dashcams may accidentally capture personal information in terms of depicted faces or license plates of cars. Hence dashcams interfere with the affected persons' right of informational

© Springer International Publishing AG 2017
J. Garcia-Alfaro et al. (Eds.): DPM/CBT 2017, LNCS 10436, pp. 183–201, 2017.
DOI: 10.1007/978-3-319-67816-0_11

self-determination. Whether these interferences with personal rights are proportionate is still controversially disputed. Compared to that, so-called *crashcams* constitute a more privacy-friendly approach, since they only record images in an event-driven manner, for example triggered by an acceleration sensor. Crashcams use a ring buffer to record video images for a fixed time period before and after an event. But even with crashcams the acquisition of personal information cannot be entirely prevented.

The admissibility of dashcams under applicable European data protection law is still disputed within the member states. While in Germany there is no leading decision by superior courts regarding dashcams yet, in Austria dashcams have been inadmissible since 2012. Furthermore in 2015 the Austrian Supreme Administrative Court in Vienna prohibited the use of a crashcam that operates with reduced image resolution to protect the privacy of depicted persons. The court did not consider an artificially lowered image resolution to be a sufficient countermeasure against the acquisition of personal information and suggested a camera system that automatically disguises privacy relevant image areas like faces and license plates. Although adequate anonymization methods exist, their computational costs prevent an integration into portable camera systems.

As of May 25th 2018 the European General Data Protection Regulation (GDPR) must be applied directly in the member states (Art. 288 TFEU, Art. 99 no. 2 GDPR). However, as the GDPR lacks a specific legal norm for video surveillance, only its very generally phrased regulations remain for application.[1] Art. 6 no. 1 f GDPR relies on a balancing of interests between the dashcam user and the affected individuals, but it does not provide further narrowing criteria.[2] Therefore it is questionable whether such a broadly defined permission as phrased in Art. 6 no. 1 f GDPR can regulate an intrusive technology like dashcams.[3] Hence the legal standard exclusively amounts to a balancing of interests. The dashcam user has a legal interest in an effective demonstration of evidence in a trial as well as in an effective prosecution of hit-and-run drivers.[4] Individuals affected can claim the protection of their personal data according to Art. 7 and Art. 8 of the Charter of Fundamental Rights of the European Union. However, this balancing of interests must also account for the technical specification of a concrete dashcam, since privacy enhancing technologies (PETs) may contribute to an adequate level of data protection (cf. recital 78 GDPR and Art. 25 GDPR).

When considering the current regulations of the member states concerning video surveillance, the GDPR may prove to be too indeterminate due to the lack

---

[1] See Bretthauer/Krempel/Birnstill, CR 2015, 239 (242) [3].

[2] E. g. § 6 b BDSG, § 50 a ff. ÖDSG, §§ 16 ff. Data Protection Act, Lithuania, § 26 Act on Processing of Personal Data, Denmark, § 6 Data Protection Act, Liechtenstein, §§ 36 ff. Personal Data Act, Norway.

[3] See Bretthauer/Krempel, in: Schweighofer/Kummer/Htzendorfer (ed.), Transparenz – Tagungsband des 17. Internationalen Rechtsinformatik Symposions, 2014, S. 525, 532 [2]; on the requirements laid down in Art. 52 of the Charter of Fundamental Rights of the EU see Rieckhoff, Der Vorbehalt des Gesetzes im Europarecht, 2007, p. 155 ff [13].

[4] E. g. Ernst, CR 2015, 620 (623) [6].

of further narrowing criteria. The use of dashcams in the private sector is then no longer covered by the GDPR. Legal certainty on an international level should not be expected within the next few years. In any case, future legal norms will most likely not define exact design specifications of a privacy-friendly dashcam, but instead state certain mandatory guidelines for such a system. It is our goal to show that privacy-friendly dashcams are possible by implementing technical measures that enforce anonymization on dashcam videos. The existence of a proof-of-concept system may then serve as input for future jurisdiction.

This article presents an approach that securely outsources the image exploitation algorithms required for an appropriate image anonymization to a dedicated, powerful computer system. For this purpose a storage medium is used that encrypts videos immediately. Access to this storage medium is only possible via a computer that is protected by data flow tracking and usage control (UC) mechanisms. These mechanisms ensure the anonymization of the dashcam video material prior to any user access. Furthermore they guarantee that the user cannot modify or delete any acquired data. This idea has been published by the authors in [16] in a preliminary and condensed version.

Related Work. The task of video image anonymization consists of two independent steps. First, image classifiers detect privacy relevant image areas like faces or license plates. These regions of interest (ROIs) are then obfuscated so as to remove all sensitive information in the actual anonymiyation step.

From the perspective of privacy protection in dashcam recordings, the most challenging image classification task is pedestrian detection. The best performances have recently been obtained using advancements of the integral channel features detector (ICF) [17,18] and also by using deep learning approaches for augmenting classification models with high-level features learnt from various tasks and datasets [8,15]. For privacy protection a detector's miss rate is the vital performance metric, and the referred detectors achieve miss rates of less than 20Furthermore, Zhang et al. [17] found that small scale and side-view persons are the largest sources of false negative detections, whereby at least persons captured in small scale are not a major privacy issue.

Anonymizing video images to obfuscate privacy-sensitive regions is an intensively researched task as well. Naive anonymization methods such as blurring or pixelization can quickly obfuscate certain image areas, but have been shown to be generally ineffective [4] while possibly reducing the utility of the remaining video images for later evaluation. More advanced image anonymization techniques like image warping [10], region-based transform-domain scrambling [5], or a combination of different filters can yield better results. As shown in [1] effective privacy filters can be found that preserve the utility of filtered video data [1].

In the field of privacy-sensitive video acquisition, real-time image anonymization on embedded devices has been proposed. With the prototype *TrustEYE.M4* Rinner and Winkler [14] present a trusted camera with integrated privacy enhancing technologies (PET). The hardware is based on a Raspberry PI, an inexpensive single-board computer, which immediately processes the data acquired by the camera before they can be stored or distributed. After detecting ROIs, a privacy filter is applied to the images before they are stored permanently, thus ensuring that only anonymized data is available. However, since the available computing power is limited, only simple detection and anonymization methods can be used. It is not yet clear whether those simple anonymization methods are capable of adequately protecting personalized image areas, while still keeping the resulting video images suitable for reconstructing traffic accidents. Sufficiently powerful image processing algorithms, which can reliably detect privacy critical image areas in real time, generally have high computational costs and thus are only of limited use in mobile camera systems. In 2015 Janard and Marurngsith implemented a face detection based on local binary patterns (LBP) on a Raspberry PI and achieved no more than 17 fps for QVGA (320×240 px) [9]. As most customary dashcams achieve a higher resolution and frame rate, it seems appropriate to outsource the ROI detection and anonymization to a dedicated computer system.

In order to outsource the anonymization of acquired video material to a dedicated computer, the dashcam has to store the videos on a separate storage medium, which is then connected to the processing computer system by the dashcam user himself. At this point it has to be ensured that the user cannot access the video files before they have been anonymized. By encrypting the video material on the storage medium and applying UC techniques [11,12] as soon as the video material is being decrypted in a controlled environment, the usage of data can be continuously supervised. UC is a generalization of access control where data usage can be restricted even after an initial access to the data has been granted. However, for this purpose the protected data has to be continuously monitored, which is why UC is often extended by data flow tracking. Data flow tracking allows to restrict data usage by expressing (in)admissible data flows instead of defining restrictions in terms of observable system events [7].

2   System Model

As explained above, the European jurisdiction assumes that dashcams cannot be operated in public places without acquiring personal information of uninvolved persons. Hence dashcam videos must be regarded as containing privacy sensitive information and must therefore be protected from illegitimate access. We propose and analyze a system model that is capable of preventing illegitimate accesses to the recorded dashcam videos until all personal information has been removed by anonymization. The basic system design consists of a customary dashcam and a storage device that stores video files and related meta data. Video images are considered to be classified until a designated declassification component, running on a separate computer, removed all personal information by anonymizing the images. On the way from the storage to the declassification component, the video data has to be properly protected. The declassified video data can then be shown to the user. Firstly, we define the protection goals for the system as well as the attacker and trust model for the considered scenario.

Protection Goals. The main assets that have to be protected are personal information embedded into the acquired video images, especially faces and license plates of cars. Furthermore many dashcams also produce meta data like time stamps and GPS locations, which may be either embedded into the original video files or stored in separate files. In any case this information has to be protected as well. The most important protection goal is the confidentiality of the video images and the embedded personal information. The system needs to protect the classified video images in the scope of the system from being viewed by unauthorized eyes. Note that at this point we abstract from the detection and obfuscation techniques that are used to detect and anonymize image areas containing privacy relevant information. The implemented image classifiers used for this task will always have an error rate, and hence might miss some of the privacy relevant image areas. However, the goal of the proposed system is to securely enforce anonymization on dashcam videos, i.e., to prevent an attacker from bypassing the mandatory classification and anonymization step, regardless of the used algorithms. What types of image classifiers can detect privacy relevant image areas with sufficient precision in order for the resulting anonymized images to be considered unproblematic in a legal sense is still an open question.

Another protection goal is the integrity of the acquired information, especially the meta data. If they should be used as evidence in court, it has to be ensured that the data has not been manipulated. Finally the authenticity of users with extended access rights, like prosecution authorities (see below), has to be guaranteed. Privacy protection goals like intervenability, unlinkability and transparency are not directly applicable to our system, since we focus on removing privacy related information altogether instead of gathering and processing them.

Attacker Model. The main attacker against our system is interested in extracting and distributing the personal information embedded into the acquired video images. This *privacy attacker* has access to the camera, the encrypted storage medium as well as the processing computer system that is used to view the anonymized videos. The system must not disclose any privacy relevant data to this attacker. This goal is substantially complicated by the fact that the privacy attacker is not an uninvolved third person, who for example steals a camera system, but the user of the camera system itself. So we obviously need to allow the user to operate the camera system and partially view the recorded images, but still make sure that no privacy related information is leaked to him. This type of ambivalence, that the user of a system simultaneously is the attacker, is a typical characteristic of UC enforced systems. Nevertheless, a dashcam system can only be privacy friendly if it is resistant against a privacy attacker.

The *modifying attacker* pursues the goal of manipulating recorded videos or meta data. For example, a modifying attacker could try to forge the GPS locations or time stamps on the video images to make the evidence more favorable for him. Unlike the privacy attacker, this type of attacker may also operate on unclassified data like meta data. Therefore a mechanism is required to specifically protect the integrity of unclassified data as well. The modifying attacker usually has access to both the storage device and the declassification system.

The third type of attacker is the *destructive attacker*, who wants to destroy unfavorable video images recorded by the camera system, for example after causing a traffic accident. Since a physical destruction of the storage medium can hardly be prevented, the destructive attacker is restricted by the assumption that he wants to delete information in a way that it is undetectable for third persons. The destructive attacker has access to both the declassification system and the storage medium, but desists from mechanical destruction.

A fourth typical attacker to be considered is the *outsider attacker*. The outsider attacker is completely unaffiliated with the persons operating either the dashcam or the declassification tool and might come into possession of one or more system components by accident. The classical example of this type of attacker is the thief who broke into the car and stole the dashcam. The outsider attacker is a special type of privacy attacker who has access to the storage medium and is interested in all saved information, be it classified or unclassified. Furthermore, the outsider attacker has no access to the declassification system.

Trust Model. In our scenario four different actors use, interact with or have an interest in the camera system. The *operator* is the actor who buys, deploys and uses the camera system in order to benefit from video footage in case of traffic accidents or similar incidents. The operator acts on his own behalf, so he must not be granted access to the classified data. Because the operator is the one who generates potentially privacy sensitive information, he is simultaneously the main antagonist of the system. He can act as privacy attacker, modifying attacker, and also as destructive attacker. Because the operator is not trusted in the first place, there is also no need to authenticate him explicitly in the system.

The *evaluator* is generally interested in the acquired video data as well as its integrity, but does not operate the dashcam himself. The evaluator is allowed to review anonymized dashcam videos for certain purposes. However, just like the operator, the evaluator must not be granted access to the classified data. An example for this actor is an insurance company that offers lower fees for dashcam users and wants to evaluate the video images after an insurance claim has been filed. In that case the insured person is the operator, whose driving behavior is assessed by the evaluator using anonymized dashcam footage. The insurance company is also interested in the integrity of the dashcam footage, in order to prevent insurance fraud. Similarly, the insured person wants to be guaranteed that the insurance company does not tamper with the recorded videos in order to escape payment obligations. Hence the evaluator is a possible privacy attacker, modifying attacker and destructive attacker. Because the evaluator is not allowed to view classified data, the exemplary insurance company cannot identify the other party in case of a hit-and-run accident, as the license plates are being anonymized. However, in that case the incident is of criminal relevance and legal action is necessary, involving a prosecution authority as a third actor.

In specific cases the *prosecution authority* has a legitimate interest in the recorded video images to serve as evidence in court. By court order it may get entitled to access the classified video data and identify depicted persons. Because the prosecution authority is granted sufficient rights to bypass the protection mechanisms, it has to be fully trusted. Hence the proper authentication and enforcement of access rights of this actor is of major importance.

The *administrator* is the actor who puts the system into operation and initially specifies the access rights for all other actors. Naturally, the administrator has to be fully trusted as well. In the following it will be assumed that the administrator only gets one-time access to the system in order to set it up. After that the system is operated in an environment that the administrator cannot influence and has no access to. Hence the administrator can be ignored for the security analysis later in Sect. 5. Nevertheless, there are some crucial measures that the administrator has to take in order to set up a secure system.

3   System Specification

In the following sections the concrete system is specified. In order to do so, the various components as well as their interaction with each other is defined. Finally a possible implementation of the developed system model is presented.

Components. The system model distinguishes between the *camera* itself and a *storage* that saves the acquired data for further processing. How the video images that contain personal information reach the system is irrelevant for the model. Hence the model can abstract from the camera and view the dashcam as consisting of only a storage device. Therefore the approach depicted in Fig. 1 can be used for any customary camera devices.

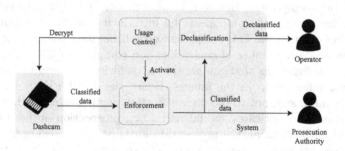

Fig. 1. System design

The storage consists of an encrypted (SD) memory card that can encrypt data on-the-fly when it is written to the storage. The encryption takes place transparently for the writing camera device. It does not notice that the data is encrypted while writing, but will not be able to read from the storage again. The cryptographic key that the memory card uses for the encryption is itself stored in a specifically secured area of the storage, which is not readable from the outside. Reading the encrypted data from the storage in plain-text is only possible after unlocking the key with a secret PIN. If the memory card is unlocked the stored data is decrypted on-the-fly when reading from the device. Hence the decryption takes place transparently for the process that is reading. Encrypted memory cards that implement these requirements are available from special manufacturers. In Sect. 3 a suitable storage device is specified. The memory device ensures that any information saved on the storage cannot be retrieved without the knowledge of the secret PIN. As a matter of principle, only trusted systems may posses the PIN that is required for decrypting the storage. Before decrypting the storage, these trusted systems ensure that neither operator nor evaluator can access any classified data in a non-anonymized fashion.

The *declassification* component reads classified videos containing privacy relevant images and applies a declassification function to generate a declassified representation of the videos. This is usually done by anonymizing the privacy relevant image areas using image obfuscation techniques. Images that have been processed by a declassification function do not contain privacy relevant information anymore and hence are considered to be declassified. At this point it is assumed that the image classifiers used by the declassification function can detect all relevant image areas. To what extent image exploitation algorithms exist that can sufficiently hide personal information in order for data protection law not to be applicable is still unclear. However, for the mere task of enforcing image obfuscation on dashcam videos, this is not relevant. Subsequently, only declassified videos are allowed to leave the system scope to be viewed by the user, whereas classified data must never leave the declassification component.

Since the only legitimate access to the storage is executed by the declassification component, all further accesses must be prevented. This could be achieved by giving the secret PIN that is necessary for decrypting the storage only to the declassification component. However, a more flexible solution is to maintain a loose coupling of the two components by introducing another component, the *usage control* component. This component establishes data connections between the storage and any number of declassification components if the latter apply declassification functions that are considered sufficiently powerful for protecting personal information in the images. Hence the secret PIN is known only to the UC component, not to the declassification components. Furthermore the UC component authenticates special users, i.e., prosecution authorities. After a successful authentication the prosecution authorities are also granted access to specific not yet anonymized data sets. The respective authority is trusted to treat the classified data in a legal and responsible manner.

The *enforcement* component constitutes the core of the system. This component supervises the classified data flowing from the storage into the system and prohibits any abusive data usage within the system. In order to do so, the enforcement component monitors all data flows within the system and prevents all the operations that could transmit classified data to an unauthorized actor. *Interaction.* Figure 2 shows the interaction between the various components as soon as an operator connects a storage device to a computer that runs the declassification system. The storage component consists of an encrypted SD memory card that contains classified data in form of dashcam footage. To decrypt the stored data a PIN is necessary, which must be well hidden from the dashcam operator. This PIN has been randomly generated during the system deployment. It is securely stored by the UC component in a protected area that the user has no access to, for example as an encrypted registry entry. Hence the storage device can only be decrypted and operated at a computer system that is equipped with a trusted UC component, i.e., a UC component that knows the correct PIN for this encrypted memory card.

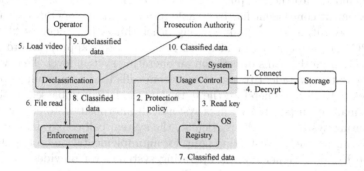

Fig. 2. System interaction

If the computer runs such a UC component, it recognizes the encrypted storage device and activates the enforcement component (step 2). This activation is performed by issuing a protection policy, uniquely identifying the device that should be protected. After the protection mechanisms are up and running, all data flows within the system are monitored by the enforcement component. Hence the UC component may now use the PIN to decrypt the storage device (steps 3 and 4). This does not actually decrypt all the data on the storage, but makes the memory card transparently decrypt the requested data for any process that is reading from the storage. From now on the classified data is accessible in plain text on the storage and can be read by any system process. If the storage is removed from the computer in this decrypted state, the memory card is automatically locked again. Therefore classified data can never be read from the storage without providing the PIN.

Preventing unwanted accesses to the classified data available on the memory card is now the task of the enforcement component. The enforcement component filters all read operations on the storage device and only allows those with an authenticated target – i.e., either from the declassification component or the prosecution authority. Hence an operator cannot access dashcam videos directly, but only through the declassification component, which is allowed to read the classified data (steps 5 to 9). Solely the protection authority is entitled to view the classified data (step 10) after an explicit authentication at the UC component. Thereby the enforcement component ensures that classified data may only flow from the storage to declassification components and the prosecution authority. The dashcam operator cannot intercept classified data at any point in the system, since the declassification components only display the video images in a declassified, i.e., anonymized representation. The enforcement component also prevents write operations on the storage for every actor, including the prosecution authority. Hence it is guaranteed that both the confidentiality as well as the integrity of the classified data is protected.

Implementation. After defining the system model some possible model instantiations are presented. In general the proposed protection techniques need to be deeply included into the computer system in order to be effective. Particularly the enforcement component has to be able to intercept any operation that leads to data flows within the system. Among other things this includes file operations, IPC and network communication. Hence it seems appropriate to enforce the protection mechanisms directly on an operating system level. That way, the operating system can identify and alter system calls that may result in possibly dangerous data flows. Therefore the data flow model encompassed in the proposed formalization (see below) uses system call interposition to enforce UC on the operating system level. In particular, the system call constraints presented in Sect. 4 can be used as a starting point for an implementation on the OS level.

While UC enforcement on an operating system level provides comprehensive, system-wide data protection, implementing a model instantiation in user space is considerably easier. On Windows, the enforcement component can be implemented as a file system filter driver that registers itself in the Windows kernel, subsequently filters all file operations requests occurring in the system, and prevents them when necessary. Even though a file system filter driver cannot monitor data flows as comprehensively as an enforcement component directly in the kernel, filtering file system operations is also sufficient if the classified data is stored in files on the storage device. The UC component can be realized as a Windows system service, which runs in the background, continuously listens for connecting storage devices, deploys respective protection policies, and takes care of further management responsibilities. The service also authenticates prosecution authorities with the system and must securely store the PIN that is needed to decrypt the memory card. This can be achieved by using the Windows Data Protection API to store the PIN as an encrypted registry entry. As soon as the UC service detects an encrypted storage, it activates the file system filter driver, and it reads the PIN, which it then uses for decrypting the storage. Any unwanted file operations on the classified data are then blocked by the filter driver.

In both cases, the software implementing the declassification component will be running in user space, since operators and evaluators use it to create and view the anonymized videos. This software has to be able to detect and anonymize privacy relevant image areas in dashcam videos. The implemented enforcement component allows classified data from the storage to flow only in this software module. Thanks to the loose coupling of the declassification components and the UC component in the system model, any suitable third-party software can be used for this task, insofar as it does not allow an unauthenticated user (everyone but the prosecution authority) to view or to export raw video data.

Furthermore for an actual implementation an encrypted memory card is necessary that meets all the requirements as specified in the previous sections. The requirements include on-the-fly encryption of data using an encryption key that is securely stored on the device itself as well as on-the-fly decryption of requested data as soon as a secret PIN is specified. Furthermore it has to be ensured that the storage device cannot be removed from the declassification system in an unlocked state. Instead the storage device has to fall back to an encrypted state in that case. Memory cards that satisfy all necessary requirements are for instance the security microSD memory cards manufactured by SwissBit[5].

Additionally, the question of how to delete recorded videos from the storage device has to be addressed. Usually dashcams store the recorded video data permanently on the memory card. Since the system prevents any modification or deletion of recorded video files, the memory card could soon run out of usable space. This problem is less severe if a crashcam is used as recording device, because due to the event-driven recording of usually one minute prior to as well as after the event hundreds of videos can be stored on a single memory card. This solution is also favorable in terms of data protection. If a continuously recording dashcam shall be used, the declassification system can be extended with a deletion mode that allows to delete all those video files from the storage, whose meta data do not show abnormalities like unusually high acceleration/deceleration. This way a full memory card can be made usable again, without allowing the deletion of possibly important video data.

4   Formalization

In the previous section we presented a system model that can enforce anonymization on classified data before displaying it to the user. In order to evaluate whether the system is actually privacy compliant by fulfilling the described UC requirements, we use data flow modeling as a more formal approach. The formalization presented in this section is based on the work of Harvan and Pretschner [7]. The authors propose a state based view on a system rather than an event based approach, which is more user-centric and has been applied by most UC formalizations. Since it would be rather tedious to explicitly state all user actions that could possibly lead to any unwanted data flow, the state based approach is more suitable for our system. Furthermore the authors propose data flow tracking as well as UC mechanisms, which simplifies the specification of formal policies that protect classified data in our system. We use the definitions and notations of [7] to express UC policies in the form of model equations, which need to be fulfilled by our system to be considered secure. These formal policies ultimately allow us to determine if a system is in fact privacy compliant.

---

[5] https://www.swissbit.com/products/security-products/overwiev/security-products-overview/.

According to Harvan and Pretschner a formal data flow model is described by a tuple $(D, C, F, \Sigma, \sigma_i, P, A, R)$. D is the set of *data* that is controlled by the system. In our case, D denotes the set of classified data at large. C is the set of *containers* available in the system, like files, system processes or network connections. $P \subseteq C$ is the set of *principals* that can trigger actions in the system, most importantly processes. Processes are containers, since they can keep data in the memory or in CPU registers. F is the set of *names* that can be used to identify containers, for example file names $F_{fn} \subseteq F$ or file descriptors $F_{dsc} \subseteq F$. The current system state is described by $\Sigma = (C \rightarrow 2^D) \times (C \rightarrow 2^C) \times (P \times F \rightarrow C)$ and consists of three mappings. A storage function $s : C \rightarrow 2^D$ gives a mapping of data stored in a container. An alias function $l : C \rightarrow 2^C$ gives a mapping of containers, which get updated implicitly whenever the storage function of a container changes. Finally a naming function $f : P \times F \rightarrow C$ maps process specific identifiers to containers. $\sigma_i = (s_i, l_i, f_i) \in \Sigma$ is the initial state of the system. Here the storage relation holds the initial representation of the controlled data. A is a set of state-changing actions that can be performed by processes. How these actions change the system state is defined by a transition relation $R \subseteq \Sigma \times P \times A \times \Sigma$, which updates an old state to a new state given a process and an action. In order to describe changes to the three mapping functions, the following notation is used. Let $m : S \rightarrow T$ be any mapping and $x \in X \subseteq S$ a variable. Then $m[x \leftarrow expr]_{x \in X} = m'$ with $m' : S \rightarrow T$ is defined by

$$m'(y) = \begin{cases} expr & \text{if } y \in X \\ m(y) & \text{otherwise} \end{cases}$$

In order to express the presented system in this formal model, there has to be a way to identify processes that reside in the scope of the declassification component as well as containers within the storage component. Hence we define the two sets $C_{storage} \subseteq (C \setminus P)$ and $C_{decl} \subseteq P$. The initial state of the model assumes that classified data only resides on the storage. Furthermore, in the beginning no aliases exist for both storage and declassification containers. This is described in Eqs. 1 and 2.

$$s_i (C \setminus C_{storage}) \cap D = \emptyset \tag{1}$$
$$\forall c \in (C_{storage} \cup C_{decl}) : l_i(c) = \emptyset \tag{2}$$

Policies. After defining a formal system model, we can specify formal UC policies that restrict the usage of classified data throughout the system. As described more in-depth in [7], policies for this model are state-based. Therefore those policies do not prohibit or allow any type of user events that might occur, but rather define what system states are illegal and need to be avoided.

The most important policy for our system is that classified data must not be processed or displayed by the user, which addresses the protection goal of confidentiality. In terms of the formal model this means that no container within the system must hold classified data, with the exceptions being storage containers, where the classified data originates from and declassification containers, where the classified data becomes declassified. Formally this policy is stated in Eq. 3.

$$\forall c \in C \setminus (C_{storage} \cup C_{decl}) : s(c) = \emptyset \qquad (3)$$

Apart from protecting confidentiality by preventing the leakage of classified data, we also want to enforce integrity by making sure that the user cannot modify or delete any protected data. This is necessary to prevent voluntary modification or destruction of evidence by a modifying or destructive attacker respectively. Since this formal model is state-based rather than event-based, there are no user events that could be filtered for write or delete requests. We can however state that within the formal system Eq. 4 needs to be satisfied at all points in time.

$$\forall c \in C_{storage} : s_i(c) = s(c) \qquad (4)$$

The policies in Eqs. 3 and 4 ensure that no unwanted data flow can occur in the system. This is regardless of any aliases that may exist in the system. However, to ease the later implementation we can explicitly forbid aliases between the storage and the declassification component, as expressed in Eq. 5.

$$\forall c \in (C_{storage} \cup C_{decl}) : l(c) = \emptyset \qquad (5)$$

State Transitions. Even though Eq. 3 is sufficient to ensure confidentiality in the system, it is rather cumbersome to quantify over the whole container set. State-based policies like in Eqs. 3 and 4 can be used to easily declare what system states are to be avoided, but they are not suitable as starting point for an actual implementation. In order to enforce these policies in an actual implementation, the data flow model must be able to interpret actions that are observed in the system in terms of information flow so as to decide whether they would put the system into an unauthorized system state. Thus, a more appropriate approach for obtaining policies that can be enforced by an implementation is to examine the actions that can trigger a system state change and restrict those actions in order to avoid unsafe system states. To do so, we need to specify the semantics of these actions in terms of data flow. The original formal model by Harvan and Pretschner was intended to model an operating system, which is why the defined actions $A = \{open, pipe, close, read, write, rename, unlink, fork, execve, kill, mmap, \dots\}$ correspond to system calls. The semantics of those actions are specified by defining the respective state transitions that are contained in the transition relation R. For example, Eq. 6 defines the semantics of the operation *read*.

$$\forall s \in [C \rightarrow 2^D], \forall l \in [C \rightarrow 2^C], \forall f \in [P \times F \rightarrow C], \forall p \in P, \forall e \in F_{dsc} :$$
$$((s, l, f), p, read(e), (s[t \leftarrow s(t) \cup s(f(p, e))]_{t \in l^*(p)}, l, f)) \in R \qquad (6)$$

According to Eq. 6, the read action modifies the storage function in a way to map every member of $l^*(p)$ to the data of the container that is read from. Hereby l^* denotes the reflexive transitive closure of the alias function, i.e. $l^*(p)$ contains all containers that have an alias relation with the calling process p. Similarly the *write* operation is defined in Eq. 7.

$$\forall s \in [C \to 2^D], \forall l \in [C \to 2^C], \forall f \in [P \times F \to C], \forall p \in P, \forall e \in F_{dsc}:$$
$$((s,l,f), p, write(e), (s[t \leftarrow s(t) \cup s(p)]_{t \in l^*(f(p,e))}, l, f)) \in R \quad (7)$$

Instead of describing the secure system states with state-based policies like in the previous section, we can also achieve a secure system model by restricting the transition relation R to those actions that do not interfere with confidentiality and integrity. Based on the policies for confidentiality and integrity (Eqs. 3 and 4), the Eqs. 8–19 describe conditions for the transition relation R that a model instantiation has to enforce in order to ensure a safe system state.

Equation 8 defines that reads on the storage are allowed for the declassification component only.

$$\forall((s,l,f), p, read(e), (\bar{s},l,f)) \in R : f(p,e) \in C_{storage} \implies l^*(p) \subseteq C_{decl} \quad (8)$$

Equation 9 defines that writes on the storage are prohibited altogether.

$$\forall((s,l,f), p, write(e), (\bar{s},l,f)) \in R : f(p,e) \notin C_{storage} \quad (9)$$

Equation 10 defines that reads on the classification component must be prohibited by the operating system.

$$\forall((s,l,f), p, read(e), (\bar{s},l,f)) \in R : f(p,e) \notin C_{decl} \quad (10)$$

Equation 11 defines that the declassification component must not write classified data.

$$\forall((s,l,f), p, write(e), (\bar{s},l,f)) \in R : p \notin C_{decl} \quad (11)$$

Equation 12 defines that files on the storage cannot be renamed. Also, no external file may be renamed to replace a file on the storage. The action $rename(n_1, n_2)$ renames the file specified by the name $n_1 \in F_{fn}$ to $n_2 \in F_{fn}$.

$$\forall((s,l,f), p, rename(n_1,n_2), (\bar{s},l,\bar{f})) \in R : f(p,n_1) \notin C_{storage} \wedge f(p,n_2) \notin C_{storage} \quad (12)$$

Equation 13 defines that files on the storage must not be deleted. The action $unlink(n)$ deletes the file specified by the name $n \in F_{fn}$.

$$\forall((s,l,f), p, unlink(n), (\bar{s},\bar{l},f)) \in R : f(p,n) \notin C_{storage} \quad (13)$$

Equation 14 defines that a fork of a declassification process must also be a declassification process. No other process can join the declassification component by forking itself. This condition is not required for $C_{storage} \subseteq (C \setminus P)$, because the storage does not contain any processes. The action $fork(rv)$ clones the current process p. The new child process is $rv \in P$.

$$\forall((s,l,f), p, fork(rv), (\bar{s},\bar{l},\bar{f})) \in R : p \in C_{decl} \Leftrightarrow rv \in C_{decl} \quad (14)$$

Equation 15 defines that a process must not execute any files containing classified data from the storage or the declassification component. The only exception is the declassification component itself. The action $execve(n)$ replaces the memory image of the current process p with the contents of a file specified by $n \in F_{fn}$.

$$\forall\big((s,l,f),p,execve(n),(\bar{s},l,f)\big) \in R : p \notin C_{decl} \implies f(p,n) \notin (C_{storage} \cup C_{decl})$$
$$(15)$$

Equation 16 defines that the declassification component must not send any classified data via IPC. This condition is similar to preventing *write* operations in Eq. 11.

$$\forall\big((s,l,f),p,kill(q),(\bar{s},l,f)\big) \in R : p \notin C_{decl} \tag{16}$$

Equation 17 defines that no process may map read-only memory that points to either the storage or the declassification component. The action $mmap(e,\texttt{PROT\_READ})$ maps the contents of a file specified by the file descriptor $e \in F_{dsc}$ to the memory of the current process p. The mapped file cannot be written to.

$$\forall\big((s,l,f),p,mmap(e,\texttt{PROT\_READ}),(\bar{s},\bar{l},f)\big) \in R : f(p,e) \notin \{C_{decl} \cup C_{storage}\}$$
$$(17)$$

Equation 18 defines that no process may map writable memory that points to the storage. The action $mmap(e)$ maps the contents of a file specified by the file descriptor $e \in F_{dsc}$ to the memory of the current process p. The mapped file can be written to.

$$\forall\big((s,l,f),p,mmap(e),(\bar{s},\bar{l},f)\big) \in R : f(p,e) \notin C_{storage} \tag{18}$$

Equation 19 defines that the declassification component must not map any writable memory itself.

$$\forall\big((s,l,f),p,mmap(e),(\bar{s},\bar{l},f)\big) \in R : p \notin C_{decl} \tag{19}$$

The above conditions define the semantics of system calls that safeguard classified data from the storage to the declassification component. As such they are a good starting point for an implementation on the operating system level. In the proposed user space implementation, the conditions in Eqs. 8, 9, 12, 13 and 15–18 are ensured by the file system filter driver. Then the operating system is only responsible for enforcing condition 10. In any case conditions 11, 14 and 19 cannot be directly enforced. They are the responsibility of the used declassification tool.

5   Security Analysis

Based on the presented formalization of a system that enforces anonymization on dashcam videos, we now analyze the system's security properties given the attacker model. Subsequently the soundness of the system model instantiation, i.e., a user space implementation complying with Eqs. 8–19, is evaluated and underlying assumptions are explained. We finally introduce configuration requirements that an administrator setting up the implemented system needs to take care of so that these assumptions hold true.

Data Protection. Regarding the data protection capabilities of the proposed system specification, the most important question is whether or not the system is robust against a privacy attacker, i.e., if the protection goal of confidentiality is fulfilled. According to the policy in Eq. 3, classified data can only exist on the storage medium as well as within the declassification component. The dashcam operator can only view any data that has previously been anonymized by the declassification component. Thus it is ensured that classified data can never leave the system scope in a classified representation, i.e., with privacy relevant information still remaining in the video images. No privacy attacker can extract any classified data from the system, which is why confidentiality is fulfilled.

For the protection goal of integrity we need to consider the modifying attacker and the destructive attacker. According to the policy in Eq. 4 it is not possible to alter or delete any classified data on the storage. Hence the system is robust against modifying and destructive attackers. The physical destruction of the storage medium has already been excluded in the attacker model.

Finally we need to analyze the protection of recorded video data against an outsider attacker, who is not related to the dashcam operator and might have acquired the camera system by theft. Hence he does have access to the storage medium, but not to the declassification system. Since the storage medium automatically encrypts any data written to it, and the shared secret required for decryption is securely stored on the declassification system, the outsider attacker is unable to extract any data whatsoever from the system.

Implementation Soundness. Before analyzing the soundness of the implemented system, some assumptions have to be made regarding the environment in which the system is deployed. The first assumption is that the system modules in question have been implemented correctly and are free of bugs, so they behave as they are specified in Eqs. 8–19. This is particularly important for the used declassification tool as it may consist of third-party software. Furthermore it is assumed that the modules cannot be modified after they have been deployed. In particular, attackers must not have any influence on their internal behavior or on the data that they process. Also attackers that have comprehensive influence on the operating system are explicitly excluded. Essentially, the latter assumptions demand that the integrity of the underlying system is ensured. Such assumptions, which require that the administrator sets up a secure execution environment, are common for instantiations of UC. We outline the prerequisites for securely deploying our declassification system in Sect. 5. Eventually we assume that the system's initial state fulfills Eqs. 1 and 2, i.e., classified data only resides on the storage medium when it is connected to the system and aliases neither exist for storage containers nor for the declassification component.

As described in Sect. 4, a secure system model instantiation has to comply with the conditions in Eqs. 8–19. In case of the proposed user space implementation, the conditions are implemented by the file system filter driver, which is responsible for the policy enforcement, and the declassification tool, which applies the anonymization to the images. According to the Eqs. 8, 15 and 17, a valid system implementation must not allow classified data from the storage to flow anywhere else but to the declassification tool. Furthermore, according to Eqs. 10, 11, 14, 15, 16 and 19, classified data must not leave the declassification tool. Only declassified data, i.e., anonymized data, is allowed to leave the scope of the declassification tool. Since at the time the storage medium is connected to the system, classified data exist nowhere but on the storage device, classified data can never exist anywhere else but on the storage component and in the declassification tool. Apparently this behavior is equivalent to what is demanded in the policy in Eq. 3, which is why the system implementation does fulfill the protection goal of confidentiality. Regarding the protection goal of integrity, Eqs. 9, 12 and 18 demand that no process, including the declassification tool, must write any data to the storage. Similarly, Eqs. 12 and 13 ensure that no process is able to delete any data from the storage. Hence the classified data that initially reside on the storage device must remain there unaltered at all times, which effectively corresponds to the policy in Eq. 4. Since both confidentiality and integrity, as defined in the original policies in Eqs. 3 and 4, are also fulfilled when restricting the system state updates according to Eqs. 8–19, model instantiations that implement those restrictions can be considered secure as well.

System Prerequisites. For the data protection analysis to be valid, we made some assumptions in the previous section. First of all we assumed that the operating system ensures the integrity of the deployed system components. This particularly means that the dashcam operator must not have administrator rights on the declassification system and his access to program executables and configuration files is restricted. Similarly the operator must not be allowed to deactivate the UC and enforcement component by setting the proper access rights for the operator's user account. The shared secret used by the UC component to decrypt the storage medium must be protected from the operator's access as well. This can be achieved, e.g., by encrypting the secret using the Windows data protection API in the context of the trusted user account. To obtain a secure system, the administrator must apply all these settings correctly on the declassification computer. It becomes apparent that the administrator as a trusted actor is of vital importance for the secure deployment of the system. While in some scenarios such a trusted actor can be identified, e.g., if an insurance company hands out dashcams to customers along with a correctly configured declassification system, it is however not yet clear how to achieve this for private individuals.

Similar to the software components, the hardware components must be physically secured as well. The operator must not get direct access to the hard drive that contains the anonymization system, or else he could easily escalate his privileges and retrieve administrator rights. This type of bypassing the operating system's security mechanisms can be effectively prevented by using a so-called trusted platform module (TPM).

6 Conclusion

We introduced a declassification system, which ensures confidentiality and integrity of privacy relevant image areas in video data recorded by a dashcam. By outsourcing the anonymization to a separate computer system, we can apply more powerful image processing algorithms so that (i) personal information can be minimized according to the state-of-the-art, and (ii) any customary dashcam along with an encrypting memory card can be enhanced with privacy protection capabilities. Dashcam operation according to data protection requirements thus seems possible under the assumptions named in Sect. 5.

As discussed in the legal considerations, the technical design of privacy-friendly dashcam solutions may play a more prominent role in future jurisdiction concerning dashcam usage. In this sense, we conceive our approach as an input for an interdisciplinary discussion of dashcams in law and computer science.

References

1. Birnstill, P., Ren, D., Beyerer, J.: A user study on anonymization techniques for smart video surveillance. In: 2015 12th IEEE International Conference on Advanced Video and Signal Based Surveillance (AVSS), pp. 1–6. IEEE (2015)
2. Bretthauer, S., Krempel, E.: Videomonitoring zur sturzdetektion und alarmierung - eine technische und rechtliche analyse. In: Schweighofer, E., Kummer, F., Htzendorfer, W. (eds.) Transparenz - Tagungsband des 17. Internationalen Rechtsinformatik Symposions. pp. 525–534 (2014)
3. Bretthauer, S., Krempel, E., Birnstill, P.: Intelligente videoberwachnug in kranken- und pflegeeinrichtungen von morgen. Computer und Recht pp. 239–245 (2015)
4. Dufaux, F.: Video scrambling for privacy protection in video surveillance: recent results and validation framework. In: Proceeding of SPIE, vol. 8063, pp. 806302–806302-14 (2011). https://dx.doi.org/10.1117/12.883948
5. Dufaux, F., Ebrahimi, T.: Region-based transform-domain video scrambling. In: Proceeding of SPIE, vol. 6077, pp. 60771U–60771U-9 (2006). https://dx.doi.org/10.1117/12.643048
6. Ernst, S.: Zur un-zulssigkeit von dashcams. Computer und Recht pp. 620–624 (2015)
7. Harvan, M., Pretschner, A.: State-based usage control enforcement with data flow tracking using system call interposition. In: 2009 Third International Conference on Network and System Security, NSS 2009, pp. 373–380. IEEE (2009)
8. Hosang, J., Omran, M., Benenson, R., Schiele, B.: Taking a deeper look at pedestrians. In: Proceedings of the IEEE Conference on Computer Vision and Pattern Recognition. pp. 4073–4082 (2015)
9. Janard, K., Marurngsith, W.: Accelerating real-time face detection on a raspberry pi telepresence robot. In: Proceedings of the Fifth International Conference on Innovative Computing Technology, INTECH 2015, pp. 136–141 (May 2015)
10. Korshunov, P., Ebrahimi, T.: Using warping for privacy protection in video surveillance. In: 2013 18th International Conference on Digital Signal Processing (DSP), pp. 1–6 (July 2013)
11. Park, J., Sandhu, R.: Towards usage control models: Beyond traditional access control. In: Proceedings of 7th ACM Symposium on Access Control Models and Technologies (2002)

12. Pretschner, A., Hilty, M., Basin, D.A.: Distributed usage control. Commun. ACM **49**(9), 39–44 (2006). doi:10.1145/1151053
13. Rieckhoff, H.: Der Vorbehalt des Gesetzes im Europarecht. Mohr Siebeck, Tbingen (2007)
14. Rinner, B., Winkler, T.: Privacy-protecting smart cameras. In: Proceedings of the International Conference on Distributed Smart Cameras, ICDSC 2014, pp. 40:1–40:5, NY, USA. ACM, New York (2014)
15. Tian, Y., Luo, P., Wang, X., Tang, X.: Pedestrian detection aided by deep learning semantic tasks. In: Proceedings of the IEEE Conference on Computer Vision and Pattern Recognition, pp. 5079–5087 (2015)
16. Wagner, P.G., Birnstill, P., Krempel, E., Bretthauer, S., Beyerer, J.: Privacy-dashcam - datenschutzfreundliche dashcams durch erzwingen externer anonymisierung. In: Informatik 2016, 46. Jahrestagung der Gesellschaft für Informatik, 26.-30. Klagenfurt, Österreich. pp. 427–440 (2016). http://subs.emis.de/LNI/Proceedings/Proceedings259/article44.html
17. Zhang, S., Benenson, R., Omran, M., Hosang, J., Schiele, B.: How far are we from solving pedestrian detection? In: Proceedings of the IEEE Conference on Computer Vision and Pattern Recognition, pp. 1259–1267 (2016)
18. Zhang, S., Benenson, R., Schiele, B.: Filtered channel features for pedestrian detection. In: 2015 IEEE Conference on Computer Vision and Pattern Recognition (CVPR), pp. 1751–1760. IEEE (2015)

DLoc: Distributed Auditing for Data Location Compliance in Cloud

Mojtaba Eskandari[1(✉)], Bruno Crispo[1,2], and Anderson Santana de Oliveira[3]

[1] DISI, University of Trento, Trento, Italy
mojtaba.eskandari@unitn.it
[2] DistrNet, KULeuven, Leuven, Belgium
bruno.crispo@cs.kuleuven.be
[3] SAP Labs, Sophia Antipolis, France
anderson.santana.de.oliveira@sap.com

Abstract. The prevalence of mobile devices and their capability to access high speed Internet has transformed them into a portable pocket cloud interface. In order to protect user's privacy, the European Union Data Protection regulations restricts the transfer of European users' personal data within the geographical boundaries of the European Union itself. The matter of concern, however, is the enforcement of such regulations. Since cloud service provision is independent of physical location and data can travel to various servers, it is a challenging task to determine the location of data and enforce jurisdiction policies. In this paper we introduce a framework, named DLoc, which enables the end-users to track the location of their data after being transferred to the cloud. DLoc does not require a network of monitoring servers (landmarks) and does not need to reside and run within the target server. It uses a proof of data possession technique to guarantee that the cloud storage service possess the particular file and estimates its location(s) in a distributed manner without requiring the collaboration of the data controller or cloud provider. Empirical evaluations demonstrate that DLoc provides a better accuracy than its rival approaches in real world scenarios.

Keywords: Smartphone · Data transfer · Privacy protection · Jurisdiction policy

1   Introduction

Steadily increasing data volumes and the rising dependency of business and social life on data ubiquity have led to massive growth of cloud storage services such as Amazon S3, DropBox, or Google Drive. These services allow users to store their data on remote servers independently of geographical location. Cloud storage services utilize a federation schema by maintaining data at different providers which then distributes and replicates the data among different cloud storage providers. This reduces vendor lock-in and increases data availability through additional redundancy.

© Springer International Publishing AG 2017
J. Garcia-Alfaro et al. (Eds.): DPM/CBT 2017, LNCS 10436, pp. 202–218, 2017.
DOI: 10.1007/978-3-319-67816-0_12

Applying such federation schema can raise issues with compliance requirements. Especially the transparent data distribution and replication on the provider-side limit the user's direct control over data flows which lead to potential violations of compliance constraints. Personal data, for instance, sometimes must not leave a particular jurisdiction while the distribution in such a case is reasonable in terms of availability, it clearly can violate privacy compliance regulations such as the EU Data Protection Regulation [12]. Russia[1] and China[2] are imposing restriction on the location of the data processing as well.

The approaches introduced to track a file in cloud are divided into two major groups. The first group propose a schema requiring modification of underlying cloud services and collaboration of cloud service providers. The second group observes the environmental parameters (from outside of the cloud) in order to estimate the location of a file in cloud. The parameters include network delay, hop counts, mode of delay, median of delay, standard deviation of delay, and population density.

The second group has a clear advantage since it does not require modifying the underlying services; however, they require a wide spread network of servers communicating to each other, pinging cloud storage servers and monitor their data transfer practices. Having such network brings a significant cost to the system. In previous work [4], we introduced VLOC, a technique which monitors the dynamics of the network delay of the cloud service and builds a model out of it and keeps updating the model. It does it through measuring RTT delay from servers which have two major characteristics: (a) they are chosen randomly, so cloud provider is not able to filter them; (b) their physical location is known to VLOC. VLOC needs to be installed on a virtual machine and be initialized with the actual location of the data center; therefore, it can be used by data controllers to monitor and verify the location of their virtual machine in cloud. Data owners need to find the location of their data in cloud and VLoc does not provide such service. In fact, we need a technique which does not require the collaboration of cloud provider or data controller in order to monitor the location of data from a client machine.

In this work, we propose a framework, named DLoc, which does not require a network of monitoring servers and does not need to reside within the cloud. The idea is to distribute the monitoring tasks to DLoc agents. Each user who subscribes for the file tracking service participates in the file tracking procedure as a DLoc agent by letting her phone to challenge the cloud storage services and share her coarse-grained location with our service. DLoc makes use of proof of data possession technique to guarantee that the cloud storage service possess the particular file in question and estimates the location of all copies of files publicly available in the cloud.

The major challenge is to minimize the number of messages going to and coming from the DLoc agents while maximizing the accuracy of location estimation. It achieves that by observing the environment and studying the algorithms

---

[1] https://techcrunch.com/2016/11/17/linkedin-is-now-officially-blocked-in-russia/.
[2] http://www.bbc.co.uk/news/technology-40106826.

used in the system and provide a measurement to evaluate the accuracy and performance.

2   DLoc

In this section, we explain how **DLoc**, Distributed Data Localization framework, works. Figure 1 illustrates a general overview of DLoc and the major steps required to track a file in cloud. There are four major entities:

- **Data owner** wants to upload a file into *Cloud Storage B* which is located in her country. She wants to assure that her file stays in that region.
- **Cloud Storages** are the storage services used as backup storage and file sharing platform.
- **DLoc agents** are actually other smartphone users who use cloud storage services as well. They challenge a given target server and collect network latency information.
- **TPA** is a third party auditor server, which coordinates the DLoc agents and handles the file tracking procedure.

The data owner runs Algorithm 1 on her phone to upload the file. This algorithm encrypts the given file with an encryption key generated by the user's device. Then, it produces a set of meta-data required by DLoc to track the file securely.

Algorithm 1, first, encrypts the given file (F) with the input key (k). Then, it generates the hash value for each block of the encrypted file (h_i). The next step is to compute MAC (Message Authentication Code) for each of hash values of the blocks (m_i) with a randomly generated key. Please note that this random generated key is the same for all blocks of the given file (M_{sk}). The encrypted file (F_c) is uploaded to the cloud and the MAC values ($M = \{m_1, m_2, \ldots, m_n\}$)

Input: F: input file; k: encryption key;
Output: F_c: encrypted file; M: set of MAC codes for F_c blocks; M_{sk}: MAC
           encryption key;

1 F_c = Encrypt(F, k);
2 M_{sk} = **new** RandomKey();
3 B_{Fc} = F_c.getBlocks();
4 **for** (b_i in B_{Fc}) **do**
5 | h_i = Hash(b_i);
6 | m_i = MAC(h_i, M_{sk});
7 **end**
8 $M = \{m_1, m_2, \ldots, m_n\}$;
9 **return** $\{F_c, M, M_{sk}\}$;

Algorithm 1. The data owner runs this algorithm on her phone in order to prepare the file for upload and provide required metadata for the tracking procedure.

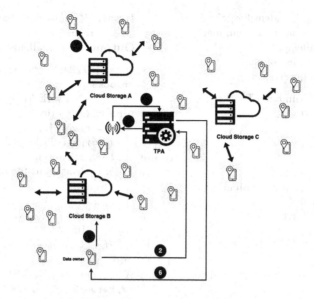

Fig. 1. System overview of DLoc.

along with the MAC key (M_{sk}) are published to the TPA. This procedure is shown by ① in Fig. 1.

When the data owner wants to track her file in the cloud, she queries the TPA (shown by by ② in Fig. 1). The TPA runs the Algorithm 2 which receives the list of DLoc agents (S), the number of required challenges (c) and the file identifier (F_{id}) which specified in the query coming from the data owner; and then it generates a list of challenge requests (R). The parameter S does not contain all the DLoc agents rather a selected subset of them. The selection policy is based on their availability, location, and the number of requests they have performed already. The number of challenges, c, is tunable; as its value grows the accuracy and also the overhead. The algorithm, first chooses c random blocks (B) of the file, then chooses a random member of DLoc agents and assigns a random block to it $\langle s_i, r_i \rangle$. In this setting, it is possible that a block is requested more than once and a DLoc agents receives more than one request. Finally the TPA sends each request to its corresponding DLoc agents, which is indicated by ③ in Fig. 1.

When a DLoc agent receives a challenge request from the TPA, it performs the Algorithm 3 shown by ④ in Fig. 1. This algorithm receives a set of requests (R'), challenges the server and provides challenge results (CR) to the TPA. This algorithm has two major tasks. First, to challenge the server whether it possesses the file or not. Second, to estimate the distance between the server and the DLoc agent in order to provide information for distributed localization. In order to challenge the server for the file possession, Since each request (r_i) contain a file block number, this algorithm queries the server for that particular block, then it computes the hash value of the block (h_i). In the meanwhile it

Input: F_{id}: file identifier; S: list of
DLoc agents; c: number of
challenges;
Output: R: list of challenge
requests;

1 $n = F_{id}.\text{getNumberOfBlocks}();$
2 $B = \{b \in \mathbb{N} | (b_i = $
$\quad RandomNumber(0, n)\big)\underset{i=1}{\overset{c}{}} \};$
3 $R = \{\};$
4 **for** (b'_i in B) **do**
5 $\quad s_i = S.\text{getRandomMember}();$
6 $\quad r_i = \textbf{new} \text{ Request}($
$\quad\quad F_{id}.\text{getURL}(), b'_i);$
7 $\quad R \leftarrow \langle s_i, r_i \rangle;$
8 **end**
9 **return** R;

Algorithm 2. Preparing the challenge messages for broadcasting to the DLoc agents.

Input: R': subset of challenge
requests;
Output: CR: challenge results;

1 $H = \{\};$ //Hash values of the
blocks
2 $N_{speed} = \text{Network.AnalyzeSpeed}();$
3 **for** (r_i in R') **do**
4 $\quad u = r_i.\text{getURL}();$
5 $\quad x = r_i.\text{getBlockNumber}();$
6 $\quad t_{start} = \text{Now}();$
7 $\quad b_i = \textbf{download}$ file-block $\#x$
from u;
8 $\quad t_{end} = \text{Now}();$
9 $\quad \Delta t_i = t_{end} - t_{start};$
10 $\quad h_i = \text{Hash}(b_i);$
11 $\quad H \leftarrow \langle x, h_i \rangle;$
12 **end**
13 $N = NormalizeNet(N_{speed}, \Delta t);$
//Network Measurements
14 $L = \text{DeviceLocation}();$
15 **return** $\{H, N, L\};$

Algorithm 3. Challenging the server.

measures the download time (Δt_i) that will be used later for distance estimation. The hash values and the measured round trip time (RTT) of the challenge request are sent to the TPA for further analysis.

There is a direct correlation between RTT value and physical distance [4]; however, there are a number of parameters involved which affect the accuracy. The major issue is that DLoc agents are located in various locations and use different network bandwidths. In order to mitigate the effect of the network variety, we take two approaches. The first one is to use an off-the-shelf technique to observe the DLoc agent network connection before challenging the server (N_{speed} in Algorithm 3). It uses an API provided by http://www.speedtest.net which encompasses a network of servers around the globe and finds a nearby server and communicate a number of packages, then it provides an observation on the network performance. The results of this API are useful to tune the weights of the RTT values in order to mitigate the effect of different network bandwidths on the estimation procedure. Moreover, due to network load, the traffic goes through different paths which causes various network delays; therefore, it lowers the accuracy of distance estimation based on RTT. In order to tackle this issue, we employ a machine learning technique, to tune the wights of parameters and adapt the estimation to the network fluctuation which is indicated by "$NormalizeNet(N_{speed}, \Delta t)$" in Algorithm 3.

Finally, each DLoc agent sends a set of the hashed value of each block (H), normalized network measurements (N) and its location (L) to the TPA (⑤ in Fig. 1). The TPA collects all the information from the DLoc agents and carries out two tasks: it verifies the challenges by running Algorithm 4 and determines the location of the server by executing Algorithm 5 which is discussed later.

Since the TPA possesses the MAC values of all blocks and their key (M_{sk}), by receiving the hash value of each block (h_j) is able to verify its integrity. Algorithm 4 receives the file identifier (F_{id}) and all collected challenge results and evaluates them. Each challenge result consists of a pair of block numbers and its hash value $\langle x_j, h_j \rangle$ which is retrieved from the server by a DLoc agent. This algorithm first computes the MAC value of the block number specified in the challenge result (m'_j) then compares it with the already stored MAC value for the same block (m_j). By doing the same procedure for all the received challenge results, we can verify the integrity of the stored file with a certain level of confidence. The confidence level depends on the number of challenge requests which may cause overheads.

Input: F_{id}: file identifier; CR: challenge results;
Output: verification result;

```
1   M_sk = F_id.getMACkey();
2   for ( c_i in CR) do
3   │   H_i = c_i.HashValues();
4   │   for ( ⟨x_j, h_j⟩ in H_i) do
5   │   │   m'_j = MAC( h_j, M_sk);
6   │   │   m_j = F_id.getMACValue(block# = x_j);
7   │   │   if ( m'_j ≠ m_j) then
8   │   │   │   return "Integrity Error!";
9   │   │   end
10  │   end
11  end
12  return "Verified!";
```

Algorithm 4. Verifying the challenges.

Computing the Location of a Point By triangulation. Computing the location of a point, p_x, on a surface is possible when we have the locations of at least three nearby points, $\{p_1, p_2, p_3\}$, and their distance from p_x. As Fig. 2 illustrates, if we draw a circle with the center of each point and the radius of their distances (d_1, d_2, d_3) from p_x, all the circles meet each other at p_x. By finding their intersection point, we can determine the location of p_x. This technique is called "*Triangulation*" [18] or "*Trilateration*" [15].

Before we utilize triangulation technique, we need to consider that since Earth is not a surface rather a sphere, the location of objects on earth is represented by the latitude (ϕ) and longitude (λ) values which are defined in polar system. The latitude of a point is the angle between the equatorial plane and the straight line that passes through that point and through (or close to) the center of the Earth. The longitude of a point is the angle east or west of a reference

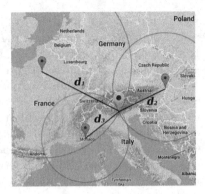

Fig. 2. Triangulation for specifying the physical location of a host by knowing the physical locations and distances from other nearby hosts.

meridian to another meridian that passes through that point [16]. In order to calculate the intersection points of the circles, we convert this coordination into the Cartesian system by utilizing Eq. 1 and for the reverse operation, Eq. 2.

$$
\begin{aligned}
x &= \lambda \cdot \cos(\phi) \\
y &= \lambda \cdot \sin(\phi)
\end{aligned}
\tag{1}
$$

$$
\begin{aligned}
\lambda &= \sqrt{x^2 + y^2} \\
\phi &= \tan^{-1}\left(\tfrac{y}{x}\right)
\end{aligned}
\tag{2}
$$

We write the equation of a circle in the following form:

$$
(x - x_i)^2 + (y - y_i)^2 = d_i^2 \quad i = 1 \ldots n
\tag{3}
$$

where (x_i, y_i) indicates the center of the circle (the location of the ith DLoc agent in our system) and d_i its radius, which is the distance between the server and the agent. In order to find intersection point of multiple circles, we do it two by two *i.e.* in pairs. However, before trying to find intersection of two circles we have to figure out if they touch each other. Suppose that we have two circles i, j; if we draw a line between the two centers (d_{ij}), compare its length with the radii $(d_i$ and $d_j)$ and employing the triangle existing conditions [17], we can conclude that whether those circles can be used for our purpose or not. We obtain the distance between the centers of two circles by measuring their Euclidean distance as the following:

$$
d_{ij} = \sqrt{(x_i - x_j)^2 + (y_i - y_j)^2}
\tag{4}
$$

The situation of the two circles is determined by the following conditions:

- $d_{ij} < \sqrt{(d_i - d_j)^2}$: One circle is inside the other so there is no intersection.
- $d_{ij} > d_i + d_j$: The circles are too far apart to intersect.
- $d_{ij} = d_i + d_j$: The circles touch at a single point.
- $d_{ij} < d_i + d_j$: The circles touch at two points.

If two circles touch at least at one point, we subtract their two equations, in 3, to get the line equation. By solving that subtraction the following equation is yielded which determines the intersection point(s):

$$(x,y) = \frac{1}{2}(x_j + x_i, y_j + y_i) + \frac{d_i^2 - d_j^2}{2d_{ij}}(x_j - x_i, y_j - y_i)$$
$$\pm \frac{1}{2}\sqrt{2\frac{d_i^2 + d_j^2}{d_{ij}^2} - \frac{(d_i^2 - d_j^2)^2}{d_{ij}^4} - 1}(x_j - x_i, y_j - y_i)$$

(5)

In order to compute the location of a point, this equation is applied on the locations of at least three nearby points and yields the intersection point which equals to the location of the first point.

2.1 Estimating the Data Location

Algorithm 5, named the localization algorithm, uses Eq. 5 and estimates the location of the data based on a set of given challenge results (CR). Each challenge result contains the location of the DLoc agent (center of the circle) and network measurement information to compute the its distance from the server (the radius of the circle). This algorithm estimates at least one location for the data. As the cloud storage provider might create multiple copies of the data on various servers, this algorithm handles this matter as well by determining the locations of all accessible copies of data.

The localization algorithm, first, creates an empty list of points (P). Then, for each given challenge result, it computes the distance from server by calling `Distance()` function. This function basically models the correlation between network delay and distance using a polynomial regression function, which is employed by VLOC as well [4]. The next major step is to calculate the intersection points of the circle of the current challenge results with the results received from the other DLoc agents. Then it verifies the circles and drops the ones which are not useful for localization according to the conditions mentioned above. There is an exception to this. Since in practice there is always a negligible error in distance estimation, sometimes the circles are close to each other but just for few meters, they do not match the condition. In order to overcome this issue, we define an error tolerance range parameter (ε) to compensate the error. The algorithm finds all intersection points amongst all the given circles and keep them in the P list. At the end, it determines the popular ranges (F_L) in which a considerable number of points are estimated. These popular ranges indicate the location of servers storing the data.

3 Empirical Evaluation

To evaluate DLoc we run experiments on 4 android devices (playing the role of servers) situated in four cities and in total, $1,422$ web hosts playing as DLoc

Input: CR: challenge results; ε: error tolerance range;
Output: F_L: locations of the file;

```
1  P = new List();
2  for ( cᵢ in CR) do
3  |    dᵢ = Distance( cᵢ.Net()); //Network Measurements
4  |    lᵢ = cᵢ.DeviceLocation();
5  |    for ( cⱼ in CR ∧ j > i) do
6  |    |    dⱼ = Distance( cⱼ.Net());
7  |    |    lⱼ = cⱼ.DeviceLocation();
8  |    |    dᵢⱼ = ‖lᵢ − lⱼ‖; //Euclidean distance
9  |    |    if ( dᵢⱼ < √((dᵢ − dⱼ)²) ) then
10 |    |    |    continue; //Ignore j
11 |    |    end
12 |    |    if ( dᵢⱼ > dᵢ + dⱼ ) then
13 |    |    |    if ( dᵢⱼ > dᵢ + dⱼ + ε ) then
14 |    |    |    |    continue;
15 |    |    |    end
16 |    |    |    inc dᵢ, dⱼ until dᵢⱼ ≤ dᵢ + dⱼ;
17 |    |    |    report "ε is used";
18 |    |    end
19 |    |    (p₁, p₂) = IntersectPoints(cᵢ, cⱼ);
20 |    |    P ← p₁;
21 |    |    P ← {p₂|p₁ ≠ p₂};
22 |    end
23 end
24 F_L = A set of the most popular ranges in P;
25 return F_L;
```

Algorithm 5. Localization procedure.

agents. As we measure the round trip time value (RTT) such role changing does not influence the final result.

We designed and implemented an android app to challenge the servers and collect network delay measurements between each DLoc agent and the nearby smartphone. Please note that in order to avoid confusion, we use the same terminology that we have explained in the approach. In other words, in the data analysis we do not consider this role changing.

This section explains the data collection process and describes the evaluation measures, the experimental results and their analysis.

3.1 Dataset Collection

In our settings there are four servers located in Trento, Turin, Eindhoven, and Leuven and there are many DLoc agents challenging them. We partially used the data collected in [4] including the address and location of numerous landmarks situated near the mentioned cities. Each DLoc agent challenges the server by utilizing an HTTP request for over 15 times a day and measures the RTT values of each challenge. In the following sections we analyze the data collected by DLoc agents and study the effect of various factors on the final results.

3.2   Evaluation Goals

The experiments are designed to answer the following research questions:

- **RQ1 Accuracy:** How accurate is DLoc to estimate the location of server hosting the file?
- **RQ2 Environment:** What are the parameters, such as number of DLoc agents, distance of the agents from the server, etc., influencing the accuracy of DLoc?

3.3   Evaluation Measure

As the main task of DLoc is to determine the location(s) of an uploaded file (data) in the cloud, to evaluate it, the distance between the actual physical location of the machine where data resides and its estimated location. We used error of average distance estimation defined in the Eq. 6 for accuracy evaluation.

$$E_{avg} = \frac{1}{N} \sum_{i=1}^{N} \|p_e^i - p_o^i\| \qquad (6)$$

where N is the number of executions of the test, p_e^i denotes the estimated physical location of the server (cloud storage) in the ith test p_o^i is the observed location (the real physical location) for that server. Finally, E_{avg} refers to the calculated average error in KM.

We evaluated the approach with challenges generated by various DLoc agents that spread widely around the servers. In order to provide a comprehensive assessment we apply a random value combination. We used a slightly modified version of cross validation technique [7] to perform such a it. We trained the system with 80% of the data and test with the remaining 20%. The operation was repeated for a 1000 times by shuffling the data each time. Moreover, we used the same setting for all 4 different servers situated in 4 cities.

3.4   Results and Discussions

The results of the experiment composed of 1000 runs in each of the four cites, i.e., Trento, Turin, Eindhoven, Leuven, are aggregated in Fig. 3(a–d), respectively. Figure 3 shows the actual location of the file hosting cloud servers, location of the surrounding DLoc agents and the location of the server hosting the file as estimated by DLoc. On the map shown in the figure, the blue, yellow and red markers represent the actual location, the estimated location and the location of the DLoc agents. As shown in the figure, DLoc estimates the location of the server with a reasonable degree of accuracy, i.e., the estimated location is within

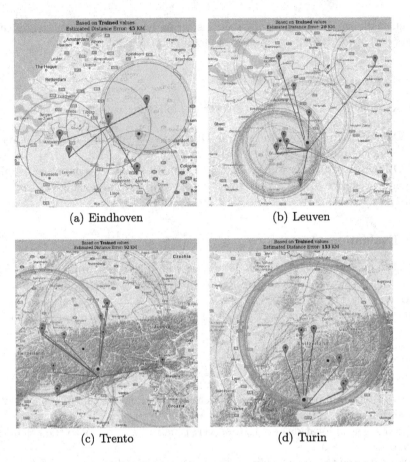

(a) Eindhoven   (b) Leuven

(c) Trento   (d) Turin

Fig. 3. Screen shots of DLoc estimating a file on the four servers situated in multiple cities. The light red markers show the locations of the DLoc agents, the blue marker indicates the actual location of the server, and the yellow marker points to the estimated physical location of the server. (Color figure online)

92 KM of the actual location for the Trento node, 153 KM for the Turin node, 45 KM for the Eindhoven node and 20 KM for the Leuven node (RQ1). Table 1 summarizes the results for each city.

Figure 4 illustrates the average error of the location determination for various number of challenges. As the results in this figure show, for the servers located in Eindhoven and Leuven, increasing the number of challenges does not have a significant impact on the estimation error while for the other two servers specially Turin, a notable change can be observed. While one of the reasons is the sparsity of DLoc agents around each server, we also study the influence of distance, between the agents and the server, on the accuracy.

To study the influence of distance on the accuracy of location estimation (RQ2), we unitized the distance into multiple ranges and performed experiments

Table 1. The summary of the results for each city.

	Eindhoven	Leuven	Trento	Turin
Min error (KM)	22.25	16.54	70.06	134.38
Max error (KM)	47.39	33.92	219.32	295.54
Standard deviation	2.22	2.02	30.67	30.54

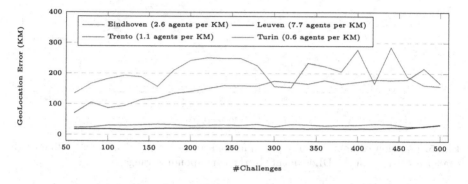

Fig. 4. GeoLocation error estimation per various number of challenges.

on all DLoc agents situated only in each individual range. Figure 5 illustrates the results of such experiment. As it shows in the range of $20-40$ KM, only in Leuven there are a number of agents surrounding the server and sent 320 challenges while there is no agent until the range of $140-160$ KM where the number of challenges increased and the accuracy slightly declined due to the distance. The similar steady move is observed for Eindhoven for the ranges of $60-80$ KM, $100-120$ KM and $140-160$ KM. Turin and Trento have a bit different story; their closest agents are in the ranges of $140-160$ KM and $200-220$ KM respectively. Moreover, the number of challenges in these ranges are quite small (20 and 85) compare to what the servers located in Eindhoven and Leuven experience in their closest range. These two reasons explain the yielded lower accuracy for Turin and Trento. Therefore, not only the number of DLoc agents influences the accuracy, also their distance from the servers has a notable effect. Which means, the closer to the server the agents are, the less number of challenges is required to track data effectively.

It worth to mention that the obtained results even for Turin and Trento are acceptable as the main usage of DLoc is to monitor the enforcement of jurisdiction regulations which, at its finest granularity, limits the data to boundaries of a country. Moreover, it can have other usage as well including quality of service measurement.

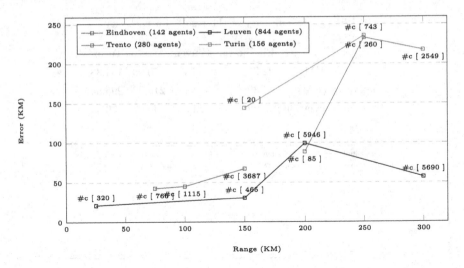

Fig. 5. Location estimation error per individual ranges. "#c" denotes the number of challenges sent from the DLoc agents in the corresponding range.

4   Security and Privacy Analysis

DLoc does not require the cloud storage provider (CSP) to modify their systems. When DLoc is running, all the CSP can realize is that a user shares her files with a number of other users and the other smartphones (DLoc agents) participating in geolocating the file are chosen randomly and can be anywhere near the server or elsewhere; therefore, the CSP is not able to impose a fake delay on the responses of the challenges it receives.

In order to bypass DLoc, there are two possible scenarios. The first one is to break into the TPA which handles the challenges, DLoc agents and prepares the results. The second scenario is to register a huge number of smart devices (DLoc agents) in the TPA and make them to collude with each other to prepare a fake delay time and fake location. Both scenarios are quite expensive for the CSP to perform. Therefore, the cost of compliance is negligible compare to bypassing DLoc.

5   Limitations

Although DLoc is promising in a real world application, there are a number of limitations need to be considered. The first limitation is dependency to the number of DLoc agents and their distance to the target server. If there is not enough DLoc agents in less than about 400 KM of a server, the accuracy of DLoc will fall down.

Moreover since the cloud provider is considered as an adversary, it can inject random delays to the outgoing traffic to reduce the accuracy of DLoc. As the location of DLoc agents are considered as trusted, such random delay can yield different measurement by each agent and increase the estimation error. However, the strength point is that by doing so the cloud provider practically cuts its quality of service; therefore, abusing such limitation is costly for the could provider.

In practice, integrating DLoc to the current cloud storage providers (*e.g.* Amazon, Google drive, etc.) without modification of their systems imposes another limitation on the user. In fact, the data owner must share the file with the other users (giving them access to the file), even if it is encrypted for them to challenge the servers, it is still a limitation.

6   Related Work

In the literature, there are a number of approaches to determine the location of data in cloud. Some focus on providing a cloud infrastructure which is able to handle the enforcement of data location policies which certainly require hardware and/or software modification in cloud services. Recently studies have drawn their attentions to finding the correlation between the network delay and geographic distance which then can be used to determine the location of an Internet node. Here we review both groups briefly with more emphasis on the second group as its more close to our work.

6.1   Server Side Data Geolocation

Krau and Fusenig propose an approach utilizing a Trusted Platform Module (TPM) on host platforms for data geolocation in clouds [9]. They assume that a certification authority stores the location of a host with its TMP's identity. Then, the owner of a virtual machine requests a certification of the host in order to transfer data. This solution is costly to implement due to the variety in cloud platforms and it requires administrative methods to perform the verification of the location.

Paladi et al. introduce a high-level architecture in cloud storage systems for a trustful location-based mechanism for data transfer control [11]. These approaches require the modification of underlaying layer of cloud services which are quite costly and difficult to be adopted by cloud providers.

6.2   Delay Based Data Geolocation

Geoping assumes that the hosts with a similar network delay are at the same location [10]. Basically, Geoping challenges the target server from a number of known landmarks and builds a set of path-delay information. To find the location of an unknown target server, it constantly pings the server from the landmarks at known paths and uses Euclidean distance and finally chooses the landmark with the best match.

Constraint-based geolocation employs multilateration, which is used by DLoc as well, where each landmark draws a circle around itself with a radius of the distance to the target server [6].

Yong et al. introduce a three layer geolocation algorithm, which employs a large database of landmarks, their relative distances and delay measurements [13]. A constraint-based geolocation algorithm to find the gross area, a distance constraint-based method to shrink the possible area, and then a mapping technique to determine a near landmark.

In order to reduce cost, *IGOD* selects a small subset of landmarks with their optimal position based on the diversity parameter [8]. Although the authors even achieved a better accuracy compare to the similar previous works, it still needs a network of fixed landmarks (*e.g.* Planet Lab) which is difficult to implement in practice.

Watson et al. demonstrate that verifying the location of data in a cloud storage has a limited accuracy [14]. They show that a collusion of the cloud provider with a number of malicious host makes it impossible for users to verify the location of their file accurately. The main drawback of this approach is that it requires a set of trusted landmarks exists in order to verify the existence of a file on a host.

GeoProof combines a proof of retrievability scheme with a delay based protocol to determine the distance between a host and a verifier [2]. They assume a tamper proof GPS device in the local network of cloud provider communicating with a third party to verify the location of data. The major drawback of this protocol is that cloud providers are not willing to have a black box attached to their local network. Moreover, the GPS signals received by the device can be faked by a malicious cloud provider.

Gondree and Peterson proposed a schema to tackle such problem by employing a latency function built based on the current network traffic observation [5]. The main disadvantage of this approach is the requirement of a dedicated network of landmarks which is quite costly. Moreover, in the model building phase the landmarks send messages amongst themselves in order to find a baseline for the Internet delay which does not quite represent the real environment. In fact, this scenario does not consider the latencies imposed by cloud mediation services such as authentication, decryption, etc. Therefore, the observation has an inherent limitation which influences the distance estimation.

Abdou et al. show that having a fixed network of landmarks can be manipulated [1]. The location of landmarks will be revealed over time and since usually delay based approaches use UDP or ICMP protocols, an adversary is able to filter them out and play with the delays of the responses in order to misrepresent its own location.

There is a parallel work with DLoc which uses network delays and a network of smartphones to estimate the physical location of a server [3]. However, the focus of DLoc is to estimate the location of data (*e.g.* a file) in the cloud. It verifies the server for the possession of user's data and tracks all available online copies of the file on all servers. Moreover, the best error rate reported in their study is 189 KM while the average error rate for DLoc in Leuven and Eindhoven is less than 50 KM and for Turin and Trento less than 150 KM. DLoc proposes a comprehensive framework which adapt itself automatically by observing the environment and remove noisy data.

7 Conclusions and Future Work

This paper introduces DLoc, which determines the location of a file transferred to the cloud. It uses a proof of data possession technique to guarantee that the cloud storage service possess the particular file and estimates its location(s) in a distributed manner without requiring the collaboration of the data controller or cloud provider. DLoc has a number of advantages compare to its rivals. First, it does not require a dedicated network of trusted landmarks which makes it quite economic to be used in a real world setting. Second, it does not require a modification to the cloud services. Third, it is able to deal with multiple copies of data. Fourth, employing machine learning techniques has made DLoc robust against network fluctuations and various types of connections. Finally, since it uses smartphones instead of fixed landmarks, it has motivation for DLoc agents to use the service and participate in the process.

In a real-world scenario where DLoc serves a huge number of smartphone users, therefore it is able to find the locations of data centers precise enough in order to report all the data centers in the world representing a physical risk to all cloud providers. Moreover, since DLoc provides measurements and statistics on where data is stored and how long does it take to be delivered, it can be used to measure the quality of service for content delivery to mobile users and help to improve it.

We are planning to include anonymization techniques to offer more protection to the DLoc mobile users, and provide test data for the Toreador project.

Acknowledgment. This project was partially funded by the European Union's under grant 317387 SECENTIS (FP7-PEOPLE-2012-ITN) and Horizon 2020 research and innovation programme under grant agreement No. 688797.

References

1. Abdou, A., Matrawy, A., van Oorschot, P.C.: Accurate manipulation of delay-based internet geolocation. In: Proceedings of the 2017 ACM on Asia Conference on Computer and Communications Security, pp. 887–898. ACM (2017)
2. Albeshri, A., Boyd, C., Nieto, J.G.: Geoproof: proofs of geographic location for cloud computing environment. In: 2012 32nd International Conference on Distributed Computing Systems Workshops (ICDCSW), pp. 506–514 (2012)
3. Ciavarrini, G., Luconi, V., Vecchio, A.: Smartphone-based geolocation of internet hosts. Comput. Netw. **116**, 22–32 (2017)
4. Eskandari, M., De Oliveira, A.S., Crispo, B.: VLoc: an approach to verify the physical location of a virtual machine in cloud. In: 2014 IEEE 6th International Conference on Cloud Computing Technology and Science (CloudCom), pp. 86–94. IEEE (2014)
5. Gondree, M., Peterson, Z.N.J.: Geolocation of data in the cloud. In: Proceedings of the Third ACM Conference on Data and Application Security and Privacy, CODASPY 2013, pp. 25–36. ACM, New York (2013)
6. Gueye, B., Ziviani, A., Crovella, M., Fdida, S.: Constraint-based geolocation of internet hosts. IEEE/ACM Trans. Netw. **14**(6), 1219–1232 (2006)

7. Hastie, T., Friedman, J., Tibshirani, R.: Model assessment and selection. In: Hastie, T., Friedman, J., Tibshirani, R. (eds.) The Elements of Statistical Learning, pp. 219–259. Springer, New York (2009). doi:10.1007/978-0-387-21606-5_7

8. Jaiswal, C., Kumar, V.: IGOD: identification of geolocation of cloud datacenters. In: 2015 IEEE 40th Local Computer Networks Conference Workshops (LCN Workshops), pp. 665–672. IEEE (2015)

9. Krauß, C., Fusenig, V.: Using trusted platform modules for location assurance in cloud networking. In: Lopez, J., Huang, X., Sandhu, R. (eds.) NSS 2013. LNCS, vol. 7873, pp. 109–121. Springer, Heidelberg (2013). doi:10.1007/978-3-642-38631-2_9

10. Padmanabhan, V.N., Subramanian, L.: An investigation of geographic mapping techniques for internet hosts. In: ACM SIGCOMM Computer Communication Review, vol. 31, pp. 173–185. ACM (2001)

11. Paladi, N., Michalas, A.: One of our hosts in another country: challenges of data geolocation in cloud storage. In: 2014 4th International Conference on Wireless Communications, Vehicular Technology, Information Theory and Aerospace and Electronic Systems (VITAE), pp. 1–6. IEEE (2014)

12. European Parliament and of the Council: General data protection regulation (2016). Final Version. http://data.europa.eu/eli/reg/2016/679/oj. Accessed 27 Apr 2016

13. Wang, Y., Burgener, D., Flores, M., Kuzmanovic, A., Huang, C.: Towards street-level client-independent IP geolocation. NSDI **11**, 27–27 (2011)

14. Watson, G.J., Safavi-Naini, R., Alimomeni, M., Locasto, M.E., Narayan, S.: Lost: location based storage. In: Proceedings of the 2012 ACM Workshop on Cloud Computing Security Workshop, pp. 59–70. ACM (2012)

15. Wikipedia: Trilateration (2014)

16. Wikipedia: Geographic coordinate system (2016). https://en.wikipedia.org/wiki/Geographic_coordinate_system

17. Wikipedia: Triangle (2016). https://en.wikipedia.org/wiki/Triangle

18. Wikipedia: Triangulation (2016). https://en.wikipedia.org/wiki/Triangulation

Inonymous:
Anonymous Invitation-Based System

Sanaz Taheri Boshrooyeh[(✉)] and Alptekin Küpçü

Department of Computer Engineering, Koç University, İstanbul, Turkey
{staheri14,akupcu}@ku.edu.tr

Abstract. In invitation-based systems, a user is allowed to join upon receipt of a certain number of invitations from the existing members. The system administrator approves the new membership if he authenticates the inviters and the invitations, knowing who is invited by whom. However, the inviter-invitee relationship is privacy-sensitive information and can be exploited for inference attacks: The invitee's profile (e.g., political view or location) might leak through the inviters' profiles. To cope with this problem, we propose *Inonymous*, an anonymous invitation-based system where the administrator and the existing members do not know who is invited by whom. We formally define and prove the inviter anonymity against honest but curious adversaries and the information theoretic unforgeability of invitations. *Inonymous* is efficiently scalable in the sense that once a user joins the system, he can immediately act as an inviter, without re-keying and imposing overhead on the existing members. We also present *InonymouX*, an anonymous cross-network invitation-based system where users join one network (e.g., Twitter) using invitations of members of another network (e.g., Facebook).

Keywords: Invitation-based system · Anonymity · Unforgeability · Cross-network invitation

1 Introduction

An invitation-based system consists of a server (administrator) and a group of members. New users join the system only by obtaining invitations from a certain number of existing members. Each invitation confirms some level of trust to the invitee. This authentication method is also known as *trustee-based social authentication*. Invitation-based systems benefit from trustee-based authentication for the initial registration of a user to the system. Afterward, any authentication technique e.g., a password, can be utilized for the further logging into the system.

Invitation-based systems are employed due to various reasons such as a limited number of server resources to cover an arbitrary number of users, improving the quality of services by constraining the number of members, securing the system against fake users, and providing data or service privacy for the system. As a well-known historical example, Google applied invitation-based registration in the early stages of its new services like Gmail, Orkut, and Google Wave [1].

© Springer International Publishing AG 2017
J. Garcia-Alfaro et al. (Eds.): DPM/CBT 2017, LNCS 10436, pp. 219–235, 2017.
DOI: 10.1007/978-3-319-67816-0_13

In invitation-based systems, the administrator knows the identity of the user's inviters to authenticate and manage new registrations. In some other cases, not only the administrator but also other members of the system are informed about the correspondence of a newcomer and his inviters. For example, in Telegram chat application, once a new user joins a group, its referee's identity is broadcasted to the group members. The user's referees are mostly among the user's acquaintances (e.g., colleagues, home mates, family members, close friends) who have many common preferences with the user. Due to this reason, information like location, religious beliefs, sexual orientation, and political views can be inferred about a user by analyzing the common features among his inviters [3,8]. Thus, the set of user's referees is privacy-sensitive information.

Related Works: Typically, trustee-based social authentication is considered as a backup authentication method, rather than the primary one. A backup authentication method is employed where the user fails to pass the primary authentication e.g., forgetting the password [4]. The account holder determines a set of trustees to the server in advance. When the user loses access to his account, the server sends recovery codes to the trustees. Upon collection of enough number (recovery threshold) of codes from the trustees, the user recovers his access. *Forest fire attack* [9] is the most significant security issue in this context where an attacker compromises a few seed accounts and exploits this to steal other accounts. The main security measures against forest fire attack are increasing the recovery threshold [10], assigning time to live to the recovery codes [10,13], keeping the identity of trustees hidden from the recovery requester [9], bit stuffing [9], and using encrypted recovery codes [13]. None of the mentioned solutions preserve the anonymity of inviters as it is not a concern in those applications. Instead, the identity of a trustee (i.e., inviter) is by default known to the server so that the server can communicate with the trustees for the account recovery procedure. On the contrary, in invitation based systems, the anonymity of trustees (inviters) is a security concern due to the inference attacks. This indicates that the existing trustee-based solutions are not applicable to invitation based systems as they disregard the anonymity of trustees.

To cope with this problem, we developed an anonymous invitation-based system named *Inonymous*. Our system overview is depicted in Fig. 1. *Inonymous* consists of three entities: A server (administrator), existing members (inviters) and a newcomer (invitee). The invitee receives invitations from a subset of existing members i.e., inviters. The invitee knows the inviters beforehand via some other means outside the network to be joined to. In the Gmail example, Google employees and their families/friends are the inviters and invitees, respectively. The invitee combines the invitations into a single invitation letter and submits to the server. If the invitation is verified by the server, the invitee joins the system. No interaction is required between inviters and the server. In contrast to the prior studies, in *Inonymous* inviters can anonymously add new users. This anonymity is not only against the server but also against the other members including inviters of the same invitee. Despite the anonymity of the inviters, the server can still verify the integrity of the invitations.

That is, a malicious invitee cannot join the system without threshold many legitimate invitations. We formally define inviter anonymity and invitation unforgeability and provide game based proofs of security. Furthermore, *Inonymous* efficiently enables the recently invited users to act as inviters. This is done instantly and without rekeying the system and contacting existing members.

Note that, while *Inonymous* guarantees the anonymity of the inviters in the phase of registration, it does not tackle with the anonymous interaction and relationship of users within the system. For example, while a user is invited to a Facebook group using *Inonymous*, his interaction with other group members might imply some information about his potential inviters. Thus, the anonymous interaction of users must be addressed independently and is out of the scope of this paper. But recall that the application of invitation-based system is not limited to the social networks e.g., a cloud does not constitute a social network while it may employ invitation-based notion to offer a limited service or storage to the recommended customers.

Additionally, we construct *InonymouX*, an anonymous cross-network invitation-based system on top of *Inonymous* which can be of independent interest. In the cross-network design, a user joins one system e.g., Twitter, by obtaining invitations from members of another network e.g., Facebook. The cross-network design is beneficial especially to bootstrap a system, for example in the case where a research group wants to hire qualified researchers from another group. A qualified researcher is the one with enough recommendations i.e., invitations from his own group.

Our contributions are as follows:

- *Inonymous* is the **first anonymous** invitation-based system that provides *inviter anonymity* and *invitation unforgeability*.
- We provide **formal security definitions and proofs** for both security objectives.
- *Inonymous* is **efficiently scalable** in terms of the number of inviters.
- We propose the **first cross-network anonymous** invitation-based system called *InonymouX* where the possibility of inter-network invitation is provided.

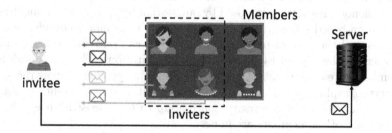

Fig. 1. *Inonymous* system overview.

2   Model

Inonymous is composed of three entities: a server, a set of existing members and a new user who is willing to join the system. The server is responsible for managing and validating users' registrations and generating certificates upon the occurrence of a new membership. The existing members are given necessary information which enables them to make anonymous individual invitations for their trusted ones. The newcomer becomes the member of the system if he obtains a certain number (denoted by t as threshold) of invitations from the existing members i.e., inviters. The invitee knows his inviters prior to joining the system. He collects and aggregates individual invitations to make a single final invitation letter. The aggregation of invitations has the main effect in inviters anonymity. Once the newcomer hands over his invitation to the server, the server is in charge to authenticate the invitation and provide necessary information for him. We assume that the system starts with at least t initially registered members (e.g., Google employees in the Gmail example), who are given credentials to join the system by the server directly. Henceforth, those existing members start inviting others.

Throughout the paper, we assume secure and authenticated channels per communication. In *Inonymous*, we seek two security objectives:

- **Inviter anonymity:** By inviter anonymity, we aim at protecting the identity of the inviters against the server and other members. The invitations should not leak any information about the inviters. We assume that the adversary is the server who may collude with a subset of a newcomer's inviters (obviously not all of them). The adversary is presumed to be honest but curious. We formally prove that the identity of non-colluding inviters remains anonymous to the adversary. Note that the newcomer is supposed to be concerned about his privacy hence does not reveal the identity of his inviters to the adversary, otherwise, the inviter anonymity is meaningless. This is defined in Sect. 7.1 as a game where the adversary controls the server and $t - 1$ inviters.
- **Invitation unforgeability:** The invitation unforgeability indicates that a user i.e., an adversary who has an insufficient number (t') of inviters $(t' < t)$ should not be able to join the system even if he acts maliciously. The adversary can join if he forges some invitations on his own. Recall that the assumption of $t' < t$ is not a restriction imposed by our system but it is a requirement in any invitation-based system. Indeed, threshold-many members collude then they can control the system in the sense that they can add an arbitrary number of users to the system by generating valid invitations. Thus, a collusion of t members threats any invitation-based system independent of how the system is cryptographically designed. We define invitation unforgeability in Sect. 7.2 as a game where the adversary controls up to $t - 1$ existing users, but the server and other members are honest.

Overview: *Inonymous* is managed by a server who owns a master value and a decryption key. The server shares the master value among the existing members using (t)-Shamir secret sharing scheme where t is the threshold value. Each newcomer requires t invitations to join the system. Each invitation is the masked version of an inviter's master share alongside with the encryption of masking value that is pseudorandomly generated. Once the invitee obtains his invitations, he can unify them into a single invitation by utilizing the homomorphic property of Shamir shares and El Gamal encryption scheme. Invitations are tied to a specific invitee using a server generated token given to each invitee.

3 Preliminaries

Negligible Function. A function f is called negligible if for every polynomial $p(.)$ there exists integer N such that for every $n > N$, $f(n) < \frac{1}{p(n)}$.

Pseudo Random Generator. A deterministic polynomial time function P: $\{0,1\}^n \to \{0,1\}^{l(n)}$ (where $l(.)$ is a polynomial) is called Pseudo Random Generator (PRG) if $n < l(n)$ and for any probabilistic polynomial-time distinguisher D there exists a negligible function $negl(.)$ such that:

$$|Pr[x \leftarrow \{0,1\}^n : D(P(x)) = 1] - Pr[y \leftarrow \{0,1\}^{l(n)} : D(y) = 1]| = negl(n) \quad (1)$$

Shamir Secret Sharing Scheme. Secret sharing is a tool by which a secret is shared among several parties such that the secret is recoverable in the presence of a certain number of shareholders. The Shamir secret sharing scheme [2,6] works based on polynomial evaluations. The secret owner selects a polynomial f of degree $t - 1$ randomly and sets the secret data S as the evaluation of that function at point 0 i.e., $f(0) = S$. Since each polynomial of degree $t - 1$ can be uniquely reconstructed by having t distinct points of that function, t Shamir shareholders are able to reconstruct the secret. Shamir shares are homomorphic under addition operation i.e., let $[s_1]$ and $[s_2]$ be Shamir shares of S_1 and S_2, then $[s_1] + [s_2]$ constitutes a share of $S_1 + S_2$.

Multiplicative Homomorphic Encryption Scheme. A public key encryption scheme consists of three algorithms $\pi = (KeyGen, Enc, Dec)$. π is called multiplicative homomorphic encryption if for every a and b, $Enc(a) \otimes Enc(b) = Enc(a \cdot b)$ where a and b belong to the encryption message space and $\otimes$ is an operation over ciphertexts. As an example, in El Gamal encryption [11], $\otimes$ corresponds to a simple multiplication of two ciphertexts. Additionally, we have $Enc(a)^c = Enc(a^c)$ where a is a plain message and c is any integer. Throughout the paper, we consider El Gamal scheme as our underlying encryption scheme.

Signature Scheme. A signature scheme [12] consists of three algorithms $\gamma = (SGen, Sign, SVrfy)$. A pair of keys (sk, vk) is generated via $SGen$ where sk is the signature key and vk is the verification key. The signer signs a message m using sk by computing $\eta = Sign_{sk}(m)$. Given the verification key vk, a receiver of signature runs $SVrfy_{vk}(\eta, m)$ to verify.

Bilinear Map. Consider G_1 and G_2 as multiplicative groups of prime order q. Let g_1 be the generator of G_1. We employ an efficiently computable bilinear map $e : G_1 \times G_1 \to G_2$ with the following properties [14]

- Bilinearity: $\forall u, v \in G_1$ and $\forall a, b \in \mathbb{Z}_q : e(u^a, v^b) = e(u, v)^{a \cdot b}$.
- Non-degeneracy: $e(g_1, g_1) \neq 1$.

Computational Diffie-Hellman Assumption. Given a cyclic group G of prime order q with a generator g, and two randomly selected group elements $h_1 = g^{r_1}, h_2 = g^{r_2}$, the Computational Diffie-Hellman (CDH) assumption [5] is hard relative to G if for every PPT adversary A there exists a negligible function $negl(\lambda)$ where λ is the security parameter, such that:

$$\Pr[A(G, q, g, h_1, h_2) = g^{r_1 \cdot r_2}] = negl(\lambda)$$

4   Construction

Inonymous consists of six algorithms: *SetUp, Token generation (Tgen), Invitation generation (Igen), Invitation collection (Icoll), Invitation Verification (Ivrfy)* and *Registration (Reg)*. Figure 2 visualizes the interaction of entities and the order of execution of algorithms in *Inonymous*. The *server* runs the *SetUp* algorithm to set the system's parameters. Every new user (invitee) must obtain a token from the server. To generate a token, the *server* runs *Tgen* algorithm. The invitee receives the token and delivers to his inviters. Tokens are used in the invitation generation and tie each invitation to its invitee (i.e., the invitations issued using different tokens cannot be used interchangeably). This makes sure that invitees cannot cheat by combining invitations that are for different purposes. Provided a token, an *inviter* executes *Igen* algorithm to make an invitation. The *invitee* aggregates the individual invitations by running *Icoll* algorithm and delivers a unified invitation letter to the server. If the *server* authenticates the invitations by running *Ivrfy* algorithm, then the user is allowed to join the system. The *server* generates data necessary for the new member to be able to invite others by executing the *Reg* algorithm. Thenceforth, the invitee who is now a new member is able to add other users to the system. Detailed descriptions of the algorithms follow (the entity running the algorithm is indicated inside square braces).

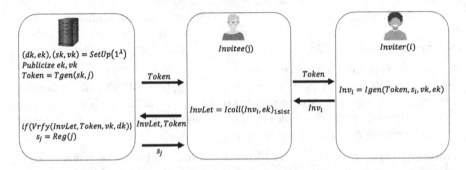

Fig. 2. The order of algorithms' execution in *Inonymous*.

SetUp(1^λ). This algorithm is run by the server who inputs the security parameter λ and generates system parameters as follows.

- Two big primes p and q such that $q|p-1$.
- g is a generator of a cyclic subgroup G of order q in Z_p^*. Let $h \in Z_p$ and
  $h \neq 0$, then g satisfies $g = h^{\frac{p-1}{q}}$ mod p.
- El Gamal encryption scheme $\pi = (EGen, Enc, Dec)$ with the key pair (ek, dk)
  denoting encryption key and decryption key, respectively. dk remains at the
  server while ek is published publicly.
- A signature scheme $\gamma = (SGen, Sign, SVrfy)$. The signature and verification
  keys (sk, vk) are generated according to $SGen$. vk is publicized.
- A pseudo random generator $PRG:\{0,1\}^\lambda \to Z_q$
- A master value $S \leftarrow Z_q$
- A randomly chosen polynomial function $F(y) = f_{t-1}y^{t-1} + ... + f_1y + f_0$ of
  degree $t-1$ whose coefficients $f_1, ..., f_{t-1}$ belong to Z_q and $f_0 = S$.

We assume that there are (at least) t users initially registered in the system.
Each registered user is known by a unique numerical index i. Each member has
the evaluation of function F on his own index i.e. the ith member is given master
share $s_i = F(i)$.

Token Generation: A new user who tends to join the system, initially must
connect to the server and obtain an index and the corresponding token. For this
sake, the server executes the token generation algorithm shown in Algorithm 4.1.
In this procedure, the server assigns the user a unique index and a corresponding
token. Indices can simply be given to the users sequentially based on their arrival
order hence the jth coming user receives the index value of j. Then, the server
computes a token as $\omega = g^r$ (line 2) where r is a randomly selected value
(line 1). The server certifies the association of user index and ω by generating
a signature on their concatenation (line 3). The server's generated certificate
constitutes the user's token (line 4). Observe that the server need not remember
any information regarding a registration attempt. Thus, generated tokens can
simply be discarded and only the last value of j (the number of token requests)
need to be remembered, *not* incurring any storage load on the server per token.

Algorithm 4.1. Tgen [Server]

Input: sk, j
Output: $Token$

1 $r \leftarrow Z_q$
2 $\omega = g^r$
3 $\eta = Sign_{sk}(j||\omega)$
4 $Token = (\eta, j, \omega)$

Invitation Generation: The user, after obtaining his token $Token$, asks his
inviters to issue an invitation letter. Each inviter uses his master share s_i to

compute an invitation letter as indicated in Algorithm 4.2. Firstly, the referee authenticates the token (line 1). Then, he computes a masked version of his master share as given in lines 2–4. δ_i is the masking value which is the output of the PRG (line 3). He also encrypts the masking value under the server's public encryption key (line 5). Note that the invitation letter is tied to the token as τ_i is the combination of the token and the inviter's master share.

Algorithm 4.2. Igen [Inviter]

Input: $Token$, s_i, vk, ek
Output: Inv_i

1   **if** $Svrfy_{vk}(\eta, j||\omega)=accept$ **then**
2     $r \leftarrow \{0,1\}^{\lambda}$
3     $\delta_i = PRG(r)$
4     $\tau_i = \omega^{s_i + \delta_i}$
5     $e\delta_i = Enc_{ek}(\omega^{\delta_i})$
6     $Inv_i = (\tau_i, e\delta_i)$

Invitation Collection: Invitation Collection ($Icoll$) is run by the new user i.e., invitee, once he obtains a set of t individual invitations. He computes the final invitation letter i.e. $InvLet$ as indicated in Algorithm 4.3. The final invitation letter is indeed the aggregation of the individual invitations Inv_i (line 3–4). For aggregation, we benefit from the homomorphic property of both Shamir shares and encryption scheme under addition and multiplication operations, respectively. The invitee re-masks the aggregated invitation letter by contributing to the sum of masking values with another randomness i.e., δ^*. The re-masking is required to cancel out the effect of Lagrange coefficients and make the final masking value independent of B_i values. Recall that the Lagrange coefficients are dependent on the inviters' indices. This way, we achieve inviter anonymity.

We expand lines 3 and 4 of Algorithm 4.3 in Eqs. 2 and 3, respectively, where B_i values are the Lagrange coefficients computed with respect to the index of the ith inviter. As indicated, T is composed of the token ω and a masked version of master value i.e., $S + \Delta$. $e\Delta$ constitutes the encryption of masking value Δ. The encryption of masking value i.e., $e\Delta$ would be required at the server for the verification purpose (see invitation verification).

$$T = \omega^{\delta^*} \cdot \prod_{i=1}^{t} \tau_i^{B_i} = \omega^{\delta^*} \cdot \prod_{i=1}^{t} \omega^{B_i \cdot s_i + B_i \cdot \delta_i} = \omega^{\delta^* + \sum_{i=1}^{t} B_i \cdot s_i + \sum_{i=1}^{t} B_i \cdot \delta_i}$$
$$= \omega^{S + \delta^* + \sum_{i=1}^{t} B_i \cdot \delta_i} = \omega^{S + \Delta} \tag{2}$$

$$e\Delta = Enc_{ek}(\omega^{\delta^*}) \cdot \prod_{i=1}^{t} e\delta_i^{B_i} = Enc_{ek}(\omega^{\delta^*}) \cdot \prod_{i=1}^{t} Enc_{ek}(\omega^{B_i \cdot \delta_i})$$
$$= Enc_{ek}(\omega^{\delta^* + \sum_{i=1}^{t} B_i \cdot \delta_i}) = Enc_{ek}(\omega^{\Delta}) \tag{3}$$

Algorithm 4.3. Icoll [Invitee]

Input: $\{Inv_i = (\tau_i, e\delta_i) | 1 \leq i \leq t\}$, ek
Output: $InvLet$

1   $r \leftarrow \{0,1\}^\lambda$
2   $\delta^* = PRG(r)$
3   $T = \omega^{\delta^*} \cdot \prod_{i=1}^{t} \tau_i^{B_i}$
4   $e\Delta = Enc_{ek}(\omega^{\delta^*}) \cdot \prod_{i=1}^{t} e\delta_i^{B_i}$
5   $InvLet = (T, e\Delta)$

Invitation Verification: This protocol (shown in Algorithm 4.4) is invoked by the server to verify the validity of a new user's invitation letter $InvLet$ corresponding to a $Token$. First, the token is authenticated (line 1). When the authentication phase passed, the server checks the validity of the invitation letter. He first decrypts the masking value (line 2) and checks whether the invitations are issued by existing members and really intended for the new user (line 3). If all the invitations are generated correctly then the verification of line 3 will be accepted (the correctness results from Eqs. 2 and 3). If all the verification steps passed successfully, then the server accepts the user's membership request.

Algorithm 4.4. IVrfy [Server]

Input: $InvLet = (T, Delta), Token = (\eta, j, \omega), vk, dk$
Output: $reject/accept$

1   **if** $Svrfy_{vk}(\eta, j||\omega) = accept$ **then**
2     $\omega^\Delta = Dec_{dk}(e\Delta)$
3   **if** $\omega^S \cdot \omega^\Delta = T$ **then**
4   return accept

Registration: When a user passes the verification phase, the server runs the registration algorithm given in Algorithm 4.5 to issue the new member's master share s_j. s_j is the evaluation of function F on the point j that was in the user's token (line 1). Hereinafter, the new user is able to invite other users to the system.

Algorithm 4.5. Reg [Server]

Input: j
Output: s_j

1   $s_j = F(j)$

---

5   *InonymouX*: Anonymous Cross Network Invitation-Based System

Consider the situation where one system e.g. Twitter offers a special service for users of another system e.g. Facebook. You may assume other scenarios as well.

We name Twitter as the *host network* i.e. the network serving a special service whereas Facebook is called the *guest network* whose users will benefit from the services offered by the host network. A user of the guest network is served by the host network by convincing the host server on being invited by adequate inviters from the guest network. To do so, one simple but cumbersome solution is to follow the regular invitation-based system i.e., each time a guest user wants to join the host network, the guest server authenticates that user and communicates the authentication result to the host server. However, this solution requires two servers keep in contact with each other and imposes unnecessary overhead on the guest server. Whereas in our proposal i.e. *InonymouX*, we provide an efficient solution for cross network invitations which is independent of two servers interaction. in *InonymouX*, the host server is given enough information to authenticate guest users by his own. The solution is as follows.

The guest network with the master value S_{guest} publicizes $g^{S_{guest}}$ alongside the signature verification key vk_{guest}. On the other side, the host network announces an encryption key denoted by ek_{host}. Members of the guest network proceed as in the regular invitation procedure where the inviters use the encryption key of host network to encrypt their masking values. Indeed, in Algorithms 4.2 and 4.3, the inviter uses ek_{host} as input. Therefore, the invitation letters received by the host server are of the form $InvLet = (T, e\Delta)$ where $e\Delta$ is an encrypted masking value under ek_{host}. The host server runs a different verification routine, which is given in Algorithm 5.1. We assume the existence of a bilinear map $e: G \times G \to G_2$ where G and G_2 are multiplicative groups of prime order q. The only difference between Algorithm 5.1 and Algorithm 4.4 is at the second verification step i.e., line 3. The correctness holds by the bilinearity of the bilinear map e, as in Eq. 4.

$$e(\omega, g^{S_{guest}}) \cdot e(\omega^\Delta, g) = e(\omega, g)^{S_{guest}} \cdot e(\omega, g)^\Delta = e(w, g)^{S_{guest}+\Delta} = e(w^{S_{guest}+\Delta}, g)$$
$$= e(T, g) \tag{4}$$

Algorithm 5.1. XIVerify [Host Server]

Input: $InvLet = (T, e\Delta), Token = (\eta, j, \omega), vk_{guest}, dk_{host}, g^{S_{guest}}$
Output: *reject/accept*

1   **if** $Svrfy_{vk_{guest}}(\eta, j\|\omega)=accept$ **then**
2     $\omega^\Delta = Dec_{dk_{host}}(e\Delta)$
3   **if** $e(\omega, g^{S_{guest}}) \cdot e(\omega^\Delta, g) = e(T, g)$ **then**
4 | return accept

---

6   Performance

In this section we aim at analyzing the running time of each algorithm. Table 1 shows the results in millisecond. We used DSA signature scheme [7] with the key size of 1024 bits. The required number of inviters i.e., t is set to 5. The running time is measured on a standard laptop with 8 GB 1600 MHz DDR3 memory

Table 1. Running time of *Inonymous* Algorithms.

SetUp	Tgen	Igen	Icoll	IVerify	Reg
842 ms	3.46 ms	37.4 ms	35.3 ms	29.4 ms	0.129 ms

and 1.6 GHz Intel Core i5 CPU. Although the running time of SetUp algorithm has a huge difference with the other algorithms, it is run only once by the server just to bootstrap the system.

7 Security

In this section, we provide security definitions for inviter anonymity and invitation unforgeability, and then prove the security of *Inonymous*.

7.1 Inviter Anonymity

Security Definition: An invitation-based system protects inviter anonymity if a new user having enough inviters can convince the server without revealing the identity of his inviters. We model this security objective as a game denoted by $InvAnonym_A(\lambda)$ played between a challenger and an adversary. The members controlled by the adversary and challenger are called colluding and non-colluding members, respectively. The adversary controls the server as well. The challenger acts as a new user who wants to join the system and is required to obtain t invitations from t different members. We assume that $t - 1$ inviters come from the colluding members (clearly it is the maximum power that can be considered for the adversary). The adversary selects two non-colluding members. The challenger uses one of them as the remaining inviter and registers into the system. If the adversary cannot guess the identity of the non-colluding inviter with more than a negligible advantage, then the system provides inviter anonymity.

Inviter Anonymity Experiment $InvAnonym_A(\lambda)$

1. The adversary outputs encryption key ek and signature verification key vk.
2. The challenger registers polynomially many users denoted by U to the system.
3. The adversary selects two users $u_0, u_1 \in U$ and generates a token $Token$. Also, the adversary outputs $t - 1$ individual invitations for the given $Token$.
4. The challenger tosses a coin and selects a bit value b accordingly. Then, the challenger generates an invitation letter $InvLet$ using u_b as one of the inviters in addition to the $t - 1$ invitations received from the adversary, and sends $InvLet$ to the adversary.
5. The adversary guesses a bit b' indicating that which of the two users u_0, u_1 is used as the inviter.
6. The output of game is 1 if $b == b'$, 0 otherwise.

Definition 1. *An invitation-based system has inviter anonymity if for every probabilistic polynomial time adversary A there exists a negligible function negl(.) such that:*

$$Pr[InvAnonym_A(\lambda) = 1] = \frac{1}{2} + negl(\lambda)$$

Security Proof: Before the formal proof, let us summarize informally. In *Inonymous*, the anonymity of inviter relies on the security of the pseudo random generator. The invited user delivers to the server (the adversary) an invitation letter of the form $InvLet = (\omega^{S+\Delta}, e\Delta)$ where S is the server's master value, $e\Delta$ is the encryption of Δ and $\Delta = \omega^{\delta^* + \sum_{i=1}^{t} B_i \cdot \delta_i}$ (δ^* is the masking value added by the invitee, δ_i is inviter's masking value resulted from a *PRG* and B_i is the Lagrange coefficient computed based on the inviter's index). The adversary may get some idea about the inviters' identity by extracting the Lagrange coefficients from Δ value (Lagrange coefficients are the function of inviters' indices). Two cases may occur. If the random values δ_i and δ^* are selected truly at random, then we know that Δ is also a random value and conveys nothing about the Lagrange coefficient B_i. Though, if δ_i and δ^* are the output of a *PRG* then the adversary may have advantages to extract the Lagrange coefficients. We denote the adversary's advantage by ϵ. If ϵ is non-negligible, it implies that we can distinguish between a *PRG* and a random number generator hence we break the security of the *PRG*. In the following we provide the formal proof.

Theorem 1. *If PRG is a pseudo random generator then Inonymous provides inviter anonymity.*

We reduce the security of *Inonymous* to the security of the employed *PRG*. If there exists a PPT adversary A who breaks the inviter anonymity of *Inonymous* with non-negligible advantage then we can construct a PPT adversary B who distinguishes between a random generator and a pseudo random generator with the same advantage of A. Assume A's success probability is

$$Pr[InvAnonym_A(\lambda) = 1] = \frac{1}{2} + \epsilon(\lambda) \tag{5}$$

B runs A as its subroutine to distinguish the pseudo random number generator from the truly random generator. B is given a vector of values in Z_q denoted by $\overrightarrow{\delta} = (\delta', \delta'')$ and aims at specifying whether $\overrightarrow{\delta}$ is selected truly at random or is the output of a *PRG*. B invokes A as his subroutine and emulates the game of inviter anonymity for A as follows. If A succeeds then B realizes that $\overrightarrow{\delta}$ is pseudo random, otherwise random.

1. B is given the security parameter λ and a vector of two values denoted by $\overrightarrow{\delta} = (\delta', \delta'')$ where $\delta', \delta'' \in Z_q$. Adversary A outputs the encryption and signature public keys ek and vk, respectively.

2. B registers polynomially many users into the system. U indicates the set of indices registered by B.
3. A outputs two users $u_0, u_1 \in U$ and a token $Token = (\eta, u^*, \omega)$. u^* is the index of the new user. A also submits $t - 1$ invitation letters i.e. $Inv_i = (\tau_i, e\delta_i)$ for $1 \le i \le t - 1$.
4. B selects a random bit b and creates an invitation letter from u_b as $Inv_{u_b} = (\tau_{u_b}, e\delta_{u_b}) = (\omega^{s_{u_b}+\delta'}, Enc_{ek}(\omega^{\delta'}))$. He finally computes
$$T = \omega^{\delta''} \cdot \tau_{u_b}^{B_{u_b}} \cdot \prod_{i=1}^{t-1} \tau_i^{B_i}$$
and
$$e\Delta = Enc_{ek}(\omega^{\delta''}) \cdot Enc_{ek}(\omega^{\delta'})^{B_{u_b}} \cdot \prod_{i=1}^{t-1} e\delta_i^{B_i} = Enc_{ek}(\omega^{\delta''+\delta' \cdot B_{u_b}+\sum_{i=1}^{t-1} \delta_i \cdot B_i}).$$
B_i and B_{u_b} denote the Lagrange coefficients. B submits $InvLet = (T, e\Delta)$ to the adversary A.
5. A outputs a bit b'.
6. If $b = b'$ then B outputs 0, otherwise 1.

Let $\vec{\delta}$ be a truly random vector. Once the adversary decrypts $e\Delta$ he obtains

$$\Delta = \omega^{\delta''+\Gamma}$$

where

$$\Gamma = \delta' \cdot B_{u_b} + \sum_{i=1}^{t-1} \delta_i \cdot B_i$$

Γ is a function of inviters indices due to the presence of Lagrange coefficients whereas δ'' is a random value completely independent of inviters. If $\vec{\delta}$ is a random vector then δ'' is also a random value from $\mathbb{Z}_q$. Therefore, in $\omega^{\delta''+\Gamma}$, Γ is indeed masked with δ'' ($\delta'' + \Gamma \mod q$ is a completely random element of $\mathbb{Z}_q$). By this masking, Δ becomes completely independent of Lagrange coefficients and A has no advantage to infer the inviters identity. Thus, A's advantage is exactly $\frac{1}{2}$ i.e.,

$$Pr[B(\vec{\delta} \leftarrow Z_q) = 1] = Pr[b = b'] = \frac{1}{2} \tag{6}$$

but if δ is the output of a *PRG* then

$$Pr[r \leftarrow \{0,1\}^\lambda : B(\vec{\delta} = PRG(r)) = 1] = Pr[b = b'] = \frac{1}{2} + \epsilon(\lambda) \tag{7}$$

where $\frac{1}{2} + \epsilon(\lambda)$ is the success probability of A as assumed in our proof in Eq. 5. By combining Eqs. 6 and 7 we have

$$|Pr[r \leftarrow \{0,1\}^\lambda : B(\vec{\delta} = PRG(r)) = 1] - Pr[B(\vec{\delta} \leftarrow Z_q) = 1]| = \epsilon(\lambda) \tag{8}$$

Equation 8 corresponds to the security definition of PRG (see Eq. 1). Thus, if $\epsilon(\lambda)$ is non-negligible then the distinguisher B can distinguish a PRG from a random generator which contradicts with the security definition of PRG. Therefore, $\epsilon(\lambda)$ must be negligible according to the PRG definition. This concludes the security proof of inviter anonymity of *Inonymous*.

Discussion: We proved inviter anonymity against an honest but curious adversary who follows the algorithm descriptions, whereas a malicious adversary breaks the anonymity of the inviters in the following attack scenario. First note that for the inviter anonymity, the adversary is the server who is colluding with $t-1$ inviters. According to the inviter anonymity game definition, the server obtains $InvLet = (T = \omega^{S+\Delta}, e\Delta)$. As we discussed, if all the inviters act honestly and use their real master shares for the invitation generation, then the adversary obtains the ω^S value. According to Shamir secret sharing scheme, even if the adversary knows $t-1$ inviters, the remaining inviter can be any of the existing shareholders, hence the inviter anonymity holds. Now, consider that the colluding $t-1$ inviters put zeros instead of their real master shares i.e., $s_1 = ... = s_{t-1} = 0$ (wlog. $1, ..., t-1$ are the indices of colluding inviters). Then, the server obtains $\omega^{S'}$ with the following value: $S' = s_1.B_1 + ... + s_{t-1}.B_{t-1} + s_t.B_t = s_t.B_t$. The adversary can simply try all the combinations of generated master shares s_t with different possible values for B_t and figure out the honest inviter's index (the possible number of values is linear in the number of remaining inviters, which in the inviter anonymity game is 2, and in practice corresponds to the number of registered users). This attack is defeated only if the inviters act honestly and follow the genuine routine of algorithms.

7.2 Invitation Unforgeability

Security Definition: In an invitation based system, the invitation unforgeability indicates that people who do not have enough inviters ($<t$) should not be able to join the system. Hence, no adversary can forge invitations by his own. We define the following game denoted by $InvUnforge_A(\lambda)$ running between a challenger and an adversary. The adversary controls a set of $t-1$ members denoted by Q. The adversary may query as many tokens as he wants and queries the challenger to check the validity of his pseudo-invitation letters. Finally, if the adversary registers to the system successfully, it shows that the invitations are forgeable, otherwise the system has invitation unforgeability. Note that we assume secure authenticated channels between entities hence we ignore the threat of eavesdropping.

Invitation Unforgeability experiment $InvUnforge_A(\lambda)$:

1. The challenger runs the setup algorithm. The adversary is given the encryption key ek, the signature verification key vk, as well as the security parameter λ.
2. The adversary registers a set of $t - 1$ users denoted by Q.
3. The adversary asks the challenger to issue a token. The challenger generates a token for the next available index j. This step may be repeated polynomially many times upon the adversary's request.
4. The adversary queries invitation verification function on the invitations of his own choice. The challenger responds accordingly.
5. The challenger outputs a token denoted by $Token^*$. The adversary outputs an invitation letter $InvLet$ corresponding to the given token.
6. If the output of $IVrfy(InvLet, Token^*, vk, dk)$ is accepted then the game's output is 1 indicating the adversary's success, 0 otherwise.

Definition 2. *An invitation-based system has invitation unforgeability if for every probabilistic polynomial time adversary A there exists a negligible function negl(.) such that:*

$$Pr[InvUnforge_A(\lambda) = 1] = negl(\lambda)$$

Security Proof. Forging invitations is information-theoretically infeasible. In fact, the adversary, in the best case, has $t - 1$ inviters hence $t - 1$ evaluations of function $F(.)$. Recall that a valid invitation letter contains the master value S i.e. $\omega^{S+\Delta}$ (S is the evaluation of $F(0)$). Since the adversary is confined to $t - 1$ points on this polynomial, he cannot reconstruct the S value in any way. Without the final share of S, $\omega^{S+\Delta}$ is a random element. Therefore, *Inonymous* has information-theoretic invitation unforgeability.

7.3 Security of *InonymouX*

InonymouX provides inviter anonymity as *Inonymous* does, hence the same proof of Sect. 7.1 applies here. However, invitation unforgeability needs a different proof, due to the publicity of $g^{S_{guest}}$, which provides computational information to the adversary. Note that a final aggregated invitation letter has the form of $T = \omega^{S_{guest}+\Delta} = g^{r \cdot S_{guest}+r \cdot \Delta}$. For an adversary who has ω and $g^{S_{guest}}$, making a valid invitation letter corresponds to solving the Computational Diffie-Hellman (CDH) problem i.e., given $g^{S_{guest}}$ and g^r compute $g^{r \cdot S_{guest}}$. Thus, assuming that CDH is hard to solve, then the invitation unforgeability holds for *InonymouX* as well. Full reduction follows.

Security Proof

Theorem 2. *If the computational Diffie-Hellman problem is hard to solve relative to G, then InonymouX has invitation unforgeability.*

234   S.Taheri.B and A. Küpçü

If there exists a PPT adversary A who breaks the invitation unforgeability with
probability $\epsilon(\lambda)$, then we construct an adversary B who solves CDH problem
with $\epsilon(\lambda)$ probability. The adversary A acts as a new user with t-1 inviters. The
adversary B plays as host and guest servers and the rest of members. B simulates
the invitation unforgeability game for adversary A to break CDH problem.

1. B is given (G, q, g, g^r, g^S) (G is a cyclic group of order q with generator g) and
   the security parameter λ. B generates signature key pair vk, sk and public
   encryption key pair ek, dk. B sends g^S, vk and ek to A. Note that S is the
   master value which is unknown to B.
2. Adversary A registers $t - 1$ users to the system. As B does not know the
   master value S, he generates random master shares for A's requests. Adversary A cannot distinguish between the real master shares and the randomly
   generated ones. Note that for every given $t - 1$ points, we can construct a
   polynomial F of degree t such that $F(0) = S$. Thus, as long as the adversary
   A has only $t - 1$ points of F, he does not distinguish whether B knows the
   master value (i.e., has generated real master shares) or is a simulator.
3. The adversary A asks for polynomially many tokens from B.
4. The adversary A outputs an invitation letter and asks B to verify it. A
   may repeat invitation verification query polynomially many times. B runs
   Algorithm 6 to answer the queries.
5. The challenger outputs $Token^*$ as (η, adv, w) where adv is an index, $\eta =
   Sign_{sk}(adv\|w)$ and $w = g^r$ (B sets w as one of the inputs given in the CDH
   game). A outputs an invitation letter:

$$InvLet = (T = w^{S+\Delta}, e\Delta = Enc_{ek}(\omega^\Delta)).$$

If $XIvrfy(InvLet, Token^*) = accept$ then B computes $w^\Delta = Dec_{dk}(e\Delta)$. As
the solution for CDH problem, B outputs

$$T.(w^\Delta)^{-1} = w^{S+\Delta}.w^{-\Delta} = w^S = g^{r.S} \tag{9}$$

If A manages to output a valid invitation letter $InvLet$, then B can extract
the solution of CDH problem from that invitation letter as indicated in Eq. 9.
Therefore,

$$Pr[B \text{ breaks CDH}] = Pr[A \text{ breaks Invitation Unforgeability}] = \epsilon(\lambda)$$

If $\epsilon(\lambda)$ is non-negligible then CDH problem is also solved with non-negligible
probability. This implies a contradiction for the hardness assumption of CDH,
hence we conclude that $\epsilon(\lambda)$ must be negligible. Therefore, invitation unforgeability of $InonymouX$ is proven.

8   Conclusion

We proposed $Inonymous$, an anonymous invitation-based system by seeking two
security objectives i.e., *inviter anonymity* against the system administrator and

existing members and *invitation unforgeability* against newcomers with insufficient inviters. We present security definition and formal proof for each security objective. The anonymity of inviter relies on the security of the employed pseudo random generator (for masking value generation) and the invitation unforgeability is information-theoretically proven due to the Shamir secret sharing scheme's security. We also proposed *InonymouX*, an anonymous cross-network invitation-based system by a slight modification on *Inonymous* so that users of one network can act as inviters for another network. *InonymouX* invitation unforgeability assumes Computational Diffie-Hellman problem. In the future, we aim to provide efficient user revocation capability as well as inviter anonymity against malicious adversaries.

Acknowledgements. We acknowledge the support of the Royal Society of UK Newton Advanced Fellowship NA140464 and European Union COST Action IC1306.

References

1. http://www.macworld.com/article/1055383/gmail.html
2. Bogdanov, D.: Foundations and properties of Shamir's secret sharing scheme research seminar in cryptography. University of Tartu, Institute of Computer Science, 1 May 2007
3. Chaabane, A., Acs, G., Kaafar, M.A., et al.: You are what you like! information leakage through users interests. In: Proceedings of the 19th Annual Network and Distributed System Security Symposium (NDSS) (2012)
4. Gong, N.Z., Wang, D.: On the security of trustee-based social authentications. IEEE Trans. Inf. Forensics Secur. **9**(8), 1251–1263 (2014)
5. Gu, K., Jia, W., Chen, R., Liu, X.: Secure and efficient proxy signature scheme in the standard model. Chin. J. Electron. **22**(4), 666–670 (2013)
6. Harn, L., Lin, C.: Authenticated group key transfer protocol based on secret sharing. IEEE Trans. Comput. **59**(6), 842–846 (2010)
7. Kravitz, D.W.: Digital signature algorithm. US Patent 5,231,668, 27 July 1993
8. Mahmood, S.: Online social networks: privacy threats and defenses. In: Chbeir, R., Al Bouna, B. (eds.) Security and Privacy Preserving in Social Networks, pp. 47–71. Springer, Vienna (2013)
9. Malar, G.P., Shyni, C.E.: Facebook's trustee based social authentication
10. Parameswari, S.M., Sukumaran, S.: Trustee based authentication mechanism for social network. Int. J. Latest Res. Sci. Technol. **4**, 84–88 (2015)
11. Rao, F.-Y.: On the security of a variant of ELGamal encryption scheme. IEEE Trans. Dependable Secure Comput. (2017)
12. Roy, A., Karforma, S.: A survey on digital signatures and its applications. J. Comput. Inf. Technol. **3**(1), 45–69 (2012)
13. Sharimila, K., Janaki, V., Nagaraju, A.: Enhanced user authentication techniques using the fourth factor "some body the user knows". In: Proceedings of International Conference on Advances in Computer Science, AETACS. Elsevier (2013)
14. Yu, J., Kong, F., Cheng, X., Hao, R., Li, G.: One forward-secure signature scheme using bilinear maps and its applications. Inf. Sci. **279**, 60–76 (2014)

Applied Cryptography and Privacy

$\mathcal{PCS}$, A Privacy-Preserving Certification Scheme

Nesrine Kaaniche$^{(\boxtimes)}$, Maryline Laurent, Pierre-Olivier Rocher,
Christophe Kiennert, and Joaquin Garcia-Alfaro

SAMOVAR, Télécom SudParis, CNRS, Université Paris-Saclay, Evry, France
{nesrine.kaaniche,joaquin.garcia_alfaro}@telecom-sudparis.eu

Abstract. We present $\mathcal{PCS}$, a privacy-preserving certification mechanism that allows users to conduct anonymous and unlinkable actions. The mechanism is built over an attribute-based signature construction. The proposal is proved secure against forgery and anonymity attacks. A use case on the integration of $\mathcal{PCS}$ to enhance the privacy of learners of an e-assessment environment, and some details of the ongoing implementation, are briefly presented.

Keywords: Attribute-based signatures · Attribute-based credentials · Anonymity · Bilinear pairings · Anonymous certification

1 Introduction

We present $\mathcal{PCS}$, a privacy-preserving certification scheme that provides the possibility of conducting anonymous authentication. This allows organizations to issue certificates to end-users in a way that they can demonstrate their possession in a series of transactions without being linked. $\mathcal{PCS}$ builds over an existing attribute-based signature scheme previously presented by Kaaniche and Laurent in ESORICS 2016 [10], called $\mathcal{HABS}$ (for *Homomorphic Attribute Based Signatures*). The objective of $\mathcal{HABS}$ is to enable users to anonymously authenticate with verifiers. At the same time, users minimize the amount of information submitted to the service provider, with respect to a given presentation policy. In [20,21], Vergnaud reported some limitations of $\mathcal{HABS}$ and proved that some of its security assumptions may fail in the random oracle model. $\mathcal{PCS}$ takes over $\mathcal{HABS}$ and addresses the limitations reported by Vergnaud. An ongoing implementation of the $\mathcal{PCS}$ proposal for e-learning scenarios, under the scope of a EU-funded project (cf. http://tesla-project.eu/ for further information), is available online[1] to facilitate its understanding and validation.

Paper Organization — Sections 2 and 3 provide additional background on the use of Anonymous Credentials (AC) and Attribute-based Signatures (ABS). Sections 4 and 5 provide a generic presentation of the $\mathcal{PCS}$ construction, as well as the main differences with respect to the previous $\mathcal{HABS}$ scheme. Section 6 presents the security analysis of $\mathcal{PCS}$. Section 7 briefly discusses a use case of $\mathcal{PCS}$ for e-assessment environments. Section 8 concludes the paper.

---

[1] Source code snippets available at http://j.mp/PKIPCSgit.

J. Garcia-Alfaro et al. (Eds.): DPM/CBT 2017, LNCS 10436, pp. 239–256, 2017.
DOI: 10.1007/978-3-319-67816-0_14

2   Background on Anonymous Credentials (AC)

In [5], Chaum introduced the notion of Anonymous Credentials (AC). Camenisch and Lysyanskaya fully formalized the concept in [3,4]. AC, also referred to as privacy-preserving attribute credentials, involve several entities and procedures. It fulfills some well-identified security and functional requirements. In the sequel, we present some further details about the type of entities, procedures and requirements associated to traditional AC schemes.

2.1   Entities

An anonymous credential system involves several entities. This includes mandatory entities (e.g., *users, verifiers* and *issuing organizations*) and optional entities (e.g., *revocation authorities* and *inspectors*) [2]. The central entity in AC is the *user* entity. Its interest is to obtain a privacy-preserving access to a series of services. The providers of such services are denoted as *verifiers*. Each verifier enforces an access control policy with regard to its resources and services. This access control is based on the credentials owned by the users. The related information is included in what is called the *presentation tokens*.

With the purpose of accessing the resources, a user has to obtain its credentials from a series of *issuing organizations*. Then, the user selects the appropriate information with regard to the issued credentials and shows the selected information to the requesting verifier, under a presentation token. The access control policy associated to the verifier is referred to as the *presentation policy*. Both the user and the verifier have to obtain the most recent revocation information from the *revocation authority* to either generate or verify the presentation tokens. The *revocation authority* may eventually revoke some issued credentials and maintain the list of valid credentials in the system. When a credential is revoked, the associated user will no longer be able to derive the corresponding presentation tokens. An additional trusted entity, denoted as the *inspector*, holds the technical capabilities to remove the anonymity of a user, if needed.

2.2   Procedures

An anonymous credential system mainly relies on the execution of the following series of procedures and algorithms:

- SETUP — It takes as input a security parameter ξ that represents the security level; and returns some public parameters, as well as the public (pk) and secret (sk) key pair of the issuing organization, denoted as (pk_o, sk_o).
- USERKEYGEN — Returns the key pairs of users. For instance, let $j \in \mathbb{N}$ represent the request of user j, it returns a key pair denoted as (pk_{u_j}, sk_{u_j}).
- OBTAIN ↔ ISSUE — It presents the issuance procedure. The ISSUE procedure is executed by the issuing organization. It takes as input some public parameters, the secret key of the issuing organization sk_o, the public key of the user pk_u and the set of attributes $\{a_i\}_{i=1}^{N}$. N is the number of attributes.

The OBTAIN procedure is executed by the user and takes as input the secret key of the user sk_u and the public key of the issuing organization pk_o. At the end of this phase, the user receives a credential C.

– SHOW $\leftrightarrow$ VERIFY — It represents the procedures between the user and the verifier. With respect to the presentation policy, the SHOW procedure takes as input the secret key of the user sk_u, the public key of the issuing organization pk_o, the credential C and the set of required attributes $\{a_i\}_{i=1}^{N'}$. N' is the number of required attributes. The resulting output of this algorithm is the presentation token. The VERIFY procedure is publicly executed by the verifier. It takes as input the public key of the issuing organization pk_o, as well as the set of attributes $\{a_i\}_{i=1}^{N'}$ and the presentation token. The VERIFY procedure provides as output a bit value $b \in \{0, 1\}$, denoting either the success or the failure associated to the verification process.

2.3 Requirements of AC Systems

An AC system has to fulfill the following requirements:

– *Correctness* — Honest users shall always succeed in anonymously proving validity proofs to the verifiers.
– *Anonymity* — Honest users shall remain anonymous with regard to other system users while conducting the presentation procedure in front of a series of verifiers.
– *Unforgeability* — Users that fail at holding an appropriate set of legitimate credentials shall not be able to generate presentation tokens for the system.
– *Unlinkability* — Honest users shall not be related to two or more observed items of the system. This requirement is often divided in two subproperties:

  • *Issue-show unlinkability.* It ensures that data gathered during the procedure of issuing credentials cannot be used by system entities to link a presentation token to the original credential.
  • *Multi-show unlinkability.* Presentation tokens derived from the same credentials and transmitted over different system sessions cannot be linked together by the verifiers.

Privacy-preserving attribute credential systems have to ensure some additional functional requirements, such as revocation, inspection and *selective disclosure*. Selective disclosure refers to the ability of the system users to present only partial information to the verifiers. Such information may be derived from the user credentials, in order to prove, e.g., that the user is at least eighteen years old to be eligible for accessing a service, without revealing the exact age.

3 Attribute-Based Signatures for AC Support

Attribute-based Signatures (ABS for short) is a cryptographic primitive that enables users to sign data with fine-grained control over the required identifying information [14]. To use ABS, a user shall possess a set of attributes and a secret signing key per attribute. The signing key must be provided by a trusted authority. The user can sign, e.g., a document, with respect to a predicate satisfied by the set of attributes. Common settings for ABS must include a Signature Trustee (ST), an Attribute Authority (AA), and several signers and verifiers. The ST acts as a global entity that generates valid global system parameters. The AA issues the signing keys for the set of attributes of the users (e.g., the signers). The role of the ST and the AA can be provided by the same entity. The AA can hold knowledge about the signing keys and the attributes of the users. However, the AA should not be capable to identifying which attributes have been used in a given valid signature. This way, the AA will not be able to link the signature to the source user. The AA should not be able to link back the signatures to the signers. This is a fundamental requirement from ABS, in order to fulfill common privacy requirements.

3.1   Related Work

Several ABS schemes exist in the related literature, considering different design directions. This includes ABS solutions in which (i) the attribute value can be a binary-bit string [9,13–16] or general-purpose data structures [22]; (ii) ABS solutions satisfying access structures under threshold policies [9,13,16], monotonic policies [14,22] and non-monotonic policies [15]; and (iii) ABS solutions in which the secret keys associated to the attributes are either issued by a single authority [14,16,22] or by a group of authorities [14,15]. General-purpose threshold cryptosystems can also be adapted in order to achieve traceability protection [7,8].

A simple ABS system can rely on using only one single AA entity. The AA entity derives the secret keys $\{sk_1, \cdots, sk_N\}$, with respect to the attribute set that identifies a given signer, denoted by $S = \{a_1, \cdots, a_N\}$. N is the number of attributes. The procedure to generate the secret keys is performed using the master key of the AA entity, as well as some additional public parameters. These elements shall be generated during the setup procedure. A message m is sent by the verifier to the user, along with a signing predicate Υ. In order to sign m, the signing user shall hold a secret key and a set of attributes satisfying the predicate Υ. The verifier shall be able to verify whether the signing user holds the set of attributes satisfying the predicate associated to the signed message.

In [10], Kaaniche and Laurent presented an anonymous certification primitive, called $\mathcal{HABS}$, and constructed over the use of ABS. In addition to common requirements such as *privacy* and *unforgeability*, $\mathcal{HABS}$ was designed with these additional properties in mind:

- *Signature traceability* — $\mathcal{HABS}$ includes a procedure denoted as INSPEC, in order to grant some entities the ability of identifying the user originating an ABS signature. To prevent common issuing organizations from tracing the system users, the INSPEC procedure is provided only to a tracing authority. This authority, typically an inspector, shall hold a secret key. The *Signature traceability* is important to guarantee accountability and prevent fraud.

- *Issuer unlinkability* — When a user requests multiple authorities to issue credentials with respect to a set of attributes, common ABS authorities can link the set of credentials to one user through the corresponding public key. $\mathcal{HABS}$ includes an issuance procedure to avoid this situation.
- *Replaying sessions* — To mitigate the possibility of replay attacks (common to ABS setups), $\mathcal{HABS}$ forces its verifiers to generate for each authentication session, a new message. Such a message shall depend on the session data, e.g., the identity of the verifier and a timestamp.

In [20,21], some of the requirements imposed by $\mathcal{HABS}$ were questioned by Vergnaud. The concrete realization of the $\mathcal{HABS}$ primitive was proved unsatisfactory with regard to the expected unforgeability and privacy properties under the random oracle model. The privacy-preserving certification scheme presented in this paper addresses such limitations. We present next the revisited primitives and procedures, and answer some of the claims reported by Vergnaud in [20,21].

4 The $\mathcal{PCS}$ Construction

4.1 System Model

The $\mathcal{PCS}$ construction relies on a series of modified algorithms with regard to the original $\mathcal{HABS}$ construction reported in [10], involving several users (i.e., signers). To ease the comparison to the initial approach, we denote by $\mathcal{PCS}$ the modifications, and by $\mathcal{HABS}$ the main algorithms originally defined in [10].

- $\mathcal{PCS}$.SETUP – It runs the original $\mathcal{HABS}$.SETUP algorithm. It takes as input the security parameter ξ and returns a set of global public parameters. All the algorithms include as default input such global public parameters.
- $\mathcal{PCS}$.KEYGEN – This algorithm returns the key pairs of either users or issuing organization. The key pairs are denoted (pk_u, sk_u) for the users, e.g., (pk_{u_j}, sk_{u_j}) for a user j; and (pk_o, sk_o) for the issuing organization.
- $\mathcal{PCS}$.OBTAIN $\leftrightarrow$ $\mathcal{PCS}$.ISSUE – The $\mathcal{PCS}$.ISSUE algorithm executed by the issuing organization takes as input the secret key of the issuing organization sk_o, the public key of the user pk_u, and a set of attributes $\mathcal{S} \subset \mathbb{S}$. $\mathcal{S} = \{a_i\}_{i=1}^N$, where N is the number of attributes. $\mathbb{S}$ is the attribute universe. The algorithm returns a signed commitment C over the set of attributes $\mathcal{S}$.

The $\mathcal{PCS}$.OBTAIN algorithm is executed by the user and corresponds to the collection of the certified credentials from the issuer. The user can verify the correctness of the received signed commitment over the provided attributes. In case the user wants to conduct the verification process, the $\mathcal{PCS}$.OBTAIN algorithm takes as input the signed commitment C, the secret key of the user sk_u and the public key of the issuing organization pk_o. It returns a bit $b \in \{0, 1\}$ with the result of the verification (either success or failure).

- $\mathcal{PCS}$.SHOW $\leftrightarrow$ $\mathcal{PCS}$.VERIFY – It enables the verifier to check whether a user has previously obtained credentials on some attributes from a certified issuing organization, to get granted access to a service with respect to a given access policy. The verifier has to send a blinded group element M based on a random message m sent to the user. Following the $\mathcal{HABS}$ construction, and in order to avoid replay attacks, each authentication session is personalized with a nonce — for instance, the identity of the verifier concatenated with a timestamp. By using the credentials, the user signs the nonce. To do so, the user selects some attributes satisfying the signing predicate Υ ($\Upsilon(\mathcal{S}') = 1$) and signs the value of M. The resulting signature Σ is sent to the verifier.

The $\mathcal{PCS}$.SHOW algorithm takes as input the randomized message M, a signing predicate Υ, the secret key of the user sk_u, the credential C and a subset of the user attributes $\mathcal{S}'$, such as $\Upsilon(\mathcal{S}') = 1$. The algorithm returns a signature Σ (or an error message $\perp$).

The $\mathcal{PCS}$.VERIFY algorithm takes as input the received signature Σ, the public key of the issuing organization(s) pk_o, the signing predicate Υ and the message m. It returns a bit $b \in \{0, 1\}$ with the result of the verification, where 1 denotes *acceptance* for a successful verification of the signature; and 0 denotes *rejection*.

4.2   Security Model

We present in this section the threat models assumed to validate the requirements of $\mathcal{PCS}$. We first assume a traditional *honest but curious* model for the verifier and the issuing organization entities. Under such a model, the verifiers and the issuing organizations are honest in the sense that they provide proper inputs and outputs, at each step of their respective algorithms, as well as properly performing the computations that are supposed to be conducted; but they are curious in the sense that they may attempt to gain some extra information they are not supposed to obtain. We assume the honest but curious threat model against the validation of the privacy requirements of $\mathcal{PCS}$, i.e., with respect to the anonymity and unlinkability properties. We consider as second threat model the case of malicious users trying to override their rights. That is, malicious users that misuse some of the steps of their associated algorithms, e.g., by providing invalid inputs or outputs. We assume this second threat model against the unforgeability requirement of $\mathcal{PCS}$ provided below.

4.2.1   Unforgeability

The unforgeability requirement expects that it is not possible to forge a valid credential — in case of the ISSUE algorithm (respectively, the presentation token of the user – in case of the SHOW algorithm). This requirement ensures that colluding users will not be able to frame a user who did not generate a valid presentation token. The unforgeability requirement is defined with respect to three security games, as presented in [10]. Each security game is defined between an adversary $\mathcal{A}$ and a challenger $\mathcal{C}$, that simulates the system procedures to interact with the adversary.

Definition 1. Unforgeability — $\mathcal{PCS}$ *satisfies the unforgeability requirement if for every Probabilistic Polynomial Time (PPT) adversary $\mathcal{A}$, there exists a negligible function ϵ such that:*

$$Pr[\boldsymbol{Exp}_{\mathcal{A}}^{unforg}(1^{\xi}) = 1] \le \epsilon(\xi)$$

where $\boldsymbol{Exp}_{\mathcal{A}}^{unforg}$ is the security experiment against the unforgeability requirement, with respect to the MC-Game, MU-Game and Col-Game games, as presented in the original $\mathcal{HABS}$ construction [10].

The aforementioned security games are defined as follows:

- MC-Game – $\mathcal{A}$ is allowed to conduct an unbounded number of queries to the $\mathcal{PCS}$.ISSUE algorithm for different sets of attributes with respect to a fixed user public key and issuing organization secret key (i.e., the secret key of the issuing organization is not known by $\mathcal{A}$). To successfully win the MC-Game, the adversary shall obtain a valid credential C^* for a challenge set of attributes $\mathcal{S}^*$, and this shall be accepted by the $\mathcal{PCS}$.OBTAIN algorithm.
- MU-Game – given a user public key pk_u, a set of attributes $\mathcal{S}$ and a credential C over $\mathcal{S}$ for pk_u, the adversary $\mathcal{A}$ can conduct an unbounded number of presentation queries — as a verifier — for any signing predicate Υ such that $\Upsilon(\mathcal{S})$ equals one. To successfully win the MU-Game, $\mathcal{A}$ shall obtain a valid presentation token for a credential C accepted by an honest verifier.
- Col-Game – given two pairs of public and secret keys (pk_{u_1}, sk_{u_1}) and (pk_{u_2}, sk_{u_2}), two disjoint and non-empty sets of attributes $\mathcal{S}_1$ and $\mathcal{S}_2$, and two credentials C_1 associated to $\mathcal{S}_1$ for pk_{u_1} and C_2 associated to $\mathcal{S}_2$ for pk_{u_2}, the adversary $\mathcal{A}$ shall be able to generate a valid presentation token for a key pair (pk_{u_j}, sk_{u_j}) for $j \in \{1, 2\}$ with respect to a signing predicate Υ such that $\Upsilon(\mathcal{S}_j) \ne 1$.

4.2.2 Privacy

The privacy requirement covers the anonymity, the issue-show and the multi-show requirements, as defined in Sect. 2. We introduce three security games based on an adversary $\mathcal{A}$ and a challenger $\mathcal{C}$, similarly to the $\mathcal{HABS}$ construction [10]. We assume that $\mathcal{A}$ does not directly run or control the $\mathcal{PCS}$.OBTAIN $\leftrightarrow$ ISSUE or $\mathcal{PCS}$.SHOW $\leftrightarrow$ VERIFY algorithms, but may request the results of these algorithms to the challenger $\mathcal{C}$ in charge of such algorithms.

Definition 2. Privacy - $\mathcal{PCS}$ *satisfies the privacy requirement, if for every PPT adversary $\mathcal{A}$, there exists a negligible function ϵ such that:*

$$Pr[\boldsymbol{Exp}_{\mathcal{A}}^{priv}(1^{\xi}) = 1] = \frac{1}{2} \pm \epsilon(\xi)$$

where $\textbf{Exp}_{\mathcal{A}}{}^{priv}$ is the security experiment against the privacy requirement, with respect to the PP-Game, MS-Game and IS-Game games, as presented in the original $\mathcal{HABS}$ construction [10].

In the aforementioned indistinguishability security games, $\mathcal{A}$ is given two pairs of public and secret keys $((pk_{u_1}, sk_{u_1})$ and $(pk_{u_2}, sk_{u_2}))$ and a set of attributes $\mathcal{S}$. The adversary can conduct an unbounded number of presentation queries — as a verifier — for any signing predicate Υ satisfied by $\mathcal{S}$; or a subset of $\mathcal{S}$ for two fixed credentials C_1 associated to $\mathcal{S}$ for pk_{u_1} and C_2 associated to $\mathcal{S}$ for pk_{u_2}. To successfully win one of the following security games, $\mathcal{A}$ should be able to guess, with a probability greater than a half:

- PP-Game – which key pair (pk_{u_j}, sk_{u_j}) for $j \in \{1, 2\}$, was used in the presentation procedure, with respect to a fixed signing predicate Υ and a chosen set of attributes $\mathcal{S}$.
- MS-Game – whether the same key pair (pk_{u_j}, sk_{u_j}) for $j \in \{1, 2\}$ was used in two different presentation procedures with respect to a chosen signing predicate Υ and a set of attributes $\mathcal{S}$.
- IS-Game – which key pair (pk_{u_j}, sk_{u_j}) and related credential C_j for $j \in \{1, 2\}$, was used in the presentation procedure, with respect to a fixed signing predicate Υ and a set of attributes $\mathcal{S}$.

Notice that the PP-Game and IS-Game formalize the notions of anonymity. The MS-Game formalizes the unlinkability requirement.

5   Concrete Construction

In this section, we complement the elements provided in previous sections to conclude the concrete construction of $\mathcal{PCS}$.

5.1   Access Structures

Definition 3 (Monotone Access Structure [1]). *Let $\mathcal{P} = \{P_1, P_2, \cdots, P_n\}$ be a set of parties. Let $\mathbb{A}$ be an access structure, i.e., a collection of non-empty subsets of $\{P_1, P_2, \cdots, P_n\}$. Then, a collection $\mathbb{A} \subseteq 2^{\{P_1, P_2, \cdots, P_n\}}$ is called monotone if for all $B, C \subseteq 2^{\{P_1, P_2, \cdots, P_n\}}$, it holds that $B \in \mathbb{A}$, $B \subseteq C$ and $C \in \mathbb{A}$. The sets in $\mathbb{A}$ are known as the authorized sets. The remainder sets, not in $\mathbb{A}$, are known as the unauthorized sets.*

Definition 4 (Linear Secret Sharing Schemes (LSSS) [1]). *A secret sharing scheme Π over a set $\mathcal{P} = \{P_1, P_2, \cdots, P_n\}$ is called linear (over $\mathbb{Z}_p$) if:*

1. *The share assigned to each party forms a vector over $\mathbb{Z}_p$;*
2. *There exists a matrix M with l rows, called the sharing generating matrix for Π, such that for each $i \in [1, l]$, we can define a function ρ, where $\rho(i)$ corresponds to the party associated to the ith row of M. If we consider the column vector $v = (v_1, \cdots, v_k)^T$, where $v_1 = s \in \mathbb{Z}_p$ is the secret to be shared,*

such that $v_t \in \mathbb{Z}_p$ and $t \in [2, k]$ are chosen at random, then $M \cdot v$ is the vector of l shares of s according to Π. The share $\lambda_i = (M \cdot v)_i$ shall belong to the party designed by $\rho(i)$.

Assume Π is an LSSS for the access structure $\mathbb{A}$. Let S be an authorized set, such that $S \in \mathbb{A}$ and $I \subseteq \{1, 2, \cdot, l\}$ is defined as $I = \{i : \rho(i) \in S\}$. If $\{\lambda_i\}_{i \in I}$ are valid shares of a secret s according to Π, then there shall exist some constant $\{w_i \in \mathbb{Z}_p\}_{i \in I}$ that can be computed in polynomial time, such that $\sum_{i \in I} \lambda_i w_i = s$ [1].

It is known that any monotonic boolean formula can be converted into a valid LSSS representation. Generally, boolean formulae are used to describe the access policy, and their equivalent LSSS matrices are used to sign and verify the signatures. The labeled matrix in Definition 4 is also known in the related literature as monotone span program [11, 14].

Definition 5 (Monotone Span Programs (MSP) [11, 14]). *A Monotone Span Program (MSP) is a tuple $(\mathbb{K}, M, \rho, t)$, such that $\mathbb{K}$ is a field, M is a $l \times c$ matrix (where l is the number of rows and c the numbers of columns), $\rho : [l] \rightarrow [n]$ is the labeling function and t is the target vector. The size of the MSP is the number l of rows. Since ρ is the function labeling each row i of M to a party $P_{\rho(i)}$, each party can be considered as associated to one or more rows. For any set of parties $S \subseteq \mathcal{P}$, the sub-matrix consisting of rows associated to the parties in S is denoted as M_S. The span of a matrix M, denoted as $span(M)$, corresponds to the subspace generated by the rows of M, i.e., all vectors of the form $v \cdot M$. An MSP is said to compute an access structure $\mathbb{A}$ if for each $S \in \mathbb{A}$ then the target vector t is in $span(M_S)$. This can be formally described as follows:*

$$\mathbb{A}(S) = 1 \iff \exists v \in \mathbb{K}^{1 \times l} : vM = t$$

5.2 Bilinear Maps

Consider three cyclic groups $\mathbb{G}_1$, $\mathbb{G}_2$, and $\mathbb{G}_T$ of prime order p, such that g_1 and g_2 are the generators of, respectively, $\mathbb{G}_1$ and $\mathbb{G}_2$. A bilinear map $\hat{e}$ is a function $\hat{e} : \mathbb{G}_1 \times \mathbb{G}_2 \rightarrow \mathbb{G}_T$ such that the following properties are satisfied:

- (i) for all $g_1 \in \mathbb{G}_1, g_2 \in \mathbb{G}_2$ (i.e., bilinearity property);
- (ii) $\hat{e}(g_1, g_2) \neq 1$ (i.e., non-degeneracy property);
- (iii) there exists an efficient algorithm that can compute $\hat{e}(g_1, g_2)$ for any $g_1 \in \mathbb{G}_1$ and $g_2 \in \mathbb{G}_2$ (i.e., computability property).

5.3 Complexity Assumptions

For our construction, we shall consider the following complexity assumptions:

- **q-Diffie Hellman Exponent Problem (q-DHE)** – Let $\mathbb{G}$ be a multiplicative cyclic group of a prime order p. Let g be a generator of $\mathbb{G}$. Then, the q-DHE problem can be stated as follows: given a tuple of elements

$(g, g_1, \cdots, g_q, g_{q+2}, \cdots, g_{2q})$, such that $g_i = g^{\alpha^i}$, where $i \in \{1, \cdots, q, q + 2, \cdots, 2q\}$ and $\alpha \xleftarrow{R} \mathbb{Z}_p$, there is no efficient probabilistic algorithm $\mathcal{A}_{qDHE}$ that can compute the missing group element $g_{q+1} = g^{\alpha^{q+1}}$.

- **Discrete Logarithm Problem (DLP)** – Let $\mathbb{G}$ be a multiplicative cyclic group of a prime order p. Let g be a generator of $\mathbb{G}$. Then, DLP problem can be stated as follows [18]. Given the public element $y = g^x \in \mathbb{G}$, there is no efficient probabilistic algorithm $\mathcal{A}_{DLP}$ that can compute the integer x.
- **Computational Diffie Hellman Assumption (CDH)** – Let $\mathbb{G}$ be a group of a prime order p. Let g be a generator of $\mathbb{G}$. The CDH problem, whose complexity is assumed stronger than DLP, is stated as follows: given the tuple of elements (g, g^a, g^b), where $\{a, b\} \xleftarrow{R} \mathbb{Z}_p$, there is no efficient probabilistic algorithm $\mathcal{A}_{CDH}$ that computes g^{ab}.

5.4   Resulting Construction

Find below the revisited set of algorithms that conclude the $\mathcal{PCS}$ construction:

- SETUP — It takes as input the security parameter ξ and returns the public parameters *params*. The public parameters are considered an auxiliary input to all the algorithms of $\mathcal{PCS}$.
  Global Public Parameters params – the SETUP algorithm first generates an asymmetric bilinear group environment $(p, \mathbb{G}_1, \mathbb{G}_2, \mathbb{G}_T, \hat{e})$ where $\hat{e}$ is an asymmetric pairing function such as $\hat{e} : \mathbb{G}_1 \times \mathbb{G}_2 \to \mathbb{G}_T$.
  The random generators $g_1, h_1 = g_1^{\alpha}, \{\gamma_i\}_{i \in [1,\mathcal{N}]} \in \mathbb{G}_1$ and $g_2, h_2 = g_2^{\alpha} \in \mathbb{G}_2$ are also generated, as well as $\alpha \in \mathbb{Z}_p$ where $\mathcal{N}$ denotes the maximum number of attributes supported by the span program. We note that each value γ_i is used to create the secret key corresponding to an attribute a_i. Let $\mathcal{H}$ be a cryptographic hash function. The global parameters of the system are denoted as follows:

$$params = \{\mathbb{G}_1, \mathbb{G}_2, \mathbb{G}_T, \hat{e}, p, g_1, \{\gamma_i\}_{i \in [1,\mathcal{N}]}, g_2, h_1, h_2, \mathcal{H}\}$$

- KEYGEN — It returns a pair of secret and public keys for each participating entity (i.e., issuing organization and user). In other words, the user gets a key pair (pk_u, sk_u) where sk_u is chosen at random from $\mathbb{Z}_p$; and $pk_u = h_1^{sk_u}$ is the corresponding public key. The issuing organization also gets a key pair (pk_o, sk_o). The issuing organization secret key sk_o relies on the couple defined as $sk_o = (s_o, x_o)$, where s_o is chosen at random from $\mathbb{Z}_p$ and $x_o = g_1^{s_o}$. The public key of the issuing organization pk_o corresponds to the couple $(X_o, Y_o) = (\hat{e}(g_1, g_2)^{s_o}, h_2^{s_o})$.
- ISSUE — It is executed by the issuing organization. The goal is to issue the credential to the user with respect to a pre-shared set of attributes $\mathcal{S} \subset \mathbb{S}$, such that $\mathbb{S}$ represents the attribute universe, defined as: $\mathcal{S} = \{a_1, a_2, \cdots, a_N\}$, where N is the number of attributes such that $N < \mathcal{N}$.
  The ISSUE algorithm takes as input the public key of the user pk_u, the set of

attributes $\mathcal{S}$ and the secret key of the issuing organization sk_o. It also selects an integer r at random and returns the credential C defined as:

$$C = (C_1, C_2, \{C_{3,i}\}_{i \in [1,N]}) = (x_o \cdot [pk_u^{s_o \mathcal{H}(\mathcal{S})^{-1}}] \cdot h_1{}^r, g_2{}^r, \{\gamma_i{}^r\}_{i \in [1,N]})$$

where $\mathcal{H}(\mathcal{S}) = \mathcal{H}(a_1)\mathcal{H}(a_2)\cdots\mathcal{H}(a_N)$ and $\gamma_i{}^r$ represent the secret key associated to the attribute a_i, where $i \in [1, N]$.

– OBTAIN — It is executed by the user. It takes as input the credential C, the secret key of the user sk_u, the public key of the issuing organization pk_o and the set of attributes $\mathcal{S}$. It returns 1 if Eq. 1 is true (0 otherwise).

$$\hat{e}(C_1, g_2) \overset{?}{=} X_o \cdot \hat{e}(g_1^{sk_u \mathcal{H}(\mathcal{S})^{-1}}, Y_o) \cdot \hat{e}(h_1, C_2) \tag{1}$$

– SHOW — It is also executed by the user. The goal is to authenticate itself. The rationale is as follows. The user sends a request to the verifier to get granted access to a service. The verifier sends a presentation policy to the user. The presentation policy is given by a randomized message M, a predicate $\varUpsilon$ and the set of attributes that have to be revealed by the user. The user signs the message $M = g_1{}^m$ with respect to the predicate $\varUpsilon$, satisfying a subset of attributes in $\mathcal{S}$. As introduced in Sect. 4, m is different for each authentication session.

In the following, we denote by $\mathcal{S}_R$, the set of attributes revealed to the verifier, and $\mathcal{S}_H$ the set of non-revealed attributes, such as $\mathcal{S} = \mathcal{S}_R \cup \mathcal{S}_H$. The signing predicate $\varUpsilon$ is represented by an LSSS access structure (M, ρ), i.e., M is a $l \times k$ matrix, and ρ is an injective function that maps each row of the matrix M to an attribute. The SHOW algorithm takes as input the user secret key sk_u, the credential C, the attribute set $\mathcal{S}$, the message m and the predicate $\varUpsilon$ such that $\varUpsilon(\mathcal{S}) = 1$. The process works as follows:

1. The credentials of the user are randomized by choosing an integer $r' \in \mathbb{Z}_p$ at random, and conducting the following operations:

$$\begin{cases} C_1' = C_1 \cdot h_1{}^{r'} = x_o \cdot [pk_u^{s_o \mathcal{H}(\mathcal{S})^{-1}}] \cdot h_1{}^{r+r'} \\[2mm] C_2' = C_2 \cdot g_2{}^{r'} = g_2{}^{r+r'} \\[2mm] C_{3,i}' = C_{3,i}' \cdot \gamma_i{}^{r'} = \gamma_i{}^{r+r'} \end{cases}$$

The resulting credential C' is set as follows:

$$C' = (C_1', C_2', \{C_{3,i}'\}_{i \in [1,N]}) = (x_o \cdot [pk_u^{s_o \mathcal{H}(\mathcal{S})^{-1}}] \cdot h_1{}^{r+r'}, g_2{}^{r+r'}, \{\gamma_i{}^{r+r'}\}_{i \in [1,N]})$$

2. As the attributes of the user in $\mathcal{S}$ satisfy $\varUpsilon$, the user can compute a vector $v = (v_1, \cdots, v_l)$ that also satisfies $vM = (1, 0, \cdots, 0)$ according to Definition 5.

3. For each attribute a_i, where $i \in [1, l]$, the user computes $\omega_i = C_2'^{v_i}$ and calculates a quantity B that depends on $\{C_{3,i}'\}_{i \in [1,N]}$ such that $B = \prod_{i=1}^{l}(\gamma_{\rho(i)}')^{v_i}$.

4. Afterwards, the user selects a random r_m and computes the couple $(\sigma_1, \sigma_2) = (C_1' \cdot B \cdot \mathsf{M}^{r_m}, g_1^{r_m})$. Notice that the user may not have knowledge about the secret value of each attribute in Υ. If this happens, v_i is set to 0, so to exclude the necessity of this value.

5. Using now the secret key of the user, it is possible to compute an accumulator on non-revealed attributes as follows:

$$A = Y_o^{\frac{sk_u \mathcal{H}(\mathcal{S}_H)^{-1}}{r_m}}$$

The user returns the presentation token $\Sigma = (\Omega, \sigma_1, \sigma_2, C_2', A, \mathcal{S}_R)$, that includes the signature of the message M with respect to the predicate Υ, and where $\Omega = \{\omega_1, \cdots, \omega_l\}$ is the set of committed element values of the vector $\boldsymbol{v}$, based on the credential's item C_2'.

- VERIFY — Given the presentation token Σ, the public key of the issuing organization pk_o, the set of revealed attributes $\mathcal{S}_R$, the message m and the signing predicate Υ corresponding to $(M_{l \times k}, \rho)$, the verifier checks the received set of revealed attributes $\mathcal{S}_R$, and computes an accumulator A_R such that $A_R = \sigma_2^{\mathcal{H}(\mathcal{S}_R)^{-1}}$. Then, the verifier picks uniformly at random $k-1$ integers $\mu_2, \cdots, \mu_k$ and calculates l integers $\tau_i \in \mathbb{Z}_p$ for $i \in \{1, \cdots, l\}$, such that $\tau_i = \sum_{j=1}^{k} \mu_j M_{i,j}$, and where $M_{i,j}$ is an element of the matrix M. The verifier accepts the presentation token as valid (i.e., it returns 1) if Eq. 2 holds true:

$$\hat{e}(\sigma_1, g_2) \stackrel{?}{=} X_o \hat{e}(A_R, A)\hat{e}(, h_1, C_2') \prod_{i=1}^{l} \hat{e}(\gamma_{\rho(i)} h_1^{\tau_i}, \omega_i)\hat{e}(\sigma_2, g_2^m) \tag{2}$$

6 Security Analysis

Theorem 1. *Correctness* – $\mathcal{PCS}$ *is correct if for all* (params) $\leftarrow$ SETUP(ξ), *all pairs of public and secret keys* $\{(pk_o, sk_o), (pk_u, sk_u)\} \leftarrow$ KEYGEN(*params*), *all attribute sets* $\mathcal{S}$, *all credentials* $C \leftarrow$ ISSUE ($\mathcal{S}, sk_o, pk_u$), *all claiming predicates* Υ *such as* $\Upsilon(\mathcal{S}) = 1$ *and all presentation tokens* $\Sigma \leftarrow$ SHOW ($C, sk_u, \mathsf{M}, \Upsilon$), *we have* OBTAIN ($C, sk_u, pk_o, \mathcal{S}$) $= 1$ *and* VERIFY ($\Sigma, m, \Upsilon, pk_o$) $= 1$.

Proof. The correctness of Theorem 1 relies on Eqs. 1 and 2 (cf. Sect. 5.4). The correctness of Eq. 1 is straightforward by following the bilinearity requirement of pairing functions (cf. Sect. 5.2), summarized as follows:

$$\begin{aligned}
\hat{e}(C_1, g_2) &= \hat{e}(x_o \cdot [pk_u^{s_o \mathcal{H}(\mathcal{S})^{-1}}] \cdot h_1^r, g_2) \\
&= \hat{e}(g_1^{s_o}, g_2) \cdot \hat{e}(h_1^{sk_u s_o \mathcal{H}(\mathcal{S})^{-1}}, g_2) \cdot \hat{e}(h_1^r, g_2) \\
&= \hat{e}(g_1, g_2)^{s_o} \cdot \hat{e}(g_1^{sk_u \mathcal{H}(\mathcal{S})^{-1}}, h_2^{s_o}) \cdot \hat{e}(h_1, g_2^r) \\
&= X_o \cdot \hat{e}(g_1^{sk_u \mathcal{H}(\mathcal{S})^{-1}}, Y_o) \cdot \hat{e}(h_1, C_2)
\end{aligned}$$

Recall that the correctness of the presentation token is validated by the verifier. It verifies if the received token $\Sigma = (\Omega, \sigma_1, \sigma_2, C_2', A, \mathcal{S}_R)$ holds a valid signature of message M, based on the predicate Υ. For this purpose, the verifier checks the set of revealed attributes $\mathcal{S}_R$ and computes an accumulator A_R of the revealed attributes' values, using σ_2, such as $A_R = \sigma_2^{\mathcal{H}(\mathcal{S}_R)^{-1}}$, where $\mathcal{H}(\mathcal{S}_R) = \prod_{a_i \in \mathcal{S}_R} \mathcal{H}(a_i)^{-1}$. The value of σ_1 can be expressed as follows:

$$\sigma_1 = C_1' \cdot B \cdot M^{r_m}$$

$$= C_1' \cdot \prod_{i=1}^{l} (\gamma_{\rho(i)}')^{v_i} \cdot g_1^{r_m m}$$

$$= x_o \cdot pk_u^{s_o \mathcal{H}(\mathcal{S})^{-1}} \cdot h_1^{r+r'} \cdot \prod_{i=1}^{l} (\gamma_{\rho(i)})^{(r+r')v_i} \cdot g_1^{r_m m}$$

To prove the correctness of the presentation token verification, let us denote $(r + r')$ by R, and the first side of Eq. 2 by $\circledS$, such that:

$$\circledS = \hat{e}(x_o \cdot pk_u^{s_o \mathcal{H}(\mathcal{S})^{-1}} \cdot h_1^{r+r'} \cdot \prod_{i=1}^{l} (\gamma_{\rho(i)})^{R v_i} \cdot M^{r_m}, g_2)$$

$$= \hat{e}(x_o, g_2) \cdot \hat{e}(pk_u^{s_o \mathcal{H}(\mathcal{S})^{-1}}, g_2) \cdot \hat{e}(h_1^{R}, g_2) \cdot \hat{e}(g_1^{r_m m}, g_2) \cdot \hat{e}(\prod_{i=1}^{l} \gamma_{\rho(i)}^{R v_i}, g_2)$$

$$= \hat{e}(g_1, g_2)^{s_o} \cdot \hat{e}(g_1^{sk_u \mathcal{H}(\mathcal{S}_R \cup \mathcal{S}_H)^{-1}}, g_2^{\alpha s_o}) \cdot \hat{e}(h_1^R, g_2) \cdot \hat{e}(\sigma_2, g_2^m) \cdot \prod_{i=1}^{l} \hat{e}(\gamma_{\rho(i)}^{R v_i}, g_2)$$

$$= X_o \cdot \hat{e}([g_1^{sk_u}]^{\mathcal{H}(\mathcal{S}_R)^{-1} \mathcal{H}(\mathcal{S}_H)^{-1}}, h_2^{s_o}) \cdot \hat{e}(h_1, g_2^R) \cdot \hat{e}(\sigma_2, g_2^m) \cdot \prod_{i=1}^{l} \hat{e}(\gamma_{\rho(i)}, g_2^{R v_i})$$

$$= X_o \cdot \hat{e}(g_1^{\mathcal{H}(\mathcal{S}_R)^{-1}}, [Y_o^{sk_u}]^{\mathcal{H}(\mathcal{S}_H)^{-1}}) \cdot \hat{e}(h_1, C_2') \cdot \hat{e}(\sigma_2, g_2^m) \cdot \prod_{i=1}^{l} \hat{e}(\gamma_{\rho(i)}, \omega_i)$$

$$= X_o \cdot \hat{e}(A_R, A) \cdot \hat{e}(h_1, C_2') \cdot \prod_{i=1}^{l} \hat{e}(\gamma_{\rho(i)} h_1^{\tau_i}, \omega_i) \cdot \hat{e}(\sigma_2, g_2^m)$$

Given that $\tau_i = \sum_{i=1}^{k} \mu_j M_{i,j}$, then the last equality is simplified to:

$$\sum_{i=1}^{l} \tau_i(v_i R) = R \sum_{i=1}^{l} \tau_i v_i = R \cdot 1 = R$$

and the term $\hat{e}(h_1^R, g_2)$ leads to $\hat{e}(h_1^R, g_2) = \prod_{i=1}^{l} \hat{e}(h_1^{R \tau_i}, g_2^{R v_i})$ ☐

Theorem 2. Unforgeability – *The $\mathcal{PCS}$ scheme ensures the unforgeability requirement, under the CDH, q-DHE and DLP cryptographic assumptions.*

Sketch of proof. To prove that $\mathcal{PCS}$ satisfies the unforgeability requirement, we show that an adversary $\mathcal{A}$ who does not own an appropriate legitimate credential, is not able to generate a valid presentation token. Thus, $\mathcal{A}$ cannot violate the statements of Theorem 2 by reaching the advantage $Pr[\mathbf{Exp}_A^{unforg}(1^\xi) = 1] \geq \epsilon(\xi)$.

Theorem 2 is based on the security games presented in Sect. 4.2 for the unforgeability requirement, namely MC-Game, MU-Game and Col-Game. We recall that the $\mathcal{PCS}$ scheme mainly relies on the $\mathcal{HABS}$ mechanism [10] for the $\mathcal{PCS}$.OBTAIN $\leftrightarrow$ $\mathcal{PCS}$.ISSUE and $\mathcal{PCS}$.SHOW $\leftrightarrow$ $\mathcal{PCS}$.VERIFY algorithms. It is, therefore, similarly resistant to forgery attacks under the CDH, q-DHE and DLP assumptions.

For the first game, namely MC-game, $\mathcal{A}$ may try a forgery attack against the CDH assumption, considering that the credential element C_1 is a product of an accumulator over the set of user attributes, the secret key of the issuing organization x_o and a randomization of the public group element h_1. Knowing that this randomization is required for deriving the remaining credential elements, $\mathcal{A}$ is led to violate the CDH assumption. In [20, 21], Vergnaud details a forgery attack against the $\mathcal{HABS}$ construction. The assumption is to imagine a situation in which $\mathcal{A}$ overrides the granted rights by multiplying the first credential element C_1 such that $C_1 = C_1 \cdot X_u^{-\mathcal{H}(\mathcal{S})^{-1}} \cdot X_u^{\mathcal{H}(\mathcal{S}')^{-1}}$, where X_u is the public key of the user, $\mathcal{S} = \{a_1, \cdots, a_N\}$, $\mathcal{S}' = \{a_1, \cdots, a_M\}$ and $N < M$. This attack does not affect the $\mathcal{PCS}$ construction, since the secret key of the issuing organization is used during the generation of the credential element C_1. This protects the $\mathcal{PCS}$ construction from the attack reported by Vergnaud against $\mathcal{HABS}$ in [20,21].

By building over the previous attack, Vergnaud also states in [20,21] that an adversary $\mathcal{A}$ can override the granted rights by conducting a collusion attack (i.e., Col-Game) based on two different credentials C_{u_1} for pk_{u_1} and C_{u_2} for pk_{u_2}. The use of the secret key of the issuing organization for the derivation of the credential element C_1 also makes unfeasible this forgery attack against $\mathcal{PCS}$.

Similarly, and under the MU-Game, Vergnaud states in [20,21] that an adversary can try a forgery attack against the $\mathcal{HABS}$ construction, by eavesdropping the communication of a presentation protocol for a signing predicate Υ and a public key (pk_u); then, by impersonating the same user during the following sessions under the same predicate Υ. In fact, $\mathcal{A}$ can compute $\sigma_1' = \sigma_1 - \sigma_2(m'-m) = C_1' \cdot B \cdot g_1^{m r_m}$, for some known r_m. This attack does not affect the $\mathcal{PCS}$ construction, since the signing message m is properly randomized, and only the corresponding group element $\mathsf{M} = g_1^m$ is provided to the signer.

Finally, $\mathcal{PCS}$ is also resistant to replay attacks. The randomness elements appended by the challenger, for each request addresses the issue. Therefore, the $\mathcal{PCS}$ scheme ensures the unforgeability requirement, under the q-DHE, CDH and DLP assumptions, with respect to MC-Game, MU-Game and Col-Game.

Theorem 3. *Privacy* – $\mathcal{PCS}$ *satisfies the privacy requirement, with respect to the anonymity and unlinkability properties.*

Sketch of proof. Theorem 3 relies on the security games introduced in Sect. 4.2, namely PP-Game, MS-Game and IS-Game. They assume an adversary $\mathcal{A}$ trying to distinguish between two honestly derived presentation tokens for different settings with respect to every security game. As in the original $\mathcal{HABS}$ proposal [10], each specific setting of the $\mathcal{PCS}$ construction randomizes the secret keys of the users, as well as the presentation tokens.

During the PP-Game, since a new presentation token for the same message M and the same access predicate Υ is computed from random nonces, generated by $\mathcal{C}$, both presentation tokens are identically distributed in both cases. Then, an adversary $\mathcal{A}$, against the issue-show requirement — with respect to IS-Game — has an access to the *Issue* oracle for generating users' credentials. However, an honest user produces a different presentation token for each presentation session $\mathcal{PCS}$.SHOW, by using the randomness introduced by the user while generating the presentation token. As such, the probability of predicting j is bounded by $\frac{1}{2}$. In [20,21], Vergnaud identifies an anonymity attack against $\mathcal{HABS}$ with respect to the PP-Game and the IS-Game. Vergnaud states in [20,21] that an adversary $\mathcal{A}$ can compute $A^{\mathcal{H}(S_H)r_m} = g_2^{sk_{u_j}\mathcal{H}(S_H)^{-1}r_m^{-1}} = g_2^{sk_{u_j}}$ for some known r_m and $j \in \{1,2\}$, in order to identify the signing user. This attack does not affect the $\mathcal{PCS}$ construction, since the secret key of the issuer is used during the generation of the credential element C_1.

Similarly, the MS-Game relies on a *left-or-right* oracle, where an adversary $\mathcal{A}$ cannot distinguish the oracle's outputs better than just flipping a coin. In fact, both presentation tokens for the same message M and the same access predicate Υ sent to different users, such as $\Upsilon(\mathcal{S}_{u_1}) = \Upsilon(\mathcal{S}_{u_2}) = 1$, are statistically indistinguishable. Using the previous attack against the $\mathcal{HABS}$ construction, Vergnaud states in [20,21] that the adversary can check whether two presentation tokens $\Sigma^{(1)}$ and $\Sigma^{(2)}$ were generated using the same pair of public and secret keys (sk_{u_j}, pk_{u_j}), by computing two group elements $T_1 = C_1'^{(2)}/C_1'^{(2)}$ and $T_2 = C_2'^{(2)}/C_2'^{(2)}$, hence evaluating the equality between two bilinear maps values $\hat{e}(T_1, g_2)$ and $\hat{e}(g_1^{-1}, T_2)$. This same attack does not affect the $\mathcal{PCS}$ construction, since C_1' and C_2' are no longer provided with the presentation token. Indeed, the adversary $\mathcal{A}$ cannot distinguish two different presentations tokens with probability $\mathbf{Adv}(\mathcal{A}, t) \neq \frac{1}{2} + \epsilon$. As such, $\mathcal{PCS}$ is unlinkable, ensuring as well the privacy requirement.

7   E-assessment Use Case for $\mathcal{PCS}$

E-assessment is an innovative form for the evaluation of learners' knowledge and skills in online education, where part of the assessment activities is carried out online. As e-assessment involves online communication channel between learners and educators, as well as data transfer and storage, security measures are required to protect the environment against system and network attacks. Issues concerning the security and privacy of learners is a challenging topic. Such issues are discussed under the scope of the TeSLA project (cf. http://tesla-project.eu/ for further information), a EU-funded project that aims at providing learners with an innovative environment that allows them to take assessments remotely, thus avoiding mandatory attendance constraints.

In [12], the security of the TeSLA e-assessment system was analyzed and discussed w.r.t. the General Data Protection Regulation (GDPR) [6] recommendations. To meet such recommendations, it is necessary to ensure a reasonable level of privacy in the system. TeSLA implements several privacy technological filters. For instance, a randomized system identifier is associated to each learner. This identifier is used each time the learner accesses the TeSLA system, hence ensuring pseudo-anonymity to every learner — full anonymity not being an option in TeSLA for legal reasons. Yet, a randomized identifier alone cannot protect the learners against more complex threats such as unwanted traceability. The system can still be able to link two different sessions of the same learner. To handle such issues, the $\mathcal{PCS}$ construction is being integrated along with the security framework of the TeSLA architecture.

Available as a multi-platform C++ source code at http://j.mp/PKIPCSgit, and mainly based on existing cryptographic libraries such as PBC [19] and MCL [17], the construction is available online to facilitate understanding, comparison and validation of the solution. For the time being, the integration of $\mathcal{PCS}$ in TeSLA is expected to allow learner-related tools to prove they are authorized to access a resource without revealing more than needed about the identity of the learners. For example, learners can be issued with certified attributes that may be required by the system verifier, such as *enrolled on engineering courses* or *conducting graduate studies*. When the learners want to prove that they own the right set of attributes, they perform a digital signature based on the required attributes, allowing the system verifier to check if a precise user is authorized, sometimes without even knowing precisely which attributes were used.

Such an approach can be easily integrated to access electronic resources on e-learning environments such as Moodle (cf. https://moodle.org/). It should be enough to prove that the learner comes from an allowed university or that the learner is registered for a given e-learning course. That way, it becomes impossible for the learning environment to follow some unnecessary information of each learner, while still letting them access specific resources of the system (e.g., anonymous quizzes and polls, to quickly validate the percentage of understanding of the learners, prior the final e-assessment). Similarly, when a learner takes the final e-assessment, the learner's work can be anonymously sent to anti-cheating tools (such as anti-plagiarism). With anonymous certification, each tool might receive a request for the same work without being able to know which learner wrote it, but also without being able to correlate the requests and decide whether they were issued by the same learner. Some further information about the integration of $\mathcal{PCS}$ into the TeSLA platform is under evaluation for testing purposes. It will be reported soon, in a forthcoming publication.

8   Conclusion

We have proposed an anonymous certification scheme called $\mathcal{PCS}$, as a building block of new privacy-friendly electronic identity systems. By using $\mathcal{PCS}$, a user can anonymously agree with a verifier about the possession of a set of attributes, such as age, citizenship and similar authorization attributes. While staying anonymous and having the control over all the released data, users can preserve their privacy during the verification procedure.

$\mathcal{PCS}$ builds over $\mathcal{HABS}$ (short for Homomorphic Attribute Based Signatures), presented by Kaaniche and Laurent in ESORICS 2016 [10]. $\mathcal{PCS}$ revisits the previous construction and addresses some security and privacy concerns reported by Vergnaud in [20,21]. Based on several security games, $\mathcal{PCS}$ handles the limitations in $\mathcal{HABS}$ with respect to forgery and anonymity. $\mathcal{PCS}$ supports a flexible selective disclosure mechanism with no-extra processing cost, which is directly inherited from the expressiveness of attribute-based signatures for defining access policies. A use case dealing with the integration of $\mathcal{PCS}$ to allow the learners of an e-assessment platform to reveal only required information to certificate authority providers has also been briefly presented. Multi-platform C++ snippets of code, available at http://j.mp/PKIPCSgit, and based on two different cryptographic libraries [17,19], are released to facilitate the understanding, comparison and validation of $\mathcal{PCS}$, with regard to $\mathcal{HABS}$.

Acknowledgements. This work is supported by the H2020-ICT-2015/H2020-ICT-2015 TeSLA project *An Adaptive Trust-based e-assessment System for Learning*, Number 688520.

References

1. Beimel, A.: Secret sharing and key distribution. Research thesis (1996)
2. Camenisch, J., Krenn, S., Lehmann, A., Mikkelsen, G.L., Neven, G., Pederson, M.O.: Scientific comparison of ABC protocols: part i - formal treatment of privacy-enhancing credential systems (2014)
3. Camenisch, J., Lysyanskaya, A.: An efficient system for non-transferable anonymous credentials with optional anonymity revocation. In: Pfitzmann, B. (ed.) EUROCRYPT 2001. LNCS, vol. 2045, pp. 93–118. Springer, Heidelberg (2001). doi:10.1007/3-540-44987-6_7
4. Camenisch, J., Mödersheim, S., Sommer, D.: A formal model of identity mixer. In: Kowalewski, S., Roveri, M. (eds.) FMICS 2010. LNCS, vol. 6371, pp. 198–214. Springer, Heidelberg (2010). doi:10.1007/978-3-642-15898-8_13
5. Chaum, D.: Security without identification: transaction systems to make big brother obsolete. Commun. ACM **28**(10), 1030–1044 (1985)
6. Europe, C.: Proposal for a regulation of the european parliament and of the council on the protection of individuals with regard to the processing of personal data and on the free movement of such data. In: General Data Protection Regulation, January 2016 (2016)
7. Garcia-Alfaro, J., Barbeau, M., Kranakis, E.: A proactive threshold secret sharing scheme handling Gen2 privacy threats. Technical report, Carleton University, March 2009
8. Garcia-Alfaro, J., Barbeau, M., Kranakis, E.: Proactive threshold cryptosystem for EPC tags. Ad hoc Sensor Wirel. Netw. **12**(3–4), 187–208 (2011)
9. Herranz, J., Laguillaumie, F., Libert, B., Ràfols, C.: Short attribute-based signatures for threshold predicates. In: Dunkelman, O. (ed.) CT-RSA 2012. LNCS, vol. 7178, pp. 51–67. Springer, Heidelberg (2012). doi:10.1007/978-3-642-27954-6_4

10. Kaaniche, N., Laurent, M.: Attribute-based signatures for supporting anonymous certification. In: Askoxylakis, I., Ioannidis, S., Katsikas, S., Meadows, C. (eds.) ESORICS 2016. LNCS, vol. 9878, pp. 279–300. Springer, Cham (2016). doi:10.1007/978-3-319-45744-4_14

11. Karchmer, M., Wigderson, A.: On span programs. In: Proceedings of the 8th IEEE Structure in Complexity Theory (1993)

12. Kiennert, C., Rocher, P.O., Ivanova, M., Rozeva, A., Durcheva, M., Garcia-Alfaro, J.: Security challenges in e-assessment and technical solutions. In 8th International Workshop on Interactive Environments and Emerging Technologies for eLearning, 21st International Conference on Information Visualization, London, UK (2017)

13. Li, J., Au, M.H., Susilo, W., Xie, D., Ren, K.: Attribute-based signature and its applications. In: ASIACCS 2010 (2010)

14. Maji, H.K., Prabhakaran, M., Rosulek, M.: Attribute-based signatures. In: Kiayias, A. (ed.) CT-RSA 2011. LNCS, vol. 6558, pp. 376–392. Springer, Heidelberg (2011). doi:10.1007/978-3-642-19074-2_24

15. Okamoto, T., Takashima, K.: Efficient attribute-based signatures for non-monotone predicates in the standard model. In: Catalano, D., Fazio, N., Gennaro, R., Nicolosi, A. (eds.) PKC 2011. LNCS, vol. 6571, pp. 35–52. Springer, Heidelberg (2011). doi:10.1007/978-3-642-19379-8_3

16. Shahandashti, S.F., Safavi-Naini, R.: Threshold attribute-based signatures and their application to anonymous credential systems. In: Preneel, B. (ed.) AFRICACRYPT 2009. LNCS, vol. 5580, pp. 198–216. Springer, Heidelberg (2009). doi:10.1007/978-3-642-02384-2_13

17. Shigeo, M.: MCL - Generic and fast pairing-based cryptography library. https://github.com/herumi/mcl. Version: release20170402

18. Shor, P.: Polynomial-time algorithms for prime factorization and discrete logarithms on a quantum computer. SIAM Rev. **41**(2), 303–332 (1999)

19. Stanford University: PBC - The Pairing-Based Cryptography Library. https://crypto.stanford.edu/pbc/. Version: 0.5.14

20. Vergnaud, D.: Comment on "attribute-based signatures for supporting anonymous certification" by N. Kaaniche and M. Laurent (ESORICS 2016). IACR Cryptology ePrint Archive (2016)

21. Vergnaud, D.: Comment on attribute-based signatures for supporting anonymous certification by N. Kaaniche and M. Laurent (ESORICS 2016). Comput. J. 1–8 (2017)

22. Zhang, Y., Feng, D.: Efficient attribute proofs in anonymous credential using attribute-based cryptography. In: Chim, T.W., Yuen, T.H. (eds.) ICICS 2012. LNCS, vol. 7618, pp. 408–415. Springer, Heidelberg (2012). doi:10.1007/978-3-642-34129-8_39

Order-Preserving Encryption Using Approximate Integer Common Divisors

James Dyer[1(✉)], Martin Dyer[2], and Jie Xu[2]

[1] School of Computer Science, University of Manchester, Manchester, UK
james.dyer@postgrad.manchester.ac.uk
[2] School of Computing, University of Leeds, Leeds, UK

Abstract. We present a new, but simple, randomised *order-preserving encryption* (OPE) scheme based on the *general approximate common divisor problem* (GACDP). This appears to be the first OPE scheme to be based on a computational hardness primitive, rather than a security game. This scheme requires only $O(1)$ arithmetic operations for encryption and decryption. We show that the scheme has optimal information leakage under the assumption of uniformly distributed plaintexts, and we indicate that this property extends to some non-uniform distributions. We report on an extensive evaluation of our algorithms. The results clearly demonstrate highly favourable execution times in comparison with existing OPE schemes.

Keywords: Order-preserving encryption · Symmetric cryptography · Cloud computing · Data analytics

1 Introduction

Outsourcing computation to the cloud has become increasingly important to business, government, and academia. However, in some circumstances, data on which those computations are performed may be sensitive. Therefore, outsourced computation proves problematic.

To address these problems, we require a means of secure computation in the cloud. One proposal, is that of *homomorphic encryption*, where data is encrypted and computation is performed on the encrypted data [32]. The data is retrieved and decrypted. Because the encryption is homomorphic over the operations performed by the outsourced computation, the decrypted result is the same as that computed on the unencrypted data.

Fully homomorphic encryption has been proposed as a means of achieving this. However, as currently proposed, it is not practical. Therefore, we believe that *somewhat homomorphic encryption*, which is homomorphic only for certain inputs or operations, is only of current practical interest.

For sorting and comparison of data we require an encryption scheme that supports homomorphic comparisons of ciphertexts. *Order-preserving encryption* (OPE) is a recent field that supports just such a proposition. An OPE is defined

© Springer International Publishing AG 2017
J. Garcia-Alfaro et al. (Eds.): DPM/CBT 2017, LNCS 10436, pp. 257–274, 2017.
DOI: 10.1007/978-3-319-67816-0_15

as an encryption scheme where, for plaintexts m_1 and m_2 and corresponding ciphertexts c_1 and c_2,[1]

$$m_1 < m_2 \implies c_1 < c_2$$

Our work presents an OPE scheme that is based on the *general approximate common divisor problem* (GACDP) [18], which is believed to be hard. Using this problem we have devised a system where encryption and decryption require $O(1)$ arithmetic operations.

1.1   Notation

$x \xleftarrow{\$} S$ represents a value x chosen uniformly at random from the discrete set S.

KeyGen : $S \to K$ denotes the key generation function operating on the security parameter space S and whose range is the secret key space K.

Enc : $M \times K \to C$ denotes the symmetric encryption function operating on the plaintext space M and the secret key space K and whose range is the ciphertext space C.

Dec : $C \times K \to M$ denotes the symmetric decryption function operating on the ciphertext space C and the secret key space K and whose range is the plaintext space M.

$m, m_1, m_2, \ldots$ denote plaintext values. Similarly, $c, c_1, c_2, \ldots$ denote ciphertext values.

$[x, y]$ denotes the integers between x and y inclusive.

$[x, y)$ denotes $[x, y] \setminus \{y\}$.

$\mathbb{R}[x, y)$ denotes the real numbers in the interval $[x, y)$.

1.2   Scenario

Our OPE system is intended to be employed as part of a system for single-party secure computation in the cloud. In this system, a secure client encrypts data and then outsources computation on the encrypted data to the cloud. Then computation is performed homomorphically on the ciphertexts. The results of the computation are retrieved by the secure client and decrypted. We intend that our OPE scheme will support sorting and comparison of encrypted data.

1.3   Formal Model of Scenario

We have n integer inputs, $m_1, m_2, \ldots, m_n$, where $m_i \in M = [0, M]$ and $n \ll M$.[2] We wish to be able to compare and sort these inputs. A secure client A selects an instance $\mathcal{E}_K$ of the OPE algorithm $\mathcal{E}$ using the secret parameter set K. A

---

[1] This relationship is typically represented as $m_1 \le m_2 \implies c_1 \le c_2$. However, this seems to introduce an insecurity, by permitting an equality test for plaintexts using two comparisons.

[2] We must assume $n \ll M$ to avoid the "sorting attack" of Naveed et al. [27].

encrypts the n inputs by computing $c_i = \mathcal{E}_K(m_i)$, for $i \in [1, n]$. A uploads $c_1, c_2, \ldots, c_n$ to the cloud computing environment. These encryptions do not all need to be uploaded at the same time but n is a bound on the total number of inputs. The cloud environment conducts comparisons on the $c_i, i \in [1, n]$. Since $\mathcal{E}$ is an OPE, the m_i will also be correctly sorted. A can retrieve some or all of the c_i from the cloud and decrypt each ciphertext c_i by computing $m_i = \mathcal{E}_K^{-1}(c_i)$.

A snooper is only able to inspect $c_1, c_2, \ldots, c_n$ in the cloud environment. The snooper may compute additional functions on the $c_1, c_2, \ldots, c_n$ as part of a cryptanalytic attack, but cannot make new encryptions.

1.4   Observations from Scenario

From our scenario we observe that we do not require public-key encryption as we do not intend another party to encrypt data. Symmetric encryption will suffice. Furthermore, there is no key escrow or distribution problem, as only ciphertexts are distributed to the cloud.

It is common in the literature [2,3] to refer to an encryption or decryption oracle in formal models of security. However, our scenario has no analogue of an oracle because another party has no way of encrypting or decrypting data without breaking the system. Any cryptological attacks will have to be performed on ciphertexts only. Therefore, we see *chosen plaintext attacks* (CPA) and *chosen ciphertext attacks* (CCA) as not relevant to our scenario. Indeed, it can be argued that any notion of indistinguishability under CPA is not relevant to OPE in practice (see Sect. 2.2). Various attempts have been made by Boldyreva and others [5,6,33,36] to provide such indistinguishability notions. However, the security models impose practically unrealistic restrictions on an adversary. See, for example, our discussion of IND-OCPA below (Sect. 2.2). It should also be pointed out that satisfying an indistinguishability criterion does not guarantee that a cryptosystem is unbreakable, and neither does failure to satisfy it guarantee that the system is breakable.

We also note that a *known plaintext attack* (KPA) is considered possible only by brute force, and not through being given a sample of pairs of plaintext and corresponding ciphertext.

Our notion of security requires only that determining the plaintext values is computationally infeasible within the lifetime of the outsourced computation. However, in some cases, we can show that the information leaked about the plaintexts is not significantly greater than is leaked by the total ordering revealed by the OPE.

1.5   Related Work

Prior to Boldyreva et al. [6], OPE had been investigated by Agrawal et al. [1] and others (see [1] for earlier references). However, it wasn't until Boldyreva et al. that it was claimed that an OPE scheme was provably secure. Boldyreva et al.'s algorithm constructs a random order-preserving function by mapping M consecutive integers in a domain to integers in a much larger range $[1, N]$, by recursively dividing the range into M monotonically increasing subranges. Each integer is assigned a pseudorandom value in its subrange. The algorithm recursively bisects the range, at each recursion sampling from the domain until it hits the input plaintext value. The algorithm is designed this way because Boldyreva et al. wish to sample uniformly from the range. This would require sampling from the negative hypergeometric distribution, for which no efficient exact algorithm is known. Therefore they sample the domain from the hypergeometric instead. As a result, each encryption requires at least $\log N$ recursions. Furthermore, so that a value can be decrypted, the pseudorandom values generated must be reconstructible. Therefore, for each instance of the algorithm, a plaintext will always encrypt to the same ciphertext. This implies that the encryption of low entropy data might be very easy to break by a "guessing" attack (see Sect. 4). For our OPE scheme, multiple encryptions of a plaintext will produce differing ciphertexts. In [6], the authors claim that $N = 2M$, a claim repeated in [10], although [5] suggests $N \geq 7M$. We use $N \geq M^2$ in our implementations of Boldyreva et al.'s algorithm, since this has the advantage that the scheme can be approximated closely by a much simplified computation, as we discuss in Sect. 3.2. The cost is only a doubling of the ciphertext size. However both [5,6] take no account of n, the number of values to be encrypted. As in our scheme, the scheme should have $n \ll M$ to avoid the sorting attack of [27]. If $c = f(m)$ is Boldyreva et al.'s OPE, it is straightforward to show that we can estimate $f^{-1}(c)$ by $\hat{m} = Mc/N$, with standard deviation approximately $\sqrt{2\hat{m}(1 - \hat{m}/M)}$. For this reason, Boldyreva et al.'s scheme always leaks about half the plaintext bits.

Yum et al. [37] extend Boldyreva et al.'s work to non-uniformly distributed plaintexts. This can improve the situation in the event that the client knows the distribution of plaintexts. This "flattening" idea already appears in [1]. In Sect. 2.3 we discuss a similar idea.

In [5], Boldyreva et al. suggest an extension to their original scheme, modular order-preserving encryption (MOPE), by simply transforming the plaintext before encryption by adding a term modulo M. The idea is to cope with some of the problems discussed above, but any additional security arises only from this term being unknown. Note also that this construction again always produces the same ciphertext value for each plaintext.

Teranishi et al. [33] devise a new OPE scheme that satisfies their own security model. However, their algorithms are less efficient, being linear in the size of the message space. Furthermore, like Boldyreva et al., a plaintext always encrypts to the same ciphertext value.

Krendelev et al. [22] devise an OPE scheme based on a coding of an integer as the real number $\sum_i b_i 2^{-i}$ where b_i is the ith bit of the integer. The algorithm to encode the integer is $O(n)$ where n is the number of bits in the integer. Using this encoding, they construct a matrix-based OPE scheme where a plaintext is encrypted as a tuple (r, k, t). Each element of the tuple is the sum of elements from a matrix derived from the private key matrices σ and A. Their algorithms are especially expensive, as they require computation of powers of the matrix A. Furthermore, each plaintext value always encrypts to the same ciphertext value.

Khadem et al. [19] propose a scheme to encrypt equal plaintext values to differing values. Their scheme is similar to Boldyreva et al. where a plaintext is mapped to a pseudorandom value in a subrange. However, this scheme relies on the domain being a set of consecutive integers for decryption. Our scheme allows for non-consecutive integers. This means that our scheme can support updates without worrying about overlapping "buckets" as Khadem et al.

Liu et al. [25] addresses frequency of plaintext values by mapping the plaintext value to a value in an extended message space and splitting the message and ciphertext spaces nonlinearly. As in our scheme, decryption is a simple division. However, the ciphertext interval must first be located for a given ciphertext which is $\Omega(\log n)$ when n is the total number of intervals.

Liu and Wang [24] describe a system similar to ours where random "noise" is added to a linear transformation of the plaintext. However, in their examples, the parameters and noise used are real numbers. Unlike our work, the security of such a scheme is unclear.

In [29], Popa et al. discuss an interactive protocol for constructing a binary index of ciphertexts. Although this protocol guarantees ideal security, in that it only reveals the ordering, it is not an OPE. The ciphertexts do not preserve the ordering of the plaintexts, rather the protocol requires a secure client to decrypt the ciphertexts, compare the plaintexts, and return the ordering. It is essentially equivalent to sorting the plaintexts on the secure client and then encrypting them. Popa et al.'s protocol has a high communication cost: $\Omega(n \log n)$. This may be suitable for a database server where the comparisons may be made in a secure processing unit with fast bus communication. However, it is unsuitable for a large scale distributed system where the cost of communication will become prohibitive. Kerschbaum and Schroepfer [21] improved the communication cost of Popa et al.'s protocol to $\Omega(n)$ under the assumption that the input is random. However, this is still onerous for distributed systems. Kerschbaum [20] further extends this protocol to hide the frequency of plaintexts. Boelter et al. [4] extend Popa et al.'s idea by using "garbled circuits" to obfuscate comparisons. However, the circuits can only be used once, so their system is one-time use.

Also of note is *order-revealing encryption* (ORE), a generalisation of OPE introduced by Boneh et al. [7], that only reveals the order of ciphertexts. An ORE is a scheme (C, E, D) where C is a comparator function that takes two ciphertext inputs and outputs '$<$' or '$\geq$', and E and D are encryption and decryption functions. This attempts to replace the secure client's responsibility for plaintext comparisons in Popa's scheme with an exposed function acting on the ciphertexts.

Boneh et al.'s construction uses multilinear maps. However, as stated in Chenette et al. [10], "The main drawback of the Boneh et al. ORE construction is that it relies on complicated tools and strong assumptions on these tools, and as such, is currently impractical to implement".

Chenette et al. offer a more practical construction, with weaker claims to provable security. However, since it encrypts the plaintexts bit-wise, it requires a number of applications of a pseudorandom function f linear in the bit size of the plaintext to encrypt an integer. The security and efficiency of this scheme depends on which pseudorandom function f is chosen.

Lewi et al. [23] devise an ORE scheme where there are two modes of encryption: left and right. The left encryption consists of a permutation of the domain and a key generated by hashing the permuted plaintext value. The right ciphertext consists of encryptions of the comparison with every other value in the domain. It is a tuple of size $d + 1$ where d is the size of the domain. Lewi et al. then extend this scheme to domains of size d^n. This results in right ciphertext tuples of size $dn + 1$. Our experimental results compare favourably with theirs, largely because the ciphertext sizes of Lewi et al.'s scheme are much larger.

The security of these ORE schemes is proven under a scenario similar to IND-OCPA [6] (see Sect. 2.2). However, under realistic assumptions on what an adversary might do, these ORE schemes seem to have little security advantage over OPE schemes. For example, in $O(n \log n)$ comparisons an adversary can obtain a total ordering of the ciphertexts, and, hence the total ordering of the plaintexts. A disadvantage of ORE schemes are that they permit an equality test on ciphertexts [7, p. 2] by using two comparisons. This could be used to aid a guessing attack on low-entropy plaintexts, e.g. [15,27]. A randomised OPE scheme, like ours, does not permit this. On the other hand, the information leakage of the ORE schemes so far proposed appears to be near-optimal.

1.6 Road Map

In Sect. 2, we present our OPE scheme. In Sect. 3, we provide the generic version of Boldyreva et al.'s algorithm and the Beta distribution approximation used in our experiments. In Sect. 4, we discuss the results of experiments on our OPE scheme. Finally, in Sect. 5 we conclude the paper.

2 An OPE Scheme Using Approximate Common Divisors

Our OPE scheme is the symmetric encryption system (KeyGen, Enc, Dec). The message space, $\mathcal{M}$, is $[0, M]$, and the ciphertext space, $\mathcal{C}$, is $[0, N]$, where $N > M$. We have plaintexts $m_i \in \mathcal{M}, i \in [1, n]$ such that $0 < m_1 \leq m_2 \leq \cdots \leq m_n \leq M$.

Key Generation. Both the security parameter space $\mathcal{S}$ and the secret key space $\mathcal{K}$ are the set of positive integers. Given a security parameter $\lambda \in \mathcal{S}$, with $\lambda > 8/3 \lg M$, KeyGen randomly chooses an integer $k \in [2^\lambda, 2^{\lambda+1})$ as the secret key, sk. So k is a $(\lambda + 1)$-bit integer such that $k > M^{8/3}$ (see Sect. 2.1). Note that k does not necessarily need to be prime.

Encryption. To encrypt $m_i \in \mathcal{M}$, we compute,

$$c_i = \mathsf{Enc}(m_i, \mathsf{sk}) = m_i k + r_i,$$

where $r_i \stackrel{\$}{\leftarrow} (k^{3/4}, k - k^{3/4})$.

Decryption. To decrypt $c_i \in \mathcal{C}$, we compute,

$$m_i = \mathsf{Dec}(c_i, \mathsf{sk}) = \lfloor c_i/k \rfloor.$$

Order-Preserving Property. If $m > m'$, then $c \geq c'$ provided $mk + r > m'k + r'$, if $k(m - m') > (r' - r)$, which follows, since the lhs is at least k, and the rhs is less than $(k - 1)$. If $m' = m$, then the order of the encryptions is random, since $\Pr(r' > r) \approx \frac{1}{2} - 1/k \approx \frac{1}{2}$.

2.1   Security of the Scheme

Security of our scheme is given by the *general approximate common divisor problem* (GACDP), which is believed to be hard. It can be formulated [9,11] as:

Definition 1 (General approximate common divisor problem). *Suppose we have n integer inputs c_i of the form $c_i = km_i + r_i$, $i \in [1, n]$, where k is an unknown constant integer and m_i and r_i are unknown integers. We have a bound B such that $|r_i| < B$ for all i. Under what conditions on m_i and r_i, and the bound B, can an algorithm be found that can uniquely determine k in a time which is polynomial in the total bit length of the numbers involved?*

GACDP and *partial approximate common divisor problem* (PACDP), its close relative, are used as the basis of several cryptosystems, e.g. [12,14,16]. Solving the GACDP is clearly equivalent to breaking our system. To make the GACDP instances hard, we need $k \gg M$ (see below). Furthermore, we need the m_i to have sufficient entropy to negate a simple "guessing" attack [26]. However, note that the model in [26] assumes that we are able to verify when a guess is correct, which does not seem to be the case here. Although our scenario does not permit it, even if we knew a plaintext, ciphertext pair (m, c), it would not allow us to break the system, since $c/m = k + r/m \in [k, k + k/M]$, which is a large interval since $k \gg M$. A number n of such pairs would give more information, but it still does not seem straightforward to estimate k closer than $\Omega(k/(M\sqrt{n}))$. Thus the system has some resistance to KPA, even though this form of attack is excluded by our model of single-party secure computation.

Howgrave-Graham [18] studied two attacks against GACD, to find divisors d of $a_0 + x_0$ and $b_0 + y_0$, given inputs a_0, b_0 of similar size, with $a_0 < b_0$. The quantities x_0, y_0 are the "offsets". The better attack in [18], GACD_L, succeeds when $|x_0|, |y_0| < X = b_0^{\beta_0}$, and the divisor $d \geq b_0^{\alpha_0}$ and

$$\beta_0 = 1 - \tfrac{1}{2}\alpha_0 - \sqrt{1 - \alpha_0 - \tfrac{1}{2}\alpha_0^2} - \epsilon.$$

where $\epsilon > 0$ is a (small) constant, such that $1/\epsilon$ governs the number of possible divisors which may be output. We will take $\epsilon = 0$. This is the worst case for Howgrave-Graham's algorithm, since there is no bound on the number of divisors which might be output.

Note that $\beta_0 < \alpha_0$, since otherwise $\sqrt{1 - \alpha_0 - \frac{1}{2}\alpha_0^2} \leq 1 - \frac{3}{2}\alpha_0$. This can only be satisfied if $\alpha_0 \leq \frac{2}{3}$. But then squaring both sizes of the inequality implies $\alpha_0 \geq \frac{8}{11} > \frac{2}{3}$, contradicting $\alpha_0 \leq \frac{2}{3}$.

Suppose we take $\alpha_0 = \frac{8}{11}$. Then, to foil this attack, we require $\beta_0 \geq \frac{6}{11}$. For our system we have, $b_0 - a_0 = \max m_i - \min m_i = M$.[3] To ensure that the common divisor k will not be found we require $b_0^{\alpha_0} \geq k$, so we will take $k = b_0^{8/11}$. Since $b_0 \sim Mk$, this then implies $b_0 = M^{11/3}$. Thus the ciphertexts will then have about $11/3$ times as many bits as the plaintexts. Now GACD_L could only succeed for offsets less than $b_0^{\beta_0} = b_0^{6/11} = k^{3/4}$. Thus, we choose our random offsets in the range $(k^{3/4}, k - k^{3/4})$.

Cohn and Heninger [11] give an extension of Howgrave-Graham's algorithm to find the approximate divisor of m integers, where $m > 2$. Unfortunately, their algorithm is exponential in m in the worst case, though they say that it behaves better in practice. On the other hand, [8, Appendix A] claims that Cohn and Heninger's algorithm is worse than brute force in some cases. In our case, the calculations in [11] do not seem to imply better bounds than those derived above.

We note also that the attack of [9] is not relevant to our system, since it requires smaller offsets, of size $O(\sqrt{k})$, than those we use.

For a survey and evaluation of the above and other attacks on GACD, see [17].

2.2 Security Models

One-Wayness. The one-wayness of the function $c(m) = km + r$ used by the scheme clearly follows from the assumed hardness of the GACD problem, since we avoid the known polynomial-time solvable cases.

IND-OCPA. The model in [6, p. 6] and [23, p. 20] is as follows: given two equal-length sequences of plaintexts $(m_0^1 \ldots m_0^q)$ and $(m_1^1 \ldots m_1^q)$, where the m_b^j ($b \in [0, 1], j \in [1, q]$) are distinct,[4] an adversary is allowed to present two plaintexts to a *left-or-right oracle* [2], $\mathcal{LR}^{(m_0, m_1, b)}$, which returns the encryption of m_b. The adversary is only allowed to make queries to the oracle which satisfy $m_0^i < m_0^j$ iff $m_1^i < m_1^j$ for $1 \leq i, j \leq q$. The adversary wins if it can distinguish the left and right orderings with probability significantly better than $1/2$.

However, Boldyreva et al. [6, p. 5] note, concerning chosen plaintext attacks: "in the symmetric-key setting a real-life adversary cannot simply encrypt messages itself, so such an attack is unlikely to be feasible". Further, they prove that no OPE scheme with a polynomial size message space can satisfy IND-OCPA. Lewi et al. [23] strengthen this result under certain assumptions.

The IND-OCPA model seems inherently rather impractical, since an adversary with an encryption oracle could decrypt any ciphertext using $\lg M$ comparisons, where M is the size of the message space. Furthermore, Xiao and Yen [35]

---

[3] Note this is our M, not Howgrave-Graham's.

[4] [6, p. 6] and [23, p. 20] do not clearly state this assumption but it appears that all plaintext values used must be distinct. This assumption clearly does not weaken the model.

construct an OPE for the domain $[1, 2]$ and prove that it is IND-OCPA secure. However, this system is trivially breakable using a "sorting" attack [27]. For these reasons, we do not consider security models assuming CPA to be relevant to OPE.

Window One-Wayness. We may further analyse our scheme under the same model as in [5], which was called *window one-wayness*. The scenario is as follows. An adversary is given the encryptions $c_1 \leq c_2 \leq \cdots \leq c_n$ of a sample of n plaintexts $m_1 \leq m_2 \leq \ldots \leq m_n$, chosen uniformly and independently at random from the plaintext space $[0, M)$. The adversary is also given the encryption c of a challenge plaintext m, and must return an estimate $\hat{m}$ of m and a bound r, such that $m \in (\hat{m} - r, \hat{m} + r)$ with probability greater than $1/2$, say. How small can r be so that the adversary can meet the challenge?

This model seems eminently reasonable, except for the assumption that the plaintexts are distributed uniformly. However, as we show in Sect. 2.3, this assumption can be weakened in some cases for our scheme.

Since the m_i are chosen uniformly at random, a random ciphertext satisfies, for $\mathbf{c} \in [0, kM)$,

$$\Pr(\mathbf{c} = c) = \Pr(k\mathbf{m} + \mathbf{r} = km + r) = \Pr(\mathbf{m} = m)\Pr(\mathbf{r} = r) = \frac{1}{M}\frac{1}{k} = \frac{1}{Mk},$$

where $\mathbf{m} \xleftarrow{\$} [0, M)$, $\mathbf{r} \xleftarrow{\$} [0, k)$. Thus $\mathbf{c}$ is uniform on $[0, kM)$. Note that this is only approximately true, since we choose $\mathbf{r}$ uniformly from $[k^{3/4}, k - k^{3/4}]$. However, the total variation distance between these distributions is $2Mk^{3/4}/Mk = 2/k^{1/4}$. The difference between probabilities calculated using the two distributions is negligible, so we will assume the uniform distribution.

By assumption, the adversary cannot determine k by any polynomial time computation. So the adversary can only estimate k from the sample. Now, in a uniformly chosen sample $c_1 \leq c_2 \leq \cdots \leq c_n$ from $[0, kM)$, the sample maximum c_n is a sufficient statistic for the range kM, so all information about k is captured by c_n. So we may estimate k by $\hat{k} = c_n/M$. This is the maximum likelihood estimate, and is consistent but not unbiased. The minimum variance unbiased estimate is $(n + 1)\hat{k}/n$, but using this does not improve the analysis, since the bias $k/(n + 1)$ is of the same order as the estimation error, as we now prove. For any $0 \leq \varepsilon \leq 1$,

$$\Pr\left(\hat{k} \in k(1 \pm \varepsilon)\right) \leq \Pr\left(c_n \geq kM(1 - \varepsilon)\right)$$

$$= 1 - (1 - \varepsilon)^n \begin{cases} \leq n\varepsilon < 1/2 & \text{if } \varepsilon < 1/(2n); \\ \geq 1 - e^{-n\varepsilon} \geq 1/2 & \text{if } \varepsilon \geq \ln 2/n. \end{cases}$$

Now, if $c = mk + r$, we can estimate m by $\hat{m} = c/\hat{k} \approx mk/\hat{k}$. Then

$$\Pr\left(m \in \hat{m}(1 \pm \varepsilon)\right) \approx \Pr\left(m \in mk/\hat{k}(1 \pm \varepsilon)\right) = \Pr\left(\hat{k} \in k(1 \pm \varepsilon)\right) < 1/2,$$

if $\varepsilon < 1/(2n)$. Thus, if $r \leq m/2n$, $\Pr(m \in \hat{m} \pm r) < 1/2$. Similarly, if $r \geq m \lg 2/n$, $\Pr(m \in \hat{m} \pm r) \geq 1/2$. Thus the adversary cannot succeed if $r \leq m/2n$, but can if $r \geq m \lg 2/n$.

It follows that only $\lg m - \lg(m/n) + O(1) = \lg n + O(1)$ bits of m are leaked by the system. However, $\lg n$ bits are leaked by inserting c into the sequence $c_1 \leq c_2 \leq \cdots \leq c_n$, so the leakage is close to minimal. By contrast the scheme of [6] leaks $1/2 \lg m + O(1)$ bits, independently of n. Therefore, by this criterion, the scheme given here is superior to that of [6] for all $n \ll \sqrt{M}$. Note that we have not assumed that m is chosen uniformly from $[0, M)$, but the leakage of the random sequence $c_1 \leq c_2 \leq \cdots \leq c_n$ is clearly $n \lg n + O(n)$ of the $M \lg M$ plaintext bits. This reveals little more than the $n \lg n$ bits revealed by the known order $m_1 \leq m_2 \leq \cdots \leq m_n$.

2.3   Further Observations

This scheme can be used in conjunction with any other OPE method, i.e. any unknown increasing function $f(m)$ of m. We might consider any integer-valued increasing function, e.g. a polynomial function of m, or Boldyreva et al.'s scheme. If $f(m)$ is this function, then we encrypt m by $c = f(m)k + r$, where $r \xleftarrow{\$} (k^{3/4}, k - k^{3/4})$, and decrypt by $m = f^{-1}(\lfloor c/k \rfloor)$. The disadvantage is that the ciphertext size will increase.

If $f(m)$ is an unknown polynomial function, we solve a polynomial equation to decrypt. The advantage over straight GACD is that, even if we can break the GACD instance, we still have to solve an unknown polynomial equation to break the system. For example, suppose we use the linear polynomial $f(m) = a_1(m + a_0) + s$, where $s \xleftarrow{\$} [0, a_0]$ is random noise. But this gives $c = a_1 k(m + a_0) + (ks + r)$, which is our OPE system with a deterministic linear monic polynomial $f(m) \leftarrow m + a_0$, $k \leftarrow a_1 k$ and $r \leftarrow ks + r \xleftarrow{\$} [0, a_1 k)$, so $f(m)$ contains a single unknown parameter, a_0. More generally, we need only consider monic polynomials, for the same reason.

If $c = f(m)$ is Boldyreva et al.'s OPE, we can invert f only with error $O(\sqrt{m})$. Therefore a hybrid scheme offers greater security than either alone.

Flattening. Another use of such a transformation is when the distribution function $F(m)$ of the plaintexts is known, or can be reasonably estimated. Then the distribution of the plaintexts can be "flattened" to an approximate uniform distribution on a larger set $[0, N)$, where $N \gg M$. Thus, suppose the distribution function $F(m)$ ($m \in [0, M)$) is known, and can be computed efficiently for given m. Further, we assume that $\Pr(\mathbf{m} = m) \geq 1/N$, so F is strictly increasing. This assumption is weak, since the probability that $\mathbf{m}$ is chosen to be an m with too small probability is at most M/N, which we assume to be negligible.

We interpolate the distribution function linearly on the real interval $\mathbb{R}[0, M)$, by $F(x) = (1 - u)F(m) + uF(m + 1)$ for $x = (1 - u)m + u(m + 1)$, where $u \in \mathbb{R}[0, 1)$. Then we will transform $m \in [0, M)$ randomly by taking $\tilde{m} = NF(x)$ where u is chosen randomly from the continuous uniform distribution on $\mathbb{R}[0, 1)$. It follows that $\tilde{m}$ is uniform on $\mathbb{R}[0, N)$, since F is increasing, and $\tilde{m} = NF(x)$, since

$$\Pr(\tilde{m} \leq y) = \Pr(x \leq F^{-1}(y/N)) = F(F^{-1}(y/N)) = y/N.$$

Now, since we require a discrete distribution, we take $\bar{m} = \lfloor \tilde{m} \rfloor$. We invert this by taking $\hat{m} = \lfloor F^{-1}(\bar{m}) \rfloor$. Now, since F is strictly increasing,

$$\hat{m} = \lfloor F^{-1}(\bar{m}/N) \rfloor \leq F^{-1}(\bar{m}/N) < F^{-1}(NF(m+1)/N) = m + 1$$
$$\hat{m} = \lfloor F^{-1}(\bar{m}/N) \rfloor > F^{-1}((\bar{m}-1)/N) \geq F^{-1}(NF(m-1)/N) = m - 1,$$

and so $\hat{m} = m$. Thus the transformation is uniquely invertible. Of course, this does not imply that $\hat{m}$ and m will have exactly the same distribution, but we may also calculate

$$\Pr(\hat{m} \leq x) \leq \Pr(\bar{m} \leq NF(x)) < \Pr(\tilde{m} \leq NF(x) + 1) = F(x) + 1/N,$$
$$\Pr(\hat{m} \leq x) \geq \Pr(\bar{m} < NF(x+1)) \geq \Pr(\tilde{m} < NF(x)) = F(x).$$

This holds, in particular, for integers $x \in [0, M)$. Thus the total variation distance between the distributions of $\hat{m}$ and m is at most M/N. Thus the difference between the distributions of m and $\hat{m}$ will be negligible, since $N \gg M$.

This flattening allows us to satisfy the assumptions of the window one-wayness scenario above. The bit leakage in m is increased, however. It is not difficult to show that it increases by approximately $\lg(mp_m/F(m))$, where p_m is the frequency function $\Pr(\mathbf{m} = m)$. Thus the leakage remains near-optimal for near-uniform distributions, where $\alpha/M \leq p_m \leq \beta/M$, for some constants $\alpha, \beta > 0$. In this case $\lg(mp_m/F(m)) \leq \lg(\beta/\alpha) = O(1)$. There are also distributions which are far from uniform, but the ratio $mp_m/F(m)$ remains bounded. Further, suppose we have a distribution satisfying $1/m^\alpha \leq p_m \leq 1/m^\beta$, for constants $\alpha, \beta > 0$ such that $0 < \alpha - \beta < 1/2$. Then $\lg(mp_m/F(m)) < 1/2 \lg m$, so the leakage is less than in the scheme of [6].

This transformation also allows us to handle relatively small plaintext spaces $[0, M)$, by expanding them to a larger space $[0, N)$.

Finally, note that the flattening approach here is rather different from those in [1,37], though not completely unrelated.

3   Algorithms of Boldyreva Type

We have chosen to compare our scheme with that of Boldyreva et al. [6], since it has been used in practical contexts by the academic community [5, p. 5], as well as in Popa et al.'s original version of CryptDB [30], which has been used or adopted by several commercial organisations [31]. However, scant computational experience with the scheme has been reported [30]. Therefore, we believe it is of academic interest to report our experimental results with respect to Boldyreva et al.'s scheme. We also discuss some simpler variants which have better computational performance. These are compared computationally with our scheme in Sect. 4 below. The relative security of the schemes has been discussed above.

In this section we describe generic encryption and decryption algorithms based on Boldyreva et al.'s algorithm [6], which sample from any distribution and which bisect on the domain (Sect. 3.1). We also present an approximation of

Boldyreva et al.'s algorithm which samples from the Beta distribution (Sect. 3.2). The approximation and generic algorithms are used in our experimental evaluation presented in Sect. 4.

3.1 Generic Algorithms

Algorithm 1 below constructs a random order-preserving function $f : \mathcal{M} \rightarrow \mathcal{C}$, where $\mathcal{M} = [0, M], M = 2^r$, and $\mathcal{C} = [1, N], N \geq 2^{2r}$, so that $c = f(m)$ is the ciphertext for $m \in \mathcal{M}$. Algorithm 1 depends on a pseudorandom number generator, P, and a deterministic seed function, S. Likewise, Algorithm 2 constructs the inverse function $f^{-1} : \mathcal{C} \rightarrow \mathcal{M}$ so that $m = f^{-1}(c)$.

Algorithm 1. Generic Boldyreva-type Encryption Algorithm

1: **function** RECURSIVEENCRYPT$(a, b, f(a), f(b), m)$
2:     $x \leftarrow (a + b)/2$
3:     $y \leftarrow f(b) - f(a)$
4:     Initiate P with seed $S(a, b, f(a), f(b))$
5:     Determine $z \in [0, y]$ pseudorandomly, so that $\Pr(z \notin [y/4, 3y/4])$ is negligible
6:                          ▷ The condition implies that y cannot become smaller than
    $3N/4(1/4)^r = 3N/4M^2 = 3M/4$, with high probability.
7:         $f(x) \leftarrow f(a) + z$
8:     **if** $x = m$ **then**
9:             **return** $f(x)$
10:     **else if** $x > m$ **then**
11:             **return** RECURSIVEENCRYPT$(a, x, f(a), f(x), m))$
12:     **else**
13:             **return** RECURSIVEENCRYPT$(x, b, f(x), f(b), m)$
14:     **end if**
15: **end function**
16: Initiate P with a fixed seed S_0.
17: Choose $f(0), f(M)$ pseudorandomly so that $f(M) - f(0) > 3N/4$
18: **return** RECURSIVEENCRYPT$(0, M, f(0), f(M), m)$

3.2 An Approximation

We have a plaintext space, $[1, M]$, and ciphertext space, $[1, N]$. Boldyreva et al. use bijection between strictly increasing functions $[1, M] \rightarrow [1, N]$ and subsets of size M from $[1, N]$, so there are $\binom{N}{M}$ such functions. There is a similar bijection between nondecreasing functions $[1, M] \rightarrow [1, N]$ and multisets of size M from $[1, N]$, and there are $N^M/M!$ such functions. If we sample n points from such a function f at random, the probability that $f(m_1) = f(m_2)$ for any $m_1 \neq m_2$ is at most $\binom{n}{2} \times 1/N < n^2/2N$. We will assume that $n \ll \sqrt{N}$, so $n^2/2N$ is negligible. Hence we can use sampling either with or without replacement, whichever is more convenient.

Algorithm 2. Generic Boldyreva-type Decryption Algorithm

1: **function** RECURSIVEDECRYPT$(a, b, f(a), f(b), c)$
2:     $x \leftarrow (a + b)/2$
3:     $y \leftarrow f(b) - f(a)$
4:     Initiate P with seed $S(a, b, f(a), f(b))$
5:     Determine $z \in [0, y]$ pseudorandomly
6:     $f(x) \leftarrow f(a) + z$
7:     **if** $f(x) = c$ **then**
8:         **return** x
9:     **else if** $f(x) > c$ **then**
10:         **return** RECURSIVEDECRYPT$(a, x, f(a), f(x), c)$
11:     **else**
12:         **return** RECURSIVEDECRYPT$(x, b, f(x), f(b), c)$
13:     **end if**
14: **end function**
15: Initiate P with a fixed seed S_0.
16: Choose $f(0), f(M)$ pseudorandomly so that $f(M) - f(0) > 3N/4$
17: **return** RECURSIVEDECRYPT$(0, M, f(0), f(M), c)$

Suppose we have sampled such a function f at points $m_1 < m_2 < \cdots < m_k$, and we now wish to sample f at m, where $m_i < m < m_{i+1}$. We know $f(m_i) = c_i$, $f(m_{i+1}) = c_{i+1}$, and let $f(m) = c$, so $c_i \leq c \leq c_{i+1}$.[5] Let $x = m - m_i$, $a = m_{i+1} - m_i - 1$, $y = c - c_i$, $b = c_{i+1} - c_i + 1$, so $1 \leq x \leq a$ and $0 \leq y \leq b$. Write $\tilde{f}(x) = f(x+m_i) - c_i$. Then, if we sample a values from $[0, b]$ independently and uniformly at random, $c - c_i$ will be the xth smallest. Hence we may calculate, for $0 \leq y \leq b$,

$$\Pr\left(\tilde{f}(x) = y\right) = \frac{a!}{(x-1)!\,(a-x)!} \left(\frac{y}{b}\right)^{x-1} \frac{1}{b} \left(\frac{b-y}{b}\right)^{a-x} \tag{1}$$

This is the probability that we sample one value y, $(x - 1)$ values in $[0, y]$ and $(a - x)$ values in $(y, b]$, in any order. If b is large, let $z = y/b$, and $dz = 1/b$, then (1) is approximated by a continuous distribution with, for $0 \leq z \leq 1$,

$$\Pr\left(z \leq \tilde{f}(x)/b < z + dz\right) = \frac{z^{x-1}(1 - z)^{a-x}}{\mathrm{B}(x, a - x + 1)}\, dz \tag{2}$$

which is the $\mathrm{B}(x, a-x+1)$ distribution. Thus we can determine $f(m)$ by sampling from the Beta distribution to $\lg N$ bits of precision. In fact, we only need $\lg b$ bits. However, using $n \leq M \leq \sqrt{N}$,

$$\Pr(\exists i : m_{i+1} - m_i < N^{1/3}) \leq \frac{nN^{1/3}}{N} \leq \frac{M}{N^{2/3}} \leq \frac{1}{N^{1/6}}$$

is very small, so we will almost always need at least $\frac{1}{3} \lg N$ bits of precision. Thus the approximation given by (2) remains good even when $a = 1$, since it is then the uniform distribution on $[0, b]$, where $b \geq N^{1/3}$ with high probability.

---

[5] We can have equality because we sample with replacement.

When the m_i arrive in random order, the problem is to encrypt them consistently without storing and sorting them. Boldyreva et al. use binary search. If $M = 2^r$, we will always have $a = 2^s$ and $x = 2^{s-1}$ in (2), so $a - x = x$, and (2) simplifies to

$$\Pr\left(z \le \tilde{f}(x)/b < z + \mathrm{d}z\right) = \frac{z^{x-1}(1-z)^x}{\mathrm{B}(x, x+1)}\,\mathrm{d}z,$$

for $0 \le z \le 1$, This might be closely approximated by a Normal distribution if Beta sampling is too slow.

4   Experimental Results

To evaluate our scheme in practice, we conducted a simple experiment to pseudo-randomly generate and encrypt 10,000 ρ-bit integers. The ciphertexts were then sorted using a customised TeraSort MapReduce (MR) algorithm [28]. Finally, the sorted ciphertexts were decrypted and it was verified that the plaintexts were also correctly sorted.

Table 1. Timings for each experimental configuration ($n = 10000$). ρ denotes the bit length of the unencrypted inputs. *Init* is the initialisation time for the encryption/decryption algorithm, *Enc* is the mean time to encrypt a single integer, *Exec* is the MR job execution time, *Dec* is the mean time to decrypt a single integer

Algorithm	ρ	Encryption		MR job	Decryption	
		Init. (ms)	Enc. (μs)	Exec. (s)	Init. (ms)	Dec. (μs)
GACD	7	50.13	1.51	63.79	11.62	1.47
GACD	15	58.04	2.18	61.28	10.86	2.46
GACD	31	58.66	2.07	63.02	12.18	2.59
GACD	63	70.85	1.94	65.20	10.61	4.22
GACD	127	91.94	2.38	61.08	11.10	6.29
BCLO	7	143.72	191.48	70.78	154.01	192.42
BCLO	15	135.04	74390.95	65.47	148.29	79255.23
Beta	7	189.52	57.87	64.77	208.16	58.27
Beta	15	202.64	124.79	63.70	218.91	121.53
Beta	31	181.14	221.92	63.64	208.22	221.83
Beta	63	176.24	477.23	66.74	193.03	466.03
Uniform	7	167.66	42.61	64.64	182.27	42.92
Uniform	15	166.98	83.40	66.29	176.14	82.53
Uniform	31	162.11	179.92	63.89	176.53	180.52
Uniform	63	156.53	409.13	63.91	173.57	412.79
Uniform	127	162.17	1237.34	65.30	170.74	1232.19

The MR algorithm was executed on a Hadoop cluster of one master node and 16 slaves. Each node was a Linux virtual machine (VM) having 1 vCPU and 2 GB RAM. The VMs were hosted in a heterogeneous OpenNebula cloud. In addition, a secure Linux VM having 2 vCPUs and 8 GB RAM was used to generate/encrypt and decrypt/verify the data.

Our implementation is pure, unoptimised Java utilising the JScience library [13] arbitrary precision integer classes. It is denoted as algorithm $GACD$ in Table 1. In addition, to provide comparison for our algorithm we have implemented Boldyreva et al.'s algorithm (referred to as $BCLO$) [6] along with two variants of the Boldyreva et al. algorithm. These latter variants are based on our generic version of Boldyreva et al.'s algorithm (see Sect. 3.1). One is an approximation of Boldyreva et al.'s algorithm which samples ciphertext values from the Beta distribution (referred to as $Beta$ in Table 1). The derivation of this approximation is given in Sect. 3.2. The second samples ciphertexts from the uniform distribution (referred to as $Uniform$ in Table 1). This variant appears in Popa et al.'s CryptDB [30] source code [31] as `ope-exp.cc`. The mean timings for each experimental configuration is tabulated in Table 1. The chosen values of ρ for each experimental configuration are as a result of the implementations of Boldyreva et al. and the Beta distribution version of the generic Boldyreva algorithm. The Apache Commons Math [34] implementations of the hypergeometric and Beta distributions we used only support Java signed integer and signed double precision floating point parameters respectively, which account for the configurations seen in Table 1. To provide fair comparison, we have used similar configurations throughout. It should be pointed out that, for the $BCLO$, $Beta$ and $Uniform$ algorithms, when $\rho = 7$, this will result in only 128 possible ciphertexts, even though we have 10,000 inputs. This is because these algorithms will only encrypt each plaintext to a unique value. Such a limited ciphertext space makes these algorithms trivial to attack. Our algorithm will produce 10,000 different ciphertexts as a result of the "noise" term. Each ciphertext will have an effective entropy of at least 21 bits for $\rho = 7$ (see Sect. 2.1). So, our algorithm is more secure than $BCLO$, $Beta$, and $Uniform$ for low entropy inputs.

As shown by Table 1, our work compares very favourably with the other schemes. The encryption times of our algorithm outperform the next best algorithm ($Uniform$) by factors of 28 ($\rho = 7$) to 520 ($\rho = 127$). Furthermore, the decryption times grow sublinearly in the bit length of the inputs. Compare this with the encryption and decryption times for the generic Boldyreva algorithms which, as expected, grow linearly in the bit length of the inputs. Boldyreva et al.'s version performs even worse. We believe this is down to the design of the algorithm, as stated in [6], which executes n recursions where n is the bit-size of the ciphertexts. We also discovered that the termination conditions of their algorithm can result in more recursions than necessary.

It should also be noted that the size of the ciphertext generated by each algorithm seems to have minimal bearing on the MR job execution time. Table 1 shows that the job timings are similar regardless of algorithm.

Of course, it is impossible to compare the security of these systems experimentally, since this would involve simulating unknown attacks. But we have shown above that the GACD approach gives a better theoretical guarantee of security than that of [5,6,33], which defines security based on a game, rather than on the conjectured hardness of a known computational problem.

5 Conclusion

Our work has produced an OPE scheme based on the general approximate common divisor problem (GACDP). This appears to be the first OPE scheme to be based on a computational hardness primitive, rather than a security game. We have described and discussed the scheme, and proved its security properties, in Sect. 2. In Sect. 4 we have reported on experiments to evaluate its practical efficacy, and compare this with the scheme of [6]. Our results show that our scheme is very efficient, since there are $O(1)$ arithmetic operations for encryption and decryption. As a trade-off against the time complexity of our algorithms, our scheme produces larger ciphertexts, ~ 3.67 times the number of bits of the plaintext. However, as pointed out in Sect. 4, ciphertext sizes had minimal impact on the running time of the MR job used in our experiments.

With regard to our stated purpose, our experimental results show that the efficiency of our scheme makes it suitable for practical computations in the cloud.

We have noted that, like any "true" OPE, our scheme cannot guarantee indistinguishability under CPA [6], unlike the non-OPE protocols of Popa and others [21,29]. However, with proper choice of parameters, we believe that its security is strong enough for the purpose for which it is intended: outsourcing of computation to the cloud.

References

1. Agrawal, R., et al.: Order preserving encryption for numeric data. In: Proceedings of the SIGMOD 2004, pp. 563–574. ACM (2004)
2. Bellare, M., et al.: A concrete security treatment of symmetric encryption. In: Proceedings of the FOCS 1997, pp. 394–403. IEEE (1997)
3. Bellare, M., Desai, A., Pointcheval, D., Rogaway, P.: Relations among notions of security for public-key encryption schemes. In: Krawczyk, H. (ed.) CRYPTO 1998. LNCS, vol. 1462, pp. 26–45. Springer, Heidelberg (1998). doi:10.1007/BFb0055718
4. Boelter, T., et al.: A secure one-roundtrip index for range queries. Cryptology ePrint Archive: 2016/568 (2016)
5. Boldyreva, A., Chenette, N., O'Neill, A.: Order-preserving encryption revisited: improved security analysis and alternative solutions. In: Rogaway, P. (ed.) CRYPTO 2011. LNCS, vol. 6841, pp. 578–595. Springer, Heidelberg (2011). doi:10.1007/978-3-642-22792-9_33
6. Boldyreva, A., Chenette, N., Lee, Y., O'Neill, A.: Order-preserving symmetric encryption. In: Joux, A. (ed.) EUROCRYPT 2009. LNCS, vol. 5479, pp. 224–241. Springer, Heidelberg (2009). doi:10.1007/978-3-642-01001-9_13

7. Boneh, D., Lewi, K., Raykova, M., Sahai, A., Zhandry, M., Zimmerman, J.: Semantically secure order-revealing encryption: multi-input functional encryption without obfuscation. In: Oswald, E., Fischlin, M. (eds.) EUROCRYPT 2015. LNCS, vol. 9057, pp. 563–594. Springer, Heidelberg (2015). doi:10.1007/978-3-662-46803-6_19
8. Chen, Y., Nguyen, P.Q.: Faster algorithms for approximate common divisors: breaking fully-homomorphic-encryption challenges over the integers. Cryptology ePrint Archive: 2011/436 (2011)
9. Chen, Y., Nguyen, P.Q.: Faster algorithms for approximate common divisors: breaking fully-homomorphic-encryption challenges over the integers. In: Pointcheval, D., Johansson, T. (eds.) EUROCRYPT 2012. LNCS, vol. 7237, pp. 502–519. Springer, Heidelberg (2012). doi:10.1007/978-3-642-29011-4_30
10. Chenette, N., Lewi, K., Weis, S.A., Wu, D.J.: Practical order-revealing encryption with limited leakage. In: Peyrin, T. (ed.) FSE 2016. LNCS, vol. 9783, pp. 474–493. Springer, Heidelberg (2016). doi:10.1007/978-3-662-52993-5_24
11. Cohn, H., Heninger, N.: Approximate common divisors via lattices. In: Proceedings of the ANTS-X, vol. 1, pp. 271–293. Mathematical Sciences Publishers (2012)
12. Coron, J.-S., Mandal, A., Naccache, D., Tibouchi, M.: Fully homomorphic encryption over the integers with shorter public keys. In: Rogaway, P. (ed.) CRYPTO 2011. LNCS, vol. 6841, pp. 487–504. Springer, Heidelberg (2011). doi:10.1007/978-3-642-22792-9_28
13. Dautelle, J.-M.: JScience. Version 4.3.1, September 2014. http://jscience.org
14. Dijk, M., Gentry, C., Halevi, S., Vaikuntanathan, V.: Fully homomorphic encryption over the integers. In: Gilbert, H. (ed.) EUROCRYPT 2010. LNCS, vol. 6110, pp. 24–43. Springer, Heidelberg (2010). doi:10.1007/978-3-642-13190-5_2
15. Durak, F.B., et al.: What else is revealed by order-revealing encryption? In: Proceedings of the CCS 2016, pp. 1155–1166. ACM (2016)
16. Dyer, J., et al.: Practical homomorphic encryption over the integers. arXiv:1702.07588 [cs.CR], February 2017
17. Galbraith, S.D., et al.: Algorithms for the approximate common divisor problem. LMS J. Comput. Math. 19(A), 58–72 (2016)
18. Howgrave-Graham, N.: Approximate integer common divisors. In: Silverman, J.H. (ed.) CaLC 2001. LNCS, vol. 2146, pp. 51–66. Springer, Heidelberg (2001). doi:10.1007/3-540-44670-2_6
19. Kadhem, H., et al.: MV-OPES: multivalued-order preserving encryption scheme: a novel scheme for encrypting integer value to many different values. IEICE Trans. Inf. Syst. 93(9), 2520–2533 (2010)
20. Kerschbaum, F.: Frequency-hiding order-preserving encryption. In: Proceedings of the CCS 2015, pp. 656–667. ACM (2015)
21. Kerschbaum, F., Schroepfer, A.: Optimal average-complexity ideal-security order-preserving encryption. In: Proceedings of the CCS 2014, pp. 275–286. ACM (2014)
22. Krendelev, S.F., et al.: Order-preserving encryption schemes based on arithmetic coding and matrices. In: Proceedings of the FedCSIS 2014, pp. 891–899. PTI (2014)
23. Lewi, K., Wu, D.J.: Order-revealing encryption: new constructions, applications, and lower bounds. In: Proceedings of the CCS 2016, pp. 1167–1178. ACM (2016)
24. Liu, D., Wang, S.: Programmable order-preserving secure index for encrypted database query. In: Proceedings of the CLOUD 2012, pp. 502–509. IEEE (2012)
25. Liu, Z., et al.: New order preserving encryption model for outsourced databases in cloud environments. J. Netw. Comput. Appl. 59, 198–207 (2016)
26. Massey, J.L.: Guessing and entropy. In: Proceedings of the ISIT 1994, p. 204. IEEE (1994)

27. Naveed, M., et al.: Inference attacks on property-preserving encrypted databases. In: Proceedings of the CCS 2015, pp. 644–655. ACM (2015)
28. O'Malley, O.: TeraByte sort on Apache Hadoop. Technical report, Yahoo, Inc., pp. 1–3, May 2008. http://sortbenchmark.org/YahooHadoop.pdf
29. Popa, R.A., et al.: An ideal-security protocol for order-preserving encoding. In: Proceedings of the SP 2013, pp. 463–477. IEEE (2013)
30. Popa, R.A., et al.: CryptDB: protecting confidentiality with encrypted query processing. In: Proceedings of the SOSP 2011, pp. 85–100. ACM (2011)
31. Popa, R.A., et al.: CryptDB, March 2014. https://css.csail.mit.edu/cryptdb/
32. Rivest, R.L., et al.: On data banks and privacy homomorphisms. Found. Secure Comput. 4(11), 169–180 (1978)
33. Teranishi, I., Yung, M., Malkin, T.: Order-preserving encryption secure beyond one-wayness. In: Sarkar, P., Iwata, T. (eds.) ASIACRYPT 2014. LNCS, vol. 8874, pp. 42–61. Springer, Heidelberg (2014). doi:10.1007/978-3-662-45608-8_3
34. The Apache Software Foundation: Commons Math: The Apache Commons Mathematics Library. Version 3.6.1, August 2016. http://commons.apache.org/proper/commons-math/
35. Xiao, L., Yen, I.-L.: A note for the ideal order-preserving encryption object and generalized order-preserving encryption. Cryptology ePrint Archive: 2012/350 (2012)
36. Xiao, L., Yen, I.-L.: Security analysis for order preserving encryption schemes. In: Proceedings of the CISS 2012, pp. 1–6. IEEE (2012)
37. Yum, D.H., Kim, D.S., Kim, J.S., Lee, P.J., Hong, S.J.: Order-preserving encryption for non-uniformly distributed plaintexts. In: Jung, S., Yung, M. (eds.) WISA 2011. LNCS, vol. 7115, pp. 84–97. Springer, Heidelberg (2012). doi:10.1007/978-3-642-27890-7_7

Privacy-Preserving Deterministic Automata Evaluation with Encrypted Data Blocks

Giovanni Di Crescenzo$^{(\boxtimes)}$, Brian Coan, and Jonathan Kirsch

Vencore Labs, Basking Ridge, NJ 07920, USA
{gdicrescenzo,bcoan,jkirsch}@vencorelabs.com

Abstract. Secure computation (i.e., performing computation while keeping inputs private) is a fundamental problem in cryptography. In this paper, we present an efficient and secure 2-party computation protocol for deterministic automata evaluation, a problem of large practical relevance. Our result is secure under standard assumptions and bypasses roadblocks in previous general solutions, like Yao's garbled circuits and Gentry's lattice-based fully homomorphic encryption, by performing secure computations over data blocks (instead of bits) and using typical-size (instead of impractically large) cryptographic keys. An important efficiency property achieved is that the number of both asymmetric and symmetric cryptographic operations in the protocol is *sublinear* in the size of the circuit representing the computed function (specifically, improving linear-complexity protocols by a multiplicative factor equal to a block size). All previous protocols for deterministic automata evaluation required a linear number of asymmetric cryptographic operations. Moreover, we use quantitative comparison techniques to show that in typical parameter settings, our protocols' latency is at least 1 to 2 orders of magnitude smaller than the protocol obtained by a direct application of both state-of-the-art general-purpose secure 2-party computation protocols. Even though not as general as in these two general-purpose techniques, our result is applicable to the class of all constant-space computations.

1 Introduction

Managing data privacy for real-life systems is a complex endeavor with many different areas in need of investigation. Cryptography research has traditionally produced cornerstone technical solutions to a large variety of data privacy problems. In some domains, like communication security, a wide variety of cryptography solutions with various dimensions of desirable properties have been produced, and a typical system designer has several valid options to choose from at development stage. Unfortunately this is not the case for other areas, many of which related to data privacy. This paper focuses on one of these areas, 2-party secure computation [22], where several solutions have been proposed, but still different types of gaps remain towards regular deployment of this technology in real-life systems. Existing solution paradigms, like garbled circuits [22] and

© Springer International Publishing AG 2017
J. Garcia-Alfaro et al. (Eds.): DPM/CBT 2017, LNCS 10436, pp. 275–294, 2017.
DOI: 10.1007/978-3-319-67816-0_16

fully homomorphic encryption [10], address a large spectrum of assumptions and satisfy many desirable properties, but do not exhaustively cover needs that may arise from real-life systems.

In this paper, we propose new cryptography solutions for 2-party secure computation based on a recent paradigm of privacy-preserving computations over encrypted data blocks [5]. We show that solutions can be exhibited for the important problem of deterministic automata evaluation, going beyond a previous result of [5] that only applied to monotone formulae over equality statements.

Automata evaluation. Deterministic automata evaluation is a well-known problem in computer science, also equivalent to regular expression matching, with several applications (most notably, pattern matching). We consider the design of secure 2-party protocols for deterministic automata evaluation, where Alice holds the (pattern) automata, Bob holds the (text) string, and one of the two parties obtains the match result, while the two parties learn no other information on the other party's input. A practical and secure 2-party protocol for deterministic automata evaluation is expected to have several interesting applications, including DNA identity testing, firewall policy checking on web traffic, keyword search on emails, etc.

Secure computation: state of the art. Secure two-party computation is a fundamental cryptographic primitive with significant application potential. In the formulation of interest for this paper, there are two parties, Alice and Bob, who would like to interactively compute a function f on their inputs x and y, respectively, such that at the end of the protocol: Bob obtains $f(x, y)$; an efficient adversary corrupting Alice learns nothing new about Bob's input y; and an efficient adversary corrupting Bob learns nothing new about Alice's input x, in addition to what is efficiently computable from $f(x, y)$. The first general solution to this problem for any arbitrary function f was presented by Yao in [22], assuming that the adversary is semi-honest (i.e., he follows the protocol as the corrupted party but may at the end try any polynomial-time algorithm to learn about the other party's input). The generality of this solution is so attractive that, even decades after their introduction, researchers are considering improvements and optimizations (see, e.g., [14,17]), thus bringing them closer to being usable in practice, at least in some specific scenarios (i.e., with the help of additional servers [1]). An important roadblock in this process is represented by the fact that Yao's protocol, using a boolean circuit representation of the function f, requires cryptographic operations for all input bits and binary gates in the circuit.

Recently, another general and powerful cryptographic primitive, fully homomorphic encryption, has been realized [10]. This primitive allows arbitrary polynomial-time computations over encrypted data and thus can be applied to construct secure 2-party computation protocols for any arbitrary polynomial-size arithmetic circuit (and therefore any polynomial-size boolean circuit). Even in this case, researchers are recently considering improvements and optimizations, trying to bring it closer to being usable in practice (see, e.g., [3]). The roadblock for garbled circuits does not apply here, when using arithmetic circuits, since in that case fully homomorphic encryption solutions typically do operate over data blocks (instead of bits). However, another roadblock on the way to efficiency appears here: the security of all known constructions of fully homomorphic encryption is based on problems whose required key lengths are significantly high and the overall scheme is only theoretically efficient, but not in practice.

Computations over encrypted data blocks, as introduced in [5], attempt to combine the best features from both cited general-purpose approaches: computing over encrypted data blocks (as in fully homomorphic encryption over arithmetic circuits), limited requirements on key lengths (as in garbled circuits), and achieving solutions for a large class of problems (as in both). The solution proposed in [5], shows secure protocols over encrypted data blocks for the class of monotone formulae over string equality statements.

Our contribution. Our main result in this paper is an efficient and secure 2-party protocol, based on computations over encrypted data blocks, for deterministic automata evaluation, thus being applicable to all constant-space computations. The security of our protocol holds under standard cryptographic assumptions and is proved based on the existence of secure 2-party protocols for simpler tasks: (a) pseudo-random function evaluation, which, in turn, were previously proved secure based on standard number-theoretic assumptions with conventional key lengths (see, e.g., [8,16]); and (b) conditional transfer [6] for string equality and AND of string equality statements, which, in turn, can be based on symmetric encryption alone, given the information shared between the two parties during the protocol for pseudo-random function evaluation. We give two instantiations of the secure 2-party protocols for these two simpler tasks, resulting in two instantiations of our main protocol with different desirable efficiency properties.

The main efficiency property is the protocol's time complexity, as we show, in our main protocol's first instantiation, that it only requires a number of cryptographic operations *sub-linear* in the size of the circuit computing the function. Specifically, it improves over the natural application of the garbled circuit technique from [22] by a factor equal to the length of alphabet symbols. In practice, depending on the alphabet required by the specific application, this can be anywhere between a small and a very large improvement. In our main protocol's second instantiation, we also show a variant that improves multiplicative constants for small alphabets, by using an alternative implementation of the secure 2-party protocol for pseudo-random function evaluation. We show a performance analysis of both variants, and comparisons with previously known protocols in the literature [9,15,18], all requiring at least a linear number of asymmetric cryptographic operations. Moreover, we use quantitative comparison techniques to compare the latency of both our protocols with the protocol obtained by a direct application of both state-of-the-art general-purpose secure 2-party computation protocols. We obtain that our protocols' latency is at least 1 to 2 orders of magnitude smaller in typical parameter settings.

Organization of the paper. In Sect. 2 we detail definitions and models of interest, including a formal definition for secure function evaluation protocols, and for tools used in our constructions, such as symmetric encryption schemes, pseudo-random functions, oblivious PRF evaluation protocols, and conditional OT protocols.

In Sect. 3 we present our main result: a practical and secure protocol for 2-party evaluation of a deterministic automata, based on building blocks such as a PRF, an oblivious PRF evaluation protocol, and a conditional OT protocol for string equality and AND of string equality conditions.

In Sect. 4 we describe a first instantiation of our main result that is particularly efficient for large automata alphabets, based on an adaptation of an oblivious PRF evaluation protocol from [16], and a simple variant of conditional OT protocols in [4,6].

In Sect. 5 we describe a second instantiation of our main result that is particularly efficient for small automata alphabets. This differs from the previous instantiation in that the oblivious PRF evaluation protocol is now replaced by a suitable combination of results from [19,20].

In Sect. 6 we discuss the practical performance of the two instantiations of our protocols, showing improved efficiency with respect to previous work, including a protocol that can be constructed by an application of the original Yao's general-purpose protocol [22].

2 Definitions and Background

In this section we give definitions and background useful in the rest of the document. Definitions in Sect. 2.1 are specific to the main problem of interest in the paper, and include deterministic automata, secure 2-party function evaluation protocols, and efficiency requirements. Definitions in Sect. 2.2 are specific to our solutions to the main problem considered, and include pseudo-random functions, and secure 2-party protocols for pseudo-random function evaluation and conditional transfer.

2.1 Secure 2-Party Evaluation of Deterministic Automata

Deterministic automata. A *deterministic automata* is formally defined as a tuple $DA = (S, s_0, F, A, \tau)$, where S is the set of automata states, s_0 is the initial state, F is a subset of S representing the set of final states, A is an alphabet, and $\tau : S \times A \rightarrow S$ is a transition function that maps any state and any alphabet element to the next state (when defined). We also denote as $|S| = s$ the number of states, as $|F| = f$ the number of final states, and as $|A| = a$ the number of alphabet symbols. An input string $x = (x_1, \ldots, x_m)$ is a sequence of alphabet symbols $x_i \in A$, for $i = 1, \ldots, m$.

The *deterministic automata evaluation* (briefly, DAE) problem consists of computing $s_i = \tau(s_{i-1}, x_i)$, for $i = 1, \ldots, m$, and then returning as output $out_{ae} = 1$ if s_m is in F (denoting that a final state is reached) or $out_{ae} = 0$ otherwise.

In the *2-party DAE* problem, the two parties, called Alice and Bob, are given as input the automata objects S, s_0, A and the parameters s, a, m; Alice is given as input F, τ; Bob holds the input string x; and at the end of the 2-party protocol, Bob obtains the output out_{ae}, defined as for the DAE problem.

Secure 2-party function evaluation protocols. The expression $z \leftarrow D$ denotes the probabilistic process of randomly and independently choosing x according to distribution D. By $\text{Prob}[z \leftarrow D : E]$ we denote the probability of event E after the execution of the probabilistic process $z \leftarrow D$. Let σ denote a security parameter. A function over the set of natural numbers is *negligible* if for all sufficiently large natural numbers $\sigma \in \mathcal{N}$, it is smaller than $1/p(\sigma)$, for all polynomials p. Two distribution ensembles $\{D_\sigma^0 : \sigma \in \mathcal{N}\}$ and $\{D_\sigma^1 : \sigma \in \mathcal{N}\}$ are *computationally indistinguishable* if for any efficient algorithm A, the quantity $|\text{Prob}[x \leftarrow D_\sigma^0 : A(x) = 1] - \text{Prob}[x \leftarrow D_\sigma^1 : A(x) = 1]|$ is negligible in σ (i.e., no efficient algorithm can distinguish if a random sample came from one distribution or the other). In a 2-party protocol execution, a party's *view* is the sequence containing the party's input, the party's random string, and all messages received during the execution.

We use the simulation-based definition from [11] for security of 2-party function evaluation protocols in the presence of semi-honest adversaries (i.e., adversaries that corrupt one party, follow the protocol as that party and then attempt to obtain some information about the other party's input). According to this definition, a protocol π to evaluate a (possibly probabilistic) function f satisfies *simulation-based security* in the presence of a semi-honest adversary, if there exists two efficient algorithms Sim_A, Sim_B (called the *simulators*), such that:

1. let $out_{S,A}$ be Sim_A's output on input Alice's input and Alice's output (if any); then, it holds that the pair $(out_{S,A},$ Bob's output$)$ is computationally indistinguishable from the pair (Alice's view, Bob's output); and
2. let $out_{S,B}$ be Sim_B's output on input Bob's input and Bob's output (if any); then, it holds that the pair (Alice's output, $out_{S,B}$) is computationally indistinguishable from the pair (Alice's output, Bob's view).

In the above, the first (resp., second) condition says that a semi-honest adversary's view when corrupting Alice (resp., Bob), can be generated by an efficient algorithm not knowing Bob's (resp., Alice's) input, and thus the adversary does not learn anything about the uncorrupted party's input. This definition also implies correctness of the protocol's output: that is, the intended recipient of the 2-party problem formulation's output does receive this output at the end of the protocol.

Efficiency requirements. We will consider the following efficiency metrics, relative to a single execution of a given secure 2-party protocol:

1. *time complexity:* time between the protocol execution's beginning and end;
2. *communication complexity:* length of all messages exchanged; and
3. *round complexity:* number of messages exchanged.

All efficiency metrics are expressed as a function of the security parameter σ, and parameters s, a, m associated with the deterministic automata and input string that are input to the protocol. In evaluating protocol latency, we will pay special attention to the number of asymmetric cryptography operations (e.g., modular exponentiations in a large group) and of symmetric cryptographic operations (e.g., block cipher executions), since the former are typically orders of magnitude more expensive than the latter (although the latter might be applied a larger number of times). As a comparison result, we will target the general solution from [22] for the 2-party secure evaluation of function $f(x, y)$, where x is Alice's input and y is Bob's input, which requires $O(|y|)$ asymmetric cryptography operations and $O(|C_f|)$ symmetric cryptography operations, if C_f denotes the size of the boolean circuit computing f. Even if we will mainly focus our efficiency analysis on time complexity, our design targets minimization of all the mentioned efficiency metrics.

2.2 Cryptographic Primitives and Protocols Used in Our Solutions

Pseudo-random function families. A family of functions $\{r_n : n \in \mathcal{N}\}$ is a *random function family* if, for each value of the security parameter n, the function r_n associated with that value is chosen with distribution uniform across all possible functions of the pre-defined input and output domains. A family of keyed functions $\{F_n(k, \cdot) : n \in \mathcal{N}\}$ is a *pseudo-random function family* (briefly, a PRF family, first defined in [12]) if, after key k is randomly chosen, no efficient algorithm allowed to query an oracle function O_n can distinguish whether O_n is $F_n(k, \cdot)$ or O_n is a random function $R_n(\cdot)$ over the same input and output domain, with probability greater than $1/2$ plus a negligible (in n) quantity. We consider *symmetric-type PRFs*, which are implemented in practice using symmetric-key cryptography primitives (e.g., block ciphers like AES), and *asymmetric-type PRFs*, which are based on a public and a secret key, usually implemented using number-theoretic functions, the most expensive often being modular exponentiations.

Secure evaluation protocols for specific functions. In our solutions, we use or build constructions of 2-party secure evaluation protocols for the following functionalities: pseudo-random function, scalar product, and real-or-random conditional transfer.

A *secure pseudo-random function evaluation protocol* (briefly, sPRFeval protocol) is a protocol between two parties: Alice, having as input a key k for a PRF F, and Bob, having as input a string x, where the description of F is known to both parties. The protocol is defined as a secure function evaluation of the value $F(k, x)$, returned to Bob (thus, without revealing any information about x to Alice, or any information about k to Bob in addition to $F(k, x)$). Efficient constructions of sPRFeval protocols, based on the hardness of number-theoretic problems, were given in [8,16].

A *secure conditional transfer protocol* for the condition predicate p (briefly, p-sCTeval protocol, or sCTeval protocol when p is clear from the context) is a protocol between two parties: Alice, having as input a message m and a string x, and Bob, having as input a string y. The protocol is defined as a secure function evaluation of the value m', returned to Bob, where $m' = m$ if $p(x,y) = 1$ or m' is computationally indistinguishable from a string random and independent from m, and of the same length as m, if $p(x,y) = 0$. Thus, an execution of the protocol does not reveal any information about y to Alice, or any information about x to Bob in addition to m', and m' only reveals m when $p(x,y) = 1$ or the (possibly padded) length of m when $p(x,y) = 0$. Also, note that if m is a pseudo-random string, then at the end of a p-sCTeval protocol, Bob does not obtain any information about the value of predicate p. The notion of a p-sCTeval protocol is a generalization of the symmetrically-private conditional transfer notion in [4], which, in turn, generalizes the conditional oblivious transfer from [6]. Specifically, it differs in formalizing privacy according to the secure computation notion. Both notions from [4,6] are, in turn, variants of the much studied oblivious transfer (OT) protocol notion from [21].

3   Secure Evaluation of Deterministic Automata

In this section we present our 2-party protocol for secure evaluation of a deterministic automata. The protocol consists of a private evaluation of Alice's deterministic automata on Bob's input string, using cryptographic primitives such as encrypted data blocks (also called pseudonyms), a symmetric-type and an asymmetric-type pseudo-random function, a secure pseudo-random function evaluation protocol, and a secure conditional transfer protocol. Formally, our protocol satisfies the following result.

Theorem 1. Assume the existence of:

1. symmetric-type pseudo-random function family prF_s
2. asymmetric-type pseudo-random function family prF_a,
3. an sPRFeval protocol for the evaluation of prF_a, and
4. an sCTeval protocol for equalities, and AND of equalities condition predicates.

There exists a (black-box) construction of a 2-party sDAeval protocol π, requiring $O(m)$ executions of the sPRFeval protocol, and $O(sam)$ applications of an sCTeval protocol, where s, a denote the number of states and alphabet symbols of the Alice's input automata, and m denotes the number of alphabet symbols in Bob's input string.

We note that the sPRFeval protocol from [8] only requires $O(1)$ asymmetric cryptography operations, and thus an execution of π based on them only requires $O(m)$ asymmetric cryptography operations, which is linear in the number of alphabet symbols input to Bob, and thus sublinear in the length $n = O(m \log a + sa \log s)$ of the input to the 2-party DAE problem. Instead, a direct application of the general solution from [22] would require $O(m \log a)$ asymmetric cryptography operations. We now prove Theorem 1 with a description of protocol π, and then show its efficiency and security properties.

Narrative and formal description of π. The description of protocol π can be divided into 4 phases: Alice's input processing, Bob's input processing, transition processing and output computation. At a high-level, π can be summarized as follows: in the first two phases, Alice and Bob compute encrypted data blocks or pseudonyms for their inputs; in the transition processing phase, Alice and Bob compute the transition steps in the DAE problem over encrypted data blocks; in the output computation phase, Alice and Bob compute the output of the DAE problem over encrypted data blocks, in a way that Bob receives the cleartext output. We now describe all 4 phases of protocol π in greater detail.

Alice's input processing. In this phase, Alice randomly chooses two keys: k_s for the symmetric-type pseudo-random function prF_s, and k_a for the asymmetric-type pseudo-random function prF_a. Then, Alice computes an initial set of encrypted pseudonyms for all s DFA states, as the output of the pseudo-random function prF_s on input the state symbol s_j and a position index $i = 0$, for $j = 1, \ldots, s$. Moreover, Alice computes an encrypted pseudonym for the a DFA alphabet symbols, as the output of the pseudo-random function prF_a on input the alphabet symbol a_h, for $h = 1, \ldots, a$. The detailed steps of this phase go as follows:

1. Alice randomly chooses keys k_s, k_a
2. For $j = 1, \ldots, s$, Alice computes $p_{S,j,0} = prF_s(k_s, (0|j))$
3. For $h = 1, \ldots, a$, Alice computes $p_{A,h} = prF_a(k_a, h)$

Bob's input processing. In this phase, Bob transforms each symbol in Bob's input string x into an encrypted pseudonym, to be computed as output of the pseudo-random function prF_a on input the symbol $x(i)$. This computation is performed by an execution of the sPRFeval protocol for each $i = 1, ..., m$, where Alice uses key k_a as input, and Bob uses x_i as input and receives $prF_a(k_a, x_i)$ as output. By the end of this phase, Bob has obtained the encrypted pseudonyms associated with all his input symbols $x_1, \ldots, x_m$. A formal description of this phase goes as follows:

1. For $i = 1, \ldots, m$,
   Alice and Bob run the sPRFeval protocol for function prF_a, where
      Alice's input is key k_a
      Bob's input is x_i
      Bob's output is $p_{x,i}$, intended to be $= prF_a(k_a, x_i)$

Circuit processing. In this phase, Alice sends to Bob the encrypted pseudonym associated with the initial state s_0 (set, wlog, $=1$), also being the current state. The invariant that Bob holds a valid encrypted pseudonym for the current state will be maintained throughout the protocol execution. Alice and Bob perform private evaluation of the deterministic automata, using the sCTeval protocol and the encrypted pseudonyms computed in the input processing phases. In the private evaluation of the deterministic automata, the execution continues in n iterations, where the i-th iteration, for $i = 1, \ldots, n$, goes as follows. First, Alice randomly chooses permutations α_i of $(1, \ldots, s)$ and β_i of $(1, \ldots, a)$, and computes an encrypted pseudonym for i-th variants of the s DFA states, as follows: the pseudonyms are outputs of the pseudo-random function prF_s on input the state symbol s_j and the position index i, for $j = 1, \ldots, s$. Then, for each symbol and state, Alice transfers the next state pseudonym to Bob, using an sCTeval protocol, where the condition is an AND of 2 equalities, defined so that Bob obtains the next state pseudonym sent by Alice in correspondence to the current state pseudonym and the current symbol pseudonym held by Bob. Alice will perform one execution of an sCTeval protocol for each of the possible current states and each of the possible symbols (in random orders according to permutations α_i, β_i), but only for one such pair is Bob holding the valid pseudonyms that meet both equalities; thus, Bob will receive the next state pseudonym only in correspondence of one such pair, in a random position, except with negligible probability. The detailed steps of this phase go as follows:

1. Alice computes $p_{S,1,0} = prF_s(k_s, (0|1))$ and sends $p_{S,1,0}$ to Bob
2. Bob sets $q_{S,0} = p_{S,1,0}$
3. For $i = 1, \ldots, m$,
   Alice randomly chooses permutations α_i of $(1, \ldots, s)$ and β_i of $(1, \ldots, a)$
   for $j = 1, \ldots, s$,
   Alice computes $p_{S,j,i} = prF_s(k_s, (i|j))$
4. For $i = 1, \ldots, m$,
   for $j = \alpha_i(1), \ldots, \alpha_i(s)$,
   for $h = \beta_i(1), \ldots, \beta_i(a)$,
   Alice and Bob run the sCTeval protocol for the AND-of-equality function, where
   Alice uses as input key k_s and pseudonyms $p_{S,j,i-1}, p_{A,h}$ and pseudonym $p_{S,j,i}$
   Bob uses as input pseudonyms $q_{S,i-1}$ and $p_{x,i}$
   Bob's output is in $\{\bot, z\}$ for some string $z \in \{0,1\}^\ell$, and
   it is intended to be $= p_{S,j,i} \neq \bot$ if $(p_{S,j,i-1} = q_{S,i-1})$ AND $(p_{A,h} = p_{x,i})$
   if Bob's output is $z \neq \bot$ then Bob sets $q_{S,i} = z$

Output computation. In the output computation phase, after the last symbol from string x is processed, Alice computes encrypted pseudonyms for the two expressions in set $\{\text{yes}, \text{no}\} = \{\text{final-state}, \text{non-final-state}\}$ and transfers each of these two pseudonyms using an sCTeval protocol, using an equality condition, defined so that Bob obtains the appropriate pseudonym sent by Alice in correspondence to the current state pseudonym held by Bob. Alice will perform one execution of an sCTeval protocol for each of the possible current states, but only for one of these states, Bob is holding the valid pseudonym; thus, Bob will receive the final-state or non-final-state pseudonym only in correspondence of one such state, except with negligible probability. The detailed steps of this phase go as follows:

1. For $j = 1, \ldots, s$,
   Alice and Bob run the sCTeval protocol for the equality function, where
   Alice sets $s_j = \text{‘yes’}$ if $j \in F$ or $s_j = \text{‘no’}$ if $j \notin F$
   Alice uses as input key k_s, pseudonym $p_{S,j,m}$, and string s_j
   Bob uses as input pseudonym $q_{S,m}$
   Bob's output is in $\{\bot, z\}$ for some string $z \in \{0,1\}^\ell$, and
   it is intended to be $= s_j \neq \bot$ if $(p_{S,j,m} = q_{S,m})$ and $\bot$ otherwise
   if Bob's output is $z \neq \bot$ then Bob returns z and halts.

Pictorial description. A pictorial description of this protocol can be found in Fig. 1. We remark that the circuit processing phase may be actually run in parallel across all $i = 1, \ldots, n$, and that the protocol in Fig. 1 can be easily adapted if we require Alice to be the party receiving the computation output, as follows. In the output computation phase, instead of obliviously transferring to Bob a yes or no string, Alice obliviously transfers a large random pseudonym for such strings, and then Bob sends back the received string to let Alice determine the output.

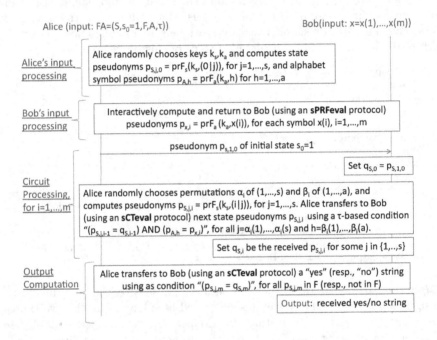

Alice (input: FA=(S,s_0=1,F,A,τ))   Bob(input: x=x(1),...,x(m))

<u>Alice's input processing</u> — Alice randomly chooses keys k_s, k_a and computes state pseudonyms $p_{s_{j,0}} = prF_s(k_s,(0\,|\,j))$, for j=1,...,s, and alphabet symbol pseudonyms $p_{A,h} = prF_a(k_a,h)$ for h=1,...,a

<u>Bob's input processing</u> — Interactively compute and return to Bob (using an **sPRFeval** protocol) pseudonyms $p_{x,i} = prF_a(k_a,x(i))$, for each symbol x(i), i=1,...,m

pseudonym $p_{s,1,0}$ of initial state s_0=1

Set $q_{s,0} = p_{s,1,0}$

<u>Circuit Processing, for i=1,...,m</u> — Alice randomly chooses permutations α_i of (1,...,s) and β_i of (1,...,a), and computes pseudonyms $p_{s,j,i} = prF_s(k_s,(i\,|\,j))$, for j=1,...,s. Alice transfers to Bob (using an **sCTeval** protocol) next state pseudonyms $p_{s,j,i}$ using a τ-based condition "($p_{s,j,i-1} = q_{s,i-1}$) AND ($p_{A,h} = p_{x,i}$)", for all j=α_i(1),...,α_i(s) and h=β_i(1),...,β_i(a).

Set $q_{s,i}$ be the received $p_{s,j,i}$ for some j in {1,..,s}

<u>Output Computation</u> — Alice transfers to Bob (using an **sCTeval** protocol) a "yes" (resp., "no") string using as condition "($p_{s,j,m} = q_{s,m}$)", for all $p_{s,j,m}$ in F (resp., not in F)

Output: received yes/no string

Fig. 1. Our sDAeval protocol

Properties of π. It is easy to calculate Alice and Bob's runtime by inspection of protocol π. Specifically, Alice's runtime is dominated by her program in m executions of an sPRFeval protocol, $(ma+1)s$ executions of an sCTeval protocol, $(m+1)s$ computations of pseudo-random function prF_s and a computations of pseudo-random function prF_a. Bob's runtime is dominated by his program in m executions of an sPRFeval protocol and in $(ma+1)s$ executions of an sCTeval protocol. We now show the security properties of protocol π, considering two cases, depending on which of the two participants is corrupted by the adversary Adv.

Security, part 1 (Adv corrupts Alice): We note that in protocol π Alice's program consists of running a polynomial number of sPRFeval and sCTeval protocols, and sending an initial state pseudonym to Bob. Since these subprotocols are secure, they admit an efficient simulator whose output is computationally indistinguishable from the adversary's view during protocol execution. By suitably composing these simulators and running some of Alice's instructions, we obtain an efficient simulator for Adv's view when corrupting Alice in π. Specifically, simulator Sim_A runs Alice's program to simulate Alice's view during her input processing phase, runs the simulator for the sPRFeval protocol to simulate Alice's view during Bob's input processing phase, runs Alice's program to simulate the sending of the initial state pseudonym from Alice to Bob, and runs the simulator for the sCTeval protocol to simulate Alice's view during the circuit processing and output computation phases. The simulation's output is computationally indistinguishable from Alice's view since an analogue property holds for the simulators for the sPRFeval protocol and the sCTeval protocol.

Security, part 2 (Adv corrupts Bob): We note that in protocol π Bob's program consists of running a polynomial number of sPRFeval and sCTeval protocols, and receiving multiple pseudo-random state pseudonyms. Since these subprotocols are secure, they admit an efficient simulator whose output is computationally indistinguishable from the adversary's view during protocol execution. For every $i = 1, \ldots, m$, sa sCTeval protocols are executed by Bob and only one results in a pseudo-random state pseudonym (different than the error symbol) as output. The position of this non-erroneous execution can be simulated as a random position in the $s \times a$ matrix, and the received pseudo-random state pseudonyms can be simulated using a random string of the same length. By suitably composing these simulators and the generation of the next-state pseudonyms, we obtain an efficient simulator for Adv's view when corrupting Bob in π. Specifically, simulator Sim_B runs the simulator for the sPRFeval protocol to simulate Bob's view during Bob's input processing phase, randomly chooses pseudonym $p_{s,1,0}$ of initial state $s_0 = 1$ and sets $q_{s,0} = p_{s,1,0}$, randomly chooses next state pseudonym $p_{s,j,i}$ and sets $q_{s,j} = p_{s,j,i}$, runs the simulator for the sPRFeval protocol to simulate Bob's view during the executions of the sPRFeval protocol in the circuit processing phase, and runs the simulator for the sCTeval protocol to simulate the output computation phase. The simulation's output is computationally indistinguishable from Alice's view since an analogue property holds for the simulators for the sPRFeval protocol and the sCTeval protocol, and since a random permutation of both rows and columns of the transition matrix at each iteration $i = 1, \ldots, m$ implies that the distribution of the position of the state pseudonym received by Bob during the protocol is random within the $s \times a$ matrix.

4   Our sDAeval Protocol: A First Instantiation

In this section we describe a first instantiation of our main result that is asymptotically more efficient than previous schemes in the literature, having, in particular, running time sublinear in the length of Bob's input string x. The instantiation is obtained by an adaptation of the family of asymmetric-type PRF and related sPRFeval protocol from [2, 7, 13, 16], and a simple sCTeval protocol for an AND of equalities between pseudo-random cryptographic pseudonyms, based

on any symmetric-type PRF. In the rest of this section, we describe these 3
ingredients, and the efficiency properties of the resulting instantiation, denoted
as π_1, of our main protocol.

A family of asymmetric-type PRFs. In this instantiation of π, the family
of asymmetric-type pseudo-random functions, denoted as prF_a, is realized as an
adaptation of the family used in [16], as we detail here. First, on input a security
parameter 1^σ, the function's parameters are generated by running the following
steps:

1. randomly choose $p_1, p_2, p_1', p_2' \in \{0,1\}^\sigma$ such that
    $p_1 = 2p_1' + 1$, $p_2 = 2p_2' + 1$, and p_1, p_2, p_1', p_2' are primes
2. set $n = p_1 p_2$
3. randomly choose an element g_1 of order n in a group Z_p^* such that
    p is the first prime such that p divides $(n-1)$
4. output: parameters (n, g_1)

Then, on input a randomly chosen key k in Z_n^* and an input string x in $\{0,1\}^q$,
the function prF_a returns $g_1^t \mod p$, for $t = 1/(k+x)$ if $\gcd(k+x,n) = 1$
and 1 otherwise. Two remarks are necessary on this definition. First, the event
$\gcd(k+x,n) \neq 1$ happens with negligible probability over the random choice
of k, assuming the hardness of factoring numbers of the same distribution as n.
Second, the length q of the input string was first thought in [16] to be limited
by the number-theoretic assumption needed to prove the pseudo-randomness of
this function family, but later [13] observed that such restriction is not needed
(see below for more details). This function family, defined in [16], is a variant
of the one in [7], in turn based on an unpredictable function from [2], the only
modification being of using a group whose order is a safe RSA modulus instead
of a group of prime order. The function from [2] was proved to be unpredictable
under a number-theoretic assumption on the underlying group (i.e., the computational q-DHI assumption). A proof from [7] can be extended to show that
this same function is a pseudo-random function under the mentioned number-
theoretic assumption. Moreover, as stated in [16], the same arguments from [2]
for prime-order groups also imply that (1) the function family considered here
in a composite-order group is pseudo-random assuming the decisional q-DHI
assumption on such groups and the hardness of factoring, and (2) the same
generic-group argument which motivated trust in the q-DHI assumption on the
prime-order groups carries to composite-order groups as well. Here, we recall a
sketch of the definition of the q-DHI assumption: all efficient algorithms, given
n and g, can only distinguish the two tuples

- $(g, g^u, g^{u^2}, \ldots, g^{u^q}, g^{1/u})$,
- $(g, g^u, g^{u^2}, \ldots, g^{u^q}, h)$

for random $h \in Z_p^*$ and $u \in Z_n^*$, with negligible probability. In later work [13], it
has been showed that no restriction of value q is needed by observing that the
function family we consider is (almost) a permutation.

An sPRFeval protocol for function prF_a. This protocol is a simplified version of the oblivious evaluation protocol from Fig. 1 of [16] for the above pseudo-random function prF_a. Specifically, this protocol evaluates the pseudo-random function f_K in Sect. 2.1 of the same paper and uses the encryption scheme in Sect. 2.2 of the same paper. The simplification is possible since we only require our protocol to be secure against semi-honest adversaries, and is thus obtained by removing the three zero-knowledge proofs of knowledge π_1, π_2, and π_3 from the protocol in Fig. 1 of [16]. The resulting protocol is an sPRFeval protocol for pseudo-random function prF_a, which will be run interactively by Alice and Bob and evaluate function prF_a on input Bob's input symbols. The proof for this fact is obtained as a corollary of the proof in [16]. As an optimization that does not affect the theorem validity, our implementation for π_1 also avoids the initial exponentiation to the k-th power of generator g_2 and just randomly chooses a symmetric key k instead. In this instantiation of π, function prF_a will also be computed non-interactively by Alice, on input relatively short strings denoting the alphabet symbols of the DA states.

An sCTeval protocol for 2 equalities conditions. We describe an sCTeval protocol for an equality condition and then one for an AND-of-equality condition. In both cases, we assume that all inputs to the equality statements are (large-size and pseudo-random) cryptographic pseudonyms. First, assume Alice wants to transfer some pseudonym p to Bob under the condition that Alice's pseudonym p_A is equal to Bob's pseudonym p_B. Based on any symmetric-type PRF prF_s with output length, the sCTeval protocol goes as follows:

1. Alice sets $k_A = p_A$, randomly chooses $r \in \{0,1\}^\sigma$, computes $u = prF_s(k_A, r)$, $v = u \oplus (p|0^\sigma)$, and sends (r, v) to Bob;
2. Bob sets $k_B = p_B$, computes $u' = prF_s(k_B, r)$; if $u' \oplus v = (m|0^\sigma)$ for some m, it returns: p; if not, it returns a special error symbol.

Note that if Alice's pseudonym p_A is equal to Bob's pseudonym p_B then Bob returns the same pseudonym p sent by Alice with probability 1; moreover, if Alice's pseudonym p_A is not equal to Bob's pseudonym p_B then Bob returns p only with negligible probability; finally, by the pseudo-randomness properties of prF_s, Alice learns no information about p_B and Bob learns no information about p_A, which implies the security of the protocol. This protocol is run s times in the output computation phase of π_1. Now, assume Alice wants to transfer some pseudonym p to Bob under the condition that Alice's pseudonym p_A is equal to Bob's pseudonym p_B and Alice's pseudonym q_A is equal to Bob's pseudonym q_B. Based on any symmetric-type PRF prF_s with output length, the sCTeval protocol goes as follows:

1. Alice randomly chooses p_1 and computes $p_2 = p \oplus p_1$
2. Alice transfers p_1 via the above sCTeval protocol for the string equality predicate, using the equality $(p_A = p_B)$ as condition;
3. Alice transfers p_1 via the above sCTeval protocol for the string equality predicate, using the equality $(q_A = q_B)$ as condition;

4. If Bob returns p_1', p_2' (and thus no error symbol) on any of these two executions, he returns $p' = p_1' + p_2'$; else Bob returns an error symbol.

Note that if both equalities are satisfied then Bob can compute $p_1' = p_1$ and
$p_2' = p_2$ and return $p' = p$ with probability 1; moreover, if at least one equality
is not satisfied then Bob returns $p' = p$ only with negligible probability. The
security of this protocol directly follows from the security of the individual single-
equality sCTeval protocols used.

Efficiency properties of π_1. Protocol π_1 only requires 3 messages between
Alice and Bob, as the sPRFeval protocols require 3 messages (where Alice sends
first), the sCTeval protocols require a single messages between Alice and Bob,
and this latter message can be combined with the last message in the sPRFeval
protocols. Alice's input processing phase requires $O(s)$ symmetric cryptography operations in Alice's executions of prF_s and $O(a)$ asymmetric cryptography
operations in Alice's executions of prF_a. Bob's input processing phase requires
$O(m)$ applications of an sPRFeval protocol, which only need $O(m)$ asymmetric
cryptography operations. The circuit processing and output computation phase
require $(sa+1)m$ applications of an sCTeval protocol, which need $O(sam)$ symmetric cryptography operations. Thus, in total, π_1 only requires $O(sam)$ symmetric cryptography and $O(m)$ asymmetric cryptography operations (instead
of $O(m \log a)$, as required in a direct application of the general solution from
[22]). An analogue improvement is observed in the protocol's communication
complexity.

5   Our sDAeval Protocol: A Second Instantiation

In this section we describe a second instantiation of our main protocol that,
although asymptotically less efficient than the first instantiation, is actually efficient for small automata alphabets, including some encountered in practice. The
instantiation is obtained by replacing the use of asymmetric-type PRFs with any
symmetric-type PRFs, and realizing a sPRFeval protocol by a suitable combinations of protocols from [19,20]. This realization uses the fact that the automata
alphabet is small (i.e., polynomial in the security parameter), and that the PRF
needs to be evaluated over any one of the a alphabet elements. In the rest of this
section, we describe this different sPRFeval protocol, and the efficiency properties of the resulting instantiation, denoted as π_2, of our main protocol.

An sPRFeval protocol for any small-domain symmetric-type function
prF_s. While in the first instantiation of π, we used a simplified version of the
oblivious pseudo-random function evaluation protocol from Fig. 1 of [16], here,
assuming that the number a of automata's alphabet symbols is small (i.e., polynomial in the security parameter, as opposed to super-polynomial), we use a
protocol that can be based on: (1) any arbitrary symmetric-type pseudo-random
function, including the already assumed prF_s, which we implement using a block
cipher (e.g., AES), and (2) any secure (1-out-of-a)-OT protocol, such as the one
in [19], which is in turn based on any arbitrary symmetric-type pseudo-random

function, including the already assumed prF_s, and any arbitrary (1-out-of-2)-OT protocol, such as the one in [20], based on the hardness of the Decisional Diffie-Hellman problem. Specifically, the new oblivious pseudo-random function evaluation protocol will be an oblivious protocol for the evaluation of function on input (i, x_i), where x_i is the i-th element from Bobs input string $x = x_1, \ldots, x_m$, for all $i = 1, \ldots, m$. This protocol goes as follows:

1. Alice computes $z_h = prF_s(h, as_h)$, for $h = 1, \ldots, a$, where as_h denotes the h-th alphabet symbol according to a standard, lexicographic, ordering;
2. Alice uses the (1-out-of-a)-OT protocol from [19] to transfer z_t to Bob, where Alice uses as input strings $z_1, \ldots, z_a$, Bob uses as input $t \in \{1, \ldots, a\}$ such that $as_t = x_j$

The resulting protocol is a sPRFeval protocol for pseudo-random function prF_s, whenever a is polynomial in the security parameter. To summarize, protocol π_1 and π_2 differ in how the design of the sPRFeval protocol, affecting the type of PRF used and the assumption on the size of the automata alphabet. In π_1, the sPRFeval protocol is designed as an adaptation of the scheme from [16], and works for a specific asymmetric-type PRF, and for arbitrary-size automata alphabets. On the other hand, in π_2, the sPRFeval protocol is designed building from a (1-out-of-a)-OT scheme from [19], works for any arbitrary symmetric-type PRF, and for polynomial-size automata alphabets.

Efficiency properties of π_2. Protocol π_2 only requires 2 messages between Alice and Bob, as the sPRFeval protocols require 2 messages (where Bob sends first), the sCTeval protocols require a single messages between Alice and Bob, and this latter message can be combined with the last message in the sPRFeval protocols. As in π_1, Alice's input processing phase requires $O(s)$ symmetric cryptography operations in Alice's executions of prF_s and $O(a)$ asymmetric cryptography operations in Alice's executions of prF_a. Bob's input processing phase requires $O(m)$ applications of an sPRFeval protocol, which need $O(m \log a)$ asymmetric and symmetric cryptography operations. The circuit processing and output computation phase require $(sa + 1)m$ applications of an sCTeval protocol, which need $O(sam)$ symmetric cryptography operations. Thus, in total, π_2 requires $O(sam)$ symmetric cryptography and $O(m \log a)$ asymmetric cryptography operations, which is asymptotically similar to a direct application of the general solution from [22], but, as later shown in the performance evaluation of our implementation, comes with considerable runtime improvements.

6 Performance Analysis

In this section we discuss the practical performance of the two instantiations π_1, π_2 of our main protocol π, showing improved latency with respect to the original Yao's protocol, as well as previous protocols in the literature. We performed two types of analysis of our protocols' on-line computation (or latency): an asymptotic analysis, with comparison with previous sDAeval protocols, and a more practical numerical analysis based on measurements of our implementations running time.

Implementation setup, metric and parameter settings. Testing of our implementations of protocols π_1 and π_2 was done on 2 Dell PowerEdge 1950 processors and one Dell PowerEdge 2950 processor, Intel(R) Xeon(R) CPU E5405 @ 2.00 GHz. We run Alice and Bob's programs on the 2 PowerEdge 1950 processors, and the testing control was run on the 2950 processor. All offline and online communication traffic was run over a dedicated gigabit Ethernet LAN. Testing control and collection of timing measurement traffic was isolated on a separate dedicated gigabit Ethernet LAN.

In our performance experiments, we mainly evaluated on-line computation time (or latency), divided into asymmetric cryptographic operations, with security parameter σ, and symmetric cryptography operations, with security parameter λ. Recall that in practice the former type of operations is expected to require computing resources greater than the latter type by orders of magnitude (slightly more than 3 orders on our machines, when setting $\sigma = 2048$ and $\lambda = 128$). In addition than σ and λ, latency was evaluated over input length parameters s (the number of DA states), a (the number of DA alphabet symbols) and m (the number of symbols in Bob's input string x).

Performance evaluation of π_1, π_2. Off-line computation performance (used for the generation of one-time public keys and parameter value settings) required 200 s in π_1 and less than 4 s in π_2. Memory used by π_1 (resp., π_2) was 337 Mbytes (resp., 2.553 Mbytes).

Practical numeric latency times of our protocols are heavily dependent on the subset of values that we consider as settings for parameters s, a, n. We considered three main cases for parameter a, reflecting related application scenarios; namely:

- $a = 2$ (binary alphabet),
- $a = 27$ (English alphabet plus one special symbol for all other alphabet symbols),
- $a = 128$ (smallest power of 2 that includes all ASCII symbols).

For these three values, we measured running times and extrapolated them into estimates of close-to-maximum values of s and n such that the overall latency of the protocols would remain below 30 s or 10 s.

The found values are captured in Table 1 below.

Comparison of asymptotic performance with previous sDAeval protocols. We compared our protocols π_1, π_2 with previous sDAeval protocols achievable from results in [9,15,18,22]. This comparison was performed by evaluation of asymptotic expressions for their latency, and is summarized in Table 2 below. (While we were able to extend the protocol from [22] to a non-binary automata alphabet size, it was unclear how to do the same with the protocol in [18], which is defined for binary alphabets.)

We remark that the number $O(m)$ of asymmetric cryptography operations in π_1 is sublinear in the total length of the input $n = O(m \log a + sa \log s)$ to Alice and Bob.

Table 1. Max s, a, n parameter values obtained for our protocols, under constraints of latency ≤ 30s (columns 2, 3, 4) and of latency ≤ 10s s (columns 5, 6, 7).

Protocol	s	a	n	s	a	n
π_1	200	2	84	200	2	28
π_1	70	27	70	70	27	23
π_1	80	128	42	80	128	14
π_2	200	2	6200	200	2	2100
π_2	100	27	1500	100	27	500
π_2	80	128	75	80	128	25

Table 2. Asymptotic latency analysis, relative to alphabet type.

Protocol	Asymmetric crypto	Symmetric crypto	Alphabet
	Operations	Operations	Type
[22]	$O(m \log a)$	$O(sm \log a \log s)$	a-ary, for any $a \geq 2$
[9]	$O(ms \log a)$	None	a-ary, for any $a \geq 2$
[15]	$O(ms \log a)$	None	a-ary, for any $a \geq 2$
[18]	$O(m \log a)$	$O(sm \log a)$	Binary
π_1	$O(m)$	$O(sam)$	a-ary, for any $a \geq 2$
π_2	$O(m \log a)$	$O(sam)$	a-ary, for any $a \geq 2$

Performance comparison with Yao's protocol. To obtain some insights on the 'computing with encrypted data blocks' paradigm underlying our sDAeval protocol, we compared our sDAeval protocols' performance with sDAeval protocols obtained by instantiating the state-of-the-art solutions in the area of general-purpose secure 2-party function evaluation (specifically, the garbled circuit paradigm, starting with [22], and the fully homomorphic encryption paradigm, starting with [10]). We expanded the quantitative performance comparison framework used in [5] to obtain numeric (as opposed to asymptotic) performance estimates and derive a comparison of these 3 approaches. It was quickly apparent that an sDAeval protocol obtained using the fully homomorphic encryption paradigm, would be the least efficient. Accordingly, we focused our analysis on comparing our sDAeval protocols obtained using the computing with encrypted data blocks paradigm with the sDAeval protocol obtained using the garbled circuit paradigm from [22].

Let π_Y denote the 2-party sDAeval protocol obtained using the garbled circuit paradigm from [22]. Then, for any 2-party sDAeval protocol π, we define the *latency ratio* for π, as follows:

$$\text{latency ratio}(\pi) = \text{latency}(\pi_Y)/\text{latency}(\pi).$$

In our analysis, we have found that the latency ratio is essentially independent on parameter m, which makes it much easier to analyze as a function of the

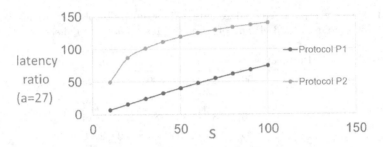

Fig. 2. Latency ratio of π_1 and π_2, with alphabet size 27, as a function of the number s of states

remaining parameters s and a. Using a combination of runtime measurements and estrapolations based on protocol analysis, we characterized the latency ratio for our protocols π_1 and π_2 in Fig. 2 below. We observe that the improvement of π_1 (respectively, π_2) over π_Y varies between almost 1 to about 1.8 (respectively, almost 1.5 to about 2.2) orders of magnitude in the shown parameter value space and further increases with the number s of states.

7 Conclusions and Open Directions

This work can be considered a next step in the direction of [5], where we have introduced a paradigm for the design of more efficient secure function evaluation protocols, performing the most computationally expensive operations (i.e., asymmetric cryptography operations) over input data blocks instead of input data bits, while maintaining efficient key sizes. This addresses performance shortcomings of the 2 main general-purpose secure function evaluation approaches in the literature: Yao's garbled circuits, which has efficient key sizes but operates on single data bits, and Gentry's fully homomorphic encryption, which operates on input data blocks when applied to arithmetic circuits, but with inefficient key sizes. In [5], we had shown efficient secure function evaluation protocols satisfying both requirements, for the class of monotone formulae over equality statements. In this paper, we show such a protocol for deterministic automata evaluation, which, being equivalent to regular expression matching, captures all constant-space computations. A first open research direction is to improve the practical performance of secure protocols for pseudo-random function evaluation protocols, which would improve the performance of the first instantiation of our protocol on practical parameter settings. A second and more general open research direction is that of finding more instances of protocols following the paradigm of computations over encrypted data blocks, possibly including large classes of polynomial-size circuits.

Acknowledgments. We thank Jonathan Katz for pointing us to a useful reference. This work was supported by the Defense Advanced Research Projects Agency (DARPA) via Air Force Research Laboratory (AFRL), contract number FA8750-14-C-0057. The U.S. Government is authorized to reproduce and distribute reprints for Governmental purposes notwithstanding any copyright annotation hereon. Disclaimer: The views and conclusions contained herein are those of the authors and should not be interpreted as necessarily representing the official policies or endorsements, either expressed or implied, of DARPA, AFRL or the U.S. Government.

References

1. Bogetoft, P., Christensen, D.L., Damgård, I., Geisler, M., Jakobsen, T., Krøigaard, M., Nielsen, J.D., Nielsen, J.B., Nielsen, K., Pagter, J., Schwartzbach, M., Toft, T.: Secure multiparty computation goes live. In: Dingledine, R., Golle, P. (eds.) FC 2009. LNCS, vol. 5628, pp. 325–343. Springer, Heidelberg (2009). doi:10.1007/978-3-642-03549-4_20

2. Boneh, D., Boyen, X.: Short signatures without random oracles. In: Cachin, C., Camenisch, J.L. (eds.) EUROCRYPT 2004. LNCS, vol. 3027, pp. 56–73. Springer, Heidelberg (2004). doi:10.1007/978-3-540-24676-3_4

3. Brakerski, Z., Vaikuntanathan, V.: Efficient fully homomorphic encryption from (standard) LWE. In: IEEE 52nd Annual Symposium on Foundations of Computer Science, FOCS 2011, Palm Springs, CA, USA, pp. 97–106, 22–25 October 2011

4. Crescenzo, G.: Private selective payment protocols. In: Frankel, Y. (ed.) FC 2000. LNCS, vol. 1962, pp. 72–89. Springer, Heidelberg (2001). doi:10.1007/3-540-45472-1_6

5. Di Crescenzo, G., Coan, B.A., Kirsch, J.: Efficient computations over encrypted data blocks. In: Proceedings of the 40th International Symposium on Mathematical Foundations of Computer Science, Part II, MFCS 2015, Milan, Italy, pp. 274–286, 24–28 August 2015

6. Di Crescenzo, G., Ostrovsky, R., Rajagopalan, S.: Conditional oblivious transfer and timed-release encryption. In: Stern, J. (ed.) EUROCRYPT 1999. LNCS, vol. 1592, pp. 74–89. Springer, Heidelberg (1999). doi:10.1007/3-540-48910-X_6

7. Dodis, Y., Yampolskiy, A.: A verifiable random function with short proofs and keys. In: Vaudenay, S. (ed.) PKC 2005. LNCS, vol. 3386, pp. 416–431. Springer, Heidelberg (2005). doi:10.1007/978-3-540-30580-4_28

8. Freedman, M.J., Ishai, Y., Pinkas, B., Reingold, O.: Keyword search and oblivious pseudorandom functions. In: Kilian, J. (ed.) TCC 2005. LNCS, vol. 3378, pp. 303–324. Springer, Heidelberg (2005). doi:10.1007/978-3-540-30576-7_17

9. Gennaro, R., Hazay, C., Sorensen, J.S.: Automata evaluation and text search protocols with simulation-based security. J. Crypt. **29**(2), 243–282 (2016)

10. Gentry, C.: Fully homomorphic encryption using ideal lattices. In: Proceedings of the of 41st ACM STOC, pp. 169–178 (2009)

11. Goldreich, O.: The Foundations of Cryptography - Basic Applications, vol. 2. Cambridge University Press, New York (2004)

12. Goldreich, O., Goldwasser, S., Micali, S.: How to construct random functions. J. ACM **33**(4), 792–807 (1986)

13. Hazay, C., Nissim, K.: Efficient set operations in the presence of malicious adversaries. In: Nguyen, P.Q., Pointcheval, D. (eds.) PKC 2010. LNCS, vol. 6056, pp. 312–331. Springer, Heidelberg (2010). doi:10.1007/978-3-642-13013-7_19

14. Huang, Y., Evans, D., Katz, J., Malka, L.: Faster secure two-party computation using garbled circuits. In: Proceedings of 20th USENIX Security Symposium (2011)
15. Ishai, Y., Paskin, A.: Evaluating branching programs on encrypted data. In: Vadhan, S.P. (ed.) TCC 2007. LNCS, vol. 4392, pp. 575–594. Springer, Heidelberg (2007). doi:10.1007/978-3-540-70936-7_31
16. Jarecki, S., Liu, X.: Efficient oblivious pseudorandom function with applications to adaptive OT and secure computation of set intersection. In: Reingold, O. (ed.) TCC 2009. LNCS, vol. 5444, pp. 577–594. Springer, Heidelberg (2009). doi:10.1007/978-3-642-00457-5_34
17. Malkhi, D., Nisan, N., Pinkas, B., Sella, Y.: Fairplay - secure two-party computation system. In: Proceedings of 13th USENIX Security Symposium, pp. 287–302 (2004)
18. Mohassel, P., Niksefat, S., Sadeghian, S., Sadeghiyan, B.: An efficient protocol for oblivious DFA evaluation and applications. In: Dunkelman, O. (ed.) CT-RSA 2012. LNCS, vol. 7178, pp. 398–415. Springer, Heidelberg (2012). doi:10.1007/978-3-642-27954-6_25
19. Naor, M., Pinkas, B.: Oblivious transfer with adaptive queries. In: Wiener, M. (ed.) CRYPTO 1999. LNCS, vol. 1666, pp. 573–590. Springer, Heidelberg (1999). doi:10.1007/3-540-48405-1_36
20. Naor, M., Pinkas, B.: Efficient oblivious transfer protocols. In: Proceedings of the Twelfth Annual Symposium on Discrete Algorithms, Washington, DC, USA, pp. 448–457, 7–9 January 2001
21. Rabin, M.O.: How to exchange secrets with oblivious transfer. IACR Cryptology ePrint Archive, 2005:187 (2005)
22. Yao, A.C.-C.: How to generate and exchange secrets (extended abstract). In: Proceedings of 27th IEEE FOCS, pp. 162–167 (1986)

Consensus and Smart Contracts

Securing Proof-of-Stake Blockchain Protocols

Wenting Li, Sébastien Andreina, Jens-Matthias Bohli, and Ghassan Karame[✉]

NEC Laboratories Europe, Heidelberg, Germany
{wenting.li,sebastien.andreina,jens-matthias.bohli,
ghassan.karame}@neclab.eu

Abstract. Proof-of-Stake (PoS) protocols have been actively researched for the past five years. PoS finds direct applicability in open blockchain platforms and has been seen as a strong candidate to replace the largely inefficient Proof of Work mechanism that is currently plugged in most existing open blockchains. Although a number of PoS variants have been proposed, these protocols suffer from a number of security shortcomings; for instance, most existing PoS variants suffer from the *nothing at stake* and the *long range* attacks which considerably degrade security in the blockchain.

In this paper, we address these problems and we propose two PoS protocols that allow validators to generate at most one block at any given "height"—thus alleviating the problem of nothing at stake and preventing attackers from compromising accounts to mount long range attacks. Our first protocol leverages a dedicated digital signature scheme that reveals the identity of the validator if the validator attempts to work on multiple blocks at the same height. On the other hand, our second protocol leverages existing pervasive Trusted Execution Environments (TEEs) to limit the block generation requests by any given validator to a maximum of one at a given height. We analyze the security of our proposals and evaluate their performance by means of implementation; our evaluation results show that our proposals introduce tolerable overhead in the block generation and validation process when compared to existing PoS protocols.

1 Introduction

The blockchain is gaining increasing attention nowadays motivated by the wide success of the Bitcoin cryptocurrency. To reach distributed agreement, the blockchain relies on consensus protocols which ensure that all nodes in the network share a consistent view on a common distributed ledger. Most existing blockchain systems rely on Bitcoin's Proof-of-Work (PoW) to reach network consensus in permission-less systems that do not require the knowledge of nodes' identities. However, PoW has been often criticized for its huge waste of energy; for instance, it is estimated that Bitcoin miners can consume as much electricity as Ireland in 2005 [16].

To remedy the limitations of PoW, the community has turned to Proof of Stake (PoS) protocols in the hope of offering a more efficient and environment-friendly alternative. Unlike PoW, PoS leverages virtual resources such as the

© Springer International Publishing AG 2017
J. Garcia-Alfaro et al. (Eds.): DPM/CBT 2017, LNCS 10436, pp. 297–315, 2017.
DOI: 10.1007/978-3-319-67816-0_17

stake of a node in order to perform leader election and maintain consensus in the network. Since the mining resources are virtual, PoS-based consensus process is instant and results in negligible costs.

Nevertheless, although many PoS variants have been proposed [7,12,15,17–19,21], PoS is still not widely deployed in existing blockchains. Namely, in spite of their efficiency, PoS-powered blockchains still account for less than 2% of the market capitalization of existing digital currencies. This is mostly due to the fact that most existing PoS protocols are vulnerable to a number of security threats, such as the *nothing at stake* and the *long-range* attacks. The former attack allows the nodes to mine conflicting blocks without risking their stake which increases the number of forks in the system as well as the time to reach consensus in the network. The latter attack (commonly referred to as history attack) consists of an adversary that aims to alter the entire history of the blockchain starting from early blocks (even from the genesis block). This can be achieved when e.g., the attacker acquires the private keys of older accounts which no longer have any stake at the moment, but that have accrued majority stake at previous block height h; the attacker can construct a fork starting from block h leveraging these accounts.

To remedy these attacks, a number of proposals suggest the reliance on deposit-based PoS [3,22] and checkpoints [12,18,19,21]. Deposit-based PoS essentially requires each validator to make a deposit in the system; this deposit will be withdrawn by the system if the validator generates conflicting blocks, thus preventing nothing at stake attacks. Checkpoints, on the other hand, correspond to previous blocks up to which the blockchain does not allow forks. This limits the impact of the long-range attack to some extent, as the earliest attack point has to be after the last checkpoint. Clearly, such solutions do not however completely prevent misbehavior in the blockchain.

In this paper, we address these problems and we propose two PoS variant protocols that are secure against the nothing at stake and the long-range attacks. Our first solution leverages a digital signature scheme that is directly linked to the registered identities of the nodes. In case blocks in parallel forks are mined by the same node, the private key of that node along with his identity will be immediately revealed. As such, this solution complements existing solutions in the area [3,12,18,19,21,22] by embedding accountability in case of misbehavior but at the expense of relying on an identity manager. Our second solution solves this shortcoming and leverages Trusted Execution Environments (TEEs) to prevent validators from signing two blocks of the same height in parallel chains. We analyze the security of both solutions and we show that they can effectively prevent malicious validators from generating conflicting blocks with nothing at stake. We also implement prototypes derived from our proposals and evaluate their performance. Our results show that our first solution only introduces an additional ∼500 ms of latency and ∼19 KB of block header payload when generating and verifying the cryptographic proofs compared to existing PoS protocols. On the other hand, our second solution does not incur any meaningful overhead compared to Nxt's PoS protocol.

The remainder of the paper is organized as follows. We overview existing PoS protocols and the main intuition behind the nothing at stake attack and the long range attack in Sect. 2. We then introduce our solutions and analyze their security provisions in Sects. 3 and 4. We evaluate the performance of our proposals in Sect. 5 and we conclude the paper in Sect. 6.

2 Background and Related Work

Blockchain is a distributed ledger technology based on a peer-to-peer network. Transactions are broadcast in the network for every node to verify. Most existing blockchains leverage consensus protocols allowing nodes to collaboratively maintain a common ledger of validated transactions.

Proof-of-Stake (PoS) is a consensus protocol dedicated for *open* blockchains—which feature open membership allowing any node to join the network. PoS defines a group of *validators* whose task is to propose the next transaction(s) to be included in the ledger. These proposals are broadcast in the network in the form of *blocks*. Blocks typically build on each other, thereby forming a chain of blocks—hence the blockchain.

Since there are multiple validators in the network, PoS introduces a computational problem for the validators to solve when generating a block to throttle the number of block proposals in the network. Typically, the block generation time is manipulated by the means of a *target* value that denotes the difficulty of the problem to be solved by the validators. Each validator who finds a PoS solution then includes the solution along with the proposed block as a *proof* that he is "eligible" to generate the block. Blocks are deemed correct if their proof is correct with respect to all correct transactions that they confirm. If multiple validators find a solution simultaneously, a *fork* occurs in the block chain.

2.1 Proof-of-Stake (PoS)

In what follows, we summarize the general operations on a validator to maintain consensus defined by a PoS consensus protocol:

IsEligible($blkhder, T, key_V, stake_V$). This qualification function verifies, given the prepared block header $blkhder$ and the target T, whether the validator is eligible to generate the next block given the account information ($key_V, stake_V$). This function aims to elect a *leader* among the validators to generate the next block.

GenerateBlock(blk, T). This routine refers to the block generation function. Given a block blk and target T, the validator first checks the predicate IsEligible and returns a proof prf whether the validator is eligible.

ValidateBlock(blk, T, prf). This routine corresponds to the block verification function. It returns true if the information in the block blk is correct and if the proof prf is valid for the predicate IsEligible.

Resolve($fork_1, \ldots, fork_n$). This routine is a fork resolution algorithm that returns a unique fork $fork_k$ to work on if multiple forks are detected.

As mentioned earlier, PoS constitutes one of the few workable candidates set to replace that largely inefficient PoW in the near future. PoS leverages virtual resources denoted by the stake of a validator to solve the computation problem. *Stakes* refer to the assets (or cryptocurrencies) owned by a node. The idea is that the more stake a validator has, the more likely he will find a solution to generate a block. Thus, PoS defines the predicate IsEligible as $f(blkhder, key_V) < T \cdot stake_V$, where $f(\cdot)$ is a deterministic function on the block header and the validator's account key. Recall that the account key and the amount of stake is publicly verifiable by all nodes in the network.

GenerateBlock returns *empty* if the validator's $\langle key_V, stake_V \rangle$ does not satisfy the statement of the IsEligible predicate; otherwise it returns a proof $prf = \langle Prf_e, Sig_b \rangle$, where Prf_e is the *eligibility proof* and Sig_b is the *block signature* of the validator. This also implies that validators do not need to search for the PoS solution exhaustively (as in PoW) since the solution only depends on the validator's account information. Meanwhile, ValidateBlock returns true if the proof prf is valid and the validator's account $\langle key_V, stake_V \rangle$ satisfies the IsEligible statement.

The community currently features a number of PoS variants. For instance, Peercoin [12], Cloakcoin [7], and Novacoin [15] use coin age as mining resources to generate blocks in their PoS protocols. Coin age is defined as the accumulated time that a node holds his stake before using them to generate a block. However, relying on coin age discourages nodes from actively participating in the consensus process, as nodes would have incentives to hoard the coins so that they have a better chance to generate a block. VeriCoin [17] uses "stake-time" based on coin age, which also takes into account the activity of the nodes in the network. The stake time starts to degrade at a certain point of time if the nodes do not participate in block generation with their stake. Blackcoin [19] and Nxt [21] only rely on the amount of stake in the consensus protocol. Nxt [21] uses a deterministic algorithm (IsEligible) to elect the leaders in order to mitigate the *grinding* vulnerability [4,10], where adversaries use computational resources to increase their probabilities of being elected as leaders. This leads to another issue that the leader of each valid block is predictable in the network, thus making it vulnerable to planned denial of service attack or selfish-mining strategies. Additionally, an adversary can still perform stake grinding by skipping an opportunity to create a block if he is able to increase his advantage over the future blocks [4]. Blackcoin [19] defines a "stake modifier" which periodically introduces some entropy to the eligibility test, but only limits the period where leaders are predictable until the next update of the stake modifier. BitShares [18] proposes Delegated Proof-of-Stake where the shareholders first vote for a group of delegated witnesses who then generate the blocks in round-robin fashion. Slasher [3] and Casper [22] are deposit-based PoS proposed by Ethereum. They require the nodes to submit a deposit in order to become a validator.

Snow white [2] offers robustness under sporadic node participation with epoch-based committees composed of selected active stakeholders. Ouroboros [11] increases the incentives for honest behavior with a novel reward mechanism. It also prevents stake grinding while keeping the leaders unpredictable using verifiable secure multi-party computation. However, this approach requires the coordination amongst the validators in the network. Algorand [6,9] is rather a Byzantine Agreement protocol [1] in a public blockchain setting that does not generate forks (with a high probability). Block proposers and voting committee members are elected based on their stake through Verifiable Random Function [13]. However, this protocol requires at least three rounds of Byzantine Agreement voting if the block proposal is honest assuming a voting committee size of 4000 nodes. If the block proposal is malicious, an empty block will still be generated after a long consensus process.

Example—Nxt's PoS: We now describe Nxt's PoS which emerges as one of the most popular PoS protocols.

In Nxt's PoS, each block contains two additional values: a *base target value* T_b and an *eligibility proof* (called *generation signature* in Nxt) Prf_e, which vary from block to block. Similar to the *difficulty* level used in PoW, the base target value aims to adjust the average block generation time to match the desired value, which is 60 s in Nxt. On the other hand, the eligibility proof Prf_e is used to check whether the current validator is eligible to generate the next block. It is computed as the hash value over the public key of validator's account and the eligibility proof of the previous block: $Prf_e^{(i)} = Hash(PubKey_V || Prf_e^{(i-1)})$.

Then, each validator has his own target value T based on the elapsed time $time_e$ since the last block and the current effective stake in his account: $T = T_b \cdot time_e \cdot stake_V$. Finally, the leading l bytes of the eligibility proof Prf_e are checked against the target T. To summarize, the predicate IsEligible is defined as follows:

$$Prefix(Hash(PubKey_V || Prf_e^{(i-1)}), l) < T_b \cdot time_e \cdot stake_V \qquad (1)$$

GenerateBlock returns a proof $prf = \langle Prf_e, Sig_b \rangle$, where Sig_b is the *block signature* $Sig_b = Sign(PrivKey_V, blkhder)$.

To verify a block, nodes first check if the block signature is valid before re-evaluating the IsEligible predicate defined in Eq. 1. Here, the block signature is required for nodes to verify validator's public key used in the eligibility proof as well as validator's stake.

In case multiple forks are detected, a *cumulative difficulty* value is defined for each block. This difficulty is computed based on the cumulative difficulty of the previous block and the base target value of the current block: $CD^{(i)} = CD^{(i-1)} + \frac{2^{64}}{T_b}$. Resolve returns a fork whose last block exhibits the highest cumulative difficulty.

2.2 The "Nothing at Stake" Attack

Despite the variety of PoS protocols, since generating a block in PoS is no more than generating one signature, validators have incentive to work on multiple forks. In other words, in order to maximize the benefits, validators could generate conflicting blocks on all possible forks with nothing at stake. This problem is commonly referred to as the *nothing at stake* attack.

This attack slows down the consensus time in the network and thus reduces the efficiency of the system. Moreover, it results in blockchain forks which weaken the ability of the blockchain to resolve double spending attacks and other threats.

Notice that the aforementioned Nxt's PoS does not address the nothing at stake problem. Namely, validators can ignore the fork resolution algorithm and generate blocks on top of multiple forks. Moreover, since the eligibility proof is deterministic for each account, one can easily predict which validators will generate valid blocks in the future. This is often referred to as "transparent forging" and opens an additional attack surface to the blockchain, allowing the attackers to selectively nit-pick the next leader to compromise.

Ouroboros [11] introduces a new reward mechanism that incentivizes the validators to behave honestly. However, it only discourages opportunistic adversaries and cannot prevent targeted attacks that would benefit from (temporarily) forked blockchain such as double-spending attack. Slasher [3] proposes to address this attack by requiring validators to provide a deposit which will be locked for a period. In case conflicting blocks at the same height are signed by the same validator, the misbehaving validator will lose his deposit. In this way, the network punishes the validators who simultaneously create conflicting blocks on multiple forks. BitShares [18] adopts a similar approach to Slasher. Here, if a validator (witness) misbehaves, they will lose their ability to generate blocks in the future. Other deposit-based PoS protocols even penalize the validators if they are voting on the "wrong" fork—assuming that there is only one correct fork at all time. Nevertheless, all such countermeasures freeze a considerable amount of stake in the network. In addition, in spite of the deposit-based mechanism, malicious validators can still profit from targeted attacks as they can create conflicting blocks with double-spending transactions whose value surpasses that of the deposit that they committed in the network.

2.3   The "Long Range" Attack

Long range attacks on PoS (also known as history attacks) refer to the case where an attacker tries to alter the blockchain history by creating a fork from an already generated block. While this attack in theory requires an attacker that controls the majority of stake in the network, long range attacks can be practically instantiated if the attacker controls/compromises accounts that have no stake at the moment, but have a large stake at some past block height h. For example, an account that had 30% stake at block height h and no stake at block height $h+1$ can still use his 30% stake to re-generate another block at height h.

This allows an attacker to create forks from past blocks that can overtake the current chain with (past) majority stake. This can be achieved by compromising the private keys of older accounts which no longer have any stake at the moment, but that have accrued majority stake at previous block height. Notice that accounts that exhibit zero stake might not be as protected as other *active* accounts—which would further facilitate this attack.

At present, most existing countermeasures [2,12,18,19,21] against long range attack use *checkpoints* to limit the range of such attacks. A checkpoint refers to a block until which the blockchain is regarded as "finalized" and immutable. A number of PoS instantiations [12,18,19] rely on a centralized checkpoint server to define a correct chain periodically; on the other hand, Nxt [21] nodes do not accept a change to a fork that differs from a block more than 720 blocks old. Similarly, Snow White's nodes [2] do not accept a (longer) chain which modifies blocks "too far" in the past. However, these approaches require nodes to be synchronized; for instance, nodes that recently join the network can hardly distinguish which chain of the forks is the correct one.

Table 1 summarizes the security of existing PoS protocols against the nothing at stake and long range attacks. We see that the existing protocols are either insecure against these attacks, or only secure under specific conditions.

Table 1. Resilience of existing PoS protocols against the nothing at stake and long range attacks. Here, ○ denotes refers to the case where a property is partially achieved.

Blockchain (PoS)	Secure against	
	Nothing at stake	Long range attack
Cloakcoin	×	×
Novacoin	×	×
Blackcoin	×	○
Peercoin	×	○
Nxt	×	○
Slasher	○	×
Vericoin	○	×
BitShares	○	○
Snow white	×	○
Ouroboros	×	○

2.4   System Model

We assume a similar system model to Nxt (cf. Sect. 2.1). More specifically, we assume a peer-to-peer system where nodes commit their virtual resources in the system; and the stake of nodes is publicly verifiable by all participants in the network.

We rely on a trusted infrastructure with which the nodes interact off-chain. In our first solution, nodes trust identity providers and their certificates. On the other hand, in our second solution, we assume that nodes trust the implementation of the trusted hardware and TEE architectures. Notice that this model can be easily adopted by permission-based blockchain, where participants can quickly agree on a set of trusted infrastructures. However, we stress that our model equally applies to permissionless blockchain deployments by relying on existing public identity providers and/or TEE supported devices.

We further assume that nodes are rational and are only interested in increasing their advantage in the system without being identified. We assume that no node controls majority stake in the network presently; this however does not prevent an adversary from compromising different accounts to accrue stake majority at a prior block height. We further assume that all participants are computationally bounded and cannot break the signature schemes or the guarantees provided by secure proof of knowledge schemes.

Whenever secure hardware and TEE are used, we assume that the adversary cannot compromise the TEE environment. For example, the adversary cannot extract the keys from the trusted applications within TEE or change the behavior of the trusted applications.

In what follows, we present two PoS solutions that are resilient against the aforementioned nothing at stake and long range attacks. To ease the presentation, we describe these solutions as extensions to the well-known Nxt PoS protocol (cf. Sect. 2.1).

3 Identity-Based PoS

As mentioned earlier, the limitation of conventional deposit-based PoS is that even if a malicious node is caught creating conflicting blocks, the punishment of losing his deposit is not severe enough to totally discourage him. For example, an attacker can launch double-spending attacks that involve huge amount of stake through the forks he creates.

We start by showing that the combined use of deposit-based PoS and identity management in the network can alleviate this limitation. Namely, we describe a solution that requires the validators to submit their identity information in a privacy-preserving fashion, while their private keys used for generating blocks are bound to their committed identity information. We show how to conceal the nodes' identities—unless misbehavior happens.

The intuition behind our solution is to bind the randomness of the DSA signature of the block to the block height value. Therefore, once a validator creates two conflicting blocks at the same block height, a node can recover the validator's private key based on the block signatures and reveal the corresponding identity accordingly. Before describing our solution, we start by introducing the building blocks that we will use.

3.1 Building Blocks

Notations. Throughout this section, we denote p, q, g as the public parameters in DSA signature scheme, where p, q are the prime numbers such that $q|p-1$. g is a generator of order q in $\mathbb{Z}_p$. We further introduce a subgroup of $\mathbb{Z}_q$ with prime order w generated by a and h; while h's discrete logarithm to the base a is not known. Each node has one DSA key pair (x, y) for his account, where

$0 < x < w$ is the private key and $y = g^x \mod p$ is the public key. Each node also publishes another public key $y' = a^x \mod q$ to the network.

Recall that DSA [20] signature is of the form of (r, s), where r is a random value whose seed k is picked randomly by the signer: $r = (g^k \mod p) \mod q$. Recall that DSA requires that k should never be re-used for signing different messages, otherwise the private key is able to be recovered from these signatures.

We denote $r \xleftarrow{\mathcal{R}} \mathbb{Z}_n$ as randomly picking an element r from $\mathbb{Z}_n$. We use H for block height value included in each block header. We distinguish this with $H(\cdot)$ which is a cryptographic hash function.

Verifiable Random Function (VRF). VRF [13] refers to a pseudo-random function which provides a publicly verifiable proof that a given number is correctly generated based a public input and a private key. We need to use VRF in our block signature construction in order to *enforce* the validators to generate the randomness k which is bound to the block height H and prove to the others. Since DSA's security also relies on the fact that k is unpredictable, we require the VRF outputs to be unpredictable too.

Dodis et al. [8] have presented an efficient VRF scheme. However, since this scheme reveals k in the verification process, which is not allowed in DSA, we need to revise and extend it with Proofs of Knowledge [14] to prove that k is correctly generated according to the VRF scheme and is also used to compose r without revealing its value.

3.2 Protocol Specification

We now detail the various procedures used in our solution.

Identity Management: Our Identity-based PoS consensus protocol only allows registered validators who have committed their identity information to generate blocks. We therefore start by defining the setup phase in this protocol.

Our scheme requires a trusted identity provider that can issue identity-linked certificates for everyone, such as the credentials of the citizen's ePass. To commit his identity, a validator first generates his anonymous account key pair (x, y). The validator provides the public key y (along with the proof of knowledge of x) to the identity provider or uses his e-Identity card. He obtains in return an encrypted identity C_{id} under y along with a certificate $Cert_{IP}$ that binds key and encryption together, issued by the identity provider or the e-Identity card respectively. Then, the validator commits his encrypted identity $(C_{id}, Cert_{IP})$ to the blockchain network. A validator will be successfully registered with his account and identity (y, C_{id}) if the certificate from the identity provider is valid.

Notice that during this process, the validator's identity is only revealed to the identity provider or protected inside the e-Identity card. Therefore, committed identities do not violate nodes' privacy. Note that we do not restrict the way how a node looks up registered validators. We can achieve this either by introducing a trusted CA service in the blockchain to verify the committed identities and issue certificates for these validators, or each node can locally perform the validation.

Block Generation and Validation: The block generation and validation process is similar to Nxt's PoS as described in Sect. 2.1. Miners have to first create an eligibility proof Prf_e to check their eligibility of generating the current block. Subsequently, a block signature Sig_b is included in the created block to authenticate the validator.

In our protocol, in order to prevent a malicious node from signing conflicting blocks, validators construct the eligibility proof and the block signature as follows: a validator first generates the randomness k and $r = g^k$ (cf. Algorithm 2), along with the proof of knowledge $C_k, C_a, \pi_1, \pi_2, [\langle C_r^i, \pi_r^i \rangle]$ that k and r are correctly computed. Here, π_1 is a proof of knowledge of equality of discrete logarithm constructed from the Schnorr Proof of Knowledge as described in [5]. This allows us to prove that e.g., two elements $y_1 = g^a$ and $y_2 = h^a$ have the same discrete logarithm a without revealing a. We describe the non-interactive variant of this proof of knowledge in Algorithm 1. $[\langle C_r^i, \pi_r^i \rangle]$ is standard proof of knowledge with probabilistic result. We skip the details of how to construct π_2 as it is standard Schnorr Proof of Knowledge.

Algorithm 1. Proof of knowledge of the same discrete logarithm

---

Input: $y_1 = g^a$ and $y_2 = h^a$ where a is not revealed.
Output: A proof s that y_1 and y_2 have the same discrete log a.
1: $r \xleftarrow{\mathcal{R}} \mathbb{Z}_q^*$
2: $t_1 \leftarrow g^r$
3: $t_2 \leftarrow h^r$
4: $c \leftarrow H(t_1 \| t_2)$
5: $s \leftarrow r - c \cdot a \mod q$
6: Send s to the verifier
    ▷ Verifier accepts if $g^s \cdot y_1^c = t_1$ and $h^s \cdot y_2^c = t_2$

Subsequently, we use k and r to create the eligibility proof $Prf_e = Hash(r, y, Prf_e^{(H-1)})$. If the validator is eligible to generate the next block, the block signature is computed as follows: $Sig_b = Sign(x, blkheader) = (r, s)$.

To validate a block, nodes first verify the proof of knowledge to see if the block signature uses the correct randomness r given the block height H. Then, the block signature is verified similarly to the DSA signature verification process. Finally, the eligibility proof is checked against the IsEligible predicate function.

In case of forks, the resolution algorithm is similar to that of Nxt. Namely, each block contains a value of cumulative difficulty and nodes will adopt the fork chain that has accrued the largest cumulative difficulty (cf. Sect. 2.1).

3.3 Security Analysis

To show the security of our protocol, it suffices to show that a node can reveal the identity of a malicious validator based on his block signatures on conflicting blocks and all nodes are able to verify whether the block signatures are correctly constructed. Notice that since the nodes' private keys are bound to their identity, nodes will protect (e.g., they will not sell) their unused accounts—thus alleviating long-range attacks.

Algorithm 2. Generate k and r used for block signature

Input: Block height H, key pair (x, y')
Output: DSA randomness k, r, and the proof of knowledge $C_k, C_a, \pi_1, \pi_2, [\langle C_r^i, \pi_r^i \rangle]$

1: $k \leftarrow a^{\frac{1}{H+x}} \mod q$ ▷ random function on H
2: $r_0 \xleftarrow{\mathcal{R}} \mathbb{Z}_w$
3: $C_k \leftarrow k \cdot h^{r_0} \mod q$ ▷ commit to k
4: $C_a \leftarrow (C_k)^{H+x} \mod q$
5: $\pi_1 \leftarrow$ PK of same discrete log on C_a and $a^{H+x} = a^H \cdot y'$
      ▷ C_a is correctly computed as C_k^{H+x}
6: $\pi_2 \leftarrow$ Schnorr PK on $C_a \cdot a^{-1} = h^{r_0 \cdot (H+x)}$
      ▷ k is correctly computed as $a^{\frac{1}{H+x}}$

◇ π_1, π_2: VRF proof of k masked by r_0

7: $r \leftarrow (g^k \mod p) \mod q$
8: **for** $i \leftarrow 1$ to n **do**
9:     $r_1^i \xleftarrow{\mathcal{R}} \mathbb{Z}_w$
10:    $C_r^i \leftarrow H(r^{h^{r_0 + r_1^i}} \mod p)$ ▷ commit to r_1^i
11: **end for**
12: $challenge \leftarrow H(C_r^1 || \ldots || C_r^n)$
13: **for** $i \leftarrow 1$ to n **do**
14:     **if** bit i of $challenge == 0$ **then**
15:        $\pi_r^i \leftarrow r_0 + r_1^i \mod w$ ▷ verify if $C_r^i = H(r^{h^{\pi_r^i}})$
16:     **else**
17:        $\pi_r^i \leftarrow r_1^i$ ▷ verify if $C_r^i = H(g^{C_k \cdot h^{\pi_r^i}})$
18:     **end if**
19: **end for**

◇ π_r^i: proof that $r = g^k$ with high probability

We first show that the block signatures generated by a malicious validator $M_{\mathcal{A}}$ on different blocks with the same block height H will recover the validator's private key, and therefore reveal his committed identity.

According to the construction of the block signature (r, s), r is deterministic and only depends on the value of the block height H and the validator's private key x. In other words, if $M_{\mathcal{A}}$ generates multiple blocks at the same height, the block signature component r will be the same. According to the DSA signature scheme, this will allow anyone to recover the validator's private key x from two signatures (r, s) and (r, s'). Since validator's identity is encrypted by his public key and committed to the network (cf. Identity Management in Sect. 3.2), any node that has recovered a validator's private key is able to reveal the corresponding identity. As a result, our block signature scheme discourages the validators from creating conflicting blocks. In addition, the proof of knowledge which comes along with the block signature proves that k and r are computed correctly according to the VRF function (cf. Algorithm 2 line 1) without revealing the value of k.

We use multiple proof of knowledge (PK) schemes to achieve this. First, the PK of equality of discrete logarithm π_1 proves that C_a is indeed C_k to the power of $(H + x)$ with the help of a^{H+x}. Then, the Schnorr PK π_2 (cf. line 4) together with π_1 proves that k is correctly computed as $a^{\frac{1}{H+x}}$. This is because if $C_a \cdot a^{-1}$ cannot cancel out a, then the prover is not able to know the discrete logarithm of $h^{r_0 \cdot (H+x)}$. Finally, based on the standard PK $[\langle C_r^i, \pi_r^i \rangle]$, the validator proves that r is correctly computed from k with the help of the committed value C_k, for $r^{h^{r_0}} = g^{C_k}$. Here, the proof of knowledge is repeated n times (line 13–19) that can prevent cheating with a high probability of $P = 1 - 2^{-n}$.

We also point out that the identity of an honest node will not be revealed, as there is at most one signature per block height, thus the randomness of the DSA signature is chosen securely. It is straightforward to show that if the attacker is able to retrieve the identity of an honest node, he has to acquire the private key of the node based on the DSA signatures.

Notice that according to [5], the VRF function $a^{\frac{1}{H+x}}$ outputs an unpredictable random number, therefore k can be used as the randomness for the DSA signature. Moreover, DSA also requires that the value of k should never be revealed. Our proof of knowledge schemes guarantee that the verifiers do not have the knowledge of k.

Finally, our eligibility proof is computed based on the randomness component r used in the block signature. This modification allows the eligibility proof remain deterministic as our r is constructed deterministically given a certain block height; moreover, it eliminates the problem of transparent forging (i.e., forger of each block is predictable in the network) as r is also unpredictable. Compared to Ouroboros [11], our construction achieves *grinding*-resilience without requiring the validators to coordinate in the network.

4   TEE-Based PoS

In the previous section, we introduced a solution that strongly penalizes misbehavior by exposing the identities of validators. Although this solution can indeed deter misbehavior of the rational nodes in the network, it requires the reliance on an identity provider. In this section, we introduce another PoS protocol that drops this requirement and leverages Trusted Execution Environments (TEEs) to enforce security.

4.1   Protocol Specification

Specification of the Setup Stage: We require all validators in the network to be equipped with secure hardware to run trusted applications within TEE. TEEs are pervasive nowadays and supported by many commodity platforms. For instance, Intel's SGX is being deployed on PCs and servers, while mobile platforms are mostly supported by ARM's Trustzone. TEEs define an isolated environment running in parallel with the rich operating system. They additionally provide standard cryptographic functionalities and restrict the memory access from the hosting OS—thus ensuring secure execution for the code running inside TEE.

We require that the eligibility proof and the block signature (cf. Sect. 2.1) are generated by a trusted application within TEE. We denote it in the following as the *trusted application*. To enforce this requirement, the validators need to prove to the network that they are hosting legitimate trusted application for block signing and their account keys are protected by the TEE and not accessible from outside of TEE. This can be achieved by distributing the trusted application as part of the client wallet application when nodes first join the network; and the account key pairs are only generated inside the TEE during the application initialization. The validators should also allow remote attestation for other nodes to verify the integrity of the deployed trusted application. Here, we require the platform certificates of validators' secure hardware to be publicly verifiable.

PoS Protocol Specification: The main intuition behind our solution is to use the trusted application to restrict the signing operations on the blocks. More specifically, we rely on TEE's monotonic counter to guarantee that there will be at most one block generated at each height of the block chain; recall that monotonic counters refer to increase-only registers that are resilient by design to replay attacks.

In our trusted application, we track the block height information of each signing request using monotonic counters. More specifically, we reserve two registers in the trusted application CTR_{ep} and CTR_{bs} which are implemented using monotonic counters. CTR_{ep} tracks the block height value submitted by the eligibility proof requests, while CTR_{bs} tracks the block height value submitted by the block signature requests.

To construct an eligibility proof, the validator submits the eligibility proof of the previous block along with the block height H of the current block to the trusted application. The latter checks whether $CTR_{ep} < H$; if so, the validator computes the eligibility proof as follows: $Prf_e = Sign(\text{``}ep\text{''}, x, H, Prf_e^{(H-1)})$, where x is the validator's private key; otherwise the request will be rejected. Meanwhile, the trusted application updates its register CTR_{ep} with the height information H. If validator's eligibility proof is lower than the target (cf. Eq. 1), the validator is eligible to generate the next block and becomes a *leader*. The validator can therefore submit a request of block signature to the trusted application with the information of the block header[1]. Similarly, the trusted application checks if $CTR_{bs} < H$ is true, then a block signature is returned to the validator as $Sig_b = Sign(\text{``}bs\text{''}, x, blkhdr)$, and the register CTR_{bs} is updated. The block validation process is similar as in Nxt (cf. Sect. 2.1). Nodes first verify if the signatures are correct. Then, they check if the validator is eligible to generate the block given the eligibility proof in his block. Similarly, we keep the fork resolution algorithm the same as Identity-based PoS. Figure 1a depicts the interaction between the validator's wallet application (which is untrusted) and the trusted application for block signature. Here, a signing request with increasing block

---

[1] The block height value is included in the block header.

height can be processed successfully while a request with the same or smaller block height will be rejected.

Protecting against Chain Switching: Notice that this aforementioned process does not restrict the validators to only work on one particular fork of the block chain. For example, while it is prohibited that a validator generates a block at height H on both fork F and F', it is allowed that a validator generates a block at height H on fork F and later on at height $H + 1$ on fork F'. The validators are allowed to do so as in some cases they might initially work on a wrong fork (i.e., that differs from the output of the fork resolution algorithm) because of network partitioning; therefore the validators are allowed to later switch to work on another fork.

In other cases when the blockchain is able to define a *correct* chain to work on, we should further restrict the node to only work on one fork and cannot switch to other forks. To enforce this requirement, we extend our protocol to identify a fork by tracking the blocks of the fork. Specifically, we reserve a register H_{fork} in the trusted application to keep the accumulated hash of all the confirmed blocks of a fork that the validator submits in the block signature requests. This accumulated hash can uniquely identify a fork as it contains the information of all the confirmed blocks in the fork.

To generate the block signature, the validator submits block headers $[blkhdr_m, \ldots, blkhdr_n]$ that were confirmed since the last block signature request to the trusted application. The latter computes and updates the accumulated hash as $H_{fork}^{(n)} = H(\ldots (H(H_{fork}^{(m-1)}, blkhdr_m), \ldots, blkhdr_n)$. This value is then included in the block signature, so that all nodes in the network are able to verify it: $Sig_b = Sign(\text{``bs''}, x, H_{fork}, blkhdr_{n+1})$.

Figure 1b depicts an example where the validator requests the block signature to the trusted application. Here, we assume that the last signed block is at height $H = 3$. We also assume there are two forks F with blocks $[blk_1, blk_2, blk_3, blk_4, blk_5]$ and F' with blocks $[blk_1, blk_2, blk_3, blk_4', blk_5']$. In the first attempt, the validator submits a signing request for fork F at height $H = 5$. The validator sends the confirmed blocks since the last signing request blk_3 and blk_4 along with the request. To this point, the trusted application records the accumulated hash of fork F up to blk_4. In the second request, the validator switches to another fork F' and requests a block signature at height $H = 6$. Block blk_5' is sent to the trusted application along with the request. As a result, the trusted application updates the register H_{fork} to include blk_5' and adds this value to the block signature. However, this block signature will not be accepted by the network, since H_{fork}' identifies a fork composed by non-existing blocks $[blk_1, blk_2, blk_3, blk_4, blk_5']$.

4.2   Security Analysis

Notice that the account private keys are protected by the TEE, which prevents an adversary from acquiring additional accounts to mount long-range attacks. Therefore, to prove that our TEE-based PoS is secure, it suffices to show that:

(i) a validator is unable to acquire more than one eligibility proof or block signature for a block at a certain height, and *(ii)* a validator is unable to acquire valid block signatures for blocks on other forks if a validator has already worked on a different fork.

We first show that validators can only acquire at most one eligibility proof or block signature for a block at a certain height. Since the account keys are unique and protected by the trusted application whose integrity is attested by the network, no one can generate a valid eligibility proof or block signature except the trusted application (recall that we assume that the adversary cannot compromise the TEE). For each signature request, the trusted application will first compare the block height with what was signed last time before advancing the monotonic counter. The TEE's monotonic counter guarantees that the recorded block height value is never repeated: an attacker can neither restart the counter nor replay a previous block height value. Therefore, TEE-based PoS ensures that a validator has only one chance to create an eligibility proof or a block signature for a block at a certain height. This additionally prevents a malicious validator from exhaustively searching the space of valid eligibility proof by changing the volatile fields of a block such as the transactions set and the timestamp. Moreover, recall that the forger of each block is predictable in the original Nxt's PoS. Here, we use digital signatures to generate eligibility proofs in an unpredictable manner—thus eliminating the problem of transparent forging.

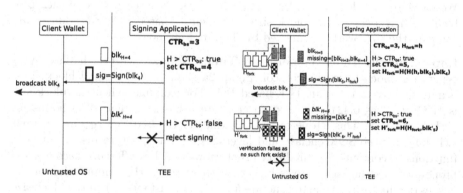

Fig. 1. (a) Misbehaved validator requests to sign the second block for another fork. (b) Misbehaved validator requests to sign the second block for another fork.

We further show that our protocol extension prevents validators from generating blocks for different forks. Suppose any two forks $fork$ and $fork'$ contain two different confirmed blocks blk_m and blk'_m at height m. Given the previous guarantee, a validator can only generate one block signature for blocks at height m. We assume it is block blk_m and therefore blk_m is included in the register value H_{fork}. Later on, the validator would like to generate a block for $fork'$ at height n. However, since blk'_m can never be included in H_{fork} (as blk_m is already included in H_{fork}), the validator cannot generate a valid block signature that includes the information blk'_m for fork $fork'$, which is required for successful block validation.

5   Performance Evaluation

We implemented both PoS variants as well as Nxt's PoS protocol [21]. To ensure a fair comparison, we use in our implementation the same block structure as in Nxt; our protocols only differ in the algorithms to compute and verify a block.

5.1   Experimental Setup

Our implementation is based on Golang. We use Intel SGX to provide hardware security support and implement the trusted application of TEE-based PoS as an SGX enclave. In all solutions, we use SHA256 as the hash function. For Identity-based PoS, we implement our own DSA signature scheme for the block signature with security parameters of 256-bit w, 2048-bit q, 2072-bit p, and $n = 80$ challenges for the proof of knowledge; for TEE-based PoS, we use 256-bit ECDSA as the signature scheme.

We deploy our validator on a server equipped with 8-Core Intel Xeon E3-1240 and 32 GB RAM. We vary the block size[2] from 1 KB to 1000 KB and measure the performance of signing and verifying a block.

5.2   Performance Evaluation

We measure the block generation time and block verification time of each protocol with respect to the block size. For Identity-based PoS, we additionally compare the size overhead induced by the proof of knowledge.

Impact on the Block Generation Time: We first measure the latency to generate a block for each protocol. Figure 2a shows that for small block sizes, Nxt is slightly faster than TEE-based PoS. For example, when the block size is 1KB, it takes 0.42 ms for Nxt to generate a block, compared to 1.7 ms for TEE-based PoS. This is due to the fact that TEE-based PoS requires context switching for the SGX enclave and leverages digital signature instead of hash functions to compute the eligibility proof. However, this difference becomes less pronounced as the block grows bigger; in these cases, the computation of the hashes dominates the time to generate a block. For instance, when the block size is as big as 500 KB, the block generation time for TEE-based PoS is equivalent to Nxt's (cf. Fig. 2c).

While TEE-based PoS is almost as efficient as Nxt, the block generation process is however slower for Identity-based PoS. Even for small block sizes of 1 KB, Identity-based PoS requires 548 ms to generate a block. This overhead is mostly due to the generation of the proof of knowledge for the block signature; in this case, approximately 98% of the time is consumed in the generation of the proof. In addition, the size of the block header also increases dramatically due to the data field of the employed proof of knowledge schemes; the size grows to 19 KB for Identity-based PoS compared to only 200 B for Nxt.

---

[2] We denote block size as size of the transaction set.

Impact on the Block Verification Time: We now assess the impact of our protocols on the resulting block verification process. Our evaluation results are depicted in Fig. 2a and d.

Our results show that TEE-based PoS and Nxt require almost identical block verification times. For instance, when the block size is 1 KB, TEE-based PoS requires 0.34 ms while Nxt takes 0.28 ms. Recall that signature verification does not need to be performed inside the SGX enclave—which explains the comparable verification time for block signature. However, verifying eligibility proof is slightly slower in TEE-based PoS, as the eligibility proof used in TEE-based PoS consists of a digital signature rather than a cryptographic hash.

As expected, the block verification for Identity-based PoS incurs considerable verification times as the operation to verify the proof of knowledge is time consuming; our results show that it takes 772 ms to verify the proof of knowledge. For block sizes of 1000 KB, this sums up to 870 ms to verify a block, which is almost 8 times slower than Nxt.

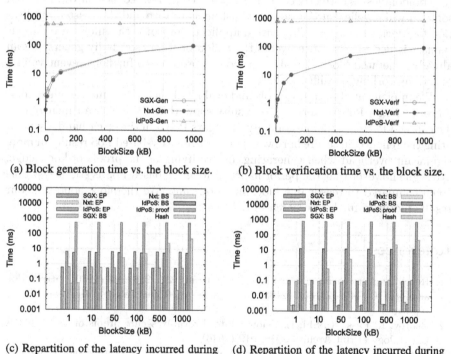

(a) Block generation time vs. the block size.

(b) Block verification time vs. the block size.

(c) Repartition of the latency incurred during the block generation.

(d) Repartition of the latency incurred during the block verification.

Fig. 2. Performance evaluation results. Each data point in our plots is averaged over 4000 independent measurements; where appropriate, we include the corresponding 95% confidence interval. EP stands for eligibility proof, BS for block signature, proof for proof of knowledge, and Hash for hash over the transaction set.

6 Conclusion

Although a number of PoS consensus protocols have been proposed for open blockchain platforms in the past five years, these protocols still suffer from a number of security shortcomings which prevents their large scale adoption in existing open blockchains.

In this paper, we propose two PoS protocols that are secure against a number of threats including the nothing at stake attack and long range attack. The idea of both protocols is to restrict the validators to generate at most one block at a given block height. Our first protocol is a software-based solution with an enhanced signature scheme which binds the randomness of the signature to the block height value. Signing multiple blocks at the same height will thus reveal validator's private key as well as his identity. The limitation of this approach, however, is the storage and computation overhead, as the block header needs to include extra information over the proof of knowledge to verify that the signature randomness is correctly computed. Our second protocol is a hardware-based solution which relies on the tamper-resistant hardware and the trusted application for block generation. The trusted application records the information about the last issued blocks and prevents the validator from repeatedly generating an already generated block. We also extend our protocol to further prevent validators from working on different forks.

We implemented both protocols and evaluated their performance when compared to Nxt's PoS protocol. Our results show that the overhead incurred by TEE-based PoS is negligible compared to Nxt's PoS. On the other hand, by obviating the reliance on secure hardware support, Identity-based PoS results in more significant overhead when generating and verifying of the proofs of knowledge. We argue however that the performance of Identity-based PoS is still acceptable when compared to reasonable block creation time. We therefore hope that our results motivate further research in this area.

References

1. Reaching Agreement in the Presence of Faults **27**, 228–234 (1980). http://doi.acm.org/10.1145/322186.322188%5Cndl.acm.org/ft_gateway.cfm?id=322188&type=pdf
2. Bentov, I., Pass, R., Shi, E.: Snow white: Provably secure proofs of stake. IACR Cryptology ePrint Archive 2016, 919 (2016)
3. Buterin, V.: Slasher: A punitive proof-of-stake algorithm. https://blog.ethereum.org/2014/01/15/slasher-a-punitive-proof-of-stake-algorithm/. Accessed June 2017
4. Buterin, V.: Validator ordering and randomness in pos. http://vitalik.ca/files/randomness.html
5. Camenisch, J., Michels, M.: Proving in zero-knowledge that a number is the product of two safe primes. In: Stern, J. (ed.) EUROCRYPT 1999. LNCS, vol. 1592, pp. 107–122. Springer, Heidelberg (1999). doi:10.1007/3-540-48910-X_8
6. Chen, J., Micali, S.: Algorand: the efficient and democratic ledger. arXiv preprint arxiv:1607.01341 (2016)

7. Cloak posa v3.0 - a trustless, anonymous transaction system for cloakcoin. https://bravenewcoin.com/assets/Whitepapers/CloakCoin-posa3wp.pdf. Accessed June 2017

8. Dodis, Y., Yampolskiy, A.: A verifiable random function with short proofs and keys. In: Vaudenay, S. (ed.) PKC 2005. LNCS, vol. 3386, pp. 416–431. Springer, Heidelberg (2005). doi:10.1007/978-3-540-30580-4_28

9. Gilad, Y., Hemo, R., Micali, S., Vlachos, G., Zeldovich, N.: Algorand: scaling byzantine agreements for cryptocurrencies. https://people.csail.mit.edu/nickolai/papers/gilad-algorand-eprint.pdf

10. Ethereum - prrof of stake faq - how does validator selection work, and what is stake grinding? https://github.com/ethereum/wiki/wiki/Proof-of-Stake-FAQ#how-does-validator-selection-work-and-what-is-stake-grinding

11. Kiayias, A., Russell, A., David, B., Oliynykov, R.: Ouroboros: a provably secure proof-of-stake blockchain protocol. Technical report, Cryptology ePrint Archive, Report 2016/889, 2016 (2016). http://eprint.iacr.org/2016/889

12. King, S., Nadal, S.: Ppcoin: Peer-to-peer crypto-currency with proof-of-stake (2012). https://peercoin.net/assets/paper/peercoin-paper.pdf. Accessed June 2017

13. Micali, S., Rabin, M., Vadhan, S.: Verifiable random functions. In: 40th Annual Symposium on Foundations of Computer Science, pp. 120–130. IEEE (1999)

14. Non-interactive zero-knowledge proof. https://en.wikipedia.org/wiki/Non-interactive_zero-knowledge_proof. Accessed June 2017

15. Novacoin - proof of stake. https://github.com/novacoin-project/novacoin/wiki/Proof-of-stake. Accessed June 2017

16. O'Dwyer, K.J., Malone, D.: Bitcoin mining and its energy footprint (2014)

17. Pike, D., Nosker, P., Boehm, D., Grisham, D., Woods, S., Marston, J.: Proof-of-stake-time whitepaper. https://www.vericoin.info/downloads/VeriCoinPoSTWhitePaper10May2015.pdf. Accessed June 2017

18. Schuh, F., Larimer, D.: Bitshares 2.0: General overview. http://docs.bitshares.org/_downloads/bitshares-general.pdf. Accessed June 2017

19. Vasin, P.: Blackcoin's proof-of-stake protocol v2. https://blackcoin.co/blackcoin-pos-protocol-v2-whitepaper.pdf. Accessed June 2017

20. Kravitz, D.W.: Digital signature algorithm (1993). US Patent 5,231,668

21. Wiki, N.: Whitepaper: nxt – nxt wiki (2016). https://nxtwiki.org/mediawiki/index.php?title=Whitepaper:Nxt. Accessed June 2017

22. Zamfir, V.: Introducing casper the friendly ghost. https://blog.ethereum.org/2015/08/01/introducing-casper-friendly-ghost/. Accessed June 2017

Merged Mining: Curse or Cure?

Aljosha Judmayer(✉), Alexei Zamyatin(✉), Nicholas Stifter(✉),
Artemios G. Voyiatzis, and Edgar Weippl

SBA Research, Vienna, Austria
{ajudmayer,azamyatin,nstifter,avoyiatzis,eweippl}@sba-research.org

Abstract. *Merged mining* refers to the concept of mining more than one cryptocurrency without necessitating additional proof-of-work effort. Although merged mining has been adopted by a number of cryptocurrencies already, to this date little is known about the effects and implications. We shed light on this topic area by performing a comprehensive analysis of merged mining in practice. As part of this analysis, we present a block attribution scheme for mining pools to assist in the evaluation of mining centralization. Our findings disclose that mining pools in merge-mined cryptocurrencies have operated at the edge of, and even beyond, the security guarantees offered by the underlying Nakamoto consensus for extended periods. We discuss the implications and security considerations for these cryptocurrencies and the mining ecosystem as a whole, and link our findings to the intended effects of merged mining.

1 Introduction

The topic of merged mining has received little attention from the scientific community, despite having been actively employed by a number of cryptocurrencies for several years. New and emerging cryptocurrencies such as *Rootstock* continue to consider and expand on the concept of merged mining in their designs to this day [19]. *Merged mining* refers to the process of searching for proof-of-work (PoW) solutions for multiple cryptocurrencies concurrently without requiring additional computational resources. The rationale behind merged mining lies in leveraging on the computational power of different cryptocurrencies by bundling their resources instead of having them stand in direct competition, and also to serve as a bootstrapping mechanism for small and fledgling networks [27,33].

In the past, concerns have been voiced that merged mining could lead to additional security risks and challenges [27]. In particular, the realistic threat of network centralization has rendered merged mining a controversial topic. Ali et al. [1] observed a critical level of mining centralization in the merge-mined cryptocurrency *Namecoin*, concluding that merged mining is failing in practice. These alarming findings were not the result of direct investigations into merged mining itself, but rather emerged as part of a report on the experiences with the real-world deployment of a decentralized PKI service on top of the Namecoin blockchain. Hence, an in-depth analysis of merge-mined cryptocurrencies based on real-world data is necessary to determine if such observed failures in practical applications are systemic to the underlying concept of merged mining.

© Springer International Publishing AG 2017
J. Garcia-Alfaro et al. (Eds.): DPM/CBT 2017, LNCS 10436, pp. 316–333, 2017.
DOI: 10.1007/978-3-319-67816-0_18

In this paper we conduct the first extensive study on the impacts of merged mining on individual cryptocurrencies. We discuss security implications and considerations regarding merged mining, while relating previous arguments from [27] to the results of our study. We seek to provide empirical evidence either confirming or falsifying these arguments and extend the discussion by providing ideas and examples for future experiments, which can lead to a better understanding and classification of merged mining.

To cover a broad spectrum of merge-mined cryptocurrencies we analyzed two established players and pioneers of the field, namely Namecoin and Dogecoin, as well as two relatively young merge-mined cryptocurrencies supporting merged mining with more than one PoW algorithm, namely Huntercoin [14] and Myriadcoin [23]. Thereby, we present the following contributions:

- We analyze the effects and implications of merged mining in four cryptocurrencies over time and comment on its adoption, the related difficulty increase, as well as other characteristic patterns.
- We introduce a deterministic mapping scheme that attributes blocks to specific miners and mining pools.
- We provide empirical evidence for centralization risks in cryptocurrencies involved in merged mining. Furthermore, we are successful in attributing merged mining activity to an apparently small set of mining pools.
- Concluding, we discuss the related security implications for cryptocurrencies implementing merged mining.

The remainder of this paper is structured as follows. Section 2 provides the necessary background information on fundamental concepts regarding proof-of-work based cryptocurrencies and merged mining. Section 3 describes the cryptocurrencies considered in our study as well as the experimental methodology. Section 4 presents the results of our empirical analysis. In Sect. 5, we discuss the security implications in relation to established claims and theoretical arguments regarding merged mining. Furthermore, we propose new research questions and conclude the paper in Sect. 6, pointing out interesting directions for future work.

2 Background

A key aspect of Bitcoin constitutes its novel distributed consensus mechanism, generally termed *Nakamoto consensus*. It leverages on proof-of-work (PoW) puzzles and the *blockchain* data structure to achieve eventual agreement on the set and ordering of transactions by an anonymous and changing set of participants. Nakamoto consensus thereby facilitates decentralized or so-called *permissionless* cryptocurrencies. The process by which consensus participants in proof-of-work cryptocurrencies search for valid PoW puzzle solutions is referred to as *mining* and the speed at which such *miners* find solution candidates for the PoW is called *hash rate*.

While efforts towards replacing the resource-intensive mining process have so far yielded various promising approaches such as [5,18,22], their viability in practice is yet to be tested at a larger scale. Furthermore, due to the high degree of adoption of proof-of-work in various cryptocurrencies and the difficulties related to changing this consensus critical component, it can be assumed that PoW will remain an integral part of the overall cryptocurrency landscape in the foreseeable future.

2.1   Attacks on the PoW Security Model

The security properties of PoW cryptocurrencies are derived from the assumption that the majority of the overall mining power belongs to honest miners. Early work in Bitcoin security modeling concluded that the mining power of all the honest miners has to be strictly greater than 50% to sustain the security of the blockchain [24,31]. Should adversaries accumulate the majority of mining power, they can control the insertion of new transactions, the transaction fee market, and the supply of newly-mined coins, as well as potentially revert already recorded transactions.

Attack strategies which can be successful even without controlling the majority of mining power, most notably *selfish mining* [10,32] and *eclipse* attacks [12,13,28] have been the topic of recent work. The success probability of such adversarial strategies depends on the mining power share (α), as well as the network connectivity (γ) of the adversary [10,28]. While a poorly connected attacker ($\gamma \approx 0.1$) is shown to require $\alpha > 0.33$ to successfully perform selfish mining attacks, an adversary connected to half of the nodes in the network ($\gamma \approx 0.5$) only requires $\alpha > 0.25$. Hence, in a conservative analysis, successful attacks on PoW cryptocurrencies are more likely when dishonest entities control more than 25% of the total mining power.

2.2   Merged Mining

Merged mining refers to the process of reusing (partial) PoW solutions from a *parent* cryptocurrency as valid proofs-of-work for one or more *child* cryptocurrencies. It was introduced as a solution to the fragmentation of mining power among competing cryptocurrencies and as a bootstrapping mechanism for small networks. Merged mining was first implemented in Namecoin in 2011, with Bitcoin acting as the parent cryptocurrency. One of the earliest descriptions of the mechanism as it is used today was presented by Satoshi Nakamoto in [33]. Apart from the source code of the respective cryptocurrencies implementing merged mining, a detailed technical explanation is presented in the Bitcoin Wiki [25].

The general idea of reusing proof-of-work such that the computational effort invested may also serve to verify a separate computation was first introduced by Jakobsson and Juels under the term *bread pudding protocols* in 1999 [15]. Previous research related to merged mining is mostly limited to the application layer of the underlying cryptocurrencies. A short description of merged mining is provided by Kalodner et al. in an empirical study of name squatting in Namecoin [16]. Ali et al. highlights that Namecoin suffers from centralization issues linked to merged mining, but provides no detailed study on the extent of the problem, nor on merged mining in general [1]. Other descriptions of and references to merged mining can be found in [2,11,27], whereas [4,19] seek to employ merged mining as a component of various blockchain-based applications.

For a cryptocurrency to allow merged mining the parent blockchain must fulfill just one requirement: it must be possible to include arbitrary[1] data within the input over which the proof-of-work in the parent is established. The main protocol logic of merged mining resides in (i) the specification and preparation of the data linked to (or included in) the block header of the parent, e.g., a hash of the child block header, and (ii) the implementation of the verification logic in the client of the child blockchain.

2.3 Mining Pools

To generate a constant stream of revenue, miners may team up and form so called *mining pools*, where they bundle their resources and share the rewards based on their contribution and according to the rules of the pool. A mining pool can be described as a *"pool manager and a cohort of miners"* [9]. To compensate the administrative effort, the mining pool keeps a small proportion of the total revenue as a fee[2]. Different reward distribution policies and related game-theoretic aspects are studied in [20,30,34]. Optimal strategies for mining pools in the context of adversarial behavior are discussed in [9,28,32]. Pool managers can have the ability to maliciously mislead their miners into participating in attacks, as happened in the case of Eligius (See Footnote 9). Although doing so might result in miners switching to another pool once they learn about the attack. The delay of these consequences however might be enough for the pool to complete the attack.

3 Methodology

In this paper we consider the following subset of cryptocurrencies exemplary for merged mining. Bitcoin, the first and currently largest cryptocurrency based on a SHA256 PoW, serves as a starting point of our analysis and acts as one of the two parent blockchains for merged mining we consider. Litecoin [21] is a fork of Bitcoin, which replaces SHA256 with the memory-hard *Scrypt* cryptographic hash function in its PoW algorithm. Litecoin's primary aim was to counter the domination of *ASICs*, i.e., hardware devices specifically-built for high-performance SHA256 hashing operations, in Bitcoin. At the time of writing it is the largest Scrypt PoW cryptocurrency.

Namecoin [26], which intends to provide a decentralized and censorship resistant alternative to the Domain Name System (DNS), was the first alternative cryptocurrency and the first blockchain to introduce merged mining, in this case with Bitcoin. While its design is heavily based on Bitcoin, Namecoin extends

---

[1] In practice, being able to include the output of a cryptographically secure hash function can be considered sufficient space.

[2] Usually between 1 and 5%.

the underlying protocol by introducing new *transaction types*, which enable the storage and management of additional information in the blockchain (e.g., DNS entries). Dogecoin [8] initially started as a non-serious project based on an internet meme but was able to attract and maintain a vivid community. It is roughly based on the Litecoin codebase and was the first cryptocurrency to introduce Scrypt-based merged mining with Litecoin.

A new generation of so called *multi-PoW* cryptocurrencies was marked by the introduction of Huntercoin [14] which supports SHA256 and Scrypt. Another notable pioneer in this field is Myriadcoin [23], maintaining five different PoW algorithms in parallel. The concept of multi-PoW aims to provide resistance to mining centralization by including different types of proof-of-work in a single cryptocurrency. Huntercoin and Myriadcoin furthermore are the first *multi-merge-mined* cryptocurrencies, as they allow merged mining with multiple parent chains, namely Bitcoin and Litecoin.

3.1   Data Set Collection

For our analysis we rely on the open and publicly-accessible ledgers (i.e., blockchains) of the examined cryptocurrencies, as they represent the most reliable source of information with regards to historical data[3]. The results presented in the rest of this paper are based on data collected from Bitcoin, Litecoin, Namecoin, Dogecoin, Huntercoin and Myriadcoin up to a cut-off date set to June 18, 2017 23:59:59 (UTC), i.e., Block 471,892 in Bitcoin, 347,175 in Namecoin, 1,224,533 in Litecoin, 1,763,524 in Dogecoin, 1,788,998 in Huntercoin and 2,089,974 in Myriadcoin.

3.2   Block Attribution Scheme

A key element for the investigation of mining power centralization issues is a correct attribution of blocks to the original miners. Hence, we devise an attribution scheme using publicly-available information contained in the *coinbase transactions* of both the parent and child blockchains as indicators. Thereby we rely on the following fields:

Reward payout addresses. The *coinbase transaction* represents the first transaction in a block and creates new currency units as reward for its miner. Assuming miners act rationally and profit-oriented, they are expected to specify one of their own addresses as output of this transaction. Hence, the reward payout addresses of blocks can be used as strong indicator in the attribution scheme.

Coinbase signatures (markers). Miners and especially mining pools often utilize the `coinbase` field of the coinbase transaction to publicly claim the creation of the respective block, by inserting their so-called *block-* or *coinbase signature*. As the latter represents a human-readable string indicating the pool name or

---

[3] While some public APIs are available for Bitcoin (e.g., http://blockchain.info/), online sources the other cryptocurrencies are scarce and not well-maintained.

an abbreviation thereof, rather than a cryptographically-strong signature, we hereafter refer to this piece of information as *marker*.

Collecting and Linking Markers and Addresses. At the time of writing there exists no global registry for markers or reward payout addresses of miners or mining pools[4]. Therefore, this information must be collected by analysis of publicly-available records including but not limited to websites of mining pools and discussion forums, as well as direct contacts with pool operators. As an outcome of this process, we are able to compile a list of block attribution indicators for 95 miners and mining pools, which operated in the observed cryptocurrencies.

Merge-mined blocks can contain up to four attribution indicators: the coinbase marker and reward payout addresses of the child chain, as well as the coinbase marker and reward payout addresses of the parent chain, which are stored in the so called *AuxPoW* header[5]. This allows to establish connections between reward payout addresses across multiple cryptocurrencies and to detect if miners switch between multiple addresses. Hence, reward payout addresses appearing in parent and child coinbase transactions of all blocks are checked for intersections. More specific: an address of the parent chain appearing in the coinbase of the AuxPow header allows to link it to the child chain address used in the coinbase transaction of the block. The child chain address in turn can appear in blocks together with other parent chain addresses, creating more links, and so on.

Attributing Blocks to Miners. A block is considered attributed to a miner if one of his markers or reward payout addresses appears in the respective fields of the coinbase transaction. However, a miner is technically allowed to use this first transaction to immediately split the block rewards to multiple outputs, this way also potentially obfuscating his identity. It is not easily possible to determine the miner of a block, unless a known coinbase marker is used or all addresses appearing in the outputs of the coinbase transaction are associated with the same miner or mining pool. If this is the case, the block is marked as *non-attributable*. A visualization of the scheme for merge-mined blockchains is provided in Fig. 1. Payout addresses appearing often in mined blocks but which cannot be linked to an identified miner or mining pool are denoted as *other unknown miners*.

However, for a permissionless proof-of-work cryptocurrency, where participants are not obliged to disclose their activity, it is not feasible for a third party to fully reconstruct a miner's history of action retroactively. Furthermore, miners may actively try to hide their identity by avoiding the reuse of payout addresses, not using any markers or using markers associated with other identities. Hence,

---

[4] To the best of our knowledge, the most detailed list of Bitcoin mining pools can be found here: github.com/blockchain/Blockchain-Known-Pools/blob/master/pools.json.

[5] Additional header in merge-mined blocks, used to verify the PoW performed in the parent chain.

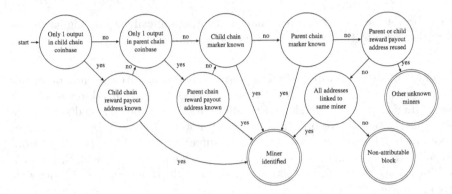

Fig. 1. Block attribution scheme for merge-mined blockchains. The process for parent chains like Bitcoin and Litecoin is analogous.

it is not possible to identify all miners and mining pools with 100% accuracy by relying only on the information present in the public ledger.

4   Merged Mining in Practice

In this section we present the results of our analysis of merged mining and provide evidence for mining power centralization issues in the implementing cryptocurrencies.

4.1   Degree of Adoption

Merged mining was introduced at block 19,200 in Namecoin (Oct. 2011), 11,163 in Huntercoin (Feb. 2014), 317,337 in Dogecoin (Jul. 2014) and 1,402,791 in Myriadcoin (Sept. 2015). The developers of Namecoin, Dogecoin and Huntercoin also disabled normal mining in the official clients at introduction. Hence, from that point forward over 99% of the blocks have been created through the process of merged mining in these cryptocurrencies. Table 1 shows the total distribution of normal and merge-mined blocks.

Table 1. Merge-mined blocks in examined cryptocurrencies.

Blockchain	Normal	Merge-mined	% of Total
Huntercoin	15,083	1,773,916	99.2
Namecoin	19,330	327,846	94.4
Dogecoin	373,927	1,389,553	78.8
Myriadcoin	1,789,994	299,981	14.4

4.2 Effects on PoW Difficulty

The main objective of merged mining is to attract more miners and hence increase the difficulty of the child blockchain [27]. By extracting the information on the PoW difficulty encoded in each block header, we are able to confirm merged mining indeed has a positive effect in this respect.

Figure 2 visualizes the development of the SHA256 PoW difficulty in Bitcoin compared to Namecoin, Huntercoin and Myriadcoin on a logarithmic scale. The PoW difficulty of the merge-mined chains rapidly increased after the introduction of merged mining. Furthermore, the behavior of Bitcoin's difficulty is, to some extent, mirrored to the merge-mined cryptocurrencies. For example, between January 2012 and April 2013 the difficulty remained stable in both Bitcoin and Namecoin, until an upward trend occurred in May 2013. The latter coincides with the wide deployment of specialized hardware dedicated to mining (ASICs) [35]. The visualization for Litecoin and Scrypt merge-mined cryptocurrencies is provided in Fig. 3. An interesting observation is that the PoW difficulty of the multi-merge-mined cryptocurrency Myriadcoin exceeded that of Litecoin, one of its parent blockchains, by 31,85%.

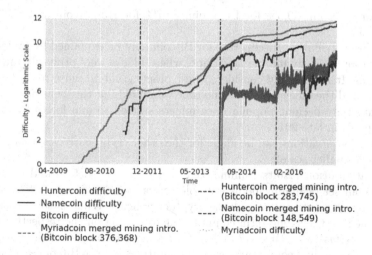

Fig. 2. Difficulty development in Bitcoin compared to SHA256 merge-mined cryptocurrencies over time on a logarithmic scale (since the launch of Bitcoin).

4.3 Impacts on Mining Power Distribution

In order to investigate the connection of merged mining and mining power centralization, we apply the attribution scheme described in Sect. 3.2 to the evaluated cryptocurrencies. A block is considered successfully mapped, if we can attribute it to either a known mining pool, or a reused reward payout address. Based on this scheme we are able to map the following percentage of blocks within the respective cryptocurrency: 59.1% for Bitcoin, 88.5% for Namecoin,

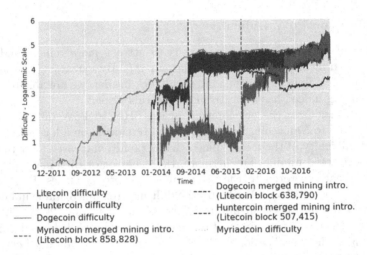

Fig. 3. Difficulty development in Litecoin compared to Scrypt merge-mined cryptocurrencies over time on a logarithmic scale (since the launch of Litecoin).

73.2% for Litecoin, 99.5% for Dogecoin, 82.7% for Huntercoin and 87.2% for Myriadcoin.

The low attribution success rate for Bitcoin may be explained by taking into consideration its early mining landscape, where blocks were primarily mined by individuals. It is generally considered best practice not to reuse reward payout addresses and the official client at the time would exhibit this behavior. The use of markers only became popular once miners started to join forces by forming mining pools in late 2011.

Similar observations can be made for the other cryptocurrecies we analyzed, albeit at a smaller scale.

The attribution results, summarized in Tables 2, 3, 4, 5, 6 and 7, suggest that a small set of mining pools are able to control significant portions of the overall mining power across multiple cryptocurrencies. While in some cases this is explained by their long-term commitment to mining on the respective chain, pools like *GHash.IO*, *BW Pool* and *F2Pool* appear to have enough capacity to concurrently conduct competitive mining operations in both Bitcoin and Litecoin (i.e., on different PoWs). In fact, F2Pool, which represents one of the largest mining pools across both SHA256 and Scrypt PoW cryptocurrencies, was able to accumulate block shares exceeding the security guarantees of the Nakamoto consensus protocol (cf. Fig. 4).

However, not all miners and mining pools currently participate in merged mining. A possible explanation is the economies of scale attributed to merged mining [27]. Since no additional computational effort is required for the PoW, the costs of merged mining, namely bandwidth, storage and validation of blocks/transactions, are the same for all miners, regardless of their mining power. In particular smaller mining operations may face the situation that their

Table 2. Bitcoin block attribution

Pool	Blocks	(%)
Smaller pools (share <1.5%)	74,753	15.8
F2Pool	35,955	7.62
BTC Guild	32,932	6.98
AntPool	26,884	5.70
GHash.IO	23,063	4.89
SlushPool	19,650	4.16
BitFury	16,070	3.41
BTCC	15,228	3.23
Other unknown miners	11,706	2.48
Eligius	11,424	2.42
BW Pool	11,075	2.35
Attributed (total)	278,740	59.1
Non-attributable blocks	193,151	40.9

Table 3. Namecoin block attribution

Pool	Blocks	(%)
F2Pool	88,795	25.6
BTC Guild	54,623	15.7
GHash.IO	34,239	9.86
SlushPool	26,726	7.70
Smaller pools (share <1.5%)	24,832	7.15
Eligius	21,144	6.09
BitMinter	18,788	5.41
EclipseMC	12,954	3.73
BTCC	11,298	3.25
ViaBTC	7,734	2.23
N3aNrkyTKY...	6,027	1.74
Attributed (total)	307,160	88.5
Non-attributable blocks	39,927	11.5

Table 4. Litecoin block attribution

Pool	Blocks	(%)
Smaller pools (share <1.5%)	284,339	23.2
F2Pool	240,691	19.7
LTm3aN5CbZ...	62,623	5.11
Clevermining	56,340	4.60
Other unknown miners	51,671	4.22
BW Pool	47,229	3.86
litecoinpool.org.	35,806	2.92
LTC1BTC/LTC.BTC.TOP	28,627	2.34
LTZaRkmkTJ...	23,342	1.91
GHash.IO	22,435	1.83
LiteGuardian	22,148	1.81
Give Me Coins	21,299	1.74
Attributed (total)	896,550	73.2
Non-attributable blocks	327,984	26.8

Table 5. Dogecoin block attribution

Pool	Blocks	(%)
F2Pool	497,013	28.2
Other unknown miners	353,671	20.1
Clevermining	187,376	10.6
Smaller pools (share <1.5%)	186,348	10.6
Litecoin pool using LT'm3aN5CbZ2Ns34...	160,644	9.11
litecoinpool.org.	113,283	6.42
BW Pool	91,265	5.18
LTC1BTC/LTC.BTC.TOP	65,228	3.70
yihaochi.com	35,745	2.03
Coinotron	34,694	1.97
GHash.IO	29,814	1.69
Attributed (total)	1,755,081	99.5
Non-attributable blocks	8,443	0.5

Table 6. Huntercoin block attribution

Pool	Blocks	(%)
F2Pool	1,142,821	63.9
litecoinpool.org.	282,136	15.8
HaoBTC	27,974	1.56
Smaller pools (share < 1.5%)	26,057	1.46
Attributed (total)	1,478,988	82.7
Non-attributable blocks	310,010	17.3

Table 7. Myriadcoin block attribution

Pool	Blocks	(%)
Smaller pools (share <1.5%)	587,986	28.1
Other unknown miners	423,684	20.3
nonce-pool	192,193	9.20
MiningPoolHub	181,168	8.67
Zpool	135,876	6.50
MJv9fLd7Qj...	64,720	3.10
LTC1BTC/LTC.BTC.TOP	48,132	2.30
Multipool	44,510	2.13
MWQVvPypce...	40,281	1.93
GHash.IO	37,916	1.81
wafflepool	33,605	1.61
Nut2Pools	31,359	1.50
Attributed (total)	1,821,430	87.2
Non-attributable blocks	268,544	12.8

additional expenditures for merge-mining another cryptocurrency exceed the expected rewards.

Resulting Mining Power Centralization Issues. The number of blocks found by a miner over a certain period indicate his actual hash rate (i.e., their mining power) during this period. Hence, we use the number of blocks generated by the largest miner or mining pool per day as an approximation for measuring the centralization of mining power[6]. Our findings are visualized as heatmaps in Fig. 4. Therein, each bar (column) represents the number of blocks mined by the largest entity on that day. We use the thresholds described in Sect. 2.1 as centralization indicators. If exceeded, the latter are known to introduce potential threats on the decentralization and security level of a PoW blockchain:

---

[6] We set the observation period to 24 hours to avoid extreme variance caused by lucky/unlucky streaks of miners since the time between found blocks is exponentially distributed, while still achieving accurate results.

– *Below 25%* (green) - Highest share is below the pessimistic threshold.
– *Greater 25%* (yellow) - Highest share is between 25% and one third.
– *Greater 33.33%* (orange) - Highest share is between one third and 50%.
– *Greater 50%* (red) - Highest share controls the majority of mining power.

In Bitcoin no single miner or mining pool has been able to aggregate and maintain more than 50% of the overall mining power for an extended period, since blocks became attributable[7]. (Table 8) However, the situation is quite different in Namecoin: here, *F2Pool* reached and maintained a majority of the mining power for prolonged periods.

Litecoin, despite being the largest Scrypt PoW blockchain, has experienced slight centralization since mid-2014, among others caused by *Clevermining* and lately *F2Pool*. Through merged mining, this situation is reflected and amplified in Dogecoin: *F2Pool* was responsible for generating more than 33% of the blocks per day for significant periods, even exceeding the 50% threshold around the end of 2016.

The effects of introducing merged mining have played out differently in the two multi-PoW cryptocurrencies we analyzed. While Huntercoin was instantly dominated by *F2Pool* and remained in this state until mid-2016, Myriadcoin appears to have experienced only a moderate impact. However, we note that so far none of the large mining pools that are active in other merge-mined chains have been observed to also operate in Myriadcoin.

Table 8. Distribution of overall percentage of days below/above the centralization indicator thresholds.

Blockchain	$\leq 25\%$	$> 25\%$	$> 33.33\%$	$> 50\%$
Bitcoin	75.7	24.3	5.43	0.03
Namecoin	11.7	88.3	66.6	30.5
Litecoin	45.0	55.0	35.9	0.75
Dogecoin	16.3	83.7	60.7	2.45
Huntercoin	1.53	98.5	96.1	81.0
Myriadcoin	87.7	12.3	6.20	0.2

Mining Power Fluctuation. The operation of a mining pool requires extensive coordination effort in terms of recruiting miners or purchasing and installing the necessary infrastructure. Hence, it usually takes time until a mining pool is able to accumulate significant mining power shares. Merged mining, however, requires only minimal effort and can be described as a "software switch". Consequently, the observable high fluctuations of mining power in merge-mined cryptocurrencies may be attributed to mining pools being able to easily start

---

[7] It is in the realm of possibility that in the early days of Bitcoin individual miners, such as Satoshi Nakamoto himself have controlled large shares of the overall mining power.

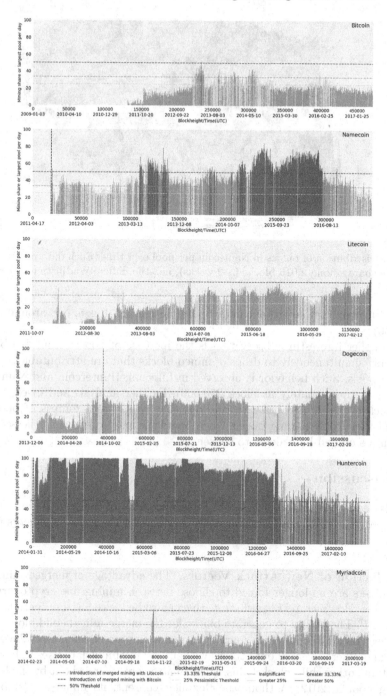

Fig. 4. Block share of largest miner/mining pool per day for Bitcoin (144 blocks), Litecoin (576 blocks), Namecoin (144 blocks), Dogecoin (1,440 blocks), Huntercoin (1,440 blocks) and Myriadcoin (1,440 blocks) since launch of the respective cryptocurrency. (Color figure online)

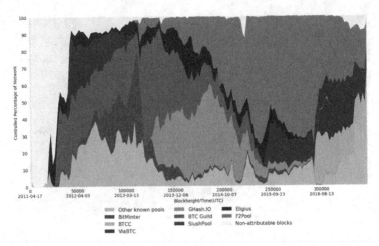

Fig. 5. Distribution of blocks in Namecoin per pool over time. Each data point resembles the share among 2,016 blocks ($\sim$ 2 weeks), i.e., the difficulty adjustment period.

or end their operation without major preparations (cf. Fig. 5, e.g. around block 300,000).

A further interesting observation is the increase of non-attributable blocks occurring simultaneously to drops of mined blocks that are attributable to large mining pools. Such behavior is observed in Litecoin, Huntercoin and Namecoin (cf. Fig. 5 approximately at block 250,000). Further analysis and investigation into such events is necessary to rule out that these are attempts of pools to conceal their total mining power when operating near or beyond the security guarantees offered by Nakamoto consensus

5   Discussion

In this section we discuss the security implications of merged mining on the ecosystem of cryptocurrencies and study how current theoretic arguments relate to our findings.

Introduction of New Attack Vectors. The advantage of merged mining is that miners are no longer forced to choose between mining one cryptocurrency or another. However, its biggest strength can also be viewed as a potential attack vector [27]. The ability to generate blocks for the merge-mined child blockchains at almost no additional cost, apart from maintaining a client node, allows misbehaving miners to carry out attacks without risking financial losses in both the parent and other child blockchains. Such an attack was carried out by the Eligius mining pool in 2012. Without their explicit consent, its miners were coerced to participate in an attack led by the pool operator, ultimately stalling the operation of the fledgling cryptocurrency CoiledCoin by mining empty blocks[8].

---

[8] cf. https://bitcointalk.org/index.php?topic=56675.msg678006#msg678006.

This attack serves as the predominant example for highlighting threats posed by merged mining on child cryptocurrencies: the miners of the pool did not suffer any financial loss and, as it appears, were not even aware of the attack, as all actions were performed solely by the operator.

However, to the best of our knowledge, it was never explicitly stated that merged mining may also facilitate attacks against a parent cryptocurrency. Consider for example a miner who is highly invested in a multi-merge-mined cryptocurrency. Due to merged mining this miner can perform attacks on one of the supported parent blockchains (e.g. selfish mining or DoS through mining empty blocks) at no additional mining cost. While such scenarios previously seemed far-fetched, as the PoW difficulty of a parent blockchain was generally considered to exceed that of a merge-mined child, this is no longer the case for multi-merge-mined cryptocurrencies (see Sect. 4.2). This highlights that *merged mining as an attack vector works both ways.* Such attacks are particularly interesting because parent cryptocurrencies cannot easily prevent being merge-mined by child blockchains.

Furthermore, we describe a *reputation attack* as a noteworthy adversarial strategy in the context of merged mining. Since block attribution to pools is currently based on markers and addresses, rather than cryptographic signatures, an adversary can fake attribution of parent blocks while still earning revenue in the child chains. We consider a scenario where a targeted mining pool $\mathcal{P}$ holds a 24% mining power share of a parent chain C_{parent}, which can be used to merge-mine a child chain C_{child}. We assume a malicious merged mining entity $\mathcal{M}$ holds only 10% share of C_{parent} and uses the C_{child} (and not C_{parent}) as its main revenue channel. In such a scenario, it would be possible for $\mathcal{M}$ to create $\approx 10\%$ of the blocks in C_{parent}. $\mathcal{M}$ could now fake the attribution of its blocks in C_{parent} by using the (public) reward address and/or coinbase marker of $\mathcal{P}$. Due to the false flag blocks attributed to $\mathcal{P}$, this pool would appear to hold 34% of the share for C_{parent}. As a result, $\mathcal{P}$ might be regarded as too large or nefarious for the parent cryptocurrency, which could in turn undermine the integrity of the parent chain as a whole. While $\mathcal{M}$ will lose all revenue in C_{parent}, it will still gain revenue in C_{child}.

Centralization Risks. Merged mining does not increase the costs to the miner in regards to solving the Proof-of-Work puzzle, which is considered to be the primary cost factor in PoW cryptocurrencies. However additional costs regarding bandwidth, storage and validation of the merge-mined blockchain's blocks/transactions are incurred regardless of the relative size or hash rate of the miner. Therefore, according to [27] merge-mined cryptocurrencies have a greater risk of centralization or concentration of mining power (economies of scale).

Our analysis indicates that merge-mined child blockchains experienced prolonged periods where individual mining pools have held shares beyond the theoretical bounds that guarantee the security of the cryptocurrency. We conclude that *current merge-mined currencies have a trend towards centralization.*

However, it is too early to tell if the centralization trend also applies to multi-merged-mining in cryptocurrencies such as Myriadcoin. Multi-merge-mined blockchains allow for more than one parent cryptocurrency and have a greater chance to acquire a higher difficulty per PoW algorithm, in comparison to the respective parent blockchain. This, in fact, may change the underlying (crypto)economic assumptions with regards to merged mining and introduces new directions for research in this field.

The theoretic implications of a dishonest miner holding a large share of the network hash rate are well known [3,12,17,28]. However, we are not aware of any recent case where such an attack has been carried out in one of the analyzed cryptocurrencies, as such evidence cannot easily be derived solely by analyzing the blockchain data structures. Rather, active measurements within the P2P network of the cryptocurrency are necessary [17]. Our analysis serves as a cautionary note – the impact of such an attack on the cryptocurrency market and the mining ecosystem are unclear. The apparent lack of cryptographically verifiable attribution information regarding the hash rate of mining pools only renders the situation worse. This bares additional risks of intended or unintended misattribution of non negligible fractions of the overall hash rate.

Furthermore, we want to point out that through the alternative use-cases of some of the merge-mined cryptocurrencies, certain attacks may also have additional implications. Namecoin for example, can be used to register and update arbitrary name-value pairs, such as DNS entries. In this case, every registered domain expires after a certain number of blocks (i.e., amount of time). Should a mining pool hold a large block share at that time, it can take over a domain name by blocking the required update (refresh) transaction to enter the blockchain in time. Once the domain name has expired, the misbehaving pool can register the domain himself.

Validation Disincentive. Not only the detection of misbehaving pools with large hash rates requires active network monitoring, but also the verification of the *validation disincentive* assumption: In [27] the authors propose that miners which participate in merged mining have an incentive to skimp on (transaction) validation, since it becomes the main (computational) cost driver in merged mining. Although not mentioned explicitly in [27], the rate of blockchain forks, i.e., stale block rate of merged mined cryptocurrencies, could be an indicator for relaxed transaction validation of miners. Since stale blocks are not directly recorded in the blockchain, the only way to acquire the required measurements is through active monitoring of the involved peer-to-peer networks, as demonstrated in [6,7]. Conducting these measurements for multiple merge-mined cryptocurrencies is topic for future work. In addition, it might be necessary to actively trigger those conditions by broadcasting incorrect transactions/blocks. However, we stress that performing such tests in live networks raises ethical and financial questions.

Long-Term Dependency. Merged mining was originally conceived as a bootstrapping technique for alternative cryptocurrencies [27,33]. To the best of our knowledge, once introduced, no cryptocurrency has abandoned merged mining – not even the child cryptocurrencies which our analysis in Sect. 4 has shown to suffer from centralization issues. Hence, we argue that although merged mining can increase the hash rate of child blockchains, *it is not conclusively successful as a bootstrapping technique.*

Results presented in [29] indicate that even if a PoW blockchain should just be used in a bootstrapping phase before switching to a different consensus algorithm, it is theoretically necessary to keep on mining infinitely long. Otherwise it would be impossible for new nodes joining the network to distinguish between the original bootstrapping chain and a longer, but malicious counterpart. In theory, this might pose a new use case for merged mining in scenarios where a blockchain is bootstrapped using PoW and then switches to a different consensus algorithm. In this case the PoW bootstrapping chain can be continued relatively cheap through merged mining by appending empty blocks.

6 Conclusion

In this paper, we assessed current theories regarding merged mining from an empirical point of view and contributed to the discussion by raising new questions and directions for future work.

We derived a simple attribution scheme and achieved to map a significant portion of the mining pool ecosystem of the analyzed cryptocurrencies, beyond what was publicly known until now. The collected information sheds some light on the long-term evolution of merged mining in different cryptocurrencies. While merged mining is a common practice in the cryptocurrency space, the empirical evidence suggests that only a small number of mining pools is involved in merged mining. These pools enjoy block shares beyond the desired security and decentralization goals. It is currently unclear and topic of future research whether new constructs, such as multi-merged mining, will succeed in resolving the outlined issues.

The multi-purpose usage of PoW in merged mining is an interesting application, not only from a resource consumption point-of-view, but also in the context of future sharding and scalability discussions. Therefore, further research and analysis regarding merged mining is required as a basis for developing and building solutions, which will be able to stand the test of time.

Acknowledgments. We want to thank Philipp Schindler and Georg Merzdovnik for valuable discussions and feedback. This research was funded by FFG - Austrian Research Promotion Agency Bridge Early Stage 846573 A2Bit, FFG Bridge 1 858561 SESC and COMET K1.

References

1. Ali, M., Nelson, J., Shea, R., Freedman, M.J.: Blockstack: a global naming and storage system secured by blockchains. In: 2016 USENIX Annual Technical Conference (USENIX ATC 2016), pp. 181–194. USENIX Association, Denver (2016)
2. Anderson, L., Holz, R., Ponomarev, A., Rimba, P., Weber, I.: New kids on the block: an analysis of modern blockchains (2016). http://arxiv.org/pdf/1606.06530.pdf. Accessed 10 Nov 2016
3. Androulaki, E., Capkun, S., Karame, G.O.: Two bitcoins at the price of one? double-spending attacks on fast payments in bitcoin. In: CCS (2012)
4. Back, A., Corallo, M., Dashjr, L., Friedenbach, M., Maxwell, G., Miller, A., Poelstra, A., Timón, J., Wuille, P.: Enabling blockchain innovations with pegged sidechains (2014). http://newspaper23.com/ripped/2014/11/http:www-blockstream-com-sidechains.pdf. Accessed 10 Nov 2016
5. Bentov, I., Pass, R., Shi, E.: Snow white: provably secure proofs of stake (2016). https://eprint.iacr.org/2016/919.pdf
6. Decker, C., Wattenhofer, R.: Information propagation in the bitcoin network. In: 2013 IEEE Thirteenth International Conference on Peer-to-Peer Computing (P2P), pp. 1–10. IEEE (2013)
7. Decker, C., Wattenhofer, R.: Bitcoin transaction malleability and MtGox. In: Kutyłowski, M., Vaidya, J. (eds.) ESORICS 2014. LNCS, vol. 8713, pp. 313–326. Springer, Cham (2014). doi:10.1007/978-3-319-11212-1_18
8. Dogecoin community. Dogecoin reference implementation. github.com/dogecoin/dogecoin. Accessed 10 Nov 2016
9. Eyal, I.: The miner's dilemma. In: 2015 IEEE Symposium on Security and Privacy (SP), pp. 89–103. IEEE (2015)
10. Eyal, I., Sirer, E.G.: Majority is not enough: bitcoin mining is vulnerable. In: Christin, N., Safavi-Naini, R. (eds.) FC 2014. LNCS, vol. 8437, pp. 436–454. Springer, Heidelberg (2014). doi:10.1007/978-3-662-45472-5_28
11. Franco, P., Bitcoin, U.: Cryptography, Engineering and Economics. Wiley, New York (2014)
12. Gervais, A., Karame, G.O., Wüst, K., Glykantzis, V., Ritzdorf, H., Capkun, S.: On the security and performance of proof of work blockchains. In: Proceedings of the 2016 ACM SIGSAC Conference on Computer and Communications Security, CCS 2016, pp. 3–16. ACM, New York (2016)
13. Heilman, E., Kendler, A., Zohar, A., Goldberg, S.: Eclipse attacks on bitcoin's peer-to-peer network. In: 24th USENIX Security Symposium (USENIX Security 2015), pp. 129–144 (2015)
14. Huntercoin developers. Huntercoin reference implementation. https://github.com/chronokings/huntercoin. Accessed 05 Jun 2017
15. Jakobsson, M., Juels, A.: Proofs of work and bread pudding protocols (extended abstract). In: Preneel, B. (ed.) Secure Information Networks. IFIP, vol. 23, pp. 258–272. Springer, Boston (1999). doi:10.1007/978-0-387-35568-9_18
16. Kalodner, H., Carlsten, M., Ellenbogen, P., Bonneau, J., Narayanan, A.: An empirical study of namecoin and lessons for decentralized namespace design. In: WEIS (2015)
17. Karame, G.O., Androulaki, E., Roeschlin, M., Gervais, A., Čapkun, S.: Misbehavior in bitcoin: a study of double-spending and accountability. ACM Trans. Inf. Syst. Secur. 18(1), 2:1–2:32 (2015). doi:10.1145/2732196. Article no 2

18. Kiayias, A., Russell, A., David, B., Oliynykov, R.: Ouroboros: a provably secure proof-of-stake blockchain protocol (2016). https://pdfs.semanticscholar.org/1c14/549f7ba7d6a000d79a7d12255eb11113e6fa.pdf. Accessed 20 Feb 2017
19. Lerner, S.D.: Rootstock platform. http://www.the-blockchain.com/docs/Rootstock-WhitePaper-Overview.pdf. Accessed 5 Jun 2017
20. Lewenberg, Y., Bachrach, Y., Sompolinsky, Y., Zohar, A., Rosenschein, J.S.: Bitcoin mining pools: a cooperative game theoretic analysis. In: Proceedings of the 2015 International Conference on Autonomous Agents and Multiagent Systems, pp. 919–927. International Foundation for Autonomous Agents and Multiagent Systems (2015)
21. Litecoin community. Litecoin reference implementation. github.com/litecoin-project/litecoin. Accessed 10 Nov 2016
22. Micali, S.: Algorand: The efficient and democratic ledger (2016). http://arxiv.org/abs/1607.01341. Accessed 9 Feb 2017
23. Myriad core developers. Myriadcoin reference implementation. https://github.com/myriadcoin/myriadcoin. Accessed 05 Jun 2017
24. Nakamoto, S.: Bitcoin: A peer-to-peer electronic cash system, December 2008. https://bitcoin.org/bitcoin.pdf. Accessed 10 Nov 2016
25. Nakamoto, S.: Merged mining specification, April 2011. en.bitcoin.it/wiki/Merged_mining_specification. Accessed 10 Nov 2016
26. Namecoin community. Namecoin reference implementation. https://github.com/namecoin/namecoin. Accessed 10 Nov 2016
27. Narayanan, A., Bonneau, J., Felten, E., Miller, A., Goldfeder, S.: Bitcoin and Cryptocurrency Technologies: A Comprehensive Introduction. Princeton University Press, Princeton (2016)
28. Nayak, K., Kumar, S., Miller, A., Shi, E.: Stubborn mining: generalizing selfish mining and combining with an eclipse attack. In: 1st IEEE European Symposium on Security and Privacy. IEEE (2016)
29. Pass, R., Shi, E.: Hybrid consensus: Scalable permissionless consensus, September 2016. https://eprint.iacr.org/2016/917.pdf. Accessed 10 Nov 2016
30. Rosenfeld, M.: Analysis of bitcoin pooled mining reward systems. arXiv preprint arXiv:1112.4980 (2011)
31. Rosenfeld, M.: Analysis of hashrate-based double spending (2014). http://arxiv.org/abs/1402.2009. Accessed 10 Nov 2016
32. Sapirshtein, A., Sompolinsky, Y., Zohar, A.: Optimal selfish mining strategies in bitcoin. In: Grossklags, J., Preneel, B. (eds.) FC 2016. LNCS, vol. 9603, pp. 515–532. Springer, Heidelberg (2017). doi:10.1007/978-3-662-54970-4_30
33. Nakamoto, S.: Comment in "bitdns and generalizing bitcoin" bitcointalk thread. https://bitcointalk.org/index.php?topic=1790.msg28696#msg28696. Accessed 05 Jun 2017
34. Schrijvers, O., Bonneau, J., Boneh, D., Roughgarden, T.: Incentive compatibility of bitcoin mining pool reward functions. In: Grossklags, J., Preneel, B. (eds.) FC 2016. LNCS, vol. 9603, pp. 477–498. Springer, Heidelberg (2017). doi:10.1007/978-3-662-54970-4_28
35. Taylor, M.B.: Bitcoin and the age of bespoke silicon. In: Proceedings of the 2013 International Conference on Compilers, Architectures and Synthesis for Embedded Systems, p. 16. IEEE Press (2013)

Atomically Trading with Roger: Gambling on the Success of a Hardfork

Patrick McCorry[1]([✉]), Ethan Heilman[2]([✉]), and Andrew Miller[3,4]([✉])

[1] University College London, London, UK
`p.mccorry@ucl.ac.uk`
[2] Boston University, Boston, USA
`heilman@bu.edu`
[3] University of Illinois at Urbana-Champaign, Champaign, USA
`soc1024@illinois.edu`
[4] Initiative for Cryptocurrencies and Contracts, Berkeley, USA
`http://www.initc3.org/`

Abstract. We present atomic trade protocols for Bitcoin and Ethereum that can bind two parties to swap coins in the event that two blockchains emerge from a single "pre-fork" blockchain. This work is motivated by a bet between two members of the Bitcoin community, Loaded and Roger Ver, to trade 60,000 bitcoins in the event that Bitcoin Unlimited's planned hardfork occurs and the blockchain splits into two distinct forks. Additionally we study several ways to provide replay protection in the event of hardfork alongside a novel mechanism called migration inputs. We provide a detailed survey and history of previous softforks and hardforks in Ethereum and Bitcoin.

1 Introduction

Bitcoin [29] is the world's first successful and most valuable cryptocurrency. In June 2017, it reached a market cap of $ 43 bn USD [10] and processed $\approx$ 250,000 transactions per day [4]. However, Bitcoin's future is uncertain; it is reaching its capacity limits, and so far the community has failed to reach consensus on how best to increase its capacity.

One proposed approach for increasing capacity, called Bitcoin Unlimited (BU), involves removing the 1-megabyte-per-block parameter that most directly effects the capacity limit [35]. A competing approach, the Core Roadmap [26], calls for a technical upgrade called SegWit [24], followed by deployment of the overlay payment network, Lightning [30]. Both approaches require changing the network's consensus rules; however there is a critical difference between them, BU is implemented as a hardfork upgrade, whereas Core relies on softforks. These two approaches are mutually incompatible: unlike a hardfork, a softfork is "forward-compatible" in the sense that blocks mined using the new rules can still be processed by non-upgraded clients (for additional details see Sect. 2.3).

If the community remains divided on which approach to support, then the result may be a schism, where each faction maintains a distinct fork of

© Springer International Publishing AG 2017
J. Garcia-Alfaro et al. (Eds.): DPM/CBT 2017, LNCS 10436, pp. 334–353, 2017.
DOI: 10.1007/978-3-319-67816-0_19

Bitcoin with mutually incompatible consensus rules.[1] Both blockchains will diverge post-fork, but share the same pre-fork transaction history. We denote the non-upgraded fork as FORK-1 and the fork with new consensus rules as FORK-2. As both forks share a common history, a party holding X coins in the pre-fork blockchain will, after the hardfork, hold X coins in FORK-1 and hold X coins in FORK-2.

In this paper we consider the scenario where, prior to a hardfork, Alice and Bob decide to bet on which of the two forks will be most valuable. After the hardfork, Alice's coins in FORK-1 are sent to Bob, and Bob's coins in FORK-2 are sent to Alice. Remarkably, this gambling scenario is inspired by real-world events: two wealthy members of the Bitcoin community, Loaded[2] and Roger Ver, have expressed the desire to arrange a 1:1 trade of coins in the event that Bitcoin Unlimited performs a hardfork from Bitcoin [23]. Roger wants to exchange 60,000 of his coins on FORK-2 for 60,000 of Loaded's coins on FORK-1. After the trade Loaded would have 120,000 coins on FORK-1 and Roger would have 120,000 coins on FORK-2 (this trade was roughly $120 million USD when proposed).

There are two previously known approaches we could employ for cross-chain trades, though both have drawbacks in this scenario. In the first approach, both parties escrow funds with a third party who facilitates the trade; several protocols have been outlined by Goldfeder et al. [14] that could mediate such a trade. The second approach, an atomic cross-chain swap smart contract, was proposed by TierNolan [33] (see Appendix A for details). Unfortunately the first approach requires a trusted third party and the second does not allow users to commit to the bet prior to the hardfork.

In this paper we introduce a novel atomic cross-chain trade where the trade can be committed prior to the activation of a hardfork, but executed after the hardfork. We construct protocols for both Bitcoin and Ethereum (the second most popular cryptocurrency with a market cap of $29 bn USD as of June 2017 and which had four hardforks in 2016). It is worth mentioning that our protocol for Bitcoin *does not require a fix for transaction malleability*, but relies on the hardforked blockchain FORK-2 implementing replay protection[3]. On the other hand, our protocol for Ethereum leverages a Hardfork Oracle contract that can detect if it is on FORK-1 or FORK-2. Our contributions are:

- The first atomic cross-chain trade protocols for Bitcoin and Ethereum that can transfer coins across both sides of a hardfork
- A novel mechanism which we call migration inputs that provides replay protection in the event of a Bitcoin hardfork.
- A detailed history of hardforks and softforks in Bitcoin and Ethereum.

---

[1] A schism has previously occurred in the case of Ethereum, whose *TheDAO* hardfork precipitated a split into Ethereum and Ethereum Classic.

[2] Loaded is a pseudonym used by a person on the bitcointalk forums.

[3] The user can choose which blockchain can accept their newly signed transaction.

2   Background

In this section we cover technical background for our protocols, a history of soft/hardforks in Bitcoin and Ethereum and a survey of replay protection proposals for Bitcoin including *migration inputs* a novel replay protection mechanism.

2.1   Bitcoin

Bitcoin is a digital currency that facilitates trading the ownership of a single asset (i.e. bitcoins). Users send bitcoins to other users by publishing transactions. All transactions are stored in a globally replicated data structure called the blockchain. A computationally expensive process called mining (i.e. Proof-of-Work) is responsible for periodically electing a leader to create and append a new block of recently authorised transactions to the blockchain. To understand our protocol we focus on a Bitcoin transaction's scripting and lock time capability.

A Bitcoin transaction contains a list of inputs and outputs. Inputs specify the source of bitcoins along with evidence that the spender is authorized to spend these bitcoins. Outputs specify the conditions that must be satisfied before its associated bitcoins can be spent. Inputs and outputs are controlled using a limited forth-like language called *script*. The most popular script is the *pay-to-pubkey-hash* script which requires a digital signature σ_A from the corresponding secret key of a specified Bitcoin address (i.e. hash of the public key $H(PK_A)$).

Scripts can include a function `CHECKLOCKTIMEVERIFY` [34] to prevent spending an output until time t. This lock time t is compared against the median time of the previous 11 block's timestamps [21]. It is worth mentioning that a block's timestamp must be greater than the median timestamp computed over the 11 previous blocks and it must not be greater than 2 hours from a node's network time. As a result, the median time is loosely-bound with current time.

2.2   Ethereum

The motivation for Ethereum (and Ethereum Classic[4]) is to store and execute expressive *smart contracts* on a peer-to-peer network as opposed to simply trading a single asset. Similar to Bitcoin, users must authorize transactions using an Ethereum account (i.e. public-secret key pairs) and miners are responsible for appending new blocks to the blockchain. Unlike Bitcoin, the transaction payload contains the code/execution instructions for the contract and the transaction's destination is the contract address[5]. Here we focus on the capability of smart contracts and how coins can be locked for a pre-determined period of time.

Ethereum smart contracts are written in Solidity which is a Javascript-like language. Prior to being stored in the blockchain this code is compiled from Solidity to EVM (Ethereum Virtual Machine) code. Transactions that contain

---

[4] Emerged in July 2016 after Ethereums's TheDAO hardfork.
[5] The hash of the transaction's nonce and the creator's Ethereum accounts address.

Table 1. Previous forks. A list of significant softforks, hardforks and blockchain splits in Bitcoin, Ethereum and Ethereum Classic.

Name	Date	Softfork	Hardfork	Split
Bitcoin				
1MB Block Size	12th Sep 2010	✓	✗	✗
182 Billion Coins	15th Aug 2010	✓	✗	✓
BIP30	15th Mar 2012	✓	✗	✗
BIP16	15th Apr 2012	✓	✗	✗
Bitcoin Core 0.8	11th Mar 2013	✗	✗	✓
BIP34	24th Mar 2013	✓	✗	✗
BIP50	16th Aug 2013	✗	✓	✗
BIP66	4th Jul 2015	✓	✗	✓[a]
BIP65	8th Dec 2015	✓	✗	✗
BIP68/112/113	4th Jul 2016	✓	✗	✗
Ethereum				
Homestead	14th Mar 2016	✗	✓	✗
TheDAO	20th Jul 2016	✗	✓	✓
Tangerine Whistle	18th Oct 2016	✗	✓	✗
Spurious Dragon	22nd Nov 2016	✗	✓	✓[b]
Ethereum Classic				
Gas Reprice	25th Oct 2016	✗	✓	✗
Die Hard	13th Jan 2017	✗	✓	✗

[a] It was discovered that a significant portion of miners who signaled for the activation of BIP66 were not fully validating blocks (i.e. spv mining). This led to a temporary blockchain split and the invalid fork was eventually discarded.
[b] The blockchain split occurred on the 24th November 2016.

EVM code are propagated throughout the network and deterministically executed by all peers using their copy of the EVM. The transaction is stored in the blockchain to ensure the contract's state is no longer reversible.

It is worth mentioning that locking coins until time t can be expressed in a straight-forward manner. Solidity supports accessing a block's timestamp using `block.timestamp` or a block's height using `block.number`. Furthermore, there is a tighter-bound on a block's timestamp as it must be greater than the previous block and strictly less than the user's local clock [28]. Next, we discuss soft and hardforks that have occurred in Bitcoin and Ethereum.

2.3 History of Forks

Cryptocurrencies have clearly defined consensus rules on which all network peers (including both miners and relay nodes) must agree in order to deterministically validate scripts, transactions and blocks. These rules define a transaction's format, the semantics of its scripting language, the rate at which new coins are minted, parameters such as the maximum block size, and many more constraints. Changing these consensus rules to upgrade a cryptocurrency requires community-wide co-ordination and approaches generally fall into two categories:

- A **softfork** introduces new rules such that a new block conforming to the changed consensus rules is considered valid by non-upgraded nodes, i.e. the proposed change is "forward compatible."
- A **hardfork** introduces new rules such that a new block conforming to the changed consensus rules is not considered valid by non-upgraded nodes.

In both cases, a fork proposal typically has a "flag day" activation time and built-in activation conditions, such as requiring a threshold limit of miners and/or validators to indicate support before the change is activated. This provides ample time for the entire community to upgrade their nodes to support the new consensus rules. However, the difference between a softfork and hardfork is how non-upgraded nodes are impacted. In the former, non-upgraded nodes will follow the majority of miners, whereas in the latter non-upgraded nodes will find themselves in a partitioned network. In practice, Table 1 highlights that Bitcoin has performed softforks (with the exception of one hardfork due to BerkeleyDB's misconfiguration), whereas Ethereum (and Ethereum Classic) have used hardforks. Next, we explore the new consensus rules introduced in Bitcoin, Ethereum and Ethereum classic.

Bitcoin. So far, Bitcoin has implemented over six softforks. These softforks range from introducing rules to prevent miners creating coinbase transactions with duplicated identification hashes [1,38], requiring all ECDSA signatures to strictly enforce DER coding [39], and introducing both absolute [34] and relative lock times [13] for individual transaction outputs. In terms of implementation, this involves storing new information in the `scriptsig` of the coinbase transaction, constraining transaction validation rules or re-defining the use of special `OP_NOP` function.

On the other hand, Bitcoin has experienced two accidental (and temporary) splits (i.e. FORK-1, FORK-2 emerged) that required miner intervention to remedy. The first split permitted a user to exploit an integer overflow bug and create 184 billion coins. This required miners to co-operatively extend a new blockchain without the coin creation transaction [5] and to enforce a soft-fork to prevent this exploit. The second split involved miners who upgraded to Bitcoin Core 0.8 accidentally creating blocks that were invalid for Bitcoin Core 0.7. Unfortunately, BerkeleyDB's configuration in Bitcoin Core 0.7 was non-deterministic and as a result was not compatible with LevelDB's configuration in Bitcoin Core 0.8. Resolving this fork required miners to immediately downgrade to Bitcoin Core 0.7 and abandon the forked blockchain. Next, the developers released Bitcoin

Core 0.8.1 that enforced the activation of a hardfork[6] after a two-month grace period for miners and users to upgrade [2,27].

Ethereum. Ethereum has executed four hardforks in response to community demand and to reduce the impact of network spam attacks. Homestead modified the gas cost for creating transactions and EVM operation codes [36], TheDAO fork reversed a theft of approximately $40 m worth of ether [16], Tangerine Whistle reduced long-term gas changes for IO-heavy operations [7] in response to a spam atack and Spurious Dragon enabled transactions to delete empty accounts by *touching* them [37]. All hardforks required peers on the network to upgrade their software to continue participating in the network.

TheDAO hardfork precipitated the creation of Ethereum Classic (market cap of $2 bn, June 2017) as a distinct fork of Ethereum [16]. One of the reasons this split occurred was that a faction of the community disagreed in principle with modifying TheDAO smart contract in order to reverse the theft. An accidental split also occurred after the Spurious Dragon hardfork as both Geth and Parity (i.e. distinct implementations of the Ethereum protocol) failed to identically implement the new consensus rules. Geth was updated to fix a bug in order to resolve the fork and of course the forked blockchain was abandoned [17].

Ethereum Classic. There have been two hardforks in Ethereum Classic. Gas-Reprice replicated Ethereum's hardfork to increase the cost for underpriced EVM operation codes in order to prevent future spam attacks [18]. Die Hard removed the *difficulty time-bomb* that was hard-coded into Ethereum [19]. So far, there have been no accidental splits.

In the next section, we highlight that Ethereum's inclusive hardfork for TheDAO allowed an attacker to perform replay attacks against unprepared exchanges before presenting a survey of replay protection proposals for Bitcoin.

Other cryptocurrencies. We briefly note that other cryptocurrencies besides Bitcoin and Ethereum, such as Litecoin and Monero, have also endured softforks and hardforks. Monero notably has committed to regularly scheduled every six months (and therefore predictable) hardforks [32].

2.4 Replay Protection

A replay attack is when the sender signs a transaction with the intention that it is accepted into one blockchain (i.e. FORK-1), but it can also be accepted into an alternative blockchain (i.e. FORK-2). Thus, the purpose of replay protection is to permit users to decide which blockchain can accept their newly signed transactions. Unfortunately, the lack of replay protection after Ethereum's *TheDAO* hardfork caused some companies to lose a substantial number of Ethereum Classic coins (ETC). For example, a Chinese exchange YUNBI lost 40k ETC as a single transaction was unexpectedly accepted in both blockchains.

---

[6] The community disputes whether BIP50 (deployed in response to BIP34's accidental split) should be considered a hardfork, and therefore to what degree Bitcoin governance has established a precedent of avoiding hardforks.

Table 2. An overview of the replay protection proposals. ◑ highlights that this feature depends on whether the proposal was introduced via a softfork or hardfork.

Proposal	Any Fork	Fork-1 First	Prior to HF	Tx Format	Softfork
Transaction version	◑	◑	✗	✗	✓
Check block at height	✓	✗	✓	✗	✓
Sighash Enum	✓	✗	✗	✓	✗
Migration Input	✓	✗	✗	✗	✗
Chain ID	✓	✗	✗	✓	✗

In Ethereum, this incident led to the Spurious Dragon hardfork which introduced `chain_id` [8]. The sender is responsible for updating the transaction's `chain_id` to state which blockchain can accept it. On the other hand, several companies in Bitcoin have co-operatively signed a letter [20] to request replay protection in any future hardfork. We provide a survey on four approaches for replay protection from the community before proposing migration inputs below.

Transaction Version. All transactions have a version number that can be incremented to inform clients that a new feature is supported. For example, a recent softfork incremented the version number from 1 to 2 when the developers introduced relative lock times.[7] Both Harding [15] and Lau [22] proposed that a single bit in the transaction version can be re-purposed as an *opt-in/opt-out bit*. The sender can update this bit to dictate which blockchain can accept this transaction. However, the Fork-1 blockchain cannot respect this new consensus rule without a softfork. As a result the sender must first create a transaction that is only valid in Fork-1 before creating a second transaction for Fork-2.

Check Block At Height. Dashjr proposed a new Bitcoin script function `OP_CHECKBLOCKATHEIGHT`. This allows the sender to specify that a block hash (at a given height) must exist in the blockchain before this transaction can be accepted [11]. It was originally proposed to prevent double-spending and blockchain re-organization attacks. However, it can conceivably be used to decide whether a transaction can be accepted into Fork-1 or Fork-2. Although, the function must be introduced via a softfork for Fork-1 and a block hash after the hardfork must be known before transactions that spend "pre-fork" coins can be signed.

Sighash Enum. One approach proposed by Zander was to change the hash-type enum (i.e. `SIGHASH`[8]) to begin with 10 instead of zero [41].

---

[7] `OP_CHECKSEQUENCEVERIFY` [13] and a new consensus rule was introduced to only check for relative lock times if the transaction version number is two or higher [3].

[8] A marker in the transaction input to specify how to construct the transaction's hash before verifying the signature. For example, the transaction hash can contain no transaction outputs, all transaction outputs, or a 1:1 mapping of inputs/outputs.

The purpose is to change the transaction format such that all signed transactions are only valid in the forked blockchain FORK-2. The full proposal can be found here [12].

Chain ID. In a similar style to Ethereum it is feasible to incorporate a `chain_id`. This value can be included explicitly in the transaction as an additional field which allows all validating peers for FORK-1 to reject the transaction as its format is not valid, whereas peers for FORK-2 can confirm that `chain_id` is part of the signed message.

Migration Input. We propose a new consensus rule for the forked blockchain FORK-2 to include an additional transaction input when a transaction is spending "pre-fork" coins. Technically, it is a sentinel 41 `byte` transaction input of zeros.[9] Of course, the previous transaction hash can be reduced from 32 `bytes` to 1 `byte` if structural changes to the transaction are implemented in the forked blockchain, and if so the overall cost per transaction is 10 `bytes`. Peers conforming to the previous consensus rules will reject this transaction, while peers with the new set of consensus rules will accept it.

Compatibility. Table 2 presents a comparison of the proposals. The criteria is based on whether the sender can dictate if a transaction is accepted into FORK-1 or FORK-2, if the sender must first sign a transaction for FORK-1 before FORK-2, if a transaction must be stored in FORK-1 prior to the hardfork, if the transaction format must be changed or if a softfork in FORK-1 is necessary.

We highlight that Sighash Enum, Migration Input and the Chain ID proposals are compatible with our protocol as no new consensus rules is required for FORK-1 while the sender can explicitly dictate if a transaction is accepted into FORK-1 or FORK-2. As well, transaction version can be used if FORK-1 performs a softfork. On the other hand, `OP_CHECKBLOCKATHEIGHT` is not compatible as the block hash immediately after the hardfork must be available and thus prevents both parties setting up the atomic trade prior to the hardfork.

3 Bitcoin Hardfork Atomic Cross-Chain Trade

To set the scene, both Alice and Bob publicly commit to the atomic trade by depositing coins into a single transaction. Next, both parties co-operatively set up the atomic trade by signing off-chain transactions before the hard-fork activation time Δ_{FORK}[10]. After the hardfork has occurred, one party (i.e. Alice) is responsible for triggering the trade. If she fails to trigger the atomic trade, then Bob can claim all coins in both FORK-1 and FORK-2. Next, we present the Bitcoin's hardfork atomic trade protocol.

---

[9] Previous transaction hash as 32 `bytes`, the previous transaction output index as 4 `bytes`, the length of the script as 1 `byte` and the sequence number as 4 `bytes`.

[10] The activation time can be determined by a publicly announced flag day (i.e. similar to Bitcoin Cash [31]). There is a signalling process outlined in BIP9 [40], but this is designed for softforks. If the signalling process is used, then this atomic trade must be set up after the new rules are locked in.

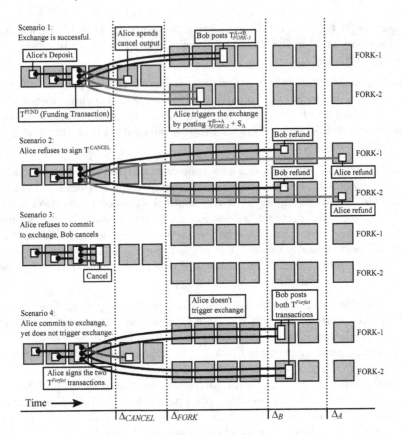

Fig. 1. High-level overview. Our protocol has four outcomes: (1). both parties successfully perform the trade, (2). Alice aborts the protocol shortly after T^{Fund} is accepted into the blockchain and both parties are refunded, (3). Bob cancels the atomic trade and both parties are immediately refunded, and (4). Alice forfeits her coins in both blockchains to Bob by not triggering the atomic trade

3.1 Proposed Protocol for Bitcoin

Table 6 presents the atomic trade protocol that permits two parties to exchange coins in the event of a hardfork. We present the establishment, off-chain setup and atomic trade aspects of the protocol below.

On-chain Establishment. Alice computes the secret S_A and hashes it $h_A = H(S_A)$ before both parties co-operatively deposit coins into a Funding Transaction T^{Fund}. This transaction has an output for Alice's deposit, Bob's deposit and an auxiliary output that we denote as Cancel Timer[11]. Both deposit outputs can be redeemed if either condition is satisified:

---

[11] Both parties deposit a sufficient number of coins in this output to cover a future transaction fee.

1. **Refund.** Each party is refunded their deposit if the trade times-out after time Δ_A for Alice or Δ_B for Bob.
2. **Transfer.** One party can claim the deposit if both parties have signed the transaction and S_A is revealed.
3. **Cancel.** A sentinel condition that cancels the atomic trade if it is redeemed simultaneously with the Cancel Timer output of this transaction.
4. **Forfeit (Alice Deposit Only).** Alice forfeits her deposit if she does not trigger the transfer by Δ_B.

Alice's refund time Δ_A must be after Bob's refund time Δ_B such that $\Delta_A > \Delta_B$. As well, both timers must be after the hardfork activation time Δ_{FORK} such that $\Delta_A, \Delta_B > \Delta_{FORK}$. This provides a grace period for Alice to reveal S_A (i.e. trigger the trade) and for Bob to find S_A to claim his coins.

The Cancel Timer output has a Cancel condition that can cancel the atomic trade if it is signed by both parties before Δ_{CANCEL}. Otherwise the output also has a Commit condition that allows Alice to single-handedly sign this output after Δ_{CANCEL}. The lock time Δ_{CANCEL} must expire before the hardforks activation time Δ_{FORK} such that $\Delta_{FORK} > \Delta_{CANCEL}$. This is to ensure the atomic trade is set up within a timely manner and before the hardfork. Finally the Funding Transaction T^{Fund} must achieve sufficient depth in the blockchain before both party's can co-operatively begin the off-chain setup.

Set up cancellation. Alice signs and sends Bob T^{Cancel}. This transaction satisfies the Cancel condition for all three outputs[12] of the Funding Transaction T^{Fund} and sends both parties their deposits The purpose of this transaction is to allow Bob to cancel the atomic trade if it is not set up before Δ_{CANCEL}. Alice can sign and broadcast T^{Commit} after Δ_{CANCEL} that spends the Cancel Timer's output (i.e. Commit condition) in order to invalidate T^{Cancel} and prevent Bob cancelling the atomic trade.

Set up trade. Alice signs and sends Bob $T^{A \to B}_{FORK1}$. This transaction spends both deposit outputs using the Transfer condition and sends all coins to Bob if the pre-image S_A is revealed and the transaction is accepted into the blockchain FORK-1 before Δ_B. Next, Bob signs and sends Alice $T^{B \to A}_{FORK2}$. This transaction spends both deposit outputs using the Transfer condition and will send all coins to Alice if the pre-image S_A is revealed and the transaction is accepted into the blockchain FORK-2 before Δ_A. As well, this transaction must incorporate relay protection such that it is only valid for the forked blockchain FORK-2. It is worth mentioning that the atomic trade can be performed after the hardfork activation time Δ_{FORK} if Alice broadcasts T^{Commit} to invalidate T^{Cancel}. However, Alice currently has an unfair advantage as she can abort the protocol (i.e. not reveal the pre-image S_A) and cancel the atomic trade without a penalty.

---

[12] Table 6 highlights that each transaction output in the Funding Transaction has a Cancel condition. For example, Alice's deposit can be spent if Cancel(PK_{A_3}, PK_{B_3}) is satisfied and the Cancel Timer can be spent if Cancel(PK_{A_2}, PK_{B_2}). is satisfied.

Set up forfeit. To overcome this fairness issue, Alice must sign and send Bob $T^{Forfeit}_{FORK1}$, $T^{Forfeit}_{FORK2}$. Both transactions spend Alice's deposit using the Forfeit condition and Bob's deposit using the Transfer condition. Of course, these transactions will send all coins to Bob in both FORK-1 and FORK-2. This allows Bob to penalize Alice for aborting the protocol (i.e. not triggering the trade before Δ_B). Furthermore, Alice must sign and send Bob both transactions before the lock time Δ_{CANCEL}. Otherwise, Bob is expected to cancel the atomic trade by signing and broadcasting T^{Cancel}.

Commit to Atomic Trade. Alice signs and broadcasts T^{Commit}. This transaction spends the Cancel Timer output using the Commit condition after Δ_{CANCEL} in order to invalidate the cancellation transaction T^{Cancel}. Thus, both parties are committed to performing the atomic trade.

Trigger Trade. After the hardfork activation time Δ_{FORK} Alice can claim both deposits in FORK-2 using $T^{B \to A}_{FORK2}$. This reveals S_A in FORK-2 and allows Bob to claim both deposits in FORK-1 using $T^{A \to B}_{FORK1}$.

Forfeit. As we mentioned previously Bob can penalise Alice if she does not trigger the transfer. He can broadcast the transactions $T^{Forfeit}_{FORK1}$, $T^{Forfeit}_{FORK2}$ after Δ_B to claim all coins in both blockchains FORK-1, FORK-2.

3.2 Distinct Keys

We highlight that the protocol is only secure if each condition in a transaciton output has a unique signing key i.e. $PK_{A_1}, ..., PK_{A_4}$. The core issue is that the message signed for a transaction output is the same regardless of the condition the signer intends to satisfy. This insecurity can be highlighted if we assume all conditions for Alice's deposit output rely on a single signing key PK_{A_1}.

Alice signs the transaction output that represents her deposit during the trade setup phase. She intends for her signature to satisify the Transfer(PK_{A_1}, PK_{B_2}, h_A) condition that sends her deposit to Bob if S_A is revealed. Unexpectedly, Bob can re-use her signature to also satisfy the forfeit condition Forfeit($PK_{A_1}, PK_{B_4}, \Delta_B$). This guarantees that he receives both deposits in the non-forked blockchain FORK-1 after Δ_B and thus he has no motivation to continue following the protocol.

4   Ethereum Hardfork Atomic Cross-Chain Trade

The key insight for this protocol is that both parties can deposit their coins into a smart contract. After the hardfork has occurred the contract can use a `Hardfork Oracle` to determine whether it is on the blockchain FORK-1 or FORK-2 before sending each respective party their coins. In this section, we discuss how to construct `Hardfork Oracles` before presenting the protocol.

Table 3. Ethereum Hardfork Atomic Cross-Chain Trade. Both parties deposit coins into the `Trade` Contract. This contract can detect if it is on FORK-1, FORK-2 using `Hardfork Oracle` contract before sending the deposits.

---

1. Alice and Bob agree on the refund lock time Δ_{REFUND} based on the fixed hardfork time Δ_{FORK}

2. Alice creates the `Trade` contract that specifies the deposits d_a, d_b required by both parties, the refund lock time Δ_{REFUND} and `Hardfork Oracle` contract's address σ

3. The contract locks both parties into the exchange once the deposits d_a, d_b are confirmed

4. **Both parties wait for the hardfork at time Δ_{FORK}**

5. Alice signs $T_{FORK2}^{B \to A}$ and claims both deposits in the forked blockchain FORK-2 before Δ_{REFUND}

   – Contract communicates with `Oracle Hardfork` contract to confirm this is the forked blockchain FORK-2

6. Bob signs $T_{FORK1}^{A \to B}$ and claims both deposits in the non-forked blockchain FORK-1 before Δ_{REFUND}

   – Contract communicates with `Oracle Hardfork` contract to confirm this is the non-forked blockchain FORK-1

4.1   Hardfork Oracle

We propose that a `Hardfork Oracle` contract can be used to distinguish whether it is on FORK-1 or FORK-2 without the need for a trusted third party. There are two approaches to realize this oracle:

Detection within contract. As mentioned in Sect. 2.4, Ethereum has implemented replay protection in the form of a `chain_id`. The simplest approach is for the contract to query `tx.chain_id` to determine if the transaction was accepted into FORK-1 or FORK-2. Unfortunately, the `chain_id` cannot yet be programmatically accessed by the contract's code.

The Ethereum Community have also proposed the concept of an oracle contract that can detect the activation of a hardfork and have provided an example for TheDAO hardfork [25]. This contract checks TheDAO's contract balance after the publicly announced hardfork time Δ_{FORK} to determine if the contract is in FORK-2 (i.e. the balance is reverted to reverse the theft) or FORK-1 (i.e. the coins remain stolen and the balance has not changed).

Detection outside contract. One approach is that the user can provide the contract evidence that a transaction with the desired `chain_id` was accepted into the blockchain after the Δ_{FORK}. This evidence can be a confirmed transaction alongside its patricia tree branch and the respective block's header. The contract can verify that the transaction is accepted in the respective block before confirming that it is in the blockchain's most recent 256 blocks. Finally, the contract can extract the chain_id from the transaction and determine if this blockchain is FORK-1 or FORK-2.

Future Hardforks. Ethereum have recently approved changes that will be included as a hardfork in the future. This includes EIP96 [6] that proposes extending block.blockhash to return hashes that are more than 256 blocks deep and EIP98 [9] that proposes removing the intermediate state value from a transaction's receipt. We highlight that a hardfork for EIP96 can be detected within a contract as block.blockhash(257) will either return 0 for the oracle contract on FORK-1 or the respective block hash for the oracle contract on FORK-2. On the other hand, a hardfork for EIP98 can be detected in a similar manner to chain_id by providing a transaction receipt, patricia tree branch and the respective block header. The contract can verify if the intermediate root's value is removed (or set to 0) to decide if it is on FORK-1 or FORK-2. We leave it for future work to determine if oracles can be built to detect gas changes or new functions (i.e. opcodes).

4.2 Proposed Protocol for Ethereum

Given a Hardfork Oracle we can perform an Atomic Cross-Chain Trade in Ethereum and the protocol is presented in Table 3. We briefly explain how to establish the atomic trade prior to the hardfork, how to perform the trade using the hardfork oracle and why the trigger is no longer necessary.

Establishment. First, Alice establishes the Trade contract and specifies the required deposits d_a, d_b, the timers $\Delta_{FORK}, \Delta_{REFUND}$, and the Hardfork Oracle's address. Finally, both parties deposit their coins into the contract before the hardfork activation time Δ_{FORK}.

Atomic Trade. Both Alice and Bob must claim both deposits from the Trade contract during the grace period between Δ_{FORK} and Δ_{REFUND}. Otherwise, either party can withdraw their deposit from the contract after Δ_{REFUND}. Notably, at the time of withdrawal, the Trade contract contacts the Hardfork Oracle to determine if this blockchain is FORK-1 or FORK-2.

Triggering Trade. The Bitcoin protocol's trigger served two purposes. The first was to ensure both deposits could not be spent until the activation of the hardfork, and the second was to ensure the trade was only conducted if the hardfork occurred. The Trade contract can enforce both purposes without a trigger as the contract can detect which fork it is on after the hardfork activation time Δ_{FORK}. Most importantly, this also removes the requirement for a synchronised clock for both FORK-1, FORK-2 in order to perform the atomic trade.

5   Discussion

In this section, we discuss the requirement for a synchronised global clock, the potential for miner censorship and bribery attacks, and the impact of transaction malleability for designing our protocols.

Synchronised Time. Unlike the TierNolan protocol, the Bitcoin atomic trade protocol in this paper does not rely on both blockchains having a synchronised block height or timestamp in order to co-ordinate and enforce the atomic trade's fair exchange. We highlight that Bob is guaranteed to receive his coins in FORK-1 after Δ_B using the forfeiture transaction $T_{FORK1}^{Forfeit}$. The only crucial timer is Δ_B in FORK-2 that dictates when Alice should reveal S_A to claim both deposits. As a result, both the block height and the median time of the previous 11 blocks is suitable for our protocol.

In Ethereum, no single party is responsible for triggering the trade and the Δ_{REFUND} timer used by the `transfer` contract is independent for both blockchains. It is feasible for miner's to slow the passage of time although this simply increases the affected party's grace period to claim both deposits.

Miner Censorship. A cartel of miners have the authority to censor transactions in both Bitcoin and Ethereum. This censorship permits miners to interfere with the atomic trade and coerce either party to share a portion of their deposit. To illustrate for the Bitcoin protocol, it is feasible for miners in blockchain FORK-2 to simply censor $T_{FORK2}^{B \rightarrow A}$ if Alice refuses to pay a bribe. At the same time, Bob can agree to pay this bribe by sending the miners a new bribery transaction which is only valid if the forfiture transaction $T_{FORK2}^{Forfeit}$ is accepted into FORK-2 after Δ_B. In Ethereum, miners can simply stop the atomic trade by preventing both parties depositing or withdrawing the contract's coins. It is worth mentioning that bribery and censorship attacks also violate the security guarantees for timelock based atomic cross-chain trade protocols/off-chain payment channels.

Hardfork Time. The hardfork's activation time Δ_{FORK} must be fixed to permit both parties to agree suitable lock times for the atomic trade. Alice must only sign the forfeit transactions if she is confident the hard-fork activation time Δ_{FORK} will not be delayed. Otherwise, the delay can result in $\Delta_{FORK} > \Delta_B$ for the Bitcoin protocol. This allows Bob to claim the deposits in both blockchains FORK-1 and FORK-2 using the forfeiture transactions. On the other hand, in Ethereum, both parties mutually agree upon a single Δ_{REFUND} and if the hard-fork is delayed until after this time then both parties are refunded.

Transaction Malleability. The atomic trade protocol for Bitcoin is designed to account for transaction malleability which is why both parties are required to co-operatively sign cancellation, trade and forfeit transactions after T^{Fund} is stored in the blockchain. If transaction malleability is fixed, then it is feasible to simplify the protocol such that only the trade transactions $T_{FORK1}^{A \rightarrow B}$, $T_{FORK2}^{B \rightarrow A}$ need to be signed off-chain before both parties co-operatively sign and broadcast the funding transaction (protocol in full paper). (see Appendix B for details). On the other hand, the Ethereum protocol is not impacted by transaction malleability as the contract can store the current state of the atomic trade and parties are not required to co-operatively authorise transactions.

Nature of the Bet. It is important to distinguish if both parties are betting that the hardfork activates at Δ_{FORK}, or if both parties are betting whether FORK-1 or FORK-2 will be more valuable if the hard-fork occurs. Our protocol is focused on the former bet as Alice only signs the forfeit transactions once she is confident the hardfork will activate at time Δ_{FORK}. If the hardfork does not occur at time Δ_{FORK}, then she forfeits her deposit to Bob. It is feasible to perform the latter bet (i.e. refund both parties if the hardfork does not occur) if Alice does not perform the final forfeiture step. However, this has a fairness issue as Alice can evaluate whether to perform the trade or to abort the protocol (i.e. not to reveal S_A) and cancel the atomic trade.

6   Conclusion

In this paper, we propose the first protocol that can commit two parties to swapping "pre-fork" coins before a hardfork activates, and then enforce the swap after the hardfork has occurred without the assistance of a trusted third party. Our protocols are inspired by real-world events as Loaded and Roger voiced interest in atomically trading 120 k bitcoins (i.e. approximately \$120 m USD at the time) to effectively gamble on the success of a future hardfork in Bitcoin.

We show how to realize the atomic trade protocols in Bitcoin and Ethereum. The former relies on the hardfork deploying replay protection and a global clock, whereas the latter simply leverages a `Hardfork Oracle` contract that allows another contract to detect if it is in blockchain FORK-1 or FORK-2. Finally, also we provided a detailed survey on the history of soft/hard forks for Bitcoin, Ethereum and Ethereum Classic, and a survey on proposed replay protection mechanisms in Bitcoin.

Acknowledgements. We thank Nick Johnson for bringing to our attention hardfork oracles, Tadge Dryja for his comments and criticisms, Roger Ver for allowing us to use his name in the paper's title, Iddo Bentov for insightful discussions and #bitcoin-wizards IRC channel for answering questions regarding forks. Patrick McCorry is supported by EPSRC grant EP/N028104/1, Ethan Heilman is supported by NSF 1350733.

A   TierNolan's Atomic Cross-Chain Trading Protocol

Table 4 presents the protocol proposed by TierNolan in 2013. The TierNolan protocol allows two parties to atomically exchange coins across two blockchains. Such protocols are called Atomic Swaps because the two transactions happen *atomically i.e.,* either swap occurs or it does not. It requires both parties to deposit coins in separate blockchains and for one of the parties to trigger the exchange.

Brief overview. Consider two blockchains, the first blockchain we denote as FORK-1, the second blockchain we denote as FORK-2. Alice wants to trade her coins on blockchain FORK-1 for coins which Bob controls on blockchain FORK-2. First, Alice picks a random value S_A, hashes it to $H(S_A)$ and deposits her coins into a transaction T_1 which is confirmed on FORK-1. Bob can claim the funds in T_1 if and only if he learns the value S_A. However if the coins in T_1 are still unspent by Δ_A Alice can refund the coins in this transaction back to herself.

Table 4. Atomic Cross-Chain Trading Protocol. This protocol allows two parties to atomically exchange coins across two distinct blockchains

---

1. Alice and Bob agree on lock times Δ_A, Δ_B

2. Alice picks random S_A, hashes it $h_A = H(S_A)$ and constructs T_1 with her deposit. This transaction has a single output:
   - **Alice's deposit:** Output script is (PK_{A_1}, Δ_A)[a] OR $(H(S_A), B)$

   This transaction is signed by Alice and published to the first blockchain FORK-1

3. Bob has knowledge of $H(S_A)$ and creates T_2 with his deposit. This transaction has a single output:
   - **Bob's deposit:** Output script is (PK_{B_1}, Δ_B) OR $(H(S_A), A)$

   This transaction is signed by Bob and published to the second blockchain FORK-2
   It is important that $\Delta_A > \Delta_B$ by a sufficient margin

4. Alice must claim Bob's deposit before Δ_B. She signs a transaction that spends T_2, includes S_A and publishes it to the second blockchain FORK-2

5. Bob must claim Alice's deposit before Δ_A. He learns S_A, signs a transaction that spends T_1 and publishes it to the first blockchain FORK-1

---
[a] The original protocol had an explicit refund transaction that Bob was required to sign. It is possible to remove this step using CHECKLOCKTIMEVERIFY.

B   Proposed Bitcoin Protocol if Transaction Malleability is fixed

Table 5 presents the Bitcoin hard-fork atomic cross-chain protocol if transaction malleability is fixed. It assumes that both parties can use replay protection to dic-

Table 5. Bitcoin's Hard Fork Atomic Cross-Chain Trade if transaction malleability is fixed. Both parties authorise the atomic trade transactions prior to signing and broadcasting the funding transaction T^{Fund}. Both trade transactions can be accepted into their respective blockchain after the hard-fork activation time Δ_{FORK}.

---

1. **Funding Transaction.** Alice and Bob agree on lock times Δ_A, Δ_B that should be sufficiently after the hardfork activation time Δ_{FORK}

2. Alice constructs a transaction we call *the Funding Transaction* or T^{Fund}. This transaction requires a deposit from each parties and has a single output:
   - **Deposits:** Trade$(PK_{A_1}, PK_{B_1}, \Delta_{FORK} + 1)$

3. Alice signs and sends Bob $T^{A \to B}_{FORK1}$. This transaction is only valid in FORK-1 and cannot be accepted into the blockchain until after the hard-fork activation time Δ_{FORK}

4. Bob signs and sends Alice $T^{B \to A}_{FORK2}$. This transaction is only valid in FORK-2 and cannot be accepted into the blockchain until after the hard-fork activation time Δ_{FORK}

5. Both parties co-operatively sign and broadcast T^{Fund} for acceptance into the blockchain

6. **Atomic Trade.** Both parties can broadcast $T^{A \to B}_{FORK1}$, $T^{B \to A}_{FORK2}$ after the hard-fork activation time Δ_{FORK}

Table 6. Bitcoin's Hard Fork Atomic Cross-Chain Trade. Our proposed protocol commits both Alice and Both to the trade prior to the hardfork's activation

---

1. **Funding Transaction.** Alice and Bob agree on lock times Δ_A, Δ_B that should be sufficiently after the hardfork activation time Δ_{FORK}

2. Alice picks random S_A, hashes it $h_A = H(S_A)$ and constructs a transaction we call *the Funding Transaction* or T^{Fund}. This transaction requires a deposit from each parties and has three outputs:

– **Alice's deposit:** Refund(PK_{A_1}, Δ_A) OR Transfer(PK_{A_2}, PK_{B_2}, h_A) OR Cancel(PK_{A_3}, PK_{B_3}) OR Forfeit($PK_{A_4}, PK_{B_4}, \Delta_B$)

– **Bob's deposit:** Refund(PK_{B_1}, Δ_B) OR Transfer(PK_{A_2}, PK_{B_2}, h_A) OR Cancel(PK_{A_3}, PK_{B_3})

– **Cancel timer:** Commit($PK_{A_1}, \Delta_{CANCEL}$) OR Cancel($PK_{A_2}, PK_{B_2}$)

This transaction must be accepted into the blockchain before Δ_{FORK} and achieve sufficient depth before performing the next step

3. **Set up cancellation.** Alice signs and sends Bob T^{Cancel}. This transaction spends all three outputs using the Cancel condition and sends both parties their deposit. He can sign and broadcast T^{Cancel} before Δ_{CANCEL} to cancel the atomic swap

4. **Off-chain setup.** Alice signs and sends Bob $T^{A \to B}_{FORK1}$, and Bob signs and sends Alice $T^{B \to A}_{FORK2}$. Both transactions spend Alice's and Bob's deposit outputs using the Transfer condition

5. **Set up forfeit:** Alice signs and sends Bob two transactions $T^{Forfeit}_{FORK1}$ and $T^{Forfeit}_{FORK2}$. Both transaction's spend Alice's deposited coins using the Forfeit condition and is valid after time Δ_B

6. **Commit to Atomic Trade.** If Alice does not sign and send the forfeit transactions before time Δ_{CANCEL} then Bob must sign and broadcast T^{Cancel}. Otherwise, she signs and broadcasts T^{Commit} after time Δ_{CANCEL}. This transaction effectively invalidates T^{Cancel} by spending the Cancel Timer output using the Commit condition

7. Both parties wait for the hardfork at time Δ_{FORK}

8. **Trigger Trade.** If Alice triggers the trade:

(a) Alice signs $T^{B \to A}_{FORK2}$, reveals S_A and claims both deposits in the forked blockchain FORK-2 before Δ_B

(b) Bob finds S_A, signs $T^{A \to B}_{FORK1}$ and claims both deposits in the non-forked blockchain FORK-1 before Δ_A

8. **Forfeit.** If Alice does not trigger the trade by Δ_B:

(a) Bob signs $T^{Forfeit}_{FORK1}$ and $T^{Forfeit}_{FORK2}$ claims both deposits in FORK-2 and FORK-1

tate if a transaction can be accepted into FORK-1 or FORK-2. As we will soon see this variation is significantly simpler compared to the protocol outlined in Sect. 3.

Briefly, both parties co-operatively create a Funding Transaction T^{Fund} and the two trade transactions $T^{A \to B}_{FORK1}$, $T^{B \to A}_{FORK2}$. Next, both parties must exchange signatures for the trade transactions before signing and broadcasting the funding transaction. Finally, both parties wait until after the hard-fork activation time Δ_{FORK} to claim both deposits in their respective blockchain.

This approach follows a similar style to payment protocols such as Duplex Micropayment Systems and Lightning as the off-chain's transactions are signed prior to the funding transaction. The order of signing off-chain transactions does not necessarily matter as these transactions are only valid if the funding transaction is accepted into the blockchain. Furthermore, it is worth highlighting that this approach does not require one party (i.e. Alice) to reveal a pre-image S_A or to sign cancel/forfeit transactions.

References

1. Andresen, G.: Block v2, Height in Coinbase, July 2012. https://github.com/bitcoin/bips/blob/6925e66aa092d97f8273e4bab15bb0d4c63f9ac9/bip-0034.mediawiki
2. Andresen, G.: March 2013 Chain Fork Post-Mortem, March 2013. https://github.com/bitcoin/bips/blob/master/bip-0050.mediawiki
3. BitcoinCore. Accept Transaction version 2 or more, June 2017. https://github.com/bitcoin/bitcoin/blob/1088b02f0ccd7358d2b7076bb9e122d59d502d02/src/consensus/tx_verify.cpp#L45
4. blockchain.info. Blockchain charts, March 2017. https://blockchain.info/charts
5. Buterin, V.: Bitcoin Network Shaken by Blockchain Fork, March 2013. https://bitcoinmagazine.com/articles/bitcoin-network-shaken-by-blockchain-fork-1363144448/
6. Buterin, V.: Blockhash refactoring, April 2016. https://github.com/ethereum/EIPs/issues/98
7. Buterin, V.: Long-term gas cost changes for IO-heavy operations to mitigate transaction spam attacks, September 2016. https://github.com/ethereum/EIPs/issues/150
8. Buterin, V.: Simple replay attack protection, October 2016. https://github.com/ethereum/eips/issues/155
9. Buterin, V.: Removal of intermediate state roots from receipts, February 2017. https://github.com/ethereum/EIPs/pull/210
10. coinmarketcap.com. CryptoCurrency Market Capitalizations: Bitcoin, March 2017. https://coinmarketcap.com/currencies/bitcoin/
11. Dashjr, L.: OP_CHECKBLOCKATHEIGHT, September 2016. https://github.com/luke-jr/bips/blob/bip-cbah/bip-cbah.mediawiki
12. Deadalnix. Add spec for UAHF, June 2017. https://github.com/Bitcoin-UAHF/spec/blob/master/replay-protected-sighash.md
13. Friedenbach, M., BtcDrak, Dorier, N., Kinoshitajona: Relative lock-time using consensus-enforced sequence numbers, May 2015. https://github.com/bitcoin/bips/blob/master/bip-0068.mediawiki
14. Goldfeder, S., Bonneau, J., Gennaro, R., Narayanan, A.: Escrow protocols for cryptocurrencies: how to buy physical goods using bitcoin. In: Financial Cryptography and Data Security. Springer (2017)

15. Harding, T.: [bitcoin-dev] Proposal: Hard fork opt-out bits, July 2016. https://lists.linuxfoundation.org/pipermail/bitcoin-dev/2016-July/012917.html
16. Hertig, A.: Ethereum Executes Blockchain Hard Fork to Return DAO Funds, July 2016. http://www.coindesk.com/ethereum-classic-explained-blockchain/
17. Hertig, A.: How Developers Are Responding to Ethereum's Unexpected Fork, December 2016. http://www.coindesk.com/developer-response-ethereum-fork/
18. Hertig, A.: The Blockchain Created By Ethereum's Fork is Forking Now, October 2016. http://www.coindesk.com/ethereum-classic-blockchain-fork-ddos-attacks/
19. Hertig, A.: Ethereum Classic Freezes 'Difficulty Bomb' With 'Diehard' Fork, January 2017. http://www.coindesk.com/ethereum-classic-diehard-fork/
20. S. Higgins. Bitcoin Exchanges Unveil Hard Fork Contingency Plan, March 2017. http://www.coindesk.com/ethereum-executes-blockchain-hard-fork-return-dao-investor-funds/
21. Kerin, T., Friedenbach, M.: Median time-past as endpoint for lock-time calculation, August 2015. https://github.com/bitcoin/bips/blob/master/bip-0113.mediawiki
22. Lau, J.: [bitcoin-dev] Anti-transaction replay in a hardfork, January 2017. https://github.com/bitcoin/bips/blob/master/bip-0068.mediawiki
23. Loaded. @RogerVer lets make a deal. At least 60k, my BTU for your BTC, March 2017. https://bitcointalk.org/index.php?topic=1836672.0
24. Lombrozo, E., Lau, J., Wuille, P.: Segregated Witness (Consensus layer), December 2015. https://github.com/bitcoin/bips/blob/master/bip-0141.mediawiki
25. Maersk, N.: The DAO Hard Fork Oracle, July 2016. https://github.com/veox/solidity-dapps/blob/TheDAOHardForkOracle-v0.1/TheDAOHardForkOracle/TheDAOHardForkOracle.sol
26. Maxwell, G.: Capacity increases FAQ, December 2015. https://bitcoin.org/en/bitcoin-core/capacity-increases-faq#roadmap
27. Maxwell, G., Wilcke, P.W.: Conversation on Bitcoin Wizards, April 2017. https://botbot.me/freenode/bitcoin-wizards/2017-04-20/?msg=84304042&page=3
28. McCorry, P., Shahandashti, S.F., Hao, F.: A smart contract for boardroom voting with maximum voter privacy. In: Financial Cryptography and Data Security. Springer (2017)
29. Nakamoto, S.: Bitcoin: a peer-to-peer electronic cash system (2008). https://bitcoin.org/bitcoin.pdf
30. Poon, J., Dryja, T.: The bitcoin lightning network, February 2015. https://lightning.network/
31. Song, J.: Timeline, The Bitcoin Cash: What Will Happen When. https://www.coindesk.com/bitcoin-cash-what-expect-fork-10000-foot-view/
32. Spagni, R.: A formal approach towards better hard fork management (2015). https://forum.getmonero.org/4/academic-and-technical/303/a-formal-approach-towards-better-hard-fork-management
33. Tier, N.: Re: Alt chains and atomic transfers, May 2013. https://bitcointalk.org/index.php?topic=193281.msg2224949#msg2224949
34. Todd, P.: OP_CHECKLOCKTIMEVERIFY, October 2014. https://github.com/bitcoin/bips/blob/master/bip-0065.mediawiki
35. ViaBTC. Miner guide: how to safely hard fork to bitcoin unlimited, October 2016. https://medium.com/@ViaBTC/miner-guide-how-to-safely-hard-fork-to-bitcoin-unlimited-8ac1570dc1a8
36. Wilcke, J.: Homestead Release, February 2016. https://blog.ethereum.org/2016/02/29/homestead-release/
37. Wood, G.: State trie clearing (invariant-preserving alternative), October 2016. https://github.com/ethereum/EIPs/issues/161

38. Wuille, P.: Duplicate transactions, February 2012. https://github.com/bitcoin/bips/blob/6925e66aa092d97f8273e4bab15bb0d4c63f9ac9/bip-0030.mediawiki
39. Wuille, P.: Strict DER Signatures, January 2015. https://github.com/bitcoin/bips/blob/6925e66aa092d97f8273e4bab15bb0d4c63f9ac9/bip-0066.mediawiki
40. Wuille, P., Todd, P., Maxwell, G., Russell, R.: Version bits with timeout and delay, October 2015. https://github.com/bitcoin/bips/blob/master/bip-0009.mediawiki
41. Zander, T.: Replay Protection Guidance, March 2017. https://bitco.in/forum/threads/replay-protection-guidance.1930/

Smart Contracts and Blockchain Identity

In Code We Trust?

Measuring the Control Flow Immutability of All Smart Contracts Deployed on Ethereum

Michael Fröwis[(⊠)] and Rainer Böhme

Department of Computer Science, Universität Innsbruck, Innsbruck, Austria
michael.froewis@uibk.ac.at

Abstract. Program code stored on the Ethereum blockchain is considered immutable, but this does not imply that its control flow cannot be modified. This bears the risk of loopholes whenever parties encode binding agreements in smart contracts. In order to quantify the issue, we define a heuristic indicator of control flow immutability, evaluate it based on a call graph of all smart contracts deployed on Ethereum, and find that two out of five smart contracts require trust in at least one third party. Besides, the analysis reveals that significant parts of the Ethereum blockchain are interspersed with debris from past attacks against the platform. We leverage the call graph to develop a method for data cleanup, which allows for less biased statistics of Ethereum use in practice.

Keywords: Smart contract · Trustless · Code analysis · Call graph · Ethereum

1 Introduction

Smart contracts are computer programs that encode agreements between parties. They can be settled in virtual currency by decentralized systems of networked nodes. This is advantageous in situations where conventional means of contract enforcement are prohibitively costly, or the parties have no access to a common arbiter or juridical system.

Like for conventional natural-language contracts, a number of conditions must be fulfilled before a party can accept being bound by the terms: the party must understand the content of the contract with the same semantic applied by a potential judge, the integrity of the contract must be guaranteed over its entire lifetime, and the contract must not contain or refer to any terms that can be changed unilaterally after the contract is signed. These three conditions can be mapped to technical requirements (in the same order): access to verifiable source code, immutability of compiled code, and control flow immutability.

If any of these conditions is violated, the party accepting contract terms must trust at least one third party in that the enforcement does not thwart the

© Springer International Publishing AG 2017
J. Garcia-Alfaro et al. (Eds.): DPM/CBT 2017, LNCS 10436, pp. 357–372, 2017.
DOI: 10.1007/978-3-319-67816-0_20

contract's designated objectives. Ethereum presents itself as a platform for *trust-less* smart contracts, and provides means to meet the above-mentioned technical requirements. However, users are free to write smart contracts in a Turing complete language, so the extent to which smart contracts meet the requirements in practice remains an empirical question.

We set out to answer this question with special emphasis on control flow immutability. We apply abstract interpretation techniques to all bytecode deployed on the public Ethereum blockchain, and synthesize the information in a complete call graph of static dependencies between all smart contracts.

We are not the first to systematically analyze smart contracts on Ethereum. Luu et al. [13] execute 19 366 smart contracts symbolically with the intention to uncover security vulnerabilities, which they find in about 8833 cases. Using source code provided by Etherscan, Bartoletti and Livio [5] manually classify 811 smart contracts by application domain (e. g., financial, gaming, notary) and identify typical design patterns. Norvill et al. [16] propose unsupervised clustering to group 936 smart contracts on the Ethereum blockchain. We are not aware of any prior work that builds or analyzes a call graph of dependencies between smart contracts on Ethereum or a similar platform.

Systemic analyses of all smart contracts on the Ethereum blockchain are impeded by the presence of a significant number of smart contracts originating from attacks against the platform. Therefore, as a second contribution, we propose a cleanup method to pre-process the smart contracts. This is necessary before any meaningful and generalizable measurements of legitimate[1] use can be made.

The paper is organized as follows. Section 2 recalls the vision of *trustless* smart contracts and derives necessary technical requirements for the trustlessness property. Section 3 briefly describes the Ethereum platform and documents our data extraction and analysis methods. Section 4 motivates the cleanup and describes how we accomplished it. Results are presented in Sect. 5. Finally, Sect. 6 concludes the paper with a discussion of limitations and implications.

2   Trustless Smart Contracts

We provide some background by reflecting on the notion of trustlessness. Section 2.1 reviews the vision of smart contracts as defined by Szabo [18]. Section 2.2 defines the technical requirements to reach the vision of trustless smart contracts.

2.1   The Vision

Smart contracts are not a very new concept. Szabo introduced the term in 1997. The idea of smart contracts is that many kinds of contractual clauses, in fact

---

[1] In a slight abuse of legal terminology, this notion of legitimacy includes *everything* except attacks against the platform as a whole.

every computable clause, can be encoded in logic. That means we can encode contract clauses in computer programs and let the program decide what happens in the course of the contract's lifetime.

This automation of contracts has many advantages, such as reduced transaction cost, less subjectivity, easier auditing, etc. It also facilitates machines to enforce in contractual agreements. Think of a car that only starts when the insurance premium is paid. The vision also comprises scenarios where machines enter contractual agreements as partners. Think of autonomous trading agents.

As long as programs encoding contracts are run on local *trusted hard- and software*, and the source code (or some human readable representation) is available for verification, no trust in other parties is needed. This rationale has been around for long. It serves, e. g., as a philosophical pillar of the free software movement.

In the real world, contracts regulate relationships between different parties who may have different interests and objectives, and do not necessarily trust each other. This raises the question of who executes the program encoding a contract? If only one party executes it, the others have to trust in its honesty. If many execute it, what happens if they disagree about the output? A simple approach, also known from paper-based contracts, is the involvement of an impartial *trusted third party*. This can happen in two ways. First, the third party computes the outcome of the contract. Second, whenever a conflict arises, the trusted third party acts as an arbiter. In both cases, all other parties must trust that the third party is fair and abide to its decisions.

Trusted third parties only shift the problem to another hopefully trustworthy party. The declared vision of smart contracts is a system where nobody has to trust a central party. Szabo argues that every algorithmic intermediary can be replaced by a *trustworthy virtual computer*. He contemplates a trustless system using "post-unforgeable transaction logs" and "mutually confidential computation" [18].

Although, in theory, it was known in 1997 that is is possible to build a trustless system based on cryptographic multiparty computation, practical universal systems remained out of reach for lack of efficiency. The advent of blockchain-based systems has demonstrated the existence of a sweet spot that offers more efficient solutions by combining off-the-shelf cryptography with probabilistic distributed consensus protocols. This has led to a renaissance of the ideas behind trustless smart contracts as well as practical freely programmable systems.

2.2   Technical Requirements of Trustless Smart Contracts

Blockchains, or more specifically their underlying consensus protocols, allow to resolve conflicts between parties over a public network without a trusted third party [15]. With the ideas behind Bitcoin, it was possible to build a more efficient version of the *trustworthy virtual computer*, called *consensus computer* [14].

Consensus computers carry out and verify computations over a public network as if they ran on local trusted hardware. Individual parties do not need to trust in any other single party in the system. It is sufficient to make behavioral assumptions about collectives of parties, e. g., that the majority follows the protocol. This brings us back to the desirable situation where we do not have to trust anyone as long as we can verify a program's source code. But now we can run programs that affect many parties, not just one.

If the programs encode contractual clauses, access to the source code is only one of several necessary requirements for trustless smart contracts. We also need *immutability of control flow*. Once we send a smart contract to a consensus computer, it is not supposed to change anymore; just akin to conventional contracts should not be altered after signing. More specifically, if a smart contract has dependencies to other smart contracts on the consensus computer (e. g., by following the common practice of code reuse through libraries, which has been adopted on practical consensus computers), those references should be hard coded in the smart contract. Especially, they should not be determined by (later) input or state of the consensus computer. In other words, once the program is deployed, the control flow must not be changed.

Observe that code immutability is necessary but not sufficient for control flow immutability; which again is necessary but not sufficient for trustlessness, because a contract's outcome may also depend on data, which can be unknown at the time of the deployment. In this work, we make first steps towards measuring trustlessness in practice using a heuristic indicator of control flow immutability.

3   Method

Now we describe the data collection and analysis process. Section 3.1 introduces specifics of the Ethereum platform and the terminology needed to understand the analysis (For details, we refer to [3, 19].). Section 3.2 explains how we extract smart contract code and build a call graph. Section 3.3 describes how we measure trustlessness of the smart contracts deployed on the public Ethereum blockchain.

3.1   Ethereum in a Nutshell

Ethereum [3, 19] can be seen as a generalization of the ideas behind Bitcoin. It is a decentralized system that updates a global state stored in an authenticated data structure called *blockchain*. Besides transferring virtual currency tokens, the Ethereum platform enables users to create smart contracts. Smart contracts are implemented as a special kind of account, which is controlled by program code. More specifically, the program in such a *code account* represents an encoding for arbitrarily complex state transitions. Those state transitions are triggered by sending transactions to the address of the code account. Parameters can be passed in the transaction's data field. Code accounts can hold private[2] state in *state variables*. All state variables are persisted in the blockchain and can be modified only by the code of the corresponding code account. Besides code accounts, there exist *user accounts* that are controlled by external parties

---

[2] Private refers to scope and write access. It does not imply any confidentiality.

(i. e., private keys belonging to public keys that define the account). User accounts are best comparable to standard Bitcoin accounts. Both account types can create arbitrary transactions and thus interact with other code accounts, create new code accounts, or transfer virtual currency tokens.

The program in a code account is executed by the *Ethereum Virtual Machine* (EVM), a stack-based virtual machine that executes bytecode. Users typically create smart contracts using a high-level programming language that compiles to EVM bytecode. A popular smart contract language is Solidity [1].

Once a smart contract is compiled to EVM bytecode, it can be deployed to the Ethereum blockchain and thus made available to others. This is done by sending a transaction without a specified recipient to the Ethereum network. The code is sent within the `init` field of the transaction. When the transaction is included in a valid block, every node that processes and verifies the block sees the transaction without recipient. If a node[3] encounters such a transaction, it passes the payload contained in the `init` field to the EVM, which executes it. The output is saved as code of the newly created code account. The address assigned to the code account is determined by the rightmost 160 bits of the Keccak hash of the *recursive length prefix* (RLP) encoded creator address and the account's nonce. The nonce of a code account is incremented as smart contracts are created.[4]

The typical payload of a smart contract creation looks as follows: (initialization code ‖ code ‖ initialization parameters), where ‖ denotes concatenation. The EVM starts by executing the payload, thus the `initialization code` is executed. The `initialization code` is responsible for setting up initial values of state variables, if needed. The `initialization code` returns the code that will be stored at the newly created address. By default, the `initialization code` loads the `code` part from the payload into memory and returns the memory address and length. But this is just a convention. The `initialization code` could also dynamically build code in memory, or even return garbage. We found that almost all smart contract creations follow the default deployment convention (see Table 1 on page 12).

When a code account is created, its code is part of the blockchain, inheriting the property that it gets harder to modify as more blocks are added to the chain. After several confirmations, the possibility of modification is negligible, therefore the code becomes practically *immutable* over time. (Recall that immutable code does not imply control flow immutability. Measuring the latter is our objective.).

Although code is practically immutable, there is a possibility to disable code accounts. The EVM has an instruction that indicates that the current smart contract should be disabled and the space used by state variables and the account itself can be freed. This operation is called self destruction.[5] After a code account has self destructed, it can still be called, but it behaves as if there is no code

---

[3] A node that follows the protocol. We make this assumption throughout the paper.

[4] For completeness: also user accounts have nonces. The nonce of an user account is the number of transactions sent by that account.

[5] EVM instruction `SELFDESTRUCT`.

available. This means a call to a self destructed smart contract returns without any effect [4]. We call smart contracts that have called self destruct at some point in time *dead smart contracts* . By contrast, all smart contracts that have not called self destruct are called *active smart contracts* .

As mentioned in Sect. 2.2, source code availability is critical to smart contracts. Whenever the semantic of a smart contract on the blockchain shall be evaluated based on higher-level source code, a verifiable mapping between bytecode, source code, and addresses is needed. We are aware of two relevant services that aim to provide this mapping on a larger scale.

Etherscan[6] is a closed source web application. Users can upload source code that runs on a certain address. The user must provide the exact compiler version and flags used to generate the bytecode at the address. Etherscan then checks if the compiled source matches the bytecode at the supplied address. If it matches, Etherscan saves the corresponding source code and considers this code account a verified smart contract. At the time of writing,[7] Etherscan hosts 1728 verified smart contracts, which is less than 1% of all active smart contracts.

Swarm [2], the other service, is a decentralized peer-to-peer system built as storage service for the Ethereum development stack. It is linked to Ethereum's virtual currency to incentivize honest participation. The idea is as follows: whenever a smart contract is deployed to the blockchain, at the same time one deploys to Swarm a metadata file containing compiler version, flags, and source code. The address of the metadata in Swarm is the hash of its content. This hash is added to the compiled bytecode, hence the bytecode itself refers to its metadata. The verification of the mapping involves the same steps as done by Etherscan, but all metadata is available and can be automatically gathered from Swarm. Although this system sounds promising, and the Solidity compiler already generates metadata and adds hashes to the compiled bytecode, we found that Swarm is barely used to host metadata at the time of writing (see "Swarm metadata" and "Swarm hashes" in Table 1).

3.2   Parsing, Data Extraction and Call Graph Creation

Our goal is to analyze smart contracts and especially the call relationships between them. We extract the call relationship information directly from bytecode because source code is barely availability, as discussed in the previous section.

To extract bytecode from the Ethereum blockchain, we built upon an existing open source blockchain parser project.[8] The project uses the JSON–RPC API, which is part of all major Ethereum node implementations,[9] to extract data from the blockchain. Although this approach is probably slower than parsing the on-disk blockchain format directly, it is more convenient and less error prone.

---

[6] https://etherscan.io/.
[7] Accessed on 19 June 2017.
[8] https://github.com/alex-miller-0/Ethereum_Blockchain_Parser.
[9] https://github.com/ethereum/wiki/wiki/JSON-RPC.

As already said, code accounts are created by transactions without recipient. To extract the code of all smart contracts, we iterate over all transactions and select those which have no recipient. The code of the smart contract can be found in the `init` field of the transaction [19]. Unfortunately, this approach is limited to smart contracts created by user accounts. smart contracts created by code accounts are not manifested as transactions in the blockchain itself, but are side effects of the transaction that invoked the contract execution. Interactions between smart contracts (calls) or creations of new smart contracts by other smart contracts are done by so called *internal transactions*. To make internal transaction visible, the execution of the smart contract code needs to be instrumented. Fortunately, the *parity* client supports a tracing mode[10] that instruments the EVM for this purpose. The tracing API also allows to analyze whether a contract self destructed during an invocation.

All smart contract creations found are written to a MongoDB[11] instance for further processing. We store the bytecode, creation block number, and destruction block number of every smart contract we found. This enables us to filter for active smart contracts in a given time range.

To analyze if a smart contract is trustless, we need to know its call relationships to other smart contracts. We want to distinguish calls to hard coded addresses from calls to addresses provided as input parameter or read from state variables. If a call destination is hard coded, we want to be able to extract it. Our target is to build a call graph of all smart contracts we parsed. To do so, we analyze the bytecode of all smart contracts to extract calls to other smart contracts.

We start by disassembling the bytecode. For that purpose, we use the *evmdis*[12] project as a starting point. Evmdis supports data flow analysis[13] on EVM bytecode. Of interest to us is the *reaching definition* analysis. Informally speaking, reaching definition means that instructions are annotated with a set of variables that are visible to this instruction. For every such variable, evmdis stores the position in code where the variable was assigned last before the instruction. Therefore, evmdis annotates every instruction with the EVM's stack layout before the execution of the instruction. Instead of actual values, this stack layout contains references to instructions that could have produced this stack entry.

We use the reaching definition annotations to find the source of call addresses. To do so, we first search the bytecode for call instructions.[14] A call instruction on the EVM consumes seven stack entries. We are interested in the address, which is stored in the second entry. What we obtain from the annotation is either a static value or a set of n instructions that could have generated the relevant stack entry. If we reach a static value, we are done. Otherwise we follow the links to the instructions that potentially produced the stack entry. We recursively follow

---

[10] https://github.com/paritytech/parity/wiki/JSONRPC-trace-module.

[11] https://www.mongodb.com/.

[12] https://github.com/Arachnid/evmdis/.

[13] Via abstract interpretation.

[14] Specifically: `CALL`, `DELEGATECALL`, `CALLCODE`.

all stack positions consumed by the instruction until we either find evidence (in the form of *indicator instructions*) that the address is derived from input parameters,[15] state variables,[16] or we find a constant pushed to the stack.[17]

The fact that we do not evaluate address calculations besides length padding sounds over-simplifying. However, this does not matter in practice for two reasons. First, if the address is not hard coded, we are not interested in its computation because it has no effect on our measurement. Second, we are not aware of any instance where smart contracts use hard coded addresses that are modified before the call. Address arithmetic is impractical on the EVM because addresses cannot be systematically assigned. Moreover, the most popular high-level language Solidity disallows address computation. Nevertheless, there remains a small risk of wrongly extracted addresses, which we handle later in the analysis.

Another thing to consider are smart contracts that cannot be analyzed at all. This may happen if a code account hosts invalid bytecode. The code provided to the EVM upon creation of a smart contract is not necessarily valid EVM bytecode. We also have to consider the time needed for the extraction of call data. Although smart contracts tend to be rather small (see "Bytecode size" in Table 1), it can take some time to follow all code paths to extract the address origin. To keep the time to extract data manageable over all code accounts, we limit the runtime of the extraction process to 30 s per smart contract. A total of 539 smart contracts where not included in our dataset because of this restriction.

With the calls extracted from the bytecode of all code accounts, we can build the desired call graph. The graph is generated by iterating over all active smart contracts in our database.[18] Vertices represent smart contracts and are annotated with the address and the block number of the smart contract creation. Edges are directed and represent call relationships (from caller to callee).

Our graph contains five special nodes. Not all active smart contracts have corresponding transactions in the blockchain: the EVM supports four[19] hard coded smart contracts. Our fifth special node is UNKNOWN. It is used whenever a smart contract has calls where no hard coded address could be extracted. In the later analysis, we treat UNKNOWN as *not* trustless because the code is not known, whereas the hard coded addresses of the EVM are considered trustless.

Another possible point of failure is the extraction of hard coded addresses, especially if arithmetic on addresses is involved. To prevent wrong addresses, we check before the creation of new edges if the called address belongs to an active smart contract. If so, we insert the edge. Otherwise we check if the address is in the set of dead smart contracts. If so, we can be almost certain that the smart contract is no longer active. If not, we either extracted a wrong address or the user deployed a smart contract with a wrong address. We ignore calls to wrong addresses as well as calls to dead smart contracts for our analysis of trustlessness.

---

[15] Reaching a `CALLDATALOAD` instruction.

[16] Reaching a `SLOAD` instruction.

[17] Reaching a `PUSH20`: an address is 20 bytes long.

[18] Using the *networkX* graph library, https://networkx.github.io/.

[19] at the addresses 0x1, 0x2, 0x3, 0x4.

As calls to addresses that do not host code return without effect, we consider such calls as trustless. Even though we do distinguish between dead and wrong to build our call graph, we learned how many smart contracts refer to smart contracts that are not longer *active* (see "Calls to dead addresses" in Table 1).

3.3 Measuring Trustlessness

The call graph is the basis for analyzing the trustlessness of smart contracts.

A simple indicator of trustlessness can be defined as follows: Let $G = (V, E)$ be the directed call graph and $\mathrm{succ}(v) = \{ w \mid (v, w) \in E \}$ with $v, w \in V$. Now,

$$
\mathrm{trustless}(v) = \begin{cases} \text{true,} & \text{if } \mathrm{succ}(v) = \emptyset \\ \text{false,} & \text{if } \textsc{Unknown} \in \mathrm{succ}(v) \\ \wedge_{s \in \mathrm{succ}(v)} \mathrm{trustless}(s), & \text{otherwise.} \end{cases}
$$

Informally, a smart contract is trustless if and only if all calls in its dependency tree have hard coded addresses, hence all code that a smart contract can execute is fixed upon deployment of the smart contract.

A disadvantage of this recursive indicator is that it does not terminate on cyclic graphs. Note that Ethereum makes it difficult (but not impossible) to produce cycles. Every smart contract is deployed in its own transaction. The address is returned after the smart contract is deployed. To introduce cyclical dependencies, one has to deploy a smart contract with a reference to a smart contract that is not yet deployed. Thus, one must be able to predict the address a smart contract is deployed to. This is possible because the address creation is deterministic. Therefore, with some effort, it is possible to deliberately create dependency loops. We found that loops do exist (see Table 1). To handle cyclic dependencies, we use a set that tracks already visited vertices when calculating the trustlessness indicator and stop the recursion. A vertex encountered twice signals that there is a cycle in the dependency graph. We consider smart contracts with cyclic dependencies as not trustless in our analysis.

4 Call Graph Cleanup

Extracting statistics from the raw Ethereum call graph can be misleading as the data is interspersed with attack debris. Here we report our cleanup procedure.

The Ethereum platform has been target of multiple attacks in the last couple of months [9,10]. Two attacks are especially notable because they led to hard forks of the Ethereum blockchain [8,12]. One of them is the infamous DAO Attack. The DAO (*Decentralized Autonomous Organisation*) is a blockchain-based venture capital fund, designated to fund new Ethereum projects. Due to a bug, an attacker was able to steal coins worth roughly 60 million USD, at the time of the attack [9]. Besides the ominious fork, the DAO Attack has left no obvious traces in the call graph of smart contracts.

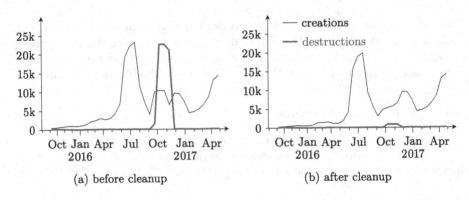

(a) before cleanup   (b) after cleanup

Fig. 1. Creation and destruction rate (moving window over 100 k blocks)

This cannot be said of the other major attack on Ethereum, a DoS (*Denial of Service*) attack which unfolded in October 2016. An attacker flooded the Ethereum network with transaction spam, using various strategies to overload and slow down the network [17]. To prepare the attack, the attacker deployed thousands of smart contracts that called other smart contracts in a tree structure. The addresses of the called smart contracts are hard coded in the calling smart contract. The leaves of the tree carried out the actual attack, e. g., by cheap contract creation via self-destruct [7].

One example of such an attack can be seen in block 2 416 461,[20] where one invocation of a smart contract caused 15 000 others to call self-destruct. The attack is easily observable in our dataset. In Fig. 1a, the spike in contract destructions in October 2016 as well as the spike in contract creations July and October 2016 are indicators of the attack. We also observed many smart contracts created and destructed in the same block, which is atypical for non-malicious uses (see "With zero lifetime" in Table 1).

The volume and patterns of smart contracts involved in the DoS attack present a significant bias for our analysis. To clean our data, we asked the Ethereum community for help and were provided with a set of 99 addresses that where *directly involved* in the attacks. 34 of them are code accounts. Directly involved means they were used for the actual attack on the network. We know that the attacker created far more code accounts than he actually used in the attack. Ideally, we want to filter *all* smart contracts created in preparation of the attack. Therefore we started to look for patterns to identify suspect code accounts.

One pattern we filter are code accounts created and destroyed in the same block around the time of the attacks[21] (see "With zero lifetime" in Table 1).

By looking at connected components in the call graph, we found 45 star-shaped subgraphs with 171 vertices each, sharing a very similar structure: one

---

[20] See TxHash: 0xf435a354924097686ea88dab3aac1dd464e6a3b387c77aeee94145b0fa 5a63d2.
[21] From 01 May 2016 until the hard fork on 18 Oct 2016.

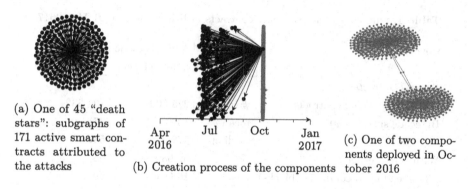

(a) One of 45 "death stars": subgraphs of 171 active smart contracts attributed to the attacks

Apr 2016   Jul   Oct   Jan 2017

(b) Creation process of the components

(c) One of two components deployed in October 2016

Fig. 2. Call graph perspective on the 2016 DoS attack (selected components)

master code account deployed in October called 170 sub-code accounts deployed earlier. Figure 2 illustrates this behavior for one selected *death star*. All of them were created between July and October 2016 by the same address.[22] This address is in the set provided by the Ethereum community. As illustrated in Fig. 2, the attackers also deployed at least two large connected components in October 2016.

Our final set of smart contracts to be excluded from the analysis is composed of all 34 smart contracts flagged by the Ethereum community, all code accounts identified by our heuristics as well as their direct and indirect neighbors in the directed call graph. We obtain a total of 95 791 code accounts that are potentially related to the attack, of which 30 668 are still active on 01 May 2017.

Observe from Fig. 1b that the cleanup largely removed the spikes in smart contract creation and destruction. There remains a suspicious spike in smart contract creations in July 2016. We conjecture that most of the smart contracts created in July 2016 are also related to the attacks. But due to a lack of evidence and the risk of false positives, we decided to not filter our data further.

5 Results

We study the Ethereum main chain from the day of its inception until 01 May 2017.[23] We report results *before* and *after the cleanup*, as described in Sect. 4. We have 225 000 active smart contracts before cleanup and 194 332 after cleanup.

5.1 Stylized Facts

Table 1 summarizes our quantitative results. General statistics include the mean and median of bytecode sizes ("Bytecode size"). Observe that the cleanup reduced both mean and median bytecode sizes. This means that the smart contracts used for the attacks were exceptionally large. We also measured the mean and median lifetime of smart contracts ("Lifetime"). It is easy to see the bias

---

[22] Address: 0x1fa0e1dfa88b371fcedf6225b3d8ad4e3bacef0e.

[23] Block number: 3 633 433.

Table 1. Summary of active smart contracts in Ethereum until 01 May 2017

Concept	Statistic	Analysis mode	
		Before cleanup	After cleanup
Smart Contracts			
Total active smart contracts	#	225 000	194 332
Bytecode size (bytes)	mean	1078	775
	median	578	542
With zero lifetime[a]	#	52 689	65
Lifetime of dead contracts (blocks)	mean	10 061	40 687
	median	0	39 001
Violate deployment convention	#	6	6
Source Code Availability			
Swarm hashes	#	29 496	29 480
Swarm metadata	#	14	14
Dependencies			
Smart contracts with calls	#	196 176	167 110
Smart contracts without calls	#	25 456	24 430
Could not analyze dependencies	#	3368	2792
Smart contracts with self loops[b]	#	1	1
Smart contracts with loops	#	30	7
Calls to dead addresses	#	14 196	1712
Calls to wrong addresses	#	6983	5487
Trustlessness			
Trustless smart contracts	#	122 375	119 493
	% of total	54.4	61.5

[a] Created and self destruct in the same block.
[b] Address: 0x938162cc5d6f4fc5d3f9edec18c93c5379d56062.

introduced by the attacks in the *before cleanup* column. The median smart contract lifetime before cleanup is 0. This is a consequence of the 52 689 smart contracts created and self destructed in the same block ("With zero lifetime"). This is a significant bias in a set of 69 875 destructed smart contracts in total. If we look at the results after cleanup, we see that mean an median are about the same, approximately five and a half days.[24] As mentioned in Sect. 3.1, we found only 6 smart contracts that violated the default deployment convention.

In terms of source code availability, we find that about 13 to 15% of all active smart contracts contain references to Swarm metadata (*Swarm hashes*). But only 14 (in absolute terms!) actually host metadata (*Swarm content*). We conclude that Swarm is not a reliable source of source code for the study period.

---

[24] Assuming 12 s block time.

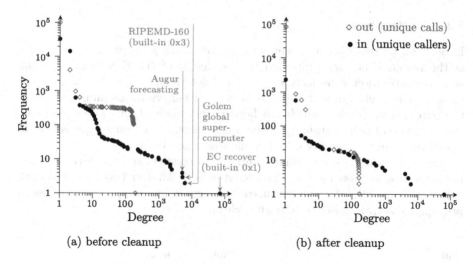

Fig. 3. Cumulative degree distributions of the directed call graph

When it comes to dependencies, we find that most smart contracts have calls (dependencies) to other smart contracts ("smart contracts with calls", "smart contracts without calls"). Our cleanup filtered very few smart contracts without calls. Many of the smart contracts used in the attacks create big dependency trees to amplify the attack, thus the result is not surprising. The row "Could not analyze dependencies" reports the number of smart contracts we were not able to extract dependency information from. Both values are around 1.5% of the total active smart contracts. As mentioned in Sect. 3.3, our call graph contains cyclic dependencies. Interestingly, most of the loops we found are related to the attacks, only 7 are left after cleanup. In Sect. 3.2 we described how we deal with calls to wrong and dead smart contracts. It is interesting to see that after cleanup, the references to self destructed smart contracts decrease significantly ("Call to dead addresses").

Another way of looking at dependencies is the degree distribution of the call graph depicted in Fig. 3. The in-degrees follow a typical Pareto shape in the cumulative log-scaled representation both before and after cleanup. We annotate the smart contract that are called from the highest number of other smart contract in Fig. 3a. Two of them are hard coded smart contracts (cf. Sect. 3.2). The distribution of out-degrees is visibly more affected by the attacks. The singularity around degree 170 can be attributed to the death stars. It disappears largely, but not completely, after cleanup. We conjecture that we might have missed 10–20 suspicious smart contracts after successfully removing several hundreds. Comparing both distributions highlights the importance of removing attack debris from the Ethereum call graph.

5.2 Trustlessness

In Sect. 2.2 we described the requirements for trustless smart contracts. Some of the requirements are supported by the design of the Ethereum platform, such as distribution, consensus, fairness, and determinism. The extent to which these requirements are met depends largely on behavioral assumptions about the participating nodes, which are beyond the scope of this paper. Here we concentrate on the immutability of the control flow, a necessary requirement for trustlessness and a property of individual smart contracts.

Figure 4 compares active smart contracts to trustless active smart contracts using the trustlessness indicator presented in Sect. 3.3 over time. We find that, before cleanup, 54% of all active smart contracts in our sample are trustless in principle. The ratio raises to 62% after cleanup.

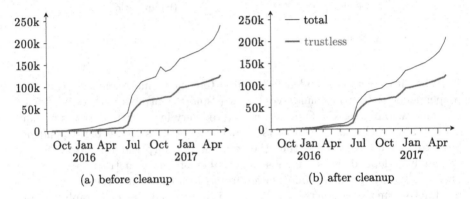

(a) before cleanup   (b) after cleanup

Fig. 4. Active smart contracts compared to active trustless smart contracts

In other words, two out of five smart contracts deployed on Ethereum do require trust in at least one third party who, in principle, can alter the control flow of the program that enforces an agreement after it is committed to the blockchain. This is not necessarily concerning, but a remarkable observation against the backdrop of trustlessness being framed as the key benefit of smart contracts and blockchain-based systems in general over conventional (centralized) infrastructures. In simple terms, there remains a gap between vision and practice.

6 Discussion and Conclusion

We have developed a measurement approach for the trustlessness of smart contracts and applied it to all the smart contracts on Ethereum. Two out of five smart contracts we found on Ethereum are not trustless according to our call graph-based indicator. This means it is hard or even impossible for users to verify these smart contracts. We also motivated the need for data cleanup when analyzing smart contract properties in order to avoid biases introduced by the large scale attacks against the Ethereum platform. Accordingly, we propose a cleanup strategy that leverages the call graph. This allows us to produce unbiased summary statistics of legitimate use of Ethereum, including indicators of bytecode size, smart contract lifetime, and source code availability.

Our approach has some limitations. It is based on the extraction of hard coded addresses from bytecode. Although it seems to be robust in practice, it is heuristic in nature with the possibility of extracting wrong information. The apparent robustness also depends on the usage conventions on the Ethereum platform. For example, if languages that allow address arithmetic gain popularity, the current approach will resolve fewer dependencies. Other limitations persist independent of the extraction of code dependencies. Currently, our approach is blind to data dependencies. Those can range from simple deactivation flags, which differ from self destruct only in the gas impact, to emulations of Turing equivalent machines inside the smart contract. This means that even if a smart contract is trustless according to our indicator, it can still encode agreements where trust in individual parties is needed. Tackling data dependencies is hard, because many use cases of smart contract need them.

Furthermore, we do not consider gas restrictions at the moment. Callers can limit the amount of work a callee can do by restricting the gas supply of the callee, this directly influences the amount of trust needed between parties.

Let us conclude with a broader outlook: Ethereum promises to fulfill the vision of trustless smart contracts. However, trustlessness is not only a property of the platform, but also of every individual smart contract. Our measurements show that many smart contracts violate necessary conditions for trustlessness in practice. We assume that many of these violations are the result of a lack of awareness rather than intentional. This raises the need for tooling that helps to avoid such mistakes, or at least increases awareness for the subject. Static analysis of source code (for example Solidity) could be used to prevent the most common trustlessness violations, such as calling addresses obtained from parameters or state variables. Furthermore, there is a relation to the verifiability of smart contracts: existing formal verifiers for Ethereum [6,11] need certain assumptions, which seem to be implied in our notion of trustlessness. Therefore, the subset of trustless smart contracts is more amenable to formal verification than general code for the Ethereum platform.

Acknowledgments. We like to thank Dr. Christian Reitwießner for answering many Ethereum related questions, Dr. Arthur Gervais for pointing out the existence of the parity tracing API and the excellent parsing script, Nick Johnson for the creation of the *evmdis* disassembler, Martin Holst Swende for the additional material on the Ethereum DoS attacks, and Clemens Brunner for proofreading and discussions. This work has received funding from the European Union's Horizon 2020 research and innovation programme under grant agreement No 740558.

References

1. Contracts - Solidity 0.4.12 documentation. http://solidity.readthedocs.io/en/develop/. Accessed 12 June 2017
2. Contracts - Solidity 0.4.12 documentation - Swarm. http://solidity.readthedocs.io/en/develop/miscellaneous.html#contract-metadata. Accessed 12 June 2017
3. Ethereum Homestead Documentation. http://ethdocs.org/en/latest/. Accessed 19 June 2017
4. Atzei, N., Bartoletti, M., Cimoli, T.: A survey of attacks on Ethereum smart contracts. Technical report, Cryptology ePrint Archive: Report 2016/1007 (2016)
5. Bartoletti, M., Pompianu, L.: An empirical analysis of smart contracts: platforms, applications, and design patterns. arXiv preprint arXiv:1703.06322 (2017)
6. Bhargavan, K., Delignat-Lavaud, A., Fournet, C., Gollamudi, A., Gonthier, G., Kobeissi, N., Kulatova, N., Rastogi, A., Sibut-Pinote, T., Swamy, N., Zanella-Béguelin, S.: Formal verification of smart contracts: short paper. In: Proceedings of the 2016 ACM Workshop on Programming Languages and Analysis for Security, PLAS 2016, pp. 91–96. ACM (2016)
7. Buterin, V.: A state clearing FAQ. https://www.reddit.com/r/ethereum/comments/5es5g4/a_state_clearing_faq/. Accessed 18 June 2017
8. Buterin, V.: Hard Fork Completed. https://blog.ethereum.org/2016/07/20/hard-fork-completed/. Accessed 18 June 2017
9. del Castillo, M.: The DAO Attacked: Code Issue Leads to $60 Million Ether Theft. http://www.coindesk.com/dao-attacked-code-issue-leads-60-million-ether-theft/. Accessed 18 June 2017
10. Hertig, A.: So, Ethereum's Blockchain is Still Under Attack. http://www.coindesk.com/so-ethereums-blockchain-is-still-under-attack/. Accessed 18 June 2017
11. Hirai, Y.: Formal verification of Deed contract in Ethereum name service. (2016). https://yoichihirai.com/deed.pdf. Accessed 31 July 2017
12. Jameson, H.: FAQ: Upcoming Ethereum Hard Fork. https://blog.ethereum.org/2016/10/18/faq-upcoming-ethereum-hard-fork/. Accessed 18 June 2017
13. Luu, L., Chu, D.H., Olickel, H., Saxena, P., Hobor, A.: Making smart contracts smarter. In: Proceedings of the 2016 ACM SIGSAC Conference on Computer and Communications Security, pp. 254–269. ACM (2016)
14. Luu, L., Teutsch, J., Kulkarni, R., Saxena, P.: Demystifying incentives in the consensus computer. In: Proceedings of the 22nd ACM SIGSAC Conference on Computer and Communications Security, pp. 706–719. ACM (2015)
15. Nakamoto, S.: Bitcoin: A peer-to-peer electronic cash system (2008)
16. Norvill, R., Awan, I.U., Pontiveros, B., Cullen, A.J., et al.: Automated labeling of unknown contracts in Ethereum (2017)
17. Swende, M.H.: The Shanghai Attacks. https://edcon.io/ppt/one/Martin%20Holst%20Swende_The%20%27Shanghai%20%27Attacks_EDCON.pdf. Accessed 19 June 2017
18. Szabo, N.: Formalizing and securing relationships on public networks. First Monday 2(9) (1997)
19. Wood, G.: Ethereum: A secure decentralised generalised transaction ledger (EIP-150 revision) (2017). http://gavwood.com/paper.pdf. Accessed 18 June 2017

Who Am I? Secure Identity Registration
on Distributed Ledgers

Sarah Azouvi$^{(\boxtimes)}$, Mustafa Al-Bassam, and Sarah Meiklejohn

University College London, London, UK
{sarah.azouvi.13,mustafa.al-bassam.16,s.meiklejohn}@ucl.ac.uk

Abstract. Bitcoin is a decentralized cryptocurrency that uses a ledger (or "blockchain") to keep track of the transactions made between its users. Because it is a fully decentralized system and anyone can join, every transaction is by necessity public. Thus, to preserve some semblance of privacy, users in the system are represented not by their real-world identities but by pseudonyms. While pseudonyms are acceptable for a standalone cryptocurrency, the emergence of other potential blockchain-based applications — e.g., using them to administer benefits and pensions — poses a need to associate certain attributes with the users of the system. In this paper, we address the question of how to register identities and attributes in a system built on globally visible ledgers. We propose a variety of possible solutions and in each case, we analyze the tradeoff our solution provides between privacy (ensuring that no one can associate the user's real-world identity with the pseudonym or other attributes they use on the ledger), usability (ensuring that verification of their attributes poses the lowest possible burden to users), and integrity (ensuring that no one can impersonate a user). We also present an implementation of one of our solution using Ethereum.

1 Introduction

Distributed ledgers, or "blockchains," have received a lot of attention for their potential applications: in addition to being used as the underlying architecture for cryptocurrencies such as Bitcoin, they have been discussed for achieving decentralized versions of identity management, DNS and public-key infrastructures, notary publics, and file storage. While centralized versions of these systems already exist, the attraction of distributed ledgers is that they minimize the extent to which users must place trust in a single entity such as a certificate authority.

In all existing deployments of distributed ledgers, users identify themselves using *pseudonyms* — or even more anonymous identifiers, as in the cryptocurrency Zcash [4] — that they create themselves. The use of pseudonyms is important for two reasons: first, all existing distributed ledgers are *transparent*, meaning their contents are globally visible, so having users reveal their real-world identities would completely violate their privacy. Second, allowing users to generate their own identifiers is necessary to preserve the openness of the system and allow anyone to join.

© Springer International Publishing AG 2017
J. Garcia-Alfaro et al. (Eds.): DPM/CBT 2017, LNCS 10436, pp. 373–389, 2017.
DOI: 10.1007/978-3-319-67816-0_21

While these "on-chain" pseudonyms are thus seemingly quite useful (and to some extent necessary) in public distributed ledgers, there are certain cases in which it may be necessary for someone to know some quality of the owner of a pseudonym, e.g., gambling services would like to know that their users are over 18. As a more involved example, we consider the case of governments administering pensions or benefits on a distributed ledger; the argument that has been made for doing this is that it could provide recipients with better visibility into their spending and reduce fraud [13], but such programs have recently come under significant scrutiny [9,19] due to the fact that they allow the government to identify its recipients on the ledger and thus track and monitor their spending. In all of these settings, we would thus like the user to not be forced to reveal to anyone the tie between their real-world identity and their pseudonym(s), but rather to have some information that proves that the real-world user associated with their pseudonym has been registered for some scheme (e.g., a pension) or is associated with some required set of attributes (e.g., is over 18).

Our focus in this paper is on the role that registration of identity can play in public distributed ledgers. While certain settings such as the ones described above might require a centralized registration protocol (e.g., only the government can decide whether or not a user is eligible for a pension), we also consider more informal notions of registration such as the so-called "web of trust." The web-of-trust concept has historically been used solely within the setting of certificate issuance, wherein users sign each others' PGP identity certificates to vouch for their authenticity, but has recently been discussed for the more general concept of identity in distributed ledgers. These decentralized settings are particularly appealing, as they remove the need for a single trusted party and provide an opportunity to improve privacy for users.

Our Contributions. In this paper, we propose methods for achieving registration in decentralized settings — such as the web of trust — in which multiple entities, in potentially flexible configurations, can act to validate attributes of a user's identity. We consider the registration of users' pseudonyms, unless stated otherwise. Our results focus on public open (or "permissionless") ledgers, but the same results would hold in the more restricted setting of "permissioned" ledgers.

Before presenting these methods, in Sect. 4 we consider both the functional and security properties that we hope to achieve. In particular, we consider how to provide *privacy* for users, so that even the registrar who sees their real-world identity and signs off on their attributes cannot subsequently link that identity to the pseudonyms that the user goes on to adopt within the ledger.

Due to space constraints, we relegate our centralized constructions to a full version of the paper. In the decentralized setting, in Sect. 5, we begin with a registration protocol in the style of the web of trust (but again, leveraging some of the key properties of distributed ledgers), and then build off of it to achieve protocols that provide better privacy and overall security.

Finally, in Sect. 6, we present an implementation of a decentralized registration protocol — that most closely resembles the web of trust, but allows for the *blinding* of attributes — as an Ethereum smart contract. In this setting, users can publish certain attributes (e.g., their Twitter handle) associated with their Ethereum address. Other users or institutions can then publish a signature on these attributes, reflecting a certain belief in its veracity. For attributes that the user may not want to directly link to their real-world identity (e.g., a particular Bitcoin or other cryptocurrency address), we provide a blind signing protocol in which users can publish blinded attributes on the blockchain and other users can sign them (and then the user can unblind them locally).

2 Related Work

In the setting of certificate issuance, our proposed systems are related to the idea of a public-key infrastructure (PKI). Some of our proposed registration protocols rely on a fixed set of specified registrars. These are related to the decentralized PKIs proposed by Fromknecht et al. [14] and the ARPKI system [3], which both distribute the process of certificate issuance to not only provide transparency into the process but also prevent misbehavior in the first place. In the more ad-hoc setting in which we allow any user to act as a registrar, our protocols are related to the idea of the web of trust.

The notion of accessing a service in a privacy-preserving manner can seemingly be achieved by anonymous credentials [7,8,11], which allow an issuer to create credentials that vouch for a user's identity or other generic attribute (e.g., their age). These credentials can then be shown to a verifier in a way that doesn't reveal anything to the verifier beyond the fact that the user possesses the attribute (e.g., is over 18 years old). The idea of issuing anonymous credentials has also been explored in the decentralized setting [15]. Our goal in this paper, however, is to allow users to not only access services but also to openly engage in existing blockchain-based systems using a registered identifier that — despite being vouched for by some registrar — cannot be linked to their real-world identity. To the best of our knowledge, this goal cannot be achieved directly by any solution based on anonymous credentials, at least not in an efficient manner: even if credentials could be issued on-chain, they would be larger than a blockchain address and issuance would consume a prohibitively high amount of gas.

Finally, a lot of recent work, both in the academic literature and in the broader community, has focused on the question of using the blockchain to establish and manage identities (see, e.g., https://github.com/peacekeeper/blockchain-identity for a comprehensive list). The ChainAnchor project [17] presents a system for identity and access control, with the purpose of having anonymous but verified on-chain identities, and of providing incentives to miners to include only transactions from verified users. While some of the techniques used are similar to our own, as they also adopt a form of registration, their focus is on permissioned ledgers and on requiring registration for all users (which is useful in, e.g., the setting of providing compliance with know-your-customer and anti-money-laundering regulations). In terms of industrial solutions, uPort [12] is a web identity management system that links an Ethereum address with a name, profile picture, and other information like an email address or Twitter account, and OneName is a similar initiative that does the same with Bitcoin addresses. MIT also recently introduced its Digital Certificates Project [20] using the Bitcoin blockchain, with the goal of making "certificates transferable and more easily verifiable." These solutions have seen some level of adoption and we borrow some useful features from each of them (e.g., we use a similar technique to achieve revocation as the Digital Certificates project), but add the benefit of additional points of comparison, and a security framework and analysis.

3   Background

3.1   The Web of Trust

The web of trust is a public-key authentication system established by PGP. In this setting, if Alice trusts that a certain key belongs to Bob (e.g., they have met in person), she can demonstrate this by signing his public key. The more signatures associated with Bob's public key, the more confident another user can be that this public key does indeed belong to him and not to someone who wants to impersonate him in order to intercept his communications.

In this system, one must of course be careful that it achieves some notion of Sybil resistance; i.e., that an adversary has not simply created alternate identities in order to vouch for their own impersonated key. To do this, users in the web of trust can form a *trust path*. For example, if Alice trusts Bob's public key, and Bob trusts Dave's public key, then there is a trust path from Alice to Dave and she can have added confidence in Dave's public key (as Bob's public key, which she trusts, was used to sign it). The shorter the trust path, the stronger the trust can be in the associated public keys.

3.2   Distributed Ledgers

Bitcoin relies on a peer-to-peer network to process transactions. Within the system, users are represented by *addresses* addr, each of which is uniquely linked to a pair of public and private ECDSA keys (pk, sk). We denote by $\mathsf{addr}(pk)$ the address associated with pk. Every time Alice wants to pay Bob using Bitcoin she generates a *transaction* $\mathsf{tx}(\mathsf{addr}(pk_A) \to \mathsf{addr}(pk_B))$ and signs it with her private key sk_A. (More generally, Bitcoin transactions can have arbitrarily many input and output addresses, in which case the transaction must be signed by all private keys associated with the input addresses, or even m-of-n multi-signature transactions, in which a transaction must be signed by the private keys associated with at least m of the input addresses.) She then broadcasts the signed transaction to the network, which checks its validity and if applicable, adds it to the *blockchain*, which acts as a public ledger of all such transactions.

To achieve more general functionality, Ethereum is a decentralized platform that operates with the same underlying blockchain technology as Bitcoin, except that it provides a Turing-complete scripting language. In Ethereum, a smart contract consists of program code, a storage file, and an account balance. The program's code is executed by the network, which is responsible for maintaining a consistent view of the state of every contract in the blockchain. Users can call the contract by sending transactions to its address, which updates the state of the contract in the blockchain. Moreover, the execution of a program's instructions induces a cost; the currency used to pay for it is called gas.

3.3 Cryptographic Primitives and Notation

Following standard cryptographic notation, we use $x \xleftarrow{\$} S$ to denote the process of sampling a member uniformly from S and assigning it to x. In particular, we use $x \xleftarrow{\$} [n]$ to denote sampling x uniformly from $\{1, \ldots, n\}$. We use $y \leftarrow A(x_1, \ldots, x_n; R)$ to denote running algorithm A on inputs $x_1, \ldots, x_n$ and random coins R and assigning its output to y. By $y \xleftarrow{\$} A(x_1, \ldots, x_n)$ we denote $y \leftarrow A(x_1, \ldots, x_n; R)$ for R sampled uniformly at random.

Both Bitcoin and Ethereum rely on ECDSA for signing. In what follows we use $(pk, sk) \xleftarrow{\$} \mathsf{Sig.KeyGen}(1^\lambda)$ to denote key generation, $\sigma \xleftarrow{\$} \mathsf{Sig.Sign}(sk, m)$ to denote signing, and $0/1 \leftarrow \mathsf{Sig.Verify}(pk, m, \sigma)$ to denote verification.

Some of our decentralized registration protocols make use of public-key encryption; here we denote the appropriate generic algorithms as $c \xleftarrow{\$} \mathsf{Enc}(pk, m)$ (for encryption) and $m \leftarrow \mathsf{Dec}(sk, c)$ (for decryption). In order to maintain compatibility with Bitcoin and Ethereum, the Elliptic Curve Integrated Encryption Scheme (ECIES) provides an encryption scheme that is compatible with ECDSA; i.e., one that allows for the encryption of ECDSA secret keys.

Finally, some of our schemes also make use of blind signatures. As initially defined by Chaum [10], a blind signature provides an interaction — denoted $\mathsf{U}(pk, m) \leftrightarrow \mathsf{S}(sk)$ — wherein a user U obtains a signature from a signer S on a message without the signer learning anything about the message. One commonly used construction is the RSA blind signature [16], which we use in our constructions due to the lack — to the best of our knowledge — of any provably secure blind signatures that are compatible with ECDSA.

4 Definitions and Threat Model

We consider a setting in which *users* maintain *attributes* about themselves and require *registrars* to vouch for these attributes. For example, in order to register the attribute "over 18 years old," a user reveals their identity to the government, who verifies their age. If they are over 18, the government registers the user's pseudonym, and they are now able to use it directly on the blockchain. For Bitcoin, we consider only the registration of pseudonyms, but in Ethereum, we consider the registration of more general types of attributes. Confirmation that the user possesses a given pseudonym may in turn be carried out by *verifiers* in order for the user to gain access to a particular service; i.e. for the users to interact with the service using their registered pseudonyms (e.g., use it to receive a pension from the government). We break this system down into four phases: (1) *setup*, in which various actors may initialize certain information about themselves (e.g., keys); (2) *registration*, in which the user interacts with the registrar(s) to register their pseudonym(s) and receive some evidence of this; (3) *verification*, in which the user interacts with the verifier to convince them that certain pseudonyms have been registered; and (4) *revocation*, in which either the registrar or (in some cases) the user revokes the registration of their pseudonym.

In order for the system to function, we must have a way for verifiers to check certain information about users without the intervention of the registrar. Let's assume, for example, that the user wants to register as an attribute the fact that they are over 18 years old so they can use a gambling service. If the registrar must intervene in order to confirm this attribute — as in the recently proposed brokered identification systems proposed in the US and UK [5, 18, 21] — then the registrar must be online at all times and can link the user's identity with their usage of certain services, neither of which is desirable. If instead this information is stored on a blockchain, then the verification step can happen in a non-interactive, or *passive*, fashion, as the verifier can simply check for themselves if the user's pseudonym has been registered or not. If evidence of the registration is not stored on the ledger, or if additional information is needed to "unlock" it (e.g., it is encrypted), then it may be necessary for the user to send additional information to — or otherwise interact with — the verifier. We capture these two functional properties as follows:

Definition 1 (Passive/active verification). *The verification process is passive if any verifier with access to the shared ledger can determine whether or not a given user has registered a particular attribute. The verification process is instead active if verifiers require additional information beyond what is available on the shared ledger.*

In order for the system to be secure, we would like to ensure that users are able to register only accurate attributes about themselves; e.g., they can register only for services, such as a pension scheme, that they are eligible to use. We must also ensure that the individual identities of users are protected and cannot be impersonated by anyone else. Once the user has completed the registration process and is interacting within the system using only their registered pseudonyms (e.g., their Bitcoin address), we should be able to ensure *privacy*; i.e., that the registrar cannot link the user's real-world and "on-chain" identifiers (even across separate attributes). We consider the different types of security we would like to achieve as follows:

Definition 2 (Attribute integrity). Attribute integrity *holds if attributes are registered only to those users to whom they belong; i.e., in the presence of an honest registrar, malicious users are unable to either register a fake attribute or one that otherwise does not belong to them, and malicious registrars are unable to impersonate an individual honest user.*

Definition 3 (Attribute privacy). Attribute privacy *holds if malicious entities (i.e., registrars and verifiers who are allowed to collude) are unable to link* *the attributes a user claims within the system to their identity. In particular, after the registration process is complete, malicious registrars are unable to distinguish the behavior of two users within the system that have different real-world identities but the same set of attributes.*

As we will see in our constructions, while revocation is useful and often necessary — as keys are frequently compromised or lost — it also tends to require active verification, as registrations cannot be deleted from the ledger (because it is immutable) and it is difficult to efficiently prove the absence of a revocation entry. To thus separate out these complexities, we analyze our protocols separately in the cases where revocation is and isn't supported.

5   Decentralized Registration

The "web of trust" reputation system can be considered a decentralized registration process in which any user can act as a registrar. The more signatures one accumulates for a particular attribute, the more *trusted* that attribute can be considered. In the PGP web of trust, however, the system still uses a central website to provide the lookup and signing services. In our constructions below, we use the blockchain to provide these two services. We also consider additional decentralized protocols that provide more robust properties or are useful in settings outside of the web of trust (see Table. 1).

Table 1. The different properties of a blockchain-based registration protocol and whether or not they are satisfied by our various constructions. No circle indicates that the property is not satisfied, a filled circle indicates it is, and a partially filled circle indicates it is partially satisfied.

	Verification		Attribute integrity	Privacy
	Passive	Active		
Basic web of trust	●		◐	
Blinded web of trust (with revocation)		●	◐	◐
Blinded web of trust (without)	●		◐	●
Multi-Casascius	●		●	●
Mix-network	●		●	●

5.1   Basic Web of Trust

One simple way of translating the web of trust into the setting of blockchains is to have users create transactions that vouch for each others' attributes. This can be done either individually or — if a user knows in advance which other users will vouch for their attribute — as a multi-input transaction.

Construction. In the setup phase, the user optionally chooses a set of peers to validate their attribute and act as registrars. We assume each registrar creates and publishes an on-chain identity addr$_R$.

In the registration phase, the user sends their identity id and address $\mathsf{addr_{id}}$ to each registrar, who determines if the address belongs to id (or just if id is a valid identity), using some off-chain mechanisms that we omit here. If it does, each registrar R_i creates a revocation keypair $(pk_{rev}^{(i)}, sk_{rev}^{(i)}) \xleftarrow{\$} \mathsf{Sig.KeyGen}(1^\lambda)$, and publishes to the blockchain a transaction $\mathsf{tx}(\mathsf{addr}(R_i) \rightarrow \{\mathsf{addr_{id}}, \mathsf{addr}(pk_{rev}^{(i)})\})$. In a basic system like Bitcoin this could involve sending a specific amount of bitcoins to both the attribute and revocation addresses, while in a more sophisticated system like Ethereum it could be a registration smart contract. Alternatively, if the set of registrars is fixed ahead of time, a user can create an n-input $n + 1$-output transaction and, after collecting signatures on it from each registrar, publish it to the blockchain.

In the verification phase, when the user wishes to prove that they have registered the pseudonym, the verifier checks for the existence of these transactions in the blockchain, and that the output address $\mathsf{addr}(pk_{rev})$ has not spent its contents. (While this may seem inefficient, if we associate with the ledger a list of unspent transaction outputs, or utxos, then it becomes significantly faster.)

Our approach to revocation here and in what follows is inspired by the approach of the MIT Digital Certificates project [20]. In the revocation phase, a registrar R_i can revoke their registration by spending the contents of $\mathsf{addr}(pk_{rev}^{(i)})$.

Security Analysis

Verification is passive, as the verifier needs to check only whether or not certain transactions are in the blockchain.

Attribute integrity is partially satisfied: restricting ourselves to the setting of on-chain pseudonyms, no registrar is able to impersonate the user, as they don't know the private key corresponding to a user's $\mathsf{addr_{id}}$. We could strengthen integrity by requiring the user to also send a signature to prove its ownership of $\mathsf{addr_{id}}$. Because the user can pick its own set of registrars, however, we cannot unilaterally guarantee that a user can't register a fake attribute, as a malicious coalition of users could act to register each other's fake identities or attributes. This is the same problem faced in the web of trust, however, and it can be mitigated by having the verifier place trust only in registrars with whom they can create a trust path of a certain (short) length (see Sect. 3.1). If malicious registrars can place themselves along this trust path with a certain proximity to the verifier, this is analogous to launching a Sybil attack, which can be prevented or detected in a variety of ways [2]. Thus, if the verifier sets a low threshold for the required length of the trust path and a high threshold for the number of registrars required to have registered the attribute, we can argue that the probability that malicious users can register fake attributes is low.

Privacy is not satisfied, as every registrar sees both id and $\mathsf{addr_{id}}$ at the same time.

5.2 Blinded Web of Trust

We provide a blinded version of the web of trust in which the user collects blind signatures from a set of nodes and the verifier then verifies the unblinded signatures. In Sect. 6, we present the results of an implementation and deployment of this approach on Ethereum.

Construction. In the setup phase, each registrar maintains as before a public on-chain identity $\mathsf{addr_R}$ linked to a public signing key pk_R.

In the registration phase, the user sends their identity id to a registrar, who determines whether or not they believe the user is eligible for the service. If they do, the user and registrar engage in the blind signing protocol $\mathsf{U}(\mathsf{addr_R}, pk) \leftrightarrow \mathsf{R}(sk_R)$ at the end of which the user obtains a signature σ such that $\mathsf{Sig.Verify}(pk_R, pk, \sigma) = 1$ and the registrar learns nothing about pk. The registrar also creates a revocation keypair $(pk_{rev}, sk_{rev}) \overset{\$}{\leftarrow} \mathsf{Sig.KeyGen}(1^\lambda)$, sends it to the user, publishes to the blockchain a transaction $\mathsf{tx}(\mathsf{addr_R} \rightarrow \mathsf{addr}(pk_{rev}))$, and maintains the mapping from id to pk_{rev}. The user repeats this process with every registrar. In the verification phase, the verifier verifies the unblinded signatures, and the user proves they control the revocation address pk_{rev} by signing a message using sk_{rev}. The verifier verifies this signature, checks the existence of the revocation transaction in the blockchain, and checks that $\mathsf{addr}(pk_{rev})$ has not yet spent its contents.

In the revocation phase, the registrar spends the contents of $\mathsf{addr}(pk_{rev})$.

Security Analysis

Verification is active, as the user must provide the signatures to the verifier. To allow for passive verification without revocation, the user could, after some delay, send pk and σ back to the registrar. The registrar would then check its own signature and, if it verifies, publish to the ledger a transaction of the form $\mathsf{tx}(\mathsf{addr_R} \rightarrow \mathsf{addr}(pk))$. The verifier would, in this case, simply check for a the transaction $\mathsf{tx}(\mathsf{addr_R} \rightarrow \mathsf{addr}(pk))$ in the blockchain to verify the registration, making it passive.

If we require revocation, however, we cannot achieve passive verification. The user would need to prove to the verifier that the coins in their revocation address are unspent, but to do that they would still need to prove that they know the secret key associated with their revocation address — as otherwise they could find and use any revocation address in the ledger — which requires active participation.

Attribute integrity is partially satisfied, as malicious registrars cannot impersonate users since they do not know the private key associated with the public key they register. While the unforgeability of the blind signature guarantees that a malicious user cannot fake the approval of an honest registrar, we cannot guarantee that malicious users and registrars cannot collude to register fake attributes. Instead, we can diminish the probability of this by requiring short trust paths and numerous registrars.

382 S. Azouvi et al.

Privacy is satisfied, as the unlinkability of the blind signature means that malicious registrars are unable to link id and pk. If we consider malicious verifiers as well, however, then the verifier could collude with the registrar and use pk_{rev} to de-anonymize the user. If we ignore revocation then privacy is (fully) satisfied.

5.3 Multi-Casascius

In this setting, we assume that the registrar consists of several entities (e.g., different certificate authorities) that are assumed to have some level of trust in each other; in particular, one registrar must be trusted by the others to correctly verify the identity of the user. As an improvement over the previous construction, these multiple entities make the registration process anonymous and provide passive verification, even in the case where revocation is necessary.

Our solution is based on the two-factor key generation protocol used to generate physical Casascius coins [6]. In this process, the manufacturer (Casascius) encodes on a physical coin a public key and a share of the associated secret key. (Traditional Casascius coins have the full secret key, meaning the manufacturer knows it and is able to spend the contents in the same way as the person who bought it.) The user who purchases the product can then fold in their own share of the secret key (which has been communicated to Casascius in the obfuscated form of an "intermediate code"), which yields the full secret key needed to spend the coins stored in the public key; thus, only the user and not the manufacturer can spend the coins. Our solution attempts to retain this property, which allows for attribute integrity, but provides a decentralized version for use in a wider variety of settings.

Construction. In the setup phase, each registrar R_i establishes some on-chain identity $addr_{R_i}$ associated with a public key pk_i, and the user creates a keypair $(pk_{pub}, sk_{pub}) \xleftarrow{\$} \mathsf{Sig.KeyGen}(1^\lambda)$. The user chooses a set of registrars with whom they want to register, as well as the order in which the registrars will proceed. (This can be thought of as either a property of the system, or as a choice made by the user that they communicate to the registrars.)

The registration phase proceeds in two phases. First, the user sends pk_{pub} and their real world identity id to R_1. This registrar verifies that the user is legitimate; if so, it picks a random secret key sk_1, sends $pk_1 \leftarrow (pk_{pub})^{sk_1}$ to R_2, and keeps (for use in the second phase) the mapping $sk_1 \mapsto pk_{pub}$. Now, for all i, $2 \le i < n$, registrar R_i picks a random secret key sk_i, sends $pk_i \leftarrow (pk_{i-1})^{sk_i}$ to registrar R_{i+1}, and keeps the mapping $sk_i \mapsto pk_{i-1}$. Upon receiving pk_{n-1}, registrar R_n also picks a random secret key sk_n and forms $pk_n \leftarrow (pk_{n-1})^{sk_n}$. It then creates a revocation keypair $(pk_{rev}, sk_{rev}) \xleftarrow{\$} \mathsf{Sig.KeyGen}(1^\lambda)$ and publishes a transaction $\mathsf{tx}(addr_{R_n} \rightarrow \{addr(pk_n), addr(pk_{rev})\})$ that acts as a registration.

In the second phase, the registrars create an *onion* to send the secret keys back to the user. In particular, R_n encrypts sk_n using pk_{n-1} and sends $c_n \xleftarrow{\$} \mathsf{Enc}(pk_{n-1}, (sk_n, \perp))$ to R_{n-1}. Now, for all i, $n > i \ge 2$, R_i folds their own secret key into the onion by sending $c_i \xleftarrow{\$} \mathsf{Enc}(pk_{i-1}, (sk_i, c_{i+1}))$ to R_{i-1}. At the end, R_1 creates $c_1 \xleftarrow{\$} \mathsf{Enc}(pk_{pub}, (sk_1, c_2))$ and sends this to the user. The user can now recover all the individual sk_i values by computing $(sk_i, c_{i+1}) \leftarrow \mathsf{Dec}(sk_{i-1}, c_i)$ for all i, $1 \le i \le n$ (where $sk_0 = sk_{pub}$), and can thus reconstruct the public key pk_n as

$$pk_n \leftarrow (pk_{pub})^{\prod_{i=1}^{n} sk_i},$$

and the private key as $sk_n \leftarrow sk_{pub} \cdot \prod_{i=1}^{n} sk_i$.

In the verification phase, the verifier checks for the existence of the transaction $\mathsf{tx}(\mathsf{addr}_{R_n} \rightarrow \{\mathsf{addr}(pk_n), \mathsf{addr}(pk_{\mathsf{rev}})\})$ in the blockchain, and verifies that the contents of pk_{rev} are unspent.

In the revocation phase, R_1 is the only registrar that can initiate revocation (as it is the only one that knows id), but R_n is the only registrar that can spend the contents of $\mathsf{addr}(pk_{\mathsf{rev}})$. Thus, R_1 starts by sending a revocation request for key pk_1 to R_2. In turn, using the mapping $sk_i \mapsto pk_{i+1}$, R_i sends a revocation request for key pk_i to R_{i+1} for all i, $2 \le i < n$. When the request reaches R_n, they can revoke the registration by spending the coins in $\mathsf{addr}(pk_{\mathsf{rev}})$.

Security Analysis

Verification is passive, as the verifier needs to check only whether or not certain transactions exist in the blockchain.

Attribute integrity is satisfied. The first registrar R_1 checks for the validity of id, so a user cannot register a fake or ineligible identity as long as R_1 is honest. Similarly, because the user sends a value pk_{pub} to the registrar that involves a partial secret key sk_{pub} known only to them, even if all the registrars collude the user is still the only entity who knows the full secret key associated with pk_n, which means they cannot be impersonated. We could require the user to send a signature under sk_{pub} to additionally prove their ownership of pk_{pub}.

Privacy is satisfied, as long as at least one registrar is honest. For all i, $2 \le i \le n$, each registrar R_i knows the mapping between pk_{i-1} and pk_i, and R_1 knows the mapping between id and pk_1. If all the registrars collude, they can thus learn the mapping between id and pk_n, but as long as one registrar doesn't collude with the others and $n \ge 3$, the user cannot be de-anonymized. Assuming that R_1 does not know which node is acting as R_n, which is plausible as it communicates directly only with R_2, R_1 cannot de-anonymize the user by observing the transactions published in the blockchain. Timing attacks can be mitigated by adding some random delays in the publication of the registration transaction. Our next protocol will completely thwart this attack.

5.4 Mix-Network

While the blinded web of trust protocol in Sect. 5.2 and the multi-Casascius protocol in Sect. 5.3 provide strong privacy guarantees, the former has the drawback that verification required active participation on behalf of the user, and the latter has the drawback that all registrars must trust the initial one to verify the identities and allows timing attacks. Here, we try to maintain the advantages of these protocols but eliminate these drawbacks.

Without adopting the time delay from our protocol in Sect. 5.2, we cannot achieve passive verification unilaterally. Instead, we consider how to provide passive verification in a setting in which multiple users register at the same time through the same set of nodes (e.g., voter registration), which also allows us to provide each registrar with the ability to verify the set of identities for themselves without violating privacy. As we will see, if k users register at the same time then this provides each user with an anonymity set of size k.

Construction. In the setup phase, each user j creates a keypair $(pk_{pub}^{(j)}, sk_{pub}^{(j)}) \xleftarrow{\$}$ Sig.KeyGen(1^λ), and each registrar R_i maintains some on-chain identity addr_{R_i}. The order of registrars is determined beforehand.

The registration phase is similar to the two-phase process in Sect. 5.3. First, each user j sends its public key $pk_{pub}^{(j)}$ and $\mathsf{id}^{(j)}$ to R_1. This first registrar then verifies that all the identities are legitimate; if not it drops the illegitimate identities and waits to receive a legitimate set of k users. For each user, R_1 then picks a random secret key $sk_1^{(j)}$, computes $pk_1^{(j)} \leftarrow (pk_{pub}^{(j)})^{sk_1^{(j)}}$, and keeps the mapping $sk_1^{(j)} \mapsto pk_{pub}^{(j)}$. It then performs a permutation π_1 on the identities and sends the public keys $\{pk_1^{(j)}\}_{j=1}^k$ and the permuted identities $\pi_1(\{\mathsf{id}^{(j)}\}_{j=1}^k)$ to R_2. For all i, $2 \leq i < n$, R_i verifies for itself the set of identities and, if they are eligible, picks for each user j a random secret key $sk_i^{(j)}$, computes

$$pk_i^{(j)} \leftarrow (pk_{i-1}^{(j)})^{sk_i^{(j)}},$$

and keeps the mapping $sk_i^{(j)} \mapsto pk_{i-1}^{(j)}$. It then applies its own permutation π_i to the mapping and sends the public keys $\{pk_i^{(j)}\}_{j=1}^k$ and the permuted identities $\pi_i \circ \cdots \pi_1(\{\mathsf{id}^{(j)}\}_{j=1}^k)$ to R_{i+1}. Finally, R_n creates k revocation keypairs $(pk_{\mathsf{rev}}^{(j)}, sk_{\mathsf{rev}}^{(j)}) \xleftarrow{\$}$ Sig.KeyGen(1^λ) and k transactions

$$\mathsf{tx}(\{\mathsf{addr}_{R_1}, \ldots, \mathsf{addr}_{R_n}\} \rightarrow \{\mathsf{addr}(pk_n^{(j)}), \mathsf{addr}(pk_{\mathsf{rev}}^{(j)})\}). \tag{1}$$

It signs each transaction $\mathsf{tx}^{(j)}$ of this form with its private key.

In the second phase, the registrars must now jointly create the transactions to publish to the blockchain, and create an onion (as in Sect. 5.3) to send the keys back to the users. So, R_n first signs each transaction $\mathsf{tx}^{(j)}$ of the form specified in Eq. 1 with its private key. It then encrypts $sk_n^{(j)}$ with $pk_{n-1}^{(j)}$ to form $c_n^{(j)} \xleftarrow{\$} \mathsf{Enc}(pk_{n-1}^{(j)}, (sk_n^{(j)}, \perp))$ and sends the set $\{\mathsf{tx}^{(j)}, c_n^{(j)}\}_{j=1}^k$ to R_{n-1}.

For all i, $n > i \geq 2$, R_i incorporates its own signature into the transactions $tx^{(j)}$, encrypts $sk_i^{(j)}$ with $pk_{i-1}^{(j)}$ to form $c_i^{(j)} \xleftarrow{\$} \mathsf{Enc}(pk_{i-1}^{(j)}, (sk_i^{(j)}, c_{i+1}))$, and sends $\{\mathsf{tx}^{(j)}, c_i^{(j)}\}_{j=1}^k$ to R_{i-1}.

Finally, R_1 incorporates its own signature into the transactions $\mathsf{tx}^{(j)}$ and, now that they have the full set of signatures needed for validity, publishes these transactions to the blockchain. It also creates $c_1^{(j)} \xleftarrow{\$} \mathsf{Enc}(pk_{pub}^{(j)}, (sk_1^{(j)}, c_2^{(j)}))$ and sends $c_1^{(j)}$ to each user j.

At the end, user j recovers the secret key shares $sk_i^{(j)}$ in the same manner as in Sect. 5.3; i.e., they compute $(sk_i^{(j)}, c_{i+1}^{(j)}) \leftarrow \mathsf{Dec}(sk_{i-1}^{(j)}, c_i^{(j)})$ for all i, $1 \leq i \leq n$ (using $sk_0 = sk_{pub}$), and computes the secret key as $sk_n^{(j)} \leftarrow sk_{pub}^{(j)} \cdot \prod_{i=1}^n sk_i^{(j)}$ and the public key as

$$pk_n^{(j)} \leftarrow (pk_{pub}^{(j)})^{\prod_{i=1}^n sk_i^{(j)}}.$$

In the verification phase, the verifier check for the existence of the transaction in the blockchain and verifies that the contents of $pk_{\mathsf{rev}}^{(j)}$ are unspent.

As in Sect. 5.3, the revocation request can be initiated only by R_1, but revocation can be carried out only by R_n. R_1 can initiate the process by sending a revocation request for $pk_1^{(j)}$ (which represents $\mathsf{id}^{(j)}$) to R_2. In turn, R_i transmits the revocation request to R_{i+1} using their partial key $pk_i^{(j)}$ and their knowledge of the mapping $pk_{i-1}^{(j)} \mapsto pk_i^{(j)}$. Once this reaches R_n, it can spend the coins in $pk_{\mathsf{rev}}^{(j)}$ to revoke the registration.

Security Analysis

Verification is passive, as the verifier needs to check only whether or not certain transactions exist in the blockchain.

Attribute integrity is satisfied, as long as one registrar is honest: every registrar verifies the set of identities $\{\mathsf{id}^{(j)}\}_{j=1}^k$ for themselves, so if one registrar is honest then it will drop any fake identities and users cannot register fake ones. As in our previous protocols, malicious registrars cannot impersonate a user as they do not have access to the private key.

Privacy is satisfied, as k-anonymity is provided as long as one registrar is honest. In particular, R_i knows only the mapping between $pk_{i-1}^{(j)}$ and $pk_i^{(j)}$, and only R_1 knows the mapping between $\mathsf{id}^{(j)}$ and $pk_1^{(j)}$. Thus, as long as not all registrars collude, $\mathsf{id}^{(j)}$ and $pk_n^{(j)}$ are unlinkable.

6   Implementation and Deployment

We now present an implementation of the decentralized registration systems described in Sects. 5.1 and 5.2; i.e., a system that allow for decentralized registration in both a standard (in which no privacy is achieved) and blinded (in which privacy is achieved) fashion. Our implementation is built on top of SCPKI [1], which implements a basic web of trust system on the Ethereum blockchain. We extended SCPKI to supported a blinded web of trust.

6.1   Overview

We have developed an identity management system based on blind signatures and deployed it on the Ethereum blockchain as a smart contract. As in SCPKI, each user has their own identity on the blockchain that corresponds to an Ethereum address. Using the methods of the smart contract, users can add attributes to their Ethereum address, sign attributes, and revoke signatures. The system also provides a way for users to search and retrieve attributes, by producing Ethereum events, which allow clients to efficiently watch the blockchain for new changes by a smart contract.

Due to the expensive fees of Ethereum data storage, data associated with attributes may be stored off the blockchain but authenticated on the blockchain. This can be done by adding an address (e.g., a URI) for the location of the data instead of the data itself along with its cryptographic hash if necessary for authenticity. The smart contract allows for the ability to store data using IPFS (https://ipfs.io/) where the cryptographic hash of the data is also its address.

The signing and verification of signature validity is performed client-side. As described in Sect. 5.2, when checking a signature, the client must also look for the existence of a revocation transaction as well as check the optional signature expiry date. Because of the incompatibility discussed in Sect. 5.2 between revocation and privacy, our implementation does not allow for the revocation of blind signatures — only standard signatures can be revoked.

6.2 Technical Specification

The smart contract is written in Solidity, a high-level language for writing Ethereum contracts, and the client is written in Python. Our open-source implementation, based on SCPKI, consists of 1502 lines of Python and Solidity code. The client is a command line console application and provides access to the smart contract's methods and functionality to search for user attributes, retrieve attributes, retrieve signatures, and verify signatures. For the blind signature, we use the RSA blind signature scheme with 2048-bit RSA keys.

Simple Signing. In the setup phase, the user generates their own Ethereum address. To obtain a simple signature the user first adds an attribute to their Ethereum address, by calling the method **addAttribute** and specifying the attribute type and data. This creates an **AttributeAdded** event on the blockchain containing the attribute properties, which can be detected by the client. Because Ethereum events are indexable, the client can easily search for attributes. In the registration phase, the registrar signs the attribute by calling the method **signAttribute** and specifying the ID of the attribute to sign and optionally an expiry date of its signature. This creates an **AttributeSigned** event containing the signature properties, including the Ethereum address of the signer. Because only the owner of the private key of an Ethereum address can create transactions originating from that address, this cryptographically proves that a specific Ethereum address signed an attribute. In the verification phase, the verifier checks the published signature on the user's attributes, checking that there are no revocations and that the signature has not expired.

Blind Signing. If a user wants to obtain a blind signature in order to anonymously register a public key, they first publish a blinded public key attribute using the method **addBlindedAttribute**, providing the data for the blinded key and specifying the ID of the registrar's public key attribute on the blockchain that the key is blinded for; i.e., specifying which registrar the user wants to blindly sign the key. This creates a **BlindedAttributeAdded** event that can be detected by the owner of the signing public key attribute. To blindly sign an attribute, the registrar calls the method **signBlindedAttribute** on the blinded public key attribute previously added by the user, providing the data of the signature, this is done client-side. This creates a **AttributeBlindSigned** event. On receiving the event, the user can then unblind the signature client-side. In the verification phase, the user shows the unblinded signature to the verifier (as described in Sect. 5.2).

6.3   Costs

In Ethereum, every operation has a cost paid using gas. As of May 2017, this cost can be translated into ether and USD using the exchange rate of 1 gas = 0.00000002 ether, and 1 ether = $192.00. Table 2 shows the cost of each operation when data is stored on and off the blockchain. Aside from the observation that operations are relatively cheap — publishing the contract is the most expensive step, at about $3, and all of the operations involving individual attributes cost a few cents — we also see that the operations that involve adding and signing attributes are significantly cheaper when the data representing attributes and blind signatures is stored on IPFS.

Table 2. Cost for operations, where all data is stored on the blockchain.

Operation	Gas	Ether	USD
Publish contract	786586	0.0157	3.01
Add standard RSA attribute	70952	0.0014	0.27
Add standard RSA attribute (IPFS)	40713	0.0008	0.15
Sign standard attribute	49904	0.001	0.19
Revoke standard attribute	28514	0.0006	0.12
Add blinded RSA attribute	60173	0.0012	0.23
Add blinded RSA attribute (IPFS)	38303	0.0008	0.15
Sign blinded RSA attribute	58012	0.0012	0.23
Sign blinded RSA attribute (IPFS)	36079	0.0007	0.13

7   Conclusions and Open Problems

In this paper, we have proposed different methods for achieving registration in public distributed ledgers. We presented a decentralized setting, where registration is potentially flexible and can be done by several entities. For each case we presented the trade-offs between security (in the form of privacy and integrity), usability (in the form of passive or active verification), and efficiency. Moreover, all our solutions use only lightweight cryptographic primitives, as opposed to approaches that adopt zero-knowledge proofs or other advanced cryptography. We have also implemented a decentralized registration process that operates on the Ethereum blockchain and evaluated its costs and efficiency.

Our system doesn't provide a mechanism for key recovery, but we view this as an important open problem and an avenue for future research, especially in the setting in which a user has accumulated many signatures on an attribute and built up a robust on-chain identity.

Acknowledgements. This project was supported in part by EPSRC Grant EP/N028104/1.

References

1. Al-Bassam, M.: SCPKI: a smart contract-based PKI and identity system. In: Proceedings of the ACM Workshop on Blockchain, Cryptocurrencies and Contracts, BCC 2017, pp. 35–40. ACM, New York (2017)
2. Alvisi, L., Clement, A., Epasto, A., Lattanzi, S., Panconesi, A.: SoK: the evolution of sybil defense via social networks. In: 2013 IEEE Symposium on Security and Privacy, pp. 382–396. IEEE Computer Society Press, Berkeley, 19–22 May 2013
3. Basin, D., Cremers, C., Kim, T.H.-J., Perrig, A., Sasse, R., Szalachowski, P.: ARPKI: attack resilient public-key infrastructure. In: Proceedings of ACM CCS 2014, pp. 382–393 (2014)
4. Ben-Sasson, E., Chiesa, A., Garman, C., Green, M., Miers, I., Tromer, E., Virza, M.: Zerocash: decentralized anonymous payments from Bitcoin. In: Proceedings of the IEEE Symposium on Security and Privacy (2014)
5. Brandão, L.T.A.N., Christin, N., Danezis, G., Anonymous: Towards mending two nation-scale brokered identification systems. In: Proceedings on Privacy Enhancing Technologies (2015)
6. Caldwell, M., Voisine, A.: Passphrase-protected private key (2016)
7. Camenisch, J., Lysyanskaya, A.: An efficient system for non-transferable anonymous credentials with optional anonymity revocation. In: Pfitzmann, B. (ed.) EUROCRYPT 2001. LNCS, vol. 2045, pp. 93–118. Springer, Heidelberg (2001). doi:10.1007/3-540-44987-6_7
8. Camenisch, J., Lysyanskaya, A.: Signature schemes and anonymous credentials from bilinear maps. In: Franklin, M. (ed.) CRYPTO 2004. LNCS, vol. 3152, pp. 56–72. Springer, Heidelberg (2004). doi:10.1007/978-3-540-28628-8_4
9. Cellan-Jones, R.: Blockchain and benefits - a dangerous mix? http://www.bbc.com/news/technology-36785872. Accessed 04 Aug 2016
10. Chaum, D.: Blind signatures for untraceable payments. In: Chaum, D., Rivest, R.L., Sherman, A.T. (eds.) CRYPTO 1982, Santa Barbara, CA, USA, pp. 199–203. Plenum Press, New York (1982)
11. Chaum, D.: Security without identification: transaction systems to make big brother obsolete. Commun. ACM **28**(10), 1030–1044 (1985)
12. Consensys: uPort: The wallet is the new browser. https://medium.com/@ConsenSys/uport-the-wallet-is-the-new-browser-b133a83fe73#.jquv8q5u3. Accessed 04 Aug 2016

13. Evenstad, L.: DWP trials blockchain technology for benefit payments. http://www.computerweekly.com/news/450300034/DWP-trials-blockchain-technology-for-benefit-payments. Accessed 04 Aug 2016
14. Fromknecht, C., Velicanu, D., Yakoubov, S.: A decentralized public key infrastructure with identity retention. IACR Cryptology ePrint Archive, Report 2014/803 (2014). http://eprint.iacr.org/2014/803.pdf
15. Garman, C., Green, M., Miers, I.: Decentralized anonymous credentials. In: Proceedings of the NDSS Symposium 2014 (2014)
16. Goldwasser, S., Bellare, M.: Lecture notes on cryptography (2000). http://cseweb.ucsd.edu/~mihir/papers/gb.pdf
17. Hardjono, T., Pentland, A.S.: Verifiable anonymous identities and access control in permissioned blockchains (2016). http://www.mit-trust.org/s/ChainAnchor-Identities-04172016.pdf
18. U.C. Office and G.D. Service: Introducing GOV.UK Verify, September 2015. https://www.gov.uk/government/publications/introducing-govuk-verify
19. Plimmer, G.: Use of bitcoin tech to pay UK benefits sparks privacy concerns. http://www.ft.com/cms/s/0/33d5b3fc-4767-11e6-b387-64ab0a67014c.html
20. Schmidt, P.: Certificates, Reputation, and the Blockchain (2015)
21. U.S.P. Service: Federal cloud credential exchange (FCCX), August 2013. https://www.fbo.gov/spg/USPS/SSP/HQP/1B-13-A-0003/listing.html

A User-Centric System for Verified Identities on the Bitcoin Blockchain

Daniel Augot[1,2,3], Hervé Chabanne[4,5], Thomas Chenevier[4],
William George[1,2,3(✉)], and Laurent Lambert[4]

[1] INRIA, Palaiseau, France
daniel.augot@inria.fr
[2] Laboratoire LIX, École Polytechnique and CNRS UMR 7161, Palaiseau, France
wgeorge@lix.polytechnique.fr
[3] Université Paris-Saclay, Paris, France
[4] OT-Morpho, Issy-les-Moulineaux, France
[5] Télécom ParisTech, Paris, France
{herve.chabanne,thomas.chenevier}@morpho.com

Abstract. We present an identity management scheme built into the Bitcoin blockchain, allowing for identities that are as indelible as the blockchain itself. Moreover, we take advantage of Bitcoin's decentralized nature to facilitate a shared control between users and identity providers, allowing users to directly manage their own identities, fluidly coordinating identities from different providers, even as identity providers can revoke identities and impose controls.

Keywords: Bitcoin blockchain · Identity proofs · Discrete Logarithm REPresentation (DLREP) · Personal Identity Management Systems (PIMS)

1 Introduction

We live in a world where the ways in which a person's identity is being used are increasingly complex. Appropriately handling sensitive personal data, such as medical, financial, and employment data, is subtle and requires care [21]. In this context, it is important to employ technical solutions that promote good security practices and that ensure that users have appropriate controls over how their data is being used. There are many [5] who advocate for a decentralized approach in which users directly manage their own identities via personal servers, Personal Identity Management Systems (PIMS). Meanwhile, blockchains, most notably Bitcoin [18], have provided new models of decentralization. In this work, we propose a sort of "light-PIMS," to be implemented on the Bitcoin blockchain. The decentralized nature of the blockchain allows us to create a neutral space where identity issuers and users share responsibility for users' identities, providing protections and the capacity for oversight for both parties.

Related Work. In 2015 MIT Media Labs introduced a system for academic certificates on the Bitcoin blockchain [20]. Taking advantage of the blockchain's

© Springer International Publishing AG 2017
J. Garcia-Alfaro et al. (Eds.): DPM/CBT 2017, LNCS 10436, pp. 390–407, 2017.
DOI: 10.1007/978-3-319-67816-0_22

persistence over time, this system gives students a convenient way of proving that they graduated, see Sect. 2. The Blockstack project [6] has implemented decentralized versions of PKI and DNS on the Bitcoin network. In [11], a decentralized scheme to issue credentials in the absence of a trusted third party is proposed using Bitcoin. This scheme incorporates zero-knowledge protections such as those we will deal in Sect. 2.3. The startup CryptID [1] has proposed a system where encrypted records of fingerprints (along with a password) are stored in the Factom blockchain, which is itself periodically committed to the Bitcoin blockchain, replacing the traditional centralized server in fingerprint scanning identification systems with a more lightweight system. We generalize these ideas to permit more flexible user identities that can contain different fields of information useful in interacting with diverse service providers. We further explore the possibilities enabled by performing these interactions on a blockchain. Some architectures propose new, application designed blockchains. For example, the proposal of IDCoins [2] relies on a custom blockchain in which the proof of work is related to the generation of GPG/PGP keys necessary to create a web of trust. The Guardtime KSI blockchain, which forms the base of an electronic records system used in Estonia [4,23], is a permissioned blockchain. In [28] a system is proposed to store user information such as the GPS data from their phone in a distributed hash table and then store pointers to this data and permissions on how it may be used or retrieved on a blockchain. The proposition of ChainAnchor [14] even allows to create a semi-permissioned structure that can be placed on top of an existing blockchain such as that of Bitcoin by changing the incentive structure of miners to promote permissioned transactions. For a survey on other proposals that touch on the relationship between blockchains and identity management, see [16,27].

Our Contribution. We propose an identity management system that will take advantage of the decentralized nature of the Bitcoin blockchain to allow for a balance between the ability for users to manage their own identities and for issuers to establish controls. The different entities of our proposal communicate via Bitcoin transactions, allowing identity issuers to outsource much of the infrastructure required for this system to the Bitcoin network, which as the most robust, most established blockchain, has strong security properties, most notably, that miner's work maintains strong integrity of its data. Privacy during identity verification is ensured thanks to the attribute-based credentials of Brands [8]. While [11] already proposes using Brands credentials in Bitcoin, their protocol could, in fact, be implemented in any blockchain without major modifications. In contrast, our proposal takes advantage of the specifics of the Bitcoin scripting language to encode identity meaning in Bitcoin syntax. Specifically, we build upon the idea of MIT Media Labs [20] that revocation can be encoded in terms of the status of a Bitcoin transaction to enable additional mechanisms for issuer oversight which are then enforced by the Bitcoin network. Particularly, in our system an issuer can limit the number of times an identity can be used, see Sect. 3.5. At the same time, we will see that our system gives a great deal of control to the user over her identity.

Note that in traditional systems the reconciliation between user control and issuer oversight is problematic; in most systems the identity is generally controlled entirely by an on-line issuer with little input from the user [5], or alternatively the issuer will sign an identity to be managed by the user, then the issuer will go offline ceding his capacity for oversight (See [9] for a further discussion on the advantages and disadvantages of these two models.)

Compared to a traditional decentralized system, we offer more integrated issuer controls. For example, compare the revocation mechanism discussed in Sect. 3.4 to the challenges encountered using revocation lists in public key infrastructures (PKIs) [17]. Additionally, we will see that our system has the following advantages compared to centralized systems:

- Our system does not require identity providers to be as "lively" as they must be in traditional, centralized systems. If an identity provider has placed controls on an identity, such as a limit on the number of times it can be used, then even if an identity issuer has a service interruption, a user can continue to use her identity and these limits will continue to be enforced by the robust, worldwide Bitcoin network. A user can even revoke her own identity without intervention by the issuer.
- By providing a common space, control over which is shared between the different actors through the mechanisms of the blockchain, we allow users to coordinate several micro-identities, only needing to trust a small portion of their identities to any given identity provider, see Sect. 3.6. While a similar coordinate scheme is possible without a blockchain, in practice it is highly impractical for a user to coordinate identities from different identity providers each of whom uses his own distinct formatting and infrastructure.

On the other hand, our system has two (potential) drawbacks. First, as authentications are encoded in Bitcoin transactions, this requires paying transaction fees to miners, see Sect. 3.7 for an estimate of these fees. Second, Bitcoin transactions are by their nature public, posing risks to user anonymity. The typical suggestion to ensure (pseudo-)anonymity in Bitcoin is to use each Bitcoin address exactly one time. An analogous idea works here, at the expense of having higher user fees, see Remark 5. Note that users have differing standards regarding the privacy that they expect in their interactions. Some users may be willing to sacrifice some anonymity in exchange for lower fees. In fact, some users, such as those that gladly link their Facebook account to their Instagram account or their favorite blogs, may even prefer that metadata on their transactions be tied to them, allowing them to create a digital presence on which they can build a reputation. See Sect. 5 for a proposal on how a reputation system can be built on top of our architecture. A user should be empowered to make choices regarding how private they want to be.

2   Background

In this section we briefly recall some of the existing ideas, in Bitcoin and in the work of Brands [8], upon which our system is built.

2.1   Bitcoin Relevant Notions

It is a particularity of Bitcoin that all bitcoins exist in the form of Unspent Transaction Outputs (UTXOs) [7, Chap. 5], [18]. Each transaction may have several inputs, each of which was an output UTXO for some previous bitcoin transaction, and it may have several outputs. Most transaction outputs correspond to a bitcoin address, the hash of the public key that can spend it or a hash of a script detailing how the coin can be reclaimed. (These are called Pay to Public Key Hash P2PKH and Pay to Script Hash P2SH outputs respectively.) Particularly, one can create P2SH outputs that can then be spend by an m of n multisig. Also relevant to our work will be OP_RETURN outputs; each such output contains up to 80 bytes of space in which the sender of a transaction can store arbitrary information. Note, OP_RETURN outputs must have zero bitcoins associated to them; as such, they are provably not usable as inputs to later transactions.

The raw transaction that is broadcast to the nodes contains the amount of bitcoin to associate to each output, the script permitting validation of each output (P2SH, P2PKH, etc.), and the scripts for each input that satisfy the requirements set up when the corresponding input UTXO was created, generally including a signature from a corresponding private key. The hash of this raw transaction becomes the transaction identifier (txid), which is included in the Merkle tree that produces a block header and is ultimately recorded in the block chain in an immutable way. Thus, the given inputs and outputs of a given transaction are provably linked together.

Financial Friction in Bitcoin Transactions. Miners are compensated by "fees." The amount paid in fees for a given transaction is the difference between the combined values of the inputs and the combined values of the outputs. Miners, who are limited in how many bytes they can fit a given block, generally choose to include the transactions with the most profitable fees with respect to the number of bytes in its raw transaction [7, Chap. 5]. When discussing our schema, we will denote the fees for a given transaction by $F_{\text{NAME-OF-TRANSACTION}}$. See Sect. 3.7 for estimations of these amounts.

In order for a Bitcoin transaction to be considered valid it must satisfy certain basic properties such as not double spending a previously spent output, having valid signatures, etc. Any block that contains an invalid transaction will be rejected by the network. In addition, the Bitcoin Core software distributions to miners suggests requirements that transactions need to satisfy in order to be considered "standard." These requirements are implemented at the discretion of each miner and thus vary slightly across the network; a miner may refuse to include a given transaction in the blocks he mines as "non-standard," but if another miner broadcasts a block with this transaction in it, he will still accept that block if the transaction is valid. In particular, for a transaction to be considered standard, each of its non-OP_RETURN output must have a minimal value so as to prevent the network from being spammed by extremely low value transactions. Any amount of bitcoin below this minimum is called "dust." As of version 0.14 (March 2017), Bitcoin Core [12] recommends that miners refuse transactions that have a P2PKH output of less than .00000546 bitcoin, currently (June 2017, 1BTC = 2720 USD) around .01 USD. We denote by $\mathcal{D}$ this minimal amount. Fees and the requirement to leave dust can greatly erode the value of a user's bitcoins if she engages in many transactions of small amounts.

2.2 MIT Media Labs Certificate Issuing Schema

We are inspired by the transaction structure used in [20]. In this system a certificate or diploma is issued to a user who completes a given program of study, encoded in a Bitcoin transaction. The transaction has a single input, from the credential issuer, so the transaction must be signed by the private key corresponding to the issuer's address. Hence, verifiers can be confident that credential was issued by an approved party. There are three outputs. The first is the Bitcoin address of the user. Then the user can authenticate herself as the holder of the credential by signing messages using the corresponding private key. The second output is to an address again belonging to the issuer. If this output is spent, the certificate is seen as being revoked. We view this revocation mechanism as a key innovation of [20], and we integrate and develop it into our system. Finally, the third output is an OP_RETURN that contains the certificate information. Note that as each of these UXTOs is thought of as having symbolic meaning, their bitcoin values are secondary; indeed, they are assigned values slightly larger than $\mathcal{D}$.

Input Addresses	Amounts	Output Addresses	Amounts
Issuer	.000155 BTC	Recipient	.000275 BTC
		Issuer (for revocation)	.000275 BTC
		OP_RETURN(Certificate info)	0 BTC
		Fees:	.0001 BTC

Fig. 1. Schema of an MIT certificate issuing transaction as in [20]. See, for example, txid: 41740ae0812e5a7804778f43c9fd1f8df50fe1bcd0545e9d627a83ab9d0d3d07

2.3 The DLREP Function

In [8], Brands proposed very efficient ways of revealing parts of an identity to verifiers, relying on discrete logarithms and hash functions. All the following is from [8]. Assume that n identity fields $X_1, \ldots, X_n$ are to be cryptographically blinded for further proofs. Let q be a prime number and G a group of order q, in which the discrete logarithm is hard. Typically, we take G to be the Koblitz elliptic curve secp256k1 where points are represented with 64 bytes (we use multiplicative notation for compatibility with [8]), namely we use the same G that is already being used for the Bitcoin signature protocol. Let $g_0, g_1, \ldots, g_n \in G$. Furthermore, there is the need (see Sect. 3) for an auxiliary random X_0 to protect unknown fields from a dictionary attack when the other fields are known.

Definition 1. *The tuple* $(X_0, X_1, \ldots, X_n) \in \mathbb{Z}_q^{n+1}$ *is called a Discrete Logarithm REPresentation (DLREP) of* $h = \prod_{j=0}^{n} g_j^{X_j} \in G$ *with respect to* $(g_0, g_1, \ldots, g_n)$.

To (non-interactively) prove knowledge of a DLREP of h to a verifier $\mathcal{V}$, a prover $\mathcal{P}$ performs the following protocol steps [8, Sect. 2.4.3]

1. $\mathcal{P}$ generates $n+1$ secret, random numbers $a_0, a_1, \ldots, a_n$ in G. Let $A = \prod_{j=0}^{n} g_j^{a_j}$, and compute c as $c = \mathcal{H}(A)$, where H is a one-way hash function.
2. $\mathcal{P}$ computes $b_j = a_j + cX_j$, $j = 0, 1, \ldots, n$ and sends them, as well as c to $\mathcal{V}$.
3. The verifier $\mathcal{V}$ checks that $\mathcal{H}(\prod_{j=0}^{n} g_j^{b_j} h^{-c}) = c$ holds.

Then, [8, Chap. 3] shows how the DLREP can be used to selectively prove properties about the X_j's, while any other information remains hidden. These techniques can be used to prove arbitrary satisfiable Boolean statements about the X_j's. For example, a prover can demonstrate that she is a French citizen AND that she is either under 18 OR over 65. $\mathcal{P}$ can prove (true) statements about her identity that contain an arbitrary number of ANDs, ORs, and NOTs in such a way that $\mathcal{V}$ only learns information that can be computed using the status of the formulas requested and information available a priori. See [8, Proposition 3.6.1] for a formal statement of this result. Brands [8] also shows that if the discrete logarithm problem is difficult, DLREP is one-way and collision-intractable, preventing an adversary from forging an identity with a given DLREP.

3   Our Proposal

3.1   Actors, Protocol Structure, and Security Assumptions

Our system will have three types of actors: **Identity Providers** ($\mathcal{IP}$), **Service Providers** ($\mathcal{SP}$), and **Users** ($\mathcal{USR}$). We borrow the following from [20]:

Definition 2. *An identity is a tuple* $(X_1, \ldots, X_n)$ *where each* $X_j \in \mathbb{Z}_q$ *stands for a different attribute, as exemplified below.*

An attribute X_j may represent a name, a date of birth, a social insurance number, medical or financial data, or some other personal information about a user. Typically, based on an identity provided by $\mathcal{IP}$, a user ($\mathcal{USR}$) wants to convince $\mathcal{SP}$ to give her access to its services.

Assumptions on Actors. We consider that both the Bitcoin addresses of $\mathcal{IP}$ and $\mathcal{SP}$ are well-established and public, $\mathsf{a}_{\mathcal{IP}}$ and $\mathsf{a}_{\mathcal{SP}}$ respectively. We will consider scenarios in which we have multiple identity providers and service providers, whose addresses are denoted $\mathsf{a}_{\mathcal{IP}_1}, \mathsf{a}_{\mathcal{IP}_2}, \ldots$ and $\mathsf{a}_{\mathcal{SP}_1}, \mathsf{a}_{\mathcal{SP}_2}, \ldots$ respectively. In contrast, $\mathcal{USR}$ may have different Bitcoin addresses $\mathsf{a}_{\mathcal{USR}}^{(1)}, \mathsf{a}_{\mathcal{USR}}^{(2)}, \ldots$ in order to obfuscate the link between her identity transactions. When discussing a given user's address generally, we write $\mathsf{a}_{\mathcal{USR}}^{(i)}$ to indicate one her addresses. Note that a user should not re-use Bitcoin addresses that she has used for non-identification transactions, in order to not link this identity with her other Bitcoin activity.

We assume that all of $\mathcal{USR}$, $\mathcal{IP}$, and $\mathcal{SP}$ are capable of sending and receiving bitcoin and that they can perform operations in secp256k1. We will explore in Sect. 3.9 further technical requirements on the ability of $\mathcal{SP}$ to track Bitcoin transactions which will depend on $\mathcal{SP}$'s security requirements. We assume that $\mathcal{IP}$ validates a user's real world identity (via a more or less rigorous verification process) and then publishes documents that are correct. Furthermore, $\mathcal{IP}$ should handle user personal data in a way that respects user-privacy. Note that $\mathcal{IP}$ does not need to stay online for the identities it issues to be used, and only participates for issuing and revocation of identities, and certain exceptional maintenance, see Sect. 3.5. Service providers accept identities issued by identity providers they wish to trust. Note that service providers may fail or refuse to provide a service, a fact which can not be managed by our protocol. They may deviate from the protocol (at the risk of impairing their reputation, see below).

Assumptions on Bitcoin Network. We will use the *public ledger* functionality of Bitcoin: it is a "bulletin board" where anyone can post messages and read messages posted. More precisely, [13,22] provide the definitions of *liveness*, i.e. every honest participant will have its posted messages seen by every honest participant after some delay, and *persistence*, which means that every posted message will indefinitely be seen at the same position by all participants. We will also rely on the security semantics of the Bitcoin transaction verification procedure which ensure no double-spending, that each non-generation transaction has inputs linked to previous transaction outputs, etc. Under some quantitative bounds on the relative power of the adversary, be it computing power in [13], and or computing and network power [22], the Bitcoin core protocol is proven to securely provide these functionalities.

The above results are theoretical and quantitative. There could be real world situations in the Bitcoin blockchain where the adversary has enough power to violate the above quantitative bounds, and also accidental cases where problems occurs like small forks, peer-to-peer failures, etc. We will discuss the impact of these possible attacks and failures in Sect. 3.9 below.

Remark 1. Note that there are other relatively well-established blockchains such as Ethereum that can also serve as a "bulletin board." However, by working in Bitcoin, we can use the linking mechanism of Bitcoin transactions, which is not natively present in the account based model of Ethereum [26]. Also, the total hash power of the Bitcoin network is substantially greater than that of Ethereum [15], which can be seen as a sign that Bitcoin has a great resilience to 51% attacks.

There are three steps for our protocol: a **Setup phase**, an **Enrollment phase**, and an **Operational phase**.

3.2   Setup Phase

Each $\mathcal{IP}$ will choose some set of $g_0, g_1 \ldots, g_n \in G$ that will serve as the base for a DLREP function. These g_j should be public and readily available. For example, $\mathcal{IP}$ could create a series of Bitcoin transactions with inputs from his address in which the g_j and the fields they represent are stored in OP_RETURN outputs.

3.3   Enrollment Phase

During the Enrollment phase, $\mathcal{USR}$ brings to $\mathcal{IP}$ the (physical, biometric, etc.) elements required to assert that her identity indeed matches all the X_j's. This can be as strong as a physical meeting, in which the user shows a passport, or as light as an authentication on a web server, depending on the policy of $\mathcal{IP}$. During this phase $\mathcal{USR}$ should provide $\mathcal{IP}$ with a Bitcoin address $a_{\mathcal{USR}}^{(i)}$ that she controls and an element $g_0^{X_0}$ to protect against dictionary attacks, where X_0 is chosen at random by $\mathcal{USR}$ so that $\mathcal{IP}$ does not learn it. Then, $\mathcal{IP}$ can form $h_{a_{\mathcal{USR}}^{(i)}} = g_0^{X_0} g_1^{X_1} \ldots g_n^{X_n}$, as in Sect. 2.3.

The Enrollment phase corresponds to a single Bitcoin transaction, TX$_{\text{PUBLISH}}$. The primary purpose of this transaction is to record $h_{a_{\mathcal{USR}}^{(i)}}$ in the blockchain; however, we see that this transaction will include other structure.

TX$_{\text{PUBLISH}}$ (**Identity Establishment**): $\mathcal{IP}$ sends amounts of bitcoin to two outputs. First a minimal amount of bitcoin $\mathcal{D}$ is sent to the user's address $a_{\mathcal{USR}}^{(i)}$; this ties the user's address to the identity. Also, $\mathcal{IP}$ sends bitcoin to a 1 of 2 P2SH multisig of $a_{\mathcal{USR}}^{(i)}$ and $a_{\mathcal{IP}}$, denoted MSIG1_2($a_{\mathcal{USR}}^{(i)}$, $a_{\mathcal{IP}}$), which we view as an **authentication token** that the user will spend upon using her identity. Moreover, either $\mathcal{USR}$ or $\mathcal{IP}$ can prevent further use of the token by $\mathcal{USR}$ by sending it to $\mathcal{IP}$ or even spending it to a random address. This should be seen as **revocation**. More precisely, when using her identity as described below in Sect. 3.4, $\mathcal{USR}$ will send transactions of a specific form that return bitcoin to the same multisig address of $a_{\mathcal{IP}}$ and $a_{\mathcal{USR}}$ leaving a transaction output for future authentications; if at any point $\mathcal{USR}$ or $\mathcal{IP}$ spend this output in a transaction that is not of the form of another authentication, then this transaction is a TX$_{\text{REVOKE}}$ and the identity is seen as revoked. Finally, an OP_RETURN contains $h_{a_{\mathcal{USR}}^{(i)}}$.

The authentication token will be used in subsequent transactions; its amount V will be calibrated to cover the costs of these transactions, see Sect. 3.7.

Note that the structure of TX$_{\text{PUBLISH}}$ is similar to that of the transactions in the architecture of [20] as shown in Fig. 1. Now, revocation can be performed by both $\mathcal{IP}$ and by $\mathcal{USR}$ as both parties can destroy the authentication token via a TX$_{\text{REVOKE}}$.

Remark 2. There are alternative zero-knowledge selective credential systems in addition to that of Brands [8]. As discussed above, one advantage of using Brands' scheme is that its cryptographic primitives: discrete logarithms (in our

Input Addresses	Amounts	Output Addresses	Amounts
TX_PUBLISH			
$a_{\mathcal{IP}}$	$V + \mathcal{D} + F_{\text{PUBLISH}}$	$a_{\mathcal{USR}}^{(i)}$	$\mathcal{D}$
		$\text{MSIG1\_2}(a_{\mathcal{USR}}^{(i)}, a_{\mathcal{IP}})$	V
		$\text{OP\_RETURN}\left(h_{a_{\mathcal{USR}}^{(i)}}\right)$	
		Fees:	F_{PUBLISH}

Fig. 2. Structure of TX_PUBLISH.

case on secp256k1) and hash functions are also primitives of Bitcoin, so we minimize the number of cryptographic assumptions necessary. Also, the commitments of Brands are small enough (a compressed elliptic curve point of 33 bytes) to fit in an OP_RETURN. In contrast this is not the case for example for the commitments of the Camenisch-Lysyanskaya scheme which produces commitments of 670 bytes [24, Table 2].

Remark 3. One can imagine cases where a hostile or hacked $\mathcal{IP}$ uses the authentication token to obtain services acting as if it were the user, possibly with the aim of harming the user's reputation. However, when spending a multisig output, it is visible which of the public keys one is signing by [7], thus such an attack would be visible and, in fact, damage $\mathcal{IP}$'s reputation.

3.4 Operational Phase

The Operational phase is made up of two further Bitcoin transactions. We think of certain outputs as being distinguished (or colored with a transferable semantic meaning in the sense of Colored Coins [10], [19, Sect. 9.2]), corresponding to the authentication token. The flow of this token will chain the transactions together and ultimately to the creation of the identity in TX_PUBLISH (see Fig. 4). We suppose $\mathcal{SP}$ informs $\mathcal{USR}$ of what statement about her identity she needs to prove to authenticate. Then we have the Bitcoin transactions:

TX_REQUEST **(Request for Service):** $\mathcal{USR}$ creates a transaction where the input is the $\text{MSIG1\_2}(a_{\mathcal{USR}}^{(i)}, a_{\mathcal{IP}})$ from TX_PUBLISH. One output is sent to $a_{\mathcal{SP}}$. One output is sent back to $\text{MSIG1\_2}(a_{\mathcal{USR}}^{(i)}, a_{\mathcal{IP}})$ and will serve as the authentication token for future transactions. $\mathcal{USR}$ proves to $\mathcal{SP}$ the required Boolean statement about the X_j's without revealing them as in Sect. 2.3 (see below for a discussion of how this proof is transmitted and stored).

TX_ACCEPT **(Acknowledgment of the Identity by $\mathcal{SP}$):** Upon validating the proof of $\mathcal{USR}$, checking that the authentication token is the result of a series of TX_REQUEST's each of whose input is the output of the previous chained back to a TX_PUBLISH, checking that TX_PUBLISH was issued by a trusted $\mathcal{IP}$, and verifying that the multisig output of the most recent TX_REQUEST has not been spent (namely that there has not been a TX_REVOKE), $\mathcal{SP}$ accepts $\mathcal{USR}$'s authentication and uses its output from TX_REQUEST to send bitcoins to $a_{\mathcal{IP}}$.

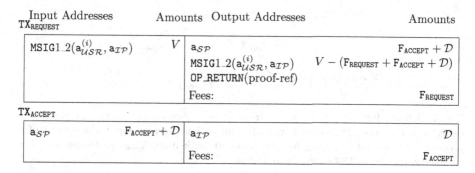

Input Addresses TX$_{\text{REQUEST}}$	Amounts	Output Addresses	Amounts
$\text{MSIG1\_2}(a_{\mathcal{USR}}^{(i)}, a_{\mathcal{IP}})$	V	$a_{\mathcal{SP}}$	$F_{\text{ACCEPT}} + \mathcal{D}$
		$\text{MSIG1\_2}(a_{\mathcal{USR}}^{(i)}, a_{\mathcal{IP}})$	$V - (F_{\text{REQUEST}} + F_{\text{ACCEPT}} + \mathcal{D})$
		$\text{OP\_RETURN}(\text{proof-ref})$	
		Fees:	F_{REQUEST}

TX$_{\text{ACCEPT}}$			
$a_{\mathcal{SP}}$	$F_{\text{ACCEPT}} + \mathcal{D}$	$a_{\mathcal{IP}}$	$\mathcal{D}$
		Fees:	F_{ACCEPT}

Fig. 3. The transactions that compose a typical authentication The inputs and outputs highlighted in red are thought of as an authentication token that chain the user's transactions together and to TX$_{\text{PUBLISH}}$.

Storage of Proofs. A careful reading of [8, Chap. 3] shows that the size of the Brands proofs required to demonstrate a given Boolean statement about an identity $(X_0, \ldots, X_n)$ scales linearly in n, but also depends on the statement being proven. We note that these proofs will generally be too large to be contained directly in an OP_RETURN. Depending on the needs of $\mathcal{USR}$ and $\mathcal{SP}$, we propose three different mechanisms by which these proofs might be transmitted and stored. 1. A user can store in the OP_RETURN of TX$_{\text{REQUEST}}$ a link to a site where the proofs are stored externally as well as a hash of the relevant contents of this site. We denote this information by proof-ref. The hash will be included in mined blocks, so the information on the site has the same protections against mutability as other information on the blockchain. This is similar to how metadata is stored in [10]. 2. A user that is very concerned about privacy, or who is proving a statement that is already sensitive, can transmit the Brands proofs entirely off-chain. 3. If one wants to avoid an off-chain storage mechanism, there are a number of non-OP_RETURN ways to store data in the Bitcoin blockchain (see [10]) such as in a vanity address or using a fake 1 of N multisig. Alternatively, one can issue a P2SH output in TX$_{\text{REQUEST}}$ with Pubkey Script OP_HASH160 $H(\text{data})$ OP_EQUAL for which the corresponding input Sig Script is simply the data itself (see txid   db195e4bfcfb3cc6d47f8d6231cb59e543c31e01d196d557457bca0fa5c1aba0). While there are still limits on how much data can be placed in a single input, through using multiple inputs, one can store larger amounts of data in this fashion in exchange for paying (much) higher transaction fees.

For the remainder of this article (and in Fig. 3) we assume that proofs are being referenced via a link and a hash in an OP_RETURN.

Remark 4. TX$_{\text{ACCEPT}}$ publicly shows that $\mathcal{SP}$ has accepted $\mathcal{USR}$'s identity proofs as valid, contributing to the reputation of $a_{\mathcal{USR}}^{(i)}$ (see Sect. 5). This is particularly useful if the proofs were conveyed off-chain or are otherwise unavailable. TX$_{\text{ACCEPT}}$ can also serve to alert $\mathcal{IP}$ that $\mathcal{SP}$ has used an identity that it provided, and can even be a basis for a payment by $\mathcal{SP}$ for the issuing of this identity.

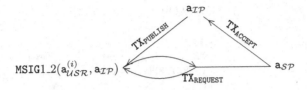

Fig. 4. Scheme for users to prove their identity to service providers. An identity is issued via a TX_PUBLISH. Subsequently, each transaction takes as input the output of a previous transaction (TX_PUBLISH for the first authentication, TX_REQUEST thereafter). For simplicity, the OP_RETURN output is not shown.

Remark 5. The transaction output of TX_REQUEST to $\text{MSIG1\_2}(a_{USR}^{(i)}, a_{IP})$ is necessary if the user wishes to reuse an identity, so that USR will have an UTXO tied to her identity to spend in a subsequent TX_REQUEST. This cyclic structure chains the various authentications together permitting a verifier to trace any of them back to the original identity issued in TX_PUBLISH. Alternatively, USR can obtain a new TX_PUBLISH attached to a different address $a_{USR}^{(j)}$ for each authentication if she wishes to maintain a more complete anonymity in her authentications. However, doing so is slightly more expensive as additional fees need to be paid for each TX_PUBLISH. Additionally, this limits the ability of a user to take advantage of the reputation system we propose in Sect. 5. (See the discussion in the introduction on user empowerment over her level of privacy and compare to [8, Chap. 5.2.1], where Brands discusses the balance between reputation and anonymity and proposes reuse solutions for his certificates.) In cases where the identity is only designed to be used one time, this transaction output is unnecessary.

3.5   Limited Use Identities and Setting Bitcoin Values

Due to the chaining of authentications, when SP verifies the continued validity of USR's identity, the number of times this identity has been used can also be calculated. Thus, if IP includes a use limit of N authentications with $h_{a_{USR}^{(i)}}$ in the OP_RETURN of TX_PUBLISH, SP can check if this identity can still be used. Then, IP should calibrate the amount of bitcoin, V, that is placed in the $a_{USR}^{(i)}$ output to cover these N authentications. As we saw in Fig. 3 that each authentication consumes $F_{REQUEST}+F_{ACCEPT}+D$ bitcoin before the authentication token is returned to the user, and this returned token needs to have a value of at least D after the last usage for the transaction to be accepted as standard, V must be at least $N(F_{REQUEST} + F_{ACCEPT} + D) + D$. Note, the fees required for a transaction to be processed in a timely fashion slowly vary based on market forces, so IP should, in practice, set V to be slightly larger than current market demands in case miners increase their fees. Then, situations requiring IP to come online and top up its users' balances can be limited to cases of extreme changes in Bitcoin fees.

3.6 Coordinating Multiple Identities

Suppose a given user has obtained identities $h_{a_{\mathcal{USR}}^{(1)}}$ and $h_{a_{\mathcal{USR}}^{(2)}}$ from more than one identity provider. We see that these identities can be coordinated.

Input Addresses $\text{TX}_{\text{REQUEST-DOUBLE}}$	Amounts	Output Addresses	Amounts
$\text{MSIG1\_2}(a_{\mathcal{USR}}^{(1)}, a_{\mathcal{IP}})$	V_1	$a_{\mathcal{SP}}$	$2F_{\text{ACCEPT}} + 2D$
$\text{MSIG1\_2}(a_{\mathcal{USR}}^{(2)}, a_{\mathcal{IP}})$	V_2	$\text{MSIG1\_2}(a_{\mathcal{USR}}^{(1)}, a_{\mathcal{IP}})$	$V_1 - (F_{\text{REQUEST}} + F_{\text{ACCEPT}} + D)$
		$\text{MSIG1\_2}(a_{\mathcal{USR}}^{(2)}, a_{\mathcal{IP}})$	$V_2 - (F_{\text{REQUEST}} + F_{\text{ACCEPT}} + D)$
		$\text{OP\_RETURN}(\text{proof-ref})$	
		Fees:	$F_{\text{REQUEST-DOUBLE}}$

$\text{TX}_{\text{ACCEPT-DOUBLE}}$

$a_{\mathcal{SP}}$	$2F_{\text{ACCEPT}} + 2D$	$a_{\mathcal{IP}_1}$	D
		$a_{\mathcal{IP}_2}$	D
		Fees:	$F_{\text{ACCEPT-DOUBLE}}$

Fig. 5. Use of the authentication tokens of two identities together. The paths of these tokens are colored in red and blue. The Brands proofs referenced in proof-ref are with respect to the DLREP of Eq. 1

Concretely, suppose a user has been issued an identity by $\mathcal{IP}_1$ consisting of $h_{a_{\mathcal{USR}}^{(1)}} = \prod_{j=0}^{n} g_j^{X_j}$ and another identity by $\mathcal{IP}_2$ consisting of $h_{a_{\mathcal{USR}}^{(2)}} = \prod_{u=0}^{m} (g_u')^{Y_u}$. A service provider will be able to verify that each of these values correspond to the respective $\text{TX}_{\text{PUBLISH}}$ transactions issued by the identity providers. Then

$$h_{a_{\mathcal{USR}}^{(1)}} \cdot h_{a_{\mathcal{USR}}^{(2)}} = \prod_{j=0}^{n} g_j^{X_j} \prod_{u=0}^{m} (g_u')^{Y_u} \tag{1}$$

is a DLREP commitment of the union of $X_0, \ldots, X_n$ and $Y_0, \ldots, Y_m$. The user can do proofs with selective disclosure using this commitment.

We preserve the chaining properties by having two transactions $\text{TX}_{\text{REQUEST-DOUBLE}}$, which takes in the authentication tokens from both identities, and $\text{TX}_{\text{ACCEPT-DOUBLE}}$, which notifies both identity providers. The amounts used in these transactions are chosen as in Fig. 5 to ensure that a user's balances decrease by no more than what would have been the case for separate authentications with the two identities, in keeping with the calibration of V in Sect. 3.5. (We will see in Sect. 3.7, $F_{\text{REQUEST-DOUBLE}} \leq 2F_{\text{REQUEST}}$ and $F_{\text{ACCEPT-DOUBLE}} \leq 2F_{\text{ACCEPT}}$, so adequate fees are paid here; the change can be split between $\mathcal{USR}$'s authentication tokens for use in case of future Bitcoin fee increases, paid to $\mathcal{SP}$, or left to the miners to increase the speed of the transaction's approvals). This schema can obviously generalize to more than two identities.

Thus, a user can obtain many "micro-identities" - from the government, from her bank, from her employer, from her health care provider - which she can manage together without having to unnecessarily share information between her identity providers. This is very much in the spirit of a PIMS [5].

Remark 6. The ability of $\mathcal{USR}$ to issue a transaction as in Fig. 5, which requires signing with the private key corresponding to the address of each identity, is already a weak way of establishing that these identities belong to the same person. However, it is possible for malicious users to pool the private keys from identities corresponding to distinct people. $\mathcal{USR}$ can provide stronger proof of the connection of her identities if she shows as part of her proof in $TX_{REQUEST}$ that h and h' share common fields, such as name or social insurance number.

3.7 Estimates of Cost

We now estimate the costs of the transactions we have introduced in the preceeding sections. As mentioned in Sect. 2, Bitcoin miners have flexibility in what fees they demand. However, the current standard fee to have one's transaction processed in a timely manner is 360 satoshis, namely .0000036 bitcoins, per byte [3]. Based on our schema, $TX_{PUBLISH}$ will contain one input, one P2PKH output, one P2SH output, and an OP_RETURN that contains one (compressed) point on secp256k1. Hence the OP_RETURN contains 33 bytes resulting in a total transaction size of roughly 267 bytes (see [7, Chap. 2] for more information on the size of the various components of a Bitcoin transaction) costing .0009612 bitcoin. At current market rates (June 2017, 1BTC = 2720 USD), this corresponds to a minimum transaction fee of approximately 2.61 USD. We compute the sizes and costs of the other transactions similarly (based on proof-ref consisting of a 32 byte SHA-256 hash and a 30 byte url when necessary):

Transaction	$TX_{PUBLISH}$	TX_{REVOKE}	$TX_{REQUEST}$	TX_{ACCEPT}	$TX_{REQUEST-DOUBLE}$	$TX_{ACCEPT-DOUBLE}$
# Bytes	267	229	334	191	479	225
Cost (USD)	2.61	2.24	3.28	1.87	5.41	2.20

Then, building off Sect. 3.5, the total cost to issue an N use identity is the value of the input issued by $\mathcal{IP}$ in $TX_{PUBLISH}$. As in Fig. 2, this is

$$\text{Cost of } N\text{-use Id} = V + \mathcal{D} + F_{PUBLISH}$$
$$= N(F_{REQUEST} + F_{ACCEPT} + \mathcal{D}) + 2\mathcal{D} + F_{PUBLISH}$$
$$\approx 5.2N + 2.6 \text{ USD}.$$

Note that Bitcoin fees have increased substantially recently as the Bitcoin community seeks consensus on how to scale block capacity. It is hoped that a solution to this issue, such as an implementation of SegWit, will reduce fees [25].

3.8   Obtaining Information About the Bitcoin Network

Note that, in the processing of an authentication, it is the service provider that must verify the status of past Bitcoin transactions. Service providers with rigorous verification requirements, such as banks and insurance companies, should run a full node or possibly a Simplified Payment Verification (SPV) client, see [7]. Note the SPV protocol, which is already commonly used by vendors who payment in Bitcoin, allows someone who downloads merely the 80 byte header of each block to verify that a transaction has been included in a block, upon being provided with information related to that transaction by a full node. Hence, a service provider running this protocol can verify that each of the $TX_{REQUEST}$'s a user has issued, chained back to $TX_{PUBLISH}$, counting the number of times the identity has been used. This process also checks that the identity has not been revoked as the SPV client sees that the network has accepted the most recent transaction, so the transaction output controlled by the multisig between USR and IP could not have already been spent in a TX_{REVOKE}. Service providers with less rigorous standards may retrieve their information from an online block explorer if they accept the additional risks of attacks on these sites.

3.9   Security Considerations in Case of Blockchain Failures

In Sect. 3.1, we place ourselves in a security model in which Bitcoin possesses certain properties of an ideal blockchain. Here we explore the consequences on our system when these properties are not satisfied.

Inconsistencies in the Bitcoin ledger: The integrity of the Bitcoin ledger serves in our system to allow issuer oversight, concretely to allow the issuer to revoke identities and to impose limits on the number of uses. On the other hand, if there is a fork, a dishonest user can to continue to use an identity which an issuer has revoked until the revocation transaction finally appears in the dominant chain. If an attacker can issue a double spend (due to an accidental fork, because the attacker has a large percentage of the mining power, etc.), then she can reuse her authentication token allowing her to exceed her usage limit.

Bitcoin network failure: We also rely on Bitcoin P2P infrastructure to propagate the transactions that make up our protocol, and we rely on being able to download information on previous Bitcoin transactions from nodes to check the state of an identity. An attack on the P2P Bitcoin network can translate into a denial of service attack on our system as one cannot issue $TX_{PUBLISH}$, $TX_{REQUEST}$, etc. if the network does not relay them or if one cannot verify relevant previous transactions. How vulnerable a service provider is to network attacks will depend on how it receives information about the network as in Sect. 3.8. Note that, regardless of this choice, user privacy is protected and impersonation is prevented by the security of Brands' protocols, see [8]. Even a service provider that obtains its information from a block explorer can assure itself of the correctness of Brands proofs and the validity of signatures.

4   Example Use Cases

In this section we propose a few use cases of our system that highlight its advantages versus existing systems.

4.1   University ID

We consider a university where the administration delivers identity credentials to students, teachers, and staff. These credentials provide certificates of various fields related to the user including their name, their status at the university (student, teacher, etc.), and their academic records. Individuals may use such identities, revealing some (or none) of these fields, to authenticate themselves to various university services such as the university pool or medical clinic.

Now imagine that a user wants to claim a discount on car insurance reserved for students with high GPAs. This student may need to coordinate her university identity with a driver's license issued by her local government. Then she can selectively reveal information to the service provider, the insurer, using the multi-$\mathcal{IP}$ protocols described in Sect. 3.6. If her status at the university changes, her university identity can be revoked preventing her from performing such authentications, even as her driver's license identity remains valid.

4.2   Network of Small Museums

We imagine a group of small museums that form a partnership in which any member of one museum is allowed a limited number of visits to the other museums. In this case, the user is a member of one of the museums, the identity provider is the museum that issued the membership, and the other museums are service providers. Then the user may selectively disclose fields such as her membership status or category of membership. More sensitive information may be included in the identity allowing the user to authenticate to tax authorities which give a tax credit for museum memberships. The limit on the number of visits is controlled through the methods of Sect. 3.5.

In contrast to the tax authorities, the security requirements of the museums may allow them to obtain the transaction information from an online block explorer, completely outsourcing the costs of transmitting and storing information to the Bitcoin network similar to how [1] uses the blockchain as a virtual server. This may be substantially cheaper and more streamlined than traditional systems (namely, either for each of the museums to invest in infrastructure that then has to be coordinated or for a single museum to set up infrastructure to manage the entire system which may create conflicts of interest and be unacceptable to the other museums). Thus, our system allows the museums to create a shared, neutral management space, maintaining transparency into exactly how the data is stored and used, that minimizes infrastructure costs.

5 Building a Reputation on the Blockchain

We see in Sect. 4.2, in the case of our museums, that little infrastructure is required of $\mathcal{SP}$. Nonetheless, $\mathcal{SP}$ must be able to compute in secp256k1, perform Bitcoin transactions, and be able to access the blockchain history, as discussed in Sects. 3.1 and 3.9. Imagine that some very lightweight service provider wants to participate in this network, but does not have the security requirements, nor the resources to justify performing these operations. For example, this may be the case of a university pool in the university ID example of Sect. 4.

As all transactions are visible in the blockchain, a user can then simply direct a lightweight service provider to her past transactions, which requires merely an Internet connection, and prove that she controls the private key corresponding to those transactions by issuing a signature. Then, if the lightweight service provider is willing to trust the larger service providers that have already accepted the user's identity (e.g. if the university pool is willing to trust the campus medical clinic in accepting that the user is a member of the university community), it is not necessary to re-validate the relevant Brands proofs. As seen before (see Sect. 3.6), a user may have had her identity established under different Bitcoin addresses and proven to different service providers in such a way that is unknown that these addresses belong to the same user. If the user has used the two identities together in a $TX_{REQUEST-DOUBLE}$, the light service provider may be again willing to trust that the other service provider has verified these two identities as corresponding to the same person. Alternatively, in situations with lower security standards (as per Remark 6), the user can issue signatures for both of the private keys corresponding to the identities used.

Moreover, the collection of transactions of a user, seen as having been accepted via TX_{ACCEPT} transactions, gradually forms a digital footprint of the user. While some users will want to avoid reusing the same $TX_{PUBLISH}$ for multiple authentications for greater anonymity, for other users this digital presence, over which the user has a great deal of direct control, can be a useful addition to the online reputation they develop, for example through social media.

6 Conclusion

The Bitcoin blockchain is a global network, and by building on top of this network, we can take advantage of its existing infrastructure to reach a global scope while minimizing overhead. Moreover, by placing an identity management system in this decentralized space, we have seen that we can strike a more equitable balance between the rights and responsibilities of users and identity issuers.

Acknowledgment. The work leading to this paper has received funding from the European Community's Framework Programme (FP7/2007-2013) under Grant Agreement n° 607049.

References

1. CryptID. Source code https://github.com/CryptidID/Cryptid. Consulted April 2017. http://cryptid.xyz/
2. IDCoins. Consulted April 2017. https://github.com/IDCoin/IDCoin
3. Predicting Bitcoin fees for transactions, Consulted April 2017. https://bitcoinfees.21.co/
4. Estonian e-residency, Consulted March 2017. https://e-estonia.com/e-residents/about/
5. Abiteboul, S., André, B., Kaplan, D.: Managing your digital life. Commun. ACM **58**(5), 32–35 (2015)
6. Ali, M., Nelson, J., Shea, R., Freedman, M.J.: Blockstack: a global naming and storage system secured by blockchains. In: 2016 USENIX Annual Technical Conference (USENIX ATC 2016), Denver, CO, USA, June 22–24, 2016. Proceedings, pp. 181–194 (2016)
7. Antonopoulos, A.M.: Mastering Bitcoin. O'Reilly Media, Sebastopol (2015). ISBN: 978-1-449-37404-4
8. Brands, S.: Rethinking Public Key Infrastructures and Digital Certificates (Building in Privacy). MIT Press, Cambridge (2000)
9. Camenisch, J., Lehmann, A., Neven, G.: Electronic identities need private credentials. IEEE Secur. Priv. **10**(1), 80–83 (2012)
10. Charlon, F.:. Open assets protocol (OAP/1.0) (2011). https://github.com/OpenAssets/open-assets-protocol/blob/master/specification.mediawiki
11. Miers, I., Garman, C., Green, M.: Accountable privacy for decentralized anonymous payments. In: Financial Cryptography and Data Security (2016)
12. The Bitcoin Core developers: Bitcoin transactions primitives code, Consulted March 2017. https://github.com/bitcoin/bitcoin/blob/0.14/src/primitives/transaction.h
13. Garay, J., Kiayias, A., Leonardos, N.: The bitcoin backbone protocol: analysis and applications. In: Oswald, E., Fischlin, M. (eds.) EUROCRYPT 2015. LNCS, vol. 9057, pp. 281–310. Springer, Heidelberg (2015). doi:10.1007/978-3-662-46803-6_10
14. Hardjono, T., Smith, N., (Sandy) Pentland, A.: Anonymous identities for permissioned blockchains, January 2016. http://www.the-blockchain.com/docs/MIT-ChainAnchor-DRAFT.pdf
15. Hay, S.: Bitcoin vs ethereum: Cryptocurrency comparison, March 2017. https://99bitcoins.com/bitcoin-vs-ethereum-cryptocurrency-comparison/
16. Jacobovitz, O.: Blockchain for identity management, December 2016. https://www.cs.bgu.ac.il/%7Efrankel/TechnicalReports/2016/16-02.pdf
17. Liu, Y., Tome, W., Zhang, L., Choffnes, D.R., Levin, D., Maggs, B.M., Mislove, A., Schulman, A., Wilson, C.: An end-to-end measurement of certificate revocation in the web's PKI. In: Proceedings of the 2015 ACM Internet Measurement Conference, IMC 2015, Tokyo, Japan, October 28–30, 2015, pp. 183–196 (2015)
18. Nakamoto, S.: Bitcoin: a peer-to-peer electronic cash system (2008). http://bitcoin.org/bitcoin.pdf
19. Narayanan, A., Bonneau, J., Felten, E., Miller, A., Goldfeder, S.: Bitcoin and Cryptocurrency Technologies: A Comprehensive Introduction. Princeton University Press, Princeton (2016)
20. Nazaré, J., Hamilton, K., Schmidt, P.: Digital certificates project. Source code https://github.com/digital-certificates. Consulted December 2016. http://certificates.media.mit.edu

21. Office of the Privacy Commissionner of Canada. Privacy and your reputation - who shapes your identity online? (2012)

22. Pass, R., Seeman, L., Shelat, A.: Analysis of the blockchain protocol in asynchronous networks. In: Coron, J.-S., Nielsen, J.B. (eds.) EUROCRYPT 2017. LNCS, vol. 10211, pp. 643–673. Springer, Cham (2017). doi:10.1007/978-3-319-56614-6_22

23. Prisco, G.: Estonian government partnerts with bitnation to offer blockchain notarization services to e-residents, November 2015. https://bitcoinmagazine.com/articles/estonian-government-partners-with-bitnation-to-offer-blockchain-notarization-services-to-e-residents-1448915243/

24. Security Team: Specification of the identity mixer cryptographic library version 2.3.0. Technical report RZ 3730, IBM Research, Computer Science Dept, IBM Research - Zurich, Switzerland, 48 pages (2010)

25. Torpey, K.: Are bitcoin miners making more money off small blocks? March 2017. https://bitcoinmagazine.com/articles/are-bitcoin-miners-making-more-money-small-blocks/

26. Wood, G.: Ethereum: a secure decentralised generalised transaction ledger, EIP-150 REVISION (030c1b5 - 10 July 2017). https://ethereum.github.io/yellowpaper/paper.pdf

27. Yang, D., Gavigan, J., Wilcox-O'Hearn, Z.: Survey of confidentiality and privacy preserving technologies for blockchains, November 2016. https://z.cash/static/R3_Confidentiality_and_Privacy_Report.pdf

28. Zyskind, G., Nathan, O., Pentland, A.: Decentralizing privacy: using blockchain to protect personal data. In: 2015 IEEE Symposium on Security and Privacy Workshops, SPW 2015, San Jose, CA, USA, May 21–22, 2015, pp. 180–184. IEEE Computer Society, Los Alamitos (2015)

Short Papers

Towards a Concurrent and Distributed Route Selection for Payment Channel Networks

Elias Rohrer[1]([✉]), Jann-Frederik Laß[2], and Florian Tschorsch[1]

[1] Technical University of Berlin, Berlin, Germany
{elias.rohrer,florian.tschorsch}@tu-berlin.de
[2] Humboldt University of Berlin, Berlin, Germany
lassjann@informatik.hu-berlin.de

Abstract. Payment channel networks use off-chain transactions to provide virtually arbitrary transaction rates. In this paper, we provide a new perspective on payment channels and consider them as a flow network. We propose an extended push-relabel algorithm to find payment flows in a payment channel network. Our algorithm enables a distributed and concurrent execution without violating capacity constraints. To this end, we introduce the concept of capacity locking. We prove that flows are valid and present first results.

1 Introduction

It seems that blockchain-based systems such as Bitcoin [9] will, due to their requirements regarding storage, processing power, and bandwidth, not be able to natively scale to high transaction rates [2]. Off-chain approaches [3,10], however, offer a way to create long-lived payment channels between two nodes. The payments transferred via a payment channel are processed locally and therefore eliminate the need to commit each individual transaction to the blockchain.

In order to enable payments between any two nodes—whether they are directly connected or not—payment channels form a network in which payments can be routed over more than one hop. Finding a route that can process a certain transaction volume is challenging, though. Related approaches [11] cannot guarantee to utilize the available capacities as they focus on finding a single path from payer to payee that meets the capacity constraints. We argue that single-path routing restricts the transferable amount and misses many payment opportunities due to bottleneck capacities in the network. Particularly, if payment channel networks may ultimately become a viable payment alternative and process large transaction volumes that exceed channel capacities, single-path routing will probably fail.

In this paper, we propose to aggregate multiple paths to a *payment flow*, which can in sum provide larger transaction volumes. We believe that algorithms from the domain of flow networks in general and the push-relabel algorithm [5] in particular are appropriate candidates for route selection in payment networks.

Our main contribution is a new route selection algorithm, which is based on the push-relabel algorithm. It can find feasible flows in a payment channel

© Springer International Publishing AG 2017
J. Garcia-Alfaro et al. (Eds.): DPM/CBT 2017, LNCS 10436, pp. 411–419, 2017.
DOI: 10.1007/978-3-319-67816-0_23

network. While it may be executed in a centralized setup, it is also safe for concurrent fully distributed execution. To this end, we introduce the concept of *capacity locking*. We show that our algorithm guarantees that routes are feasible flows and at the same time does not violate any capacity constraints. Our first results confirm that the approach is able to handle a high number of flows and transaction volumes. The results emphasize that our approach succeeds in scenarios where single-path routing schemes are bound to fail. In summary, we offer a new perspective on payment channel networks.

The remainder is structured as follows. Section 2 discusses related work. Subsequently, Sect. 3 introduces payment flows and describes the basic algorithmic design. Section 4 develops a distributed and concurrent route selection algorithm. In Sect. 5, we present and discuss first results, before Sect. 6 concludes the paper.

2   Background and Related Work

Payment channels are a new and unexplored concept. The specifications [6] of the Lightning Network [10], for example, are subject to constant change. For the sake of clarity, we abstract from any specific payment channel design [3,10].

Routing in a payment channel network poses many challenges, e. g., regarding the routing paradigm (per-hop routing vs. source routing) and the topology (hub-and-spoke vs. peer-to-peer). In this paper, we focus on route selection, i. e., finding a route in a payment channel network that meets certain constraints. Flare [11], a proposed routing system for the Lightning Network, creates a list of candidate routes from the set of channels with sufficient capacity. So far, however, Flare and current implementations [4,7,8] of the Lightning Network opt for selecting single-path routes only. In our work, we consider a payment as a flow and provide an algorithm that finds and aggregates multiple paths based on local knowledge.

We identify flow network algorithms as a promising direction to find multi-path routes. While multi-commodity flows address a similar problem, most of the existing approaches require global knowledge and/or a centralized routing coordinator. The approach in [1] allows a distributed and concurrent execution but solves the feasible-flow problem only approximately. Our distributed algorithm, in contrast, guarantees that the selected route is a feasible flow. Moreover, it can be executed concurrently without violating capacity constraints and enables route selection in a fully distributed scenario.

3   Payment Flows

Payment flows describe a flow of units between pairs of nodes in a payment channel network. Figure 1 shows an example of a payment channel network in which node s wants to send a payment to node t. We consider the payment channel network as a peer-to-peer network in which nodes communicate directly with

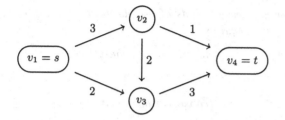

Path	Vol.
$s \to v_2 \to t$	1
$s \to v_2 \to v_3 \to t$	2
$s \to v_3 \to t$	2
maximum flow	4

Fig. 1. Payment channel network example.

each other and build an overlay network congruent with the payment channel network. That is, we aim for a decentralized route selection.

In order to process the payment, a path between s and t must exist. Every path is a concatenation of payment channels. Since payment channels have a capacity, as indicated by the edge labeling in Fig. 1, a path's transaction volume is limited by the smallest payment channel capacity of this path. While we cannot eliminate this limit, we can use multiple paths, which in sum provide a higher transaction volume.

Determining the maximum transferable amount poses a challenge. For example, simply finding all paths from source to sink and summing up their respective capacities does not suffice; paths may have common edges and thus need to share the respective capacities. For the example in Fig. 1, this naive approach would violate payment channel capacities.

The problem of finding the largest payment flow between two nodes s and t in a capacitated flow network is known as the *maximum-flow problem*. Several algorithmic solutions to the maximum-flow problem exist. In the following, we elaborate on the efficient and well-studied *push-relabel* [5] algorithm and adopt it for the route selection of payment flows in payment channel networks.

We consider a network of payment channels as a directed graph $G = (V, E)$ and a non-negative function $c : V \times V \to \mathbb{R}_{\geq 0}$. We call c the capacity function, which determines a channel's capacity $c(u, v)$ with $u, v \in V$ and $(u, v) \in E$. Moreover, nodes s and t are the source and sink of the flow. The resulting network $F = (G, c, s, t)$ is called a *flow network*.

Definition 1 (pseudo-flow, pre-flow, feasible flow). *A **pseudo-flow** on the capacitated graph (G, c) is a mapping $f : V \times V \to \mathbb{R}$ with the properties:*

$$f(u, v) \leq c(u, v), \forall (u, v) \in E \qquad \text{(capacity constraint)}$$
$$f(u, v) = -f(v, u), \forall (u, v) \in E \qquad \text{(skew symmetry)}$$

*Note that pseudo-flows do not require incoming and outgoing flows of a node to be equal. Therefore, nodes can hold **excess flow**, denoted by*

$$x_f(u) = \sum_{v \in V} f(v, u) - \sum_{v \in V} f(u, v).$$

*A pre-flow and a feasible flow are special kinds of pseudo-flows with one of the following constraints. A **pre-flow** requires*

$$x_f(v) \geq 0, \forall v \in V \setminus \{s,t\} \qquad \text{(non-negativity constraint)}$$

*and a **feasible flow** requires*

$$x_f(v) = 0, \forall v \in V \setminus \{s,t\} \qquad \text{(conservation constraint)}.$$

Definition 2 (residual capacity and residual graph). *The **residual capacity** c_f with regard to the pseudo-flow f of an edge $(u,v) \in E$ is defined as the difference between the edge's capacity and its flow:*

$$c_f(u,v) = c(u,v) - f(u,v).$$

*Then, the **residual graph** $G_f(V, E_f)$ indicates when changes can be made to flow f in the network $G(V,E)$, where*

$$E_f = \{(u,v) \in V \times V : c_f(u,v) > 0\}.$$

Note that edges (u,v) do not have to be in the original set of edges E.

Definition 3 (height function). *A mapping $h : V \to \mathbb{N}$ is a **height function** for the push-relabel algorithm, if*

$$h(s) = |V|, \qquad h(t) = 0, \qquad h(u) \leq h(v) + 1, \forall (u,v) \in E_f.$$

At the beginning, the generic push-relabel algorithm initializes node heights and flow excess, as well as the edge pre-flow values with 0. Please note that source node s, in contrast to all other nodes, is set to a height $|V|$. Moreover, s's outgoing edges are saturated according to the height function's third condition. After these initialization steps, the algorithm repeatedly selects a node u as active node and applies one of the two basic operations push and relabel. Both operations have mutually exclusive conditions, which ensure that either push or relabel is applicable at a time.

The push procedure (cf. Procedure 1) tries to push an excess δ from node u towards a neighbor v with a smaller height. The maximum possible δ is determined as the minimum between the excess flow and the residual capacity of edge (u,v). Accordingly, edge capacities and excess values are updated to reflect flow changes in the residual graph. The procedure requires that u has excess flow and that an unsaturated edge (u,v) to a neighbor v one level below u exists.

Eventually, node u will saturate all outgoing edges that lead to neighbors on a lower level. In this case, the relabel procedure (cf. Procedure 2) "raises" node u to a higher level. The procedure calculates the minimal height of its neighbor nodes and sets u's height to the level above this minimum. Therefore, the excess of node u is guaranteed to be "pushable" in the next step.

The generic push-relabel algorithms continues until the conditions fail for all nodes. That means, the highest possible transaction volume has been pushed to the sink t and all network excess has been pushed back to the source, i.e., $x_f(v) = 0, \forall v \in V$. At this point, the push-relabel algorithm has transformed the pre-flow into a maximum flow and hence solved the maximum-flow problem.

Procedure 1 push(u,v)

Conditions: $x_f(u) > 0, c(u,v) > 0, h(u) = h(v) + 1$
$\quad \delta := \min(\,x_f(u),\ c_f(u,v)\,)$
$\quad f(u,v) := f(u,v) + \delta;\ \ f(v,u) := f(v,u) - \delta$
$\quad x_f(u) := x_f(u) - \delta;\ \ x_f(v) := x_f(v) + \delta$

Procedure 2 relabel(u)

Conditions: $x_f(u) > 0, \forall(u,v) \in E : h(u) \leq h(v)$
$\quad h(u) := 1 + \min(\,h(v) : (u,v) \in E\,)$

Fig. 2. Push-relabel algorithm [5], which solves the maximum-flow and the feasible-flow problem in flow networks.

In a payment channel network, however, it is often not necessary to know the maximum transaction volume. Rather, we want to find a payment flow that can process a certain amount only. This is a slightly different problem, which is known as the *feasible-flow problem*. Fortunately, the push-relabel can easily be modified to solve the feasible-flow problem: in order to find a payment flow from source s to sink t with a transaction volume d, we can simply insert a new (virtual) node to the payment network. We call it the *pre-source* s', with a single edge (s', s) and capacity $c(s', s) = d$. The virtual edge caps the transferable amount at exactly d. Note that this slight modification of the input data enables the push-relabel algorithm, as described before, to find feasible flows in the network.

So far, we assumed only one instance of the push-relabel algorithm. If multiple flows ought to be found subsequently in the same network, the initial flow of one instance is the result of the last instance. A generalization for subsequent flows, however, is easily possible. This subsequent approach can be used to find payment flows in a centralized or federated fashion. The following section is dedicated to show how the push-relabel algorithm can be adapted to enable route selection for concurrent and distributed payment flows.

4   Concurrent and Distributed Payment Flows

In payment channel networks, it is desirable to allow a concurrent execution of the route selection algorithm. To this end, simply running multiple instances of the push-relabel algorithm in parallel is not enough: one instance for flow f_1, for example, could consume the reverse edges' residual capacity that belong to another instance for flow f_2. We call this issue *capacity stealing*.

The problem domain of finding flows $f_1, \ldots, f_k$ for k commodities with source-sink pairs $(s_1, t_1), \ldots, (s_k, t_k)$ that meet the total capacity constraint

$$F(u,v) = \sum_{i=1}^{k} f_i(u,v) \leq c(u,v),\ \forall(u,v) \in E,$$

are known as *multi-commodity flow problems*.

As our main contribution, we propose a modified push-relabel algorithm that allows to find feasible flows in a concurrent multi-commodity scenario. To this end, we introduce the concept of *capacity locking*: flow volumes are accounted for every commodity independently, while still respecting each payment channel's total capacity constraint. The capacities on the reverse edges created by a flow f_1 are therefore *locked* for another flow f_2, which prevents capacity stealing.

Definition 4 (locked capacities and new residual capacity). *Let the **locked capacity** and **total locked capacity** of flow f_i on edge (u, v) be*

$$l_i(u,v) = max(0, f_i(u,v)) \qquad and \qquad L(u,v) = \sum_{i=1}^{k} l_i(u,v).$$

*Accordingly, the **residual capacity** is redefined as*

$$c_i(u,v) = c(u,v) - L(u,v) + l_i(v,u),$$

which yields an individual residual graph $G_i(V, E_i)$ for each commodity i.

Definition 4 ensures that there is always enough residual capacity on the reverse edges available to push the existing excess back to the source. Except for this augmented definition of the residual capacity, the `locked-push` procedure (cf. Procedure 3) is similar to the original `push` procedure. Note, however, that the modified push-relabel algorithm does not necessarily yield optimal flows in the multi-commodity scenario. It guarantees *validity*, though, which makes it superior compared to other approaches from this domain [1].

In the following, we prove validity for our proposed algorithm. As the skew-symmetry and flow-conservation constraints follow directly from the definition of the algorithm, it suffices to show that it yields flows that respect the total capacity constraint.

Lemma 1. *The total capacity constraint $F(u, v) \leq c(u, v), \forall (u, v) \in E$ is never violated.*

Proof. For a `locked-push` of commodity i on edge (u, v), the change in flow volume δ is always chosen to be at maximum the remaining residual capacity of the flow on this edge. Accordingly, lock $l_i(u, v)$ cannot be greater than δ. Therefore, the locked capacity never exceeds the edge capacity for each individual edge. It follows that the total capacity constraint is never violated:

$$F(u,v) = \sum_{i=1}^{k} f_i(u,v) \leq L(u,v) = \sum_{i=1}^{k} l_i(u,v) \leq \sum_{i=1}^{k} c_i(u,v) \leq c(u,v). \qquad \square$$

In order to execute the modified algorithm in a distributed scenario, the asynchronous distributed algorithm, introduced in [5], is adapted to our needs: each node maintains a local view on flow states, channel capacities, and its neighbors' height. Furthermore, each node maintains routing information and its

---

Procedure 3 `locked-push(i,u,v)`

Conditions: $x_i(u) > 0, c_i(u, v) > 0, h_i(u) > h_i(v)$

$l_i(u, v) := \max(0, f_i(u, v)); \, l_i(v, u) := \max(0, f_i(v, u))$

$c_i(u, v) := c(u, v) - L(u, v) + l_i(v, u)$

$\delta := \min(x_i(u), c_i(u, v))$

$f_i(u, v) := f_i(u, v) + \delta; \, f_i(v, u) := f_i(v, u) - \delta$

$L(u, v) := L(u, v) + \delta; \, L(v, u) := L(v, u) - \delta$

$x_i(u) := x_i(u) - \delta; \, x_i(v) := x_i(v) + \delta$

Fig. 3. Capacity locking enables concurrent push-relabel execution without violating capacity constraints, i.e., capacity stealing.

own height. Then, every node u with positive excess tries to push its excess along an unsaturated outgoing edge to a neighbor v of smaller height. A `locked-push` can only be committed, if v acknowledges u that it is has indeed a smaller height. Alternatively, v can reject the `locked-push` and respond with its actual height. This way, u learns its neighbors' height and can trigger `relabel`, if necessary. After relabeling, u sends height updates to its neighbors. The source and sink node can determine the termination of the algorithm and communicate the result to finalize route selection. The payment flow, i.e., the selected multi path, is secured with Hashed Timelock Contracts (HTLC) in the same way as a single path. Therefore, the payment flow can be atomically resolved.

5   Evaluation

In order to evaluate our approach, we constructed a Watts-Strogatz graph with $\beta = 0.5$, $n = 200$, and a node degree of 10. Channel capacities were generated by uniform random sampling from $[0, 10]$. In the following, we compare the sequential (seq., cf. Sect. 3) and the concurrent (conc., cf. Sect. 4) algorithm. Moreover, we contrast our results with the capabilities of single-path approaches.

First, we are interested in the number of flows that each algorithm can handle. To this end, we sampled the transaction volume from $[0, 20]$ and calculated the mean success rate over 10 runs, i.e., the share of successfully found flows. The results, shown on the left of Fig. 4, indicate that both algorithms are able to find a large number of flows (relative to the network size). At some point, when network capacities are exhausted, the success rate eventually drops. Single-path approaches, in contrast, achieve in the best case a 0.5 success rate (cf. horizontal line in the plot): while the maximum channel capacity is 10, on average every second transaction volume is in $(10, 20]$ and therefore not feasible with a single path. Effectively, this reduces the utilization of the available capacities by 50%.

Second, we are interested in the transaction volume that we can achieve by aggregating multiple paths. To this end, we set the number of flows to 128, increased the transaction volume, and calculated the mean success rate. The results, shown on the right of Fig. 4, suggest that again both variations are able to route relatively large volumes. In more than 50% of the cases, the concurrent

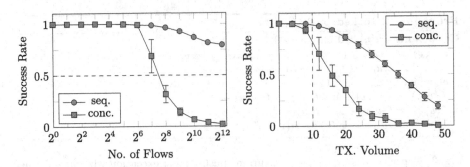

Fig. 4. Flow Network Simulation: mean success rate over 10 runs, dependant on the number of flows and transaction volume. Error bars show the 95% confidence interval.

algorithm still manages to process all 128 flows for up to a volume of 15 each. This is especially noteworthy, as a single-path approach would not be able to route a single payment with a volume exceeding 10 in our scenario (cf. vertical line in the plot). These first results illustrate that our approach is superior compared to single-path route selection schemes.

6   Conclusion

In this paper, we argued that currently deployed single-path routing schemes for payment channel networks suffer from a number of drawbacks. Most prominently, they utilize the available capacities in the network inefficiently. Eventually, single-path routes will lead to on-chain transactions as a fallback strategy and therefore subvert the idea of payment channels.

We addressed this issue by presenting a novel perspective on route selection that considers payment channel networks as flow networks. Flow network algorithms utilize the available capacity by aggregating multiple paths, which allow to route transactions of larger volume. We proposed an extended push-relabel algorithm that finds flows based on local knowledge. Thus, it is suitable for the concurrent and distributed scenario encountered in payment channel networks. We proved the validity of the flows and showed that our algorithm is indeed able to satisfy demands, where single-path based approaches fail.

References

1. Awerbuch, B., Leighton, T.: Improved approximation algorithms for the multi-commodity flow problem and local competitive routing in dynamic networks. In: Proceedings of the 26th Annual ACM Symposium on Theory of Computing, STOC 1994, pp. 487–496, May 1994
2. Croman, K., et al.: On scaling decentralized blockchains. In: Clark, J., Meiklejohn, S., Ryan, P.Y.A., Wallach, D., Brenner, M., Rohloff, K. (eds.) FC 2016. LNCS, vol. 9604, pp. 106–125. Springer, Heidelberg (2016). doi:10.1007/978-3-662-53357-4_8

3. Decker, C., Wattenhofer, R.: A fast and scalable payment network with bitcoin duplex micropayment channels. In: Pelc, A., Schwarzmann, A.A. (eds.) SSS 2015. LNCS, vol. 9212, pp. 3–18. Springer, Cham (2015). doi:10.1007/978-3-319-21741-3_1

4. Elements Project: c-lightning. https://github.com/ElementsProject/lightning. Accessed on 28 Jul 2017

5. Goldberg, A.V., Tarjan, R.E.: A new approach to the maximum-flow problem. J. ACM **35**(4), 921–940 (1988)

6. Network, L.: In-progress specifications. https://github.com/lightningnetwork/lightning-rfc. Accessed on 14 Jun 2017

7. Network, L.: lnd. https://github.com/lightningnetwork/lnd. Accessed on 28 Jul 2017

8. MIT Digital Currency Initiative: lit. https://github.com/mit-dci/lit. Accessed on 28 Jul 2017

9. Nakamoto, S.: Bitcoin: A peer-to-peer electronic cash system (2008)

10. Poon, J., Dryja, T.: The bitcoin lightning network: Scalable off-chain instant payments., January 2016

11. Prihodko, P., Zhigulin, S., Sahno, M., Ostrovskiy, A., Osuntokun, O.: Flare: An approach to routing in lightning network (2016)

Graphene: A New Protocol for Block Propagation Using Set Reconciliation

A. Pinar Ozisik[✉], Gavin Andresen, George Bissias, Amir Houmansadr, and Brian Levine

College of Information and Computer Sciences,
University of Massachusetts Amherst, Amherst, USA
pinar@cs.umass.edu

Abstract. We devise a novel method of interactive set reconciliation for efficient block distribution. Our approach, called Graphene, couples a Bloom filter with an IBLT. We evaluate performance analytically and show that Graphene blocks are always smaller. For example, while a 17.5 KB Xtreme Thinblock can be encoded in 10 KB with Compact Blocks, the same information can be encoded in 2.6 KB with Graphene. We show in simulation that Graphene reduces traffic overhead by reducing block overhead.

1 Introduction

Blockchain-based currencies [8], such as Bitcoin and Ethereum, have seen widespread adoption despite several limitations not present in traditional financial systems, such as credit cards or cash. Network delays and overhead are noticeable in blockchains. Once discovered, the propagation delay and network cost for distributing new blocks is dependent on their size, and reducing either delay or traffic is desirable.

We contribute an extremely efficient method of announcing new blocks called *Graphene*. Our protocol is applicable to a variety of blockchain-based network protocols, such as Bitcoin, Ethereum [5], Litecoin (https://litecoin.org), and Zerocash [10]. Our blocks are a fraction of the size of related methods, such as Compact Blocks [3] and Xtreme Thinblocks [11]. For example, while a 17.5 KB Xtreme Thinblock can be encoded in 10 KB with Compact Blocks, the same information can be encoded in 2.6 KB with Graphene. We use a novel interactive combination of Bloom filters [2] and IBLTs [6], providing an efficient solution to the problem of set reconciliation in the p2p network. We evaluate performance analytically and empirically via a detailed network simulation. Graphene reduces traffic overhead to about 60% compared to using Compact Blocks if blocks are sent every 2.5 min; Ethereum would see higher gains from Graphene, and the gains for Bitcoin would be lower, since blocks are sent more and less frequently, respectively.

Supported in part by an equipment grant from the Collaborative R&D Fund managed by the Massachusetts Technology Collaborative.

© Springer International Publishing AG 2017
J. Garcia-Alfaro et al. (Eds.): DPM/CBT 2017, LNCS 10436, pp. 420–428, 2017.
DOI: 10.1007/978-3-319-67816-0_24

2   Background

In this section, we review the operation of IBLTs and summarize related work.

Overview of IBLTs. We make use of Invertible Bloom Lookup Tables (IBLTs) [6], which is an efficient data structure for *set reconciliation* between two peers. Like Bloom filters [2], IBLTs allow two parties to determine, with high probability, which values from a set they share in common. But unlike Bloom filters, IBLTs enable the recovery of any missing values, which are assumed to be of fixed size and encoded as binary strings. Key-value pairs can be inserted, retrieved and deleted like an ordinary hash table. An IBLT consists of m entries, each storing a `count`, a `keySum`, and a `valueSum`, all initialized to zero.

A new value v is inserted into location $i = h(v)$ based on the hash of its value such that $i < m$. At entry i, all three fields are incremented or xored. IBLTs use $k > 1$ hash functions to store each value in k entries, which we collectively call a value's *entry set*. If table space is sufficient, then with high probability for at least one of the k entries, `count` $\equiv 1$.

Suppose that two peers each have a list of values, V and V', respectively, such that the difference is expected to be small. The first peer constructs an IBLT L (with m entries) from V. The second peer constructs V' from L' (also having m entries). Eppstein et al. [4] showed that a cell-by-cell difference operator can be used to efficiently compute the symmetric difference $L \triangle L'$. For each pair of fields (f, f'), at each entry in L and L', we compute either $f \oplus f'$ or $f - f'$ depending on the field type. When $|\text{count}| \equiv 1$ at any entry, the corresponding value can be recovered. Peers proceed by removing the recoverable key-value pair from all entries in the value's entry set. This process will generally produce new recoverable entries, and continues until nothing is recoverable.

Related Work. The main limitation we are addressing with Graphene is the inefficiency of blockchain systems in disseminating block data. A block announcement must be validated using the transaction content comprising the block. However, it is likely that the majority of the peers have already received these transactions, and they only need to discern them from those in their mempool. In principle, a block announcement needs to include only the IDs of those transactions, and accordingly, Corallo's *Compact Block* design [3] — which has been recently deployed — significantly reduces block size by including a transaction ID list at the cost of increasing coordination to 3 roundtrip times. We further detail Compact Block's operation in Sect. 3 and compare it quantitatively in Sect. 4. Xtreme Thinblocks [11], an alternative protocol, works similarly to Compact Blocks but has greater data overhead. Specifically, if an `inv` is sent for a block that is not in the receiver's mempool, the receiver sends a Bloom filter of her IDpool along with the request for the missing block. As a result, Xtreme Thinblocks are larger than Compact Blocks but require just 2 roundtrip times. Relatedly, the community has discussed in forums the use of IBLTs (alone) for reducing block announcements [1,9], but these schemes have not been formally evaluated and are less efficient than our approach. Our novel method, which we prove and demonstrate is smaller than all of these recent works, requires just 2 roundtrip times for coordination.

3   Graphene: Efficient Block Announcements

In this section, we detail *Graphene*, where a receiver learns the set of specific transaction IDs that are contained in a (pending or confirmed) block containing n transactions. Unlike other approaches, Graphene never sends an explicit list of transaction IDs, instead it sends a small Bloom filter and a very small IBLT.

PROTOCOL 1: Graphene

1: Sender: Sends *inv* for a block.
2: Receiver: Requests unknown block; includes count of txns in her IDpool, m.
3: Sender: Sends Bloom filter §and IBLT $\mathcal{I}$(each created from the set of n txn IDs in the block) and essential Bitcoin header fields. The FPR of the filter is $f = \frac{a}{m-n}$, where $a = n/(c\tau)$.
4: Receiver: Creates IBLT $\mathcal{I}'$ from the txn IDs that pass through $\mathcal{S}$. She decodes the *subtraction* [4] of the two blocks, $\mathcal{I} \triangle \mathcal{I}'$.

The Protocol. The intuition behind Graphene is as follows. The sender creates an IBLT $\mathcal{I}$ from the set of transaction (txn) IDs in the block. To help the receiver create the same IBLT (or similar), he also creates a Bloom filter §of the transaction IDs in the block. The receiver uses §to filter out transaction IDs from her pool of received transaction IDs (which we call the IDpool) and creates her own IBLT $\mathcal{I}'$. She then attempts to use $\mathcal{I}'$ to *decode* $\mathcal{I}$, which, if successful, will yield the transaction IDs comprising the block. The number of transactions that falsely appear to be in §, and therefore are wrongly added to $\mathcal{I}'$, is determined by a parameter controlled by the sender. Using this parameter, he can create $\mathcal{I}$ such that it will decode with very high probability.

A Bloom filter is an array of x bits representing y items. Initially, the x bits are cleared. Whenever an item is added to the filter, k bits, selected using k hash functions, in the bit-array are set. The number of bits required by the filter is $x = y\frac{-\ln(f)}{\ln^2(2)}$, where f is the intended false positive rate (FPR). For Graphene, we set $f = \frac{a}{m-n}$, where a is the expected difference between $\mathcal{I}$ and $\mathcal{I}'$. Since the Bloom filter contains n entries, and we need to convert to bytes, its size is $\frac{-\ln(\frac{a}{m-n})}{\ln^2(2)}\frac{1}{8}$. It is also the case that a is the primary parameter of the IBLT size. IBLT $\mathcal{I}$ can be decoded by IBLT $\mathcal{I}'$ with very high probability if the number of cells in $\mathcal{I}$ is d-times the expected symmetric difference between the list of entries in $\mathcal{I}$ and the list of entries in $\mathcal{I}'$. In our case, the expected difference is a, and we set $d = 1.5$ (see Eppstein et al. [4], which explores settings of d). Each cell in an IBLT has a *count*, a *hash* value, and a stored *value*. (It can also have a key, but we have no need for a key). For us, the count field is 2 bytes, the hash value is 4 bytes, and the value is the last 5 bytes of the transaction ID (which is sufficient to prevent collisions). In sum, the size of the IBLT with a symmetric difference of a entries is $1.5(2+4+5)a = 16.5a$ bytes. Thus the total cost in bytes, T, for the Bloom filter and IBLT are given by $T(a) = n\frac{-\ln(f)}{c} + a\tau = n\frac{-\ln(\frac{a}{m-\mu})}{c} + a\tau$, where all Bloom filter constants are grouped together as $c = 8\ln^2(2)$, and we let the overhead on IBLT entries be the constant $\tau = 16.5$.

To set the Bloom filter as small as possible, we must ensure that the FPR of the filter is as high as permitted. If we assume that all **inv** messages are sent ahead of a block, we know that the receiver already has all of the transactions in the block in her IDpool (they need not be in her mempool). Thus, $\mu = n$; i.e., we allow for a of $m - n$ transactions to become false positives, since all transactions in the block are already guaranteed to pass through the filter. It follows that

$$T(a) = n\frac{-\ln(\frac{a}{m-n})}{c} + a\tau. \tag{1}$$

Taking the derivative w.r.t. a, Eq. 1 is minimized[1] when when $a = n/(c\tau)$.

Due to the randomized nature of an IBLT, there is a non-zero chance that it will fail to decode. In that case, the sender resends the IBLT with double the number of cells (which is still very small). In our simulations, presented in the next section, this doubling was sufficient for the incredibly few IBLTs that failed.

PROTOCOL 2: CompactBlocks

1: Sender: Sends **inv** for a block that has n txns.
2: Receiver: If block is not in mempool, requests compact block.
3: Sender: Sends the block header information, all txn IDs in the block and any full txns he predicts the sender hasn't received yet.
4: Receiver: Recreates the block and requests missing txns if there exist any.

Comparison to Compact Blocks. Compact Blocks [3] is to our knowledge the best-performing related work. It has several modes of operation. We examined the *Low Bandwidth Relaying* mode due to its bandwidth efficiency, which operates as follows. After fully validating a new block, the sender sends an **inv**, for which the receiver sends a *getdata* message if she doesn't have the block. The sender then sends a *compact block* that contains block header information, all transaction IDs (shortened to 5 bytes) in the block, and any transactions

---

[1] Actual implementations of Bloom filters and IBLTs involve several (non-continuous) ceiling functions such that we can re-write:

$$T(a) = \left(\lceil \ln(\frac{m-n}{a})\rceil \left\lceil \frac{n\ln(\frac{m-n}{a})}{\lceil \ln(\frac{m-n}{a})\rceil \ln^2(2)} \right\rceil\right)\frac{1}{8} + \lceil a\rceil\tau. \tag{2}$$

The optimal value of Eq. 2 can be found with a simple brute force loop. We compared the value of a picked by using $a = n/(c\tau)$ to the cost for that a from Eq. 2, for valid combinations of $50 \leq n \leq 2000$ and $50 \leq m \leq 10000$. We found that it is always within 37% of the cost of the optimal value from Eq. 2, with a median difference of 16%. In practice, a for-loop brute-force search for the lowest value of a is almost no cost to perform, and we do so in our simulations.

that he predicts the receiver does not have (e.g., the coinbase). If the receiver still has missing transactions, she requests them via an `inv` message. Protocol 2 outlines this mode of Compact Blocks. The main difference between Graphene and Compact Blocks is that instead of sending a Bloom filter and an IBLT, the sender sends block header information and all shortened transaction IDs to the receiver.

A detailed example of how to calculate the size of each scheme is below; but we can state more generally the following result. For a block of n transactions, Compact Blocks costs $5n$ bytes. For both protocols, the receiver needs the `inv` messages for the set of transactions in the block before the sender can send it. Therefore, we expect the size of the IDpool of the receiver, m, to be constrained such that $m \geq n$. Assuming that $m > 0$ and $n > 0$, the following inequality must hold for Graphene to outperform Compact Blocks:

$$n \frac{-\ln(\frac{a}{m-n})}{c} + a\tau < 5n \qquad (3)$$

$$n > m/1287670 \qquad (4)$$

In other words, Graphene is strictly more efficient than Compact Blocks *unless* the set of unconfirmed transactions held by peers is 1,287,670 times larger than the block size (e.g., over 22 billion unconfirmed transactions for the current block size.) Finally, we note that Xtreme Thinblocks [11] are strictly larger than Compact Blocks since they contain all IDs and a Bloom filter, and therefore Graphene performs strictly better than Xtreme Thinblocks as well. In Sect. 4, we provide specific empirical results from network simulation, where we use real IBLTs and Bloom filters to evaluate Graphene and Compact Blocks.

Example. A receiver with an IDpool of $m = 4000$ transactions makes a request for a new block that has $n = 2000$ transactions. The value of a that minimizes the cost is $a = n/(c\tau) = 31.5$. The sender creates a Bloom filter §with $f = \frac{a}{m-n} = 31.5/2000 = 0.01577$, with total size of $2000 \times \frac{-\ln(0.01577)}{c} = 2.1$ KB. The sender also creates an IBLT with a cells, totaling $16.5a = 521B$. In sum, a total of $2160B + 521B = 2.6$ KB bytes are sent. The receiver creates an IBLT of the same size, and using the technique introduced in Eppstein et al. [4], the receiver subtracts one IBLT from the other before decoding. In comparison, for a block of n transactions, Compact Blocks costs $2000 \times 5B = 10$ KB, over 3 times the cost of Graphene.

Ordered Blocks. Graphene does not specify an order for transactions in the blocks, and instead assumes that transactions are sorted by ID. Bitcoin requires transactions depending on another transaction in the same block to appear later, but a canonical ordering is easy to specify. If a miner would like to order transactions with some proprietary method (e.g., [7]), that ordering would be sent alongside the IBLT. For a block of n items, in the worst case, the list will be $n \log_2(n)$ bits long. Even with this extra data, our approach is much more efficient than Compact Blocks. In terms of the example above, if Graphene was to impose an ordering, the additional cost for $n = 2000$ transactions would be

$n \log_2(n)$ bits $= 2000 \times log_2(2000)$ bits $= 2.74\,\text{KB}$. This increases the cost of Graphene to $5.34\,\text{KB}$, still almost half of Compact Blocks.

4 Evaluation

Our evaluation addresses the following question: What is the reduction in traffic from using Graphene for block announcements compared to Compact Blocks?

Simulator Assumptions. Our evaluations are based on a detailed, custom blockchain simulator using a Python-based discrete event simulator package. Our simulation models the propagation of messages across network links (ignoring effects from variable network bandwidth, TCP, etc.). Nodes accurately model any part of typical blockchain operation necessary for evaluating our metrics, including maintaining a mempool, the blockchain and its forks, and using realistic signaling.

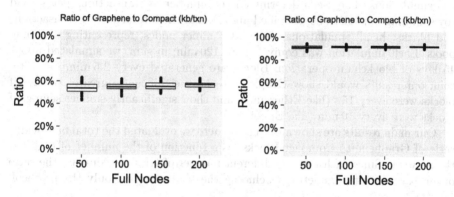

Fig. 1. When the current topology is used, Graphene reduces traffic to 60% of the cost of Compact Blocks (or to 10% for total traffic, which includes transaction data).

For Graphene and Compact Blocks, our simulator creates and decodes real Bloom filters and IBLTs, rather than merely estimating whether they might decode or return any false positives. If these data structures fail due to random chance, the nodes recover within the simulation. Because our simulation models detailed signaling and is written in a high-level language, our evaluations are based on a modest number of peers. Since our goal is a comparison between two choices, we expect that our results are representative of larger-scale scenarios.

A challenging parameter to set is the number of transactions per second offered to the network by peers. Our approach is to create kernel density estimates (KDEs) from the transaction generation patterns of real world peers. To that end, we gathered data for all Bitcoin transactions during a three-month period from http://blockchain.info. Each transaction in the dataset is labeled with an IP associated with the peer believed to have generated it, as well as the time it was released to the network. For each peer, we normalized the release times by the time of the day in which they were released. We then constructed the KDE for each peer using these normalized transactions times and gaussian kernels with one hour bandwidth. The KDE for a given peer represents a probability distribution from which we can draw transactions over the course of a simulated day. For each peer in the simulator, we randomly select one of the KDEs corresponding to a real world peer. Because these distributions have been generated from real data, they are a good approximation of the activity of real peers over the average one-day interval. On the other hand, this approach is not able to model days of the week or seasonal phenomena in transaction creation times.

Results. Each simulation is configured to use the following parameters: *(i)* Topology: a high-degree p2p graph topology. *(ii)* Block Protocol: *Compact Blocks*; or our *Graphene* protocol. *(iii)* Block capacity: 2,000 transactions. *(iv)* Full nodes: 50, 100, 150, or 200 peers. In all, we ran 8 combinations of parameters, and we ran each combination with 67 different seeds; all told, we completed 536 simulations. The seeds determined the number of transactions per second (by sampling our KDE, as described above), and the interarrival of transactions and blocks. In all simulations, we used 6 miner nodes, representing 6 mining pools. Each simulation was equivalent to 120 min; in sum, we simulated about 45 days of blockchain operation. Blocks are generated every 2.5 min, like Litecoin; our results would show Graphene to have significantly greater savings if blocks were every 15 s (like Ethereum), and show significantly smaller savings if blocks were every 10 min (like Bitcoin).

Our main results are shown in Fig. 1, where we evaluated the total bandwidth ratio of Graphene to Compact Blocks, as a function of the number of nodes in the network. Since each run is a different number of KBs, we compare the ratio of an exact set of parameters (including the seed), varying only the protocol.

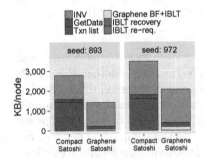

Fig. 2. A comparison of traffic, by message type, for two specific seeds for Graphene and Compact Blocks. N.b., traffic does not include transaction data.

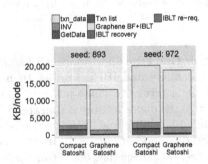

Fig. 3. Traffic by message type, for two specific seeds. Figure 2 shows the same plot without transaction data included.

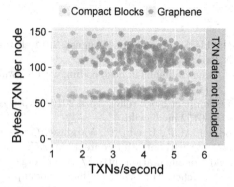

Fig. 4. Traffic sent by Graphene and Compact Blocks, where each trial's transaction rate is the independent variable. Transparency reveals some over-plotting in this scatterplot.

Boxplots show the distribution of results across all trials. Figure 1(left) shows that Graphene reduces traffic to 60% of the cost of using Compact Blocks. Note that gains reduce to 10% (i.e., are 90% of Compact Blocks) when transaction data is also included because they account for the largest portion of network traffic. However, as the number of full nodes increases along the x-axis, the ratio of total traffic in the network remains steady, suggesting that our results are representative of larger networks.

We also evaluated the sum number of bytes per message type for two example seeds, and details appear in Figs. 2 and 3. We saw that the amount of data used by Compact Blocks is much greater than Graphene's use of a Bloom filter and an IBLT. In Fig. 4, we also grouped our larger set of results according to transactions-per-second, and found that Compact Blocks generates a wide range of bytes-per-transaction, even at the lowest transactions-per-second rate. In contrast, Graphene is both more efficient and stable as load changes. Even when more transactions are generated, *Graphene uses less traffic* because the difference between the IDpool (of size m) and the block (of size n) is small, perhaps even zero, causing both its Bloom filter and IBLT to be negligible in size — see Eq. 1.

5   Conclusion

We presented Graphene, a protocol that uses Bloom filters and IBLTs for efficient block propagation. We have shown that Graphene is strictly more efficient than Compact Blocks unless the set of unconfirmed transactions held by peers is 1,287,670 times larger than the block size. Typically, the savings are significant on a per block basis. Additionally, using a detailed network simulation, we have demonstrated that Graphene reduces network traffic compared to the-state-of-the-art use of Compact Blocks.

428   A. Pinar Ozisik et al.

References

1. Andresen, G.: O(1) block propagation, August 2014. https://gist.github.com/gavinandresen/e20c3b5a1d4b97f79ac2
2. Bloom, B.H.: Space/time trade-offs in hash coding with allowable errors. Commun. ACM **13**(7), 422–426 (1970)
3. Corallo, M.: Bip152: compact block relay, April 2016. https://github.com/bitcoin/bips/blob/master/bip-0152.mediawiki
4. Eppstein, D., Goodrich, M.T., Uyeda, F., Varghese, G.: What's the difference?: efficient set reconciliation without prior context. In: ACM SIGCOMM (2011)
5. Ethereum Homestead Documentation. http://ethdocs.org/en/latest/
6. Goodrich, M., Mitzenmacher, M.: Invertible bloom lookup tables. In: Conference on Communication, Control, and Computing, pp. 792–799, September 2011
7. Hanke, T.: A Speedup for Bitcoin mining (Rev. 5), 31 March 2016. http://arxiv.org/pdf/1604.00575.pdf
8. Nakamoto, S.: Bitcoin: A Peer-to-Peer Electronic Cash System, May 2009
9. Russel, R.: Playing with invertible bloom lookup tables and Bitcoin transactions, November 2014. http://rustyrussell.github.io/pettycoin/2014/11/05/Playing-with-invertible-bloom-lookup-tables-and-bitcoin-transactions.html
10. Sasson, E.B., Chiesa, A., Garman, C., Green, M., Miers, I., Tromer, E., Virza, M.: Zerocash: decentralized anonymous payments from Bitcoin. In: IEEE S&P. pp. 459–474 (2014)
11. Tschipper, P.: BUIP010 Xtreme Thinblocks, January 2016. https://bitco.in/forum/threads/buip.010-passed-xtreme-thinblocks.774/

Short Paper: Revisiting Difficulty Control for Blockchain Systems

Dmitry Meshkov[1,2], Alexander Chepurnoy[1,2(✉)], and Marc Jansen[3]

[1] IOHK Research, Sestroretsk, Russia
{dmitry.meshkov,alex.chepurnoy}@iohk.io
[2] Ergo Platform, Sestroretsk, Russia
[3] University of Applied Sciences Ruhr West, Mülheim, Germany
marc.jansen@hs-ruhrwest.de

Abstract. The Bitcoin whitepaper [1] states that security of the system is guaranteed as long as honest miners control more than half of the current total computational power. The whitepaper assumes a static difficulty, thus it is equally hard to solve a cryptographic proof-of-work puzzle for any given moment of system history. However, the real Bitcoin network is using an adaptive difficulty adjustment mechanism.

In this paper we introduce and analyze a new kind of attack on the mining difficulty retargeting function used in Bitcoin which we call "coin-hopping". In a coin-hopping attack, a malicious miner increases his mining profits while at the same time increasing the average delay between blocks.

We propose an alternative difficulty adjustment algorithm in order to reduce the incentive to perform a coin-hopping attack, and also decrease inter-block delays. Finally, we evaluate our proposed approach and show how its novel algorithm performs better than the original algorithm of Bitcoin.

1 Introduction

Blockchain systems have attracted significant amount of interest after the Bitcoin whitepaper [1] was published in 2008. Bitcoin security relies on a distributed protocol which maintains a distributed ledger. In the protocol miners are trying to find a partial hash collision in order to generate a valid block by iterating over nonce field values.

Alternative systems may rely on other types of computational puzzles rather than finding a partial hash collision, e.g., [2,3]. Nevertheless, all of them assume some algorithm that changes the difficulty of the puzzle dynamically. An algorithm for difficulty readjustment is required in order to make an open blockchain system working stable in the face of participants joining and leaving the system (resulting in constantly changing available computational power for puzzle solving), and also to stabilize mean latency between blocks.

The difficulty readjustment algorithm in Bitcoin assumes that the total computational power involved in the mining process does not significantly change

J. Garcia-Alfaro et al. (Eds.): DPM/CBT 2017, LNCS 10436, pp. 429–436, 2017.
DOI: 10.1007/978-3-319-67816-0_25

from epoch to epoch. In contrast, real networks show that a significant variance in computational power happens over long periods. For example, as we show in this paper, due to continuous non-linear growth of computational power in the Bitcoin network the mean delay between blocks differs from the expected value by 7%. Noteworthy, exponential growth of computational power, often observed in practice, is the absolute worst scenario (regarding the mean block delay divergence) for Bitcoin's difficulty readjustment algorithm [4].

In this paper we also consider a new type of miner behavior with regards to difficulty readjustment which provides unfair advantage to the miner, and also makes inter-block delays worse. We call the discovered strategy the coin-hopping attack following the "pool-hopping" term raised in [5]. In this attack, an adversarial miner is switching from mining one coin to another in the beginning of an epoch, then he is switching back in the beginning of next epoch when difficulty becomes lower. We show how adversarial mining profit is increasing for Bitcoin's difficulty readjustment function, and how inter-block delays grow as a result of coin-hopping attack.

As a solution for the significant variance in computational power and also in order to reduce incentive of the described coin-hopping strategy, we propose an alternative difficulty readjustment procedure. We show that the proposed solution is better suited for exponential growth of the total mining power. It also reduces profit and negative side-effects of coin-hopping attacks.

1.1 Related Work

In this section we provide an overview of known formal and informal studies on dynamic nature of difficulty parameters in Bitcoin. Following the well known paper of Garay et al. [6], generalizing the Bitcoin backbone protocol in a static difficulty setting, a newer paper from the same authors [7] is providing a positive answer on whether basic security properties of the Bitcoin backbone protocol (common prefix, chain quality and chain growth) are hold in case of dynamic difficulty, in a cryptographic setting with an arbitrary adversary. Nevertheless, studying concrete attacks against the real protocol is still needed.

The Timejacking attack [8] allows an attacker to first shift the network time at a victim node (which is calculating network time by averaging timestamps it gets regularly from neighbors), and then force the victim node to reject a block with a specially crafted timestamp (other nodes are accepting). The time wrapping attack [9] is exploiting the fact that Bitcoin is using difference in timestamps between last and first block of an epoch, not the last block of an epoch and the last block of a previous epoch. By using specially crafted timestamps for the last block of each epoch, an attacker can produce more blocks for a time window, with more work contributed to his chain. The difficulty raising attack, introduced in [10], allows an attacker to discard n-depth block, for any n, and for any computational power of the attacker, with probability 1 if he is willing to wait long enough.

The paper [4] is introducing an alternative difficulty readjustment function designed to work better than Bitcoin's not just for almost constant mining power but also when the power is growing exponentially with time.

1.2 Structure of the Paper

The paper is organized as follows: in Sect. 2 we provide a detailed view of Bitcoin's readjustment function. In Sect. 3 we introduce the coin-hopping attack, followed by the definition of an improved difficulty readjustment function, described in Sect. 4. Section 5 provides experimental results for new algorithm evaluation.

2 Bitcoin Mining

The concept of Bitcoin mining was introduced in Sect. 4 of the Bitcoin whitepaper [1], and then discussed in detail in the papers [4,7]. A Bitcoin miner generates a block by iterating over a *nonce* value and calculating the hash of a block with the nonce value included. For a block $\mathcal{B}$ to be valid, a value of a hash function has to be less than the current *target* T, $hash(\mathcal{B}) < T$, where $hash$ is an ideal cryptographic hash function. Hardness to find a block could be expressed also via *difficulty* D as $D = \frac{1}{T}$. If output of the $hash$ function is μ bits long then the probability to generate a block by doing q requests to the hash function is $\frac{T \cdot q}{2^\mu} = \frac{q}{D \cdot 2^\mu}$. We define miner's *hashrate* R as $R = \frac{q_s}{2^\mu}$, where q_s is number of queries done by miner s per time unit. The probability to generate a block within a time unit is then $\frac{R}{D}$. In our analysis we assume that number of blocks mined over long period of time is proportional to hashrate of a miner. However, there are known strategies to mine a disproportionally high number of blocks, such as [11], and the strategies are in correspondence with a general result in [6], which is introducing *chain quality property*. The property sets an upper bound on number of blocks an adversary can generate over a sufficiently long period, however, this number can be higher than the relative hashrate of the adversary; the result got under an assumption of static difficulty. Adversarial manipulations with difficulty can be combined with selfish mining and other strategies to achieve disproportionally high number of blocks, making previous results worse, but this is out of scope of this paper: here, we study manipulations with difficulty in isolation.

Every M blocks ($M = 2016$ for Bitcoin) the difficulty is recalculated as

$$D_{i+1} = D_i \cdot \frac{M \cdot |\Delta|}{S_m},$$

where $|\Delta|$ is the expected time interval between blocks and S_m is the actual time spent to generate M blocks. For the Bitcoin network, the observed time interval of ≈ 9 min 20 s is less than the planned value of $|\Delta| = 10$ min due to continuous growth of the computational power of the network. Difficulty recalculation interval $M = 2016$ has been chosen to recalculate difficulty every 2 weeks on average. The epoch length is big enough to see the computational power of the network being changing over it: mean delay is close to the planned $10\,\text{min}$ right after target recalculation, whereas at the end of an epoch it is less than $9\,\text{min}$ on average.

The next section describes an attack against the recalculation algorithm.

3   Coin-hopping Attack

We consider the following attack involving an adversarial miner $\mathcal{A}$:

- There are at least 2 possible coins (C_1, C_2) $\mathcal{A}$ can contribute to. Without a loss of generality, we assume that each of them provides about the same profitability of the mining activity.
- $\mathcal{A}$ is mining coin C_2 before the beginning of an epoch A. At the beginning of A he is switching to mine coin C_1.
- Without the contribution of miner $\mathcal{A}$ the total mining power of the C_2 network for the epoch decreases.
- For an epoch B right after epoch A, the difficulty of C_2 is to be readjusted to a lower value. So $\mathcal{A}$ starts mining C_2 again with a lower difficulty.

We call this strategy a *coin-hopping attack*.

To calculate the profit the adversarial miner gains from this attack, we use Bitcoins' difficulty recalculation function and assume a constant network hashrate (with respect to the rest of the network, without the adversarial miner). We denote the hashrate of miners not participating in the coin-hopping attack as R_0 in both C_1 and C_2, and we denote the hashrate of the adversarial miner as $R_a = R_0 \cdot p, 0 < p < 1$. Before epoch A the adversary is mining coin C_2, thus the difficulty of the C_2 network is $D_0 = (R_0 + R_a) \cdot |\Delta|$ (see Sect. 3.1 in [4]). During the epoch A the difficulty of the C_2 network is still D_0, and $\mathcal{A}$ switches to mine coin C_1 at a difficulty $D_1 = R_0 \cdot |\Delta|$ calculated from honest miners hashrate R_0 only. During the epoch B the adversary starts mining of C_2, now at difficulty D_1, while honest miners on chain C_1 continue to mine it with higher difficulty D_0. After that $\mathcal{A}$ continues to switch between chains C_1 and C_2 always mining on the chain with lower difficulty D_1, spending $R_0 \cdot |\Delta|$ computational power per block, whereas honest miners spend $(R_0 + R_a)|\Delta|$ computational power per block.

Every epoch honest miners with hashrate R_0 will generate $\frac{M \cdot R_0}{R_0 + R_a}$, blocks, whereas $\mathcal{A}$ will generate $\frac{M \cdot R_a}{R_0}$ blocks. If $\mathcal{W}$ is block reward, the additional profit of the adversary is calculated as the difference of what he mines based on the lower difficulty in contrast to the difficulty he would mine at without hopping between the coins:

$$\mathcal{W} \cdot M \cdot \frac{R_a}{R_0} - \mathcal{W} \cdot M \cdot \frac{R_a}{R_0 + R_a} = \mathcal{W} \cdot M \cdot \frac{R_a^2}{R_0 \cdot (R_a + R_0)}$$

$$= \mathcal{W} \cdot M \cdot \frac{R_0^2 \cdot p^2}{R_0 \cdot (R_0 \cdot p + R_0)} = \mathcal{W} \cdot M \cdot \frac{p^2}{1 + p}$$

Remarkably, under such an attack the mean time between blocks in both chains C_1 and C_2 will be

$$T_a = \frac{T}{2}\left(\frac{R_0 + R_a}{R_0} + \frac{R_0}{R_0 + R_a}\right) = T\left(1 + \frac{p^2}{2(1+p)}\right) \tag{1}$$

which is bigger than the planned time T.

4   Improved Difficulty Adjustment

The difficulty adjustment algorithm employed by Bitcoin works as designed: if the hash rate of the network is constant, it yields to the desired block rate. However it does not achieve the desired block rate in other situations, and is vulnerable to the attack described in 3. In this section we propose an alternative difficulty adjustment algorithm.

1. It should be resistant to known types of attacks based on difficulty manipulation.
2. It should lead to an almost constant desired block rate for random fluctuations in the network hashrate.

We propose a difficulty adjustment algorithm based on the well-known linear least squares method [12], we name it *linear algorithm*. In the simplest case of pair linear regression $y = kx + b$, coefficients may be calculated as follows:

$$\begin{cases} k = \frac{\overline{xy} - \overline{x}\,\overline{y}}{\overline{x^2} - \overline{x}^2} \\ b = \overline{y} - k\overline{x} \end{cases}$$

Difficulty of the $i-th$ epoch D_i can be caclulated from the observed difficulties of previous N epochs $D_{i-1}, ..., D_{i-N}$ as follows:

$$\begin{cases} k = \frac{4 \cdot \sum_{n=i-N}^{i-1}(D_n \cdot n) - 2 \cdot (2 \cdot i - N - 1)\sum_{n=i-N}^{i-1} D_n}{4 \cdot \sum_{n=i-N}^{i-1}(D_n) - N \cdot (2 \cdot i - N - 1)^2} \\ b = \frac{2 \cdot \sum_{n=i-N}^{i-1} D_n - N \cdot k(2 \cdot i - N - 1)}{2 \cdot N} \\ D_i = k \cdot i + b \end{cases}$$

Note that for accurate difficulty prediction we use N last observed difficulties, rather than just one, as implemented in Bitcoin, but it is still possible to use this algorithm right after the second epoch of the history.

The next section provides an evaluation of the linear algorithm.

5   Evaluation

In this section we present simulation results. They show that the linear algorithm proposed in Sect. 4 outperforms Bitcoin's algorithm in all the three experiments. The first experiment is about exponential difficulty growth, which is the worst case for the original algorithm, as the previous study [4] shows. The second one is comparing two algorithms on real difficulty data from Bitcoin history. In the third experiment we compare the algorithms for a case of the coin-hopping attack. For all the experiments, $N = 4$ (we use data from last 4 epochs to calculate a difficulty value for a new epoch).

5.1   Exponential Difficulty Growth

First, we observe exponential difficulty growth, which occurs in practice in the Bitcoin network. Exponential difficulty growth is the absolutely worst case possible for Bitcoin [4]. In the experiment we consider a situation where network hashrate is increasing by 10% each epoch (more complicated research of exponential difficulty growth can be found in [4]). Figure 1 presents how Bitcoin and linear algorithms perform over epochs.

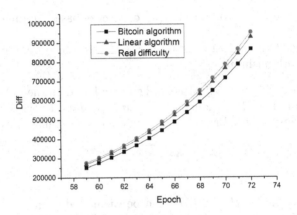

Fig. 1. Real difficulty values (red), values calculated by Bitcoin (black) and linear (blue) algorithms (Color figure online)

Note that the difficulty calculated from Bitcoin algorithm is always significantly lower than the real one. This leads to average delay between blocks of about *9* min *5* s, which is ≈10% lower than the planned *10* min value. Difficulties calculated by the linear algorithm are also always lower than the real ones, but closer to them. Mean delay between blocks when linear algorithm is used is about *9* min *45* s, which is closer to the planned value. Concretely, the algorithm currently used in the Bitcoin network has an average error of about 9.1%, while our algorithm has an error of about 1.9%.

While a difficulty readjustment algorithm proposed in [4] leads to better results for exponential difficulty growth with a constant rate, we note that our algorithm is simpler and can be implemented with integer arithmetic only.

5.2   Real Bitcoin Data

We compare the real Bitcoin network data with difficulty values calculated by the algorithm used in Bitcoin, and we do the same with values calculated by the linear algorithm.

Results show that in average Bitcoin algorithm has an error of about 12.3% while our approach has an error of about 8.4%. Thus our approach performs about 33% better than the approach currently used in the Bitcoin network.

5.3   Coin-hopping Attack

We consider the coin-hopping attack as described in the Sect. 3, with an attacker possessing 20% of total computational power of network. The attacker repeatedly turns on and then turns off his mining to manipulate difficulty and produce more blocks. Figure 2 represents difficulty over epochs for this scenario.

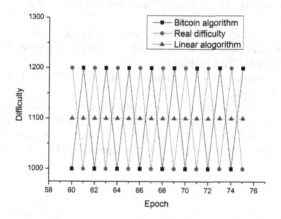

Fig. 2. Real difficulties (red), difficulties calculated from Bitcoin (black) and linear (blue) algorithms in the coin-hopping attack (Color figure online)

Note that the difficulty calculated with the Bitcoin algorithm is always in antiphase with the real one. The Bitcoin difficulty update algorithm leads to *10* min *10* s mean delay between blocks, which is in good correlation with the Eq. 1. The linear algorithm also leads to bigger than planned mean delay between blocks of *10* min *5* s, which is about two times lower difference in comparison with the algorithm of Bitcoin. Obviously, the profit of the attacker then is also 2 times lower.

Thus the linear difficulty control algorithm, proposed in Sect. 4 is better than the one used in Bitcoin for the coin-hopping attack scenario, both in terms of block rate and attacker's profit.

References

1. Nakamoto, S.: Bitcoin: a peer-to-peer electronic cash system (2008). https://bitcoin.org/bitcoin.pdf
2. Miller, A., Juels, A., Shi, E., Parno, B., Katz, J.: Permacoin: repurposing bitcoin work for data preservation. In: 2014 IEEE Symposium on Security and Privacy (SP), pp. 475–490. IEEE (2014)
3. Biryukov, A., Khovratovich, D.: Equihash: asymmetric proof-of-work based on the generalized birthday problem. Ledger **2** (2017)
4. Kraft, D.: Difficulty control for blockchain-based consensus systems. Peer-to-Peer Networking and Applications, pp. 1–17 (2015)
5. Rosenfeld, M.: Analysis of bitcoin pooled mining reward systems, arXiv preprint arXiv:1112.4980. https://arxiv.org/pdf/1112.4980.pdf
6. Garay, J., Kiayias, A., Leonardos, N.: The bitcoin backbone protocol: analysis and applications. In: Oswald, E., Fischlin, M. (eds.) EUROCRYPT 2015. LNCS, vol. 9057, pp. 281–310. Springer, Heidelberg (2015). doi:10.1007/978-3-662-46803-6_10
7. Garay, J.A., Kiayias, A., Leonardos, N.: The bitcoin backbone protocol with chains of variable difficulty. IACR Cryptology ePrint Archive. https://eprint.iacr.org/2016/1048
8. The timejacking attack (2011). http://culubas.blogspot.com
9. ArtForz, The time wrapping attack (2011). https://bitcointalk.org/index.php?topic=43692.msg521772#msg521772
10. Bahack, L.: Theoretical bitcoin attacks with less than half of the computational power, arXiv preprint arXiv: 1312.7013
11. Eyal, I., Sirer, E.G.: Majority is not enough: bitcoin mining is vulnerable. In: Christin, N., Safavi-Naini, R. (eds.) FC 2014. LNCS, vol. 8437, pp. 436–454. Springer, Heidelberg (2014). doi:10.1007/978-3-662-45472-5_28
12. Lawson, C.L., Hanson, R.J.: Solving Least Squares Problems. SIAM, Philadelphia (1974)

Secure Event Tickets on a Blockchain

Björn Tackmann[(✉)]

IBM Research – Zurich, Zurich, Switzerland
bta@zurich.ibm.com

Abstract. Concert tickets "are" nowadays unique identifiers that are printed on paper as barcodes, and scanned at the entrance gate. While this system is convenient and secure for the concert organizer, it bears risks and inconveniences for the ticket owner.

We developed a prototype system in which concert tickets are managed as assets on a blockchain. The system prevents ticket theft as well as fraud such as selling invalid tickets, or selling multiple copies of a ticket, by leveraging the consistency features of the blockchain.

We implemented the system based on Hyperledger Fabric V1. We developed a smart contract that manages the tickets as assets on the blockchain. We also developed a client application that runs on a smart phone and allows to seamlessly transfer tickets between two users using their phones, as well as the control at the entrance gate.

1 Introduction

Concert tickets, and those for most other events, are nowadays usually printed on cheap paper, and often customers also have the option to print their ticket at home. The unforgeability of those tickets is not guaranteed physically but through a unique identifier that is printed on the ticket, often as a barcode. At the entrance gate, the code is scanned, and the customer is granted access if the same code has not been used before.

While convenient and secure from the concert organizer's perspective—proper handling of the identifiers makes forging tickets impossible—this system bears risks and inconveniences for the ticket owner. "Ticket selfies" posted online can lead to ticket theft [6], fraudsters can extract the barcode from the picture and reproduce the ticket. Fraud related to re-printing tickets or selling invalid tickets has become a serious concern in recent years [1]. Furthermore, there is no secure way to re-sell spare tickets, because a buyer has no way to check whether the barcode on the ticket is valid, and in particular there is no way to check whether the same ticket has been re-sold to multiple other buyers.

One standard solution to the problem is to personalize tickets and bind them to the owner's name [6]. However, beyond complicating the entrance check at the venue through the necessary ID check, this severely complicates re-selling the ticket. The question we asked in this work is: Can we use blockchain technology to achieve the convenience of standard tickets, but with the improved security of ID-based ones?

© Springer International Publishing AG 2017
J. Garcia-Alfaro et al. (Eds.): DPM/CBT 2017, LNCS 10436, pp. 437–444, 2017.
DOI: 10.1007/978-3-319-67816-0_26

The setting. There are three different types of parties involved in the scenario. The first ones are *ticket sellers* that sell and deliver tickets for certain events to customers. The second ones are the *customers*, which may also want to re-sell the tickets among each other. The third type of party are *event organizers* that check the tickets for validity, and provide access to the event.

Blockchain systems. The concept of a blockchain was made popular by the cryptocurrency Bitcoin [8]. Conceptually, a blockchain is a list of *blocks*, each one containing a (short) sequence of transactions, which are linked by including a *hash* of block $n-1$ as part of block n. The chain is extended through some type of *consensus* mechanism depending on the particular blockchain system under consideration, and the entire chain of blocks therefore describes a sequence of transactions. Summarizing the above, the core idea of a blockchain is that it guarantees a globally consistent view on a sequence of transactions as long as the preconditions of the consensus are satisfied.

For Bitcoin, the consensus mechanism is based on a specific type of proof of work, and each transaction allows a party that has been the recipient of a previous transaction to distribute the received value to other parties. Each party is identified by a (often ephemeral) cryptographic identity, and the complete blockchain keeps track of which identity owns which amounts of currency.

Our solution in a nutshell. The core idea of our solution is to store the unique identifiers of concert tickets together with the cryptographic identity of the current owner on the blockchain. Each transaction can then either generate a new ticket, or transfer a ticket to a new owner, or invalidate a ticket, when the current owner decides to use the ticket to enter the event venue. All actions change the state of the ticket on the blockchain.

We developed a solution that is based on Hyperledger Fabric as a blockchain, uses digital signatures to protect all transactions, and allows users to manage, sell, and use the tickets with an application on their smart phone. We implemented the solution using in a simple Blockchain setup and with the client applications running on a commodity smart phone.

Related work. After the rise of Bitcoin, several new blockchain systems have been developed. While Bitcoin is restricted to its purpose as a cryptocurrency, later systems such as (most prominently) Ethereum [2] allow for generic smart contracts. The blockchain platform that we use in this work, Hyperledger Fabric [7], also supports generic smart contracts, but with different trust assumptions.

Other blockchain systems for managing assets have been published, such as Chain [3]. More recently, a commercial ticket trading application was announced [4], but we could not find any details on the actual implementation of the system that would have allowed a serious comparison.

2   Preliminaries

Algorithms may be randomized unless otherwise indicated. Running time is worst case. If A is an algorithm, we let $y \leftarrow A(x_1, \ldots; r)$ denote running A

with random coins r on inputs $x_1, \ldots$ and assigning the output to y. We let $y \leftarrow_\$ A(x_1, \ldots)$ be the result of picking r at random and letting $y \leftarrow A(x_1, \ldots; r)$.

Digital signatures. A *digital signature scheme* DS specifies the following. A probabilistic key-generation algorithm DS.keygen that takes as input the security parameter and produces a pair $(sk, pk) \leftarrow_\$ $ DS.keygen of (private) signature key sk and (public) verification key pk. Second, a (possibly probabilistic) signature algorithm DS.sign that takes as input a secret key sk and a message m and outputs $s \leftarrow_\$ $ DS.sign(sk, m), a signature. Third, a (deterministic) verification algorithm DS.verify that takes as input public key pk, message m, and signature s, and produces a Boolean $b \leftarrow$ DS.verify(pk, m, s).

Hyperledger Fabric. Hyperledger Fabric [7] is a permissioned blockchain platform with a modular architecture. In particular, the consensus mechanism and the identity provider are *pluggable* and can be instantiated according to the application scenario. The smart contracts, which are referred to as *chaincode* in Fabric, can be implemented in common programming languages. The current version is Fabric V1, which is also the version that we use in our system.

One crucial aspect of Fabric V1 is a separation of roles into *ordering service*, *peers*, and *clients*. A *client* invokes a transaction by generating a transaction proposal and sending it to peers for so-called endorsement. The *endorsing peers* run the chaincode and manage the chaincode state in a key-value store. When receiving a transaction proposal, the peers execute the transaction, track the read- and write-accesses to the key-value store, and sign the read-/write-sets (i.e., the effects of the transaction on the key-value store) including version information to manage concurrent accesses. These endorsements, i.e. the signed read-/write-sets, are sent back to the client.

After collecting sufficiently many endorsements (this can be managed on a per-chaincode basis), the client sends them to the *ordering service*. This service implements the consensus aspect known from other blockchain architectures; its purpose is to receive endorsed transactions, order them, and create the chain of blocks that contain the sequence of transactions. The ordering service has signature keys with which the blocks are authenticated.

The *committing peers* take the output of the ordering service and apply effects of the *valid* transactions[1] to the local key-value store. Usually endorsing peers are also committing, but a peer can be only committing and not endorsing. The pre-ordering execution of transactions makes sure that although the chaincode can be non-deterministic (e.g., access system state), the effects of the transaction are agreed and consistent.

The separation of roles has several advantages. First, the ordering service is separated from the execution of the chaincode; this makes the actual consensus method pluggable and also reduces the computational burden on the consensus nodes. Second, each chaincode can have its own set of peers that execute it. (Sets for different chaincodes may intersect.) The per-chaincode endorsement policy allows to adapt to the specific setting of each application. Third, clients

---

[1] Endorsed transactions can be invalid if they use outdated values.

do not need to keep the state of the blockchain, since the blocks are signed by the ordering service, and the chaincode state is managed collaboratively by the peers.

3 Design

For the purpose of this prototype, we consider a simplified scenario in which there is only a single ticket seller. (We describe a more general solution in Sect. 6.) Each party, the ticket seller, the customers, and the organizers, are identified by a digital signature key pair.

System structure and components. The ticket seller s has a signature key pair (sk_s, pk_s) that is used for enrolling new tickets to the blockchain; this action is protected by requiring each enrollment request to be signed with the key sk_s. Each customer c has a signature key pair (sk_c, pk_c) that is needed for re-selling the ticket to other customers and for presenting it at the entrance gate. Each concert organizer also has a key pair (sk_o, pk_o) that is used for invalidating tickets at the entrance gate.

The core component of the system is the chaincode that is executed on the blockchain, and that tracks the owner and state of each ticket. The chaincode is provisioned with the public key pk_s of the ticket seller.

Chaincode. Each ticket on the blockchain is a tuple $(id, pk_c, pk_o, st, age)$ of ticket identifier $id \in \{0,1\}^*$, signature public key $pk_c\{0,1\}^*$ of the customer owning the ticket, signature public key $pk_o \in \{0,1\}^*$ of the concert organizer, ticket state $st \in \{0,1\}$, where $st = 1$ means that the ticket is valid and $st = 0$ means the ticket has been invalidated, and ticket age $age \in \mathbb{N}$. The chaincode then allows for the following actions:

Enrolling a ticket: Takes as input ticket identifier $id \in \{0,1\}^*$, organizer public key $pk_o \in \{0,1\}^*$, owner public key $pk_c \in \{0,1\}^*$, and signature $s \in \{0,1\}^*$. If there is no ticket id and DS.verify$((\text{enroll}, id, pk_o, pk_c), s, pk_s) = 1$, then store the tuple $(id, pk_o, pk_c, 1, 0)$.

Re-selling a ticket: Takes as input ticket identifier $id \in \{0,1\}^*$, buyer public key $pk_b \in \{0,1\}^*$, and signature $s \in \{0,1\}^*$. If a ticket id exists, with owner key pk_c and state $st = 1$, then check DS.verify$((\text{sell}, id, pk_b, age), s, pk_c)$ and, if this check verifies, change the tuple $(id, pk_o, pk_c, 1, age)$ to $(id, pk_o, pk_b, 1, age + 1)$. Storing the ticket age prevents replay attacks when one user owns the same ticket multiple times.

Invalidating a ticket: Takes as input ticket identifier $id \in \{0,1\}^*$, owner public key pk_c, and signature s. If a ticket id exists, with owner key pk_c, organizer key pk_o, and state $st = 1$, then check DS.verify$((\text{invalidate}, id, pk_c, age), s, pk_o)$ and, if the check verifies, change the tuple $(id, pk_o, pk_c, 1, age)$ to $(id, pk_o, pk_c, 1, age)$.

Seller application. The seller application allows enrolling new tickets on the blockchain. On input ticket identifier $id \in \{0,1\}^*$, organizer public key pk_o, and owner public key pk_c, the seller application signs an enrollment request $s \leftarrow_\$ \text{DS.sign}((\text{enroll}, id, pk_o, pk_c), sk_s)$ and sends the request and s to the blockchain.

Client application. The client application supports two basic functionalities: re-selling the ticket to a different customer, and presenting the ticket to an organizer for invalidation.

For re-selling a ticket, the owner obtains the public key pk_b of the intended buyer b (see Sect. 5 for our implementation of this step), signs a re-selling request $s \leftarrow_\$ \text{DS.sign}((\text{sign}, id, pk_b, age), sk_c)$ and sends the request together with s to the blockchain.

For presenting a ticket for invalidation, the ticket owner has to provide the ticket identifier id and the public key pk_c to the organizer. To ensure that only the valid ticket owner can present the ticket, we also require a signature s on the ticket identifier id with respect to the owner public key pk_c. As (in our implementation) this signature is transferred through a QR code, to prevent "selfie attacks", we additionally include the current time t into the signed message.

Organizer application. At the entrance gate, the organizer obtains from the client the ticket identifier id, the public key pk_c, and a signature on the ticket identifier and the current time. He checks whether the time is sufficiently accurate and the signature is valid, creates a signature $s \leftarrow_\$ \text{DS.sign}((\text{invalidate}, id, pk_c, age), sk_o)$ and sends the invalidation request together with s to the blockchain.

4 Security Discussion

The security of the described system rests on two main pillars: the consistency guarantee of the blockchain and the unforgeability of digital signatures. In a nutshell, the consistency of the blockchain guarantees that each ticket only makes valid state transitions: that it can only be enrolled if no ticket by the same identifier exists, that it can only be sold by the current owner and if it is valid, and that it can only be invalidated if it belongs to the claimed owner. The unforgeability of the digital signatures in turn ensures that requests sent to the blockchain can only be generated by the relevant party; only ticket sellers can enroll tickets, only current ticket owners can sell them, and only the assigned organizers can invalidate them.

While a full security analysis is beyond the scope of this short paper, some aspects should be discussed in more detail, which we do below.

Ticket theft from posted images. The main countermeasure against reproduction of tickets from images posted on the Internet is that the ticket is bound to the user identity on the blockchain, and the presentation of the ticket at the entrance gate incorporates the identification of the user through a digital signature on the ticket state. If this signature would only contain static data, however, it would again be prone to attacks of the same type.

The signature for presenting the ticket to the organizer is therefore computed on a message that also includes the current time. This scheme works well if one can assume the clocks of all devices to be approximately synchronous— which seems reasonable given that today's smart phones usually get the time information from the mobile network. (It still seems to make sense to allow the organizer to override this check.) The scheme prevents "selfie attacks" if the selfies are not taken immediately before the concert.

Better security could be achieved by a challenge-response authentication method between the organizer and the ticket owner. However, as this requires either mobile network connectivity (which may not be available), or an ad-hoc wireless connection between the devices (which requires additional capabilities of the devices), or cumbersome handling in case of mutual QR code scanning, we chose the less secure time-based scheme in our prototype.

"Double re-selling" tickets. Paper-based tickets allow a re-seller to sell copies of the same ticket to different buyers. As our solution stores the owner together with each ticket, and the blockchain guarantees atomicity of transactions, such a "double re-selling" attack is not possible.

Sale of non-valid or invalidated tickets. While for today's paper ticket system it is easy to print tickets with invalid identifiers, this is not the case in the blockchain-based solution, where only legitimate tickets are stored on the ledger. Furthermore, the invalidation of a ticket is also a transaction on the blockchain. Re-selling invalidated tickets is not allowed by the chaincode, and the atomicity guaranteed by the blockchain ensures a consistent state of each ticket.

Invalidating without user consent. The organizer is supposed to check the user signature, but the invalidation message can actually be generated by the organizer without the owner's consent (given he knows id and pk_c, none of which is secret). The reason for not checking the user signature in the chaincode is that the concert organizer could anyway (physically) prevent the ticket owner from entering the concert venue—this is not an "attack" that can be prevented by blockchain technology. The purpose of the `invalidate`-request is to set $st = 0$ for the ticket and to prevent re-selling the invalid tickets to other customers.

Necessity of blockchain. From a theoretical perspective, the described application does not require a blockchain: for each particular ticket, the assigned organizer must be trusted to allow the ticket owner to enter the event venue. Consequently, one could alternatively implement the above scheme by running the *chaincode* part of the system under the organizer's control (instead of on a blockchain), and having each concert organizer run its own instance of the system.

From a practical perspective, however, using a blockchain allows the concert organizer (which also has a risk of having its servers compromised) to outsource the application to multiple providers *without fully trusting any one of them*. Furthermore, it seems reasonable for multiple concert organizers to run such a system together; this allows to increase resilience (e.g., against compromised servers) by distributing the trust in their infrastructure and improve customer experience by having all tickets be managed in a single application.

5   Implementation

We use Hyperledger Fabric V1 as a blockchain platform. For simplicity, the test platform uses the "solo orderer", a single node that orders the transactions; this can easily be switched to other consensus methods without affecting the remainder of the system. The digital signatures are ECDSA with curve `secp256`, as this curve is supported by the required platforms.

Chaincode. The chaincode is written in plain Go using the standard Fabric bindings and the provided LevelDB key-value store. For efficiency, we store the data in a redundant way; for each ticket we store the current state as described in Sect. 3, and for each user we store the list of identifiers of tickets he owns.

Client and organizer application. The application used by clients and organizers is programmed in Swift and runs on iOS devices. The data transmission in the selling and checking steps is implemented by generating and scanning QR codes. A ticket buyer b simply presents a QR code that contains the signature public key pk_b to the seller; the seller scans it and generates the `sell`-request. As already described above, a ticket owner c presenting a ticket to a concert organizer also does this through a QR code; in this case, however, the code contains the public key pk_c, the ticket identifier id, and a signature of c.

Access to the blockchain is implemented via a REST proxy. The client application generates the signed request and sends it to the REST proxy. The REST proxy then acts as a client in the blockchain and takes care of endorsing the transaction and submitting it to the ordering service. Note that this does not affect the security, as all requests are still signed by the client application—the REST proxy only has to be trusted for liveness, it cannot violate consistency.

Efficiency and scalability. All operations performed by the clients can easily be implemented on commodity smart phones. Each transaction requires the generation of one ECDSA signature on the respective client device and its verification in the chaincode running on the blockchain. Each ticket verification at the concert venue also requires one transaction on the blockchain. While especially for large venues with several thousand attendees this appears prohibitive on today's permissionless blockchains, the significantly greater transaction throughput of permissioned systems such as Fabric is expected to be sufficient.

6   Next Steps

We consider several modifications to the prototype to better exploit (and exemplify) the flexibility of the Fabric platform.

Use membership services to authenticate seller. While the current authentication via signature keys generated in the client application is reasonable for customers, provisioning the chaincode with the seller public key makes the scheme inflexible. This can be resolved by using Fabric membership services and providing the ticket vendors with certificates issued by the membership services. The chaincode then checks within the `enroll`-request whether it came from a certified vendor.

Flexible endorsement. The Fabric endorsement mechanism can be used to have each concert organizer run an *endorsing peer* that endorses the tickets for the respective venues. Thereby it can be assured that the ticket vendor cannot create new tickets without the respective organizer's consent.

Inter-ledger payment. The current prototype does not include any payment—the ticket re-selling is designed to easily allow transfer of tickets while the two trading customers are in the same place, and payment can occur in cash. Support of interledger transactions [5] may allow for atomic ticket transactions.

Analytics, privacy, and restricted contracts. The current version of the system keeps a transaction graph in which the individual customers are pseudonymous—as in Bitcoin—but otherwise the information is public. This allows for "mining" the graph. An obvious extension is to employ privacy-preserving techniques to better protect privacy. The current policy of unlimited re-selling could also be restricted, e.g. by bounding the number of steps per ticket or re-sales per identity, such as to curb commercial re-selling.

7   Conclusion

The presented prototype application shows how blockchain technology can solve ticket-fraud crime, an urgent real-world problem, without degrading the user experience. Tickets can be traded easily in a person-to-person scenario by simply scanning a QR code from the receiver's smart phone, and entrance control at the venue also amounts to scanning a QR code, as in today's system. In contrast to today's system, however, the blockchain backend guarantees to the customers that tickets they obtained are indeed valid and not counterfeit or copied.

Acknowledgements. I thank Andreas Kind for fruitful discussions during the conceptualization and development of the prototype. I thank Marcel Begert for creating the sleek design of the client application. I thank Yacov Manevich for providing support in building the infrastructure.

References

1. AXS: Ticket selfie equals ticket theft, unless you have id-based, digital tickets (March 2016). https://www.theguardian.com/money/2016/mar/21/online-ticket-fraud-social-media-users-warned-twitter-facebook-get-safe-online
2. Buterin, V., Di Lorio, A., Hoskinson, C., Alisie, M.: Ethereum: A distributed cryptographic ledger (2013). http://www.ethereum.org/
3. Inc, C.: Chain core (2017). https://chain.com
4. Guts, B.V.: Guts tickets (2017). https://guts.tickets
5. Interledger W3C Community Group: Interledger (2017). https://interledger.org
6. Jones, R.: Social media users warned over rise in online ticket fraud (December 2015). http://solutions.axs.com/ticket-selfie-equals-ticket-theft-unless-you-have-id-based-digital-tickets/
7. Foundation, L.: Hyperledger fabric (2017). https://www.hyperledger.org/projects/fabric
8. Nakamoto, S.: Bitcoin: A Peer-to-Peer Electronic Cash System (2009)

Author Index